OXFORD MEDICAL PUBLICATIONS

A TEXTBOOK OF
PSYCHOSEXUAL DISORDERS

But after Silence spake
Some Vessel of a more ungainly Make;
'They sneer at me for leaning all awry;
What! did the Hand then of the Potter shake?'

OMAR KHAYYÁM, *The Rubaiyat.*

A TEXTBOOK OF
PSYCHOSEXUAL DISORDERS

CLIFFORD ALLEN
M.D., M.R.C.P., D.P.M.

Second Edition

LONDON
OXFORD UNIVERSITY PRESS
NEW YORK   TORONTO
1969

Oxford University Press, Ely House, London W.1

GLASGOW NEW YORK TORONTO MELBOURNE WELLINGTON
CAPE TOWN SALISBURY IBADAN NAIROBI LUSAKA ADDIS ABABA
BOMBAY CALCUTTA MADRAS KARACHI LAHORE DACCA
KUALA LUMPUR SINGAPORE HONG KONG TOKYO

First Edition 1962
Second Edition 1969

Printed in Great Britain
by Billing & Sons Limited, Guildford and London

CONTENTS

PART SIX. PROSTITUTION

PART SEVEN. THE PREVENTION, TREATMENT, AND PROGNOSIS OF THE PSYCHOSEXUAL DISORDERS

PART EIGHT. THE MEDICO-LEGAL ASPECTS OF PSYCHOSEXUAL DISORDERS

PREFACE TO THE SECOND EDITION

This book was written as an attempt to collect together psychosexual disorders into a group of psychiatric diseases which should form part of the accepted corpus of reputable medicine. The fact that some are unpleasant is immaterial since one does not practise medicine for pleasure but to alleviate or cure those affected.

It is gratifying that a second edition should be called for so soon, but not surprising, however, since it is the only textbook of psychosexual disorders in any language.

The classification which is used here was formed on a proper psychological foundation, based on the parts of the instinct, and seems to bring some meaning into what had previously been a morass of confusion. It appears to have stood the test of time; where there have been advances new facts have easily fitted into the framework.

The predecessors of this work stressed the necessity for much more research, and the discovery of causation of psychosexual abnormalities. It was insisted that they were often responsive to treatment when others were proclaiming the hopelessness of anything other than castration, segregation, or sublimation.

The possibility of cure is now generally accepted as valid, and recognized even in the law courts. The work of those who were interested in the treatment of these diseases may have contributed a little to this; similarly they may have contributed to the change of feeling which has allowed alteration in the law.

Psychosexual disorders are definite diseases and are the cause of great unhappiness. It is true that in a more tolerant society there is no reason why they should be socially castigated, and most people now accept that it is cruel to persecute and condemn those who suffer from them; just as with any other disease. The need for prevention and treatment lies not so much in any antisocial element (although, of course, a small number, such as sadists, are dangerous to others) but because the sufferers cannot enjoy a normal life.

No attempt has been made to pile up an unwieldy mass of facts to confirm what seems already proved. Where proof and descriptions seem adequate the book has not been expanded; where new knowledge has been revealed, or wider descriptions made possible, no hesitation has prevented expansion.

All the relevant statistics which can be discovered in the literature have been recorded, but where there are no recent statistics I have not abandoned the older ones; since even if they are less valuable they give some idea of the facts until research reveals something better. Unfortunately not a great deal of work is being published on these matters.

No one realizes the inadequacies of this book more than I do, but it is to be hoped that others will be encouraged by it to expand this branch as the prevalence of the disorders demands.

I wish to thank Sir Solly Zuckerman for kindly allowing me to quote extensively from his classical work on monkeys and apes. Also the late Professor Kinsey and his colleagues for the use of three diagrams from their book, *Sexual Behavior in the Human Male*.

I am grateful to the librarians of the University of Liverpool, the British Medical Association, The Royal Society of Medicine and the Royal Medico-Psychological Association for valuable help with books and publications. Finally to Dr. J. C. Gregory of the Oxford University Press for many helpful suggestions.

CLIFFORD ALLEN

PART ONE

THE SEXUAL INSTINCT AND ITS DEVELOPMENT

INSTINCT AND ITS RELATION TO
SEXUAL ABNORMALITIES

Psychosexual illness is the result of aberration of instinct, and it is essential therefore that before we examine the nature of the aberrant we should know more of the normal and its development. As instincts are by no means easy to study in man, it is desirable that we should draw as much as possible from those facts which have been ascertained from animal observation, particularly from the sub-human primates (the monkeys and apes). It is then possible to pass on to the obliquities of sexual behaviour with some hope of understanding.

I propose therefore to examine instinct in sub-human and human, paying particular attention to maturation and development, and it is hoped by this method to throw a clearer light on the subject than by making wild analogies and basing one's conclusions on facts which have little or no relation to them at all.

There is no doubt that instinct originates in reflex behaviour, and that it is but a series of complex reflexes coupled one to another. The reflex itself is not such a simple matter, as Sherrington and his school have shown, as was once believed. Nor is it fixed and unalterable, since those more urgent reflexes are able to dominate the less urgent. Moreover, it has been shown that the reflexes are alterable through the influence of internal and external environment—for example, toxins such as strychnine and tetanus toxin, and variation and frequency of stimuli from outside. It is probable, nevertheless, that a simple reflex response is sufficient to explain the sexual behaviour of the insects, or at least the simple combination of reflexes such as Loeb described as 'tropisms'. It was Herbert Spencer who first made the brilliant suggestion that an instinct is but a combination of reflexes; this has also been supported by Loeb and more recently by the behaviourists led by Watson.

In the animals higher up in the evolutionary scale the only difference seems to be that there is a greater integration of all the inherited and acquired responses (which produces 'consciousness'), and the animal usually shows the presence of an instinct not only by excitement (which occurs in lower animals) but by a variation of behaviour suitable to the particular environmental conditions which aid or hinder it performing its instinctive needs. It is obvious that the more highly evolved is the animal the greater the variation of its responses, and it is this possibility of variation in its neuronic reactions that forms the basis of psychical or mental behaviour. In the lower animals there is a complete parallelism or somatic and 'psychical' (if one can call such fixed responses as one finds in insects 'psychical'), but in animals such as the sub-human primates (monkeys and apes) and in man himself there is usually a parallelism between the psychical and the somatic development but it is by far from being so exact. An example of this we shall see in that a full-grown ape which is sexually mature as far as its somatic development is concerned is, if it has been allowed to grow to maturity in solitude, frequently mentally immature and is quite unable to perform its sexual functions as it should. It can be seen from this simple fact how wild deductions from the lower animals tend to lead us astray and are unhelpful when applied to the sub-human primates or man.

Psychological wars have raged as to the number of instincts; there are schools which say that the number of instincts is so large that it is impossible to enumerate them in the human. An adherent of this school is William James. Again, there is another school which says that the number is not large and can be enumerated and described as MacDougall has described them. The school of Sigmund Freud, the work of whom is practically limited to the study of human beings, gives man two intertwined instincts, which are 'life instincts' (from which originate the sexual instinct) and 'death instincts' (from which originates aggression and hate). Freud's view, which is undoubtedly a profoundly philosophic one (but which is not based very soundly on fact or even accepted by all of his adherents), is that organisms originated from inorganic matter, but that the original organisms found life so difficult to live that they dissolved gratefully back into an inorganic state and this dissolution, or rather urge for dissolution, was the death instinct. Wave after wave of living things tried to live and gave up, as it were, in despair, but at last the life instinct grew more powerful than the death instinct and creatures finally lived without allowing their death instincts to triumph until they had passed through at least a brief span. How the life instincts conquered the death instincts is not completely explained, but possibly this was by exteriorizing it and destroying others rather than themselves. Moreover, there is doubt whether the death instincts are primarily aggressive instincts directed against the self, or whether they are externally directed aggression which has tended to become reversed [see CHAPTER 3]. We do not yet know. Nevertheless, there is no doubt that the aggression can frequently be directed against the self with devastating results. Those who doubt this will be converted by Menninger's remarkable work in which he collects scores of instances of every type from 'focal suicide' to complete self-destruction. This theory of life and death instincts is a very fascinating one, but a study of the protozoa does not confirm it since the amoeba, for instance, seems to show an urge for immortality rather than dissolution. In spite of these difficulties, it does appear possible that one can explain a great deal of human and infra-human behaviour by the theory of an aggressive and amorous instinct.

A point which tends to differentiate these long chains of reflexes from the simple reflex is that these chained reflexes (or instincts) are not necessarily present at birth and take some time to reach maturation, and in some cases do not do so until certain environmental factors are present. This is really a matter of complexity, since the complex responses of walking and balancing are known to be purely reflex yet take some time to mature, and even the simple plantar reflex is not flexor at birth. *It is important, however, that an instinctive response should be allowed to react when it appears spontaneously, since if it is not allowed to do so it has to be learned laboriously at a later date.* A kitten, for instance, has the instinct to chase small moving objects and knows instinctively how to kill mice if they are presented to it at the proper time. If, however, it is allowed to develop *past* the proper time, by feeding it on milk and keeping mice out of its environment, then it will chase mice but will not show any inborn knowledge of how to kill them. The tremendous importance that this simple fact has with regard to sexual anomalies will be shown later.

An important factor which has been shown by Spalding to influence the behaviour of birds is *imprinting*. How far this is present in human beings is still undetermined. If it is, then we must accept that it will be very explanatory regarding some human behaviour, such as fetishism.

Spalding found that young birds have a tendency to follow the first moving object seen at a certain time in their development. This has been confirmed by Konrad Lorenz and his school. Goslings incubated from eggs will follow a man and adopt him as their mother. They will then show fear of female geese, and will not afterwards learn to follow their parents.

F. Schutz, a collaborator of Lorenz, working at Seewiesen in West Germany, investigated this. Mallard ducks were hatched in an incubator and then reared in different ways: some were given a foster-mother of another species; some were kept with a male or female of another species, and some were kept isolated. Control birds brought up with their own species were used to check the result.

Observations over several years showed that the controls (28 males and 39 females) all mated with their own species. All the females reared with another species finally mated with their own, but not so the drakes. In a few the actual foster-mother or foster-sister was chosen, but usually it was another duck of the foster-species. Of the 19 drakes kept in isolation for more than five days, and then brought up by a foster-mother, seven were sexually imprinted by the foster-species. This is curious because it was thought that imprinting was only possible within three or four days of a duckling's life.

Some of the imprinted ducks were faithful to the foster-species for four years, even when real mating was not possible owing to bodily differences. A few weakly imprinted males were eventually captured by ducks of their own species, and birds reared with a mixture of their own species and others usually mated with their own kind (exceptions were only 2 in 21).

If this imprinting occurs in humans, as it may well do, it can be used to explain such anomalies as heterochromophilia, described later. Thouless suggests that it may be so. This is what he says:

The sex instinct, for example, has a critical period following adolescence which is favourable for falling in love with a member of the opposite sex which is a process closely parallel to imprinting in animals. Imprinting at an earlier stage may also provide a clue to one of the causes of sexual perversions amongst human beings in which the behaviour of the sex instinct is released by an inappropriate object. Certainly the human sexual response is not irreversible, as Lorenz states that the effects of imprinting are. Falling in love with one person does not, amongst human beings, preclude the possibility of subsequently falling in love with another, whatever the poets may say. But neither does it apparently in all monogamous animals. Lorenz reports occasional infidelity amongst jackdaws, and a general habit of remarriage after the death of a mate, although this is not found amongst some birds.

I must confess scepticism at Thouless' suggestion that imprinting is related to falling in love at puberty. Imprinting is a special example of conditioning which occurs only at the maturation of an instinct, neither before nor after. The likely cases of imprinting in human beings seem always to have arisen in infancy, although they manifest themselves later as symptoms. Imprinting in heterochromophilia does not seem reversible and the white man brought up by a coloured nurse continues to seek a coloured mate thus fulfilling Lorenz's conditions.

It is possible that the critical period in human imprinting occurs during two periods: in early infancy and again at puberty. This would accord with Ernest Jones' theory in libidinal development which will be described later. Such a recapitulation of the instinctual development would explain the falling in love at adolescence, but also where a man had a black children's nurse and cannot later free himself from the influence of her colour.

The mechanism of imprinting may occur in those cases where unlikely animals are friendly because they have been brought up together, and so have been imprinted that they are nest-mates of the same species. A polecat—which normally eats rats—may be brought up with a white rat without regarding it as a meal, although it will attack at once and eat a strange rat introduced into the cage. Something of this sort may occur when a child moulds its personality on its parent, as I describe elsewhere, but the subject is too new and unexplored to be more than a matter for speculation at the moment.

We may take it as a general rule that the psychical side of a reaction develops previously to the physical. The immature animal incapable of fighting effectively from the physical point of view will still growl and make a show of fighting as though the spirit were willing even if the flesh is undeveloped. It is even probable that the physical development depends somewhat on the willingness of the animal to attempt behaviour for which it is not yet physically fitted, and its growth in strength results to some extent from its play-fighting activities.

Since most animals appear to reach psychical maturity before they reach physical maturity, it would not be surprising if we should find that this occurs with regard to the sexual instinct as well as with other instincts. We shall see that it is highly probable that this is so, and that the animal will attempt sexual activities *before* it is capable of performing them physically.

The work of Charlotte Bühler suggests that maturation is a delicate matter which pervades the whole of psychical development. Each step in mental growth is dependent on a previous step, and if there is an omission in the chain, grave development with regard to the complete development may result. This is in exact accordance with the work of the animal observers, who have noticed that the higher mammals, particularly the sub-human primates, cannot reach proper social and sexual maturity without living in an environment in which they are able to make constant contact with others of the same species.

Again, although the psychical and physical development can occur more or less independently, it appears probable from the work of Broster, Vines, Patterson, Greenwood, Marrian, Butler, and Allen on the psychical changes which may accompany abnormal development of the adrenal glands that the proper psychical development is to some extent dependent on normal endocrine growth and that endocrine development may similarly to some extent be dependent on normal sexual maturation. It is not intended to go deeply into abnormal endocrinology in this work, since most of the patients who suffer from sexual anomalies do *not* show any abnormality of their glandular mechanism, but a brief chapter will be devoted to endocrine influence, for completeness.

Apart from gross endocrine dystrophies it seems possible that the instincts could be distorted from normal by four factors. These are as follows:

1. Reversion to a previous evolutionary type—the so-called atavism.
2. Genetic factors such as mutations.

3. Developmental anomalies such as the one quoted above—i.e. lack of a suitable object at the time of maturation.
4. Environmental influences such as the reflexologist calls 'conditioning'.

REVERSION TO A PREVIOUS EVOLUTIONARY TYPE

Darwin's brilliant discovery of evolution naturally led to the application of evolutionary principles to problems of mental and social abnormality. The fact that an Alsatian dog, which is closely related to the wolf, for example, should suddenly lose the gentler behaviour produced by domestication and attack its master as a wolf might do is eminently satisfactory to those who would explain behaviour in this way. This point of view was exploited at great length by Cesare Lombroso. He said:

The born criminal shows in a proportion reaching 33 per cent. numerous specific characteristics that are almost always atavistic. Those who have followed us so far have seen that many of the characteristics presented by savage races are very often found among born criminals. Such, for example, are: the slight development of the pilar system; low cranial capacity; retreating forehead; highly developed frontal sinuses; great frequency of Wormian bones; early closing of the cranial sutures; the thickness of the bones of the skull; enormous development of the maxillaries and zygomata; prognathism; obliquity of the orbits; greater pigmentation of the skin; tufted and crispy hair; and large ears. To these we may add the lemurine appendix; anomalies of the ear; dental diastemata; great agility; relative insensibility to pain; dullness to the sense of touch; great visual acuteness; ability to recover quickly from wounds; blunted affections; precocity to sensual pleasures; greater resemblance between the sexes; greater incorrigibility of the woman (Spencer); laziness; absence of remorse; impulsiveness; physiopsychic excitability; and especially improvidence, which sometimes appears as courage and again as recklessness changing to cowardice. Besides these there is great vanity; a passion for gambling and alcoholic drinks; violent but fleeting passions; superstition; extraordinary sensitiveness with regard to one's own personality, and a special conception of God and morality. Unexpected analogies are met even in small details, as, for example, the improvised rules in criminal gangs, the entirely personal influence of the chiefs; the custom of tattooing; the not uncommon cruelty of their games; the excessive use of gestures; the onomatopoeic language with personification of inanimate things; and a special literature recalling that of heroic times, when crimes were celebrated and the thought tended to clothe itself in rhythmic form. This atavism explains the diffusion of certain crimes such as paederasty and infanticide, whose extension to whole communities we could not explain if we did not recall the Romans, the Greeks, the Chinese, and the Tahitians, who not only did not regard them as crimes but sometimes even practised them as a national custom.

Although this is an impressive list, it is wholly to be discounted. The 'born criminal' is a myth and the stigmata of degeneration which are put forward so confidently occur rarely in any except a few mental defectives.

There is no evidence in any case that such stigmata necessarily accompany instinctual anomalies, and many mental defectives show no evidence of atavism in their instinctual endowment, nor do they show abnormal reactions to their environment. We can explain the universality of paederasty and infanticide in other ways. Moreover, certain sexual anomalies, which are obviously due to abnormal instinctual responses, are sometimes contradictory. Excessive sexuality might be explicable as a reversion to a previous evolutionary type, but this would be negatived by impotence. Again, some abnormal responses such as fetishism are obviously not related to the racial evolution at all. In spite of this there is a certain shadow of truth in Lombroso's ideas, as we shall see.

GENETIC FACTORS

An effort has been made, chiefly from eugenic quarters, to explain such illnesses as insanity and criminality (presumably including perversions) from the genetic point of view. The idea that these are limited to a certain stratum of society has been mooted and the suggestion has been made that these responses, which are presumably based on instinctual reactions, are due to an inborn abnormality. This is not far removed from Lombroso, except that the instinctual anomaly is believed to be carried by a gene and is, of course, not so wholesale and widespread as Lombroso would have it to be.

It is very difficult to accept such a thesis. No doubt there is a social problem group, and possibly it is composed of individuals from the same families throughout generations, but this may show, not an inherited reaction of abnormal nature, but a peculiar response to a wretched environment from which it is more or less impossible to escape. In view of this it is worth noticing that the idea of a social problem group with a genetic basis, which was put forward so confidently and enthusiastically by the geneticists some twenty years ago, has been quietly dropped and is never heard of now. One might ask, unkindly, can it be that there has been some mysterious mutation in the genes which carried it; or have the geneticists discovered that it is untenable, and quietly forgotten an unfortunate mistake? There is no doubt that an inherited endocrine anomaly (for instance, adrenogenital virilism) could deprive the individual of a specific stimulus, but could not do more than influence the sexuality other than towards diminished heterosexuality or producing mild homosexuality. Moreover, unless such traits were recessive the anomaly would tend to die out.

The idea is frequently put forward that the sexual anomalies are inherited as such—that they are, in fact, the persistent instinctual vestiges of phylogenetic development. One can see similar vestiges in the circular

B—PSY. D.

movements of the domesticated dog before it lies down. This is believed to be the effort to crush down grass, &c., to make itself a nest, although quite superfluous in a world of carpets and floors. Again, there is the curious instinctual vestige of the lizards on the Galapagos Islands (*Amblyrhynchus cristatus*). Darwin himself noticed that they were feeders on seaweed but reluctant to swim otherwise. When they are hungry they venture a long way out to sea in a bold manner, but when they are on shore they resist being driven into the water and absolutely refuse to do so of their own accord. They try every means to avoid their pursuer and even allow themselves to be forced into a corner on a jutting rock rather than dive into the sea. They can then be picked up and thrown into the water. If, however, this is done they scramble back again at the feet of the tormentor, even though they can easily escape by swimming a few feet away. Such a strong vestige is obviously a large controlling factor in the animals' behaviour, and while we do not for an instant deny the existence of such instinctual remnants, yet it seems improbable that the sexual anomalies could possibly be derived from them. The conclusive answer is that the instinctual vestiges although redundant are definitely not harmful to the race, whereas sexual anomalies, such as the perversions, are by definition unbiological and unlikely to fertilize the female. They are therefore definitely deleterious to the propagation of the species and would in any environment be bred out and disappear in a few generations. It is then certain that they cannot be instinctual vestiges but must be produced by, or in, the development of the individual. The geneticist's answer to this, of course, is that the trait is a recessive one, but this is doubtful, and such recessive traits which affect the propagation of the species are rare in any case.

It is possible that in such reactions as sadism we could explain the behaviour by postulating a mutation, but sadists are often very gentle to some individuals and it seems difficult to imagine an inherited reaction which was so limited.

Perhaps the most valuable point against psychosexual anomalies being controlled genetically is the fact that no one has ever been able to tie them to any physical evidence. If there is any genetic basis for psychosexual anomaly then it manifests itself only in instinctual deviations without concomitant physical signs.

Valuable work by Dixon and Torr regarding oral smears, which reveal the chromosexual sex, shows that no matter how abnormal the individual the chromosexual always corresponds with the physical sex. Thus, if genetics has any relationship to psychosexual illness it is not in such conditions as homosexuality, but in the more bizarre ones, like fetishisms, which are universally admitted to be more likely psychogenetic.

In general we can deduce with some confidence that if psychosexual anomalies are inherited they must be recessive, that there is no palpable evidence of any form of inheritance, and that they are more probably explicable by other factors.

DEVELOPMENTAL ANOMALIES

It is a biological truism that 'ontogeny repeats phylogeny', or simply that every animal in its individual development passes through phases which recapitulate the evolution of the species to which it belongs. It 'climbs up its family tree'. This has been known and accepted widely with regard to the physical side, and the presence of branchial cysts as due to the gill-slits, the thyroglossal remnants, the pineal body, the appendix, and so on is accepted by every surgeon as evidence of this view. It has not been understood nor accepted so widely when the psychical development is regarded, and as this possibility of inhibited development is very useful to explain instinctual anomalies, I shall review it at length. It is important, as I have already pointed out, to realize that an animal develops in three directions and in the normal these are synchronous. These parallel lines of development are: physical, intellectual, and emotional. The physical development by which the animal grows in size, strength, and sexual powers is obvious and need not be laboured. The intellectual development whereby the growing animal acquires a greater ability to cope with its environment and to understand it is again obvious. It is the emotional[1] development which is so frequently disregarded. Too often in the past it has been treated as though the emotional development was either endowed at birth as a complete entity, or else developed suddenly at puberty and the child or animal was an unfeeling machine before. We shall trace the development of the instinctual behaviour (particularly as regards sex) both in the sub-human primate and in man, and it will be observed that the individual passes through definite stages. It is obvious that, if the child repeats its phylogeny, it will tend to be more instinctual in its responses the younger it is and less so as it grows older. If the emotional (i.e. instinctual) development is delayed it will display reactions unsuitable to its environment at a later period. Moreover, its emotions will tend to be more intense. It is these points of inhibited feeling Freud has called 'fixations'. Moreover, since in cases where the instinctual response is inhibited a previously more successful instinctual response tends to be used, the animal or man appears to show a return of his emotion to an earlier stage of development, which Freud calls 'regression'. This theory of fixations and regressions, which will be considered later, tends to be confirmed by the work of Bühler on the maturation of

[1] *Note:* Emotions are the accompaniments of instinctual responses; they are probably produced by the somatic resonance of the instinct.

responses by children (although Bühler takes a wider view of the development of instinctual responses than Freud).

It is a pity that the views of Freud were greeted by such abuse and not subjected to a more careful scientific examination. This undoubtedly was due to the fact that he devised his own terminology to a great extent, and many who would have accepted his facts if they had been presented in another way were distressed by what appeared to them to be complex jargon. This is particularly so with regard to what he describes as libidinal development. It is a pity also that he stressed the emotional side of instinctual behaviour rather than the motorial side. What he describes as the development of the libido can be understood more easily as the maturation of various instinctual or reflex responses. Since the nervous system is built up by more and more complex reflex behaviour, this conception would have been much more comprehensible to those with a biological education had he described it in this way. The omission of an essential step (which Freud calls a fixation) naturally interferes with the genesis of the instinctual structure. A motor analogy would be for a child to use a knife and fork when it had never learned to use a spoon. Again, it would have been entirely comparable with the work of Hughlings Jackson if he had described a regression as the utilization of an abandoned developmental mode of behaviour through the destruction or frustration of a later developed one. This is entirely comparable to the 'release phenomena' so familiar to every neurologist.

As many of Freud's views as are found valuable will be used here, but they will be examined in a critical light (just as those of any other). The great contribution which he has made is that the development of the instinctual life of man is exactly comparable with that of the sub-human primate (although actually Freud formulated his views before the monkey and ape had been sufficiently studied to influence them). In one of his earlier papers Freud made some valuable generalizations and definitions regarding instinct, and although I do not necessarily agree entirely with them, it is worthwhile quoting some. He says:

The aim of an instinct is in every instance satisfaction, which can only be obtained by abolishing the condition of stimulation in the source of the instinct. But although this remains invariably the final goal of every instinct, there may yet be different ways leading to the same goal, so that an instinct may be found to have various nearer or intermediate aims, capable of combination or interchange.

This is confirmed somewhat by animal observation, and Bata has observed frogs at mating time attempting to copulate with pieces of floating wood.

He says of the object of an instinct that it 'is that in or through which it can achieve its aim'. He believes that 'it is the most variable thing about an instinct and is not originally connected with it, but becomes attached to it only in consequence of being peculiarly fitted to provide satisfaction'.

It is doubtful whether this is true in all cases, but no doubt if Bata's frogs obtained more satifsaction from a piece of wood than a female frog they would have sought pieces of wood. In most cases the object is the most biological one, and it eases the tension which occurs when an unsatisfied instinct is present. As Freud says, the function of the nervous system is to master stimuli, and this function is seen in both the simple reflex and the complex instinct.

Freud (in the same paper) states that instincts may undergo certain vicissitudes. They may be: (1) reversed into the opposite; (2) turned round upon the subject; (3) repressed, and (4) sublimated.

The first two are of immense importance in this work, but it will be necessary to await the section on sado-masochism and scoptophilia before we examine them in detail.

ENVIRONMENTAL INFLUENCES

One may presume that, given normal surroundings and allowed to develop naturally, the healthy animal (i.e. without endocrinopathies) will develop normally sexually. It should develop no fixations, nor should it regress in any way, but pass from one developmental stage to another until it attains maturity, mates, and propagates its species. Given a normal animal, the only factor which can influence its development therefore is some failure in the environment. We shall notice that, at least in the ape, the environment must be a social one and that the animal brought up in solitude is an abnormal animal. It is well worth noticing, however, before we pass on to the higher mammals, that environment does in some of the lower animals actually determine the sex of the animal. In such animals as the marine annelid *Bonellia* the animal starts off as a free-swimming larva which attaches itself to a female if it chances to meet one and there, attached to the proboscis, *it develops into a male*. If, however, it fails to meet a female it grows up solitary and *develops into a female*. No doubt this is a very efficacious way of determining the biological equality of the number of members of each sex. It is wise therefore, when considering the higher animals, not to be too contemptuous of the influence of the surroundings.

The work of the Russian reflexologists, particularly that of Pavlov, and to a lesser extent of Bechterew, has shown the importance of environment. Moreover, being conducted on the physiological plane, it has been more accessible and convincing to clinicians who would have been less interested in psychological experiments.

The whole of this work is really based on the single fact discovered by Pavlov—that a stimulus which is ordinarily indifferent can be attached to a reflex (or instinct) and could be thus used to initiate the reflex (or instinct) instead of the usual stimulus. He found that any stimulus, visual, tactile, auditory, olfactory, thermic, &c., would suffice. Moreover, he was able to study the laws and conditions which led to this process of conditioning. There is no doubt from his experiments that to produce a conditioned reflex it was necessary to repeat the stimulus a number of times, each time reinforcing it by feeding, &c., but from his description of the effect of the flooding of his laboratories and taking his dogs through a storm there seems no doubt that the dog could be conditioned to fear water by one single but very intense experience. This seems to be very important and is comparable with what is frequently discovered clinically with human beings.

This view is not confined to me alone. Mary Cover Jones states:

These idiosyncrasies in emotional conditioning have usually been attributed to the use of extremely potent unconditioned stimuli, involving emotional trauma. It has been shown that, when mild emotional stimulation is used, repeated associations are necessary to secure the response, the number being comparable to that required in conditioned-reflex experiments with children involving motor experiments (Krasnogorski, Mateer). Guthrie suggests that the strength of lasting quality of a conditioned stimulus may depend upon the number of conditioners involved rather than an increased strength (through repetition) of the individual conditioners. He writes: 'It is entirely possible that if Pavlov could have controlled all the stimuli instead of a very few, conditioning would be definitely established with one trial instead of fifty or more.' It is thus suggested that the complete conditioning which results from one emotional shock may be due to the effect of associating a large number of intra-organic stimuli with the unconditioned stimulus.

In general it is not one single experience but the continuous conditioning during childhood which influences the later behaviour. It is important to realize that this conditioning is not a laboratory matter, but that every single thing which happens during each moment of its life from the time of birth may be conditioning the child's future conduct. The most important agents in this process are undoubtedly the parents—particularly the mother—so that it is not surprising that the parental attitude and behaviour are of supreme importance. It is by the acquistion of reactions from the parents and later from the teacher that the child learns to deal adequately with its environment. It is usually a beneficent influence, but since it is so intense it is easily turned into harmful directions.

In the monkeys and apes, imitation, and in the human, imitation and speech, are methods of acquisition of behaviour, but these appear later than the appearance of response to conditioning. Nevertheless, they appear at an early age so that it is quite possible for the young child to see something which it imitates or misunderstands so that it fears it (e.g. parental intercourse) or else is told something which is misinterpreted. That this process of speech can be combined with conditioning through the repetition of being told something again and again, and produce a lasting effect, has been shown by Healy. He quotes a case of a child who was told of sex and sexual expressions by a girl who stole when in her company. After this she had a vivid mental imagery of this girl and felt that she had to steal. She said: 'The only bad girl I ever knew was Annie. Ever since I saw her steal scissors I have got it in my mind. I see her as if she was telling me what she was doing. *I see her standing right beside me. If I read a book and it is about a girl I see her like a picture.*' Again: 'Annie used to live in the same house with us. She lived in the basement. She swore something terrible; such words I can't tell them to you. I never think about them. Only what she told me comes into my mind, and I can see all those three times I saw her stealing. They always come into my mind before I take things. When I am busy it does not bother me and sometimes, when it comes into my mind, I take a book and read and it goes away. But sometimes it stays, and I can't think of what I am reading, and then I take things off my mother.' This girl was aged 11 years and the existence of the girl who had so influenced her was confirmed. There seems no doubt that she had been conditioned to steal apparently through the sexual instinct.

Imitation through 'fashion' has been frequently blamed for abnormal sexual behaviour, but this is unlikely. It is true, however, that the sexual instinct is variable and frequently a variance of toleration occurs. This cannot influence the origin of abnormal instincts, although it may lead to their suppression through fear. On the other hand, in evironments where abnormal sexuality is encouraged instincts which would have been suppressed in other less encouraging surroundings are often released. It is customary for the stern moralist to blame the influence of effete civilization and the corrupting effect of great cities for abnormal sexuality. It seems to me highly improbable that this is so, and anyone who cares to read the rural newspapers will find that similar, if isolated, conduct occurs just as frequently in the country as in towns. Nevertheless, it must be admitted that the more superficial evidences of sex may be influenced by fashion, which is often more prevalent in big cities than in the country. Thus the wearing of very short skirts by girls, or excessively long hair by boys, for example, may originate in this way. It is likely, also, that fashion may diminish inhibitions based on conditioning by deconditioning them.

How far literature, television, the cinema and the stage, as well as contact with other young people in clubs, &c., may have such an effect with regard to abnormal sexuality has never been statistically determined. Since to normal young people normal sex is more pleasurable than abnormal, it is very doubtful whether it could have a fraction of the effects feared by the stern moralists.

If we deduce everything which we can from the psychological studies of instinct which is likely to assist us in understanding the psychosexual abnormalities we must realize that an instinct consists of four factors: (1) *the stimulus*, (2) *the strength of the urge*, (3) *the mode of expression*, (4) *the object*.

The Stimulus

The stimulus is that part of an instinctual object which initiates action. The whole instinctual object may not do so, nor is one object as good as another. Let us take an example. In sex, for instance, a man finds his instinctual object in someone of the opposite sex. But any woman does not necessarily act as a sexual stimulus—the women must display certain characteristics which, even in normal men, vary and are peculiar to the men to some extent. One man is attracted to the girl without cosmetics and dressed in tweeds and brogues, whereas another man tends to be most attracted by a girl in the most complicated creations of Dior and adorned with the utmost skill of the cosmetic art. Again, one man is attracted to fair girls and another to brunettes, and so on. It is when this stimulus of the sexual instinct deviates too far from the normal (i.e. usual) that we have those curious sexual aberrations which we know as fetishisms.

The Strength of the Urge

The instinctual urge may vary in different people according to various factors which we shall study later. Probably there is some basic endocrine reason which primarily conditions the strength, but other facts are involved also. This variation in sexual urge and its power to manifest itself in physical effects is particularly to be seen in the sexual instinct. It is a matter of common knowledge that whereas some people feel strong sexual urges, sufficiently strong to cause them to perform crime in some cases, others feel little or no urge at all. Again, others may feel desire but are unable to translate it into physical results. This variation of the sexual urge we believe to be the basis of such aberrations as impotence and nymphomania.

The Mode of Expression

The mode of expression of the instinct (or its aim, as Freud calls it) is the manner in which the instinct is utilized. In sex we can say that it is the way in which sexual satisfaction is obtained. In the normal the sexual energy should be dissipated in copulation, and this is the usual mode of exhibition. A certain amount of pleasure may be obtained by the instinct exhibiting itself in devious directions—in the normal in kissing, stroking, and so on. This should reach the culminating point of intercourse. We shall find, however, that in the psychosexual abnormalities the mode of expression of the instinct is abnormal and that the sexual energy is dissipated in unbiological channels. It is this in conjunction with the abnormal object which produces a perversion.

The Object

The instinctual object is that towards whom or which the instinct is directed. In the normal human being it is a person of the opposite sex and of about same age. This person provides (as we have pointed out above) a stimulus which causes an instinctual urge to him or her. In the perversions it is found that the object may be someone of the same sex, but frequently it is not, and then it may be someone of the opposite sex, an immature person, or even an animal. The use of a dead person as a sexual object is a fetishism, since it is the abnormal stimulus rather than the object which is at fault, but may be related also to sadism.

It will be seen that by aberrations of the various parts of the instinctual mechanism we can understand the whole nature of the perversions and abnormalities and can appreciate that they are an illness and not a mysterious condition which is indulged in to give uncanny pleasure unobtained by normal people—in fact the pervert gets only the same sexual pleasure by devious and complicated means.

REFERENCES

BAKER, J. R. (1926) *Sex in Man and Animals*, London.
BECHTEREW, V. M. (1933) *The General Principles of Human Reflexology*, London.
BLACKER, C. P. (1937) *A Social Problem Group?* London.
BROSTER, VINES, PATTERSON, GREENWOOD, MARRIAN, BUTLER, and ALLEN (1938) *The Adrenal Cortex and Intersexuality*, London.
BÜHLER, C. (1935) *From Birth to Maturity*, London.
CREED, R. S., DENNY-BROWN, D., ECCLES, J. C., LIDDELL, E. G. T., and SHERRINGTON, C. S. (1932) *The Reflex Activity of the Spinal Cord*, Oxford.
DIXON, A. D., and TORR, J. B. D. (1958) Chromosomal sex and abnormal sexual development, *Brit. med. J.*, **2**, 388.
FREUD, S. (1922) *Beyond the Pleasure Principle*, London.
—— (1922) *Introductory Lectures on Psychoanalysis*, London.
—— (1925) Instincts and their vicissitudes, in *Collected Papers*, p. 60, London.
—— (1925) *Collected Papers*, London.
—— (1930) *Three Contributions to the Theory of Sex*, New York.
FROLOV, Y. P. (1937) *Pavlov and His School*, London.
HEALY, WILLIAM (1919) *Mental Conflicts and Misconduct*, London.
JAMES, W. (1890) *The Principles of Psychology*, London.
JONES, MARY COVER (1933) Emotional development, in *Handbook of Child Psychology*, 2nd ed., ed Murchison, C. Worcester, Mass.
KOFFKA, K. (1936) *The Growth of the Mind*, London.
LOEB, J. (1918) *Forced Movements, Tropisms, and Animal Conduct*, Philadelphia.
LOMBROSO, CESARE (1911) *Crime, Its Causes and Remedies*, London.

McDougall, W. (1928) *Outline of Psychology*, London.
Menninger, K. A. (1938) *Man Against Himself*, New York.
Pavlov, I. P. (1927) *Conditioned Reflexes*, London.
—— (1938) *Lectures on Conditioned Reflexes*, London.
Sherrington, C. (1906) *The Integrative Action of the Nervous System*, New York.
Spencer, Herbert (1881) *The Principles of Psychology*, London.
Thouless, R. H. (1960) *General and Social Psychology*, London.
Watson, J. B. (1928) *The Ways of Behaviorism*, New York.
—— (1929) *Psychology from the Standpoint of a Behaviorist*, Philadelphia.
—— (1930) *Behaviorism*, New York.

2

THE INSTINCTUAL DEVELOPMENT IN
THE SUB-HUMAN PRIMATE

The scientific study of the behaviour, particularly the sexual behaviour, of the sub-human primates started about 1913. The work of Lashley and Watson first drew attention to the sexual behaviour in the young Rhesus monkey. This work was later confirmed by Bingham, who made a very careful study of four chimpanzees, and by Zuckerman, who was fortunate in having opportunities of studying the whole primate life in the London Zoological Gardens.

Zuckerman was able to observe the young primates from birth onwards and his descriptions are very complete. He observed sexual behaviour at an early age, and, as a biologist, seems more or less to have expected to do so. He says:

Moreover, instead of the month that in the rat or guinea-pig separates weaning from sexual maturity, the monkey has about five years—the ape about nine—of prepubertal social life during which its activities are not directed by internal physiological 'drives', but by the multitude of exteroceptive stimuli presented by the social activities of its fellows. It is thus not surprising to find that the young ape or monkey reproduces all the activities of its elders, and that, so far as is physically possible, every sexual response of the sub-human primate is exhibited before puberty. At puberty these responses are given force, apparently by the sexual hormones, and their previously playful character is replaced by the seemingly purposive quality of most of the responses of mature animals.

The first external phenomenon of which a sub-human primate has any sensory experience is hair. As a baby monkey or ape is born it is pulled by its mother to her breast, and its fingers immediately clutch and hold her fur. The type of behaviour that would be designated 'maternal care' is notably absent at first. Unaided, the young animal finds the nipple by 'trial and error'. For about the first month of its life it lives entirely upon milk, and is carried by its mother wherever she goes. When the mother is sitting, the young animal is generally held close to her body, with its feet clutching at the hair of her belly and its hands buried in the fur of her chest. When she moves the baby hangs on in the same way, slung, as it were, beneath her. Usually it holds on by its own unaided efforts, but sometimes the mother clasps it with one 'arm', while she hops along on three 'legs'. When she is sitting she may embrace her baby with both arms. The baby manifests a strong interest in fur. It crawls over the mother's fur; within a week it may scratch its own body. I once observed a monkey, a week old, vaguely exploring with its hands the fur of its father, who was sitting close to its mother. Sometimes the mother monkey behaves as though she were irritated by having her fur clutched. A pig-tailed macaque in the London Gardens persisted in pulling away the hands and feet of her infant wherever they clasped.

It is of interest to note that the grasp reflex which enables the baby monkey to hold on to its mother is present at birth in the human infant and may appear at a later date in the adult, after it has disappeared, if the prefrontal lobes of the brain are damaged. This is a good example of the emergence of a previous mode of reaction as described in the influence of development. The grooming which Zuckerman noted later develops into a more or less sexual reaction, since the monkey tends to groom its mate. It is curious that Malinowski found that the Trobriand islanders groomed and 'de-loused' each other as an act of affection between lovers, &c. There seems no evidence that the suckling of the infant monkey is a sexual function as Freud believes it is in the human, but it is difficult to obtain evidence for or against such a thing. There is no doubt that the sub-human primate uses its mouth to express affection in a sexual sense when it is more mature.

Whether suckling has any significance from the sexual point of view we cannot be sure, but other reflexes soon emerge which are undoubtedly sexual in nature. For example, Lashley and Watson observed an erection in a Rhesus monkey when it was 2 months old. This was caused by the grooming of its mother, who stimulated it by picking over its genitalia. Zuckerman believes that the rhythmical pelvic movements which he observed when a monkey was 13 days old 'may represent the earliest motor expressions of sexual mechanism'. This was seen on the day the monkey first walked.

Zuckerman was able to observe the behaviour of a pig-tailed monkey from birth onwards. He describes it as follows:

A young pig-tailed monkey was born in the London Gardens on the 5th of July, 1928. As its vague movements became co-ordinated, it began to explore and move over its mother's fur—thus superimposing a social relationship of grooming upon their physiological relationship. Its mother's response to this increase in the range of its activities has already been noted in a preceding paragraph. She often reacted by pulling the young animal's hands and feet from wherever they clutched. The young monkey did not leave its mother's arms until it was three and a half weeks old, when it began to crawl along the floor and perches of its cage. As it became stronger, and its movements more certain, the range of its independent activities increased, and it began to extend its social interest to monkeys in neighbouring cages. Rhythmical shaking movements which it made when hanging on the wire of its cage and when standing on the perches, were the earliest distinct patterns of behaviour that it exhibited. These movements usually appeared sporadically during the course of ill-defined play activity, and from the beginning showed a striking resemblance to the exhibitions of vitality and dominance of more mature animals. When it was about six months old, it was seen on its perch varying such movements with similar movements accompanied by erection, which were unmistakably of a copulatory nature. The overt difference between the two kinds of movement was very slight, and over a long period the two alternated with each other. . . . In the course of its ill-defined play activities the young animal frequently explored and picked over its mother's fur. Its sexual interest was first manifested by the attention it paid to the ano-genital region, not only of its mother, but also of its immediate neighbours, from whom it was separated by wire partitions. During its explorations of its mother's body, and often in the midst of play-fighting activities, it would suddenly stop and peer at her pudendal region. As it climbed over her body, it sometimes held on to her hindquarters, its feet clasped round her thighs and its hands clutching the fur on either side of her tail, remaining in that position for a moment or two before proceeding in its climb. When it was about six months old, it mounted its mother in response to her repeated presentation, and about a month later this activity was first seen to be accompanied by erection and by pelvic thrusts. About this stage it was often observed presenting both to its mother and to neighbouring animals. Sometimes, when it mounted her, its mother pulled it off; at other times she seemed to incite it to cover her. At this time the young animal still took the breast, was still occasionally carried in the ventral position and always slept in its mother's arms. Their mutual relationship was therefore compounded of at least three elements; the maternal one, which involved nursing; the social one, which consisted in mutual picking, play activities, and the protection she afforded it; and the sexual one in which the young animal was, in a sense, its mother's mate. Its age of eight months corresponded, from the point of view of tooth eruption, to that of a child of about two years. It cannot, of course, be supposed that the behaviour of this young animal was typical of the behaviour of all monkeys at the age of eight months. It was behaviour from which almost all inhibitory social forces had been removed. It is conceivable that it would not have been exhibited had the young animal's powerful father shared the same cage.

In spite of the concluding remarks, it would appear that the young male would have been initiated into sexual behaviour, either by its mother or some other female, at such moments as its father's attention was directed elsewhere, and as a male monkey or ape frequently has a harem rather than one mate it is impossible for it to prevent such behaviour occurring. This is shown clearly when the baby is a female rather than a male. The young males who have not yet succeeded in wresting a female from the old males soon find it an object of sexual interest and use it as a sexual object. It is initiated into sexuality even if it is a female, provided that the father is removed. Hediger, from his observations, supports the view that much sexual behaviour must be learned. He states, 'Behaviour regarding mating and raising of the young does not seem to be innate in the most highly developed primates; a great deal has to be learned individually'. Zuckerman observed the behaviour of the mother pig-tailed monkey with a female child. He says:

The mother pig-tailed monkey gave birth to another baby, a female, twenty-three months after the birth of the young animal whose development has just been described. As before, the father was moved to another cage on the day of the birth. The sexual development of the young female followed a course similar to that of its brother. When about seven months old it responded to its mother's presentation by mounting. When it climbed too high on her rump, the older animal pulled it down.

The mother was really initiating the baby in sexual behaviour, although in this case it was, of course, homosexual. It is important to notice that this early sexual behaviour is not so evident in the ape. This is no doubt because of the slower sexual development in apes, whose prepubertal life is much longer and lasts about nine years. Even in apes there is a considerable amount of infantile sexual interest, and Zuckerman and others have noticed that they show great interest in each other's genitalia. In apes presentation becomes a common response only about puberty and not in early childhood as in the monkeys.

Presentation occurs in both sexes. It means the turning of the anogenital region in the direction of another. It was first observed by Darwin and is basically a sexual response. Kempf noticed that it is not only in sexual situations that this response occurs. He found that it was made to obtain food and protection as well as sexual satisfaction and was called by him 'prostitution'. It is unlikely to be a reasoned reaction, however, but a sexual response which has been conditioned to other behaviour. The observations of Bingham and Zuckerman confirm this view. It becomes much more pronounced during oestrus, when the animal is more sexually excitable. Comparable behaviour can be observed in bitches on heat when they try to attract the males by the same means. Hamilton suggested that sexual responses may have a number of meanings. Thus (1) to seek sexual satisfaction, (2) to assume female sexual position as a defensive measure, (3) to seek to lure on an enemy by assuming a female sexual position. To these Bingham adds (4) an exhibitionist display for interested observers. The monkey and ape are exhibitionistic to some degree, and Bingham noticed that sexual play and intercourse became intensified if there were spectators present. They will also hang lianas, cloths, or leaves on themselves as an adornment—this behaviour Köhler believes is sometimes an attempt at protection from the rain or cold, but is probably usually exhibitionistic. Monkeys and apes frequently display homosexual behaviour, both when immature and mature. Zuckerman describes this as follows:

Two animals will be sitting near each other, their heads will turn, their eyes meet, and immediately they may begin to smack their lips. This social response may then be extended by the animals rising, and by one presenting to the other. Then follows more pronounced smacking of the lips, sometimes a rhythmical series of low deep grunts, and the animals will either groom each other or mount each other, or do both. The females of a harem also exhibit homosexual behaviour—one female assuming the attitude of the male in mounting another. Since the females of different harems do not come into contact with each other, feminine homosexual behaviour occurs only in harems containing more than one female. Females also assume the male position and mount young males, and on rare occasions adult females have been observed mounting bachelors attached to their harems.

It is important to note that these animals were not in a state of deprivation but belonged to a colony of Hamadryas baboons on Monkey Hill at the London Zoological Gardens. Maslow *et al.*, apparently unaware of the extensive biological researches, and comments on them in previous editions of this book, have recently suggested that there is a parallel between the weak homosexual and his dominant partner, and dominance and subordination in monkeys. They think that presentation in the monkey is abandoning the male role. This was, of course, suggested some thirty years ago.

When the sub-human primate develops sufficiently and is able to chew it is weaned. It is difficult to find material on the subject of weaning, but it is probable that it is a gradual process and the breast is not suddenly withdrawn. It appears more probable that the young primate chews occasional fruits and then slowly substitutes them for the breast. Whether the aggressive reactions are present before the growth of the teeth or appear with their growth is not known. There is no doubt that biting is used as a mode of showing affection. and Bingham noticed that his chimpanzees frequently gently held his hand in their teeth to show their love for him. He noticed that excitement in the young chimpanzee frequently produced an erection. This excitement could be induced by the sight of food, by play, and so on. This erection has on occasion led to masturbation. It is not common amongst the primates, and Köhler denied that it existed amongst his apes at Teneriffe, although he did observe an immature ape masturbate on one occasion but thought that it was accidental. This view is supported by Hamilton. Bingham noticed that any excitement might overflow into sexual excitement and found that on one occasion one of his chimpanzees masturbated after being measured and on another occasion in the presence of food. A female he noticed used a leaf and pieces of mango fruit as well as pebbles. He says:

In these scattered observations on masturbationary practices there is evidence of experimental procedure similar to that previously described in mutual relations. The variety of methods employed by the female chimpanzee is especially significant. Even the behaviour of the male when he was irritated obviously revealed variety. . . . That masturbatory behaviour occurs under different emotional circumstances, the facts tend to indicate. That experience may significantly condition the behaviour there can be little doubt.

Zuckerman noticed that the sexual activity of the young male baboons was very diverse.

They employ sexual approach in obtaining access to each other and to entice a fellow for play. They masturbate and they mount each other. They mount and are mounted by adult males and by adult females, their hetero-sexual activities not provoking aggressive responses from the overlords. They engage in manual, oral and olfactory ano-genital examination with animals of their own age and with adults of both sexes. They frequently end a sexual act by biting the animal with whom they have been in contact. This end to sexual activity, which is not usually seen in the behaviour of adults, often appears to be playful, the young animal running away from his partner as soon as he has delivered the bite.

It seems probable that the monkey and ape, living in contact with others of their species, have so many sexual outlets that a masturbationary one is unnecessary; it is, however, the way it discovers its sexuality. The only prohibition which is applied to him is the superior force of his com-panions, and if that can be avoided homosexual and heterosexual activities, even if immature and not carried to their culmination, are not prevented.

There is no doubt that the excretory functions are closely related to the sexual ones, as one might expect since they have the same nerve supply. The young male and female have been observed to display erections following defaecation and urination. Moreover, in temper-tantrums the excitement may be discharged in excretory activities as well as in a sexual direction. In temper the young primate frequently empties its bladder and rectum. It does not appear that there is any definite stage in which the young primate's instinctual activities are directed towards excretion, rather that in moments of intense emotion all instinctual outlets may be activated. There does not seem to be any delay in the acquisition of control of excretory functions, but this, of course, does not occur in the ape as it does in the human primate, since it is of no consequence where or when the monkey or ape empties its bladder or bowels.

After the emptying of the bladder and bowel it has been observed that the young primate sometimes practises coprophagia. It appears to start (if Bingham's observations are correct) as a seemingly deliberate action and not due to chance.

Heuvelmans states that coprophagia in primates kept in captivity occurs when the animals have insufficient meat. The ape in nature is able to eat small mammals, insects, and so on which it cannot obtain when caged. He states that coprophagia is a frequent source of illness or death in captive specimens. The truth is, probably, that there is insufficient known of the habits of wild primates to make a firm statement, but that possibly coprophagia may occur accidentally, or when the animal suffers from dietetic insufficiencies.

An interesting point regarding the olfactory element in sexual stimulation in monkeys has been investigated by Michael and Keverne. This is the influence of pheromones, or perfumes produced by the stimulation of hormones.

Perfumes of this nature have been known for some time to act as sexual excitants. Insects, for example, will fly for miles to mate when stimulated by the scent of the female. In porcines the boar produces an odour which makes the female stand rigidly to facilitate mating; female cats crouch and permit treading, and dogs are attracted to oestrous bitches.

It would seem from the work of Michael and Keverne that Rhesus monkeys are attracted to females on heat by the body scent produced by oestrogens. They found that male monkeys were not interested in females when their nostrils were occluded, but when olfaction was restored they would push down a lever 250 times to gain access to the female.

The close relation of excremental odours and body odours may be related in sexual stimulation. Moreover, it is possible, as these authors point out, that although the olfactory influence is below the level of consciousness it may still influence behaviour in human beings.

A social environment is very necessary for the proper development of normal sexual responses, and the animal which is allowed to grow up in solitary confinement does not display the same sexual behaviour as the young primate which has had the advantage of contact with its fellows. It would appear that, like the kittens mentioned on page 5, the instinctual responses must be allowed to develop at the moment of maturation and if inhibited then they must be *learned* or reacquired instead of being inborn. If the young monkey or ape is not allowed to have a social surrounding it tends to be unable to show proper sexual activities at the time when it first meets a female. In spite of its terrific strength the sexual instinct is sensitive to environment. Moss and Louttit have both shown that it is possible to inhibit sexual behaviour in lower mammals such as guinea-pigs by giving electric shocks whenever the animals attempt to copulate. This is obviously the result of Pavlovian conditioning. It would seem in the case of primates that the sexual patterns, although present, must be mutually adjusted, and this can only be produced by the contact with a suitable mate at the correct time. Bingham, for instance, found that two mature primates failed to copulate satisfactorily when initially mated, although the female was more satisfactorily adjusted than the male. This adjustment of copulatory behaviour is also seen in dogs, and a dog which has been brought up away from females frequently fails to penetrate the bitch, as every dog-breeder is aware. It would seem then that in the primates, and in the higher mammals generally, impotence is either the result of conditioning or else that the male has had no opportunity of making contact with a suitable female and making what are conveniently described as copulatory adjustments. The young monkey or ape does not wait, however, until puberty to indulge in sexual behaviour but long before this arrives, while still immature and unable to fertilize the female, the young male attempts copulation with her.

Bingham gives a tentative list of copulatory antecedents or behaviour which precedes or leads to copulation. He says that the following are usual:

1. Clinging, cuddling, and embracing.
2. Explorations and manipulations; manual and oral contacts as in boxing, pulling, pushing, and picking; nuzzling, sucking, licking, and biting.
3. Flight, retreat, and evasion often leading to 1.
4. Play threats, erect advances, and fighting leading to 1 or 2.
5. Tantrums and borderland behaviour between fleeing and fighting which encourage responses from a companion similar to 1 or 2.
6. Orientation, coquettish play, and secretive play serving as invitations to a companion which leads to 1 or 2.
7. Erection reflexes in male or female which appear early and under various kinds of non-sexual excitement.
8. Stimulation of genitalia by contacts involving individual adjustments.

This copulatory play is confirmed by Yerkes and Yerkes in their classic work on the great apes in which they say: 'Copulatory play is both varied and frequent in immature animals. Homosexual, heterosexual, exhibitionistic and masturbationary activities occur.' Moreover, Köhler observed similar activities in his animals at Teneriffe. It would appear then that we must accept Zuckerman's view that the sexual patterns are present in young primates long before puberty, and that the presence of the endocrine stimulation at puberty tends to canalize the superabundant energy, which is frittered away in non-productive sexuality before, into strictly reproductive sexuality. It must be noticed that oral activities such as 'nuzzling, sucking, licking, and biting' are frequent copulatory precursors or even substitutes (although this latter is doubtful). The male primate will frequently stimulate the female by mouthing its genitalia, and this may even take the form of behaviour which, in the human, would be regarded as cunnilingus. Bingham says (describing such behaviour):

In the excitement that followed my appearance, Wendy was rolling her head and shoulders on the floor while she supported herself on her feet and elbows. In this manoeuvring before me, she brought her upturned buttocks under Dwina's face who grasped her flanks in both hands, and took her external genitalia in her lips. Wendy became quiet when oral contact was made with her genitalia, but nothing further developed. Cunnilingus seems to have developed since the animals left New Haven.

The opposite of cunnilingus, fellatio, does not seem to have been a part of the sexual responses of the animals, but generalized mouthing of the genitals does occur. The animals in which the cunnilingus was observed were immature apes.

The stimulus to heterosexual intercourse appears to be, in the case of the male, the pudenda of the female and it is a visual rather than olfactory or other stimulus, which leads to excitement. Some female primates during oestrus have engorgement of the skin around the sexual organs, which becomes known as the sexual skin, and this is attractive to the male. In spite of this, or the lack of it, the male is always more or less susceptible to sexual stimulation, even when it is immature, and the female is receptive even when it is not on heat and its sexual skin is not engorged. The close inspection of the sexual regions is common both as a frank sexual act and as a sign of affection as in grooming. Köhler believes that it is closely related to grooming and remarks:

We are at present in the dark as to the reason for the popularity of this investigation of the skin, hair, and hindquarters, which is carried on with the greatest eagerness and attention—and is a pleasure shared equally by the active and passive parties in the process. I am inclined to rank this manifestation, together with the constant urge towards nest building, amongst those characteristics of species of which the title 'instincts' does not help us forward in theoretical explanation, it being merely the label for a complex of equally peculiar biological riddles. The skin treatment is distinctly *social*, no chimpanzee shows so much interest in his own body if he is alone.

The riddle is solved if we accept Zuckerman's suggestion that social conduct is itself only a manifestation of sexuality.

Amongst what may be described as exhibitionist behaviour should be the sex dance which the male indulged in preparatory to copulation. Bingham believes that this dance has non-sexual as well as sexual significance. It consists of an erect swaggering waddle quite different from the usual mode of locomotion. No doubt its function is to intimidate and prepare the female for sexual submission to the dominant male. Freedman and Rosvold performed some interesting experiments on three intact male macaques and four females who had had their ovaries removed. They found that anxious females were least active sexually; they presented least and were mounted less frequently; were likely to be avoided and threatened, or attacked more by the males. Anxiety in the female was more likely to be evident during anoestrus and, reciprocally, aggression in the male was greatest. During the height of oestrogen-induced sexual receptivity the female was least anxious and the male corresponding least aggressive; copulatory activity increased, and there was a marked decrease in the distance maintained between the members of the coupling pairs.

This supports the view I have previously put forward, that anxiety tends to inhibit sexual activity and vice versa as will be seen in hyposexuality in man.

Apes copulate in either of two positions. They may use a ventro-ventral position as is usual with humans or more commonly a dorso-ventral position as is usual in the other mammals. A great deal of mouthing takes place according to some observers, and both Hamilton and Kempf observed behaviour similar to human kissing, but this was not seen by Bingham. Hamilton describes the mating of a female Rhesus monkey and male Cynomolgus monkey in which this occurred. He says:

She observed his approach from her shelf, and as he ascended towards her smacking his lips, she, too, smacked her lips. As soon as the male clambered on the shelf the female assumed the sexual position, viz.: hind legs fully extended to an almost vertical position; forelegs sharply flexed; tail erect; body inclined forward and downward from the hips; head sufficiently extended and rotated to enable the female to direct her gaze upward and backward. The male grasped the female at the angles formed by the juncture of hips and body with a hand on either side, and mounting her, clasped her legs just above the knees with his feet. He leaned forward and downward during copulation, smacking his lips violently. The female seemed to invite contact with his mouth, for she persistently thrust her smacking lips towards the male, until he leaned still further downward and touched her lips with his own. Shortly before copulation ceased, the male uttered a series of shrill little cries, and greatly increased the vigour of his copulatory movements. As soon as he dismounted the female, he took her tail in one hand and elevated it, then with his free hand examined her vaginal labia, at the same time closely inspecting them with nose and eyes.

As the primate reaches maturity he grows more serious and directs his energies more in aggression and sexuality than before. Yerkes and Yerkes describe this as follows:

Maturity, as contrasted with childhood and adolescence, is characterized by increasing quiescence and seriousness of attitude. The excess energy which at earlier ages finds expression in play and seemingly random activity tends now to be directed into the more specialized avenues of reproduction. There is a marked lessening of fooling, indiscriminate expressions of curiosity, and a correlated narrowing of interests which seem to be accompanied by increased irritability and development of stolidity, or, frequently in captive specimens, laziness and sloth.

Köhler noticed the same thing and thought that his apes became more indolent as they became more mature. He said that they often 'lay about in a sort of slumber nearly the whole day and only roused themselves under the stimulus of meal times, or some intervention from outside'. It is, of course, probable that in the wild state there is almost always a continuous 'intervention from outside' to prevent them from becoming too slothful.

Most primates, except possibly the Hoolocks and Siamangs, live in small family groups which are conveniently called harems. The family group is under the control of one dominant male who is the overlord. Until a primate is mature he acts as a sort of camp-follower, and most harems have one or two immature bachelors who are tolerated by the overlord as long as they do not attempt to claim sexual favours from his females. In fact he may even protect them from aggression. If the immature bachelor attempts sexual behaviour with a female he is chased away, or, if caught, bitten. The old male is completely despotic and does not hesitate to quell a quarrel with teeth or blows. He keeps his harem only by his strength, and as soon as the immature bachelors reach maturity he is challenged and may have to fight to keep his sexual position. Soko-lowsky describes the behaviour of the old male as being very dominant. He says:

He never indulged in games or sport, but preserved his austerity which was respected by the others. The sexual appetite of this male was very interest-ing to note. He was very exacting in this respect, and demanded intercourse every day with his females. For this purpose he sprang down, and seized one of the females who even if she struggled at first had to yield finally to his superior strength and submit to copulation. When he saw the young male attempt inter-course with the females, he sprang on the couple, and drove the young male off with bites and blows. The young male succeeded in effecting intercourse only when he waited until the old male was asleep, and then made sexual advances to the females who acceded. From my observation the old male exercised his power and strength in a despotic manner, and demanded sexually implicit submission.

It would seem that the sexual instinct is developed before the aggressive one, or before the physical means of aggression appear sufficiently for the ape to be aggressive. Nevertheless, aggression is closely linked with sex. This aggressive response may become turned on to the female and a so-called sadistic attack be made. This appears to be caused mainly when the female in a state of sexual skin engorgement presents a number of times and the overlord has mounted her as frequently as he wishes.

The aggressive responses are more frequently turned on to young bachelors who infringe the overlord's privileges or against other overlords. This occasionally occurs in a queer manifestation known as sexual fights. Zuckerman describes these sexual fights which occurred in the London Zoo, but whether they occur similarly in the wild state is improbable. He states:

The normal behaviour of most unmated male baboons suggests their passive indifference to the presence of females within the colony. On rare occasions, however, the atmosphere suddenly changes and every male appears to be trying, at the peril of his life, to secure a female in an attack upon a harem. The behaviour of one male influences another, and there have been few 'sexual fights" on Monkey Hill in which most members of the colony have not been engaged. Though mated animals have never been known to initiate a 'sexual fight', almost all of them have been observed participating once such a fight has begun. The 'sexual fights' on Monkey Hill have been so serious that they have been responsible for the deaths of thirty female baboons. After each of the serious fights had ended in the death of the female round which it raged, the colony settled down in a state of balance which, as subsequent events proved, contained all the seeds of further disruption.

The sexual fights apparently started a long time before hostilities broke out by the overlord showing signs of weakening in his aggression and avoiding his fellows. It did not apparently start by an attack of a number of bachelors gathered together for that purpose, but rather by one bachelor who challenged the overlord. The whole colony became electrified, and the overlord was too taken up with repelling the immature bachelors and family parties to take much notice of the bachelor who had captured his mate. Fighting took place for some days during which the female, who was entirely passive, was captured and recaptured again and again. The immature bachelors fought together in isolated groups and the wretched female, who was continuously ill-treated, and even unable to obtain food, finally succumbed to her miseries. The baboons were unable to appreciate that the female was dead and still treated her as a sex object. Zuckerman noticed that in one case a body continuously changed hands for twenty-four hours (before it could be removed) and that its owners carried it around by holding the waist, grooming it, examining its ano-genital region, and frequently copulating with it. This behaviour is comprehensible when we are able to appreciate that animals are unable to understand the meaning of death in the sense that we understand it, and lack of movement and response is not so strange in the case of the dead female, since a live female in these sexual fights is not responsive but allows herself to be dragged about and bitten without any attempt to struggle free. It is not surprising therefore that the animals utilize the dead body, and are unable to realize that the female is unable to be used as a mate. Although it is not relevant here, it is of interest to note that this lack of understanding and appreciation of death is seen also in the nursing of a dead baby which is continued until the infant is nothing but decomposing skin and bones. The mother does not nurse her dead infant from an excess of maternal affection but merely because the instincts which urge her to do so are mechanical and applied to the situation without appreciation of the alteration caused by death.

The observations of Washburn, de Vore, and Hall on baboons in natural surroundings showed that they develop normal, well-organized social groups with a dominance order and violence demonstrated only to predators outside. A cheetah, or other dangerous animal, would be repulsed by the males in combined attack. The females and young are protected by this outer circle of aggressive males.

Observations on restricted groups with no possibility of externalizing aggression coincide more with human behaviour in similar conditions, particularly when frustrated economically in slums &c.

The united aggression found in human beings against a stranger trying to invade their group, particularly if he is of another race or colour, is very reminiscent of the behaviour of primates. Moreover, it is significant that the greatest fury is produced when a female of the group is interested in the outsider.

Perhaps the most curious of primate behaviour is the 'masochistic' reaction first described by Tinklepaugh. It seems probable that this behaviour is 'artificial' to some extent, since it occurred only in captivity when the aggressive instinct was inhibited by obstacles from its proper outlet (i.e. attack). The behaviour was curious and worth noting. Tinklepaugh had the opportunity of observing an immature Rhesus monkey called Cupid which was placed in the same cage as a female macaque called Psyche. The male was at first dominated by the female, and although she frequently presented he did not mount her until after a fortnight had passed. He grew larger during the year and he and she finally presented normal sexual relations. All went well until two and a half years after they were first put together, when two young female Rhesus monkeys called Eva and Topsy were introduced. The male curously enough objected strongly to them, and although his mate, Psyche, had been removed, he attacked them both so viciously that they had to be removed. He showed sexual interest at the return of his original mate. It was impossible to reconcile this male monkey to the new females, and it still showed itself hostile to them even when it had been isolated and sexually deprived for a few weeks. Tinklepaugh believed that the monkey had built up a monogamous attachment and resented any attempt to break it down. Undeterred, nine months later Tinklepaugh tried again, and by muzzling Cupid tried to get him to accept Topsy. After a fortnight Topsy became attractive to him and their relations were normal. At this time Topsy was removed and his former mate, Psyche, returned to his cage. His attitude to her was normal, but he spent some time gazing at the cage where Topsy had been placed and seemed less attracted sexually to Psyche. Now a fortnight later Psyche was removed and Topsy reintroduced. Cupid mounted her but then immediately jumped off *and began to bite his own hind feet*. (Note: he had done this in play from the first time he had been observed.) This was noticed to be repeated and the sexual act was never completed. Tinklepaugh says: 'Suddenly, and with no previous signs of anger or particular emotion, Cupid lurched to the end of his chain and began to bite himself. In a few seconds he tore huge jagged rents in his already lacerated legs. Then, as though in intense pain, he jumped into the writer's arms.' (This latter outburst was caused by separation from both females in order to dress his wounds.) He was later returned to his original mate and resumed normal sexual activities with her, but remained in what in a human being would be described as psychotic depression. He sat motionless and uninterested and if interfered with would bite his legs. He continued to do this for months, so that Tinklepaugh finally decided that the only way to prevent him doing it was to whip him. He did so and the animal ceased to injure itself. It mated with Psyche and Eva and was leading a normal sexual life fourteen months later, but when it became excited there was still a tendency gently to bite its hind legs. Zuckerman says that similar behaviour is still very common amongst caged monkeys of all species. He noticed it in a male Japanese monkey and in a female pig-tailed monkey. He believes that it is the reaction to a natural dominant display. It is not unreasonable to suppose that the dominant reaction stimulates the biting reflexes and since the monkey must bite something it bites itself. The reversal of aggression from the external world on to the subject has been observed by others and is confirmed by Haslerud. He found with six adult chimpanzees and five children chimpanzees the animals responded to frustrating situations in a similar way to those described by Tinklepaugh and Zuckerman. He states 'Frustration may be revealed among other ways by hesitation at work on the task, reluctance to resume the task after a frustrated attempt, or various amounts of violence or emotion directed towards environmental objects *or towards the animal itself*' (my italics).

It has been noticed that the primate treated a dead female or a dead baby without any apparent appreciation of it being different from a live animal. It would seem that, similarly, primates have difficulty in appreciating the nature of other animals, although it appears that there is a comprehension of the sex. Bingham noticed the responses of a primate to a cat and the variation in these responses as the ape reached maturity. When it was young the ape showed only an aggressive response and made movements and so on which dominated it. On the other hand, when it was older it took a predominant sexual interest in it. He says of this latter:

Dwina (i.e. the ape) sat down close to the cat exploring its fur and picking at ears and tail. Presently she pushed her pelvis against the cat, holding the position momentarily, then continued backwards until she was lying on her back. With her head raised so that she could look forward she drew the cat on her ventral surface. She sat up several times and repeated the sitting and lying contacts. Once she turned over on knees and elbows and pushed backwards at the cat. This dorsal presentation was repeated at least once. As the activities progressed Dwina manifested increasing interest in the cat's tail. Two or three times while lying on her back, she pulled only the tail conspicuously to her genitalia. Once she did the same while crouching in dorsal presentation. I have never seen more pronounced sexual behaviour in Dwina.

It would appear then that the ape was able to use the cat as a sexual object or at least as the substitute for a mate. Unfortunately Bingham does not say whether this female ape had been kept in contact with the others or was in a state of sexual starvation when this observation was made. This behaviour with animals is not isolated and R. M. Yerkes observed similar behaviour with a female gorilla.

From the foregoing it should be easy to appreciate that the sub-human primate passes through at least two stages of psychosexual development. They are of interest because before they were known three similar stages were described in the human primate and will be considered when the emotional development of man is described.

Stage One

The stage of immaturity is one in which the young sub-human primate tends to show great diversity of activity, particularly that which is directly or indirectly connected with sexuality. It shows activities which have been described as auto-erotic and which I have described as autosexual (thus bringing it into line with homosexual and heterosexual in terminology) such as solitary masturbation, and exploring its own body. It also shows homosexual activities by mutual masturbation and frank homosexual relations with its fellows of the same sex. Amongst these are exhibitionistic, sadistic, and masochistic behaviour. It also shows a great interest in its excretory functions. All activity tends to begin with the mother and if it is not inhibited this activity is sexualized and encouraged by her.

Stage Two

In this stage the sub-human primate becomes mature and limits its activities to aggression and sexuality. The aggression is of course utilized to gain food and females. The mature male procures a mate or mates by its strength and by taking the female or females from other males. He ceases to show indiscriminate curiosity and to fritter away energy in constant movement. On the contrary he grows stolid and determined. He retains his energy either for food-seeking or other modes of aggression and for sexuality. It seems that all his energy has been canalized into these two activities; since this occurs after puberty it appears that this is the result of the endocrine activity.

The development and behaviour of the sub-human primate has been described so fully, partly because it throws a great deal of light on the development of the human primate and partly because it tends to show what instinctual reactions one can expect to find hidden under the surface if one examines the human mind. These instinctual reactions which we have so frequently to conjecture from the observations of others and ourselves form what we call in human primates the 'unconscious mind'. Since man has evolved from the lower primates it is not surprising if we find that there is some structural similarity in his mind to the minds of the lower primates, or even higher mammals below the primates. Whether this is so or not it is a fact that there is no single act of behaviour amongst those which we know in human beings as sexual perversions which is not to be seen either in the development, or in the maturity in the sub-human primate. These diverse sexual activities are not allowed to dominate those which lead to the fertilization of the female as they do in human perverts but they are there all the same. It is not unreasonable, therefore, at this stage for us to assume that sexual perversions are a residue of the phylogenetic development, which may or may not be a normal part of normal ontogenetic development, but which has made its appearance due to some abnormal factors probably of an environmental nature. This view, which was put forward in 1940, has since been amply confirmed by Beach and others.

REFERENCES

ADIE, S. J., and CRITCHLEY, M. (1927) *Brain*, **1**, 142.

BINGHAM, H. (1928) *The Sex Development in Apes*, Baltimore.

FREEDMAN, L. Z., and ROSVOLD, H. E. (1962) Sexual, aggressive and anxious behaviour in the laboratory macaque, *J. nerv. ment. Dis.*, **134**, 18–27.

HAMILTON, G. V. (1914) *J. Anim. Behav.*, **4**, 295–318.

HASLERUD, G. M. (1938) Frustration in chimpanzees, *Character and Pers.*, **7**, 132–9.

HEDIGER, HEINI P. (1962) in *Social Life of Early Man*, ed. Washburn, S. L., London.

HEUVELMANS, B. (1958) *On the Track of Unknown Animals*, London.

KEMPF, E. J. (1917) *Psychoanal. Rev.*, **4**, 127–54.

KÖHLER, W. (1925) *The Mentality of Apes*, London.

LASHLEY, K. S., and WATSON, J. B. (1913) *J. Anim. Behav.*, **3**, 114–39.

LOUTTIT, C. M. (1929) *J. comp. Psychol.*, **9**, 305–16.

MALINOWSKI, B. (1929) *Sexual Life of Savages*, London.

MASLOW, A. H., RAND, H., and NEWMAN, S. (1960) Some parallels between sexual dominance behaviour of infra-human primates and the fantasies of patients in psychotherapy, *J. nerv. ment. Dis.*, **131**, 202–12.

MICHAEL, R. P., and KEVERNE, E. B. (1968) Pheromones and sex, *Nature (Lond.)*, **218**, 5143.

MOSS, F. A. (1924) *J. exp. Psychol.*, **17**, 165–316.

SOKOLOWSKY, A. (1923) *Urol. cutan. Rev.*, **27**, 512–15.

TINKLEPAUGH, O. L. (1928) *J. comp. Psychol.*, **8**, 197–236.

YERKES, R. M. (1927) *Genet. Psychol. Monogr.*, part **2**, 377–551.

YERKES, R. M., and YERKES, A. W. (1929) *The Great Apes*, New Haven.

ZUCKERMAN, S. (1932) *The Social Life of Monkeys and Apes*, London.

3

THE INSTINCTUAL DEVELOPMENT
IN MAN

If we could calculate our knowledge of the emotional and instinctual development and its modifications by environment by the innumerable books which have been written on the child and its growth we should find most of our problems solved before we began. Unfortunately the majority of works have been inspired by the intellectual rather than the instinctual development, and interesting though the intellect may be, it does not help us to understand other than strictly conscious behaviour and throws little light on psychopathology.

In the human child we find the same confusing admixture of inherited and acquired factors so that it is inevitable that those who study it become divided into two schools based upon the influence of heredity and environment.

It is difficult for a psychologist studying behaviour not 'to put himself into the place of the animal' and anthropomorphize its behaviour. This is a thousand times more difficult in the case of an adult studying a child, and has been the cause of innumerable errors in the past. The school which has been most careful to avoid these errors has been the behaviourist school, so that I will use the observations they have made as far as possible to check those derived from elsewhere.

In spite of every precaution it is difficult always to know when we have the maturation of an inborn reflex, the utilization of reflexes which have matured in the past and are now being taken over by some fresh instinctual urge, or the appearance of some conditioned reflex due to the influence of environment on some inborn response. Unfortunately we have the most puzzling conditions in the erotic and aggressive instinct in which we are especially interested in this study. We might ask ourselves, for instance, whether in the human primate the sexual instinct (or perhaps better the sexual responses which appear before puberty) is 'sexual' from the beginning? Or is it a series of non-sexual patterns which later become utilized by the sexual urges just as the reflexes of locomotion become utilized? Or is it conditioned to its object by environment? Or are all activities, as the psychoanalytical school insists, innately sexual? There is evidence for each and all of these views and we must refrain from straining any one to fit a basic theory.

In spite of the conjectures and theories derived from retrospective material we know nothing which can be confirmed from other sources regarding the infant before birth. Does it think? If we accept the behaviourist's definition of thinking as subvocal speech or behaviour it might be difficult to imagine the child, which has not yet learned to speak, as thinking, although it seems not unreasonable to imagine it thinking as far as other small mammals think, if indeed they do. Does it feel? The child can react to pain at birth and possibly may be able to do so before birth. Minkowski observed foetuses taken from the uterus from two to two and a half months and found that they exhibited movements of the head, trunk, and limbs. The movements were slow, asymmetrical, uncoordinated, but responsive to change of position and cutaneous stimulation.

THE BEHAVIOURIST THEORIES

The behaviourist school entirely neglects 'consciousness' and merely studies reactions. It is believed that the child has certain innate reactions which are present at birth. It gains other reflex and instinctual responses by the maturation of inherited mechanisms. These inherited mechanisms are altered to adapt the child to its environment by the process which Pavlov has described as conditioning. Nothing else is needed.

The observation of innumerable infants from the time of birth has given us a certain number of facts regarding the child's equipment from the moment of birth. There is no doubt that the new-born child can sneeze, hiccough, cry, void urine and faeces, and erect the penis. This latter may be caused by warmth, a full bladder, stroking its penis, and other unknown stimuli. The most important reflex it possesses at birth is the sucking reflex which rapidly matures into the suckling instinct, and it soon finds the breast by trial and error. Apart from this the child can make at, or soon after birth, various movements of the limbs, head, and eyes.

It is obvious that the child possesses at birth all those reactions (except perhaps the capacity to bite) which can be utilized later in normal or abnormal sexual behaviour, but it is difficult from a purely objective point of view to know whether these 'sexual responses' (as erection of the penis, for instance) are activated by sexual or aggressive instincts or an admixture of both, or whether they are merely neutral reflex behaviour which is sexualized at a later date. There is no doubt that the child can often be found to be manipulating its penis or vagina during the early months following birth or more commonly at the end of the first year.

Watson says:

After observing a number of infants, especially during the first months of life, we suggest the following group of emotional reactions as belonging to the original and fundamental nature of man: *fear, rage,* and *love* (using love in approximately the same sense as Freud uses *sex*).

He found that the child tended to show fear, which was shown by 'catching of the breath', sudden closing of the eyelids, and crying, when there was (1) a loud noise, (2) sudden loss of support. Rage can be produced by hampering the child's movements such as holding its arms by its sides and is manifest by crying and screaming, breath-holding and slashing movements of the arms. He found that love was produced by

the stroking or manipulation of some erogenous zone, tickling, shaking, gentle rocking, patting and turning on the stomach across the attendant's knee. The response varies: if the infant is crying, crying ceases, a smile may appear, attempts at gurgling, cooing and finally, in slightly older children, the extension of the arms, which we should class as the forerunner of the embrace in adults.

Recent work has thrown a great deal of light on conditioning and much that is valuable in connexion with this study has been revealed. Firstly, regarding the time when conditioning can first be produced in the human child. The work of Kasatkin and Levikova has shown that a child can be conditioned to differentiate between two sounds in the first three months. Marquis experimented with ten infants who were fed only after they had heard a buzzer. After a week signs of conditioning appeared and the child started to make sucking movements as soon as it heard the buzzer. The cerebral cortex is not myelinated until at least ten days after birth, so that the conditioning must have been, in these cases, subcortical. Work in the Russian laboratories of Krasnogorski shows that it is easy to condition children until 4 years of age, but later it is not so reliable. Nevertheless, it is possible to condition human beings even after they have become adults. This is clearly shown by Hudgins' experiments. This worker found that it was possible to condition the pupillary reflex to react to verbal stimuli (as well as light), and no doubt this could be applied just as easily to other reflexes. Research work such as this does show that the modern psychologist's insistence on the importance of infantile environment is not exaggerated, and since the conditioning is subcortical, and presumably hypothalamic, the experiences must be capable of influencing the endocrine mechanisms and fundamental reactions much more than those influences to which the child is subjected at a later date.

It is a pity that the behaviourists have had no opportunity of studying individuals minutely from the objective point of view until later life, but few behaviouristic studies go beyond the first year. Watson says:

A good deal of organization and development takes place after two hundred days. Some very complex situations have yet to be faced, such as masturbation (and in boys especially, the first masturbation after puberty); the first menstruation in girls; complex situations connected with family life, such as quarrels between the parents, corporal punishment and the death of the loved ones, all of which have to be met for the first time. We know from observation that these do become hitched up to emotional reactions; whether they are original or transferred does not appear from our studies.

I would like to put forward some views which are to be regarded as supplementary to those of others rather than to replace them. Firstly it seems to be a universal rule in instinctual behaviour that *a new and un-encountered situation or object can be dealt with only in terms of a previously encountered situation or object*. A dog in a puzzle-box, for instance, tends to utilize previously acquired reactions to free itself. It scratches or bites and never gently paws the locks because it has never learned or acquired the behaviour of gently pawing something to perform an act. It is only gradually that the scratching changes to a different and more appropriate type of reaction. The child's first instinctual reaction must be to birth, but we know so little objectively of the child's reactions to birth that we have to disregard it. The next situation is the instinctual suckling with the object being the nipple and milk. Is it surprising if the law stated above is true that the child tends to suck any fresh object which comes into its ken? It may suck its toes, its thumb, or anything else which it meets *because it has no capacity to do anything else with them.* Having only encountered the suckling situation it has no instinctual knowledge of any other type of behaviour and such must be acquired by trial and error and conditioning. It is not surprising therefore that sucking may remain the dominant reaction if the child fails to find other and more suitable reactions. This would explain much of the oral behaviour of perverts.

Again, the only fluid with which the child has any instinctual knowledge is its mother's milk. The fluid the child has only one reaction towards—that is to suck it into its mouth. When the child encounters other fluids such as bath water, urine, and semi-fluid stools it does not seem unexpected that it follows its instinct (which says to it: 'swallow the stuff') and swallows it.

A persistence of this behaviour would again explain many of the abnormal acts such as coprophilia which is found in young children. Similarly, when the biting reflexes appear the child has an instinct to bite. It has no instinctual object and so bites what is nearest to it—i.e. the nipple. It has already instinctual knowledge of nipples, but of no other things.

Again, when sexual patterns start to appear, and from animal and infantile observation it seems that they do so before puberty, it is not surprising that they should be directed against the mother, since this is the first woman of whom the child has any instinctual or acquired knowledge at all.

The manner in which the mother reacts to the child and the way in which she conditions it must be the pattern in which the child will react to all women it will meet in later life. Similarly with the father when the child is old enough to differentiate him from the mother (since it is reasonable to suppose that it is not possible for it to do so before it has reached a certain amount of maturity).

There is no doubt that all this suggests a certain lack of definition in the instinctual aims and objects, but this is true of the sub-human primate and of man himself. There is not the unfailing precision in the higher type of mammals such as one finds in the solitary wasp which kills the same type of caterpillar in the same way by stinging it in more or less the same spot and stores it in the same type of nest, and so on, all by instinctual or inherited dispositions. The fluidity of behaviour found in higher animals allows them to adapt themselves to novel situations but carries with it the danger of malformation as well.

The infant has to adjust itself to the parents and probably the process I have described as 'moulding of the personality', or acquiring reactions from those about it, starts very early. This I do not think is the same thing as the Freudian introjection, which is limited, more or less, to the oral stages: but continues right on through the child's life until puberty, when the youth tends to rebel against his parents, and refuses to accept them any longer as models.

This moulding means that the child unconsciously starts behaving like the parents and acquiring their responses. It is a process, similar but less restricted in time, to the imprinting described by Spalding and confirmed by Lorenz.

It can easily be seen how valuable such a process is since it eliminates a great deal of the danger of trial and error, as well as the wearisome repetition of active learning. Anyone who has seen a tiny girl trying to use a sweeping brush, or a little boy his father's plane, cannot fail to realize that the child is reacting in a parental way. No doubt this process is partly conscious, but the basis appears to have been formed unconsciously.

Like all instinctual, innate, reactions it is valuable as long as it is applied in the right environment, but fails if this is unsuitable. To be satisfactory it is necessary that the child has both its parents and feels affection for them. If it is deprived of the proper environment, as when the father dies or the child is brought up in an orphanage, it will be in danger of being imprinted with the wrong reactions, and this, I believe, is the cause of some conditions, such as homosexuality.

The small child has, as Watson suggests, a variety of difficult situations to face, and we have as yet had little opportunity to study them objectively. Knowledge gained from the Child Guidance Clinic does help us a little, and it is mainly from this that the following account is written.

The child has really little opportunity to adjust itself to one situation before it has to prepare itself for another. No sooner has it adapted itself to its mother and father and perhaps brothers and sisters than it is forced to enter a new situation and adjust itself to school life. It probably does so by utilizing the reactions which it has learned from its father and mother. If it has had a normal home it has adequate reactions, but if it has been frightened or bullied at home it behaves as though it will be bullied at school. There is no doubt that school life is one of adjustment to aggression, just as the small monkey or ape has to adjust itself to an environment of aggression also. It is, however, modified more than the ape's world by the intervention of adults.

Also, at school it has to adapt itself to novel sexual situations and it is instructed in masturbation in most cases by its companions. Usually this is homosexual and exhibitionistic, sometimes sadistic and masochistic, in its nature. A certain number of children are, unfortunately, instructed in sex prematurely by adults, and, again, of course, mentally deformed by ridiculous teaching by those who should know better on the evils of normal sexual manifestations such as masturbation.

The growing child also is forced to adapt itself to an adjustment of leaving its parents, since in many countries the custom of the child leaving home and living in boarding-school exists. Hollingworth says:

Emancipation from the family is now left among modern civilized peoples to private discretion. Since voluntary habit-revision in any phase of conduct is always difficult, the result of this policy is that many persons pass through adolescent years without being rid of their cradle habits, or as Watson calls them: 'nest habits'. Others are permanently distorted in their attitudes by the struggles which they wage against the blind forces of parental possessiveness.

The work of Bowlby and his school suggests that separation from the mother between the age of six months and two years can have a very serious effect on the young child. Others have suggested that some, although no doubt slighter, response can be produced by such separation at a later age. Indeed, it is believed that children who go to boarding-schools tend to become home-sick (depressed and neurotic) for a longer or shorter time, and that some permanent effect may remain, so that the child is less affectionate to his parents, more self-centred and more emotionally interested in his companions. Such reactions could form the basis of homosexual attachments and probably do in some cases.

It is at adolescence that this struggle reaches its acme and the child comes to adjust itself to adult sexuality. Hollingworth says further:

It is clear both from common observation and from statistical study that adolescence is the period when impulses to mate come to their full development. Data collected by Hamilton show that the peak for frequency of love affairs is reached, in persons of good intelligence, in the years between thirteen and twenty-one. This general statement holds for both sexes, though girls rise to their peak of frequency more sharply and a little earlier.

Hollingworth believes that the taboo on sex was established amongst primitive peoples because of the economic state of adolescence which made it impossible to support a wife during that period. This has, unfortunately, grown more and more acute in the struggle of civilization. She points out that dangerous methods are frequently used to inhibit the sexual desires of adolescents.

In the case of boys, the attempt has often been made to shame their natural desires by presenting them with the idea that women are sacred and too fair and fine to be regarded with any but the most worshipful thoughts. It is suggested to the boy that in considering women he should always have his mother and sister in mind, and should speak, act and think in terms of mother and sister in his approach to women. These are, however, very unrealistic habits of thought, and if taken seriously may do great harm to the adolescent boy. Cut off from the natural attitude towards 'good' girls, he cannot but discover sooner or later that not all girls are 'good', and that there are many women whose business is to solicit from him that very behaviour which he has been led to consider 'bad'. A schism is likely to be set up in the boy's emotional life between 'good' and 'bad' women which will render it possible to approach none but the latter in a natural manner, since the former have been identified with mother and sister.

The female is sometimes 'protected' in a similar way by making men frightening and sinister so that she may never be able to make a proper mating either.

It is believed that the child is not objectively heterosexual before the development of the sexual machinery and reproductive power. Hughes obtained 1,029 replies to a questionnaire and discovered that the average age in which sex consciousness appeared was $12\frac{1}{2}$ years. Hollingworth believes that it is during adolescence that the emotional attitude of heterosexuality becomes normally established, and that the four or five years following puberty are the best years for its development. The member of the opposite sex about the same age is the most potent stimulus. Age, beauty of face, in some cases of body, limbs or features, manner of dressing, intelligence, and (probably by 'education') various moral attributes such as honesty and ambition are most attractive. Woodworth believes that the novel and forbidden are very attractive also.

In her very valuable paper Hollingworth points out how this strong growth of the erotic instinct at puberty can become distorted by environmental pressure. She compares the adolescent with an animal in a trap and points out that he or she is puzzled in the same way as Thorndyke's animals were confused in puzzle-boxes and insists that:

Supposed methods of preventing the development of the sexual impulse, such as segregation from young members of the opposite sex, taboo and threats, do not suppress the growth of the impulse, but merely determine that it cannot achieve its biologically determined objects. The craving due to normal development does not cease but impels the organism to trial and error activity, in the course of which any set of habits may be learned that will give release or partial release from the craving.

We must go to the Tuamotuan to see sex as it should be: without the connotation of 'filthy' which spoils it in 'civilization'. It is accepted as a normal healthy part of life from the beginning, as 'all things created by Tane are good and beautiful'.

Clifford Gessler says in his book, *The Dangerous Islands*, of the sex dances of the young people:

The dancers are the young unmarried people whose trial matings are a recognized custom. They range in age from fourteen to eighteen or nineteen. By the time the Tuamotuan is twenty, he or she usually is ready to settle down and raise a family. But society in this still relatively primitive land concedes what among us is considered 'advanced modernity'—the right of youth to its period of experimentation. It is not merely a matter of letting youth have its play time. The people of Tepuka believe it is necessary for normal development. It is a custom as old, probably, as the Polynesian people; as old, perhaps, as the lost Central Asian race from whom, in the dim beginnings of humanity, both they and we may have evolved.

Elsewhere he points out that shy maidens are not allowed to shrink away from normal sex (possibly shy young men are encouraged in other ways), but are taken away by the young men and introduced to what is believed is good for them. There are no frigid spinsters in Tuamotu!

Numerous observers have noted that if animals such as rats are segregated from members of the opposite sex and develop with those of the same sex, homosexual behaviour tends to occur.

Investigation of the behaviour in adolescents in both normal and 'reformatory' schools in which segregation occurs shows that this rule applies just as exactly in humans as in the lower mammals. In man, however, a certain amount of self-manipulation and masturbation replaces the homosexual behaviour of the rat.

Apart from segregation I believe that the sexuality can be injured by lack of success in sexual behaviour at the time of puberty, or painful results from attempted sexual behaviour (such as gonorrhoea). It would appear that this can cause the adolescent to fall back on previous reactions by Hughlings Jackson's principle of the dissolution of the nervous system, and in this way some abandoned infantile reaction returns as lower reflex systems return with the destruction of the higher centres. Or possibly the behaviour may appear as a substitution for heterosexuality, since the latter has been painfully conditioned. In any case it must be admitted that the first act of coitus is tremendously important and insufficient study has been made of it and its results.

The importance of the first intercourse being normal is shown in the case of a woman who attended a clinic under my care. She was suffering from depression, and while undergoing treatment it was discovered that she could obtain sexual pleasure only from having intercourse *a posteriori*. On further investigation it was found that she first had intercourse with her husband when they were engaged, and for some reason this position was the first adopted. This tremendous influence of the first intercourse was pointed out many years ago by Binet, and recently more modern authors have drawn attention to it also.

There is no doubt that the behaviourists and their related schools have done an enormous amount of spade-work which is yet to be applied to psychological medicine, and this point of view is a valuable one in check-ing the observations and discoveries of other schools and correcting their theories. It would be absurd, however, to pretend that they are in any way complete, and there is still a great deal of behaviour to be studied in an objective manner.

PSYCHOANALYTIC THEORIES[1]

In 1909 Freud first made clear his theories regarding the emotional growth of the child and its relations to the perversions. These theories created a certain amount of hostility at first but have since been studied and compared with animal behaviour, and to a certain extent substantiated by it. Levy-Suhl points out that only in man and the elephant is there such a delayed puberty, and suggests that this is due to the fact that both are survivors of the glacial periods, and this has been confirmed to some extent by the work of Bolk. There is still a great deal of study and confirma-tion to be done, particularly regarding the subdivisions which Freud has made in the broad outlines of his sexual theories.

His book, *Three Contributions to the Theory of Sex*, was firstly a study of the perversions and their nature occurring in the human being, and then a correlation of them with infantile behaviour which Freud believed to be sexual, and lastly a study of puberty and its sexual transformations. Many of Freud's views regarding the emotional development of the child have been modified and added to by Karl Abraham and Melanie Klein, so that the modified theory rather than the original will be described here. The psychoanalysts believe that the child's emotional interest is from the beginning sexual in nature. This Freud has conveniently named 'libido', and parts which are highly sexualized he says have a strong 'libidinal cathexis'. The emotional development passes through a number of stages

[1] The theories of Adler and Jung have not been used here because they are insufficiently explanatory. No doubt Adler's views on aggression can be used to give a basis for sadism, but they are insufficient for the other psychosexual abnormalities. Indeed, he never really wrote much on them.

Jung, if one had approached him, might have 'interpreted' sexual abnormality with reference to innumerable myths which entail its forms, but this would explain nothing, except the psychology of those who composed them long ago. Moreover, like Adler, he wrote little which really concerns deviations.

according to which organ is enveloped in libido. How far each stage is a maturation, and how far it is due to conditioning, Freud does not say, but it is possible according to him for the main bulk of libido to become 'fixated' at one of the earlier stages—apparently due to conditioning or to 'regress' if obstructed in its development.

Freud first suggested that the sexual development of the child was in three stages. This accords somewhat with what appears to be the nature of the sexual development in the sub-human primate. In the monkey and ape there is apparently complete agreement amongst biologists that the development occurs in two stages: firstly, a stage of diverse sexual activity which we shall see also occurs in the human; secondly, a stage of mature sexuality in which the animal abandons much of its infantile behaviour and reacts in an adult and somewhat heterosexual manner.

In the child Freud believed that there were three stages, and they were all completed before the age of 7 years. Firstly, the stage of polymorphous perversity in which the emotional interest (libido) is concentrated on the child's own body. This Freud called the narcissistic stage, and it consists of all the stages before the Oedipus stage. Then there is an Oedipus stage in which the child concentrates all its affection on its mother and hates its father. I suspect that Freud has not carried this sufficiently far back and believe that the child feels rivalry with the father for the mother's love from the moment it is sufficiently mature to formulate the existence of a male parent. It tends to identify itself with its mother and so reacts in a feminine manner (i.e. it is homosexual), so that this stage is one of homosexuality. When the child has successfully passed through this stage and is able to feel affection for its father it reaches the adult sexual stage which is, of course, one of complete heterosexuality, taking for its object some woman outside the family not identified with the mother in any way.

These stages have been divided, or rather the first stage has been divided, into a number of other minor stages, and these are named by the organ or action of that organ upon which the sexual emotion or libido is concentrated during its development.[1]

STAGES OF LIBIDINAL DEVELOPMENT

The First Oral Stage

This is present at birth when the child starts suckling. It obtains all its (sexual) pleasure from suckling, and indeed this is its only function. If the child cannot suck the breast it sucks its thumb or anything else. The sexual theory of sucking was not an original view, as Freud acknowledged, since it had previously been formulated by Lindner. Freud says of this sucking:

[1] It is impossible here to do justice to the whole intricate system of psychology elaborated by Freud. For a simple account see my *Modern Discoveries in Medical Psychology*.

Thumbsucking, which manifests itself in the nursing baby and which may be continued till maturity or throughout life, consists in the rhythmic repetition of sucking contact with the mouth (the lips), wherein the purpose of taking nourishment is excluded. A part of the lip itself, the tongue, which is another preferable skin region within reach, and even the big toe—may be taken as objects for sucking. Simultaneously there is also a desire to grasp things, which manifests itself in a rhythmical pulling of the ear lobe and which may cause the child to grasp a part of another person (generally the ear) for the same purpose. The pleasure-sucking is connected with the entire exhaustion of attention and leads to sleep or even to a motor reaction in the form of an orgasm. Pleasure-sucking is often combined with a rubbing contact with certain sensitive parts of the body, such as the breast and external genitals. It is by this road that many children go from thumbsucking to masturbation.

Abraham points out in this case that there are three definite characteristics of this infantile sexuality. Firstly, the instinct is not directed on to another but is concentrated on the self, i.e. it is autosexual or auto-erotic. Secondly, it is not a separate phenomenon but dependent on the function which is important for the preservation of life—i.e. suckling. The pleasure in sucking is therefore the pleasure which is manifested in the gratification of an instinct even though not derived from its proper function. Thirdly, it is attained by the stimulation of a specially sensitive zone (such zones are known as 'erogenous zones') that is to say, the lips. This erogenic quality differs in different children, since some suck more than others, but whether this is an inborn or an acquired tendency is not known.

Freud and Abraham pointed out that kissing, a normal adult method of showing erotic emotion, is related to this sucking, and indeed it is intimately related to sexual intercourse since, as we noticed in the case of apes, even in the sub-human primates (as well as in man) kissing is frequently an accompaniment of intercourse.

SCHEME OF LIBIDINAL DEVELOPMENT
(Partly after Abraham)

Stages of libidinal organization	Stages of object love
1. Earlier Oral Stage (Sucking)	Auto-erotism (without Object) } Pre-ambivalent
2. Later Oral Stage (Cannibalistic)	Narcissism (Total Incorporation of Object)
3. Earlier Anal-sadistic Stage (Expulsion)	Partial Love with Incorporation
4. Later Anal-sadistic Stage (Control)	Partial Love
5. Urethral Stage	Partial Love
6. Earlier Genital Stage (Masturbatory)	Object Love with Exclusion of Genitals
7. Final Genital Stage	Object Love Post-ambivalent

It is assumed that up to the appearance of the teeth the emotions which are felt by the child are purely erotic ones. With the appearance of the teeth there is the capacity for aggression and the emotion of hate or aggression appears.

The Second Oral Stage

This is the stage of eating. The child probably naturally rids itself of a great deal of its urge to eat by the biting of hard objects and hard food such as rusks. It is believed by Melanie Klein that the child first tends to turn this hatred on to its parents—its mother first of all, and in fantasy consumes its mother. This produces feelings of guilt and fear and ideas of retribution from the hated mother. Abraham thought that the cannibal-istic delusions of the manic-depressive were derived from this source. It seems possible that if the child grows teeth, as is often the case, before the time of weaning, it might tend to feel instinctual urges to devour the breast, and women frequently complain that the child, at the end of the breast-feeding period, does bite them.

I believe that in some cases the child works out a rudimentary type of Oedipus situation in the oral stages. Deprived of the maternal breast for some reason he fantasies that his father has had it instead, and develops thoughts of attacking and biting off his penis for taking it away. This pro-duces all sorts of retaliatory fantasies of having his own penis bitten off.

The importance of this mechanism is that it sometimes appears to be related to subsequent impotence since sexual pleasure and oral pleasure derived from breast sucking is equated and is felt to be punishable.

Freud believes that the process of introjection or identification with the mother (and later the father) takes place by some fantasy of consuming the parent. It is by this identification that he believes that the boy identi-fies himself with his mother, and if he does not later identify himself with his father he remains homosexual.

Since the child has developed hatred it tends to mix this hatred with affection and to show a mixture of both as an emotional manifestation. This is known by the term which Bleuler coined, 'ambivalence'. It tends to be manifested in the display of biting as an erotic motif even in normal people and particularly in children who frequently say: 'I love you so much I could gobble you up' and similar phrases. [1]

The next stage is the anal stage. Freud believes that the libido or

---

[1] Those who would suggest that oralism is a symptom discoverable only in abnormal people might consider what is revealed unconsciously in poetry. Christina Rossetti, for example, writes:

> Did you miss me?
> Come and kiss me.
> Never mind my bruises,
> Hug me, kiss me, suck my juices
> Squeezed from goblin fruits for you,
> Goblin pulp and goblin dew.
> Eat me, drink me, love me:
> Laura, make much of me.

emotional interest becomes shifted from the mouth to the anus. Again it is not clearly stated whether this is in the process of maturation or whether it is a process of conditioning.

The First Anal Stage

The first anal stage is concerned with the process of expulsion. The child obtains its sexual pleasure from the expelling of faeces, and if we are to believe Melanie Klein this expulsion is to remove the (fantasy) consumed parents and free the child from them. There is no doubt that little children do obtain pleasure in passing their faeces (as indeed do some adults). This interest in faeces may make the child wish to consume them. Abraham calls this the stage of 'partial love with incorporation'. He says:

In the stage of 'partial love with incorporation', as we have seen, the love object is represented by one part of itself. The small child has an ambivalent attitude towards that part (penis, breast, excrement, &c.) that is, he desires it and rejects it at the same time. It is not until he has completely given up his tendency to incorporate objects—a change which according to our scheme does not happen until the fourth stage—that he adopts a contemptuous attitude towards those parts, and especially towards excrement. In this stage excrement becomes for him the representative of everything that he does not want to keep.

The Second Anal Stage

In this stage the child is believed to obtain its sexual pleasure from the retention of its faeces, and so this is the 'stage of control'. Abraham believes that this is the stage of partial love.

The Urethral Stage

The next stage is the urethral stage, and curiously enough the psycho-analysts have not divided this stage into two. They speak merely of the urethral stage, and believe that the child obtains sexual pleasure from the passage of its urine. One might have believed, by analogy from the anal and oral stages, that the urethral stage would be divided into at least two stages: (1) a stage of expulsion, and (2) a stage of retention; but these have never been described, although they may exist.

The Phallic Stage

With the urethral stage the sexual interest which has been concentrated on the mouth and then the anus is believed to reach the genitalia. It is not surprising therefore that it should be displaced from the urethra on to the genitalia proper, and that the child should start to obtain its sexual pleasures from the manipulation of its penis or vagina. This is the stage of masturbation and of 'object love with the exclusion of the genitals' according to Abraham. That is to say that, although the child obtains its sexual pleasure from manipulation of its own genitalia, it does not recognize the genitals of those it loves.

Final Genital Stage

In this stage the child is able to love some love object completely and so to have normal intercourse when it becomes adult. It must be recognized that all these stages are supposed to occur before about the age of 7 or even earlier, but only if the child passes successfully through them is it able to attain adult emotional sexual behaviour in later life.

It is obvious that although this elaborate scheme explains a great deal of the sexual perversions and abnormalities, it is inadequate without the addition which Freud made. That is to say, that the child is in its earliest years 'polymorphous-perverse' and able to enjoy sexual pleasure in the most diverse manners. For example, Freud says:

It is instructive to know that under the influence of seduction the child may become polymorphous-perverse and may be misled into all sorts of transgressions. This goes to show that it carries along the adaptation for them in its disposition. The formation of such perversions meets but slight resistance because the psychic dams against sexual transgressions, such as shame, loathing and morality—which depend on the age of the child—are not yet erected or are only in the process of formation. In this respect the child perhaps does not behave differently from the average uncultured woman in whom the same polymorphous-perverse disposition exists. Such a woman may remain sexually normal under usual conditions, but under the guidance of a clever seducer she will find pleasure in every perversion and will retain the same as her sexual activity. The same polymorphous or infantile disposition fits the prostitute for her professional activity, and in an enormous number of prostitutes and women to whom we must attribute an adaptation for prostitution, even if they do not follow this calling, it is absolutely impossible not to recognize in their uniform disposition for all perversions the universal and primitive human.

This is a very useful and explanatory theory, but one wonders whether perhaps the ingenious and overwide explanation should be the correct one. The fact that a child can be 'misled into all sorts of transgressions' would suggest that there was the possibility that it had a capacity to acquire perverse sexuality just as readily as that it had an inherent faculty such as polymorphous perversity.

Freud believes that all these infantile activities are forgotten, or rather are repressed, so that it is very rare for anyone to remember them. He believes that there is a latent period following infancy until puberty when the endocrines reawaken sexuality and canalize it into the seeking of a definite object.

After the age of 7 the child has its sexuality more or less mapped out, and Freud believes that it tends to react like an adult. He points out that the new sexual aim which appears at puberty, in the boy, is the capacity to discharge his sexual products and that this causes enhanced pleasure. He suggests that the role of the erogenous zones now is to produce tension and the desire for more pleasure, so driving on the motor acts which tend to bring the coitus to a close. He names this pleasure obtained from the erogenous zones 'fore-pleasure', and it is to be contra-distinguished from that which is obtained at the end of the sexual act and which he calls 'end-pleasure'. He believes that many of the perversions can be explained by a lingering of the fore-pleasure which gave an abnormal amount of gratification in the infantile period.

It is a pity that adolescence has not been studied more widely by the psychoanalytical school, but so much attention has been given to infantile sexuality that it has been crowded out. This is particularly to be noted in the teachings of Melanie Klein, whose brilliant investigations have been driven earlier and earlier into the nature of infantile thinking and whose work has fascinated analysts to the exclusion of just as valuable studies of puberty. The fact that the pubescent child is not an easy subject may have something to do with this neglect. The best and most authoritative paper on puberty is that of Ernest Jones. He suggests that the appearance of maturity is shown by (1) intellectual growth, (2) greater integration of the mind with a heightened capacity for inhibition, (3) less egocentricity, (4) diminished dependence due to the breaking of infantile attachments, and (5) physical changes. The important point which he makes, however, is that before these changes can come about the child has to pass through a recapitulation of its infantile sexual stages. He believes that:

At puberty a regression takes place in the direction of infancy, of the first period of all, and the person lives over again, though on another plane, the development he passed through in the first five years of life. . . . Put in another way, it signifies that the individual recapitulates and expands in the second decennium of life the development he passed through during the first five years of life just as he recapitulates during these first five years the experiences of thousands of years in his ancestry and during the prenatal period those of millions of years; I believe this to be true of other mental aspects than purely sexual ones, though it is in the latter sphere that it is most definitely observed. It is, of course, obvious that by the word 'recapitulates' one does not mean simply 'repeats' any more than in speaking of the embryo recapitulating his infra-human ancestry we mean that he literally repeats it.

He shows clearly that there are features of adolescence which can be explained on this theory, and states:

That the auto-erotic phase belongs to the earlier stages of adolescence rather than the later is familiar enough knowledge. With it goes the tendency to introversion and a richer life of secret fantasy, together with the greater pre-occupation with the self and the varying degrees of shyness and self-consciousness, which are so often prominent features during adolescence. The ano-sadistic phase varies in intensity, but it is characteristic enough for the nice gentle lad of ten to change into the rough and untidy boy of thirteen, to the great distress of his female relatives; extravagance, procrastination, obstinacy, passion for collecting, and other traits of anal-erotic origin often become especially prominent at this age. The narcissism may be shown in either a positive or negative way; the bumptiousness, conceit and cock-sureness of youth are as well recognized characteristics of this stage in development as are the opposite ones of self-depreciation, uncertainty and lack of confidence; the two sets commonly alternate in the same person. The homosexual phase is more often positive than negative and is far commoner during adolescence than at any later age; that it varies enormously in intensity in different individuals is of course well known.

Elsewhere he points out that the instinctual variations at puberty are due to the fixations at the infantile period, and that the boy who has difficulty in passing through the masturbationary stage of puberty has had a fixation in a similar stage during infancy.

When it comes to criticizing the Freudian viewpoint it is by no means easy to do so. The whole system of philosophy which Freud has constructed is so intimately bound together that to destroy one point one must destroy the whole. There are a few comments which might be made, however. For example, Freud's view that the instincts are composed of death instincts and life instincts from the first seems to me to be unfounded. The fact is that it is impossible to discover the nature of the emotions from observation of the normal or abnormal child, but they can be shown only by the study of retrospective material unearthed by analysis. Now if we study a psychotic by this means (and the psychotic is supposed to have regressed as far as possible) we find that far from having any love, his unconscious mind is full of aggression. He may be bound to his mother but it is not by love but hate that he is bound. It would appear to me therefore that *the new-born child is born in a state of hate and has no other emotion but hate in its repertoire*. It cannot, of course, demonstrate this hate until it acquires means to do so by growing teeth and nails, but as soon as it does possess such means it shows its hate unmistakably.

This view, which was put forward some twenty years ago, has recently been supported by Lorenz on phylogenetic grounds. He states:

Intra-specific aggression is millions of years older than personal friendship and love. During long epochs of the earth's history there have been animals that were certainly extraordinarily fierce and aggressive. Nearly all reptiles of the present day are aggressive and it is unlikely that those of antiquity were less so. But the personal bond is known only in teleost fishes, birds and mammals, that is in groups that did not appear before the Early Tertiary period. Thus intra-specific aggression can certainly exist without its counterpart, love, but conversely there is no love without aggression.

Dart, an anthropologist, believes that primitive man evolved from *Proconsul* purely because of his aggression. In the study of the playing of children and their emotions made by Melanie Klein there appears to be much more hate exhibited than love since (if we accept her interpretations which have not met with universal approval) the objects which children destroy with such gusto are symbolic of parents and brothers or sisters. She states, 'The idea of an infant from six to twelve months trying to destroy its mother by every method at the disposal of its sadistic tendencies—with its teeth, nails and excreta and with the whole of its body, transformed in imagination into all kinds of dangerous weapons—presents a horrifying, not to say an unbelievable, picture to our minds.' It would appear that these children—who are nearer to the new-born child —lack a great deal of the postulated erotic instinct, or at least that it is more difficult to discover. This hate is slowly transmuted into love, and it is in this transmutation that development occurs. Perhaps no one ever succeeds in transforming it completely, but the more highly developed the individual the more of the hatred he has changed to love.

One might ask again: Are the stages described by Freud produced by maturation or are they the product of conditioning? There seems a considerable amount of evidence that these stages do really exist. First, because we can observe similar if abbreviated stages in the sub-human primate, and secondly, because there is endocrine evidence such as the work of Broster *et al.* on the effect of endocrine dystrophies and the result of the restoration of hormone balance in cases of hyperadrenalism. If this is so, do the divisions such as the various oral and anal stages exist? This is not half so certain, and it is difficult by any objective experimental procedure to reveal them, nor can the animal observers help us in this matter.

Fortunately we are not trying to destroy the Freudian philosophy but examining it as a means of explaining and treating the abnormalities of sex. It must be admitted that the Freudian theory of infantile sexuality accords exactly with the behaviour of the sub-human primates, at least as far as its broad outlines are concerned. It is completely explanatory and it would be absurd not to utilize these theories, at least in conjunction with the behaviourist theories, to explain the difficult phenomena of sexuality.

We may mention here the exhaustive investigations which Kinsey, Pomeroy, and Martin have performed in America. This tremendous project is an attempt to study human behaviour from the biological point of view without preconceived theories and uninfluenced by ethical considerations. As might be expected these research workers met with a certain amount of opposition but this has been overcome. The completed studies comprise over 100,000 interviews of both male and female subjects and their first volume is based on 5,300 case-histories of individuals between the ages of 4 and 90 years. The material obtained has been sorted into groups according to various factors such as race, marital status, age and educational level, religious adherence, and so on. The sexual behaviour is considered with regard to early sexual growth, total sexual outlet, masturbation, nocturnal emissions, premarital, marital, and extramarital intercourse, homosexuality, and animal contacts as well as prostitution, and 'petting'.

These writers came to many interesting conclusions such as the fact that although the nature of sexual activity may change there is never complete cessation until the erotic life ceases with senility; that sublimation is so subtle or so rare as to be rather an academic possibility than a demonstrated actuality; that there is little or no change in attitude or sexual pattern after the middle teens; that variation in position in intercourse occurs much more frequently in the more intellectual group than in the duller types, and so on.

Many of the observations made in animal studies were confirmed; for example, Kinsey, Pomeroy, and Martin point out that the young boy is erotically excitable long before he is physically capable of intercourse, which compares with what has been seen in the sub-human primates. Some of the sources of excitement are not sexual in nature but become more and more sexualized towards puberty. The large percentage of what would once have been regarded as 'abnormal' or perverse behaviour in pre-adolescent sex-play suggests that there is strong evidence of Freud's polymorphoperversity in young boys. Other important facts are found in the division of society into social groups which develop their own codes of sexual behaviour, utterly at variance with similar groups in a different level of society, the toleration of premarital intercourse and condemnation of 'petting' in some groups with the exact opposite in others, and so on.

The frequence of many forms of what have previously been regarded as uncommon and perverse behaviour must sooner or later cause some alteration in the law. Even 'abnormal behaviour' such as is found in animal contacts was found by these writers to be much more common than previously believed.

There can be no doubt that importance of work of this kind, which fills in many of the lacunae left by previous researches made by Hamilton, Davis, Dickinson and Beam, Finger and others, cannot be overestimated. It is impossible to record all these extensive researches in brief and in any case much will have to be confirmed. Many of the conclusions are not applicable to sexual life in England since, as the writers themselves point out, the *sexual mores* are not only different in various nations but show considerable variation in upper and lower levels of the same society. Nevertheless in general one can say that the conclusions reached seem to uphold the statements made in my *Sexual Perversions and Abnormalities* (1940) and show that clinical experience on much smaller numbers has not been misleading.

There is no doubt, whatever point of view from which they are regarded, that the sexual perversions are the product of incomplete development, both phylogenetically and ontogenetically. They are reminiscences both of the racial and individual growth. This is evident both from studies of the mind from the external behaviouristic point of view and internally by psychoanalysis. The word 'perversion' suggests a deliberate, 'volitional' deviation from normal sexuality; that being offered the chance of normal genital satisfaction the pervert wilfully chooses to take the path of abnormality. *Nothing is further from the truth.* In many cases we shall see that there is no sexual satisfaction from, or ability to indulge in, normal sexual life. The pervert is forced into abnormal behaviour by the same forces which drive on the normal man to normal sexual behaviour. He does not obtain excessive sexual satisfaction from his abnormality—as many people, particularly laymen, seem to think—but merely the same modicum of pleasure that the normal man obtains so much more easily by his normal sexuality. Those who are completely developed have no interest in perversions; satisfaction from the sexual act is so full that to suggest a perversion to the completely adult person is like offering a man a stone when he asks for bread.

It is worth reminding the reader that the normal sexual act is one upon which the greatest emphasis is laid upon the copulatory behaviour itself. This should give the complete psychical and physiological satisfaction. It must be admitted that, in a certain number of cases, the sexual act occurs without the emphasis being on copulation, but the act itself is still biologically satisfactory—i.e. capable of fertilization. It is only when the emphasis shifts further still and there is no possibility of fertilization from the abnormal mode of obtaining satisfaction that we recognize a perversion.

NORMAL SEXUAL BEHAVIOUR

The difficulty in writing a section such as this is the problem of delineating the norm. Human beings are so variable, so influenced by tradition and social circumstances that one must be very careful in what one accepts or excludes.

Physiologically, sexual intercourse consists in the interaction of a number of reflexes. The initial ones are psychic reflexes and are activated mainly by 'the distance receptors'—visual and olfactory stimuli, but other senses may take part.

The young man sees the girl (normally it has been found that attraction is towards someone of approximately the same age, race and so on) and is attracted by her form, colouring and perhaps her perfume. It is difficult to prove by statistics but it would seem that the man looks first at a girl's face and then at her breasts, the girl looks at the man's face, then his physique and, if possible, any suggestion of his sexual organs visible. The result of these stimuli is that the young people are sexually excited. He may develop an erection even at this early stage and the girl may have a moist exudate of the vagina; but these may not occur until later, in the next stage, when there is physical stimulation.

Given opportunity the protagonists make physical contact and the psychic reflexes are reinforced or substituted by physical ones. This is the 'fore-play' in which the man excites the girl by kissing (incidentally exciting himself more at the same time) and then by touching the nipples and clitoris. The girl may reciprocate by stimulating him, touching his penis, and stroking his body. This fore-play may last a few minutes to as long as an hour (according to Kinsey) but probably the shorter duration is more usual. Having become sufficiently excited the man penetrates the girl's vagina with his penis and the external tactile stimuli are in turn replaced for the girl by the presence of the penis within the vagina. This is increased by his movements in which the penis passes to and fro.

Intercourse lasts a varying length of time but is usually a matter of minutes and then the mounting excitement culminates in the climactic excitement which forms the orgasm. Some sexologists insist that this is controllable and that the man should control his termination to coincide with that of the female. Although ideally orgasm should occur in both participants at the same time it is doubtful how far this is under the control of volition. The orgasm in the male is simultaneous with ejaculation. It seems possible that in some women, at least, there is a sucking motion of the vagina which draws the sperm up towards the cervix and the ejaculation in the male usually occurs when the penis is deeply penetrating. Thus the sperm has a good chance of reaching the uterus. This, however, was not found by Masters and Johnson in their extensive and careful researches. Orgasm, in both sexes, should be a moment of intense pleasure. It has even been suggested that there is a clouding of consciousness at the pinnacle of pleasure but this seems doubtful, at least in most cases.

Following the orgasm there is usually a period of quiescence when the couple may lie for a varying period with the man's penis still *in situ* until the erection dies away, which it does in time. In general there is usually a sense of relief and well-being following coitus. There is often deep sleep and, unless there is anxiety, the participants awake with a feeling of refreshment. Masters and Johnson, who have done extensive research on sexual reactions, confirm the general account given here but divide the responses in intercourse into four: (1) the excitement phase, (2) the plateau phase, (3) the orgasmic phase, and (4) the resolution phase. The masculine responses seem more abrupt and he has a refractory period following orgasm.

Their work confirms what others have found regarding various concomitants of coitus, such as erection of the nipples and increase in size of the breasts, flushing of the skin, myotonia, hyperventilation, tachycardia, elevation of the blood pressure and involuntary sweating.

It is not intended to give a complete and minute account of physical reactions here and those wishing for more information should consult their book.

The position in which intercourse is had is by no means stereotyped. No doubt if the matter is considered superficially it would be thought that the normal position is obvious. The ordinary educated European or American will think that it is the traditional ventro-ventral relationship with the woman below and the man on top, and that anything else is to be gravely suspect. He will be astonished to learn that this is not always practised by man's nearest biological relatives—the apes—nor is it used by innumerable races of human beings and that with them some different position is adopted. It is dubious whether the ventro-ventral position was that of choice amongst the ancients. Horace in his *Satires* suggests other positions and Ovid in his *Art of Love* advocates a ventro-ventral position with the partners lying side by side and so on.

Not all nations use the position in which the woman lies supine on her back and, according to Malinowski, for example, the Trobrianders prefer one in which the man squats before the woman who places her thighs each side of his body. During intercourse the man pulls the woman up so that they develop a partially erect squatting position.

On the island of Yap the natives have intercourse in the sitting position with the woman stooping over the man.

The Somalis, whose environment and upbringing seem to make them rather sadistic, adopt a ventro-ventral position in which the woman's body is arched so that intercourse is somewhat painful. The Arabs are said to use one where either one or both of the woman's legs are over the man's shoulders.

Ovid's side-by-side intercourse is used by the Masai, and other nations. Usually in such cases it is face to face, but sometimes ventro-dorsal, the man entering the woman from the rear.

In some societies the man stands behind the woman who bends forward or squats on her hands and knees (this is the common position for coitus in the apes and one might have expected it to be much commoner with human beings).

According to Ford and Beach, on Truk 'for quick copulation a standing position is used in which the woman is said "to rest her foot on the man's shoulder".'

Other positions used are for the man to lie on his back and for the woman to sit astride his body. She may either face him or face away from him. It is obvious that in such a position she must play the active part.

All this does not exhaust the matter and those interested should consult Oriental literature such as the Indian *Kama Sutra,* the Japanese *Hikatsu-sho* (The book of secrets) and the Islamic *The Perfumed Garden of Nefzawi* for refinements which I cannot consider here.

Doubtless, although one particular position is usual in different nations it is not stereotyped and variations are practised by different individuals. In general one finds that it is usual for the female to take the under position but in some cases she lies above. According to Kinsey and his collaborators 35 per cent. of older people and 52 per cent. of younger ones stated that they had intercourse in which the female lay above the man. This is believed by analysts to show female dominance. If this is so it is surprising how frequently this occurs. It is certain that some women prefer this position because they cannot have an orgasm in any other. Kinsey believes that this does not necessarily show female dominance but that the woman is less inhibited, can diminish her inhibitions by avoiding a usual technique and is able to move more spontaneously.

In view of all this it must be accepted that no particular sexual position can be accepted as normal, but that human beings use different ones according to their nationality, social *mores* and psychological inclinations. No doubt any variation may have a stimulant effect at times. What then are the criteria of normality?

It seems to me that the essential criterion of normal intercourse is that it is one which tends to fertilize the woman. Intercourse is biologically for this one purpose and any pleasure, excitement, sense of well-being and so on which it produces is merely coincidental and an incitement to do what Nature needs done.

There is one further stipulation, however, which must be made. That is that coitus must not be injurious to either party. One could not consider, for example, sadistic intercourse to be normal, although the unfortunate female victim may be impregnated if she is gravely hurt. It is useless to argue that possibly the more primitive of man's ancestors—the hominids, the Neanderthals and so on—may have used a sadistic approach. This is purely a matter for speculation, no one knows what their sexual techniques and behaviour may have been and speculation on this point is futile but, in any case, no matter how roughly the female may have been treated it is obviously essential that she should not have been injured.

One might have put forward a criterion of normality as being dependent on the nubility of the sexual partner, but here we are on dangerous ground. Our minds have been so conditioned by modern customs that we are likely to forget that all the great heroines of romance were 'under the age of consent' and according to modern English law the romantic heroes would be in danger of prosecution for interfering with a minor. Thus Helen was of the mature age of 12 when Paris abducted her, Juliet was aged thirteen, and so was Chloe. Galatea was an old lady of fifteen or sixteen!

It has been shown again and again that the psychic element in behaviour tends to mature before the physical—it is easy to see small boys attracted to women in a manner which, if they were older, would be called 'in love'.

Obviously without the prohibitions which our society inflicts on sexual actions there would be much earlier open sexual activity. In support of this is Kinsey's statement that he found 29 females who had had coitus before adolescence.

Similarly with regard to women past the menopause. It would be a brave man who insisted that because she is past child-bearing it is abnormal for a woman to have intercourse. Indeed, some people have sexual relations until they are at an advanced age. Kinsey found that a small percentage (10 per cent.) of females between 56 and 60 years of age still had orgasms with intercourse.

In our civilization the woman is tacitly expected to be passive. This is not so in other societies. For instance, the Trobriander and Trukese expect her to be as active as the man and these virile natives would regard with contempt the passivity which we and such nations as the Colorado and Lepcha Indians expect.

We can summarize therefore that normal sexual intercourse consists in a sexual relationship which, other things being equal, tends to fertilize the female without injury to either party.

APHRODISIACS

It may not be out of place to make here a brief comment on aphrodisiacs. These have fascinated mankind for centuries; and range from the consumption of substances believed potent through sympathetic magic—such as oysters—to alkaloids and endocrines.

Some substances which are commonly believed to have aphrodisiac properties are very toxic and tragedies have resulted from their use. An example of this was the death of two girls who were given cantharides in chocolates by the manager of a chemical firm for which they worked. He had the mistaken belief that these girls would be overwhelmed with an uncontrollable sexual desire and would turn to him for relief. Unfortunately he had no idea of the proper dose, and although he gave a minute quantity of the alkaloid cantharidin, this was much too large. The two girls developed enteritis and nephritis with subsequent death. The manager was found guilty of manslaughter, and was given a term of imprisonment.

Another tragedy resulted from the administration of carbon tetra-chloride by a man to his mistress. This was supposed to enhance 'love play' but the woman died. She was found naked on a divan holding a cloth and a bottle of the fluid. The case was first tried at the Surrey Assizes but the jury could not agree. It was subsequently tried at Lewes Assizes. The judge, Mr. Justice Hilbery, took a severe view. He said to the prisoner: 'You knew from your experience that it excited her passions, so that coition with her was exciting to you. It was for that selfish reason you caused her to inhale it. Unfortunately it did not stimulate her passions but irritated the lung and stomach nerves. Her heart stopped and she died.' He sentenced the prisoner to fifteen months' imprisonment.

The curious thing about this case is that carbon tetrachloride is *not* an aphrodisiac. Its action is similar to that of chloroform but is much more toxic. If it is administered the effect is inebriation. No sexual stimulation is produced. This woman would have been just as excited sexually by an alcoholic drink.

It is dubious whether there is anything which acts as an aphrodisiac. Probably the best sexual stimulant is a healthy physique and an attractive sexual partner. Alcohol is not an aphrodisiac but may lead to sexual behaviour by the fact that it depresses the central nervous system and diminishes sexual restraint.

REFERENCES

ABRAHAM, K. (1927) *Selected Papers on Psychoanalysis*, London.
BOLK, L. (1926) *Das Problem der Mannerscheudung*, Jena.
BOWLBY, J., AINSWORTH, M., BOSTON, M., and ROSENBLUTH, D. (1956) *Brit. J. med. Psychol.*, **24**, 3–4.
BROSTER, L. R., *et al.* (1938) *The Adrenal Cortex and Intersexuality*, London.
FORD, C. S., and BEACH, F. A. (1951) *Patterns of Sexual Behavior*, New York.
FREUD, S. (1930) *Three Contributions to the Theory of Sex*, New York.
GESSLER, C. (1937) *The Dangerous Islands*, London.
HOLLINGWORTH, L. S. (1933) The adolescent child, in *Handbook of Child Psychology*, ed. MURCHISON, C., Worcester, Mass.
HUDGINS, C. V. (1944) *J. genet. Psychol.*, **58**, 3–51.
HUGHES, W. (1926) *J. soc. Hyg.*, **12**, 262–73.
JONES, E. (1926) *Brit. J. Psychol.*, **13**, 31–47.
KASATKIN, N. I., and LEVIKOVA, A. M. (1935) *J. exp. Psychol.*, **18**, 1–19.
KINSEY, A. C., POMEROY, W. B., and MARTIN, C. E. (1948) *Sexual Behavior in the Human Male*, Philadelphia.
KINSEY, A. C., POMEROY, W. B., MARTIN, C. E., and GEBHARD, P. H. (1953) *Sexual Behavior in the Human Female*, Philadelphia.
KLEIN, MELANIE (1932) *The Psychoanalysis of Children*, London.
KLEIN, M. (1948) *Contributions to Psychoanalysis*, 1921–1945, London.
LEVY-SUHL, M. (1934) The early sexuality of man as compared with the maturity of other mammals, *Int. J. Psycho-Anal.*, **15**, 59.

LLOYD, C. W. (1964) *Human Reproduction and Sexual Behaviour*, London.
LORENZ, K. (1966) *On Aggression*, London.
MALINOWSKI, B. (1929) *The Sexual Life of Savages*, London.
MARQUIS, D. P. (1931) *J. genet. Psychol.*, **39**, 479–92.
MASTERS, W. H., and JOHNSON, V. E. (1966) *Human Sexual Response*, London.
MUNROE, R. L. (1957) *Schools of Psychoanalytic Thought*, London.
ROSSETTI, CHRISTINA (1862) *Goblin Market and Other Poems*, London.
WATSON, J. B. (1929) *Psychology from the Standpoint of a Behaviorist*, New York.

4

THE INFLUENCE OF THE
ENDOCRINE GLANDS

The behaviour of those suffering from psychosexual illness is frequently so puzzling and bizarre, so urgent and reckless, that those who have no insight into the psychological causation are driven to some explanation in terms of their limited understanding. The commonest explanation in such a case is that there is some disease of the glands, some endocrine anomaly, as the basic cause.

Such a view has been put forward in the following words. 'For our part we are reluctant to believe that there is no organic aberration. When we consider the tremendous compulsion which must lie behind this perverted impulse to drive these individuals onwards in defiance of the savage penalties which lie in wait for them, to say nothing of the attendant personal disgrace, and when we remember that they are often men of great intelligence and ability, of sound judgement, and outside their perversion, of the highest character, it is impossible to believe that they are not victims of some freakish alteration in that obscure but compelling chemistry that plays so large, if unsuspected, a part in shaping our personalities and destinies.' Although this was written by the editor of a prominent medical paper some twenty years ago the same theme is reiterated in different works almost as much today in some quarters.

In view of this tendency to refer all psychosexual illness, whether evidence is discoverable or not, to endocrine origin, it is worth while studying the effect of the hormones, particularly the sexual ones, on behaviour. Such a review must be somewhat superficial and no attempt can be made to usurp the function of the endocrinologist. However, it is hoped to cover the field sufficiently, in the case of both animals and human beings, to give some idea of the relationship of the endocrines to behaviour.

THE RELATION OF THE ENDOCRINES TO
ANIMAL REACTION

It would appear that hormones have considerable influence on the behaviour of nearly all animals but this is most apparent on those phylogenetically above the fishes. Indeed the periodicity of the reactions of some fish seem indicative of endocrine influence.

Beach in his valuable book (to which we are indebted for much of the material in this section) considers the problem from the following points of view:

1. Courtship and mating.
2. Oviposition, parturition and parental behaviour.
3. Migration.
4. Generalized aggression, social dominance, or submission, and territorial defence.
5. Conditioning and other types of learning,

and a number of other points of view not relative to the subject of this book.

He assembles the literature and considers information on: 1, normal behaviour, 2, the effect of hormones on normal conduct, 3, the effect of removal of a gland (castration, &c.), 4, the effect of substitution of the

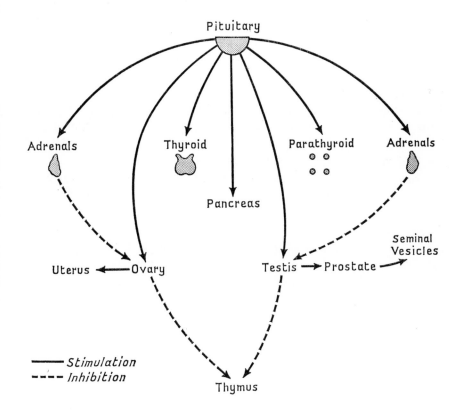

The main endocrine interrelationships illustrated diagrammatically. For simplicity, the reciprocal influence of other endocrine glands on the pituitary is omitted: but removal of such glands, e.g. thyroid and ovary, leads to hyperplasia of the pituitary, and to an increased secretion of its 'trophic' hormones, e.g. thyrotrophic, gonadotrophic, &c. The adrenals are shown as inhibiting the gonads; but in children precocity may result from adrenal tumours.
(Simpson, S. L. (1959) *Major Endocrine Disorders*, 3rd ed., London.)

missing hormone or hormones following such an operation. He produces references to observation and experiments on fish, amphibia, reptiles, and mammals up to human beings.

Normal Behaviour

In some fishes the breeding cycle coincides with periodic activity of the ovary and appears to be under endocrine control. This seems to be true of the amphibia, reptiles, and birds. There is no doubt that it is true of mammals. Beach states, 'In general it seems beyond doubt that sexual receptivity occurs in the females of these species when follicular development is approaching the maximum.' This is especially marked in the primates.

That such behaviour is due to hormone influence is shown by its production by artificial stimulation by feeding, injection or implantation of suitable endocrine substances.

Removal or Regression of Testes or Ovaries

The effects of this vary with the species but if the gonads are removed before puberty then the normal mating pattern does not occur. However, the effects of castration in adult life are less certain and more variable. Beach states, 'Aristotle was conversant with the fact that post pubertal castration in the male does not necessarily result in the total elimination of sexual behaviour, for he wrote, "If the full grown bull be mutilated, he can still to all appearances unite with the cow".'

The prepubertally castrated male chimpanzee may show sexual responses and even vigorous mating activity during adulthood. One is stated to have had ten copulations during an hour's test with a receptive female. However, it appears in general that there is a tendency towards diminution and disappearance of the sexual urge after a time in the castrated monkey. This apparently influences the responses. Michael, for example, ovariectomized five female Rhesus monkeys and observed their behaviour with males for periods between 91 and 329 days. He found that removing the ovaries stopped mounting and grooming. Normal behaviour returned and even surpassed preoperative levels with oestradiol and cholesterol implants. Progesterone alone produced no effect but with oestrogen mounting diminished sharply. He concludes, 'These results indicate that both sexual activity and grooming activity between heterosexual pairs of adult rhesus monkeys are markedly influenced by the endocrine state of the female. It appears that the notion that the primate's brain is emancipated from the influence of gonadal hormones has been overestimated.' Evidently the effect is more severe in the female than the male. Castrated female fish show no mating activity, nor do amphibia, reptiles or birds. However, some female chimpanzees permitted copulation for many months after gonadectomy, although their behaviour was less frequent and less prolonged.

Effects of Hormone Administration

The diminution or disappearance of sexual behaviour in both sexes following castration can, in general, be corrected by the administration of the proper hormones. This would appear to prove conclusively that the endocrines do certainly play a large part in such sexual reactions.

Oviposition, Parturition, and Parental Behaviour

This form of behaviour also appears to be controlled by endocrine factors at least to a large extent. However, since it is unrelated to the subject of this book it will not be discussed in detail.

Migration

It has been suggested by Rowan that migration is the result of endocrine cycles. This view has been attacked because castration does not necessarily prevent the migratory journey, and various other factors such as the response to light, fat condition, and so on are believed to be of influence. In some cases no doubt a social factor is of importance—as when birds migrate in flocks.

Aggression

There appears no doubt that the aggressive responses are heightened by the endocrines. In many species, as is well known, these are correlated with the breeding cycles. This can be seen in fish, birds, and mammals. It is common knowledge that deer, for instance, are dangerous at such times.

The effects of castration have been known, probably from neolithic times when animals were first domesticated, to diminish aggression. It seems to have the effect in all species of diminishing the aggressive responses. In a lizard, *Anolis carolinensis*, the removal of the ovaries makes the female, which is usually less aggressive, fight as savagely as the male. In this case presumably the female hormones produce an inhibiting influence.

Replacement of the missing male hormone during a period of sexual quiescence, or in castrated animals, appears to produce increased aggression. The same effect can be evoked in females in some species by the injection of androgens.

Probably dependent on the animals' aggression is the social dominance or submission. This is the so-called 'peck order' which has been noticed amongst birds such as hens. Androgens administered to a hen low down in the 'peck order' (i.e. which is submissive to others and permits itself to be chased away from food, &c.) will rapidly raise it to a higher position in the hierarchy. A similar state of affairs has been noticed in ring doves.

In apes the administration of methyltestosterone increases the dominance. In females the position of dominance depends on the ape's sexual condition. It can be increased in a spayed female by the administration of oestrogen.

Territorial defence, which again is dependent on aggression and dominance, is found to be related to the endocrine condition and can be increased by testosterone.

Conditioning and Other Types of Learning

A considerable amount of work has been done on this problem and it might be hoped that some conclusive result had been attained, but unfortunately the results given by various workers are so contradictory and unexpected that no certain deductions can be made. Pavlov believed that the sex hormones stimulated the brain but there is no certain proof of this. Neither conditioning nor maze learning seems so definitely related to castration, nor the administration of endocrines, that any proper deductions can be drawn from them.

Reversal and Bisexuality of Mating Behaviour

There is no doubt that in the lower animals, particularly invertebrates, sex reversal is very common and in some (such as the marine snail, *Credula*) the reversal occurs normally. This also happens in some annelid species. In some fish the females may spontaneously change into the male, and even be able to fertilize females. Frogs and toads have been known to change sex. Birds have changed from male to female and vice versa.

Castrated mammals in which glands of the opposite sex have been implanted tend to change behaviour and in the case of hemicastrated guinea-pigs in which a heterogeneous gland had been implanted the behaviour is said to vary according to the sex of the animal with which it comes into contact (i.e. it behaves bisexually). Goy points out, however, that 'After castration, ejaculation, intromission, and erection disappear from the mating repertoire sooner than any of the other components. Consequently the expression of these reflexes is considered to depend more heavily upon the presence of adequate amounts of androgen. Mounting and pelvic thrusting may persist for months or even years after castration although their frequency of expression certainly declines. Thus some components like ejaculation depend almost entirely on androgen for their manifestation. Others, such as mounting, can be displayed in the complete absence of androgen and only the frequency of display is influenced by the hormone.'

The effect of administering a heterogeneous endocrine in some cases results in behaviour appropriate to the hormone. This seems to be magnified if the animal had been previously castrated.

However, this is not invariably true. For example, Goodale records that a sexually inactive capon implanted with ovarian tissue commenced to crow and tread hens. He found that the behaviour of capons with ovarian grafts is more like that of the normal cock. This has been confirmed by others. A similar effect has been seen with castrated male rats. Beach comments, 'It is evident that despite the possibility that estrogen may lower the sex drive in the normal male, castrated males of the same species will nevertheless show increased sexual behavior under the influence of ovarian hormones.

'Animals may show bisexual behavior although only one type of hormone has been given. Male lizards show masculine and female mating patterns after being given testosterone. Hens, after implants of testosterone propionate, crow, circle, and tread hens yet may also squat and receive the cock. Castrated female rats may similarly show both mating patterns after injections of testosterone. However, it has been noticed that male mice may show both male and female reactions after being given yohimbine. In fact, it is dangerous to draw too extensive conclusions even from this since in normal untreated animals both sexual patterns may appear. This has been noticed in rats, guinea-pigs, and apes.'

Beach concludes his summary of this type of reaction in these words: 'The general impression that one gains from a survey of the literature tends to throw some doubt on the concept of sex reversal which depends on complete sex specificity both of the behavioral mechanisms and of the gonadal hormones. A somewhat more reasonable hypothesis would seem to be that in many if not all vertebrate species both males and females are equipped by nature to perform at least most of the elements in the overt mating pattern of the opposite sex. In some species, and particularly in the female, the heterologous reactions may occur under appropriate external stimulation without any alteration in the normal endocrine balance. In other instances the copulatory performance of the opposite sex is activated only by increasing the concentration of the heterologous hormones. But even here nothing has been "reversed". Rather a previous refractory and relatively inactive behavioral system has been rendered more responsive to external stimulation. And be it noted that under such conditions the homologous sex pattern is often simultaneously activated, so that bisexual behavior results.'

ENDOCRINE INFLUENCES IN HUMAN BEINGS

It is by no means so easy to study the part played by the hormones in human beings as in animals. We are unable to experiment freely and must observe the fortuitous occurrence of disease and its effects. This necessitates the collection of series of cases, not always sufficiently similar to provide satisfactory conclusions. We can utilize our scrutiny of the effects of treatment and replacement therapy, but this in itself is not always satisfactory. The endocrine system acts like a system of checks and balances which influence the metabolism of the body, and in a general way the psychical responses. The hormones do this by inhibition and stimulation which slows or accelerates the physical machinery or some part of it. We cannot always be sure what is happening since not only are the endocrine glands controlled by the midbrain and the pituitary, but far from each gland being responsive only to those influences they influence each other so that there is a constant wave and counter-wave of reciprocity passing and re-passing to and fro amongst them. A complicated system of cybernetics is continuously in action.

As if all this were not sufficient other factors are at work also. Firstly no other animal lives in such a complex social environment as the human being with the influence of conditioning, and perhaps other forms of learning, starting from its earliest days. This makes it difficult to be sure that certain behaviour is instinctive (due to inherited reactions), purely endocrine (due to circulating hormones), conditioned or learned, or a combination of two or all of these, and possibly other, at present unknown, influences.

There is, moreover, a possibility, which is not usually considered, that the brain can inhibit or stimulate the endocrines due to social or other influences. It is difficult otherwise to understand why Terman and Miles should notice that intellectual boys who have been forced by circumstances to devote their interest to studying should be immature physically and have, for example, poor bodily hair development whereas boys who have had little such influence are more mature physically. Again psychiatrists have noticed that homosexuals with poor hair development sometimes become more hirsute; grow hair over the upper abdomen and chest, &c., during treatment. This has been my own experience and more than one patient has spontaneously drawn attention to such growth.

Prepubertal Responses

Since the endocrine machinery, as we have pointed out, is so complicated it seems only too probable that it can be gravely thrown out of gear by some defect before it has become properly stabilized or accelerated to a normal speed. This is indeed true, and the onset of endocrine anomalies before puberty may produce a profound effect on the body. Since this book is mainly concerned with sex we shall not dwell on the gross anomalies in such a disease as cretinism, but they are obvious enough and familiar to us, although fortunately rare in England.

Disease of the adrenal gland such as tumour or hypertrophy of the cortex will cause sexual precocity in the case of the male and masculinization of the female early in life. For example, Wilkins and his co-workers described the case of a boy aged three with sexual precocity who had a sister who was a pseudohermaphrodite. In rather older boys the so-called 'infant Hercules' may result from adrenal disease. This may also result from interstitial-cell tumours of the testis. The penis becomes enlarged and body and facial hair appears. Sexual precocity may also occur in hypothalamic tumours. In the adrenal and hypothalamic types the sexual urge may be strong enough to lead the boy to seek sexual satisfaction with girls.

In the case of the female tumours or hypertrophy of the adrenal cortex may result in masculinization with enlargement of the clitoris suggestive of pseudohermaphroditism which may start in foetal life. Virilism with facial hirsuties is another result obvious in later life.

On the other hand sexual precocity in girls may show itself as early as in the first year of life. The child may show precocious development of the labia majora, vagina, uterus, and breasts, and commence menstruation. Such a condition is found most often in ovarian tumours, but can be produced by pineal or hypothalamic tumours.

In eunuchs there has been castration before puberty. This has been done in Eastern countries so that the victim could serve in harems; in Rome so that the choir boys could retain their infantile voices (the 'castrati'); in Rumania and Russia for religious beliefs, as in the 'Skoptzy'. It is unusual to see eunuchs in England unless there has been a surgical removal of the gonads for disease, for example, bilateral tuberculosis of the testes, or carcinoma.

In eunuchoidism, disease, usually mumps, which causes bilateral orchitis, may produce atrophy; in other cases trauma, other infections, and perhaps genetic factors may be causal. The sufferer has the appearance of a eunuch, but retains infantile testes. In such cases the genitalia are smaller than usual, and the testes may be very small indeed. The pubic and axillary hair is typically feminine in distribution and the body and limbs hairless. The skin is fine, white, and feminine in type. The victim shaves infrequently, if at all. The patients are usually tall and thin with little bodily fat. My own observations confirm Simpson's view that the idea that eunuchs are fat is a mistake. The voice tends to be higher than normal, but is not ludicrously so. Simpson states, 'I have not seen genital homosexuality among eunuchs, but their gentle sympathetic nature, coupled with an absence of interest in heterosexuality, may lead them to positions of prominence in boy and male adolescent social activities'. This is contrary to my experience since a certain number (perhaps 2–3 per cent.) seen by me seem to have drifted into homosexuality.

Female eunuchs and eunuchoids tend to be tall and slim with poor breast development. The writer has not noticed any sexual abnormality amongst women with glandular anomalies, except in adrenogenital virilism, but this may be due to the fact that their role is more passive and the absence of glandular stimulation naturally leads to acceptance of passivity.

It is a curious thing, contrary to Simpson's statement quoted above, that Burton noticed that the eunuchs he saw on his voyages were harsh and aggressive. He states, 'The Agha's (eunuch's) character is curious and exceptional as his outward conformation. Discontented with humanity, he is cruel, fierce, brave, and capable of any villainy. His frame is unnaturally long and lean, especially the arms and legs, with high shoulders, protruding joints, and a face by contrast extraordinary large: he rides to admiration, his hoarse, thick voice investing him with all the circumstances of command.' This, betrays, no doubt, the powerful effect of training and social circumstances. My own experience, which admittedly comprises very few eunuchs, is that they are not aggressive in this way, but sometimes socially assertive. Eunuchoids often show no distinctive personality traits, and one could not detect their abnormality without physical examination.

Puberty

No one can claim exactly what triggers off puberty. Pituitary activity is suggested by some, but this merely places the problem a little further back and does not explain what starts it. The process is a slow maturation rather than the cataclysmic explosion of popular belief. Beach gives the following developmental changes involved as: '(1) The anterior pituitary must produce and release the gonadotrophic hormones which stimulate the gonads to gametogenesis and to hormone secretion. (2) The ovaries and testes must be sensitive to pituitary gonadotrophins, and must be capable of forming mature germ cells and elaborating and releasing gonadal hormones. (3) The accessory sex structures (fallopian tubes, uterus, vagina, epididymis, seminal vesicles, prostate, and penis) must respond in normal adult fashion to the hormones secreted by the gonads. (4) The secondary sex characters which are under hormonal control must be reactive to secretions of the gonads or the pituitary as the case may be. (5) The behavioral mechanisms responsible for courtship, mating, and parental care must be fully organized and responsive to the appropriate endocrine products.'

At puberty in the human there is a general growth of the body, including the skeleton and internal organs. The female's ovaries show increased growth accompanied by maturation of the Graafian follicles and discharge of ova. The uterus starts to grow and the breasts become obvious. In both sexes hair appears on the pubes and in the axilla. In males the deepening voice, growth of the genitals, increased muscular development and appearance of facial hair form a distinctive syndrome.

The flooding of the blood by the sexual hormones at puberty has also a profound psychological effect. We have seen that in the ape it turns the male from random sexuality into the serious business of intercourse and aggression. It is suggested that the most important result in the human is *an increase in awareness*. Yet in our society there is an element of frustration because this awareness is not supposed to comprise sexuality and the youth of both sexes is not expected to interpret the sexual urges. We have already discussed Jones' view regarding regression at this time (which must be activated by the surge of endocrines) but probably this is in psychologically healthy young people, in most cases, a transient phase.

The pubescent of both sexes feels discontented, dissatisfied (and consequently easily aroused to quarrels), unstable, inferior, and liable to violent attachments. There is usually a wish to be accepted as an adult and any suggestion that this is not so will easily lead to angry outbursts. This is in accord with the appreciation that aggression in animals is increased by endocrine influence. The rioting of students in 1968 which first appeared in France, particularly in Paris, and spread to England and other countries, shows the vast fund of aggression which is general in young people. Not surprisingly, those who behaved so violently were unable to give a reasonable explanation of the causes of their behaviour, except that they were dissatisfied with university conditions, and wished for the abolition of examinations.

In some cases the nature of the urge is consciously understood and the young girls who hang about army camps, &c., are not entirely unaware of the nature of their desires!

The picture of puberty and adolescence in our society seems to be one which shows sexual frustration, at least to some extent. This is no doubt due to socio-religious restraints. The frustration may be relieved in both sexes by masturbation, but may sometimes burst out in outrageous behaviour. Possibly the drinking which is occasionally seen in young people may be some sort of substitute for sexual behaviour. The congregating of youths into gangs may be due in part to Jones' adolescent regression, but such behaviour must be activated by hormone activity. Indeed it occasionally terminates in the raping of some girl—conduct which may appear incomprehensible to authority. However, both this and the behaviour of girls who more or less invite seduction, or rape, must be considered as the result of the overwhelming sexual urge which is so obvious at the time.

The onset of the menses is caused by the pituitary follicle-stimulating hormones. This brings about growth of the ovarian follicles which in turn stimulate the breasts and uterus by means of an oestrogenic ovarian hormone. When the oestrogen rises high enough the endometrium retrogresses, bleeding takes place and the oestrogen diminishes. After the rhythm is established the pituitary secretes a luteinizing hormone which causes the follicle to secrete a second ovarian hormone—progesterone. The proper levels of oestrogen and progesterone cause the follicle to ripen and rupture. The resulting corpus luteum secretes further progesterone, possibly stimulated by yet another pituitary hormone, prolactin. Thus the cycle continues.

The menstrual cycle affects behaviour and some women display behaviour which can be related with it. Often they show increased sexual desire just before or just after menstruation. However, Swyer states that it shows no definite character, but varies from one individual to another. One symptom, that of premenstrual tension, seems definitely related to endocrine activity; and appears to be caused by sodium and water retention due to progesterone.

Postpubertal Responses

The general impression is that directly after puberty the sexual impulses are strongest and that they tend slowly to diminish as the individual grows older. This has been confirmed by Kinsey's work.

The effect of castration in both male and female is particularly instructive. The eunuch and the eunuchoid rarely produce effective responses to the female unless treated by testosterone. In that case, however, all the while they are under effective therapy they may behave normally. Many cases have been recorded in the literature, but the following is an interesting one. I treated a handsome young man who worked as a draughtsman in a factory. He was very popular with the opposite sex because of his good looks, but never able to use his sexual opportunities because of his eunuchoidism. His doctor was advised to give him injections of testosterone (it was before the use of implants). He did so and the young man was able to behave normally. However, the physician wearied of the labour of weekly injections and ceased them. The young man lost his sexual capacity and returned in despair. His sexuality returned completely on recommencing the injections. Not all such cases respond so satisfactorily.

The male castrated after puberty may suffer from a loss of feeling of well-being which is understandable enough since the testicular secretions may affect the responses of the pituitary, the adrenal, and thyroid glands.

The effect of castration seems much less obvious in the case of the female, and indeed, even if she is castrated before puberty she may be able to enjoy intercourse.

The castrated male, particularly if he has already had sexual intercourse, does not necessarily lose all his sexual impulses and capacity after the loss of his gonads. In fact such an operation may have little effect.

Lange in a very wide study of castration based on 306 cases (242 complete castrates and 64 partial ones) in mainly young men recorded that in 99 castrates 55 lost potency immediately, 22 lost it gradually, and 26 retained it. Beach states, 'The literature is replete with reference to complete retention of sexual function in individuals who have been castrated for many years'. An example of this was recorded by Feiner and Rothman who described a man who had had his testicles removed for tuberculosis and who was having a normal sexual life with his wife, with weekly coitus, *thirty years later*. They suggested that the testes were only necessary for procreation and not for potency.

The so-called 'chemical castration'—the use of oestrogenic hormones—to diminish the libido may fail just as signally as surgical castration in the male. I once gave evidence in a case of a schoolmaster who was accused of indecent assault on his pupils. This man had been sentenced three times previously and had been treated with enormous doses of stilboestrol and oestrogen. In spite of the fact that he had considerable hypertrophy of the breasts and atrophy of the testes and penis he still had sufficient sexual urge to interfere with his pupils, running the risk of the disgrace he had suffered three times previously. Obviously in spite of the physical change his libido remained unchanged.

Although castration seems to have little effect on the desire or orgasmal capacity of the woman she is strongly affected by virilism of adrenogenital origin. The ketosterones in such cases appear to diminish or even reverse her sexuality. In 24 cases of virilism I found eight were homosexual and sixteen heterosexual. Two had all their interest centred on themselves. After adrenalectomy, of the heterosexuals eight felt increased heterosexuality, seven showed no change, and one was unknown. One of those who concentrated interest on herself (autosexual) showed no change and one died. It would appear therefore that adrenogenital virilism has a profound effect on the mind as well as on the body. This seems to be due to the inhibitory effect on the ovarian functions.

The Climacteric

This manifests itself by adiposity, virilism, hypertension, impaired carbohydrate tolerance, thyroid changes, mammary atrophy, hypersensitivity to adrenaline (and hence hot flushes), anxiety, emotionalism, nervous tension, irritability, migraine, irregular menstruation, and a tendency to pruritus. It is not easy to discover how much all this is due to hormone imbalance and how much is psychological. However, the libido may be unaffected or may suddenly cease. It may even be increased for a time. Many women continue enjoying a satisfactory sexual life long after the menarche.

Women have a particular tendency to develop depression at the time of the climacteric—involutional depression. The fact that many of those suffering in this way do not show obvious glandular imbalance, and the cure which may result from electrical convulsive therapy or monoamine oxidase inhibitors suggests that this is not a simple glandular sequel, but is probably due to complex interaction between the psyche and the endocrines. (It may even be related to the postpartum psychoses occasionally seen in women.) The reciprocal influence of psychosexual and somatosexual responses has never been sufficiently studied in this connexion. The cure of psychoses in women suffering from adrenogenital virilism confirms the relationship.

It has been suggested that there is a male climacteric which tends to appear about ten years later than the female one. The symptoms are similar to the female one with hot flushes, anxiety, fatigability, loss of sexual powers, and inability to make decisions. In suitable cases response to treatment by testosterone is claimed. However, it does not seem to affect conduct to much extent.

Enlargement of the prostate occurs in the male in later life. A great deal of sexual misconduct has been attributed to it, probably wrongly. The prostate does not appear to be an endocrine gland; but is affected by hormones—for example, it atrophies following castration. If the enlargement of the prostate which occurs in old men affects conduct it is probable that this does so in one of two ways. It may cause urinary infection and frequency, thus constantly drawing attention to sexual feelings, or it may produce local pressure which appears to increase sexual urges. Prostatectomy seems to reduce the libido (possibly by removing these factors), but it is difficult to understand how an enlarged prostate could cause, for example, exhibitionism.

The Function of the Hormones

I have given a very brief and admittedly sketchy outline of endocrine influence, and we are now in a position to draw conclusions from it. It is now possible to consider a little more carefully the effect of hormones.

It would seem that they act either as stimulant or inhibitory agents. I have already pointed out that the testes lie dormant, at least in some respects, until stimulated by pituitary activity at puberty. Then the gonadal activity arouses the already prepared physical conditions. Obviously the areas where hair grows—the face, body, axillae, pubis—are waiting for the stimulant action of the hormones; but the effect is local, and not general, and it is only those areas which become hirsute and not the whole body.

The inhibitory effect can be seen in such a disease as adrenogenital virilism which prevents ovarian function so that the patient either does not menstruate or ceases if this has already commenced. (There is, of course, a very complex system of inhibition in the endocrine system just as there is a similarly complex system of stimulation.)

The effect of the hormones on the brain appears to be parallel to that on the body. Just as the pattern of hair growing is already laid down, waiting for the moment of stimulation, although it looks similar to those areas which will finally be glabrous, *so the psychic patterns are already present in the brain, and ready for endocrine stimulation.* Probably in the higher mammals, such as man, the patterns are acquired by environmental influences, and are built on the instinctual basis by conditioning. There seems to me nothing strange that these acquired patterns should be activated by the hormones at puberty. No doubt the basic instinctual patterns may be capable of development in the direction of male or female by conditioning. In fact, it seems that in the lower animals in some, if not in all, cases there are present patterns of behaviour suitable to either sex. The paradoxical reactions in lizards which I have already described shows that the effect is certainly not entirely specific in them. I have seen such a paradoxical reaction in a homosexual man who had been given oestrogens to diminish his sexual feelings, and complained that they stimulated his abnormal longings intolerably. Curiously enough testosterone may thus stimulate a homosexual's homosexuality.

From such facts we are forced to appreciate that the sexuality is not dependent on hormone influence at all but is basically a pattern laid down in the psyche. The hormones can either stimulate or diminish this antecedently-instituted behaviour construction.

I must insist therefore that the hormones act merely as a force, as, for example, the steam in a boiler, which can make a dormant machine work or keep it continuing to do so. The steam may be used to activate a brake, but in general it is a motive force. Such a motive force can no more influence the pattern of behaviour than the steam in a boiler can direct the engine which it drives. Those who are simple enough to believe that abnormal sexual conduct is invariably due to glandular anomaly are in the position of those who think that every steam-engine breaks down because there is an insufficient head of steam, neglecting the possibility of pistons seizing, valves sticking and so on.

Having established that the hormones form a mere driving force (or

F—PSY. D.

in some cases a braking one) we might legitimately ask, what sort of psychic patterns do they affect?

There is no doubt that the inherited patterns of behaviour which we call instincts are the most obvious target. Mating, maternal behaviour, aggression, &c., are so clearly activated by the glands and interfered with by hormone withdrawal that there is no possibility of dispute. However, is there any possibility that the acquired reactions I have suggested may also be activated? I believe that there is.

I have shown in the section on the instinctual development in man, and shall discuss more fully in that on homosexuality, that there is a possibility, either by conditioning or Freudian introjection, that the male child may become over-attached to the mother rather than the father and so develop female psychological reactions. It would seem possible that these antecedently developed responses can be activated by the hormones at puberty and so 'sexualized'. This is the case with the homosexual who has acquired female reactions from his mother and so acts like a paradoxical lizard, seeking males and trying to mate with them. This may sound at first glance, a little fantastic, but it explains as nothing else the curious fact that testosterone will accentuate homosexual desire.

There seems every reason why such a theory should be accepted. The instinctual reactions in the lower animals are so fixed and invariable that it is not easy to build a variation on them, although this may be done in some cases by conditioning. However, in man the instincts are very fluid and adaptable, easily influenced by conditioning and other forms of learning. An abnormal behavioural superstructure is easily erected. If we influence the basic instinct we influence the whole superstructure. The man who has acquired feminine reactions on the basis of his sexuality and who has this sexuality exaggerated by hormones will utilize the only reactions which he has—the acquired feminine ones—and so behave homosexually.

However, I must admit that this is mainly speculative and I wish to close this section by emphasizing once more that:

1. The hormones can act only as a driving or inhibiting force.
2. They do not initiate reactions in themselves, but only start or stop machinery which is already installed.
3. In all animals there is an element of bisexuality.
4. Castration does not necessarily abolish sexual reactions and does not make a heterosexual animal or person homosexual.
5. The hormones are a valuable adjuvant, but by no means the whole picture.
6. There is a possibility that reactions acquired on the basis of instinctual ones can be aggravated by endocrine influence.

These conclusions are supported by clinical and biochemical evidence: for example, Swyer has reviewed the evidence for endocrine causation of psychological maladjustments and came to the following conclusion: 'The capacity for sexual response is not primarily dependent upon sex hormones, and the direction of sexual development is influenced mainly by psychological and environmental conditioning. The levels of sex hormones appear to do little more than modify the intensity of sexual activity. There is no convincing evidence that human homosexuality is dependent upon hormonal aberrations. The use of sex hormones in treatment of homosexuality is mainly disappointing.'

Again, Garrone and Mutrux, in a study of 50 patients with a diverse variation of sexual abnormalities, sought to discover evidence of supra-renal or testicular dysfunction by determining the urinary excretion of total 17-ketosteroids and their different fractions, 3-a-steroids, form-aldehydogenic corticoids, 'total corticoids', and 17–21–dihydroxy-20-ketosteroids. With a few exceptions of dubious significance the daily excretion of these steroid metabolites did not differ from that of normal men of similar age.

In reviewing this work the *British Medical Journal* stated: 'The conclusion was therefore reached that this group of patients did not provide any evidence of endocrine disturbance such as could account for their disordered sexual behaviour. *This was a careful and extensive study, which adds materially to the now almost overwhelming evidence against endocrine causes, and therefore for psychological causes, of these behavioral disorders.*' (My italics.)

REFERENCES

BEACH, F. A. (1948) *Hormones and Behavior*, New York.
BRITISH MEDICAL JOURNAL (1957) 9 March, leading article.
BURTON, R. (1919) *Pilgrimage to Al Madinah and Mecca*, London.
GARRONE, G., and MUTRUX, S. (1956) *Schweiz. med. Wschr.*, **86,** 1001.
GOODALE, H. D. (1918) Feminised male birds, *Genetics*, **3,** 276–299
GOY, R. W. (1964) Reproductive behaviour in mammals, in *Human Reproduction and Sexual Behaviour*, ed. LLOYD, C. W., London.
JONES, E. (1926) *Brit. J. Psychol.*, **13,** 41–7.
MEDICAL PRESS AND CIRCULAR (1946) 12 June.
MICHAEL, R. P. (1963) Some aspects of the endocrine control of sexual activity in primates, *Proc. roy. Soc. Med.*, **58,** 8.
SIMPSON, S. L. (1959) *Major Endocrine Disorders*, 3rd ed., London.
SWYER, G. I. M. (1954) *Reproduction and Sex*, London.
SWYER, G. I. M. (1954) *Practitioner*, **172,** 374.
TERMAN, L. M., and MILES, C. C. (1936) *Sex and Personality*, London.

5

THE NATURE AND CAUSATION OF
THE PSYCHOSEXUAL DISORDERS

The terminology of the psychosexual disorders has been as confused as the classification. In the past it has been the custom to classify them in a haphazard manner without any proper basis so that one would be classified by the mode of expression of the instinct (such as sadism), whereas another would be classified according to the nature of the object (such as homosexuality), and so on. It is true that the psychoanalysts have done much to clarify the position and have produced a great deal of terminology of their own, but it is based upon a theory of causation and this is always unsatisfactory in medicine.

The classification used in this book is founded upon a division of the instinct into various parts. It will be remembered that in Chapter 1 it was pointed out that an instinct could be divided into its stimulus, its mode of expression, its strength of urge, and its object.

We find in the psychosexual disorders that it is the modes of expression and the objects which are at fault. To the normal adult person the mode of the sexual instinct is genital copulation and the object one of the opposite sex and about the same age. To the homosexual sadist, for instance, the mode of expression is to inflict pain, and the sexual object is one of the same sex. We shall find that the perversions are a combination of abnormal modes of expression and sexual objects to produce different behaviour.

The utter confusion of the whole terminology is so obvious that it does not need labouring. The following lists shows the derivation of the terminology, which is not only drawn from almost every language but is very sketchy and incomplete, and proper terms[1] are missing from many perverse sexual acts and behaviour. No doubt it would have been better if the term 'perversion', which suggests a wilful abandonment of normal conduct, could have been abolished entirely but, unfortunately, as it has become so familiar that it cannot be satisfactorily replaced by 'paraphilia', it has been reluctantly decided that, at least for the moment, it is wiser not to attempt to make drastic changes in terminology, no matter how desirable.

[1] There is no term for those who obtain sexual pleasure from mouthing, although there is a term for the process in either sex. There is no term for those who consume the secretions of others, nor for the process, although coprophagia can be stretched to do so.

1. HOMOSEXUAL. Attraction between those of the same sex. The word is derived from the Greek word, *homós*, and not the Latin, *homo*, a man. Sex comes from the Latin, *sexus*, which probably stems from *secare* to divide (in this case into male and female).

3. HETEROSEXUAL. Attraction between those of different sexes. This is from the Greek, *heteros* meaning the other or different, and the Latin, *sexus*.

3. SADISM. Obtaining sexual pleasure from acts of cruelty. This is a French word derived from Donatien Alphonse François, Count (usually called Marquis) de Sade, 1740–1814, who invented the word himself to describe his inclinations.

4. MASOCHISM. The seeking of sexual pleasure from what would normally be painful. The derivation is from Leopold von Sacher-Masoch, 1836–95, an Austrian novelist whose novels showed this abnormality in their themes.

5. SODOMY. Anal intercourse. The word comes from the name of the town, Sodom, which is usually associated with Gomorrah, 'the cities of the plain', (according to the Bible) destroyed for abnormal practices but now believed to have been demolished by the explosion of an oil well.

6. BUGGERY. This has a similar meaning to sodomy. It is derived from the French. The suggestion is usually made that it comes from *bougre* which was first used to mean a Bulgarian, then a heretic, and finally one who practised anal intercourse. Other derivations seem possible, such as *bougie*, a candle.

7. FETISHISM. The substitution of some abnormal and unsuitable sexual object totally unfitted for a normal sexual aim. This is from the Portuguese, *feitiço* meaning a charm or magic. Ultimately the word derives from the Latin, *factitius* 'made by art'.

8. SCOPTOPHILIA. Obtaining sexual pleasure from watching other people. It is derived from the Greek, *skopein*, to watch and *philos* loving.

9. VOYEUR. One who looks (at sexual happenings) from the French verb, *voir*, to see, and ultimately, from the Latin *videre*, with a similar meaning.

10. FELLATIO. The obtaining of sexual pleasure from the application of the mouth to the sexual organs. The origin is from the Latin, *fellare*, to suck.

11. EXHIBITIONIST. Obtaining sexual pleasure from showing the genitalia. This stems from the Latin, *exhibere*, to display.

12. FROTTEUR. Obtaining sexual pleasure from rubbing against someone else. This is from the French verb, *frotter*, to rub. (Frotteur is sometimes used in modern French in a non-sexual way for a polisher; also for a part of a machine which rubs against another.)

13. COPROPHAGIA. Dirt eating. Derived from the Greek, *kopros*, dung, and *phago*, to eat.

It is proposed to describe the modes of instinctual expression (or aims) in the order of temporal appearance during infantile development, and it must be remembered, of course, that this behaviour becomes abnormal only when it is so related to sexual conduct that it replaces the copulatory termination. Nevertheless, the more the instinctual expression tends to become sidetracked and diverted from copulation the less biological the intercourse (i.e. the less likely is intercourse to end in the proper culmination of impregnation). Each activity can be active or passive, as we have explained, by the principle of reversal or substitution of self for the sexual object. How the instinct becomes permanently reversed is not definitely known, but this may be favoured by the inability to discover the proper object and direct the instinct upon it during childhood, and various aberrations of emotional development due to environmental factors (early death of father, or a doting mother, &c.).

Classification of Abnormal Modes of Sexual Expression (*Sexual Aims*)

I. Abnormal Orificial Sexuality
1. (*a*) Oralism ⎫
   (*b*) Analism ⎬ . . . Active and Passive forms both exist
   (*c*) Other forms ⎭
2. Coprophagia . . . . Both forms probably exist
3. Sado-masochism
4. Frotteurism . . . . Active and Passive
5. Scoptophilio-exhibitionism

Again, whether the abnormal modes of expression are fundamentally erotic as Freud and the psychoanalytical school insist, or whether they are merely patterns of behaviour which become sexually conditioned through environmental circumstances we do not yet know for certain, nor does there seem to be any way of proving it.

The sexual objects can be classified in a similar manner into five different classes.

Classification of Sexual Objects

1. Heterosexual . . . . Object of the opposite sex
2. Homosexual . . . . Object of the same sex
3. Infantosexual . . . . An immature person
4. Bestiosexual . . . . An animal
5. Autosexual . . . . Oneself

These can be utilized by any or all modes of expression, or sexual, aims to produce a perversion. I have shown in the following diagram how this can occur.

Any combination of the sexual object with the sexual modes of expression can take place, thus giving the possibility of a large number of different perversions, some of which are rare and hardly ever occur, some appear only in the fantasy of perverts, but most of them are common. For the sake of clarity only heterosexual and homosexual combinations have been shown here.

In this book I have no intention of describing perverted practices in detail. To do so serves no useful purpose and throws no light on the causation of them. It is much more important to understand the origin and mechanism than to study the individual behaviour. Those interested in details should refer to Placzek's work.

Diagram to Show the Way in which the Modes of Expression (or Sexual Aims) can be Directed towards Different Sexual Objects

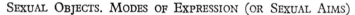

SEXUAL OBJECTS. MODES OF EXPRESSION (OR SEXUAL AIMS)

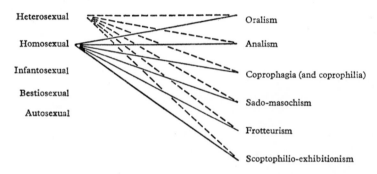

It is possible to classify the perversions either from the point of view of the mode of sexual expression or from the point of view of the sexual object. Since it is usual to speak of heterosexual, homosexual, and so on, it seems more convenient to use the object as the descriptive and to use the mode of expression as the sub-term, so that I shall speak of heterosexual sadism for the cruelty of men to women, homosexual sadism for the cruelty of men to men, infantosexual sadism for the cruelty to children, and bestiosexual sadism for cruelty to animals &c.

Autosexuality I shall use somewhat as Freud used the term narcissism, but since Freud's term carried with it a whole train of his theories it is perhaps better to use a term which is neutral and carries no particular connotations. It will perhaps be convenient to discuss the abnormal modes of instinctual expression first and to show their meaning; then to discuss the objects to which they are directed and to examine them as closely as possible.

I regard the perverts divisible into three degrees:

1. Those who commit perversions in fantasy only.
2. Those who perform perversions only under abnormal conditions (i.e. when drunk or under the influence of drugs, &c.).
3. Active perverts.

I shall deal with the abnormalities of the sexual object mainly from the point of view of the male, since to attempt to interpret the case of both sexes at once leads to useless complication. In the female the mother usually becomes replaced by the father and positive emotion is transferred to him, leaving negative emotion on the mother. *It seems to me that the whole psychology of the female is more complicated than the Freudian school yet admits,* and there is no really satisfactory explanation why the reversal of instinctual urges occurs so much more easily in the female, replacing sadism by masochism, nor why fetishims occur so rarely in women. That women, however, are not entirely averse to other psychosexual abnormalities is shown by a notorious divorce case in which these featured. The wife not only committed adultery with various men but apparently indulged in abnormal behaviour also. Lord Wheatly, the trial judge, commenting on some photographs (apparently taken by means of a polaroid camera with a time switch) stated that they seemed from the contents and positions to be more the type of photographs carried by a woman with a sex perversion than a man with a sex perversion.

REFERENCES

DAILY TELEGRAPH (1963) 9 May.
PLACZEK, F. (1931) *The Sexual Life of Man*, London.

PART TWO

DISORDERS OF SEXUAL
EXPRESSION

6

ABNORMAL ORIFICIAL SEXUALITY, COPROPHILIA, AND COPROPHAGIA

SEXUAL ORALISM

Definition

The obtaining of sexual pleasure from the application of the mouth to the sexual organs. It is a common perversion both heterosexual and homosexual. Whether the female does the act to the male or the male to another male the act is known as fellatio. (Hence, by the way, the value of our exact terminology—heterosexual oralism and homosexual oralism.) When the mouth is applied to the female genitalia it is known as cunnilingus.[1]

Psychopathology and Occurrence

From the biological point of view mouthing or sucking is the most primitive and forceful of all inborn reactions. The new-born child is able to suck at birth and anything placed on the lower lip evokes the sucking reflex which rapidly appears to be transformed into the suckling instinct. By a series of reflexes the child nuzzles at random until by 'trial and error' it discovers the right spot (i.e. the nipple), and thereto clamps itself and sucks with might and main.[2] This is not only true of the higher primates but of all mammals. Sucking, tonguing, nuzzling, and licking are all food responses in the young animal. There is no doubt that oral reflexes are early conditioned sexually—perhaps in some cases by kissing (unless as Freud thinks, the reverse is true) or because sex is encountered as a new situation which can only be explored by such responses as the child already possesses. How far it is to be regarded as the persistence of an infantile reaction or as a conditioned reflex it is difficult to be certain, but we can bring a great deal of proof to show that it is highly probable that this is the real origin. Moreover, since this proof is entirely behaviouristic it is very convincing. David Levy made observations on children which suggested to him that the sucking of the fingers, &c., indulged in by children was caused by inadequate sucking of the breast. He says:

---

[1] There is no term for those who obtain sexual satisfaction from sucking, unless one adopts the psychoanalytical terminology which drags after it a whole train of yet unproved theories. It is therefore proposed to call those who do so 'oralists' and the process 'oralism'. Similarly with anal behaviour.

[2] Cameron has shown that a new-born child can suck harder than a grown man.

For example, an infant feeding at breast or bottle, on a time-schedule of 20 minutes per feeding, would be changed to a schedule of ten minutes per feeding. Counting time spent at breast or bottle, as its minimum sucking time, the infant would, on a schedule of six ten-minute feedings, for 24 hours suffer a diminution of sucking time of 60 minutes per 24 hours, or one-half of its previous sucking activity. In such instances it would be found within a day or two of the change the finger-sucking habit would follow. Similar studies made of children of the same family showed that finger suckers contrasted with non-finger suckers in regard to one factor, the amount of sucking activity.

This reaction has been confirmed by René Spitz (quoted by Lorenz).

This observation shows that the child has an instinctual urge to suck and unless the sucking motor activity is released in breast sucking it will liberate it by some other sucking activity. J. J. Carlson observed that calves which had been fed at the udder and then fed from a bucket developed ear-licking and habits similar in nature to the finger-sucking of children. On Levy's instigation Professor H. D. Goodale made inquiries and found that the calves of dairy cattle (which are not allowed to suckle at the udder for long because of the necessity of conserving the milk) frequently licked and sucked folds of skin or tails, whereas the calves of cattle raised for beef (which were allowed to suckle at the udder) never behaved in this way. Those dairy-cattle calves which were not allowed to suck other calves, and which were penned separately, sucked themselves, unless muzzled.

Levy experimented to determine finally the importance of deprivation of sucking at the nipple in the origin of sucking habits. He took a litter of four dogs and divided them into two sections. Two dogs were allowed to suck at the nipples, whereas the other two were fed by a tube and then with a bottle with a very large teat which needed no sucking. The nipple-sucking puppies were allowed in twenty days 1,609 minutes and 1,480 minutes respectively, whereas the bottle-fed puppies took only 278 and 264 minutes in the same time. The bottle-fed puppies tended to lose weight. The first nine days the pairs were kept in separate kennels. On the second day the bottle-fed dogs started sucking at each other, particularly the lower abdomen. This continued, and the paw, and on some occasions, the penis was sucked. The bitch-fed dogs showed no similar activity even when attempts were made to produce it.

It is impossible to give in full these very illuminating experiments, but actual differences in 'personality' were noted between the breast-fed and bottle-fed pups. There is no doubt that suppression of suckling led to a persistence of the motorial factor in sucking, in their social behaviour (aggression and passivity) and accessory movements, and general motor restlessness. The so-called accessory movements are particularly important, since they show how easy it is to add an ancillary behaviour to breast-feeding or sucking (thus throwing great light on the origin of fetishism).

For example, the forepaw of one pup was moved rhythmically for some time: when it was feeding at a later date it was found that rhythmical movements of this paw tended to initiate sucking. Thus, as Levy says:

Employment of accessory movements during the feeding period opens up a field of investigation in the response or motor side of the conditioned reflex. In contrast, the Pavlov experiments in conditioned reflexes are performed by associating a neutral with an unconditioned reflex, i.e. combinations of stimuli on the receptor side of the reflex.

Levine has extended and confirmed the work of Levy by observing the effect of depriving albino rats of the breast in some cases and delaying weaning in others. He found that there was an effect on the 'personality' of the rats if they were not weaned at the proper time (i.e. at 21 days) and were allowed to continue suckling up to 35 days. 'The behaviour under examination was the capacity to learn to avoid an electric shock by traversing through a swinging door into a safe compartment at the sound of a buzzer.' The ones which were allowed to suckle excessively took longer to learn to avoid the pain than those which were weaned early. He states: 'These data, therefore, tend to support, in general, Levy's conclusions that one of the consequences of excessive maternal contact is emotional instability.'

It is interesting to notice that suckling has such a marked effect on such a low type of mammal as the rat, and one might even conjecture that the effect of excess is to keep the animals immature, or, in Freudian terminology, fixated at an earlier stage.

From the psychoanalytical point of view fellatio is clearly differentiated from cunnilingus. According to Melanie Klein the child tends to identify the breast and penis at an early age, and no doubt the primary function of suckling is a large factor in the frequency with which this perversion is discovered as a fantasy, and indeed as a reality, in women.

Otto Fenichel gives the meaning of fellation as varying and over-determined (i.e. caused by a number of unconscious wishes). He suggests the following:

(1) *Coitus* displaced upwards, (2) A *revenge* on a man who possesses the envied organ, (3) By way of a fantasy of impregnation—*pregnancy*, and (4) an *identification* with the man. 'I possess the penis I took from you.' In this latter there is a suggestion of incorporation and introjection.

Again he says:

Preference for the oral zone as an instrument of sexual gratification seldom occurs as a thorough-going perversion, to the exclusion of other modes of sexual gratification. The first impression given is that of a partial fixation, a vestige of the earlier libidinal organization, which persists alone with analogous vestiges. However, psychoanalytic studies show that the mouth often becomes a substitute for the genitals, if genital activity is inhibited by castration fantasies. This is clear in those cases of fellation which, on analysis, are seen to be the equivalents, or denial of, biting off the penis. But in cunnilingus, too, as we have mentioned above, both sexes are influenced by the fantasy of a concealed female penis.

Although in all cases these factors *may* be found, it seems more likely that in every case fellatio from the woman's point of view is plain regression to an oral level. Indeed this holds for homosexual passive oralism also. It simply represents suckling at the breast. From the point of view of the man, as in homosexual oralism, the active partner seems to have a similar wish reversed. He turns round his wish and desires that someone should suckle at his breast (i.e. penis) and hence the act of fellatio. There is the possibility, of course, that the passive protagonist of oralism in the case of the male submitting to fellatio, may be suffering from a very early fixation which occurred before the child had an opportunity of differentiating himself from the mother and that the lack of differentiation has caused this behaviour rather than a manifestation of reversal. In any case reversal probably means this latter.

The frequency of oral practices revealed by the researches of Kinsey *et al.* is higher than might be expected. It varies according to the educational level, being lowest in those of poorer intellect. Application of the male mouth to female genitalia varying from about 4 per cent. in the lower types to 40 per cent. in the highest, and of the female mouth to the male genitalia from about 7 to 42 per cent. In homosexuality there is not so much variation in the high educational levels—e.g. active frequence is about 13 to 21 per cent. but in the lower levels 14 to 46 per cent.

Oralism is an attempt to deal with sexuality in terms of breast suckling. This seems most reasonable and most in accord with the developmental knowledge and the best summary of it at our disposal. It also explains why both passive and active participants obtain pleasure from their behaviour. If this is so it is not surprising that a certain amount of fixation occurs in some people and this shows itself in oral behaviour. It is therefore to be regarded as evidence of incomplete development and immaturity.

Cannibalism

The eating of human flesh, unless under the extremities of starvation, is an extreme instance of oralism. In our culture it is practically unknown. It appears to occur: (1) associated with psychotic excitement; (2) in primitive cultures: and (3) for superstitious or religious reasons.

Biologically, one finds that many animals have no objection to eating the flesh of their own kind, sometimes even their young; and, since animals have little instinctual differentiation between their own species and others (as demonstrated, for example, by imprinting, and apes nursing kittens, &c.) there seems no reason why they should appreciate the nature of cannibalism.

Apes, however, do not indulge in it, and yet there is a strong basis of evidence that primitive man did so. Not only animal bones, but human ones, have been smashed open to obtain the marrow, and this has been discovered with most specimens right up through the Pleistocene with the Zinjanthropus to the Neanderthal. Indeed, Alberto Blanc has drawn attention to the fractures round the foramen magnum in prehistoric skulls which seem to indicate a ritual fracture of the skull to obtain the succulent brain. One anthropologist has suggested that the difference between apes and man is that man practised cannibalism!

This has persisted to some extent until recent times and the rationalization for such behaviour in primitive peoples was the sympathetic magic of Frazer, by which eating a part of a strong man endowed one with his strength.

Greek myth is full of cases of cannibalism, and it is now accepted that the Maeniads in the Dionysian frenzy tore human beings to pieces and ate them raw.

All this suggests that there is a strong unconscious urge towards cannibalism which, indeed, is often shown in the fantasies of patients. I have had patients who have had fantasies of biting and consuming their mother's breasts, biting off someone's penis, and eating it, &c., as Klein pointed out some time ago.

Action is rare, even in the psychotic, but Wertham records a case which he saw of a man aged 65 who stranged a little girl, aged 12, and lived for 9 days, *in a state of sexual excitement,* eating her flesh which he fried with onions. This man was a paranoid psychotic and behaved strangely, at times shouting out that he was Christ. He was believed to have killed at least ten children, some of whom he castrated, and he inflicted injuries on himself, including pushing needles into his body. In spite of his obvious mental illness he was refused reprieve and sent to the electric chair.

The following is a case, although the man was prevented from indulging in it, which demonstrates the intention of cannibalism.

Charge of Murdering Second Girl. Man of 71 for Trial

When Tom Lionel Burns, 71, retired motor driver, York Street, Barrow-in-Furness, Lancs., appeared on remand there yesterday charged with murdering Lavinia Murray, five, he was further charged with the murder of Sheila Barnes, also five. He was committed for trial at Lancaster Assizes in October, 1958.

Mr. E. C. MacDermott, prosecuting, said the girls disappeared on the evening of June 11th. On 15 June their 'horribly mutilated' bodies were found in the house in which Burns had lived alone since his wife went to hospital in 1956.

Medical evidence was that they died on the evening of June 11. Lavinia who lived at Cheltenham Street, Barrow, and Sheila of Ainsley Street, had been playing with two other girls at the back of a house in York Street at about 6.30 p.m.

A detective called at Burns's house on the morning of June 15th. He saw that someone had been digging a hole in his shed about 3 ft. long, 1 foot deep and 1 ft. wide. Burns asked the detective not to go upstairs because of 'sentimental reasons'. As he got to the top of the stairs the officer heard Burns say: 'I'm . . . now'. The unclothed body of one child was lying on a wicker basket and the unclothed body of the other on a mattress with a knife nearby. Burns had said, 'Sex made me do them in'. Mr. MacDermott said that Burns had made a signed statement. He said he was playing the piano when the girls walked in and listened to him. He showed them scales and they played.

They went into the kitchen and he asked them to undress. They laughed and took it as a joke. He helped them to undress and he kissed them. He then lost all control. He cut the girls' throats and carried them upstairs. 'Yesterday I cut the foot off one of them and was going to roast and eat it.'

Unfortunately in such a brief account nothing is given of his previous life. However, it is clear that the children's bodies were horribly mutilated and that there was an oral element—roasting and eating the flesh— in his behaviour. The only unusual factor appears to be the age of the man and the curious fact that there was no history of sadism previously. No doubt the separation from his wife (who was in hospital) had some relation to his conduct. He was found unfit to plead and so was not tried at the Assizes.

It is noticeable that this man attributes his behaviour to sex, so probably he felt some sexual excitement associated with it.

Jack-the-Ripper, who certainly suffered from sadistic sexuality, was a person who practised cannibalism, at least in fantasy, even if not in reality. Professor Francis Camps has published recently-unearthed material regarding this man.

Here is one of the letters he sent to the authorities.

Received Tues. 16 Oct.

'From hell'

'Mr. Lusk,

I send you half the kidney I took from one woman, presarved it for you, tother piece I fried and ate it was very nice. I may send you the bloody knif that took it out if you only wate a whil longer.

Signed

Catch me when you can, Mr. Lusk.'

The illiteracy may have been assumed, but it is curious that he stated that he ate half this kidney *fried*, since in Wertham's case the human flesh was fried with onions.

It may, of course, be objected that this letter is merely intended to shock the police, but in any case it shows the fantasy in the man's mind, and surely his behaviour had been sufficiently shocking without this addition.

Pictures of the woman Eddowes killed by Jack-the-Ripper show slashes on the face, with a detached right ear and cut nose, but the worst wound was inflicted on the abdominal wall, where there was a jagged slash starting at the vagina and ending between the breasts. This suggests (as Dr. Sequera and Dr. Saunders insisted) that the man had no anatomical skill. As far as is known this case was the only one of the women he killed in which cannibalism took place.

Wertham insists that in our culture the eating of human flesh (in the absence of starvation) is diagnostic of psychosis. I cannot comment from my own experience since these cases are extremely rare, and I have never seen a patient who indulged in it. If this is true, then Jack-the-Ripper was definitely insane and his extreme oral sadism the result of his illness.

Although acts of cannibalism are rare in our culture, even in the psychotic, they undoubtedly occur in fantasy. For example, the Marquis de Sade, in one of his novels, *Juliette*, described a Russian of gigantic stature who was enormously rich. He had a castle in a lonely spot in Italy and kept a harem of 200 girls aged five to twenty. These served his sexual purposes until, at a suitable time, they were killed and eaten by him. This story is somewhat ridiculous, but the Russian is certainly representative of the Marquis himself, and this is what he would have liked to do had he been able. It is possibly significant that he became enormously fat in his later life.

An instance of cannibalistic behaviour in a modern culture is to be found in the Japanese treatment of war prisoners. According to Wilson and Pitman, 'A captured Japanese order reveals details regulating the obtaining, and eating, of the flesh of an American airman. An accused Japanese officer described how his general was annoyed at an evening party over the shortage of meat, and suggested getting some more by means of an impending execution of an American pilot. The "meat" arrived promptly, and was duly cooked, but nobody "relished the taste".

'This was not an isolated incident. At another officer's party at which similar "meat" was devoured, the admiral asked a major for a little liver from the next pending execution. There were many cases of Australian, American, and Japanese dead being cut up and eaten. The only counter-order issued was that which forbade the eating of their own dead. Otherwise they generally practised cannibalism from choice and obviously from a very atavistic and ritualistic compulsion.'

Murry, who made a study of witchcraft, states that cannibalism occurred in some cases in the belief that it protected the witch against being

G—PSY. D.

compelled to reveal information under torture. It happened apart from this, however, and she states 'Many accusations against witches included the charge of eating the flesh of infants. This does not seem to have been altogether unfounded, though there is no proof that the children were killed for the purpose. Similar forms of cannibalism as a religious rite were practised by the worshippers of Bacchus in ancient Greece.'

It must not be forgotten that eating human flesh under the guise of eating the god is to be found in many primitive religions. Later this turned into a sacrifice and animals were substituted. The Holy Communion in the Christian Church is celebrated by eating bread, which is actually named as flesh, and drinking wine which is called blood. This appears to be either a residue of some ancient cannibalistic custom or else symbolic of it.

Vaginal Inflation as a form of Oralism

This is an abnormal form of sexual behaviour which is unfamiliar to many medical men. It was suddenly brought to notice in America in April 1946. The death of a girl aged 17, who was five months pregnant, was recorded. She had been married previously and had left her husband to live with a young teamster aged 25. They had been together for two months in a cheap hotel when one evening they decided to get drunk, and after having drunk over a pint of whisky between them had intercourse. After it the man drew a deep breath and blew into the woman's vagina. She suddenly collapsed and died before a doctor arrived. A post-mortem examination showed there was 'Thrombosis of the uterine sinusoids, following trauma, injection or admission of air into the sinusoids, with pulmonary embolism and thrombosis. Passage of air or other clotting agents into the brain, with cerebral embolism.' The man was put on trial for murder, but this, however, was dismissed and he was freed.

A very similar case was recorded in England during July 1946. It was that of a girl aged 17 who was also pregnant. She was accosted by an American corporal whilst playing darts in a public house. They left together and she permitted him to make love to her on a bench. Afterwards they went to some bushes and intercourse took place. Five minutes later he cupped his hands and blew into the vagina two or three times. The girl started groaning and collapsed, dying soon after. This man was indicted for murder and was in a very dangerous position, since the pathologist had never heard of air embolism produced in this way and thought that the girl had been strangled because of some marks on her throat. Further evidence, however, and the opinions of other pathologists, established that this was a case of air embolism. The prisoner was therefore found not guilty.

It is well known that the injection of air into the uterus may produce death and in many cases this has been recorded. The danger must be greatly increased when the air is under pressure since no death seems to have been recorded when the child has been heard to cry before birth. It seems very improbable that injection of air into the vagina is pleasurable, and the impulse—apart from oralism—on the part of the man is psychologically obscure (unless it is the reverse of suction). Whatever the basic motivation may be there is no doubt that it is orally connected, and related to other forms of such behaviour. From the examples given here it is obvious that there is great danger to the female and she is foolish to submit to it. The possibility of a murder charge on the part of the man makes this type of conduct a risky form of 'enjoyment'.

CASE No. 1

A Case of Oral Fetishism

This case was that of a young man aged 25 who complained that he felt depressed. He was not sexually stirred by young women but felt tremendously excited by seeing a girl smoke a cigarette. He obtained his sexual pleasure in this way, and would frequent cafés for hours in the hope of seeing a girl light one. He also stammered, but had improved by speech therapy.

His family history was not good. His father, a clergyman, was alive but was very neurotic and egotistic. His mother had died from carcinoma. A paternal grandfather committed suicide. One uncle had a cyclic manic-depression with two-yearly intervals, and one uncle was nearly unfrocked by the Church for offences against girls.

The patient himself was a frank and rather a charming young man. He said that he felt his fetishism an intrusion into his life and sincerely wished to be rid of it. Moreover, since he also was ordained this fetishism was likely to interfere with his profession as a clergyman.

Apparently smoking was early implanted in his mind in conjunction with sex. As a young boy he associated them together and got an erection, and this occurred again when he first started smoking. He had formerly been excited at the sight of boys smoking, but lately this had changed to girls.

He remembered that he had masturbated from an early age until he was 11 years old, when he ceased. He was told at the age of 12 years that he stammered because he masturbated. He managed to stop it until he was aged 15, when his mother was ill, and then he started again. From childhood he had had the habit of oscillating pieces of paper, pyjama strings, handkerchiefs, &c., in his hand, and had lost himself in fantasy while doing it (this was apparently a masturbation equivalent). When he was 9 years old he was sent to a school which was kept by two old ladies and was fascinated by the canings they gave those who disobeyed them. He was said to have been the worst boy in the school and was expelled. As a small boy the sight of the choir-boys excited him when he went to church. He was made to feel very guilty about smoking when he was caught trying it at the age of 10, and this escapade was treated as a very heinous sin. The atmosphere in which he was brought up was a strictly religious one, and his mother acted up to her beliefs. His father was somewhat hypocritical and he was quick to notice it as a child. The patient's relationship to women was unusual and abnormal even when he was little. The charladies who worked at his home always stirred deep emotional responses, and they were either tremendous friends or else bitter enemies. This was his reaction to a foreign girl who stayed with his mother. He had quarrelled with her bitterly for some time, but finally became engaged to her, although she was much older than he was.

As a child he seems to have been very emotional and screamed loudly for little. When he did so his mother used to say 'That is Satan!' and he actually believed that this was a separate entity which invaded his personality. His father used to go to religious meetings, and when he returned was always in a bad temper and quarrelled with the aunts who lived with them. He fantasied imaginary friends, but this shocked his parents, who insisted that he should not pray for them. He was brought up in complete ignorance of sex except what stray bits he was able to deduce from the Bible. He said: 'I learned it from the Bible "to lie together", "to lie with a beast", and so on. A boy told me of menstruation. We were brought up in absolute ignorance, but my father would blurt out sudden sex knowledge and told me that I came from my mother.'

He had dreams of watching men smoke cigarettes and his fetishism had homosexual roots. Apparently these men represented his father. He then realized that his attachment to his elderly fiancée was because she was so closely linked with his mother. There seems to have been considerable hostility to his mother since he showed it very clearly to his aunts, with whom he constantly lost his temper and had terrible quarrels when he was young. It is not surprising, therefore, that he was more strongly homosexual than most boys and fell deeply in love with a master at school and then with an officer at camp where he went for a holiday.

As the analysis proceeded it became apparent that he had some reason for hostility to his father, who seems to have been a very selfish and egotistic man. He became involved with another woman soon after his wife's death, and this enraged the patient: as soon as he was engaged to this one, however, he fell in love with another woman, but was eventually persuaded to marry the first woman, but he was not happy with her.

When the patient was a boy his brother was circumcised. He felt that this was done as a preventative against masturbation, and was very jealous indeed and felt he should have it done also. He brought up a certain amount of excrementary memories and sadistic fantasies. He remembered that when he oscillated a piece of paper (as described above) he had fantasies of being a tremendous orator with enormous crowds hanging on his words, and so on.

There was no doubt that at the bottom of his illness there was a strong homosexual element. When he was training for the priesthood he went on a holiday with a fellow student and they slept together. There was some sexual play with the result that they had erections, and this so profoundly shocked them that they terminated their holiday. Moreover, there was a strong sadistic element also. This sadistic strain seemed linked to the smoking, since he was told as a small boy that smoking was very injurious to the health and he could not dissociate the idea. Alcohol was attractive to him, and he thought a great deal of people drinking it and injuring their health also. This I was able to link up with his mother, who read a great deal to him when he was a child. She, being very religious, chose what she considered were uplifting works, which, however, were greatly concerned with the behaviour of those who had left the straight and narrow path—particularly those who drank heavily and behaved cruelly. Also at school the mistress read stories in which floggings appeared frequently. These ideas became fixed in his mind, and he frequently thought of them while masturbating.

Masturbation he said he discovered by watching the milking of a cow (but knowing that masturbation occurs first about the time of weaning and is used to substitute the pleasure derived from suckling, one wonders if this is not a fantasy). For some reason he associated eggs with sucking also.

As might be expected, his sadistic fantasies and memories had their counterpart in masochistic ones, and he produced numerous memories of hurting himself and deriving pleasure from it.

It became apparent after some time that his fantasy construction took on the following form:

Girls smoking—boys smoking—mother smoking—cigarette—penis—egg—breast. He had a fantasy of sucking a penis and said that an egg in an eggcup reminded him of a penis.

He also revived memories of the thought of eating human beings. He had already expressed the idea that the Roman Catholic view of communion was horrible ('eating a person'), and felt that at some time in his childhood he had had some thought of eating his mother and of her eating him.

As is usual in such cases, he worked out some sort of Oedipus situation with the hostile emotion detached from his mother in the treatment, and frequently expressed his hatred for his father. There was evidently some early confusion of mother and father, since he said that when he was little he had an idea that women had penises as well as men.

Ten months after he had started his analysis he went abroad for his holiday and was in contact with his elderly fiancée. This caused a marked regression. His case was, of course, a difficult one to treat since his position rather prevented him indulging in any sort of normal sexual experimentation. Moreover, I felt that it would be unwise to tell him to break off his engagement. (In these cases it is always wiser to undermine the attachment to the mother which is the basis of engagements of this type, rather than attempt to destroy them in a frontal attack.)

His unfettered associations continually strayed towards the idea of the breast and milk. He said: 'When I was told that there was a breast of lamb for lunch it always made me feel queer. The desire to smoke is more than a wish to suck the breast: in my case it is a wish to absorb the mother.' He also started to link the idea of cruelty with intercourse, and said that he had the idea that his father hurt his mother when he had intercourse with her. There was also a strong idea of having hair in his mouth which kept recurring, and apparently this was the result of some infantile experience, but although this was strong enough to penetrate consciousness, it never caused a 'hair-cutting fetish' such as occasionally one finds in which there is a compulsion to cut off girls' hair.

At this time, about a year after the commencement of his treatment, he started to fall in love with a girl he had met at church socials. She was much smarter and younger than his fiancée and naturally more suited for his mate. Unfortunately she was somewhat attached to someone else, and the conflict between them produced some signs of neurosis in her. She finally wrote to him and said that she felt her friendship with him was making her ill and that they must give each other up. He was naturally disturbed at this. About the same time a prostitute spoke to him in the train, but he did not follow up her suggestions. Then he decided himself that his engagement with his elderly fiancée was unsuitable and broke it off. This brought a feeling of relief. He noticed that he felt much attracted to women, and that he was beginning to notice their breasts. This was something which he had never done before. Moreover, he started to notice that the legs could be an attractive shape also.

Finally, just over a year after the beginning of his treatment, he managed to persuade the young girl with whom he was in love to accept his proposal of marriage. This, incidentally, rid her of her conflict and she lost her own neurotic symptoms. It put the final seal on his own recovery. He married this young lady and was offered a post abroad. This he accepted and wrote to me after eighteen months stating that he was leading a perfectly normal married life and that he had had no symptoms at all since he had finished treatment.

Such a case as this is of great interest. Firstly, it shows that it is unusual to have a fetishism in pure culture, and such sexual malversions are thoroughly intermixed with perversions (i.e. sadism and homosexuality) and the roots of other malversions (hair-cutting).

This young man's malversion seems to have been caused by the accentuation of his mammary experiences by his mother's reading of sadistic material and his unsatisfactory father. It would seem that the whole family was a hotbed of abnormality and the uncles and parents created a disturbing atmosphere, and one full of conflicts, which could hardly fail to influence the emotional development of a sensitive child. The gradual disappearance of his fetishism and slow growth of his adult personality under the encouragement of analysis was most interesting to watch, and his marriage and acceptance of work abroad (away from all the family interferences and influence) was a final proof of the success of treatment.

CASE No. 2

A Case of Obsessional Neurosis with Oral Elements

This case was that of a young man aged 25. He had had a considerable amount of psychotherapy before he came into my care, but had not responded in any way. He complained of anxiety, obsessional fears, and of being able to obtain sexual pleasure only by sucking a baby's comforter (dummy).

He came from a family which seems to have been the worst possible environment. His father, a retired civil servant, was an obsessional neurotic and spent his whole time in the observance of religious ritual, but in a purely obsessional manner and without any feeling. For example, he refused to miss a prayer meeting when his son was dying and his wife had no one to support her. He spent many hours preparing to do anything, and always insisted on being at a station at least half an hour before the time due to leave. If he had to fill up a form he always insisted that it was filled up meticulously without the possibility of a comma out of place. He told the truth in an obsessional way, and on one occasion ruined his son's chance for a scholarship by so doing.

His mother was in hypochondriacal hysteric. She complained for many years that she had serious disease of the heart, and even convinced many doctors that this was so. When she found this inconvenient she developed gastric and hepatic pain. By means of these pains and diseases she managed to keep the whole family subservient to her.

The patient was the middle one of three sons. The eldest son had had prolonged psychotherapy at the Tavistock Clinic. He had various aches and pains and, before treatment, had managed to convince a surgeon that the testicular pain he complained of was due to tuberculous disease and the testicle was removed. The younger brother seems to have met the emotional blizzard after it had blown out its full force, but even he was affected somewhat, and before he could bring himself to get married had to have a term of psychotherapy. He managed to obtain a lectureship and earn a good salary. He was the only son who obtained anything other than a living wage, since the eldest brother earned only a few pounds weekly as a clerk and the patient about the same as a school-master.

When the patient first came to the Tavistock Clinic he complained that he had had throughout his whole life an overwhelming interest in babies' dummies. Before the age of puberty he had phobias of venereal disease and deafness. These persisted until puberty, when the ideas of venereal disease ceased to worry him. The deafness still troubled him, and he tried frantically to learn details about the telephone so that he could be sure of hearing on it. He knew nothing of sex and never masturbated, but when he was aged 13 years he had a nocturnal emission and was very frightened.

He had managed to struggle through the London Matriculation before he left school. School itself was a perpetual torture to him since he felt that he was bullied because he worked hard and that he should try to be a tougher, more manly boy; but when he did this and worked less arduously he was bullied by his parents for not being top of the class. When he left school he entered a commercial firm, but lived in terror of the manager, who occasionally lost his temper and shouted. His obsession regarding listening on the telephone complicated his business life. After some time he left his firm and worked for a while with an estate agent, but again his obsessionalism and his telephone difficulties led to complications. He then decided that the only outlet was some sort of academic career and managed to obtain a Board of Education grant to become a school-teacher. He went to college, but his life then became a misery because he worried that someone might steal his instruments in class, that he might have his books stolen, that some female student might interfere with him (there was a very aggressive girl in his year), and then he would not know how to deal with her. In one case another student did quarrel with him and he indulged in a half-hearted fight for which he was worried with terrible guilt. He then followed his elder brother's example and had psychotherapy, but although he was under two physicians for about two years they did not penetrate deeply into his unconscious and their treatment had no effect whatsoever. He had never consciously masturbated in his life, but one of these physicians suggested that it was about time he started and he followed the suggestion. His masturbation was accompanied by fantasies of babies' dummies, and it is characteristic of him that whenever he met some difficulty he started to go round to various chemists' shops in order to buy a baby's dummy, preferably from a pretty shop assistant. He had had some sort of diluted affair with a girl in which their love play consisted in him being given a baby's dummy.

He started treatment under me at the end of 1935. He was then a student working for his B.Sc., but had failed on more than one occasion. He felt that his anxieties took up so much of his energy that he was unable to work successfully. He spent most of his day in what he called 'solving problems'. This occupation was really obsessionally ruminating on what line of conduct he should follow in various situations—such as if someone stuck a pin in him while he was writing his examination. Almost at the first moment when he started treatment he showed negative transference and commenced by complaining that his difficulties were much too deep to be likely to respond to psychotherapy and that I should not be able to do him any good. This was traced to his father, and he at once started to produce hostility to him. He then brought up early memories. He remembered that he masturbated at the age of 4 and sucked rolled pieces of paper. He had sought some affection from his father and had been rebuffed and took to this behaviour as an outlet. He found an old baby's dummy and sucked it until the age of 8. This conduct worried him for years, and apparently the fears he entertained of having venereal disease at the age of 13 years were due to guilt from his behaviour. He started off his analysis by bringing up terrific hatred to his father, who had a very puritanical religious outlook, and thought that children had original sin and needed watching throughout the whole of their lives. There were in his mind vague ideas which suggested the onset of a psychosis. He was very keen to start arguments with his father, and this made him feel, he said, like an aggressive Christ, or: 'Whipping the Pharisees out of the Temple'. His father had always taught him that any form of fighting was wicked, and it was partly through this that he had such a miserable time at school. It was not until he was aged 16 that he was able to abandon this concept and then succeeded in turning on a boy who was bullying him. It soon became apparent that he was dawdling over his degree because this tended to infuriate his father, who he said had 'a degree complex', and set an inordinately high value on them. He proved difficult to analyse, so that it was not surprising that two other analysts had already failed with him. I refused absolutely to be side-tracked by his interminable problems and made him realize that they were only a transference manifestation, and that in bringing them up continually he was only trying to utilize tactics which had infuriated his father. The output of hate which he produced was incredible, and at first it was all concerned with his father. As the analysis proceeded the extent of his fetishism became more and more apparent. He said that at various times when he was worried regarding his degree he had visited more than sixty chemists and bought babies' dummies at them and five babies' feeding-bottles also. He explained this by saying: 'At the age of 3 or 4 I met his great barrier of lack of sympathy and turned back to dummies as a consolation. If you are not adult you cannot deal with adult problems. I am still at the age 4 state.'

He had a strong wish to attack the Church and clergy. This was easily traced to a wish to attack his father. It became apparent that he had during his childhood made various attempts to grow up, but on each occasion he had clashed with his neurotic parents. These memories brought up still more hate for his father, which he released obliquely by telling of his hatred and fury with one of the doctors who had previously treated him and fantasizing fighting with him when he encountered him. As the analysis proceeded it became apparent that he was expressing more and more hate regarding his mother. This was a distinct progression, since when he first came for treatment he had felt hostile to his father but had regarded his mother as all that was perfect. Numerous painful memories appeared—for example, when he was about 3 years old the boy next door had taught him how to direct urine against the fence. His mother, however, saw these activities and reprimanded him as though his infantile urinary activities were cardinal sins. Moreover, she more or less refused to allow him to play with boys other than his brothers after this. Although the main stream of hostility now seemed to be directed towards his mother, it by no means left his father entirely. As is usual in these cases, it seemed that the hostility released from the mother was used again in working out an Oedipus situation. He produced a great deal of castration material and said: 'I'd like to slice up his penis like an onion. At my digs on Saturday I was given sliced onion and it was distasteful to me. I have a desire to think of my father as having no penis at all. I want to cut if off so that it is flush and is 'tidied up''. To have a penis hanging is so untidy.' (Surely this is the extreme of obsessional tidiness!) All this release of hostility produced a great deal of transference which seemed mainly related to his father. The obsessional worry regarding a girl student interfering with him during his examinations he related back to his mother. 'It is the thought of my mother castrating me—she wanted to make me a eunuch child!'

The rage expressed by him against his family took on almost incredible proportions. The unearthing of his castration feelings released tremendous hatred to his father and later to his mother, since he spent one session after another in pouring out fury against them after it appeared. Naturally this caused strong transference which had to be dealt with as soon as it arose. In a case such as this it is dangerous for the analyst to allow large accumulations of transference, for it may lead to physical assault on the analyst or suicide of the analysed. Even when transference was being watched and dealt with as soon as possible there were still abundant hostile fantasies directed towards me. He said: 'I feel I would like to kick you in the testicles. It would lay you out. Also carving off your genitals. The carving off of your legs and leaving of your genitals in place would please me. I should like to cut off your head and leave an artery squirting like a fountain.' In many cases he expressed hatred and anger regarding his brothers, but when he did so it seemed that he was using them as substitutes for his detested parents.

The release of all this fury did him a great deal of good and he managed to turn his emotions towards girls in a more normal way. When he masturbated he noticed that he was fantasying having intercourse with girls instead of having the dummy fantasies which had occupied his mind previously. At this time, about six months after he had started treatment, he happened to see one of the physicians who had analysed him previously and this aroused terrific hatred towards him. It was easily discovered that this hatred was really originating from his parents, because, like the physician, they had done nothing for him. Although there was still a strong tendency to regress in the old fantasies when he met difficulties, he was undoubtedly working much better. He then started to realize that the anthropomorphized criticism which made his life a misery and which he called 'The Criticizer' was really only the introjected mother. He had been subjected to his mother's criticism from his earliest years and had identified himself so strongly with her that he had started criticizing himself and continued this ever since. This criticism made his life a misery and compelled him to do things again and again in order that they should be exactly right. He defined it very clearly himself by saying: 'I feel that it is a hostile guilt conglomeration derived from my mother and father.' Nine months after he started treatment he succeeded in gaining his degree, for which he had been working unsuccessfully for his finals three years longer than necessary. The degree was only a third-class one, but when one realizes that the patient was seriously ill the whole time he was working for it, one must admit that it was a triumph for psychotherapeutic method even to attain this. Although he was now in a position to earn his living he was by no means cured, since he was still not sexually normal. I now set out to cure this and worked hard at his remaining psychotic residue. He contemplated entering the Church for a short time, but this identification with his father was really not possible owing to the intense hatred for him and his father's unsatisfactory personality. After trying to extract a grant from the authorities he gave it up as a bad job. This was probably as well, since he attended a few lectures on theology and they put him in a fury against the lecturers and the subject.

He then started to appreciate more and more the hatred for his mother, and realized also that this was the basis of his undoubted masochism. He said: 'I feel a desire to be tortured. I feel I must be tortured in order to have a mother. I cannot have a mother without being tortured, so I want to be tortured.' Many monotonous months passed by in which he continued to pour out almost unending hatred for his mother, so that one wondered at the multitude and variety of his fantasies. He managed in spite of this to obtain and successfully keep a post of assistant master at a private school. Many of his ideas were regarding suckling, and as one might have expected there was great hatred for the breast. He said: 'I hate the idea of suckling at the breast. She (my mother) has dirty underclothes and dirty corsets. Her breath smells. Her breasts hang down, coarse breasts, dirty chemise. I loathe the breasts; they represent all dirtiness, filth, and smell. The idea of suckling nauseates me. I want to spit them out and cut them off. Wash them and squeeze them the right shape. They represent tyranny. She forces her breasts upon me. She wants to be suckled and resents me not wanting to suckle. Altogether breasts disgust me. I prefer men to women. They are so coarse. I can see my mother's breasts all large, dirty, and greasy. I peck at them and never really suckle them. The idea of getting fluid out of my mother is revolting. I feel physically sick at the idea. I should feel defiled— she represents disease. I never suckled at a woman's breasts and my whole interest is in women's breasts. I have never suckled at a woman's breasts, but I fantasy suckling at a girl's breast. She says, "Please suckle at my breast, I want you to." I feel that during the first six months of my life I had a wet nurse because I was so weak. I think of suckling at the breast, but I feel nausea. The breast looks objectionable. One reason why I dislike girls is because they have breasts. The nipple is forced into my mouth. I don't want it and feel humiliated. No milk comes and it has only clear fluid. I suckle this dry nipple. A feeling of the clear fluid, then milk comes into your mouth. Sucking, then relaxing. The sucking rhythmically is like intercourse. Kissing is like sucking at the breast. There is a pleasurable sensation. A great big breast pointed like a horrible thing is like a nightmare lowered into my mouth. My whole life is a series of dummies and breasts. I live in a world of breasts, everything represents breasts to me. Breasts burst and blood and pus come out. I feel it going down my throat. I'll get cancer. [He had at this a somatic reaction and actually felt the sensation of something unpleasant going down his throat.] Breasts produce pus and cancerous hairs, and I am forced to drink it down. Breasts are like two big boils. Pus, mucous-blood, black poison blood going down my throat. It goes all over my face. It gets in my nose and ears. I hate all women. It is impossible to have a proper relation with women when you want to cut them all up.'

It must be remembered that these were fantasies which repeated themselves again and again, but they may have had some foundation in actuality since his mother did tell one of the physicians who treated the patient before me that she was unable to feed the patient because she had inverted nipples.

As he produced all this curious material he rapidly improved. He gave in his resignation at the school where he was working because the headmaster refused to support him in his insistence that proper discipline should be enforced. He obtained a better post at another school. He has managed to live as a more or less successful schoolmaster but has always needed some psychological support. He has never married, not, as he says, owing to his poor financial position, but because he is afraid that he will lose his position. This is not entirely a fantasy since his headmaster did try to replace him with a more efficient master. Although to some extent an emotional cripple due to this childhood he manages to find some enjoyment in life.

It would seem that his fetishism and psychotic symptoms were undoubtedly the result of his environment. The experiences at the breast started his hostility, but these would have been dealt with adequately had he not been subjected to a loveless and impossible environment produced by an obsessional father and an hysterical mother. The result was that his elder brother was made so obsessional that only prolonged treatment seems to have saved him from developing schizophrenia. The patient was made so fetishistic that he nearly reached disaster, but the younger brother who met the emotional blizzard when it was abating has managed to turn his neurosis into his work and concentrated so on it that he has been elected to a Chair and makes a successful Professor. The patient is now freed from the breast and is sexually normal but his life is too precarious for him to attain sexual happiness after so many vicissitudes.

CASE No. 3

A Case of Bestiosexual Oralism

A man aged 30 years, very tall and thin, who complained when first seen of being tired and always fatigued. He had suicidal ideas and had threatened it. He felt that he was a failure and must have nothing to do with girls.

Family History

His family history seems to have been more or less normal. His father had died of heart-failure some months before he came for treatment. He had been a miller and corn merchant. The patient, the eldest, lived with his mother aged 60, his brother aged 27, and sister aged 24.

Personal History

He had had a poor personal history. As a child he had been very nervous and shy. As he said, 'I invited aggression', and consequently was bullied a great deal. He was tremendously attached to his mother. He stated: 'When I was a small kid I was desperately fond of my mother. I was more fond of her than any man is of his wife.' He was apparently very aggressive as a child but later became quieter. He was very lonely when he went to boarding-school and missed his mother a great deal. He realized, as he said, 'I was a mother's darling', and was terribly shocked at the way the other boys talked of the facts of life. Sex disgusted him. He hated this school and asked his father to remove him, but he refused. This was a shock to him, but he sulked his way through school and to pass the time worked hard. He had no sympathy with the other boys and felt that in playing games they made animals of themselves. He only played such games as were compulsory. He had no idea that one should build up one's body, and everything about the body was disgusting to him. He had a contempt for bodies in general. There was a great deal of sensitiveness and he said: 'If I could fight a chap my hate went into my fist. If I could not it went inside and hurt me for years after. I was very shy and could not look people in the eye if I did not know them well.' During his last term he tried to stand on his dignity and in consequence the other boys gave him a rough time. He left school definitely hostile to it. After leaving his mother suggested that he should take up art and become an artist. Although in no way suited for such a profession he meekly accepted and was sent to the Slade school where he did not show any promise. He was impressed with the girls there, but made no advances to them. Although he had been hostile to school he had absorbed a futile sort of Sir Galahad type of reaction to women from it, and when he came in contact with girls treated them as too elevated to regard. He failed at the Slade school and was advised to seek another avocation. He felt very guilty about this and thought that he had wasted his father's money. In consequence he made no attempt to find another profession but asked to be taken into his father's business. This was arranged, and for a time he travelled as a representative in the corn business. The fact that it was necessary to represent the goods he was selling in the best possible light made it seem to him that he was telling lies and he felt guilty about this also.

He had various futile attractions to girls, but always feared them too much to make any advances. There were a number of strong sexual fantasies, but these he tried to suppress as unclean and worried a great deal because when in the company of girls he thought sometimes of them sexually. He said: 'I always think with women that I am not man enough for the job', and again, 'When there is no sex in it women are very charming companions.' He confessed that he had never actually taken a girl out alone, but if he were quite sure that he would never fall in love with one, only then could he take one out. He preferred plain girls to pretty ones, since the latter got him 'worked up'.

He became more and more seclusive and finally decided to commit suicide. He went to his father, told him that he had put his affairs in order and intended to make arrangements to commit suicide. This greatly alarmed his father, who persuaded him to do no such thing. Soon after his father died, and the patient was so engrossed with the necessity of putting his father's affairs in order that he had no time for suicide. Six months later, however, as he did not feel any better and life still seemed as bad he decided to do so again. His relative discovered his intentions, sent him to his own doctor, who referred him to me.

The patient was given deep psychotherapy and responded well. He soon felt considerably better. At the fourth session he produced a curious dream. It was as follows: 'I was not quite satisfied about a ewe lamb having maggots. I turned her over on her back and dealt with the maggots but noticed that the udder was developed. I sucked the teats.'

His associations to this were that he really had a ewe lamb (since his father's death he had had a small farm) and this lamb really had maggots. He admitted with great shame that he had suckled at a ewe's teats and obtained great sexual excitement from doing so. It first started when he was 18 years old and had some goats. He suckled at their udders. Anything with teats aroused his lust. He associated them with a woman's breast, but apparently the real thrill came more from the anticipation rather than the actual behaviour. There was tremendous shame about it, and he said that if he were caught at it he would commit suicide.

After the production of this dream he brought out considerable hatred to his brother, who was in normal mental health and was more successful than the patient. Following this he had another queer dream which may have significance: 'I dreamed that I was in a room struggling with Napoleon and broke off the tip of his sword. I was fearful of being stabbed in the chest and turned round and was stabbed in the back.'

Apparently this hostility to his brother went back to a very early period, since he remembered that when at the age of 6 years his brother was upset out of a pram he felt he was to blame. After this he 'got nerves' and 'saw things' on the stairs.

Bringing the suckling fantasy to full consciousness had greatly diminished his urge in that direction, but not entirely. He dreamed that he was putting a calf to a cow shortly afterwards. His dreams tended towards feeding, for the same night he dreamed: 'I kissed the little girl I had kissed before. She offered me a smoke. She had some chocolate and I took a piece when she was not looking.'

He also expressed his horror at the thought of sexual intercourse and thought that if he had an erection when in the company of a girl that the girl was insulted and he had degraded her. The jokes about sexual intercourse were 'filthy jokes', so the whole process must be filthy. (The nature of sexual intercourse was explained to him in an adult way.)

He then had another very significant dream. 'My brother and sister and I with another girl were swinging on a maypole. We were bending our middles out. The others bulged out neatly but I did not. My brother caught hold of me by the testicles and swung me round. I called out "Oh". There was something wrong with my watch. The girl put her arm round my body and touched the watch. Then she changed into another girl. I got my head on the upper part of her chest. I had an emission and woke up.' He associated the catching hold of the testicles with a book he had read on castration in Abyssinia. 'It filled me with horror—I would sooner be killed.' It is significant that when he put his head on the upper part of the girl's chest in the dream he ejaculated, and this shows how the breasts were still associated with sex in his mind. This slowly altered, and his next dream was a normal one of having a girl in bed with him and having an emission. The girl was the maid at my consulting-room. That following was also normal: 'My brother and sister and I were sitting on a bench with our legs each side of it. We were pretending to row. We stopped and I nearly had an emission.'

In his dreams he seemed to pass rapidly through homosexual and excremental stages and dreamed such dreams as washing his anus and so on, but there were still some dreams with suckling motives in them, but sometimes disguised and much less attractive than before. He gave one: 'I was with an old workman and we did some work and got dry. We suckled from an animal's udder. It did not taste nice and we soon stopped.' Slowly, however, the heterosexuality triumphed. He next dreamed: 'I was at a sale. There was a young heifer and I put my hand on its udder, but it did not appear right and I did not suckle. Some boys and I were interested in cattle and went to the farmhouse. A dairymaid came to the door and I asked for a sack. She said that there was one in the yard at the back. The auctioneer was Scotch and so was everyone else. I put my arm round the girl's waist and put my cheek on hers. She asked me to stop it and then asked the auctioneer to stop it.' In a further dream he dreamed that he touched the udder of a cow but did not suckle it. He then produced a curious dream. 'A girl I knew before she was married was flirting with another fellow. It was at the seaside. I spreadeagled her on the ground. She was naked to the waist and her breasts looked like men's muscles. I said: "You ought not to behave like this. It's all right to put your hand round her waist but you ought not to do it." She started to cry. I felt I wanted to kiss her and she kissed me.'

At this time, after two months' treatment, he noticed that he felt much more sexual with girls and in their company was bothered by erections. His oral dreams slowly disappeared. The next one was of farmers eating their lunch and going home to get his own. This was followed by one of being served by a waitress who attracted him in a café. He produced more hostility to his father, and on one occasion had a burst of rage in which he leaped to his feet and stood towering over me and threatened to attack me. This settled down when it was pointed out that he was showing negative transference, and afterwards he felt very much better. He felt much less hostile to his brother also.

He broke off treatment after three months because he said that he felt perfectly well. I usually like such patients to continue some time after they have lost their symptoms to avoid relapse, but in spite of this premature cessation he continued well for three years and had no recurrence of his suicidal urges. His subsequent history is not known.

REFERENCES

BENJAMIN, H. (1946) A case of fatal air embolism through an unusual sexual act, *J. clin. Psychopath.*, **4**, 815–20.

BLANC, ALBERTO (1962) Some evidence of the ideologies of early man, in *Social Life of Early Man*, ed. Washburn, S. L., London.

CAMPS, F. E. (1966) More about Jack the Ripper, *Lond. Hosp. Gaz.*, **69**, 1.

FENICHEL, O. (1934) *Outline of Clinical Psychoanalysis*, London.

KAHN, E., and LION, E. G. (1938) Clinical note on a self-fellator, *Amer. J. Psychiat.*, **95**, 121–3.

KINSEY, A. C., POMEROY, W. B., and MARTIN, C. E. (1948) *Sexual Behavior in the Human Male*, Philadelphia.

KLEIN, M. (1932) *The Psychoanalysis of Children*, London.

LEVINE, S. (1958) Effects of early deprivation and delayed weaning in avoidance learning in albino rats, *Arch. Neurol. Psychiat. (Chic.)*, **79**, 2.

LEVY, D. M. (1934) The sucking reflex in dogs, *Amer. J. Orthopsychiat.*, **4**, 218.

LORENZ, K. (1966) *On Aggression*, London.

MURRAY, M. A. (1956) *The God of the Witches*, London.

WERTHAM, F. (1949) *The Show of Violence*, London.

WILSON, C., and PITMAN, P. (1961) *Encyclopaedia of Murder*, London.

SEXUAL ANALISM

Definition

The use of the anus for sexual purposes.

Psychopathology and Occurrence

From the biological point of view it is presupposed that every male animal has an inborn endowment which directs its activities towards the normal object of sexual expression—i.e. the vagina. To miss the normal object and to become conditioned to the use of some other aperture is not beyond the bounds of possibility; this crude substitution by accidental or deliberate conditioning is the best explanation which the behaviourist can offer. In analism, however, the sexual pleasure is not only obtained by the active partner, but by the passive one also. This the behaviourist believes is the result of conditioning and this view is upheld to some extent by Havelock Ellis and Krafft-Ebing, who have both suggested that anal intercourse needs considerable experience before any pleasure is obtained by the passive party. This is probably so since homosexuals have stated to me that they could not indulge in analism because of the pain which they experienced. However, there is no doubt that the passive party can obtain full sexual satisfaction in this manner, and in the case of the passive homosexual man, will ejaculate at the moment when the active partner reaches his sexual climax.

Analism is not confined to homosexuals: even when the sexual partner is a woman and the normal sexual object is obtainable some abnormal men choose the anus. This shows that there can be analism without homosexuality of an overt type although it is frequently a concomitant of that condition. This abolishes the *faute de mieux* theory which is sometimes put forward regarding homosexual behaviour.

It should not be forgotten that the nerve supply of the sexual organs, as well as the anus, is derived from the embryological cloaca so that analism is not so biologically outrageous as it appears at first sight.

According to Ford and Beach the natives of New Guinea regard anal intercourse as not only normal but essential. They state: 'Keraki bachelors of New Guinea universally practice sodomy, and in the course of his puberty rites each boy is initiated into anal intercourse by the older males. After his first year of playing the passive role he spends the rest of his bachelorhood sodomizing the newly initiated. This practice is believed by the natives to be necessary for the growing boy. They are convinced that boys can become pregnant as a result of sodomy, and a lime-eating ceremony is performed periodically to prevent such conception. Though fully sanctioned by the males, these initiatory practices are supposed to be kept secret from the women. The Kiwai have a similar custom: sodomy is practised in connection with initiation to make young men strong.'

This custom is interesting because it is found amongst all the members of the tribe, and not merely amongst a few homosexuals. The passive initiates later become the active participants, and this homosexual custom does not appear to interfere in any way with heterosexuality when the bachelor marries. It would seem, therefore, that amongst such people the final attainment of normal heterosexual object sexuality is delayed but not prevented. These people are not fixated but take an inordinate time to become mature.

Plenty of other primitive people show similar behaviour. For example, the Mochicas, who lived in the pre-Inca kingdom of Chimor in Peru, have left a large amount of pottery (which, incidentally, was made by the females) depicting their daily life. Some of it is very erotic and indicates that sodomy was a tribal pleasure.

From the psychoanalytical point of view anal intercourse is due to a fixation and regression to the second stage of libidinal development where for some reason the child obtained sexual pleasure from anal contacts and tended to seek for this pleasure unconsciously afterwards. It is, of course, associated with homosexuality and the Oedipus stage of development with its related castration fears and wishes.

In spite of the fact that analism is sometimes associated with heterosexuality it is much more commonly found in relation to homosexuality and this, in view of its relation to the Oedipus situation, castration fears, and so on, is much what one would expect. The exact frequency of its occurrence does not seem to be known and unfortunately Kinsey and his collaborators have not studied it. From clinical experience it would seem to be the form of sexual outlet of about 20 per cent. of homosexuals. Its heterosexual occurrence must be very small—less than 0·1 per cent. one would judge clinically.

That this clinical experience is probably correct is shown by the fact that Kinsey *et al.* found in the technique of homosexual sex play of 2,102 pre-adolescent boys 17 per cent. indulged in anal activities.

It is, perhaps, not without significance that many patients suffering from paranoid psychoses and other forms of schizophrenia complain that they are assaulted by electricity applied to their anus, foreign bodies forced into it at night, and so on. No doubt their psychoses release ideas which would otherwise remain unconscious. Sometimes elaborate delusional constructions are built up to explain this belief. The more deteriorated the patient the franker and more fantastic the conceptions. An example of this association of homosexuality with schizophrenia is shown in the study made by Bieber *et al.* with a group of heterosexual and homosexual patients. They found that among the heterosexuals, one-fifth were diagnosed as schizophrenics, about one-half were psychoneurotic and the rest had character disorders. With the homosexuals one-fourth were schizophrenic, one-third were psychoneurotic and the rest had character disorders.

Possibly a large number of people who have treatment by rectal washouts, colonic irrigation, and so on, obtain more psychological than physical relief from this form of therapy. That this is so is suggested by the fact that an advertisement for colonic irrigation which appears in one of our great daily newspapers states that this treatment is 'very stimulating'.

The vast numbers of purgatives, laxatives, suppositories, and similar medicaments sold by chemists show that even amongst people who pass for normal there is a great deal of interest in this region.

A certain amount of horse-play amongst young men often conceals analism as the following incident demonstrates. (The account is from the medical press.)

Medico-Legal Incident at a Garage

At a Glasgow inquiry on April 2 the circumstances of the death of a 12-year-old boy were considered. The boy was in the habit of frequenting a garage near his home and watching the work in progress. At the time of the incident the manager and foreman of the garage were out, towing a car, and only two apprentices were present. One of these was blowing up tubeless tyres with compressed air.

The deceased was said to have remarked 'blow this airline up your backside and see how it feels'. The apprentice to whom he made this remark then went to the door leaving him with the other apprentice. When he came back the boy was lying on the ground and the other youth was kneeling at his feet and they seemed to be struggling together. The exact position of the airline was not observed. The boy's trousers were not displaced. The deceased complained of being unable to breathe and it appeared that air had been forced into his rectum.

He was removed to hospital and preliminary needling of the peritoneal cavity resulted in the escape of a large quantity of air through the needle. At laparotomy the muscular coat of the intestine was found to be bruised and split in many places. There was a perforation of the transverse colon and the peritoneum was soiled with faeces. The boy died soon afterwards and necropsy confirmed these findings, showing also mediastinal and scrotal surgical emphysema. In addition there were two bruises in the rectum, but no external injury.

An engineer said that the compressor produced air at pressures varying between 120 and 150 lb./sq. in. (8·4–10·5 kg./sq.cm.). He estimated that about 14,000 c.c. of air would be released in one second from the nozzle in question. He said that a variable amount of air could enter a man's rectum if the nozzle was placed near the seat of the trousers, depending on distance and closeness of weave of the cloth.

Six years after this fatal incident occurred another similar one was reported in the daily press. There is no evidence that the participants had any knowledge of the previous case, or surely they would never have indulged in such dangerous behaviour. The fact that they did so shows how thought runs in complex controlled channels.

Prank at Work Nearly Cost Youth His Life

An apprentice who was 'blown up' by an air-pressure gun in horseplay at a factory would have died without immediate treatment, it was stated in court at Gateshead yesterday. The apprentice asked a surgeon not to 'split' on his work-mates.

For 48 hours the life of Brian Hillier, 17, was said to have been in danger. He is now making satisfactory progress.

Inspector Gerald Carr, prosecuting, said: 'The incident took place at the factory of International Boiler and Radiator Ltd. on the Team Valley Trading Estate. It was totally irresponsible conduct. For 48 hours Hillier was in the greatest danger of losing his life. The compressor gun was pointed at his back by Clark while he was washing his hands, and the others talked to him to hold his attention. The air travelled into his intestine, and he fell shrieking in agony. It was planned as a factory prank. There was no intention to harm Hillier, but it was a near tragedy. The gun had a pressure of 90 lb per square inch. The apprentice saw his stomach go up as if it had been inflated.

Since young men frequently appear to have anally-controlled thinking one would have thought that it would have been wise of the manufacturers of such pressure guns to affix a warning to them stating the danger of directing them against the human body.

Case No. 4

A Case of Anxiety Neurosis due to Analism

This case shows the effects of analism on marriage. The husband was not seen by me but the wife, my patient, consulted me regarding symptoms of anxiety. She stated that she was continually frightened, and had to lock herself in her room at night. There was trembling of the hands and feet, and considerable insomnia. She felt tense and 'worked up' all the time. Her eyes had become slightly more prominent for the past six or seven years.

She came from a normal family: her father died of arteriosclerosis when she was aged 4 and this caused her mother's death twenty years later. There were three brothers all alive and well. Her father had had a bad temper and one brother was somewhat nervous but otherwise there was no history of neurosis. As a child the patient was not nervous and was physically healthy. At the age of 12 years she overworked at school and her eyes watered a great deal. This caused her to be taken off work and told not to read by electric light. On leaving school she lived at home, but when the Second World War started she worked as a voluntary telephone operator in a dockyard.

At the age of 18 years she married her husband who was a Chief Officer on a ship and was called up for the R.N.V.R. She had a miscarriage in 1943 but became pregnant again in 1944. Her doctor at that time told her not to have intercourse during the latter half of her pregnancy. Her husband (possibly because of this) asked her to allow him to commit sodomy. She was reluctant to allow it because she was a Roman Catholic and in any case it was repugnant to her. He finally compelled her to submit. In 1945 she had a further child but it died at birth. A third child was born in 1946. After this her husband seemed to wish to have anal connexion more than ever. She had an operation for a retroverted uterus which was not followed by pregnancy although no contraceptives were used. Her husband was still demanding anal intercourse and even after he had had normal relations would insist that she permit him to enter her anally. She had seen a priest about it but he could do nothing. Her husband would not see a doctor to discover whether he could be helped in his abnormal desires.

On examination she showed a definite tremor of the hands and feet, her upper eyelid lagged and showed white above the iris, but the pulse was not accelerated nor was her thyroid enlarged. It was felt that she might have very early hyperthyroidism or her symptoms might be due to anxiety but whichever it was the cause appeared to be strain and worry.

She had left her husband and had decided not to return to him. Since he would not accept medical advice there was nothing one could do other than give her a sedative and reinforce her wish not to live with him further.

SEXUAL URETHRALISM

Definition

The use of the urethra for sexual purposes.

Psychopathology and Occurrence

This abnormality would be of little importance since patients rarely complain of it clinically, except that those who stimulate the urethra frequently lose half of the objects which they use and they slip into the bladder. It is cases of this type which are recorded in the surgical journals and anyone curious enough can find that almost every type of small object has been extracted from both male and female bladders, although naturally the anatomy of the male urethra make this accident less common. (There is even a case in the literature of a snake needing to be removed!)

I once had a clergyman under my care. This man had had a catheter in his bladder which needed to be removed surgically. There is no doubt that he was in the habit of passing it frequently in order to obtain sexual satisfaction. Since the ordinary normal person finds catheterization uncomfortable, if not actually painful, it is not surprising to find that he was not only fixated at a urethral level but was sado-masochistic also. He delighted in taking photographs of himself, and a woman, naked and with him pretending to thrash her with a whip, chain her up and so on. Apparently he never injured her in any way so the whole behaviour was on a fantasy level.

It is urethralism which leads some women to pester doctors to catheterize them and no doubt they obtain some urethral satisfaction from the procedure.

The psychopathological basis possibly depends firstly on the close association of the urethra with the nerve supply of the genitalia, which makes it easy for stimuli from it to be linked with sexual pleasure, and secondly, as in the case of the clergyman quoted above, there is a masochistic element which makes the discomfort or pain enjoyable.

OTHER FORMS OF ABNORMAL ORIFICIAL SEXUALITY

The use of other orifices as sexual apertures is not usual, but the submammary fissure, the axilla, and intercrural folds are sometimes used. Although frequently sought as a method of avoiding impregnation and therefore a heterosexual activity this form of behaviour does sometimes occur, and may be encountered, in homosexual practices. It is usually the result of conditioning and as such rarely gives the passive partner any satisfaction. It is merely catalogued here for completeness.

COPROPHILIA AND COPROPHAGIA

Definition

Coprophagia is used here to mean the consumption of secretions or excretions. It is a term frequently used to mean dirt-eating such as is found in the insane, but even amongst these it is common to find that some secretion rather than earth is consumed.

Psychopathology and Occurence

The consumption of secretions or excretions is undoubtedly performed in order to obtain sexual pleasure and is usually subsidiary to the sexual act. What, one might ask, is the cause of this remarkable conduct? Biologically the behaviour of animals does not throw a great deal of light on the matter. The sub-human primate and lower animals will consume secretions or excretions which would appear unattractive to a civilized man, but this seems to be from gustatory rather than sexual reasons. Again, races like the Australian aboriginal or the Eskimo will eat things (the Eskimo, for example, will consume nasal mucus or dirt from between his toes) which could be distasteful to a white man, but in this case it is presumably from the piquancy of the taste rather than a sexual adjuvant that he does so.

Coprophagia, as a perversion, seems to be traceable back to the consumption of milk at the breast. The child, as we have already pointed out, tends to deal with fresh situations by the responses which it already possesses—those which it has inherited or acquired. When the newly born child voids its urine and faeces reflexly it is probably unaware of the act. The mother, however, makes every effort to condition it to the use of the pot and it attempts to deal with these newly encountered substances on the basis of its inherited and acquired responses: viz. to treat them like the one secretion with which it had had to deal—milk. It at once attempts to place the new substance, as it does everything else, in its mouth. Apparently coprophagia is a persistence of this behaviour.

From the psychoanalytic point of view coprophagia is a combination of oral and anal eroticism. The child has not freed itself from the oral modes of obtaining pleasure and combines this with anal sources of satisfaction. It is therefore found to smear, eat, and take pleasure in faeces which it regards as of great value.

It is well known that small children will put in their mouths coal and anything else they can reach. This may be related to coprophagia or may merely be a residue of the oral exploration which enables the new-born child to search about with its mouth until it finds the breast.

Pica—the eating of inedible and often most unpleasant substances by the psychotic and mentally defective is quite common. It is really incredible the things which are consumed. I once had under my care a deteriorated schizophrenic who ate handfuls of rotten leaves as long as he was unobserved. The result of this diet was that he had violent diarrhoea. Similarly idiots often have to be watched constantly or they will eat anything at hand. Less often normal children will eat inedible matter. The following case was recorded in the daily press. There was no evidence that any form of mental deficiency or mental illness was present.

'Connie Holland, 10, was taken to hospital at Salem, Oregon, when she developed a fever and started spitting pebbles. Doctors have removed 50 small pebbles from her stomach and intestines, but believe there are about 150 still inside her.'

She had apparently been swallowing them at intervals for six months. A doctor said she might have been trying subconsciously to compensate for a mineral deficiency. Connie said: 'They tasted good'!

The theory of an attempt to compensate for mineral deficiency is improbable because the child appears to have been perfectly normal apart from her perverted appetite. It is, indeed, astonishing that this theory should interminably reappear against all evidence. As long ago as 1920 Still pointed out that children who ate dirt were suffering from a neurosis. He found they ate mud, mortar, coal, cinders, and gravel. Usually the habit began in the second year of life and persisted from eight months to two years when it disappeared spontaneously.

The time of appearance may be of importance because apparently it occurs shortly after the child is weaned. Since coprophagia is, in those who are not defective or psychotic, a habit of childhood it suggests that when it appears in adult life it is a regression to an earlier phase of development.

The 'cravings' of pregnant women may be a related phenomenon. It has been suggested by Drummond and Wilbraham that it may be an attempt to obtain an increased amount of vitamin C which is demanded by pregnancy. That this is improbable has been pointed out by Yudkin who showed that the pregnant woman is not merely satisfied by fruit containing the required vitamin, but wishes one which is out of season.

Harries and Hughes give a list of 187 'cravings' for substances other than food out of 991 cases of such patients. These are as follows:

Coal	35	Petrol	10	Soil	7
Soap	17	Metal polish	10	Chalk	4
Disinfectant	15	Tar	10	Cinders	4
Toothpaste	14	Paraffin	9	Charcoal	4
Mothballs	10	Wood	8	Others	30

Most women are very secretive about their 'cravings' and some felt a sense of shame at having them. The usual time was from the first to the fourth month of pregnancy.

Posner, McCottry, and Posner found out of 196 cases of 'cravings' ten women admitted urge to commit pica.

The women state that in many cases it is the smell of such substances as disinfectant and petrol which appealed to them, and it is not clear whether it was sufficient to smell or actually to eat the substances. Nevertheless the craving was in most cases overwhelming at the time.

Harries and Hughes suggest that 'the expectant mother takes light refreshing snacks of those substances which "go down well" in order to counter the sickness and nausea which accompany pregnancy'. One of their cases stated that it was the desire for something to crunch. Other suggestions are that there is a need for increased calcium.

It would seem that none of these explanations is satisfactory. Only soil and chalk out of the list above would provide calcium and none vitamin C. The probability is that pregnancy (perhaps by the alteration of hormone balance) arouses urges which have been suppressed since childhood and these appear in the conscious mind as 'cravings'. Geophagy, or the eating of earth, may be a manifestation of true mineral deficiency or a demonstration of coprophagia. According to Lips it is widespread. He states: 'Geophagy, which is the practice of eating earth, is found in many places, including South America, China, and Indonesia. The Tatu of California mix their maple flour with red clay. "Stone butter", or "mined flour" was eaten in times of need in Germany and Russia. During the seventeenth century the noblewomen of Spain developed such a craving for the tasty earth of Ertemoz that State and Church had to lay heavy penalties on this "vice".'

Coprophagia is not common as an isolated perversion, but is frequently found as an ancillary to others. For example, an interest which perverts frequently show in urination may be of similar origin, although from the strict psychological point of view it is derived from the urethral eroticism described by Sadger.

This interest in urine and urination may become so evident that it forms a definite perversion and has been known as undinism. In this the sexual pleasure is often obtained by witnessing the act of urination by someone of the same or opposite sex. In some cases pleasure is obtained by being urinated upon by the loved one or in urinating on him or her, but this is a rarity. I once saw a man who had three times been prosecuted for loitering in public lavatories. The police believed that he was there to find homosexual prostitutes but he told me, before I gave evidence in his defence, that he went there to see men pass water. Unfortunately the magistrate was quite unable to comprehend such a condition and he was punished. I have seen similar cases, one in a man of excellent character, who was decorated for exceptional bravery in war, but in those cases it was associated with perverse or neurotic symptoms as well.

Like all these perversions there is the possibility of sexual pleasure in witnessing it in the child or in animals (a patient confessed to me that he obtained distinct sexual pleasure in watching his dog urinate or defaecate—he had also shown oral perversions), but in actual fact as a definite perversion in which the sexual climax is reached these latter are so rare as to be almost non-existent.

It seems probable to me that all these cases show a residue of the pleasure which the child obtained from mammary secretion activated by fixation and regression.

There is the probability that coprolalia is only a diluted form of coprophagia, but this is difficult to prove. I have had experience, however, of a patient who did not obtain sexual pleasure unless using bad language whilst indulging in the sexual act.

These patients are not common and rarely consult the psychiatrist. No doubt there are other activating forces—such as the wish to do something forbidden, sadistic elements—in the impulse to swear. If this is so it is clearly the persistence of an infantile attitude. This behaviour is half-way between the perversions and the fetishisms and is better regarded as a perversion-fetish.

PORNOGRAPHY AND POISON PEN LETTERS

Pornography or 'writing dirt', showing 'dirty pictures' and so on is perhaps best discussed here although they are not the same as coprophilia nor necessarily activated by the same psychological forces.

Pornography, or as the law calls it, 'an obscene libel' is anything written, photographed, drawn or otherwise produced which has a corruptive influence. For nearly a hundred years Lord Justice Cockburn's definition stated in Hicklin's case in 1868 has held sway. He stated that: 'The test of obscenity is this, whether the tendency of the matter charged as obscenity is to deprave and corrupt those whose minds are open to such immoral influences and into whose hands a publication of this sort may fall.'

Such a definition has infuriated writers down the years, and indeed, although written with a high seriousness this very book might have been prohibited under it. However, judges have begun to modify it in their judgments and now Parliament has passed an act to bring the law more in accordance with modern thought. Here the concern is towards the psychological factors which cause obscene productions rather than their effect on society.

Pornography is probably based on empathy and various wish-fulfilling fantasies. It is, possibly, somewhat comparable to exhibitionism on paper. There appears to be a certain amount of sexual pleasure to the writer or artist in producing the matter since it is observable that writers such as Sacher Masoch and the Marquis de Sade dwelt continuously on their own complexes. It is improbable that this would be so satisfying to them unless there was the thought that someone was reading or studying their productions and was feeling similar excitement, or was defending himself against such excitement by being shocked. So a considerable amount of empathy (i.e. identifying oneself with the reader) must occur. Since we talk of 'dirty books' and 'dirty postcards', &c., it is obvious that there must be equation with coprophilia in this matter also. Most pornography is concerned with either an over-frank account of the male or female body, or the sexual act. The latter is either normal or abnormal. Possibly, therefore, there may be voyeuristic elements present as well.

Sometimes the complaint has been of the use of 'four-letter words' in literature, as being objectionable; the words themselves being considered somehow obscene.

The interesting thing is that these words are all of Anglo-Saxon origin, and were the only ones in use, amongst even the highest in the land, until the Normans conquered England. Then the polite speech became the invaders' language; only the scullions, and serfs used the old one, which in time became prohibited for a gentleman, and so 'dirty speech'. No doubt the ecclesiastical use of Latin reinforced this attitude. It is amusing to think that if England had conquered Normandy instead of vice versa, the 'four-letter words' would be the accepted ones and those derived from Latin the obscene. Actually in French today *outil* (i.e. 'tool') is a polite word whereas *penis* is considered rude!

The lawyer always puts forward the fact that the writer or artist has made money from his publication and is satisfied with this as the sole explanation. No doubt he may make some money, but this is surely not the whole reason for his behaviour. There are easier and safer methods of obtaining money without the danger of prosecution. The monetary gain is merely the top storey, as it were, of a building which has foundations far below.

Whatever the deeper psychological motivation, which appears to be very complex, there is no doubt that the attempts by the law to suppress obscenity invariably fail. Indeed, the history of pornography shows that frequently a work is published, suppressed for its tendency to corrupt, later released, and often recognized as a work of art.

The so-called 'hard core' obscenity probably does not lead to overt antisocial behaviour. Rape, for example, is much more often caused by alcohol than by pornography. The latter may, however, form the subject of masturbation in those too timid to be able to find a girl friend.

It is an interesting fact that, as Loth points out, 'Denmark is the only country in the West which had no anti-obscenity enforcement at all. It is also the only country in the West without any "hard core" obscenity, without "girlie-magazines", or sex-comics.' This is a fact which should be of interest to those who wish to go to such lengths to abolish pornography.

There is no evidence whatsoever that pornographic material does injury to children (which is the usual reason for its suppression). This is shown by the experiments performed by Dr. O. Elthammar of the Child Psychiatric Department in Stockholm. He showed a group of children aged between 11 and 18 years films depicting violence and sex, including one called *491*, which showed a girl being raped by a group of intoxicated louts, and forced to have intercourse with a dog.

None of the children was frightened either during or after the film. A proportion of older girls (aged 15 to 18) did admit to being shocked, but apparently the younger viewers (aged between 11 and 13) were quite undisturbed.

Curiously enough two adults, who saw the experiment, one a grandmother, and the other a mother, were so upset that they needed psychological treatment for a month afterwards.

It would seem, if one accepts these experiments as valid, that the usual view should be reversed, and that obscene material is that which is likely to upset adults and leave children undisturbed!

In general, one might suggest that it is violence which disturbs children, and the depiction of sex does not interest them much, yet the law seems unperturbed by the showing of violence on the screen, or its description in books, whereas the least suggestion of sex leads to demands for its suppression.

Investigation into the responses of sex criminals does not lead to the view that they are especially responsive to excitement by pornography. A research team at Indiana University examined the attitudes of 1,500 sex criminals and compared them with 888 criminals convicted of other offences. They found that 28 per cent. of the sex criminals were strongly aroused, but 34 per cent. of the controls were similarly excited. Only 36 per cent. of normal men were aroused slightly or not at all, but, again, 43 per cent. of the sex criminals were not excited either. It would appear then that sex criminals are no more affected by pornographic material than normal men and it is not responsible for sexual crimes.

Levitt, who has done a great deal of work on this problem, has found that some photographs which are generally accepted as unobjectionable, and such as appear frequently in men's magazines, are more exciting sexually than many frankly pornographic ones. As he suggests, those eager to suppress pornography because they fear the effect of it exciting sexuality may actually be attacking the wrong material.

This is confirmed, if it is really meant that pornography should be suppressed because it causes sexual crimes, by the fact that Dr. Anders Groth, a Danish psychiatrist, reporting on behalf of the Government Commission on Sex and Enlightenment appointed in 1961, found that since the abolition of the antipornographic laws a year ago sex crimes have dropped by 25 per cent.

This has occurred in spite of the fact that the sales of pornographic material have grown enormously and there is an increased interest in sexual experiments, particularly amongst intellectuals.

It appears from these facts that sexual crime is not caused by pornography, or even aggravated by it, and tends rather to be induced by the suppression of outlets which can be provided by it.

Poison Pen Letters

The so-called 'poison pen' letters are usually of two kinds, although they may be combined. The first is a slanderous assertion that respectable people, usually the husband or wife of the recipient, are misbehaving sexually with someone else; the second is filled with sexual and excremental words, or suggests sexual behaviour which the sender would like to take part in either with the recipient or some other person.

The letters containing slanderous assertions appear most often to be sent by the frustrated type of individual; the bitter, envious spinster or, rarely, by the shy, frightened man who would not dare to approach a woman. There is, no doubt, a wish to hurt the person addressed. They are an indirect attack and probably the sexual angle is used partly because of their own frustration and partly because it is most hurtful.

The obscene letter is really the equivalent of a small child shouting out 'dirty' words to shock adults. Freud pointed out that for a man to tell a girl a 'smutty story' is a symbolical sexual assault. The intention of such letters is to shock or excite. Immaturity and frustration appear to be the fundamental elements in causation. Exhibitionism and an unconscious sadistic emotion are probably present to a certain extent. Since the letter writer prefers obscenity to real sexual approaches frigidity or impotence may be present.

Graffiti

Although this applies to any writings (usually on walls) it has come to mean those on lavatories. Since these are confined to readers of the same sex as the writer they are obviously homosexually orientated. Indeed, their content often shows this. Although some betray a frank sexual interest many are excremental and are anal-erotic in nature. They are probably equivalent to the child smearing excrement.

Graffiti of this nature were found at Pompeii and it is demonstrated how little human beings have changed in two thousand years that those made today show no real difference.

It it usually believed that graffiti are made more frequently by men, but according to a survey done by the Sanitaryware Manufacturers' Council in 1965 women are just as responsible. This survey was an extensive one and made with the help of 250 local authorities.

Mr. Batchelor, the Council's director, stated, 'We found that women scribble just as much as men. With the women the writing is just crudity; at least some of the men's is witty. And women use lipstick that's hard to remove or they scratch the messages with nail files.'

Telephone Persecutions

One occasionally encounters cases of young men who engage telephone operators and others in obscene conversations. As such men are rarely sent for treatment there is little opportunity to study their psychology. However, one can conclude without much doubt that their behaviour is based on psychological factors similar to the letter writers. They are immature, and frustrated with a result that the coprophiliac element replaces proper sexual advances.

That there is a sad lack of humour in all these productions is only to be expected since humour is a way of expressing the forbidden without damage to the conventions. These patients are expressing themselves by breaking the conventions and so have no need of it.

REFERENCES

BIEBER, I., DAIN, H. J., DRELICH, P. R., GRAND, M. G., GRUNDLACH, R. H., KREMER, M., WILBUR, A. H., BIEBER, C. B., and BIEBER, T. B. (1962) *Homsexuality*, New York.

DAILY TELEGRAPH (1958) 28 July.
DAILY TELEGRAPH (1964) 5 September.
DRUMMOND, J. C., and WILBRAHAM, A. (1939) *The Englishman's Food*, London.
ELTHAMMAR, O. (1967) *Emotionella reaktioner inför film hos 11–18 arsgrupper*, Stockholm.
FORD, C. S., and BEACH, F. A. (1951) *Patterns of Sexual Behavior*, New York.
GEBHARD, P. H., GAGNON, J. H., POMEROY, W. B., and CHRISTIANSHON, C. V. (1965) *Sex Offenders*, New York.
HARRIES, J. M., and HUGHES, T. F. (1958) Enumeration of the 'cravings' of some pregnant women, *Brit. med. J.*, **2**, 39–40.
LIPS, J. E. (1949) *The Origin of Things*, London.
LOTH, DAVID (1961) *The Erotic in Literature*, London.
POSNER, L. B., McCOTTRY, C. M., and POSNER, A. C. (1957) *Obstet. and Gynec.*, **270**, 9.
SADGER, J. (1910) *Jb. Psychoanal. Path. Forsch.*, **2**, 409.
STILL, G. F. (1920) *Common Disorders and Diseases of Childhood*, London.
VON HAGEN, V. W. (1965) *The Desert Kingdoms of Peru*, London.
YUDKIN, J. (1956) 'Cravings' in pregnancy, *Lancet*, i, 645.

7

SADO-MASOCHISM

This is a complex condition which may be conveniently divided into (1) sadism and (2) masochism. It must be realized, however, that such a division is never found in nature and that there is always a certain admixture of both conditions in clinical cases. It is believed that sadism is the primary state and that masochism is produced secondary to it. Obviously, therefore, sadism is more likely to appear in pure culture than masochism. Some writers use the terms active and passive algolagnia for sadism and masochism. There seems to be no advantage in these terms.

SADISM

Definition

The obtaining of sexual pleasure from acts of cruelty. This appears to shade off from apparently non-sexual cruelty to obvious sadism. It may be classified according to degrees as: (1) Cruel acts with concomitant pleasure which is not appreciated either at the time or later as being sexual in nature. (2) Cruel acts without ejaculation but with slight or full sexual satisfaction sometimes accompanied by erection. (3) Acts of cruelty accompanied by full sexual satisfaction and followed or accompanied by erection or ejaculation.

Psychopathology and Occurrence

The aggressive instinct which is the root of all cruelty is present at birth. We have seen that in the human child it is possible to arouse aggressive responses either at, or soon after, birth by restricting movement. It is not until the growth of the teeth and nails, however, that the child is able to give vent to its aggressive impulses in any effective way. It would seem therefore that these impulses originate in infantile aggression directed against the mother, and more particularly her breasts. Biting seems the architypical sadistic behaviour, although it may be directed against a sadistic object often derived by conditioning. Possibly the cutting which is frequently found in sadism is an extension of scratching with the nails.

Those who retain a sentimental view of the blue-eyed innocence of the child naturally find it difficult to imagine the possibility that the ruthless ferocity of the sadist originates at that time, but must be convinced when it is realized that children and adolescents are sometimes responsible for savage and brutal murders. Bender and Curran of the New York Bellevue Hospital have published a valuable study on *Children and Adolescents who Kill*. Burt, Ellis, Tredgold, Hall, Lemke, Orbison, Dittrick, Stark, Petrova, Zhelikhovsky, Solovieva, Bridgman, &c., all report murders by children and adolescents. These become of importance in our understanding of the origin of sadism when we appreciate that sadistic behaviour is a murder in miniature, or conversely that murder is the ultimate sadism.

The findings of Bender and Curran are interesting because they are not purely psychoanalytic, and there is a paucity of literature on this subject independent of special theories. They state that:

In our analysis of the overt expression of death wishes in small children we may expect that rivalry for the attention of a parent or parent substitute against other adults or against siblings or other children will be the fundamental problem. This is the normal or usual situation and finds expression in fantasy, verbalization, play and social relationships. It is a remarkable fact that it rarely finds expression in any really menacing behaviour. However, it may become dangerously exaggerated by one of the following situations:

(1) When the family rivalry situation becomes intensively severe due to some external factor.

(2) When the rivalry situation occurs in a family situation not normal to the child, such as in a foster home where the positive emotional (love) responses are not strong enough to curb the aggressive tendencies.

(3) Where the organic factors make the child feel inferior and helpless and in need of greater love, of which he is deprived.

(4) Where educational difficulties become insurmountable in a child with adequate insight to sense the inferior status into which he is forced.

(5) Where the familial behaviour pattern is one of severe aggressivity in parents and the child must protect himself against them with the only reaction pattern he knows.

All these factors are of interest inasmuch as they are conditioning stimuli which tend to cause an aggressive response in the child just as much as flogging will cause a dog or a horse to become vicious and savage.

From the psychoanalytical point of view sadism is due to the externalizing of the death instincts and the libidinization of the various orifices and organs. The child develops oral sadism when it grows its teeth and nails. It then displaces its sadistic emotion on to the anus and excremental functions, then the urethra and penis. A great deal of the psychoanalytical theory is concerned with the various transitions of the aggressive instinct, with its fixation to different organs and the manifold manoeuvres of the mind to master and divert the emotion into safe channels. It is when these fail that sadism becomes obvious and menaces the safety of the patient by influencing his behaviour into antisocial directions.

There is a tendency when reports of sadistic acts are studied, when one reads of terrible mutilations inflicted upon living persons, of almost unimaginable torments of pain, of what Karpman calls 'a journey through the inferno of human brutalities', to imagine that the sadist is a sub-human killer, a wild beast without mitigating characteristics. From this, no doubt, was born the medieval conception of the werewolf—so impossible was it in those uninstructed times to realize the nature of this illness. Judges, in their allocutions during the trials of sadists, frequently give this impression. In spite of the eloquence of the judiciary this view is entirely wrong. The sadist is not usually universally dangerous. His aggressive emotion replaces affection in others; he maims and kills only those who, if he were normal, he would love. He has missed the cultural phase which changes hate into love and is unable to express himself except in cruelty. In addition he is impotent in many cases, but if he does attain potency it is only by fantasy, or the reality, of the infliction of pain.

Some animals show reactions which seem to be sadistic; the female spider which kills the male at the moment of congress, the fox which ravages the whole of a hen-run but eats none, the irascible bull which charges the harmless passer-by in the other end of his field, the fighting of seals, deer, and other animals at mating time, and so on, all have a nuance of cruelty in them but it is not wise to draw conclusions regarding human beings from the behaviour of animals. Otherwise one might compare the sadist with a rogue elephant.

Freud first of all believed that sadism was a primary instinct but later on developed the view that man was born with a death-instinct which made him wish to destroy himself. Freud's view is so well condensed by Melanie Klein that we cannot do better than quote it here. She states: 'In his book, *Beyond the Pleasure Principle*, Freud put forward a theory according to which at the outset of the life of the human organism the instinct of aggression, or the death-instinct, is being opposed and bound by the libido, or life-instinct, the eros. A fusion of the two instincts ensues, and gives rise to sadism. In order to escape from being destroyed by its own death-instinct the organism employs its narcissistic, or self-regarding libido to force the former outwards, and direct it against its object. Freud considers this process as fundamental for the person's sadistic relations to his objects. I should say, moreover, that parallel with this deflection of the death-instinct outward against objects, an intra-psychic reaction of defence goes on against that part of the instinct which could not be thus externalized. For the danger of being destroyed by this instinct of aggression sets up, I think, an excessive tension in the ego, which is felt by it as an anxiety, so that it is faced at the very beginning of its development with the task of mobilizing libido against its death-instinct. It can, however, only imperfectly fulfil this task, since, owing to the fusion of the two instincts, it can no longer, as we know, effect a separation between them. A division takes place in the id, or instinctual levels of the psyche, to which one part of the instinctual impulses is directed against the other.' Reich and later Fenichel criticized this view and pointed out the dangers of the supposition of an unanalysable primary biological urge. I believe, by analogy with animals, and by considerable experience with human beings, that the view suggested on page 50 of this book—that is, that outward aggression is primary—is the correct one. Many analysts, e.g. Klein, write as if they believe this true although without directly contradicting the Freudian theories. The sadistic impulses manifest themselves at an early age and appear to be directed against the breast. The frustrations inherent in life probably aggravate these impulses unless they are very severe—complete frustration one suspects favours a reversal of the impulse and the production of masochism. It is felt that the cases I have treated support this view and show that aggression is directed against the breast (but it must be admitted that criminal sadists are rare in psychotherapeutic practice—they seldom demand treatment since their antisocial feelings naturally make them suspicious of help).

It is easy to see how the sadist uses hate as the emotional currency where the normal man uses love; the normal man displaces a large amount of affection from the mother on to his mate and as a result has a desire to love and caress the breasts and genitalia which naturally ends in coitus. The sadist wishes to injure the breasts and so, equating the breasts with the genitalia, finally the genitalia.

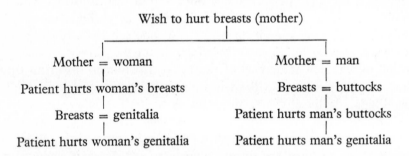

Wish to hurt breasts (mother)

Mother = woman	Mother = man
Patient hurts woman's breasts	Breasts = buttocks
Breasts = genitalia	Patient hurts man's buttocks
Patient hurts woman's genitalia	Patient hurts man's genitalia

The paths by which homosexual sadism is attained are rather complicated but are reached by transposition of a man for the mother. The buttocks are equated with the breast (indeed this is a common psychopathological finding) and so pain is inflicted on the buttocks. Less often this is continued to injury of the genitalia, and no doubt reinforced by various paternal complexes, and the consequences of father-hate also.

The Freudian view is that masochism (the death wish) is primary but this is later inverted and externalized. The result of this is the production of sadism. However satisfactory this may be from the philosophical point of view, it is unhelpful as a working hypothesis. In fact, it is my view that aggression is always primary and that sadism is invariably the original impulse. Masochism is merely the reversal of frustrated aggression and so *ipso facto* cannot be the original urge. This view explains much more than the Freudian one and is of much more value in psychopathology. Since these theories are not put forward as mere metaphysics but to help to understand these difficult patients it seems better that we utilize this simple view and this will mainly be done here.

I do not pretend to have exhausted the multitudinous possibilities of sadism, but merely demonstrated certain possible transitions which make it appear in the patient's relations with men and women. Cruelty to children or animals (infantosexual or bestiosexual sadism) are, however, developed in the same manner.

There is no doubt that there are strong obsessive-compulsive elements in both sadism and masochism. The essence of the obsessive-compulsion is its persistent intrusion of ideas or acts into consciousness, which appear independent of volition, and result in a powerful urge to perform some act: not until it is done does the patient feel a relief of tension. There is, of course, an element of obsessive-compulsion, diluted to a large degree, in normal sex. For some time following there is feeling of peace and freedom but the tension grows again and so the act must be repeated. Thus the whole cycle is constantly reiterated and nothing except physical force can stop it.

The manner is which sadists repeat their conduct in spite of the great risks which they run in doing so suggests that there is a deep-seated compulsion behind it. Thus Karpman points out:

The sadomasochistic behaviour is only a pale symbol of the behaviour whose place it takes. Being only a substitutive form of satisfaction, it can give but temporary and partial release. This effected, there soon arises again the necessity for further activity, and the process is repeated endlessly because the real satisfaction is never achieved. The sadomasochistic neurosis thus shares with the obsessional neurosis the compulsion to repetition. It is a question of an undischarged affect, the abreaction is attempted in the specific scene of the neurosis (Freud).

This compulsive, or repetitive, principle is common to all sadists although sometimes some other act (such as arson) can be substituted for the cruelty.

The only objection one can find to the suggestion of obsessive-compulsion is that all sex is a repetitive act and sadism is only a diverted form of normal sex. One would therefore expect it to be repetitive. On the other hand, the sadist does seem more aware of his impulses, more compelled to satisfy them, than the normal man and the suggestion of a compulsion does seem legitimate. Also the normal man is dissuaded by certain moral

I—PSY. D.

considerations whereas the compulsive, in some cases, does not seem so hindered.

Occasionally, in ignorant quarters, the suggestion is made that sadistic episodes are controlled by the moon, and that lust murders are more frequent at the new moon, or full moon, whichever suits the whims of the conjecturer. This is, of course, the old idea which gave lunacy its name. It is, incidentally, absolutely without foundation and the product of super-stition.

An attempt will be made to discuss the different types of sadism described above and to give examples of them.

Cruel Acts Unassociated with Appreciated Sexual Feeling

This type of sadism has, in the past, often been a concomitant of various religions. Torquemada and his fellow inquisitors who burned men alive as an 'act of faith' (auto-da-fé), Aztec priests who tore out their victims' hearts in honour of Huitzilopochtli, the god of war,[1] Muslims who carelessly slit the throats of the captives who did not accept their beliefs, are all examples of this type of reaction. The most appalling of them was the Eastern custom of impaling. This was the hammering of a sharpened stake up through the anus into the man's abdomen and thorax until it emerged in the neck. This sometimes led to an agonizing death prolonged for hours or even days. Similarly, and perhaps more naturally, sadistic reactions are released by war. The terrible massacres of the past—Tamberlane, for example, slaughtered 230,000 victims and Eichmann killed four million Jews in the Second World War—demonstrate the persistence of sadism in spite of civilization. Bestiosexual sadism is commonly dissociated from obvious sexual feeling and myriads of birds and beasts which are ruthlessly shot, the creatures, deer, foxes, badgers, otters, &c., which are hunted and chased, the bulls which are killed in pageantry, and even the hares which are coursed, are all demonstrations of man's innate wish to hurt and kill.

Sadistic tortures given the sanction of law seem even more inexcusable than those evoked by obvious illness. Count Joseph-Marie de Maistre describes an execution by breaking on the wheel as follows, 'A prisoner or a murderer or a blasphemer is given over to him [i.e. the executioner]. He seizes him and stretches and ties him on a horizontal cross; he lifts his arm and a horrible silence falls. Nothing is heard but the cry of the bones cracking under the heavy rod and the howling of the victim. Then he unties him and carries him to the wheel; the shattered limbs get twisted

---

[1] According to Prescott's *Conquest of Mexico* a soldier of Cortes had the patience to count the skulls in one *teocalli* and found them to number 136,000. These were from victims, mostly prisoners of war, whose chests had been opened by a flint knife and their hearts torn out whilst still alive as a sacrifice.

in the spokes; the head hangs; the hair stands out; and from the mouth, gaping open like a stove, come only now a few bloody words which at intervals beg for death.'

Sometimes apparently plausible excuses can be put forward for brutality and the so-called 'colour bar' is a common one. The complaint is that the Negro, or Indian, is taking away the white man's work, is attracting his girl friend, or, as is said in the Southern States of America, merely 'getting uppity'. Sometimes brutal attacks and lynchings are organized by associations such as the Ku Klux Klan or, in England, by Fascist groups. However, it is obvious that these excuses for ill-treatment do not hold water, and the Negro or Indian rarely behaves in a manner which cannot be dealt with properly by the law. The way in which mob violence can flare up with such slight provocation and its aggravation by propaganda by such organizations shows that there is a very prevalent unconscious desire for a sadistic outlet. Curiously enough the situation has been reversed to some extent recently. The Negro has become inflamed and rioted with the occasional murder or accidental death. Such a thing would be impossible except for the large amount of aggression which is usually suppressed until evoked by circumstances. Alarm is expressed that crimes of violence are increasing. It is impossible to discuss this at length here, but undoubtedly the basis of many crimes of violence is sadism. The greater prevalence is unlikely to be due to an increase in the primary instinct. Therefore it must be due to the fact that something has diminished the inhibitory or repressive forces which should keep the sadistic impulses in check or transmute them into more social behaviour. It appears that this undermining may be due to the recent war to some extent (for example, I possess a newspaper cutting, showing a Commando knifing a German sentry in the neck, published in a daily illustrated journal); changes in social *mores* (thirty years ago it was accepted that 'An Englishman fought with his fists' but now daggers and 'flick knives' are frequently shown on the films); separation of the father, on whom authority depends, for various reasons, and so on. It is noteworthy that the young men who display violence now were children during the war and often did not see their fathers for long periods.

Although most animals tend to protect their young even at the expense of their own lives, infanto-sexual sadism is frequently shown by parents to their children. Indeed, most children who are murdered are killed by their parents. The 'battered baby syndrome' is curiously similar to sadistic murder. In this a tiny child (usually under the age of 5 years) suffers from ungovernable violence which may be from either parent. This recurs in episodes without premeditation. Although help for the injured child may be sought the parent denies all knowledge of how the injuries could have arisen. There is a strong suspicion that the parents who are re-

sponsible for the battered babies have themselves suffered from parental
ill-treatment as small children. It is curious that this is an example where
women may show sadism. Children may be injured, although not
physically, by psychological ill-treatment from threats, bullying, and
frightening tales or fantasies. It would seem, however, that education can
diminish this sort of sadism, probably by the effect of public opinion.

In general this seems to be having an effect. For example, in England
in 1950 there were 946 cases of children removed from parental care by
Court order, but in 1964, 610; in 1965, 540; in 1966, 398; and in 1967, 381.

As he has slowly attempted to overcome his sadism man has turned, as
he always does, from reality to fantasy to do so. This has resulted in the
priest threatening hell-fire and eternal torment, 'where the worm dieth
not and the fire is not quenched' instead of tormenting his victim with
hot irons. Similarly, now that everyday cruelty is less tolerated the
fantasies of the ordinary man have turned to 'tough' films and plays,
romans policiers, gangster, and crime stories, as a relief. It is to be noted
that the sexual motif is not always entirely suppressed: for example, in
a popular novel, which had a very large sale, the story described the
kidnapping of a millionaire's daughter by a gangster, who repeatedly
raped her until, when finally rescued she was so demoralized that she
committed suicide.

The association of cruelty with oral activities, as characterized by
human vampires of such stories as 'Dracula', has a peculiar impact which
suggests that it activates repressed fantasies. This is not surprising since
this story, at least, is based on Transcaucasian folk-tales. The horror
which such stories arouse does not depend on the thought of someone
sucking one's blood, although this is unpleasant, but on something deeper.
It may be that the thought of blood-sucking is so common, although
deeply repressed, that its representation in a story or film causes an
emotional arousal. From personal observation the reactions of an audience
attending the play 'Dracula' seemed to be a mixture of horror and amusement. Yet if one considers it detachedly there are many more terrible
tortures than merely sucking blood which leave people unmoved. Amusement is a defence against the repressed.

This tendency towards sadism even pervades literature which has some
chance of survival—e.g. the novels of Hugh Walpole have a strong
element of cruelty in them, the most obvious being *The Man with Red
Hair*, but it is to be found in others also. Characteristically Walpole was
the gentlest and kindest of men which suggests that he repressed his
sadism in his ordinary life.

In general one may say that human beings, in spite of the horrors of
war and 'sport', are trying to turn away from cruelty, as far as their
nature allows, and the disgust with which overt sadism is viewed by most

people does show an attempt at its psychological suppression, not only as an individual trait but as a national or universal one.

Cruel Acts Associated with some Sexual Pleasure

Cruelty is sometimes vaguely associated with sexual pleasure although not to the full extent nor overtly so. This is commonly seen in domestic life in which a man ill-treats his wife in a brutal fashion. One might imagine that the woman would leave him and seek a happier life elsewhere, but often she does not do so. Again, if she once left him and then they became reconciled one might think that he would treat her better in the future. But no, the woman returns to her torturer and the man, as if he did not value her, continues his ill-treatment.

The explanation is, of course, that this is the pattern of their sexual lives; the man is a sadist to a slight degree, and no doubt feels a certain amount of sexual pleasure in his brutalities, whilst the woman enjoys her injuries in a masochistic manner. It is difficult to know how much sadism to children is associated with frank sex but probably a large percentage must be. That this is a major problem is shown by the fact that the American Humane Society thinks that there is a yearly incidence of 3,000 to 4,000 cases of sexual abuse in New York alone. This is said to be a conservative estimate and probably applies to all other large cities.

There is often a certain amount of sexuality in the way in which school-masters have treated, and occasionally still treat, boys. Schoolmasters are often homosexual and sometimes this homosexuality is admixed with sadism. The unsuitable master is rapidly being eliminated and in many schools it is an offence for him to thrash boys, but not long ago a mother complained to me that her son was being repeatedly and unreasonably flogged at school. It is easy to find examples in other kinds of life—the initiation ceremony which greets boys at work is a common example.

The importance of this variety is rather in its effect on the sexual behaviour of the sadist than on his victim—since it is unusual for him to inflict a serious injury. Being too weak to be manifest in overt, illegal behaviour the impulse tends to dissipate itself in fantasy. For example, *schadenfreude*, or the enjoyment of the miseries of others, is typical of this type of reaction, but much more frequently there is an active fantasy. Thus these patients constantly occupy themselves with day-dreams of torments; these it is who circulate rumours of atrocities in war time and delight in reading murder trials in time of peace. The psychological studies of rumour have shown with what monotony nuns have their breasts cut off, men are castrated, and children violated. This fantasization of sexual cruelty leads to a diminution of the normal sexual impulse so that it is not unusual to find that either these patients are completely impotent or, if they are capable of sexual performance, obtain little or no pleasure from intercourse. They are often worthy persons who resent this intrusion of unpleasant fantasies into their thoughts, and are unhappy at their sexual condition. Fortunately they are likely to benefit from treatment by psychotherapy.

A type of behaviour which may fall into this group or may be actively sadistic is that of the man who performs some relatively harmless injury—the cutting of a girl's hair, staining of her dress with ink, or burning of her coat with a cigarette. Since these are done in places where they are unlikely to be detected, in buses or cinemas, the act is not usually punished. Included in such behaviour is the pinching of girls' buttocks and even breasts. I had always believed that it was more prevalent in Latin countries but am assured that it is quite as common here—in fact, on some Underground railway stations girls complain that it makes their lives a misery. Men who behave like this very rarely come to the psychiatrist's knowledge—probably they do not obtain full sexual pleasure from their behaviour but rather a mild half-recognized sexual excitement.

It is of interest to note that the Marquis de Sade, whose name is attached to this form of perversion, was a sadist of either this or of the preceding class. He seems to have used cruelty as a stimulant rather than a substitute for sexual intercourse. Born in 1740 into an aristocratic family he was a man of considerable position. His doting grandmother brought him up and he said that 'her blind affection for me fostered all the defects I have just confessed'. He saw little of his father as a child, and was educated at the Jesuit Clermont College in Paris. Later he was commissioned in the in the King's Own Infantry Regiment.

De Sade soon showed that he delighted in the company of prostitutes, and a few months after his marriage he was imprisoned for fifteen days for excesses in a bawdy house. Then came the case of Rose Keller in 1768. This woman was persuaded to go with him to a country house and was there severely flagellated. His family was able to prevent him getting into serious trouble, but the king ordered him to stay on his estates.

In June 1772 the Marseilles affair followed. Here he assembled four girls with whom he dealt in turn: he flagellated one and masturbated his male servant at the same time: then he gave one cantharides in sweets and tried to persuade her to allow him, or his servant, to commit sodomy, but she stated later that she refused: he tried to persuade one of the girls to flog him with a cat-o'-nine-tails, but she was too tender-hearted to do so. He had intercourse with another girl after flogging her and his servant committed sodomy on him; then he committed sodomy on another girl, and his servant sodomized him. This sort of thing either occurred, or was requested, with all of the girls. His behaviour led to a court case, since two of the girls had been made ill by the sweets contaminated with cantharides and aniseed.

The result of this was that the Marquis was confined to Miolans prison, but he escaped in April 15th, 1773, and lived on his estates. There he did not behave normally. He engaged five young girls as servants and locked them in separate rooms; he attempted to flog and violate them in the night. All except one refused to stay on. This caused police action and again he was arrested. He was condemned to Vincennes prison for sixteen months and then the Bastille for five and a half years. There he wrote a number of books, the best known are *The 120 Days of Sodom, Aline and Valcour, Nouvelle Justine, Juliette or the Prosperities of Vice.* He died in Chartenton Asylum.

De Sade's literary work shows, as one might expect, his sexual deviations: they are pervaded with cruelty, masochism, anal perversions, exhibitionism and voyeurism, coprophagia, coprophilia, incest, and the like.

Various *avant-garde* writers have suggested that de Sade was a great psychologist, but this is nonsense. He described those perversions with which he was familiar, either by hearsay or practice, but he was quite unaware of the psychological mechanisms which lay behind them. No doubt, had he been more normal, he would have been an interesting eighteenth-century novelist, but the fact that he peppered his work with deviations does not make him a great writer. In fact, most people find it wearisome.

It is interesting to know that although his writing is filled with murders, when he was released from incarceration during the French Revolution he could not stomach the cruelty which was a daily happening. He was one of those who enjoy abnormal behaviour only associated with sex. Dissociated, as by the guillotine, he was revolted by it. He was really a polymorphous pervert with the accent on sadism.

Acts of Cruelty Associated with Full Sexual Pleasure and Accompanied or Followed by Erection, Ejaculation, and Orgastic Sensations

The patient in this sort of sadism is frequently a quiet type unsuspected by his associates; although if his life-history is examined carefully nearly always some psychopathic traits are discovered. As a rule sadistic conduct does not suddenly appear in a normal person.

There are large numbers of men who use rough or cruel behaviour as a part of their preliminary sexual play, but usually this is introductory to intercourse and not a substitute for it. They do not frequently do the woman any serious injury.

As I have pointed out alcohol will release perversions which would not otherwise be apparent, and this is true of sadism. The attacks upon young women, frequently after dances, by men who admit that they have been drinking, which fill the Sunday newspapers of the less reputable type, are cases of sadism in which the aggressor's abnormality has been released by alcohol, but which was insufficient to overwhelm his consciousness and allow him to proceed to murder. The frequency with which this occurs shows that it is far from being an insignificant problem.

The lust murder is the most characteristic of this type of sadism. I believe that when murder occurs it happens either (1) accidentally through the sadist allowing his 'love play' to go too far—he is overwhelmed by the emotion which his cruelty produces and almost before he has realized it he has killed the woman; or (2) deliberate killing for the sexual sensation. This is the type of Peter Kürten, discussed below. It seems probable that the first type, once successful, can turn into the second and no doubt this explains why there is frequently a long interval between the first sadistic murder and those which follow, but after the second the act is repeated rapidly until the sadist is arrested. This interval is to be seen in the case of Seefeld, the homosexual mass murderer, Haarmann, the Hamburg murderer, and Kürten, the Dusseldorf assassin. The interval between the first and second killing may be partly accidental since in the case of Kürten he was in prison a long time and so had little chance of hurting anyone.

In the accidental type of sadistic murder there is little evidence of premeditation, but in the repetitive murders considerable precautions may be taken by the assailant.

The typical lust murder is characterized by:

1. Periodic outbreaks, due, of course, to the patient's recurring compulsion or paroxysmal sexual desire.

2. Nearly always cutting or stabbing, particularly of the breasts or genitalia, frequently with sucking, licking, or mouthing of the wounds, sometimes with biting of the skin. In some cases there is a desire to drink the blood and eat the flesh.

3. Sometimes erection and ejaculation is followed by violation of the dying or injured victim, but often these physical manifestations take place without any attempt at intercourse.

4. Karpman suggests that there is an affective storm, or cataclysm of emotion, which clouds consciousness at the climax of sadistic behaviour. There seems no definite evidence of this, and by analogy with normal intercourse, I can see no reason why there should be such psychological obscuration. If it does occur it is of brief duration and often the aggressor makes his escape from the scene of the crime, removes blood stains and so on without difficulty. Probably the idea of psychological obscuration is the product of the impossibility of a normal person to comprehend the terrible acts of the sadist, but we must remember that, no matter how revolting, the

behaviour is pleasurable and the product of intense sexual excitement.

5. His behaviour is usually normal until the next paroxysm.

The sexual object may be heterosexual, homosexual, infantosexual, bestiosexual, or polymorphous so that any person or living thing, no matter of what sex, may be the victim. Frequently one method is chosen and one implement is used for the injuries, but this is not invariable. Sometimes the implement is retained and used again and again.

It may be of interest if I record some of the most outstanding cases of lust murders, but unfortunately careful psychological studies have not been made of them and accurate details are not available even to the genuine student. Nevertheless, such accounts as I have are valuable and throw some light on the condition.[1]

The case of Neville Heath is typical of the heterosexual sadistic murderer. It is a comparatively slight one when one compares it with those of Gilles de Rais, Haarmann, or Peter Kürten but no doubt this was because Heath was detected early in his career and prevented from continuing his lust murders.

Heath's parents were respectable people and he was a man of good education, with an excellent school record as an athlete (which incidentally shows the futility of those remarks regarding the influence of sport on character beloved of Speech Days at school). When he left school he obtained work as a warehouse clerk and at the same time joined the Territorials for some months. However, he soon embarked on a campaign of petty crime; he was a sneak thief, confidence trickster, and perpetrator of minor fraud. He was very attractive to women—he had fair wavy hair and a fresh complexion. He was also a pathological liar and delighted in posing as being an Army or Air Force officer. In fact during his career he did hold commissions in the Army, the Air Force, and the South African Air Force, but was court-martialled for misconduct and cashiered. He was first dismissed from the R.A.F. in 1937 and after that settled down to a life of fraud. Apprehended, he was tried for offences at Leicester, Peterborough, and Stamford and placed on probation. This was not successful and in 1938 he was tried at the Old Bailey and sent to Borstal for three years, on several charges. In 1942 he went to South Africa but soon reverted to his old posings. He told people he was 'Bruce Lockhart, the Cambridge Blue' and courted a girl of a good South African family. Her brother found out that he was masquerading but in spite of this he persuaded her to marry him. This marriage was not happy and after two months she returned to her family. He obtained a commission in

[1] Owing to lack of space it is impossible to give complete accounts of cases such as those of Heath and Haigh. Those interested will find excellent ones in Lindesay Neustatter's *Mind of the Murderer*.

the South African Air Force and proposed to another girl. Finally he was court-martialled for the third time, and in spite of the girl's pleas, deported.

After he left South Africa he returned to London but continued his masquerading. He appeared in public places as 'Lt.-Col. Jimmy Armstrong, D.F.C., A.F.C., of the South African Air Force', and of course, wore the appropriate uniform and insignia. He gravitated to the nightclubs of Chelsea and South Kensington where he was likely to meet rich women and which were the home of psychopaths, alcoholics, and drug addicts.

Up to now, as far as is known, he had shown nothing other than pathological lying and swindling, but it is said that already he showed some sexual abnormality since he had a handkerchief fetishism and frequently stole handkerchiefs from girls.

On 30 June 1946, however, he took a woman to a hotel at Notting Hill and tied her hands and feet with handkerchiefs he had stolen from other women. How far she was acquiescent it is difficult to say, but one might suspect that she was to this extent although not to what happened later. His sadistic feelings appear to have been beyond his control since he flogged her seventeen times, so savagely that the riding quirt he used had pieces of skin adherent. He also mutilated her (presumably the breasts and genitalia although the reports do not state clearly what was done) using his teeth on various parts of the body. The woman was then left dead and he disappeared.

About a month later, whilst living at Bournemouth, he made the acquaintance of a young girl who was staying there on holiday. He dined with her and left the hotel with her afterwards. She never arrived back at her own hotel because he enticed her into one of the chines (deep valleys characteristic of the place) and murdered her. She died of throat wounds, but was terribly mutilated and lacerated in a similar way to the previous case, and her body was also marked with teeth.

Heath was asked to visit the police station because he bore a strong resemblance to the man being sought for the Notting Hill crime, and whilst he was there the sister of the girl he had just murdered in Bournemouth walked into the station with her father. She bore a likeness to the dead girl and the detective noticed that Heath recoiled. He was interrogated further and then arrested.

The trial was of great medico-legal interest although Heath was charged only with the murder of the woman at Notting Hill. The defence pointed out that the medical witnesses for the prosecution, although they had great prison experience, were doctors who were not specialists and had never worked in mental hospitals. The medical evidence for the defence was that the prisoner was suffering from moral insanity and at times was unaware of what he did. The prosecution insisted that he was not insane.

The judge summed up the different medical opinions and told the jury that they must keep to the Macnaughton Rules. Heath was found guilty and sentenced to death.

It was stated that he showed no remorse, and a few minutes before being hanged when given a single whisky made the cynical remark that it might have been made a double!

There are a number of interesting points in his case. Firstly, he came from a respectable middle-class home (compare this with the home of Peter Kürten) and apparently did not show abnormality until puberty. He then developed a handkerchief fetishism. He was a pathological liar and swindler and even when he had the chance of a career, by being commissioned in the Forces, he could not maintain it. His sadism first became apparent in the Notting Hill murder, but it is believed that he had made previous attempts not mentioned in the trial. The second murder followed soon afterwards, instead of the usual long gap, but one wonders if the 'first' murder was only the first detected. It is to be noted that between the two murders he slept with a girl he had promised to marry and was very gentle with her. (This is comparable with Kürten's treatment of his wife.)

It is unfortunate that the facts of this, and similar cases, are kept in the official archives and not available for psychiatric study. Heath, however, refused to discuss his case with the prison doctors (which must have made it very difficult for them to form an opinion on him!) so that probably nothing similar to Kürten's case could be published.

However, from such facts as are available for examination it is obvious that Heath was a psychopath with a long history of stealing, he was a handkerchief fetishist and this was linked up with his sadism, and he showed considerable narcissism. His masquerading in uniform and his way of life generally—he habitually wore an Air Force tie, for example— were all indicative of considerable self-love. The complete lack of remorse is a very characteristic trait. In fact the total absence of emotion even to the point of making a cynical joke at the foot of the gallows suggests that there may have been a latent schizophrenic element in his mental structure. No one can read the accounts of sadists such as he was without realizing how closely related sadism and this type of psychosis must be. The only difference seems to be that consciousness is undistorted in the sadist whereas it is completely aberrant in the schizophrenic so that reality in the case of the psychosis is grotesquely falsified.

There is no evidence that Heath was other than a heterosexual sadist, but there are cases in which there appears to be such a store of repressed fury that nothing, man, woman, child, or beast, is safe. Fortunately such cases are extremely rare and naturally their behaviour attracts attention, but frequently they do terrible harm to the community before detection.

CASE No. 5

A Case of Heterosexual Sadism

The case of Patrick Joseph Byrne demonstrates how the extremity of sadism approximates to schizophrenia. He was an Irish labourer whose early life appears obscure. However, there was a long history of sexual abnormality. 'Peeping Tom' activities led to his discovery by two girls when he looked into their bedroom some time in 1958. Later he had entered a girl's room, in a block of cubicles of the local Y.W.C.A., by going through the garden. He sat on the girl's bed and talked with her. Although his intention was to get in bed with the girl, when she asked him in a friendly way to go he went without giving trouble.

On December 23rd 1959 he became intoxicated during his lunch-hour and when he returned to work on a building the foreman ordered him to come down from the scaffolding and go home. He left at approximately 4.30 p.m.

In his statement he said that he saw a girl enter the hostel and thought that he would like to peer into her window. He saw her wearing a red pullover and underskirt. She was combing her hair. Entering the building he watched her through a glass panel over the door. When she did not take off any more clothes he got bored and was just going to leave when she opened the door. She said, 'Let me get the warden'. This was about 6.30 p.m.

Byrne said, 'Give me a kiss', and before she could say 'No', he kissed her. He went on, 'She tried to shove me away but couldn't and for a second I got her round the waist. She screamed and I put my hands round her neck. She went backwards inside the room with me squeezing her throat and then fell backwards. Her head bounced on the floor and I was lying on top of her kissing her and squeezing her neck at the one time. I heard a couple of small noises in her throat but kept on kissing her. After a while I knelt up and I had a strong urge to have a good look at her. I was fully sure she was dead because I had the whole power of my back squeezing her throat.'

The statement says he did 'various other things'. He then became tired of playing about with her and saw a table knife. He then mutilated her in various ways, including scoring round the chest, lower down the body and down the back. He then cut her head off. He said that he was very excited and thought that 'he ought to terrorize all women . . . to get my own back on them for causing my nervous tension through sex'.

After mutilating the girl he left a note because 'I thought I might be had for rape but not for murder'.

When he left the room he saw another lighted window but the girl in this room did not attract him. However, another girl did apparently because she seemed to be washing. He said, 'I watched her for a while and stood close to the window. I only looked at her face and the urge to kill her was tremendously strong. I thought I would take her quietly and quickly and picked up a big stone from the garden. I think I first got a brassiére from the clothes line and then wrapped it round the stone.'

He switched off the light and waited outside the inner door. 'I heard her call out something about 'Who's there?" The door opened and I struck at her with the stone in my hand. The stone swung out of my hand and she screamed.'

He then ran back to his lodgings and 'stood by the mirror talking to myself and searching my face for signs of a madman, but I could see none'. He felt he ought to commit suicide. Then he thought of his mother and Christmas, and was unable to do it. However, he did consider going to Northern Ireland where the police carry guns and try to provoke one to shoot him. That night he slept with his cousin because he was afraid to sleep alone.

At the trial the Home Office pathologist said that the cause of death was manual strangulation; there was no evidence of recent sexual intercourse. The three medical witnesses at the trial were agreed that Byrne was not insane within the Macnaughton Rules: he knew what he was doing and that what he was doing was wrong. They also agreed that he was suffering from some disease or abnormality of the mind, and so on their evidence one of the requirements of Section 2 of the Homicide Act of 1957 was fulfilled. It was said that as a result of sexual immaturity Byrne was a sexual psychopath, and because of this he had impaired mental responsibility.

Mr. Justice Stable, in his summing up directed the jury that Section 2 of the Act was not intended to protect a man who strangles a woman 'under the influence of overwhelming, violent, and perverted lust. . . . If there is nothing else then I say the vicious, depraved tendencies, thought, desires, lusts, and conduct do not bring the accused within the Section and that does not constitute such abnormality of mind as substantially to impair his mental responsibility for his acts'. Furthermore, the Section did not cover any impairment of control through alcohol.

[Section 2 (1) of the Act states 'Where a person kills or is party to the killing of another, he should not be convicted of murder if he was suffering from such abnormality of mind (whether arising from a condition of arrested or retarded development of mind or any inherent causes or induced by disease or injury) as substantially impaired his mental responsibility for his acts and omissions in doing or being a party to the killing'.]

Byrne was convicted and appealed against his conviction on the grounds that the judge had misdirected the jury. On his behalf it was argued that the judge should have left it to the jury to decide whether a sexual pervert came within Section 2 of the Homicide Act. The judge had said in effect that if the jury were to look at the facts of the case and decide it was nothing but sexual perversion, then they need not worry about Section 2.

Delivering judgment the Court of Criminal Appeal stated that whether the accused was suffering from any abnormality of the mind was a question for the jury. Medical evidence was important, but the jury could take other matters before it into account also. Once the jury was satisfied that the accused was suffering from abnormality of the mind, the crucial question arose whether that abnormality was such as substantially impaired his mental responsibility for his acts. This was a question of degree and essentially one for the jury.

In the view of the Court, the judge's direction that the defence of diminished responsibility was not available amounted to a direction that difficulty or even inability of an accused person to exercise will-power to control his physical acts could not amount to such abnormality of mind as substantially impaired his mental responsibility. This direction was wrong. Moreover, on the evidence he was plainly on the borderline of insanity, or partially insane. Properly directed, the jury could not have failed to conclude that the defence of diminished responsibility was made out. However, in view of the accused's tendencies, the sentence of life imprisonment must stand for the lesser crime.

The decision of the Court of Criminal Appeal was obviously a sensible one and removed the possibility of other judges giving a similar direction which would have made nonsense of the Act.

Psychologically the case of Byrne is of great interest. One cannot help thinking that a careful psychiatric investigation would have discovered that he had felt rejected as a child and his voyeuristic and sadistic tendencies probably arose from this. The alcohol, as in so many other sadistic offences (for example that of Peter Griffiths who took a child from a hospital in Blackburn and smashed it to death against a wall) merely acted as a factor in the release of repressed impulses. It is a thousand pities that publicans cannot be made to appreciate the danger of serving alcohol to men who appear abnormal. In the case of a sadist such as Byrne cure was most unlikely, and his sentence of life imprisonment should not be shortened to a period of years, but should mean confinement for his whole life.

A somewhat similar case to that of Byrne occurred a little while ago in America. Here a man entered a nurses' hostel and killed a number of girls one after another, but, unfortunately, details of the criminal's psychology are not available.

Heterosexual sadism, although fairly common in the male, rarely occurs in the female—the emotion is nearly always reversed into the less obvious masochism. The demon woman who destroys and tortures her lovers appears more in the fevered imagination of novelists and dramatists than in reality. Nevertheless there is a type of woman who enjoys men killing themselves for the love of her, but this is the result of autosexuality rather than true sadism. The woman relishes the reputation of her fatal beauty more than the thought of the pain she inflicts. It has been suggested that Catherine de Medici and Lucrezia Borgia were of this type, but this is not very easy to verify and other factors—such as the desire for power—may have been present, if such women really did kill ruthlessly. In general, sadism, as in masochism in women, appears rather as a behaviour disorder than as a sexual neurosis, and there is not the paroxysmal periodic indulgence with an orgastic climax in their case. Rather is there a persistent deviation of conduct without any apparent acme of pleasure. No woman of the Peter Kürten type seems to have been recorded in history and we may be fairly certain that none ever existed. It must be admitted, however, that even in women there is some evidence of sadistic pleasure, since in some cases of poisoning the criminal appears to enjoy the suffering of her victim. This is not quite comparable with sadism found in men for there is no sexual climax and the whole cruelty is of a more passive type—the poison having been administered the poisoner stands by and observes the agonies. But in any case this seems very rare since most female poisoners have avoided observing the suffering and death of their victims.

The terrible case of Fritz Haarmann, the so-called 'Hanover Mass Murderer' is worth recording because it it unlikely that a similar example of homosexual sadism will ever be described. He killed between thirty and forty boys and youths, and sold their flesh for food, in the tragic times following the First World War. When questioned he admitted 'Es können dreissig, es können vierzig sein, ich weiss das nicht' (he remembered thirty or even forty, but apparently he had killed so many that he could not be sure of how many more!).

Haarmann was the son of a psychopathic father: a locomotive stoker who gave up his work after his son was born and afterwards lived mainly on his wife. He was bad tempered, grumbling, appallingly mean, and constantly discontented—in fact, a typical inadequate psychopath. The mother was prematurely aged and a silent woman who became bed-ridden after the birth of Fritz, her sixth child. One of his brothers, Wilhelm, was sent to a reformatory school following an offence against the daughter of a neighbour, and the three Haarmann daughters were all loose. Only the eldest son was a hard-working, although small-minded, respectable foreman.

Almost as soon as he could walk Fritz is said to have shown two characteristics: dressing up and playing at being a girl, and (as is so common with homosexuals) he hated his father. On the other hand he loved dolls, sewing and helping with the housework: he was afraid of other boys.

At first he went to a Church school and then to a preparatory school for non-commissioned officers at Neu Breisach. There he appeared a well-developed, but rather fat boy with a regular-featured, almost good-looking face. Scholastically he did not do well, but was a good soldier.

On 3 September 1895 he had some sort of a fit which was attributed to sunstroke suffered during manoeuvres. This resulted in his release from military service and he returned home. His father tried to persuade him to work in a small cigar factory. However, at the age of seventeen he was accused of interfering with children and sent to the Provincial Asylum at Hildesheim. It was not considered there that he was responsible for his acts. Indeed, Dr. Schmalfuss, the psychiatrist, considered that he was feeble-minded. This experience made him afraid of mental hospitals for the rest of his life. Six months later, whilst the Christmas tree caught fire (one wonders whether he set it alight!), he escaped. He then worked, first as a boat-builder in Zürich, and then with an apothecary. After two years he returned home where he constantly quarrelled with his father. Then he apparently impregnated a girl and was going to marry her, but broke it off. She gave birth to a still-born child.

After this he joined the Army and served in the smart Jägar Battalion in Colmar, in Alsace. The officers were pleased with him and one made him his batman. Like many similar characters he enjoyed military life, and liked the senseless routine. However, he developed further symptoms which were diagnosed as neurasthenic, and he was invalided with a 'very good' character, and a pension which he drew until he was finally arrested.

Again he returned home and there were further quarrels with his father. He was examined by Dr. Andrae who, on 14 May 1903, stated that he was morally lacking, unintelligent, rough, easily amused, revengeful, and selfish, but not mentally ill. There were no grounds for his incarceration in a mental hospital. During the next twenty years he spent about seven in prison for theft, fraud, burglary, and indecency. In fact he passed the whole of the First World War in prison, and was released in 1918.

Haarmann emerged into a world which he understood: with cheating, black-market dealings, and thefts. He worked as a police spy and informer and noticed that there were a large number of homeless, rootless, orphaned boys wandering through Hanover. In brief, he enticed them to his room, killed them, and sold their flesh as smuggled meat.

He was discovered by the finding of human skulls on the bank of the Leine and these were related to the disappearance of 600 young people in the town in 1924.

Haarmann was arrested for indecency at the railway station and his room was searched. Enough evidence was found to make it possible to charge him. His trial caused a sensation and he was convicted and beheaded.

His case shows a certain similarity to that of Peter Kürten. There is the same unstable family history; the psychopathic father, and more or less normal mother; the over-sexed sisters, and like Kürten, Fritz Haarmann started crime early, continuing it with periods in prison until he commenced his terrible final career. It would seem that both could indulge in sexual relations; but, whereas Haarmann was homosexually orientated, Kürten was polymorphous.

His behaviour in selling the young men's flesh for food no doubt satisfied his oral tendencies (besides providing him with a useful income) which is to be noticed in most sadists of no matter what type. He showed the lack of emotion of the typical sadist, also, since on some occasions he had pieces of bodies concealed only by a sack in the room where he discussed business. In fact, the walls were spattered with blood and he often carried away pails of blood concealed under a cloth.

Haarmann was a dull, but probably not defective type of man. Long before his conviction for murder he showed, in addition to his sadism, that he was psychopathic and had no moral inhibitions. Many psychiatrists would be satisfied to attribute his behaviour to hereditary influences, but the terrible home environment (which was so similar to Kürten's) would be sufficient to explain his behaviour to others, including myself.

The best example of infantosexual sadism (which also contained a homosexual element) is the classical one of Gilles de Rais, who was a companion to Joan of Arc. He distinguished himself by killing two hundred boys before he was executed in 1440. He said at his trial:

I do not know why but I, myself, out of my own head without the advice of anyone, conceived the idea of acting thus, solely for the pleasure and delectation of lust; in fact I found incomparable pleasure in it, doubtless at the instigation of the devil. This diabolical idea came to me eight years ago; that was the very year in which my relative the lord of Suze died. Now being by chance in the library of his castle. I found a latin book on the lives and customs of the Roman Caesars by the learned historian called Suetonius; the said book was ornamented by pictures, very well painted, in which were seen the manners of these pagan emperors, and I read in this fine history how Tiberius, Caracalla, and other Caesars sported with children and *took singular pleasure in martyring them*. Upon which I desired to imitate the said Caesars and the same evening I began to do so following the pictures in the book . . . for a time I confided my case to no one; but later I took the mystery to several persons, among others to Henriet and Pontou, whom I trained for this sport. The said individuals aided in the mystery and took charge of finding children for my needs. The children killed at Chantoce were thrown into a vat at the foot of a tower, from which I had them taken out on a certain night and put into a box to be transferred to Machecoul and at Nantes in the Suze mansion, they were burned in my room except for a few handsome heads I kept as relics. Now I cannot say exactly how many were thus burned and killed but they were certainly to the number of six score per year.

This confession is of interest, even five hundred years later, for the psychological light which it throws on the condition. It is curious that the sadism was released by seeing pictures in a book but perhaps there were previous cruel feelings which he did not appreciate (there were many sadistic outlets in medieval times). There is no mention of pity or remorse which, again, is characteristic. Similarly, once the children had been killed their corpses were valueless to him and discarded as worthless rubbish. (This is very similar to the rejection of articles of clothing used in festishism after they have served their purpose.) The attribution of these obscure impulses to diabolical intervention seems partly an excuse and partly due to the superstition of the time. No doubt those who enjoy repression would suggest that such books as Suetonius should be banned but, although such a view was held by Kürten, it is probably entirely wrong—no normal person would be changed into a sadist by reading a book (in fact, were it so most of our classical scholars would be killers and our universities a shambles!). The criminal sadist has usually started on this path before he reaches adult life and his impulses are as easily released by other means.

Bestiosexual sadism is rare in England but cases do occasionally occur. Such a case was recorded in the press in which a 'cat-strangler' killed as many as three cats nightly for some time. He did so by means of a running noose and then hung the bodies up on fences or railings. This form of sadism is occasionally seen when the cruelty takes the form of ham-stringing cattle or horses. Sometimes such behaviour is, of course, a form of revenge perpetrated by someone with a grudge against the owner, but even so there is a strong sadistic tone to the form which it takes.

In classical times bestiosexual sadism was revealed in religious ceremonies. This is shown in the worship of Dionysus. He was frequently represented as a bull and in some rituals the bull was torn to pieces by the frenzied priestesses-maenads. This occurred particularly in the Cretan form of the religion. Frazer states: 'Indeed, the rending and devouring of live bulls and calves appear to have been a regular feature of the Dionysiac rites. It is believed by many classical scholars that even this is not the original ritual and that the god was previously portrayed by a man. The practice of eating the flesh of the god and drinking his blood seems to have persisted even until now', and further, 'The custom of tearing in pieces the bodies of animals and of men, and then devouring them raw has been practised as a religious rite by savages in modern times.'

This interpretation is supported by Graves.

It is interesting that these rites occurred in the worship of a goddess, who presumably represented the mother, and that the animal sacrificed was a strong savage animal such as a bull which seems to have symbolized the father. Whether this was an exhibition of some unconscious manifestation of an Oedipus emotion one cannot say, but undoubtedly it shows how near the surface bestiosexual sadism has persisted until quite lately.

One of the most interesting polymorphous sadists from the psychological point of view was Peter Kürten. His case was studied exhaustively by Karl Berg, to whose book I am indebted for the facts given here. Kürten was, of course, the Düsseldorf murderer whose career of assassination filled Europe with horror at the time.

His family history was a very bad one and most psychiatrists would attribute his later behaviour to his heredity and upbringing. His grandfather on his father's side was a poacher, drank, and served penal servitude for theft. His paternal grandmother was said to be alcoholic. Some of the father's brothers had bad reputations for alcoholism and violence.

The maternal grandfather was respectable and the mother's brothers and sisters appear to have been decent citizens.

The father was an irascible, violent drunkard who served a prison sentence for incest with his eldest daughter. The mother appears to have been a normal type and she separated from the husband after this imprisonment. Kürten had ten brothers and sisters. Two died young and one was killed in the First World War. One sister married and become a good housewife. Two sisters were described by Kürten as being over-sexed and even to have made incestuous advances to him. Two brothers served long prison sentences.

Kürten first noticed pleasure at the sight of cruelty when he saw a dog-catcher hurt dogs, at the age of 9 years. This man also showed him how to interfere with them sexually. This developed, and at 13 when he compressed the neck of a squirrel he was catching to sell for pocket money he had an ejaculation. At his age he knew all about sexual matters having seen his parents having intercourse. He tried to have intercourse with a schoolgirl but she resisted too much. He therefore tried to violate animals and did commit bestiality with a sheep but the orgasm was produced by stabbing it. At 15 and 16 he stabbed sheep for the agreeable sensation it produced, but had no ejaculation. Then he embezzled money and lived with a girl until he exhausted it. He had normal intercourse but stimulated himself by pinching her. He commented that he had intercourse only a few times in a month, and realized that this was strange in a young man. He then fell in with a woman and her daughter of 16. He found that he was unattracted to the girl but had intercourse with the woman which succeeded only when he ill-treated her. Finally he threatened to kill her, she reported this to the police, and he was given a week's imprisonment. He had a long sentence for theft from 1900 to 1904, but when he came out he fired some shots at this woman and whilst doing so ejaculated. He also shot at a girl, was chased and captured. He was given a year's imprisonment as a result.

During his imprisonment, instead of having the usual sexual fantasies of relations with women he imagined situations in which he wounded people and in that way succeeded in producing ejaculations. The thefts which he committed after his release from prison he stated were the result of sheer want.

In 1913 he committed his first murder. He had entered a house at night to steal and saw a child of ten asleep in bed. He strangled her and thrust his fingers into her genitals (rupturing the vagina into the rectum). He then cut her throat with a small, sharp knife.

After this murder he committed arson (he had previously set fire to a barn, a hayloft, and two hayricks in 1904), and struck people with an axe. He was in prison from 1913 to 1921. He then obtained a steady job and met a woman who had served five years' penal servitude for shooting a man whose mistress she had been, but who had discarded her. Kürten did not attract her because she knew that he went about with other women, but he threatened to kill her unless she submitted and they had premarital intercourse. He married her in 1923. Another girl was threatening to bring an action against him because of rape but his wife dissuaded her. The wife appears to have been forbearing, even though during their married life she knew that he was unfaithful to her.

In 1925 he attempted to strangle a girl but she escaped. A similar attempt occurred in 1926, but again he failed. In these cases he seems to have ill-treated the girl *after* he had had relations with her. From 1927 to 1929 he abandoned most of his sadistic violence and substituted arson for it. He set fire to various buildings, ricks, and so on no less than *eighteen* times.

In 1929 he seems to have settled down to a life of sadism. In February he attacked a woman with scissors, and stabbed and killed a man. In March he stabbed and killed a child and attempted to strangle a girl. In July he tried three times to kill girls by throttling. In August he killed two girls and two children, besides stabbing three girls and a man. He also tried to strangle a girl and thrust her into the river. In September he tried to kill a girl with a chisel and attempted to strangle another. He succeeded in killing two girls with a hammer. In October he killed one girl with a hammer and twice tried to kill others. In November he strangled and stabbed a child with scissors. In 1930 in February he attempted strangulation of a girl and made similar attempts on two others in March. He had three major attempts and a number of minor ones, all without success, in April, one girl being attacked with a hammer. In May he attempted to murder a girl by strangulation and failed. He was then arrested.

This case shows a number of interesting points. Firstly, the extremely bad heredity; one who believes heredity to be the main factor would have plenty here to account for his abnormality. On the other hand, Kürten himself believed that his bad early environment was the cause of his terrible behaviour. His drunken, incestuous father; the cramped, dreary, penurious environment; the early revelation of sex and the experience of cruelty could hardly fail to have a deep-seated effect on him. We have noted previously that Bender and Curran gave certain conditions in which children commit murder. Kürten's environment seems to have provided most of them, particularly that of (5), i.e. where the familial behaviour pattern is 'one of severe aggressivity in parents and the child must protect himself against them with the only reaction pattern he knows' (see p. 118).

As a matter of fact, according to Kürten himself, he did commit murders as a child. He told Karl Berg that at the age of 9 years he was playing with other boys on logs in the Rhine and pushed a boy off so that he was drowned. He did this again later and this boy was also drowned. Berg does not state whether these stories were confirmed, but whether they were true or not they show the direction of his thinking as a child.

Kürten was most stimulated by the flow of blood and killed mainly for this. He did admit that he had a constant desire to kill and had he had the means would have slaughtered masses and caused catastrophes.

The substitution of arson for killing in 1927–9 seems to support the psychoanalytic view that fire is related to sexual feeling, and it is interesting to notice that on a number of occasions he attempted to burn the corpse with petrol.

Another point which is curious, particularly in view of the popular belief that 'the murderer always returns to the scene of his crime', is the fact that Kürten frequently did go back either to the corpse, before it was discovered, or to the place where he had murdered, or else to the victim's grave. He did this because he obtained sexual excitement from doing so. In some cases, e.g. when he visited the graves of his victims, he obtained an orgasm; and again when he set fire to the corpse it produced an orgasm.

Kürten usually did not attempt to violate his victims but did so on some occasions. His potency was weak unless stimulated by stabbing and this accounted for the fact that he did this whilst indulging in intercourse with the dying victims.

The polymorphous form of his sadism—his ability to be sexually stimulated by cruelty to man, woman, child, or animal—indicates to my mind a deep-seated hostility to his father and mother, and perhaps his brothers and sisters also. This is hardly to be wondered at when one understands his upbringing: his life in one room with a drunken father, the common sight of violent intercourse—he says, 'Had they not been married one would have had to think of it as rape'—and the complete lack of love in his life.

How far his perversion indicates an extreme regression it is difficult to say, but he undoubtedly indulged in blood-drinking which some would think indicated a fixation at the breast level (blood being equated to milk). He was certainly very narcissistic and was a great dandy in his dress, particular in his appearance, dressed his hair and shaved carefully, and so on. He is said to have shown occasional masochism.

It is interesting to note that he never showed any sadistic cruelty to his wife, although he threatened her before marriage, and was not always kind afterwards. Nevertheless whilst he was battering in girls' skulls, stabbing with scissors and knives, setting fire to corpses and strangling, he lived with his wife in comparative tranquillity.

In general one might summarize Kürten's abnormality as being partly the result of an inherited, passionate, violent nature which was stimulated by his early environment, particularly by a brutal father, sexual propinquity, lack of affection in childhood, and extreme poverty. He was condemned to death, made a dignified final speech, and went composedly to the block.

The false confessions of murder which occasionally appear, usually associated with some much-reported crime, are an example of sadistic fantasies. These frequently cause considerable trouble to the police since it is sometimes difficult to decide how far the man confessing has obtained his facts from the press or whether he is actually a criminal. Unfortunately men who make these confessions (it is almost invariably men) are frequently dismissed by the police, and told not to make a nuisance of themselves in future, or else summoned and fined a few shillings. *It is most essential in all such cases that the man should be remanded for psychiatric examination since these men are potential murderers.* I pointed out this many years ago after a young man made such a confession and was disregarded. He took a long knife and stabbed a girl to death on Dartford Heath a few days later.

A similar case was recorded some time ago. A young soldier 'confessed' to the murder of a woman in Leeds. The woman's husband had already admitted he had done it (although he tried to retract his confession when the soldier came forward) and was finally condemned to death. It was found, however, that the young soldier had made two serious attempts to kill other women, one of whom was so severely injured that she was unable to give evidence. He was medically examined, found to be suffering from schizophrenia, and ordered by the judge 'to be detained during Her Majesty's pleasure'.

Another case was that of a man called Rowland convicted at Manchester Assizes in 1946 of murdering a prostitute. Before he was hanged a man named Ware, who was in prison, confessed to the murder, but a rehearing was refused. Rowland was hanged, but four years later Ware confessed to the police that he had killed a woman. She recovered from her injuries, however, and Ware was tried for attempted murder: he was found guilty and committed to Broadmoor.

An examination of criminal records would easily reveal many other cases so that this is not such a rarity as to be unworthy of notice. We have few ways of detecting potential murderers so that when a sadist does betray himself by his fantasies it is as well to act before he puts them into practice.

SADISM AND THE PSYCHOPATHOLOGY OF MURDER

The problem of murder is one which is frequently related to one of five psychiatric conditions which are conveniently considered here. Since they are often confused it is worth while examining them together. These are: (1) psychopathy, (2) sadism, (3) schizophrenia, (4) the explosive crisis, and (5) adolescent instability. No doubt basically the first four are closely related and probably in some cases it is not possible to make a clear line of demarcation between them. Possibly, also, the causation of these four are linked together, if not more or less identical.[1]

[1] This brief classification does not pretend to exhaust all the possibilities but rather to

The psychopaths I have seen have all had a great deal of unconscious hatred in their minds. I would suggest that just as one finds psychoses are founded in deep-seated hostility, one can regard psychopathy as akin to them except that the symptoms—hallucinations, delusions, feelings of influence or reference, depression or elation—are absent or replaced by personality deviations. The claims of those who find lysergic acid curative in psychopathy suggest that this is not an inborn disease.

It would appear then that the psychopath is a person who has never acquired the psychological prohibitions which prevent a normal person from behaviour injurious to others. Although the word 'psychopath' has frequently been used loosely and incorrectly to cover almost any psychiatric condition here it is meant to cover a precise state of antisocial behaviour uninfluenced by the threat or reality of punishment. Thus will the charming psychopath borrow money with no intention of returning it, the inadequate psychopath live outrageously on the charity of others, and the violent psychopath knock down a weak old woman whom most people would wish to protect. They all have this fundamental element of being antisocial: there is no prohibition in their minds that such behaviour is wrong *and should not be tolerated by themselves*. Indeed, the violent psychopath will kill human beings as indifferently as a normal man will tread on a noxious insect—in fact he will feel less compunction.

A typical case of this was found in the behaviour of Peter Manuel who murdered seven people, including two entire families, but showed no compunction or remose at all. His total monetary gain was only £50 and there was no overt sexual motive. No evidence was produced to show that he found any pleasure in killing. He merely killed because the people concerned stood in his way of obtaining money, and it was easier to kill than not to do so. No suggestion of insanity was put forward. In fact, half-way through his trial he became dissatisfied with the barristers who were defending him and decided to conduct his own case. This he did with spirit and perspicacity, using the legal formulae and customs (which, no doubt, he had picked up in court) with discretion and skill. Nevertheless, he was convicted and hanged.

The only way in which such murders resemble sadistic ones is in their repetition.

The sadist, on the other hand, appears to have little in the way of psychic prohibitions to his conduct and in this he resembles the psychopath. In fact we might believe with some reason that he is a psychopath

---

examine those murders which seem closely related to sadism. There may be many other types; for example, murders which occur when men are driven to the ultimate extremity, as in the case of Crippen who had a bullying, overbearing wife; in cases of blackmail where there is the impossibility of going to the police; when the victim is guilty of some crime he cannot reveal. These murders, however, seem less spontaneously connected with sadism but rather the result of desperation.

with the addition of an abnormality which gives him positive pleasure in the infliction of pain. Moreover, as we have seen his aggression is mainly directed against those parts of the woman which a normal man wishes to caress sexually: the breasts, the vagina and so on. These are often torn, cut, lacerated and damaged in some way. Other accompaniments of sadism, including blood-drinking and eating of the flesh, may be present, as I have noted. In between his outrages the sadist may appear to be normal in his behaviour but he may be psychopathic, and get into trouble for small thefts, or pyromania (incendiarism). The following interesting case was reported in the press.

A recent case of sadistic murder was that of Ian Brady and Myra Hindley. This pair were known to have been concerned with the killing of three young people, two children and a youth, and were suspected of two others.

Ian Brady was the illegitimate son of a tea-shop waitress and was sent at an early age to foster-parents in the Gorbals district of Glasgow. He was known to have a furious temper and behaved curiously, even as a child. He built miniature 'prisons' in which he immured cats, and waited until they died. Then he buried them secretly and ceremoniously at night in the local church-yard. He started stealing early and was sent to Borstal. The court ordered that he be returned to his mother who was living near Manchester. There he obtained work as a butcher's assistant (one wonders whether this was for some conscious or unconscious sadistic reason) and later as stock clerk for a chemical company.

There he met Myra Hindley, a girl a year or two younger than himself, who worked as a shorthand typist. She set her cap at him and they soon started to go out together. He introduced her to his interests in the Marquis de Sade, and various perversions. They finally lived together, but did not marry because he converted her to his disbelief in marriage and dislike of children.

Myra Hindley had come from a poor family, and had been sent a few doors away to live with her grandmother when her younger sister was born. She had been a bright child who resented her poverty, and was very upset when a friend was drowned so that she became interested in Roman Catholicism, but dropped this when she met Brady.

The first victim, as far as is known, was little John Kilbride, a bright, trusting, little boy, who was last seen in the local market where he was trying to earn a few pennies by running errands. Whether he was tortured or not before his death is not known. He was aged only 12 years.

The next child murdered was little Lesley Ann Downey, aged 10, and she was apparently tortured, and pornographic photographs taken of her before she was killed.

The last murder was that of Edward Evans, **aged 17**, with an axe. He was homosexual and had apparently been enticed for the few pounds he had in his wages, and for sadistic reasons. In this case Brady tried to involve his brother-in-law, David Smith, by having him present at the killing, but Smith, a petty criminal, became terrified and reported the matter to the police.

A search of their house revealed blood from the murder of Evans and a plan for the murder. This led to the discovery of a left luggage ticket hidden in the spine of Myra Hindley's prayer-book. The deposited luggage was two valises in which were tape recordings, and photographs. The tape recordings were of the torturing of the little girl and the photographs of pornographic poses she was compelled to endure with Brady.

The brutal killing of Evans by chopping his head with an axe, Brady's callous remark, 'That's it. It's the messiest yet', and the final strangling of the wounded boy with a piece of electric wire, the cool cleaning up and drinking a cup of tea after the terrible business was finished, together with the dreadful tape recordings, horrified the nation.

The bodies of John Kilbride and Lesley Ann Downey were discovered buried on the lonely Yorkshire moors, but two other children who disappeared at about that time have never been unearthed.

There are a number of interesting psychological factors in this case. It is easy to see how Brady became abnormal: he was illegitimate, brought up with other children (who probably despised him for his bastardy) in a poor district, in poverty. It is not surprising that he hated children and showed this, at first, by projecting it on to cats, but later his basic hostility emerged in actual killing of young people. His early delinquencies, stealing and wounding a boy with a knife, suggest that he was psychopathic long before he murdered.

Myra Hindley, also, had a difficult childhood and could hardly have avoided feeling she was displaced by her sister. Moreover, the marriage of her parents broke up later (her father was away at the war most of her childhood), and one might suspect was never very happy.

Women usually feel protective towards children. Why then did Myra Hindley help Brady to kill them? I suspect that it was akin to *folie à deux* which is sometimes found in schizophrenia. She accepted Brady's emotional distortions without questioning them.

No doubt the photographs and tape recordings were preserved by Brady because like Kürten he found that by going back to the scene of the crime (or sound of it) he recovered the sexual thrill of the killing.

He changed from killing little children to the youth Evans, aged 17, because there was such an outcry when the children were missed. However, he needed more assistance than Hindley was able to give him in the case of a strong young man, and so wished to involve Smith who, although a petty criminal, was not a sadist and became terrified at what he saw.

It may be confidently stated that had Brady not been apprehended he would have continued killing, just as Kürten did.

The 'Boston Strangler' is an interesting example of multiple murder for no apparent reason. This man killed eleven persons, the youngest aged 19 and the oldest 75, all female, within 17 months during 1963–4. He managed to persuade these women to admit him to their flats or houses and strangled them leaving his characteristic 'trade-mark'. This was a piece of clothing tied round the neck like a grotesque neck-tie. The under-clothes were pulled up round the upper part of the body and the women were invariably raped.

Although this man's activities were given every publicity and women living alone were told to maintain the greatest security, never open their doors to strangers and admit nobody, some cheerfully disobeyed and were killed—as if they were unconsciously seeking such a fate.

The man, who was finally caught, was known as The Measuring Man because he persuaded girls to strip to be measured for work as a model. From this he progressed to tying girls on their beds and raping them, and finally to strangling them as well. He was discovered because he confessed to a friend.

A curious point is that, although this man was an obvious sadist, his wife complained that he insisted on having intercourse four times a day or five or six times a day during the week-ends.

It is impossible to know the nature of this man's impulsion but it is permissible to guess that he had some hostility towards women (which made him strangle them) combined with a tremendous sexual urge. This may suggest some basic oedipal situation. His habit of tying a piece of clothing round his victim's neck to strangle her, and then making the ends into a grotesque bow-tie, he himself related back to the fact that his little daughter, Judy, had worn a removable plaster cast for a hip disease. He used to tie the tapes which held this on into bows because it made it look prettier.

The schizophrenic type of murder is characterized by senseless violence. The resemblance to the sadist is that the schizophrenic is so disorganized mentally that he may behave just as ruthlessly as the psychopath and show absolutely no remorse afterwards. In fact, he may not even show any interest that he has done a murder. Usually the violence is excessive and not directed against the sexual organs or secondary sexual parts (the breasts). It is quite senseless. A typical schizophrenic murder was committed by Peter Griffiths who took a child from a ward in a Blackburn Hospital and smashed it to death against a wall in the grounds. Apparently Griffiths had had a large amount of alcohol to drink and this released his schizophrenic behaviour. He had a father who had been confined in a mental hospital with paranoid schizophrenia, and who remained 'queer' afterwards. There was a record of juvenile delinquency, and he had a bad Army record with two convictions for desertion. In general he was a ne'er-do-well who had never stayed at one job for long. A history of a broken love affair shortly before the murder was given at his trial. All this points to schizophrenia, although his behaviour after the murder showed a skilful evasion of detection. He was found guilty of wilful murder and hanged.

Such behaviour is quite different from psychopathy and sadism. The senseless fury, released by alcohol, is shown by the fact that he did not know the child, and had no reason to kill it, there was no sexual element in banging it to death against a wall. The prepsychotic personality, again, was different from the sadist's although closer to that of the psychopath.

An indication of sadistic fantasies which otherwise might be overlooked may be shown by hobbies, such as the collection of weapons. Those who collect firearms, guns, revolvers, or daggers, knives, &c., may sooner or later use them. This does not apply, of course, to collectors of mediaeval cross-bows or broadswords, but modern guns or knives.

The following is a very typical case and one could easily find many other similar ones. In 1966 Ian Spencer, aged 33, was convicted of murdering a girl aged 14 one evening after she had left a sailing club. At his trial he was said to have 'gloried in weapons and knives'. The girl was stabbed to death with a 'flick-knife'. There was no robbery or financial profit from the killing.

Would it be surprising if this man, who collected knives, had fantasies of using them on some unfortunate human being? It is obvious that he must have done so. Similarly, those who collect modern pistols, guns, and revolvers have the same sort of ideas.

The explosive murder seems first to have been described by Wertham in 1949, under the title of 'catathymic crisis', but the name used by Williams, 'explosive crisis' seems more descriptive, and will be used here.

In such cases the murderer is a person who has managed to repress a great deal of emotion which has never been able to reach the surface. It forms a focus of violence. The consequence is that he has been able to present a more or less normal aspect to the world. This finally breaks down, and the potential murderer then passes through five stages until he reaches the catathymic crisis or explosion. Wertham describes them as:

1. The stage of initial thinking disorders which follows the original precipitating circumstances.
2. The stage of crystallization of a plan, when the idea of a violent act emerges into consciousness.
3. The stage of extreme tension culminating in the violent crisis in which a violent act against oneself or others is attempted or carried out.

4. The stage of superficial normality beginning with a period of lifting of tension and calmness immediately after the violent act.

5. The stage of insight and recovery with the re-establishment of an inner equilibrium.

Williams regards the condition from another angle and suggests that the murderer projects his complex on to someone else. The result of this is that, sooner or later, the emotion explodes into action, and the other person is killed in an outburst of violence as an attempt to abolish the projected emotion. The murderer kills his victims so that he can kill what he has projected.

This explains, for example, such cases as those men who kill prostitutes. Firstly he finds his own sexual feelings unacceptable because he has been brought up to the idea that sex is unclean, disgusting and horrible. He projects his sexual feelings on to prostitutes; and so feels that they are disgusting, dirty and horrible because of their sexual behaviour. He cannot, however, suppress his sexual urges indefinitely, and is finally driven to go with one, but kills her in an outburst of fury because of the attributes he has projected on to her. (He may, alternatively, commit suicide as did the clergyman in Somerset Maugham's story 'Rain', who tried to reform a prostitute, became sexually attracted to her; and, when he discovered what was happening, killed himself.) Naturally, not all explosive murders are directed on to prostitutes, and other people can be used as an emotional target.

Williams describes this type of murderer very clearly. He states: 'Certain elements of an intolerable internal situation are projected into a victim, the aim being to get rid of these elements into someone else; then kill and destroy them in that person in order to prevent any re-entry of them into the self. Thus the victim is often only the scapegoat upon whom a desperate internal situation is worked out. Many murderers do not know their victims, and have no conscious hatred for them.'

This sort of murder seems related to the schizophrenic one, but whereas the schizophrenic usually already shows some evidence of his diseased mind observable in his general behaviour, the explosive murderer could only be detected by investigating his inner emotional state.

That all murders due to projection are not explosive ones is shown by the fact that sometimes a murderer specializes, as it were, in killing prostitutes.

Wertham had an opportunity of analysing a man who later killed three persons and he stated from his analysis that the man, 'From early childhood on . . . had an abnormal attachment to his mother. His fixation of the mother-image was only vaguely known to him from its manifestations. He never was conscious of its extent or its connection with his wishes, fears and deeds. The mother-image, distorted in his mind, and loved and hated at the same time, prevented him from making a normal love adjustment to other women without leading to a dominant homosexual pattern. He acted as if he wished to keep indefinitely an overwhelming pure love for his mother. He renounced the mother-image and sought it at the same time. While not even writing to his mother, whom he had helped financially when he was making only fifteen dollars a week, he repeatedly showed friendliness for older women who were like mothers to him. He would leave these mother-substitutes as abruptly as he had left his mother. His unconscious striving to escape the overpowering influence of the image of the mother led to the development of hostility towards her and her substitutes. The opposite of love is not hate, but indifference. He never could be indifferent to his mother. His love prompted him to hate her (Orestes complex).'

The fifth type of murder considered here is really quite different from those I have described. That is the killing due to adolescent instability. I gave evidence in a typical case of this nature. It was that of a young man who was educated and brought up by more or less wealthy people, but whose natural parents would not permit him to be adopted. He was, however, very fond of his foster-mother who had been very good to him. She unfortunately misunderstood the statement of an eye specialist she had consulted and thought that she was going blind. The young man, then aged 19, borrowed a revolver from a neighbour, ostensibly to practise with it, went indoors and quite calmly shot her dead. He then went and gave himself up, but expressed no remorse to the police or anyone else because he felt that he had done the right thing in putting her out of her misery. He was in no way a psychopath, and in other matters was not ruthless in obtaining his own ends. There was no history of sadism. In fact, he gained nothing from the murder.

On examination he was found to be physically undeveloped and his genitalia were small, there was no hair on his chest or upper abdomen, and he had smooth white skin. Obviously he was physically immature and this matched his psychological immaturity also, because, although intellectually normal, he was emotionally not adult in any way. He was seen by me and two other medical men: they said he was suffering from hysteria and I considered that he was a latent schizophrenic. A plea of manslaughter was accepted by the judge and he was given five years' imprisonment.

Not enough was known of his mental mechanisms to understand why he committed the murder, but it was suspected that he had transferred hostility from his real parents (? mother), who would not let him be adopted, and yet did not make him really welcome when he visited them, and unconsciously killed his foster-mother as a substitute. The only similiarity to sadistic murders and psychopathic ones in such a case lies in the lack of remorse. There was really insufficient evidence to diagnose either hysteria or schizophrenia in his case.

A somewhat similar case which terminated more happily was that of a young man and his wife who consulted me. The wife complained that the previous evening whilst sitting at her dressing-table brushing her hair he had entered the room, and tried to strangle her. In proof she showed the extensive bruising round her neck. The young man, in his early twenties, said that whilst sitting downstairs reading the evening newspaper he had had a thought 'Go upstairs and strangle your wife'. This was an idea; not an hallucination or some urge based on a delusion, merely a thought. He did not know why he had wanted to do what he did. There had been no quarrel or trouble between them.

Fortunately as he told me, 'She was too strong for me.', and was able to fight him off.

Physically he was very immature, but showed no other evidence of physical disease. He denied any symptoms of schizophrenia, had never had hallucinations, delusions, compulsions, feelings of influence or sensations of unreality, and was doing his work satisfactorily. He was frank and open in his answers, and agreed readily to go to hospital in case he repeated his behaviour successfully later on.

I have always regarded any action, whether homicidal or suicidal, as indicative that the behaviour was serious, in contradistinction to fantasy, which often is not put into practice. This case therefore alarmed me, and I was concerned for his wife's sake, if not for any other young woman he might murder as a substitute for her. Arrangements were therefore made that he should attend a large London hospital, specializing in psychiatry, for admittance. To my horror the wife telephoned me the next day and told me that his behaviour had not been regarded seriously, and he was to attend as an out-patient. This seemed too dangerous to permit, and I made other arrangements for him to enter a different hospital at once.

Unfortunately as I saw this young man only once I had no chance to investigate the psychopathology, but no doubt his wife was being used as a substitute for his mother. His instability, probably due to physical immaturity, seems to place him, even though rather late, into this category. I have never seen this type of behaviour in older men. It is characterized by unemotional compulsive or impulsive action dissociated from any feeling of remorse or shame. *If encountered it should be treated with the greatest seriousness.*

The psychopathology of the five conditions seems to me to have a great deal in common. In sadism it appears that the super-ego shows agenesis and consequently it is inadequate to control the violence of the id. The ego seems more or less intact and the sadist is aware of the fate which awaits him if he is caught (his sense of reality—which is the ego function—is functioning). On the other hand the psychopath shows dysgenesis of the super-ego which, also, in this case, cannot control the id (although this is more the aggressive than the sexual elements) but, since the psychopath is unable to respond to punishment and, indeed, hardly seems aware of it, it would seem that his ego is damaged in some way. The schizophrenic has a harsh, over-severe, super-ego which crushes down his instinctual forces (the id) until they burst out into the ego (his sense of reality) and shatter it. Schizophrenia is not merely splitting of the mind—it is destruction of the sense of reality or ego. The psycho-analyst would say that with explosive murder the behaviour was due to the murderer's repressed id which, in certain circumstances, gets beyond control of the super-ego, and is released with sudden violence. It is thus related to the schizophrenic type, but the emotion does not shatter the ego, which remains intact.

This has been supported by the work of Megargee who has suggested that murderers are divisible into two classes; undercontrolled and over-controlled. He has shown that a large proportion of those who commit violent crimes have no previous history of assaults, and are well controlled generally. It is only when disturbed that the emotion bursts out.

Blackburn compared 38 extremely assaultive patients with 25 moder-ately assaultive ones. He found the extreme assaultive group contained fewer with a criminal record. This, again, upholds Megargee's ideas. Adolescent instability appears to be dependent on an inadequacy of both the super-ego and ego, but insufficient to produce psychopathy. Possibly it merely shows delayed growth of these mental functions since it seems that most of these unstable young men ultimately adjust themselves to normal life.

Psychopathologically it would seem that the sadistic murderer is more regressive than the explosive one. The murdering sadist identifies the victim with his mother and enjoys injuring her, destroying her breasts and vagina. The explosive murderer, on the other hand, is projecting a part of himself on to the person he murders and this is a more sophisti-cated mechanism. However, where they approximate there seems to me a possibility that one type of behaviour could turn into the other: as when a sadist beats a girl for pleasure, but this releases so much excitement that he loses control explosively and kills her. This may have occurred in the case of the murderer, Heath, previously described.

It seems to me that with more research some of these cases may be detected before a murder is committed. Deep-seated emotion, such as these men have repressed, sometimes leaks out, as it were, into conscious-ness and influences behaviour to some extent. For instance, as previously discussed, I have noticed that some cases of explosive murder occur in men who collect weapons, such as rifles, revolvers; and, particularly, knives and daggers. They may do this harmlessly for some years before they finally murder someone in an explosive outburst.

Ultimately any form of murder probably rests on the externalization of deep-seated aggression, no matter what is the mechanism involved. However, since emotion is meant to deal with the outside world, it must be admitted that murder is more 'natural' than suicide, although, obviously such violence is unacceptable in a social setting. It would seem that, although there appears to be some immediate cause for the murder in most cases, probably in every one there has been some sort of trauma in infancy, which forms the original basis for the subsequent behaviour.

Little has been written comparing these five conditions by the Pavlovians and it is difficult to understand them in terms of conditioning since in some cases, at least, to all outward appearances these patients have had a normal upbringing.

In general one can understand them best from the behaviourist point of view by remembering that instincts are chain reflexes. In sadism we have the instinct *in puris naturalibus*, but in other conditions there is a conflict between the urges, which is resolved by the prepotent one—the aggressive—finding expression; just as pain will overcome the scratch reflex, for example. This explains the sudden violence of the psychopath, who has his instinct only slightly inhibited; the explosion of the catathymic crises, where the inhibitory forces are stretched beyond their capacity, and the senseless outbursts of the schizophrenic aggravated by apparently innocent stimuli.

This belief, that there are forces which hold most people's sadism under control, but are disordered in others, has recently been demonstrated in a convincing manner by Milgram. He persuaded volunteers to manipulate an apparatus labelled 'Shock Generator' which had thirty switches from 15 to 450 volts, with notices on them 'slight shock' to 'danger; severe shock'. They thought that by moving the switches they were passing a current through another volunteer (who was really an accomplice). This person acted as if in severe distress as the current apparently grew stronger and stronger.

Twenty-six of the forty subjects completed the whole series in spite of the apparent pain and suffering resulting. Many showed considerable emotional disturbance as demonstrated by their comments, profuse sweating, tremor, stuttering and nervous laughter.

Obviously there was strong resistance to hurting the other person and only the encouragement of the experimenter persuaded them to continue. This resistance must come from forces in their minds, either caused by conditioning or some other way.

This, no doubt, explains why murders are so frequently caused by alcohol. The repressive forces are undermined and the sadistic or other drives released. Thus Hunter Gillies found that out of 70 murders in the west of Scotland the following causes were present:

Alcohol	.	.	.	.	.	33
Psychopathy	.	.	.	.	.	22
Schizophrenia	.	.	.	.	.	11
Melancholia	.	.	.	.	.	1
Alcoholic psychosis	.	.	.	.		1
Mental subnormality	.	.	.	.		1
Teenage fight	.	.	.	.	.	1

The reason why these different cases have been discussed at length is that there seems to be constant confusion between them and obvious sadistic murders are frequently labelled psychopathic and so on.

Yet, with proper diagnosis of the murderer when the opportunity arises to see him prior to his crime, many tragedies could, and should, be prevented; and this is a matter for the psychiatrist who should have sufficient insight to recognize the potentially dangerous, if alert to the possibility.

I make no apology for having discussed murder at such length under the title of sadism. Probably in every murder there is an element of sadism, and some conscious or unconscious satisfaction in the injury or pain which is inflicted before death. The two subjects are so interconnected that those who try to separate them are merely splitting hairs.

How far suggestion is related to murder is as yet an unsolved problem but it does appear related in some cases. This is shown by the fact that multiple murders have occurred three times in 1966 in America. The first was performed by a man who managed to obtain entrance into a nurses' home and killed a number of young women. The second, a few months later, was done by a student who took a high-powered rifle, fitted with a telescopic sight, into a tower and killed one person after another before he was shot. He was found to have a small brain tumour, but a psychiatrist who saw him stated that it was unconnected with his behaviour. The third case was that of a student who entered a beauty salon and forced four women and a little girl to lie down with their heads together, and their bodies projecting like the spokes of a wheel. He then shot them in their heads.

The women were unknown to him and he stated that his reason for the murders was that 'he wished to make a name for himself'.

Somewhat similar murders occurred in 1968 in New South Wales, one after the other, when men held the police at bay with guns. The first man held his wife and baby prisoner and resisted for 8 days. The second shot his mother-in-law dead and withstood rifle fire and tear gas for 24 hours. The third shot his aunt dead and barricaded himself in an iron shed. He surrendered in 8 hours. The cases all occurred within 3 weeks.

Whatever the motive and condition of the murderers the subsequent ones seem to have been influenced by the first. Since, however, suggestion does not influence normal men in this way, it is reasonable to suppose that

L—PSY. D.

it does so only when there is fundamental basis of unconscious sadism which can be activated.

Sado-masochism, like other sexual abnormalities, is 'catered' for by prostitutes, as is shown by the following case which was recorded in the press, 1 June 1947.

Mayfair Flat Find

Birches, canes, ropes and a number of unusual sketches were among the articles exhibited at Marlborough Street court when A—— T—— denied an allegation that she managed a disorderly house at her address in New Bond Street, Mayfair.

Evidence was given that special observation was kept on premises in which she occupied a flat, and in which, it was said, two other women had flats.

The police alleged that altogether five known women, including A—— T——, used the premises, and that she had brought men to the house to meet the other girls.

A—— T——, who said she had removed her things from the flat since her arrest, as she was leaving the West-end, was fined £20 with £10 10s. 0d. costs.

It is not clear from this report whether the flagellation was used by the men on the prostitutes or vice versa. Possibly it was alternated as the occasion required.

There seems to be a definite demand for this sort of sexual stimulation and in the recent Denning Report it was recorded that prostitutes charged a pound each for each stroke of the cane. This suggests that sado-masochism is much more prevalent than many people realize.

It is a curious fact that when the House of Lords rejected the part of a former Bill to abolish the death penalty, an attempt was made to appease their lordships by retaining hanging for certain types of murder—one of these being sadistic murders. This is particularly surprising in view of the fact that sadists are the most abnormal of all paraphiliacs and the most nearly related to schizophrenics. If there is any type of murderer who should be treated as insane it is the sadist, yet so much horror does his behaviour produce that retaliatory emotions are at once awakened.

A similar view must be taken of the periodic attempts to bring back the cat-o'-nine-tails and make flogging a part of the legal code. Nothing of reformative value would result (as statistics clearly show) and there is the possibility that it would have the opposite effect. We must appreciate, moreover, that behind such demands there is often an element of sadism in those who wish to see them put into action. In fact, retribution probably is largely composed of unconscious sadism, and we should watch this wish in ourselves with considerable suspicion.

The contradictory nature of the response to a threat of punishment—even of being executed—is shown by the fact that when the death penalty was inflicted for theft and all executions were public, pick-pockets abounded amidst the crowd that witnessed them and usually had a good haul!

Often there is a strong element of refusal to regard reality in criminal behaviour which prevents the criminal appreciating that *he* will ever be caught, and this negatives the deterrent effect of punishment.

CASE NO. 6

A Case of Impotence associated with Sadistic and Masochistic Tendencies

This case was that of a young man, aged 29, who complained that, although he was able to obtain a good erection he could not maintain it long enough to penetrate the woman. His only sexual outlet was masturbation. In addition to these symptoms he had some more sinister ones: a feeling of being dissociated from other people and of being two persons in one.

The father and mother were alive and well. There had been a great deal of parental quarrelling in which he felt hostile to his father. In addition to the patient there were a brother aged 34 and a sister aged 27.

As a child the patient was shy until he was aged ten years, and rather quarrelsome. At his primary school he did not do very well but much better at a Grammar school. On leaving he did not know what career to follow and so went to the School of Slavonic Studies to learn Russian. Then he studied law for two and a half years. Finally he worked in a Shipping Office where he was successful and liked his duties.

His sexual life started with masturbation which caused him more anxiety than most boys. He was never homosexual nor wished to be. When he started to go out with girls he was excited by them until he persuaded them to go to bed. Then he failed to penetrate and was humiliated by his lack of success. His fantasies were mainly of thrashing girls or of being thrashed by them. This sometimes led to masturbation and orgasm. He had tried the experiment of thrashing himself but this alarmed him considerably. Between the age of 20 to 24 he stopped masturbating altogether since he did not then appreciate that it was normal. The fantasies became much more powerful during this period. He remembered as a small child that he had had fantasies of a man beating him. In adult life he had occasional fantasies of a man beating him in addition to those of women.

He was treated by analysis and it was soon apparent that there was a very strong attachment to his sister. This seems to have been reciprocated since his sister had told him that she had dreamed of intercourse with him. She seems to have had a great influence on him. Just before her birth he had been in hospital with a mastoid operation and was taken home by his father because he did not appear to be recovering in hospital. This stress was followed by his sister's birth.

He had a number of dreams of a man attacking him and it became apparent that there was considerable hostility towards his father (no doubt aggravated by the parental quarrelling in which he took his mother's side). He also had homosexual dreams and once had a fantasy that 'I feel I'd like to have my penis amputated'. He also once said spontaneously 'Being thrashed reminds me of being a child at the breast'. The idea was also developed that the fantasy of thrashing his mother or sister was only a defence against his intense feeling of affection for them. Then he expressed intense hostility towards his father which resulted in some minor depression. Suicidal fantasies emerged and he said that he had considered what it would be like to throw oneself under an Underground train. Needless to say, he was made to appreciate the nature of the transference to avoid such a tragedy happening.

He worked through his Oedipus complex. His hostility towards his father diminished and his attachment towards his sister, which on one occasion caused a tremendous abreaction with tears, slowly died away. The castration element in his dreams died with his Oedipus complex.

He had lived at home with his parents, but realized that this was holding him back and inhibiting his sexual development. He therefore took a flat where he was able to entertain his girl friends without supervision.

Then he had intercourse, not very successfully, in a wood, but was haunted by a fear of interruption all the time. Finally he found a girl who liked him and was able to have successful intercourse with her in his flat. This continued for some time but he decided that he did not wish to marry this girl who was herself not very stable.

Finally he appeared quite normal and able to have satisfactory intercourse when the opportunity occurred. There was a slight tendency to have some recurrence of the sado-masochistic fantasies when he had no sexual outlet but he felt that sufficient psychological work had been done to allow him to continue developing normally and ceased treatment. In all he was seen once a week for eight months and it was felt that a satisfactory outcome with such a difficult case in this time was gratifying. The vague schizophrenic symptoms, feeling of detachment, and of being more than one person, disappeared in the course of treatment and left him completely integrated.

REFERENCES

ALLEN, CLIFFORD (1936) Mental disease in general practice, *Clin. J.*, **65**, 199–204.

DE BEAUVOIR, SIMONE (1962) *The Marquis de Sade*, London. (Translation of Simone de Beauvoir's essay, 'Faut-il brûler Sade?', in *Les Temps Modernes*, December 1951, and January 1952.)

BENDER, L., and CURRAN, F. J. (1940) Children and adolescents who kill, *J. crim. Psychopath*, **1**, 297–322.

BERG, K. (1938) *The Sadist*, ed. GODWIN, G., trans. ILLNER, O., and GODWIN, G., London.

BLACKBURN, R. (1968) Personality in relation to extreme aggression, *Brit. J. Psychiat.*, **114**, 821–8.

BOLITHO, W. (1931) *Murder for Profit*, London.

BRIDGMAN, O. (1929) Four young murderers, *J. juv. Res.*, **13**, 281–7.

BRITISH MEDICAL JOURNAL (1959) 11 July.

BURT, C. (1931) *The Young Delinquent*, London.

CABANÈS, A. (1913) *Le Cabinet Secret de l'Histoire*, Paris.

DAILY TELEGRAPH (1946) 27 September.

—— (1958) 30 May (Case of Peter Manuel).

—— (1958) 7 July (Case of Tom Lionel Burns).

DAWES, C. W. (1927) *The Marquis de Sade*, London.

DEBORDES, J. (1939) *Le Marquis de Sade*, Paris.

DITTRICK, P. (1935) Peculiar act which can be construed as murder, *Med. Klin.*, **1**, 1034.

ELLIS, H. (1901) *The Criminal*, London.

EVENING STANDARD (1937) 8 February.
FENICHEL, O. (1934) *Outline of Clinical Psychoanalysis*, London.
—— (1935) Zur Kritik des Todestribes, *Imago*, **21**.
FRANK, GEROLD (1966) *The Boston Strangler*, New American Library.
FRAZER, J. (1954) *The Golden Bough*, London.
FREUD, S. (1930) *Collected Works*, **3**, 255–68, London.
—— (1930) *Three Contributions to the Theory of Sex*, New York.
GILLIES, HUNTER (1965) Murder in the west of Scotland, *Brit. J. Psychiat.*, **III**, 1095–1100.
GODWIN, G. (1949) *The Trial of Peter Griffiths*, Edinburgh.
HALL, G. S. (1904) *Adolescence*, New York.
KARPMAN, B. (1934) Obsessive paraphilias, *Arch. Neurol. Psychiat. (Chic.)*, **32**, 577.
KLEIN, M. (1948) *Contributions to Psychoanalysis*, London.
LELY, G. (1952) *The Marquis de Sade*,
—— (1961) trans., BRONN, ALEC, London.
LEMKE, N. (1937) Criminal responsibility in a fifteen-year-old murderer, *Allg. Z. Psychiat.*, **105**, 257.
MEGARGEE, E. L. (1966) Uncontrolled and overcontrolled personality types in extreme antisocial aggression, *Psychol. Monograph.*, **80**, 611.
MILGRAM, S. (1963) *J. abnorm. soc. Psychol.*, **67**, 371.
NEUSTATTER, L. (1957) *The Mind of the Murderer*, London.
ORBISON, T. J. (1933) Murderers' row, *Calif. west. Med.*, **39**.
PETROVA, A. E. (1938) Murder committed in period of puberty, *Z. Nevropat. Psihiat.*, **2**, 673.
REICH, W. (1933) *Charakter-Analyse, Technik und Grundlagen*, Vienna.
STARK, J. (1932–3) Jugendliche Mörder und Totschläger, *Arch. Psychiat. Nervenkr.*, **98**, 307.
TREDGOLD, A. F. (1914) *Textbook of Mental Deficiency*, London.
WAGNER, M. S. (1932) *The Monster of Düsseldorf*, London.
WILLIAMS, A. H. (1964) The psychopathology and treatment of sexual murderers, in *Pathology and Treatment of Sexual Deviations*, ed. ROSEN, I., London.
ZHELIKHOVSKY, S. W., and SOLOVIEVA, M. V. (1938) *Z. Nevropat. Psihiat.*, **2**, 673.

MASOCHISM

Masochism is the seeking of what would normally be painful for sexual reasons. It is linked with a desire to be humiliated or dominated, enslaved, bound, or degraded.

This perversion was felt by Krafft-Ebing to be a feminizing of the man since love of service, and willingness to be subjected, is a very feminine trait but it is, as Freud and Havelock Ellis have pointed out, a reversal of the wish to hurt. I have suggested that it is for this reason that it is common to find sadism to some degree in the masochist and masochism in the sadist (although not so likely as sadism in the former). The perversion from the behaviourist point of view is the reversal of the wish to hurt (see examples in the chapter on the sub-human primates).

Freud rather complicated matters from the psychoanalytical position by his postulate of primary masochism. He suggested that in the beginning the death-instinct was stronger than the erotic or life-instinct. Not until the will to live overcame it could life begin. Hatred could then be turned outwards and something external destroyed instead of the organism destroying itself. However, a secondary reversal with sexualization can occur and this is the masochism which we know. Psychopathology, however, is not a form of delightful speculation but, like other forms of pathology, needful to understand cases and of the greatest help in treatment. The theory is useless and cumbersome in treatment and it is best to adhere to his original views.[1]

He divided masochism into three types and as these are valuable we shall use his division. They are (1) an erotogenic, (2) a feminine, and (3) a moral type.

Fenichel has summarized these very conveniently as follows:

The existence of erotogenic masochism may be attributed to the fact that, since all sensations in the human organism may be sources of sexual excitement, the path of pain also may. Erotogenic masochism is, then, a sexual component impulse *sui generis*. Constitutionally and environmentally determined experiences may reinforce this particular instinctual source and adapt it to serve, in the form of perversion, as a substitute for sadistic impulses warded off from a sense of guilt. Feminine masochism—usually developed from the erotogenic—in the male sex manifests itself as a utilization of the pleasure, as part of the accentuated feminine attitude.

Erotogenic Masochism

This is the equivalent of the active sadism but in reversal. There is actual sexual excitement attached to the pain and this may reach a crescendo with orgastic pleasure, and in the male, ejaculation. Freud, rather than anyone else, has attempted to explain the basic mechanisms behind masochism. In his paper 'A Child is being beaten' he divides the beating fantasy in girls into three phases and that of boys into two. He gives this for girls:

1. My father beats a child whom I hate.
2. I am beaten by my father (repressed).
3. A teacher (father substitute) is beating boys.

Bergler suggests that Freud's two phases in the boy are incomplete and that there are also three phases in the case of the male. These he thinks are:

1. Sadistic aggression against the breasts of the mother in the pre-oedipal period.
2. Turning, because of the guilt, of the aggression against the boy's own

---

[1] It would probably have been desirable to use the same type of classification for masochism as has been used in the section on sadism, but since Freud's grouping has been generally accepted it has been used here.

buttocks, which are identified with the breasts of the mother, 'transcription' of executor power from mother to father.

3. Renewed 'transcription' from father to mother, as a defence against unconscious homosexuality.

Again Hiddema and Heymans suggest that in females the fantasy of being beaten is not at first of the patient being the victim, but of some other child, such as the brother or sister; the identity of the beater is vague but is an adult. Later it proves to be the father. In the second stage the beaten child is the patient. The behaviour is sexualized and being beaten is identified as fantasy coitus with the father. In the third phase the beaten child is not the patient, but someone else and, again, the beater is no longer the father. Possibly such changes occur in fantasy but do not seem of importance.

These schemes seem needlessly complicated and perhaps are a vestige of Freud's first confused conceptions of the psychological mechanism involved. It would seem that much the same mental processes as are seen in sadism can be used to explain what we have accepted as being only its reversal. If we are honest we must agree that we do not yet know exactly how this reversal is brought about, but by analogy with the production of depression (which is very similar) it would seem that this is favoured by frustration so strong that there is complete impossibility of any outlet for the aggression, and so by identification.

I believe that a sufficient explanation of the mechanism is given by the following phases, at least in the male.

1. Wish to hurt mother.
2. Wish to be hurt by mother.
3. Wish to be hurt by women in general.

There is no doubt that the frustration is some way produces partial or complete identification with the mother. Identification usually occurs when there is a strong positive attachment as well as aggression so that the original emotion is probably ambivalent. This identification is clearly shown in those masochists who are also transvestists and must be dressed in female clothes in order to enjoy their perversion. (This was very evident in the case of Cecil George Cornock who was accustomed to make his wife beat him whilst he was dressed as a woman, and who was afterwards found dead in a bath. The resulting trial caused considerable public interest.) This assumption of female clothes means that they are dressing as the mother, in order to obtain the sexual pleasure. It is to be noticed that in most masochistic males there is a wish to be hurt by a woman but that homosexual masochism is by no means a rarity. In the case of homosexuality the mechanism is carried one step further by equating the mother with a man. (This mechanism is demonstrated in the section on homosexuality and is very obvious in that condition.) Thus:

1. Wish to hurt mother.
2. Wish to be hurt by mother.
3. Mother equals man.
4. Wish to be hurt by a man.

A most perfect case of sado-masochism which demonstrates the principle of the reversal of the instinct and shows the original direction of it (against the mother) is shown in the following example.

CASE No. 7

M.S. age 12. Schoolboy, He was treated by me because of behaviour disorders. His mother was a normal woman although rather 'showy' and childish in her dress and manner. The father had had an attack of mental illness—apparently schizophrenia—a year previously. The boy's sister, aged 10, was attending for night terrors and refusal to eat. He had been a normal birth and a full-term child but had always seemed bad tempered and 'highly strung'. His mother complained that at present he bit people. He had been free from this until his father's illness a year before, and a motor accident when he had been concussed eighteen months previously. Since these incidents he had been frightened and nervous. He frequently lost his temper with his mother, who promised him things but did not fulfil her promises because the father's erratic temperament made him forbid her to allow him what had been promised. When this occurred the boy rushed at his mother to bite her and did so when he could. If he was unable to get at his mother to bite her *he bit himself instead*.

This perfect example of sado-masochism shows the hatred directed against the mother, and when it could not be discharged reversed on to himself. Observation of children frequently shows this type of behaviour. To become a perversion it would have to be carried further forwards. Firstly it would have to be linked with the sexual instinct. No doubt this would occur at puberty, and secondly it would have to be displaced on to other women if the perversion was to be a heterosexual one, or the mother substituted by men if it were to be a homosexual one. Unfortunately the later history of this boy is not known.

It is of interest in the study of erotogenic masochism to consider the author whose works gave the title to this malady.

The only biography of Sacher-Masoch in English which I can discover is that by James Cleugh. This is not very satisfactory because it gives little of his childhood and relations with his parents: it is written somewhat in the style of a novel with conversations which the author could not possibly have known.

He was descended from a family, originally Spanish, which settled in Prussia in the sixteenth century, and two hundred years later moved to

Galicia. His father was Chief of Police in Lemberg, and married a noble Polish lady of the family of Masoch. The Emperor allowed him to combine the names into Sacher-Masoch: his son was born in 1836.

The boy was brought up by a Ruthenian nurse who told him folk-tales, often blood-curdling in nature, and he stated in later life that he was impressed by his paternal aunt who was of Slav extraction and of commanding personality. Once when asked to put on her slippers he kissed her ankle and was rewarded by a kick in the face. Another time he saw her making love to a man other than her husband.

He witnessed an abortive revolution, with much bloodshed, when ten years old, and later had a similar experience in Prague. There he was educated and at the behest of his father studied law. Later the family moved to Graz and he was granted the degree of Doctor of Laws at the university.

He started writing history, but soon commenced publishing the novels on which his reputation rests. His sexual life demonstrates all along his urge to be hurt and for his loved one to betray him with another man. First he became involved with a masterful woman, the wife of a doctor, who was ten years his senior, and had given birth to children, named Anna von Kottowitz. She was unfaithful, as he wished, but as a result contracted syphilis, which was then incurable, and the affair ended.

Then he met another woman, Fanny Pister, who went with him on a trip to Italy with him travelling, at his own request, as the valet. She treated him badly, to his great delight. This affair formed the basis of his later work, *Venus in Furs*, and the contract mentioned in it declaring him her slave was actually signed (he was very fond of such documents).

This affair broke up and he had various liaisons, first with a French actress, by whom he had a child, and other women, all with the same masochistic elements.

Eventually he married a woman named Aurora Rümelin and lived with her for some years. They had children, but she tired of his appeals for her to be unfaithful, and his constant wish to be flogged. He then had a prolonged affair with a German secretary, Hulda Meister, with whom he was living when he finally became insane. He appears to have developed a psychosis which commenced when he killed a kitten and told Hulda of the delights of murder. It was necessary to confine him in a mental hospital where he died in 1905.

We can deduce a few possibilities from the scanty facts known about his childhood which may suggest some of the causes for his illness. Firstly, his father was Chief of Police and in those days in Germany and Austria officials were very overbearing, but we do not know his relationship with his parents. His nurse nourished him on blood-curdling folk-tales which may have affected him and the example of his commanding aunt who, according to him, was unfaithful to her husband, may have influenced his relations with women. Again, at about puberty, he saw actual blood-shed and this may have excited a young boy. All these are possibilities: insufficient is known to make any certain statements, but the fact that his psychosis was orientated towards injuring and killing surely suggests that there was a great deal of repressed aggression in his case. The works of Sacher-Masoch, however, are trivial: his characterization is superficial and uninteresting; the plots of his novels are more or less non-existent, but where the vestige of one is present it is artificial and mechanical; the style is puerile and irritating; his approach to cruelty, humiliation, slavery, and furs displays the coy excitement which aged spinsters show towards the mention of sex. The whole of his books seem directed to enble him to develop his favourite beating fantasies. In short, one can say that no normal person would read his novels for pleasure, although a psychologist might do so under the duress of duty, and but for his abnormality we may be sure that they would have disappeared into the oblivion which awaits all but outstanding literary work. Nevertheless it is worth quoting from him since almost any quotation gives such clear evidence of his abnormalities—masochism and fur-fetishism. The fol-lowing is a passage from *Venus in Furs* which is the story of a young man who becomes enamoured of a beautiful red-headed woman who accepts him as a slave and who takes him, dressed as a servant, on a trip through Italy subjecting him to various humiliations, floggings, and unfaithfulness, on the way.

'A woman who wears a fur,' exclaimed Wanda, 'is nothing more nor less than a big cat, a very powerful electric battery!'

'That is so, and that is how I explain the symbolism which has made fur represent power and beauty. It is in this sense that, long ago, monarchs adopted it and tyrannical nobles reserved it for themselves by means of sumptuary laws, and great painters used it as the symbol of queens of beauty. Thus we find that Raphael and Titian could find no more precious frame for their loved one than a sombre fur.'

'Thanks for your erotic dissertation, but you haven't told me all. You attribute some other meaning quite peculiar to fur.'

'Undoubtedly, I have said more than once that pain has a rare charm for me, that nothing impassions me so much as the tyranny, the cruelty, and, above all, the infidelity of a beautiful woman. In my imagination I can see this woman, this strange ideal of a hideous aesthetic, this soul of a Nero in the body of a Phryne.'

'From what I can see, that lends something commanding and imposing to a woman.'

'But that is not all: you know that I am an ultra-sensualist, that with me every conception proceeds first from the imagination and feeds on chimeras. At an early age I was developed and excited in this sense, for at ten years of age I was given the lives of the martyrs to read. I remember I read with a horror, which was a veritable ravishment for me, how they languished in prison, were stretched on the rack, pierced with arrows, boiled in pitch, thrown to wild beasts, crucified, and endured the greatest atrocities with a sort of joy. To suffer, to bear cruel tortures, seemed to me henceforth a species of pleasure, and particularly so if these tortures were inflicted by a beautiful woman; and it is thus for me and for always, all poetry and all infamy were concentrated in woman.'

He continues in this strain for 192 pages through various floggings and humiliations. There is no mention of normal sexual congress in the book (even by obliquity and allowing for the period in which he wrote), and indeed, the hero never goes to bed with the beautiful but cruel Wanda so we may conjecture that Sacher-Masoch was probably impotent to normal sexual stimulus.

The admixture of fur-fetishism demonstrates the point which we have made previously that usually perversions are found in conjunction with some other abnormality; it being very rare to find one in pure culture, and probably the fur-fantasy is traceable back to some material image. The pleasure with which he details the different forms of torture shows the thrill he must have had in writing this passage. The fact that, as he states, he obtained much pleasure from 'imagination and chimeras' is also characteristic of masochism, perhaps because of the difficulty of obtaining adequate satisfaction from reality, although an excessive indulgence in fantasy is common in all perversions.

Masochism is called by the French le vice anglais, but it is difficult to prove whether it is more prevalent amongst the English than amongst any other nation—it was said, for example, to be very common amongst the Germans before the Hitlerian régime. This is unfortunate since it would be valuable in regard to aetiology if one could relate it to the flogging at public schools, &c. The Latins as a rule treat their children more kindly than the Nordics, and one might expect that it would have been unlikely that it should be so prevalent amongst them. Probably the solution is that of naming a discreditable thing by the label of a neighbour —e.g. the sheath is called in France la capote anglaise.

Occasionally a masochist injures himself enough to need medical care as, for example, the case recorded by Fulghum in which a barber repeatedly cut his scrotum in order to obtain sexual pleasure, and on one occasion caused serious haemorrhage and on another the injury was followed by severe sepsis.

When the masochistic behaviour results in actual damage to the genitalia this is usually associated with masturbation, and is possibly related to guilt and the need for punishment. Often, of course, the injury may be accidental but no doubt there is, in some cases, an unconscious desire for injury—a castration complex—to relieve the tension. The multitudes of rings, bottles, and what not which surgeons remove from the penis show the frequency with which this occurs and the universality of the milder forms of masochism. Sometimes this becomes quite fantastic as in Schischoff's case, where a farmer had the belt of a threshing-machine round his penis for the purpose of masturbation and was unable to remove it. These forms of self-inflicted pain must have a masochistic basis. Sometimes the masochism does not cause direct injury but inflicts something which leads to humiliation. I have treated, for example, a young man who had overwhelming urges to shave off his eyebrows. This led to him being an object of disdainful comment by girls and curiosity by men. Yet, in spite of his universal humiliation he could not stop himself. Sometimes the impulse was not appeased by shaving off, or plucking out his eyebrows, but made him cut or pull out tufts of hair. After a bad period he looked truly grotesque and unhappy. He would not have sufficient treatment to remove his masochism (which was probably really a perversion-fetish of hair plus injury) but it was possible to see the causation. He hated his father who was an Irishman—his mother was English—and who had treated him badly. The injuries he inflicted on himself are those which he would have liked to inflict on the hated father. His mind seemed to be a veritable furnace of hate which was expressed only in the humiliations to which he exposed himself.

Sometimes masochism leads to even more terrible situations which may result in the death of the victim. Such a case was revealed in the tragic death of a young man whose skeleton was discovered in a sewage inspection pit at a disused site which had been a prisoner-of-war camp during the war. The inspection pit had been closed by a manhole cover which was so heavy it was very difficult to lift. The skeleton was chained and padlocked to a steel ladder at the bottom of the pit.

The announcement of this discovery in the press on 26 January 1960 caused considerable speculation, and some public indignation, since it seemed as if this skeleton was that of a prisoner who had been maltreated and murdered. However, such an idea was dispelled by the discovery that the dead man was a young actor who had twice been discovered chained to railings. At the inquest the pathologist stated that the man either lost, or did not possess, the keys of the self-locking padlocks and when chained up could not use the hack-saw which was discovered in the pit near him. Experiments showed that it was possible to lower the concrete lid of the pit from the inside. It was therefore evident that this unhappy young man had shut himself in the pit, chained himself to the ladder, and then found that he was a prisoner in the darkness with no hope of calling attention to his situation. His father gave evidence at the inquest and stated that his son had meningitis at the age of 14 and had been seen by a psychiatrist at the age of 15. He was taken from a public school because he was not able to make progress there and finally worked in a repertory stage company as an actor for a time. After the first two chainings he saw a psychiatrist who thought he was suffering from a personality disorder and sexual perversion.

It must be made clear that the masochist welcomes only the pain of his own seeking, and does not enjoy all pain. In fact he suffers impersonal pain just as acutely as the normal person and avoids it in the same way.

Feminine Masochism

Masochism, owing to the stress which Krafft-Ebing laid upon female passivity and acceptance of pain, has tended to be regarded as a feminine trait. It must be emphasized, however, that feminine masochism is very different from that found in the male. The male masochist deliberately, periodically seeks a situation in which he can be tied up, humiliated, and flogged. It is quite clearly a sexual situation and reaches an affective crescendo with erection and ejaculation as its culmination. Feminine masochism is entirely different.

Masochism in women does not appear as a frank perversion; in fact, apart from homosexuality and its ancillary reactions, perversions are not markedly apparent in women at all. In the woman masochism is not a periodic reaction but a permanent and continuous one. It is broken only when the conditions under which she lives become intolerable, but even so she tends to drift back into them. Examples are, for instance, the wife who lives for years with a drunken husband who ill-treats her, but who never appears able to break free from him and liberate herself from the misery of her existence. Again, the intelligent girl who drifts into prostitution and is unable to withdraw from the degradation of her life. Some feminine avocations appear to pander deliberately to the woman's masochism—the harsh conditions in which they live in some religious communities, for example.

If one were asked to summarize the difference between male and female masochism one might say that in the man masochism appears as a definite, obvious, outstanding neurosis which occurs periodically whereas *in the woman it is more a way of life, a behaviour problem rather than a neurosis.*

This does not, however, mean that actual masochistic practices do not occur in the woman, and when they do they tend to resemble erotogenic masochism—e.g. it is not uncommon for surgeons to discover, or be asked to remove, foreign bodies from the urethra. These are often of such shape and size that they could not have been introduced without considerable pain. Although this might be classed as a urethral perversion yet there must be a masochistic element present and this explains why the act was done. (Geyerman even records the discovery of a snake in the bladder!)

Similarly, Laforgue points out that many women who pester surgeons for operations, particularly hysterectomy, are masochistic and much unnecessary surgery results from the failure to realize it.

Self-mutilation and window smashing, which often leads to severe and dangerous wounds, occur frequently with female patients in mental hospitals. It has been studied by Offer and Barglow, who thought that it was due to the seeking of attention, gaining of prestige, and reduction of tension. They believed that it was a reversal of aggression on to the self, and there was tendency for the behaviour to become contagious so that a number of patients in the same ward would indulge in it.

McKerracher, Loughnane, and Watson studied patients in Rampton Special Hospital which is used mainly for the subnormal and psychopathic patients. They found that self-mutilation and window smashing occurred more frequently during the week-ends when there was less to occupy the patients. They put forward the view that there was a certain self-conditioning in the behaviour since when it was indulged in there was a relief of tension which 'stamped-in' the conduct, and led to its repetition. How far it is justifiable to compare psychopathic patients of this sort with those who are normal except for masochism it is difficult to say.

From the psychoanalytical point of view feminine masochism is produced by the discovery of the anatomical difference between the boy and girl. Rado and Deutsch both support Freud's view that it is the discovery of the girl that she has no penis that turns her aggression inward rather than on to others. Deutsch says that 'the hitherto active-sadistic libido attached to the clitoris rebounds from the barricade of the subject's inner realization of her lack of the penis . . . and most frequently of all is deflected in a regressive direction to masochism'. Rado's belief is that the discovery that she has no penis makes the girl feel that she is deprived of sexual enjoyment compared with the boy, and this destroys for ever the pleasure she had derived from masturbation. The extreme suffering which she experiences excites her sexually and so provides a substitute gratification. The suffering has become sexualized and is henceforth the mode of sexual pleasure.

This view is supported by Marie Bonaparte but is criticized severely by Karen Horney. She points out that feminine masochism is to some extent a conditioned reaction. The Russian woman in the time of the Tsars was taken as the perfect example of masochism since she felt that if her husband did not beat her he did not love her, but—as Horney points out—under the Soviet régime the Russian woman has become aggressive and self-assertive.

It is easy to scoff at the psychoanalytical point of view, and indeed, in my experience the penis-envy so stressed by this school is not so evident as the members of it suggest; yet Adler has insisted on the feminine wish for masculinity (masculine protest) and no doubt the discovery of her lack of it may, in some cases, be a blow to her narcissism.

I am inclined to agree with Horney when she states:

The problem of feminine masochism cannot be related to factors inherent in the anatomical-physiological-psychic characteristics of woman alone, but must be considered as importantly conditioned by the culture-complex or social organization in which the particular masochistic woman has developed. The precise weight of these two groups of factors cannot be assessed until we have the results of anthropological investigations using valid psychoanalytical criteria in several culture-areas significantly different from ours. It is clear, however, that the importance of the anatomical-physiological-psychic factors has been greatly over-estimated by some writers on the subject.

The development of masochism in the female is not very easy to understand and it is evident that Freud himself was not entirely satisfied with his interpretation. Helene Deutsch gives a careful study of the mechanisms which she believes to be at the bottom of it but we must regard these with some scepticism. She says:

This activity thrust of the girl is usually met by an attitude on the part of the father that exerts an inhibiting influence on her active drive. In this function the father is representative of the environment, which later will again and again exert this inhibiting influence on the woman's activity and drive her back into her constitutionally predetermined role. This attitude of the father contains another element of decisive importance in feminine development. He appears, without being conscious of it, as a seducer, with whose help the girl's aggressive instinctual components are transformed into masochistic ones. The masochistic ingredient in relation to the father appears in active games with him, which later assume an increasingly erotic character. It is enough to observe the little girl's fearfull jubilation when the father performs acrobatic tricks with her that are often painful, when he throws her up in the air, or lets her ride 'piggy back' on his shoulders. When this seduction on the part of the father is lacking, the girl will encounter difficulties in her feminine development.

There is no doubt that girls at puberty do have a fantasy and dream life in which there is a strong masochistic element. These are, to some extent, the equivalent of the erotic dreams of boys, although the sexuality is often less clearly directed or defined. As Deutsch says:

Girlish fantasies relating to rape often remain unconscious but evince their content in dreams, sometimes in symptoms, and often accompany masturbating actions. In dreams the rape is symbolic; the terrifying male persecutor with knife in hand, the thief who steals a particularly valuable object, are typical and frequently recurring figures in the dreams of young girls.

She describes a rape fantasy which is very suggestive as to the origin of this type of response:

Another very frequent rape fantasy is a sort of masochistic orgy within a triangular situation. In this characteristic fantasy a female figure forces the girl to submit to sexual acts performed by men whom the female figure urges on. The female figure ties the girl, gags her, and prepares the red-hot objects; these are applied by the men to the girl's genitals. Sometimes the female figure introduces a number of men who one after the other abuse the girl sexually. Compulsion by a woman plays the principal part in these practices. The superficial elements of these fantasies are easy to grasp: the pain decreases the guilt feeling produced by the pleasure, the rape frees the girl from responsibility; the compulsion exerted by the woman, who represents the mother, is a counterweight to the latter's prohibitions.

Such fantasies explain the cases of girls who make false accusations of having been raped (a patient I once saw had twice had men imprisoned for alleged such assaults) or else place themselves in situations where it may actually occur.

One would think that the rape-fantasy would be sufficient basis for masochism in women since it would explain the acceptance of pain from either a man or a woman, but Deutsch insists that when masochistic perversions exist in women their basis is a wish to be beaten. This they agree to suffer either from monetary reasons if they are prostitutes or else as 'love sacrifices' to sadistic lovers.

Moral Masochism

Freud has pointed out that moral masochism is most distant from sex. He says:

The third form of masochism, the moral one, is chiefly remarkable for having loosened its connection with what we recognize to be sexuality. To all other masochistic sufferings there still clings the condition that it should be administered by the loved person; it is endured at his command; in the moral type of masochism this limitation is dropped. It is the suffering itself which matters; whether the sentence is cast by a loved or by an indifferent person is of no importance; it may even be caused by impersonal forces or circumstances, but the true masochist always holds out his cheek wherever he sees a chance of receiving a blow.

It is possible that numerous psychiatrists would refuse to recognize this latter as a real perversion (i.e. sexually connected). Probably the most perfect example of sexually-coloured masochism without amounting to active perversion is to be found in the hero of Somerset Maugham's novel, *Of Human Bondage*. This tells the story of a young medical student's attachment to a woman who persistently betrays and treats him badly. This strikes the balance between Freud's moral masochism and active sexual perversion. It is possible that the book was partly autobiographical.

For some unknown reason moral masochism appears to be commoner in the East than in Europe or America. The fakirs who lie on beds of nails, who thrust skewers through their cheeks, who hold an arm in one position until it withers, and so on are all examples of moral masochism.

The history of every religion is redolent of it and perhaps it is because the Orient is more favourable for moral and mystical speculation than the Occident that it appears there.

Moral masochism, which clearly reveals that it is a reversal of aggression that has been prevented from externalizing itself, is very clearly shown in Buddhism. Buddha preached that it was wicked to kill anything; even a harmful or dangerous insect or snake. When the Buddhist wishes to protest he is unable, through this teaching, to injure his aggressor and consequently is left only with publicly injuring himself. This has been clearly shown in such examples as in Vietnam where nuns and priest have practised self-immolation by pouring petrol over their robes and setting fire to them.

This contrasts strongly with those who adhere to less inhibiting religions, such as Mohammedanism, which do not hesitate to attack their enemies and rarely, if ever, commit suicide in this horrible way.

Significantly, where excessive mysticism is favoured masochism appears—e.g. in the Jesuits, and similar sects, who still practise flagellation.

Indeed, Roman Catholicism occupies a place between Modammedanism and Buddhism. The Catholic, although he preaches universal peace, has never hesitated to become involved in war; yet, on the other hand, the martyrs have subjected themselves to humiliation and pain. Some have indulged in degrading practises, such as kissing lepers' sores, and others, such as Origen, have castrated themselves, or worn hair shirts, starved and tortured their bodies, &c.

It is difficult to know, apart from a basis of masochism, why such behaviour should be regarded as showing any more holiness than living a healthy life and devoting oneself to helping others.

Berlinger has tried to resuscitate the conception of moral masochism on the basis that it is neither a manifestation of the death instinct nor a reversal of sadistic feeling which has failed to be externalized, but suggested that it is 'a disturbance of object relations, a pathologic way of loving'. He states: 'Masochism is the search for love, or, in sexual perversion, for sexual pleasure, through the troubled medium of displeasure which was originally forced upon the subject and thereafter bends the search for gratification of erotic needs in the specifically masochistic direction.'

He further emphasizes (in his own italics) that *'Masochism is the sadism of the love object fused with the libido of the subject'*. I do not find such a view helpful and it appears to me as a mere re-statement that the patient finds the ill-treatment administered by someone he loves pleasurable— which is where we started.

Moral masochism is harmless except in as far as it drains away energy which should be directed down normal sexual channels. Moreover it

M—PSY. D.

must have caused an incalculable amount of misery in the world and distorted lives which otherwise might have been happy and normal.

In all forms of masochism, in addition to the more obscure mental mechanisms, we find the same obsessive compulsive elements which we discovered in sadism. I have, for example, seen a middle-aged man who had such strong hand-washing compulsions that he had washed away the entire skin of his hands and wrists. They appeared to be like anatomical specimens prepared to show the muscles and must have been exquisitely painful. In spite of this nothing but physical force could prevent the continuation of his compulsive behaviour. It is this factor which causes the repetition of masochistic acts in the same way as it does sadistic ones. Perhaps it is not surprising that the Jesuits, which are a sect practising flagellation, were founded by St. Ignatius, who developed various 'exercises' which obviously have an obsessive compulsive basis.

Like other forms of sexual deviation, masochism is exploited by the underworld and a special language evolved. For example, those suffering from masochism or fetishism are termed 'kinky', and the knee-high boots with spike heels fashionable at the moment are called 'kinky boots' although probably only one woman in a thousand who wears them realizes the meaning of the word. The word *bondage* is a term describing the tying up for sado-masochistic purposes, and the like. (Note the significance of Somerset Maugham's title mentioned above.)

The elaborate theories and classifications discussed do not seem to include ritual masochism. I would class masochism not only into: (1) masochistic behaviour in which the patient persuades someone else to beat him, insult him and so on, but (2) ritual masochism. In this the patient does not enlist the help of others, but inflicts the misery on himself. Such cases rarely come to light except when the patient dies through some accident. The typical one is that in which a young man trusses himself up, sometimes so that he is suspended and can swing freely to and fro. Naturally he indulges in this in some place, an attic or storeroom, where he is unlikely to be interrupted. There, when a rope slips and obstructs his breathing, he is unable to summon help. Later he is missed and his body is discovered tied up. Sometimes foul play is suspected.

The desire to be tied so that the masochist can swing is commonly found and is believed to act as a sexual stimulant in some way, probably because of the rhythmical movement. In some cases binding alone is exciting.

Many puzzling cases of this nature are discussed by coroners, often without proper understanding, but usually with a correct verdict of accidental death being reached.

The case of the young man whose skeleton was discovered chained up in an inspection pit of a sewer described on page 164 is typical of ritual masochism. This case would have been more puzzling had the young man not behaved in this way previously. Possibly skeletons discovered in obscure places sometimes originate through such accidents but in these cases ropes, and not chains have been used, and when they rot away with the man's flesh no clue is left as to what has happened.

This ritual masochism is curious, but may be related, in a reversed way, to ritual sadism when the victim is killed in some special manner (for example, in the case of Jack-the-Ripper) and perhaps, also, to the ritual suicides found in transvestism.

Masochism and Suicide

Since masochism is aggression turned back on to the individual (whereas in sadism it is turned outward) we should expect to discover that there were types of suicide similar to those murders I have discussed associated with sadism. These are: (1) psychopathic, (2) masochistic, (3) explosive, and (4) adolescent instability.

The violent psychopath does not usually commit suicide because his emotion is directed outward and, having no inhibitions, he is more likely to kill others than himself. There are occasional cases, however, where men commit suicide as freely as they have murdered, without any apparent emotion. It is not easy to prove that these are psychopathic because a suicide destroys the evidence of his condition, and we cannot study his subsequent behaviour as we can a murderer's.

The masochistic type of suicide is demonstrated because the person chooses the most painful and terrible means of dying. It seems, for example, that those people who pour petrol over themselves and set themselves on fire may be of this type. Since the reversal of aggression often produces depression such suicides are often associated with that form of psychosis.

Again, the schizophrenic suicide, meaningless, sometimes performed in odd ways, is common enough. Other evidence of schizophrenia, such as hallucinations, delusions, feelings of influence, and similar complaints, may indicate what was wrong.

The explosive type of suicide in which the patient destroys himself suddenly and violently is fairly common. In this type the hated object is not projected, as in murder, but is killed in the patient himself.

Adolescent instability may lead to suicide just as easily and more frequently than to murder. The story is often that of a young man, sometimes a student, who appears to have everything to live for, commits suicide for no apparent reason. This type occurs very commonly at universities and is constantly being reported.

There must be a tremendous human wastage due to self-murder and often this means the loss of valuable members of the community. It seems that here is a field which needs investigating and would yield valuable results in prevention. Something is being done but not nearly sufficient.

In general, masochism has much less social importance than sadism since masochists never attack others and never perform murders. The perversion is a harmless one usually and only causes trouble when it drains away so much sexual energy that the patient is impotent, or entails behaviour resulting in self-injury.

REFERENCES

BERGLER, E. (1938) Preliminary phases of the masculine beating fantasy, *Pyschoanal. Quart.*, **7**, 514–36.
BERLINGER, B. (1958) The role of object relations in moral masochism, *Psychoanal. Quart.*, **27**, 38–56
BONAPARTE, M. (1951) *De la Sexualité de la Femme*, Paris.
CLEUGH, JAMES (1951) *The Marquis and the Chevalier*, London.
DAILY TELEGRAPH (1960), 26 January (Case of skeleton in inspection pit).
DEUTSCH, H. (1944) On some aspects of masochism, *Int. J. Psycho-Anal.*, **25**, 150–5.
—— (1946) *The Psychology of Women*, London.
FARBEROW, N. L., and SHNEIDMAN, E. S. (1961) *The Cry for Help*, London.
FENICHEL, O. (1934) *Outline of Clinical Psychoanalysis*, London.
FREUD, S. (1919) A child is being beaten, in *Collected Works*, **2**, 191–7.
GEYERMAN, P. T. (1937) Medical curiosities—snake in the bladder, *J. Amer. med. Ass.*, **108**, 1409.
HIDDEMA, F., and HEYMANS, C. (1961) Masochism: a case report, *Psychiat. Neurol. Neurochir.*, **64**, 434–8.
HORNEY, K. (1935) The problem of feminine masochism, *Psychoanal. Rev.*, **22**, 3. 241–57.
LAFORGUE, R. (1960) À propos du rôle joué par le médecin au service de la névrose de ses malades, *Maroc méd.*, **39**, 1306–8.
LEWINSKY, H. (1944) On some aspects of masochism, *Int. J. Psycho-Anal.*, **25**, 150–5.
MCKERRACHER, D. W., LOUGHNANE, T., and WATSON, R. A. (1968) Self-mutilation in female psychopaths, *Brit. J. Psychiat.*, **114**, 829–32.
OFFER, D., and BARGLOW, P. (1960) Adolescent and young adult self-mutilation incidents in a general psychiatric hospital, *Arch. gen. Psychiat.*, **3**, 194–204.
RADO, S. (1933) Fear of castration in women, *Psychoanal. Quart.*, **3–4**, 425–75.
SACHER-MASOCH, L. (1925) *Venus in Furs*, trans. WARNER, G., Boston.
SCHISCHOFF, L. (1935) Autoalgolagnia, *Urol. cutan. Rev.*, **39**, 40–3.

8

FROTTEURISM AND SCOPTOPHILIO-EXHIBITIONISM

FROTTEURISM

Definition
Contact with another person in order to obtain sexual excitement.

Psychopathology and Occurrence
The infantile reaction to cuddle and rub against the mother seems to become a perversion in some cases, and when it does so the sexual satisfaction is obtained by rubbing against persons in crowds and so on. It is not uncommon to find young men who feel intense sexual excitement when caressing a girl and ejaculate when doing so. Should they attempt intercourse they have a premature ejaculation or else are impotent. From the behaviourist point of view this is really a condition of over-excitation, and indeed it may be found to occur temporarily in those who have been deprived of intercourse overlong.

As far as I can discover the psychopathology of frotteurism has been rather neglected by the psychoanalyst, perhaps because it does not fit in well and coincide with the Freudian philosophy. It is to be considered, as Freud himself has written upon it, as a 'fore-pleasure', or one of the sensations which increase sexual tension and urge the partners on to the final culmination of the sexual act. Frotteurs rarely come to the psychotherapist, since their behaviour does not usually lead them to perform antisocial acts and they are able to satisfy their desires in crowds, &c., without getting into trouble with the police. However, this is not always the case and occasionally one reads in the press of men who are unwise enough to press up against the same girl more than once, as in a crowded Underground train, and are the subject of a complaint. It would seem, in most cases, that, if the man conducts his behaviour with some degree of discretion, he can only be denounced with difficulty. We do not therefore know a great deal about the psychopathology. In my experience it is an uncommon perversion and rarely occurs alone—in fact in the many perverts seen and treated by me there has been no case of pure frotteurism. This is confirmed by the fact that the medical literature on frotteurism is comparatively sparse. Indeed, no psychiatric papers of any value seem to have been published on it during the past ten years.

The following is a typical case in which frotteurism occurs in association with other sexual abnormality. A young man aged 25 consulted me complaining of lack of sexual desire, poor sensation, and weak erections. His parents were normal and he had one sister married. As a child he had been spoiled by his mother; commenced masturbation at the age of 6 and this continued until puberty. At the age of 10 years he exposed himself to a little girl. From that time he obtained sexual pleasure and excitement by pressing against women in the cinema. Since puberty he had exposed his penis under his coat when he did this but not so that the woman could see it. Two years later after doing this he experienced a great deal of pain in the penis and scrotum and this had worried him. He felt that he might have injured himself, and a year later he had intercourse twice, without much success or pleasure.

This case is of great interest. The patient had excessive love as a child, but when this was withdrawn he started to masturbate. His exhibitionism was an attempt to seek love, and his consequent frotteurism and 'masked exhibitionism' were also attempts to obtain affection. A dream which he had clearly showed that the woman from whom he sought love was his mother.

Frotteurism may occur when there is no other sexual outlet. In Brazil, for example, as in most Latin countries, respectable girls had, in the past, no opportunity for harmless forms of love-making. This was replaced by frotteurism. Thus Ressencourt states:

Notwithstanding, there are open to Brazilian girls curious substitutes for dating, petting, and even premarital intercourse. The basic substitute is what is known in Brazilian slang as bowling or *bolinagem*—from the verb *bolinar*, which means in this sense to lean upon or to rub up against a person. Originally and specifically, the verb *bolinar*—to bowline—was a nautical term, in Portuguese and several other languages, signifying to draw a sail tight against the wind with the bowline rope: in English we have it only in the noun form bowline, indicating the rope itself.

Bolinagem, in Brazilian social lore, is a surreptitious manner of caressing engaged in by and between men and women under a great variety of possible circumstances: on crowded buses and street cars and elevators, at public gatherings, in fact, whenever convenient. This surreptitious rubbing is done in such a clever way as to appear accidental: no words are spoken, no change of facial expression takes place, and no outward familiarity is evidenced in any manner. It is a game that is usually played by two, but either person may be active or passive as wish and opportunity afford. Many girls and women play this game with strange men, for there seems no harm in it whatever.

There are many possible variations in the game; rubbing elbows, arms, shoulders, limbs, feet, buttocks, &c.—the most popular being when a man presses himself close against a woman's buttocks from directly behind, especially on a moving bus. If in any way repulsed or called to account, a man can always say, with a look of hurt surprise, 'Why, I beg your pardon, madam, for pushing. The bus is so crowded!'

A favourite spot for one particular use of this game is the cinema matinée. Many 'teenage girls are permitted by their elders to attend the neighbourhood movies in the afternoon if there are two or more to go together in force. Well, 'teenage boys make a practice of looking for attractive girls to sit next to at these matinées: and they play this game of *bolinagem* by rubbing elbows and legs—with the hope that it may go much further than that. Sometimes furtive friendships are formed in this way, and a girl and boy will make a kind of date to meet again another day in a certain section of the audience; and in time intimacies may develop to the point at which the pair masturbate each other with a cloak draped across their laps.

This account has been quoted at length because literature on frotteurism is rare and it gives such a revealing description. Moreover, it shows that the social suppression of sexuality by instilling shame and fear into women—the Brazilian *pudor*—merely resulted in its evasion by what is really perversion.

Dr. A. C. Pacheco e Silva Filho of São Paulo, who has worked in the United States as a psychiatrist, informs me in a private communication that this account given by Ressencourt is not now valid. He feels that the sexual behaviour of young Brazilians differs little, if at all, from that of any other nation. They merely indulge in the 'petting' so familiar in America and England amongst youngsters.

Ressencourt wrote some years ago and customs change so rapidly that what was true then may have disappeared now. This may be due, as Dr. Pacheco e Silva Filho points out, to the fact that the Brazilians are now freer in their sexual *mores* than any other Latin country.

Freud, I feel, may not be entirely correct in regarding frotteurism as a component instinct (i.e. part of the fundamental sexual responses), since over a hundred years ago Darwin pointed out:

Hence we long to clasp in our arms those whom we tenderly love. We probably owe this desire to inherited habit, in association with the nursing and tending of our children, and with the mutual caresses of lovers. With the lower animals we see the same principle of pleasure derived from contact in association with love.

CASE No. 8

A Case of Exhibitionism, with some Symptoms of Frotteurism

This case was one of a young man aged 25 who was a clerk in an insurance office. His mother had died when he was aged $7\frac{1}{2}$ and he was brought up by a stepmother. His father had died three years before he came under my care. An older brother died at the age of 21, but he had a sister aged 23 still alive. She was normal, except that she had had neurotic symptoms.

Two and a half years previously he had placed his hand on a girl's thigh while in a train and this had led to prosecution, but he was discharged as a first offender. Five months previous to the date when first seen he had exposed himself to two ladies in a train, was prosecuted, but again bound over. He was finally discovered doing this again in a train and was then placed on probation, but only on condition that he had psychotherapy. Such an attitude on the part of the magistrate showed a very sensible and kindly point of view which fortunately was rewarded in the patient's treatment.

He was perfectly frank and open and related his sexual life without any signs of emotion. He had been expelled from school at the age of 17 for mutual masturbation with another boy which was discovered. He had found out previously how to masturbate and had done it alone, but did not appreciate the sexual nature of the act. He had had, when seen, intercourse with girls twice. Once not with any satisfaction, but later more satisfactorily. He stated that he had sexually handled the lift girls at his place of employment, and had obtained sexual satisfaction from this and from rubbing against them. He said that he had given this up since he had become a member of the Oxford Group. It was soon discovered, however, that the religious aura of the Oxford Group had practically no influence in restraining his behaviour. This clearly shows, by the way, how little religion can be used as a deterrent to sexual urges. He had quarrelled with his parents before he met the Oxford Group, but under this influence he made up his quarrels with them. He had had clashes with his father from almost his earliest childhood. The father was a rather stiff-necked Nonconformist and did his best to suppress rather than canalize his budding sexuality. At the age of 7 years he showed an interest in a young girl aged 7, but his father said that he must either love the girl or love him (the father) and discouraged his early interest. He soon showed, in this rather loveless home, a tendency to exhibit himself—at the age of puberty he exposed himself to a girl in the shop his father owned and was reported by her to him. The result of this was a thrashing. At the age of 16 he had some sexual interest in his sister and this ended by his sister masturbating him.

There were constant quarrels at home between his stepmother and his father, and his father blamed the patient for provoking them. This may have been justified, since he did hate her and felt that his father's marriage had been a mistake. He found consolation in 'religion', but even there sexuality intruded and he touched the breasts of a girl with whom he used to discuss religion.

Almost from the first it was apparent from his dreams that he had death wishes to his father and incestuous feelings to his mother and sister. Moreover, there was a certain amount of sadism in his fantasies which was apparently the result of the hatred he felt towards his father. He said: 'Even when I was aged 7 I had fantasies of the little girls at school. Also of using two horses in a plough and removing their insides and of slitting up a negro and taking out his inside.'

As might be expected, it was impossible to cure him at one fell swoop, and after a few sessions he confessed that he had again exposed himself to a girl. This, by the way, shows how tolerant one must be; since psychotherapy naturally takes some months to make much difference to the patient, it must be expected that he will show some of his abnormal behaviour before he can be sufficiently influenced to prevent it, even in such a case as this where severe imprisonment would have followed discovery by the police. It was discovered that his exhibitionism was not merely a heterosexual one but had its roots in homosexuality also. This is frequently found with the perversions, and a perversion which appears to be heterosexual can often be found to be homosexual in origin. This to my mind shows that the perversion originated in the emotions to the mother or surrogate.

As the analysis proceeded the patient talked more and more of his mother, stepmother, and sister, and there was a diminution of the urge to expose him- self, although one might have expected it to have been increased, since a girl with whom he had been going out had given him up. He showed a certain amount of positive transference to his mother, although releasing hostility to his stepmother. Apparently the reason why he chose trains to expose himself in was due to the fact that he always went on holidays with his mother and sister as a small boy, and presumably the excitement of the holidays conditioned him to them. He never produced much in the way of castration material which he should have done if the Freudian theory of exhibitionism is correct. The only time this appeared was when he had a dream of shaving off his moustache. After two months' treatment he still had exhibitionistic dreams—mainly very clear and frank ones—but he was refraining from exhibiting himself in a way which would have been impossible to him before. Moreover, he felt more secure and less anxious. This was not to last, and he had another outburst of exhibitionism in which he exposed himself twice in one week. He talked excessively of his sexual adventures, of exhibitionism and frotteurism with girls in the past. His exhibitions seemed to be changing in spite of his outburst, and he said: 'I feel I want to touch girls rather than expose myself to them.' At this time he started to have voyeurist dreams and said that as a child he had had a strong desire to see other boys' penises. He had one further lapse when he attempted to expose himself to a girl in the Underground but ejaculated before he could do so. He then fell in love with a sympathetic young lady and forswore exhibitionism for her. This is the first time that he appears to have felt real adult love for a girl and was prepared to give up things for her. Strong voyeurist and exhibitionistic dreams continued to appear, but he was slowly realizing that these feelings were really directed against his mother and sister. With the realization of this he behaved better to them and their relations were very much improved.

He was discharged after having lost his exhibitionist urges for two months and has behaved perfectly normally since.

This case clearly shows that the exhibitionism was the result of lack of affection as a child. His mother dying at a critical period left him to the mercy of a stepmother whom he disliked. His narrow, religious father gave him no proper affection and was inclined to regard the sexual interest of his young son as original sin. No doubt his excessive interest in the Oxford Group was the result of an attempt to overcompensate for his guilty feelings, although it in no way influenced his behaviour. The successful result shows the value of even a short course of psychotherapy of six months' duration in such cases.

REFERENCES

DARWIN, C. (1938) *The Expression of the Emotions in Man and Animals*, London.
FREUD, S. (1924) *Collected Works*, London.
RESSENCOURT, E. (1955) Sex life in Brazil, *Int. J. Sexol.*, **8**, No. 4.

SCOPTOPHILIO-EXHIBITIONISM

Definition

Scoptophilia is the obtaining of sexual pleasure by watching other people. It is usually manifested by observing people undress, as in the so-called 'Peeping Toms', or else in those who observe courting couples in order to watch them having sexual intercourse.

Exhibitionism is exposing oneself to obtain sexual pleasure. It usually occurs in males and consists in the exposing of the genitalia. Intercourse in public (see above) does not usually occur.[1]

Psychopathology and Occurrence

Scoptophilia appears to be derived from the infantile desire to look. We have seen that the young monkey soon started to be absorbed by the appearance of its mother's genitalia, and the curiosity of young children—particularly regarding sexual matters—cannot fail to be observed by those who do not blind themselves.

I cannot give any other behaviouristic explanation than that given above, and I know of no experiments which throw any objective light on the origin.

The psychoanalyst has a long and complicated theory to offer. From this point of view scoptophilia is a wish to deny castration. Fenichel says:

In the unconscious of voyeurs the same tendencies may be found as in exhibitionists. The experiences of childhood on which the voyeurs are fixated, as a rule resemble the primal scene (i.e. intercourse between father and mother). The painful element which this fixation is intended to overcome and repress is again the same—the danger of castration. The influence of fixations of such a nature is most clearly seen in those cases in which gratification is obtained only if the sexual scene which they wish to witness is subject to certain definite conditions: these conditions represent either a repetition of the childhood experiences which are the foundation of their perversion, or attempts to deny the absence of a penis in women. Abraham reported the case of a pervert who obtained gratification only under the following conditions: a man and a woman must have intercourse in an adjacent room; the patient would begin to cry; the woman would leave the man and rush to the patient.

I have seen a similar case where the patient did not wait for chance sexual relationships he could watch, but arranged situations where he could see his wife having intercourse with other men. The psychopathology of this is not certain, but in this case it seemed probably to stem from some infantile memory of watching his parents (the so-called 'primal scene'). The patient was a middle-aged clergyman who encouraged his wife to commit adultery with other men and secretly observed what occurred. He realized that this was wrong, but his compulsion was so

---

[1] In some of the ancient religions the priest did have intercourse with maidens in public, so this form of the perversion may have become obsolescent. An example of a nation practising this form of religious exhibitionism is that of the Picts and the people who lived in Thessaly before the coming of the Achaeans.

strong that he was unable to resist. In normal sexual relations with his wife his urge was weak and his performance unsatisfactory.

East states, regarding this form of scoptophilia, 'Voyeurism calls for police action if a concealed observer of courting couples indulges in his secret pleasures so recklessly that he is detected and assaulted by his victims. But more serious cases occur. A middle-aged man led a normal sexual life as far as could be ascertained until his wife died. He lived then with his grown-up daughter and induced her to bring men home for an immoral purpose so that he could watch the incidents which took place between them.' East makes no mention of having investigated the psychopathology of this behaviour and it is probable that he had no opportunity to do so.

The fact that the voyeur arranges for his wife or daughter to have intercourse with the other man probably satisfies his inner urge to see his mother in that situation with his father and should be regarded as similar to that of a scientist who arranges the conditions of an experiment instead of waiting for chance to produce what he desires.

I believe that most such cases are based on infantile memories but other factors may be important. For instance, Sabeine Spielrein described a peeping perversion based on a very early repression of genital and manual sexuality.

(It is interesting to see the enormous trouble these perverts had to go to in order to obtain what normal people get so easily.)

I cannot accept the Freudian view *in toto*, and it seems improbable that the whole of scoptophilia is related to the castration fears as Fenichel suggests. It seems likely to me that the wish to look at someone is the manifestation of love, and it is not said without some truth that a man 'cannot keep his eyes off' his beloved. This seems literally true, and the wish to look at a woman is a sign of sexual attraction rather than related to any elaborate theory of castration (this does not mean, of course, that one is denying castration fears—the fact that they exist is only too clear to anyone who has worked at psychotherapy). Gordon Holmes, however, has shown that ocular fixation is a reflex and this in itself demonstrates how primitive the instinct really is. There is no doubt that this is not the whole story, since in scoptophilia *all* the sexual pleasure comes from looking at the females naked or the sexual act. This would suggest that it was the direct fulfilment of an infantile wish to do so which was repressed and was now seeking frank satisfaction.

In the case of those who watch mating couples one is tempted to suggest that there is considerable identification. The scoptophiliac in this case is one who is sexually deprived for some reason (perhaps through excessive shyness, lack of attraction to women, or some similar reason) and obtains pleasure from watching others do what he would wish to do himself. The immense trouble which such a man will go to in order to obtain his wish is shown by a case which was recorded in the press some time ago. A man was killed whilst hanging outside a train. At the inquest it was revealed that he and another man were in the habit of travelling a considerable distance in order to watch couples in the hope that they would see intercourse. The man had been struck by a passing train whilst climbing about outside and so was killed.

It would seem in many cases that there is often a basis of sexual inadequacy which induces the behaviour. For example, Gebhard *et al.* in their statistical analysis of types state that 'a large number (possibly a majority) of habitual peepers generally have inadequate sexual lives' and again 'All in all the picture is one of somewhat stunted heterosexuality'. In such a case scoptophilia is a poor substitute for intercourse.

The type of scoptophilia which consists of viewing women in a state of nakedness or semi-nakedness is catered for socially to some extent by the theatre. Many vaudeville entertainments are merely a frame in which the charms of beautiful girls may be exposed to the voyeurs of the audience, the 'strip-tease' 'fan-dances', 'bubble dances', and similar 'entertainments' being dependent on the same psychological mechanisms.

Kinsey and his co-workers have pointed out that scoptophilio-exhibitionism forms an important part in pre-adolescent sex play, whether it be homosexual or heterosexual in nature, and found that out of a total of 1,843 boys 43 per cent. had indulged in some sexual activity and 99 per cent. had used scoptophilio-exhibitionistic activity in it. Out of 2,102, 44 per cent. had indulged in homosexual play, in which exhibitionism played a part in 99·8 per cent.

Exhibitionism is the counterpart of scoptophilia. As I have pointed out, exhibitionists are more commonly men than women. In fact women exhibitionists are very rare, although I have treated one woman who had this perversion along with various obsessional anxieties, and Harmann and Schroder have also published a case of feminine exhibitionism. Attempts have recently been made to introduce a fashion for women to wear topless bathing dresses, and even frocks, totally exposing the breasts. On 21 August 1964 three women were fined in London for indecency through wearing such clothes. Previous cases had occurred in America and France. This might suggest that women may be more exhibitionistic than is usually realized, but how far this is an attempt to inspire sexual attraction rather than an end in itself, it is difficult to say. It is, perhaps, significant that two of the women in London were theatrical artistes and the one in France a fashion model.

Curiously enough, although baring the breasts occurs in primitive cultures, as in parts of Africa and in Bali, it has been fashionable in sophisticated civilizations only occasionally in the past: in Minoan Crete, for example, the women wore no top to the dresses, but sported a sort of waistcoat, mainly as a decoration. Breasts were exposed, by respectable women, also, during some periods in ancient Egypt and, for a short time, in France after the revolution. Courtesans, for obvious reasons, have always been prepared to expose their nipples in public.

The commercial motive is obvious, also, in the innovation of 'topless waitresses' (i.e. without covering on the upper part of the body) who have been introduced into some American restaurants and clubs. It is improbable that these girls obtain pleasure from the exposure, but profit from the high wages obtained and, possibly, occasional prostitution. In exhibitionism the desire is to show the genitalia in men, and in women the nipples as well as the genitalia have sexual significance. Goodhart, a biologist, has suggested that the nipples in women have particular significance inasmuch as the areola round them is the human equivalent to the sexual skin in monkeys (which becomes engorged at oestrus). It is this which gives them their erotic significance. He states:

> Women may like to remember that there are probably sound and long-standing biological reasons for this otherwise not easily explained hesitation about exposing their nipples and areolae to the public view. The breasts do form an important part of a woman's biological equipment for courtship, and it is a question not so much of morals as of tactics to consider at what stage in the proceedings they are to be deployed to the best advantage.

It is important to realize that the mere showing of the genitalia is not sufficient, and to suggest that an exhibitionist join a nudist colony is to invite indignation! The genitalia must be shown to a member of the opposite sex and the sexual excitement is greater if she is emotionally stirred in some way—shocked, &c. The exhibition is usually performed in some favourite spot such as a railway carriage, a lonely lane, &c. Not unusually ejaculation takes place at or after the exhibition (or the patient may masturbate; sometimes masturbation in public occurs as well as showing the genitalia).

Kopp made a character study of 100 sexual offenders at the New Jersey State Hospital, Trenton, U.S.A. and concluded that they fell into two groups. The first (which is what is considered the usual) was the man who was passive, receptive, over-conscientious, unusually modest, and had a strict moral code. He was frightened and ashamed at what he had done and blamed it on alcohol or sudden impulse.

The second type was the man who was loud, brash, and attention-seeking. He boasted of his conquests; swore openly to shock people and tried to show how clever he was.

Both types were dominated by women and resented it. In Kopp's opinion, genital exposure is an attempt to reverse roles and dominate the female.

It is not easy to be certain that there is a third type, but I have occasionally met exhibitionists who did not fit into either of these two groups. They firmly denied that they had ever committed any offence: it was all a mistake. They were merely passing urine against a tree out of sight and some officious woman complained to the police &c. Such men seemed to have a more normal personality, although usually dominated by females.

Fenichel gives the cause of exhibitionism as follows:

As far as psychoanalytical material on exhibitionists is available, it shows that the exhibitionistic behaviour represents an eternal denial of castration. This denial has a double meaning; on the superficial level, the exhibitionist, by showing his penis, demands that everybody should confirm the fact that he has one; on a deeper level, he demands that the women and girls to whom he exposes his penis should expose themselves. Behind the manifest exhibitionistic act, then, is concealed the latent wish to look; thus the exposure is seen to be a magic gesture to show women what the exhibitionist wishes to see—that they have no penis. In exhibitionists, we have the first example to allay castration anxiety—due to the Oedipus complex—by means of a simple hypertrophy of one of the infantile component sexual impulses. The harking back to the pre-genital exhibitionist pleasures of early childhood—made possible, surely, only by the fixation of this component impulse—thus serves regressively the purpose of repressing genital conflict.

I cannot feel altogether satisfied with this explanation. No doubt such cases do exist but the psychoanalysts believe that the castration anxiety is much greater in women than in men—in fact the discovery that they have no penis converts women from sadistic to masochistic reactions. *If this is so one might expect women to be more sexually exhibitionistic than men, but they are less so.* (Exhibition on the stage is planned not to give the actresses pleasure but to please the scoptophiliacs in the audience.)

Levitan describes how a man, who lived with his mother, became exhibitionistic when she went blind. He recovered and was free from his urges for five years. At the end of this time his wife became pregnant and he was promoted foreman at the works where he was employed; the behaviour started again.

Although Levitan explains this as due to a castration complex it is difficult to accept such an explanation, since surely his wife's pregnancy in itself was a denial of it and promotion to be foreman, although an additional anxiety, was a further refutation of his lack of masculinity.

I have dealt with this castration theory to some extent under the section on scoptophilia. It is sufficient to point out here that, although I am reluctant to utilize facts regarding lower animals to provide us with material on which to judge human beings, there is a very valuable point regarding the sexual behaviour of the newt which shows that sexual pleasure is related to looking and exhibiting. Moreover, it shows that the scoptophilio-exhibitionistic urge is a biological one, and in some animals can alone satisfy the sexual desire. Baker says of the newt:

In the breeding season the male acquires bright colours along the sides and a large crest grows out along the back. Finding a female, he deposits near her a bundle of sperms, held together by some sticky substance. He then devotes himself to swimming about and actively displaying his charms before the female. If the latter is sufficiently aroused by his antics, she swims to the bundle of sperms, picks it up, and forces it into her egg-tube so that fertilization may be effected. *The male's desires are satisfied by the sight of her performance of this process.* (My italics.)

Attempts have been made by some writers to explain exhibitionism on grounds other than psychological. For example, Arieff and Rotman, who made a study of 100 cases of exposure, suggested 'a phylogenic explanation appears to be the most plausible at present'. It is obvious that they could not have gone deeply into the patients' psyche—as indeed their paper indicates they failed to do.

Naville and Dubois-Ferrière have described an elaborate classification of types of exhibitionism. This they think is due to various causes such as: (1) hypersexuality, (2) hyposexuality, (3) feeble-mindedness, (4) chronic psychosis, (5) epilepsy, (6) psychopathy, (7) post-febrile deliria, (8) nudism, and (9) accidental. Nobody would, of course, deny that exhibitionism may occur in any of these conditions, or a dozen other ones, but this gives not the slightest clue as to why it happens.

We all know that organic diseases may release psychological conditions which would otherwise be hidden (as, for example, delirium), but what we wish to know is the dynamic factors, not what releases them, although these may be of secondary importance.

Karpman, who has had very wide prison experience with patients suffering from psychosexual illness points out, I believe rightly, that 'organic defects play a minor role in the development of exhibitionism'. If this is true, and the exhibitionists seen by me have been normal men physically, then the release of such impulses by organic factors must be rare.

Naville and Dubois-Ferrière do not explain in their long paper why these patients exhibited themselves rather than ran amok with a chopper, committed suicide, or did any of the thousand and one similar things which a confused man is capable of doing. I insist that the exhibitionistic tendencies were already there and were released, not originated, by the illness. (This is not to deny, of course, that exhibitionism may not be seen in epilepsy. For example, Juillet *et al.* described two cases; one, a soldier aged 19, who following a trivial remark by an officer removed his clothes and walked about the barracks naked. His E.E.G. revealed 'a focus of spikes in the right temporal region' when he was in hyperpnoea.

The second case was that of a man aged 27 who had committed acts of exhibitionism in the Underground. His E.E.G. was within normal limits, but an injection of cardiazol provoked 'a left temporal discharge of slow spikes', followed by a generalized convulsive episode. During the confused stage he made an attempt to expose his genital organs.

Such cases are not of much value since they reveal only the trigger mechanism and not the underlying psychological motivation: moreover, the vast majority of exhibitionists show no evidence of epileptic attacks or abnormal E.E.G.s.)

It seems probable that the driving force is a psychological one and that when the inhibitions are diminished, either by physical illness, loss of psychological control, or increase of the sexual drive beyond restraint, then exhibitionism occurs.

It is felt that Rickles was nearer to the truth when he suggested that there was a strong obsessive–compulsive element present (most of perverse behaviour, in fact all sexuality, shows a certain similarity to obsessional behaviour—the slowly growing imperious desire, the performance of the act, the relief for a long or shorter period, and then the renewed urge starting the cycle again).

Rickles suggests, I believe correctly:

Most of the cases that I have observed have had a pathological degree of repression. Mother or wife domination of an already timid, unassertive man has led the man to the place where he exhibits himself as a means of proving he is virile, he is attractive and there is one thing that his mother can't do for him. The desire to assert his masculine superiority becomes so great that it cannot be controlled. The significance of the act is more defiance than acquisitive. The compulsion to defy conventions sometimes reaches the point where one finds the exhibitionist pleased when he is arrested. It seems to give him satisfaction to know that he is capable of doing something which will classify him as a criminal.

In cases of exhibitionism caused by compulsion neurosis, the exposure is usually repeated in the same vicinity and at the same time of the day. It is for this reason that the police are able to pick up these people so easily. The act may take place in a department store, a church, or a bus—but it will almost certainly be repeated in the same environment. Other types such as the depraved are very much more apt to pick a secluded spot and are capable of controlling their choice, of time, place, and person: so are less often arrested.

Karpman believes that patients have prodromal symptoms before exhibiting and feel 'restlessness, excitement, fearfulness, apprehension. There may be physical symptoms, as oppression, headache, hotness, perspiration, diarrhoea, pricking in the urethra, palpitation, vertigo, vague feeling of increasing sexual excitement'.

It is improbable that there is any mystery about such sensations: they are those of combined sexual excitement and fear of consequences because the patient knows that such behaviour would meet with disapprobation.

Exhibitionism is the seeking of love. It can be seen in the love dances of the ape and the sexual dances of the Polynesian. The mating of all animals shows it to some degree. In man it is a frank sexual approach— too frank in civilization to obtain success. This is clearly shown by the fact that a patient of mine became exhibitionistic only after having a refusal of marriage, and another after anxiety had caused such prematurity that he abandoned attempts at heterosexual intercourse. The sexual excitement in both scoptophilia and exhibitionism may culminate in ejaculation before it is possible to do more than peer or exhibit. It is not that these are 'fore-pleasures' as Freud suggests, but that the sexual act cannot be attempted because ejaculation has already taken place and the climax reached. Like other examples of premature ejaculation, of course, it may be the result of excessive excitation and occur in those who have suffered sexual deprivation for some long period. This is, however, not to be regarded as a perversion, since it is rapidly removed by a normal heterosexual life.

Arieff and Rotman suggest that exhibitionism is the most common of all sexual offences and state that it forms 35 per cent. of those admitted to the Chicago Municipal Psychiatric Institute. Of their 100 cases they found the peak age was in the third decade, and 84 per cent. of cases occurred before the age of 40. All offenders were male. Only 4 per cent. were Negroes. Seventy-four per cent. exposed themselves in broad daylight. Of 78 of the cases 36 were Roman Catholic, 34 Protestant, 5 Jewish, and 3 Christian Scientists. Of these, 32 attended church regularly, 29 had completed less than 8 grades at school, and 2 were illiterate, 25 had reached the eighth grade, and 21 had had 2 years at high school, and 12 had had college work. Of the 100 patients 62 were single and 38 married. Marital adjustment was poor, although 23 had children. Sixty-six had a history of previous antisocial incidents other than exhibitionism. Six had schizophrenia, 13 were mentally defective, 1 was an alcoholic paranoid, 1 had dementia paralytica, and 1 senile dementia, 13 had a constitutional psychopathic state, 26 had a compulsive neurosis, 16 had borderline mental deficiency, 15 were dull, and 4 had a borderline schizoid state. Alcoholism was the contributing factor in 28 cases, 38 patients admitted guilt, 24 denied it. Six stated they were dazed at the time the act was committed. Eleven admitted sexual pleasure, 15 said they had marital dissatisfaction. Lack of home harmony was present in 12 cases. In 10 instances the patient was the only child. Twenty-one patients had had no previous heterosexual experience; 8 admitted practising perversions; 31 stated they masturbated even when heterosexual adjustment had supposedly been made.

N—PSY. D.

Gebhard *et al.* say that it is worth noting that not infrequently the exhibitionist may expose himself to unsuitably young girls which hints at a feeling of inadequacy in relationships with adult females.

Radzinowicz and Turner found that out of 1,985 sexual offenders 490 were exhibitionists, and these were composed of 80 per cent. of first offenders; the other 20 per cent. were recurrent cases. Taylor found that exhibitionists formed about a third of all sexual offenders. The same thing has been noticed at the Portman Clinic. American workers have confirmed this for their own country. It must be agreed, then, that exhibitionism forms a large and important section of sexual cases coming before the courts.

I once had an interesting case of exhibitionism which was activated by inhaling amphetamine sulphate. The patient was an ex-naval officer, aged 47, who stated that he came from normal parents and was the middle child of a family of three (the other two being girls). His childhood was happy but he was a reserved boy. At school he did well. On leaving he entered the Royal Navy and served for thirteen years. He had been married twenty-three years and this was happy except that he felt he was more highly sexed than his wife. This had become more marked since she had had to have a hysterectomy for fibroids some six years previously. For the previous nine years he had had an urge to expose himself but had done so only in front of his wife.

During the past five years he had used amphetamine sulphate (which had been prescribed for nasal catarrh) as a form of intoxicant. After sniffing this for some time he became excited, his genitalia shrank up, and he paraded about the house naked. His wife said that he appeared then to be in a mild maniacal condition and would stand before an open window in icy weather. Once she found him wearing some of her jewellery during one of these spells. He drooled at the corners of his mouth and appeared to have uncontrollable excitement.

The only incident in his past which seemed to have a bearing on his behaviour was that when he was a young Naval officer he had been to a show in France where a woman paraded, naked except for some jewellery. This had made a great impression on him.

Physically he was normal but because he had a horror of hirsutism he had shaved off all his bodily hair.

He agreed that he would make a great effort to stop using the amphetamine inhaler and co-operate. He was treated by a frank discussion of the nature of his illness, and by sedation. His wife was persuaded to let him have intercourse whenever he needed it.

In spite of his apparent willingness to co-operate he did not do so and would not attend for psychotherapy. The last that was heard of him was that he had gone to a Turkish bath in the middle of the day, inhaled his amphetamine, and failed to attend an important meeting at the firm where he was personnel manager.

Such a case shows the release of unconscious urges through intoxication, the parading naked before his wife presumably being an urge to seek her love in some way. There is a deeper element in wearing her jewellery which suggests that he was unconsciously identifying himself with a woman. The recent increase in addiction due to amphetamine has not increased exhibitionism, so obviously it acts merely as an excitant or intoxicant.

One of the dangers of exhibitionism is that it may produce psychic trauma in the victim. This is particularly serious since most of those to whom it happens are young girls. Thus of 786 cases, 389 (49·5 per cent.) were girls under 16 years of age, 71 (9 per cent.) were between 16 and 21 years of age and 326 were 21 years of age or over. 44·1 per cent. of exposures were to solitary adult females and 24·7 per cent. to two or more children together, at least one being a girl.

Although the effects of exhibitionism to an adult female are probably exaggerated it can frighten children sexually and have a permanent effect upon their later-life.

Exhibitionism may occur with persons of the same sex—I have known cases of homosexual exhibitionism in which the genitalia have been exposed to other men, and again of infantosexual exhibitionism (both homosexual and heterosexual varieties occur), e.g. a schoolmaster who exposed himself to boys on trams.

I have not found in exhibitionism the sadistic element which Freud suggested was part of the motivation—except in so much as the patients like to observe some sexual reaction—shock or horror—in the person to whom they expose themselves. The exposure of the genitalia, or of masturbation, is very specifically the converse of voyeurism in which the peeping is to see nudity or sexual intercourse.

Scoptophilio-exhibitionism is, more than any other perversion, the result of cultural influences, mainly religious ones. Curiously enough these have increased in the last hundred years. For example, 90 years ago the Rev. Francis Kilvert wrote in his diary of the beauty of a teenage girl sun-bathing naked on the beach at the Isle of Wight; and, annoyed by bathing trunks, discarded his and bathed naked himself. A similar freedom is permitted on some beaches in Scandinavia.

Westbrook says:

If you live among men and women who are practically nude they soon fail to attract attention. Everyone is attired alike; it is part of everyday life. Let a nude male or female garb themselves in trousers or petticoats, with the rest of the people nude, and one notes how soon sexual curiosity becomes excited. That which is exposed never creates curiosity: it is that which is hidden. I recall hearing a lady missionary bound for the Bismarck Archipelago who was most distressed by the thought of leaving her husband's side before she became used to the sight of nude men and women. She accustomed herself to the horrifying spectacle by peering through the portholes of the ship as it lay at anchor, herself unseen.

This beautiful example of abnormal sexuality is related by one un-interested in modern psychology.

CASE No. 9

This is an exceptional case inasmuch as the patient was not dominated by a house full of overbearing females as in those described by Rickles, but was happily married and of previously fine character.

The patient was of Welsh origin and came from a normal, though poor, family without psychopathic traits. As a child he was not nervous, did well at school, and won a scholarship to a Grammar School, where he remained until he was aged 14. He then worked in a colliery until he was aged 20. Owing to the depression in his home town, at the time, he joined the Army and served in the Guards. He served on through the War and saw much active service. His behaviour was good under fire and he won the Military Medal for bravery in the field. In 1945 he was invalided with the rank of sergeant, of an exemplary character, from the effects of war wounds.

In 1946 he joined the police and gained a commendation during his service for catching some thieves when he was in civilian clothes off duty. In the police he had the reputation for being a conscientious and hard-working officer, well liked by both his superiors and equals.

In 1941 he had married and had two children who were aged 12 and 10 years old when he was first seen. Both he and his wife insisted that the marriage was happy in every way; his wife was not the dominating type but kind and under-standing. They were both sexually contented and he had intercourse about twice a week.

Then, in 1960, this happily married man of exemplary character suddenly started exposing himself to schoolchildren, was identified and arrested.

At first sight such a lapse from his previous behaviour was difficult to understand, but careful investigation threw a light on its causation. The patient had been involved in a motor cycle smash when working as a traffic policeman some six months previously. This was due to a mistake in the garage when a tyre was put on wrongly and burst when he was going along. He was flung from the machine and suffered from a brief concussion. His doctor, a fine type of general practitioner, advised him very properly to take a rest from his work in order to recover. This the patient resolutely refused to do since he was much too over-conscientious to give up his work when he felt that he was capable of continuing. However, the concussion affected his memory, and although he was able to continue work, it was at a great strain. Most unfortunately he was then put on duty which entailed even more anxiety—he had to deal with accidents in which fatal injuries had occurred, and on one occasion gave evidence at the Old Bailey on six of these in a fortnight. His meticulousness in finding the exact details in every case caused him enormous anxiety and he started to sleep badly. His memory became worse.

Finally he consulted his doctor again, this time suffering from nervous symptoms, including a psychogenic rash. He was told that it was imperative that he reported sick and asked for leave. This he again refused to do.

Although this man drove himself on with obsessional ruthlessness owing to his terrific sense of duty he must, unconsciously, have felt that he had to do something to end the strain. Incredible though it may seem, instead of resigning, or asking for a change of work, or using some conscious means of escape from the intolerable position, he started the exhibitionism, although he must have known from his experience in the police that exhibitionists are always caught, and indeed, must have wished to be caught, to end his strain.

Fortunately the magistrates who tried his case were sympathetic and he was placed on probation. Even so, after fifteen years service he lost his position and his pension.

This shows how unwise it is to state that any certain psychopathology invariably applies to some particular type of case. This man used his exhibitionism not as a demonstration of masculinity, nor as a denial of castration, nor as a reminiscence of the primal scene, but as an escape mechanism to end a situation which was beyond his capacity.

REFERENCES

ARIEFF, A. J., and ROTMAN, D. B. (1942) Psychiatric inventory of 100 cases of indecent exposure, *Arch. Neurol. Psychiat. (Chic.)*, **47**, 495–8.

BAKER, J. R. (1926) *Sex in Man and Animals*, London.

CAMBRIDGE DEPARTMENT OF CRIMINAL SCIENCE (1957) *Sexual Offences*, London.

CHRISTOFFEL, H. (1936) Exhibitionism and exhibitionists, *Int. J. Psycho-Anal.*, **2, 17**, 321–45.

DANA, J. (1935) *Gods Who Die*, New York.

EAST, W. N. (1924) Observations on exhibitionism, *Lancet*, ii, 370–5.

—— (1949) *Society and the Criminal*, London, H.M.S.O.

FENICHEL, O. (1934) *Outline of Clinical Psychoanalysis*, London.

GEBHARD, P. H., GAGNON, J. H., POMEROY, W. B., and CHRISTENSON, C. V. (1965) *Sex Offenders*, London.

GOODHART, C. B. (1964) A biological view of toplessness, *New Scientist*, **407**, 558–60.

HARMANN, K., and SCHRODER, G. E. (1936) Un cas d'exhibitionisme chez une femme, *Acta Psychiat. (Kbh.)*, **10**, 547–64.

JUILLET, P., DAMASIO, R., RIGAL, J., CADOUR, E., and SAVELLI, A. (1963) Exhibitionism and the E.E.G., *Ann. Méd. lég.*, **42**, 197–204.

KARPMAN, B. (1957) *The Sexual Offender and his Offenses*, New York.

KOPP, S. B. (1962) The character structure of sex offenders, *Amer. J. Psychother.*, **16**, 64–70.

LEVITAN, H. L. (1963) An exhibitionist, *Psychoanal. Quart.*, **32**, 246–8.

NAVILLE, F., and DUBOIS-FERRIÈRE, H. (1938) Étude sur l'exhibitionisme, *Schweiz. Arch. Neurol. Psychiat.*, **19**, 79–84, 575.

RADZINOWICZ, L., and TURNER, J. W. C. (1957) *English Studies in Criminal Science*, **9**, London.

RICKLES, N. K. (1942) Exhibitionism, *J. nerv. ment. Dis.*, **95**, 11–17.

RICKLES, N. K. (1950) *Exhibitionism*, London.

TAYLOR, F. H. (1947) Observations on some cases of exhibitionism, *J. ment. Sci.*, **93**, 631.

PART THREE

DISORDERS OF THE INSTINCTUAL OBJECT

9

THE HETEROSEXUAL AND HOMOSEXUAL PERVERSIONS

THE HETEROSEXUAL PERVERSIONS

Definition

Perversions performed with one of the opposite sex.

Psychopathology and Occurrence

These perversions are heterosexual only inasmuch as the object is one of the opposite sex. The pervert does not treat his sexual partner in a normal adult heterosexual manner (i.e. loving, protective, copulatory, &c.) at all. On the contrary he treats her in various ways which we have seen are derived mainly from the infantile reaction patterns which have in some way persisted into adult conduct and replaced normal copulatory behaviour.

It is obvious that these reaction patterns must have originated in childhood—one has only to look at sexual oralism to realize that. Moreover, this behaviour has, in every case, been directed against the mother. She is the original conditioner and from her all the child's acquired reactions have originated.

It is this fact which gives us the clue—without psychoanalytic help it might have been guessed—that the instinctual object, even when it is heterosexual, is not the equivalent of the adult instinctual object but is really a substitute for the mother. We might guess, behaviouristically, that in the case of women the father is the first substitute for the mother and that other men are used to substitute him, since it is impossible to explain homosexual oralism otherwise.

It must be admitted, however, that if the sexual object is some sort of maternal substitute, the behaviour to this sexual object is wildly exaggerated as though one could see the deviation which was occurring in childhood, but the patient has progressed a long way down the path of abnormality.

I shall not discuss heterosexual perversions individually since they attain such importance that they merit individual consideration—in such sections as those on sadism, masochism, exhibitionism, &c., they are considered separately. No apology is made for the large amount of space devoted here to homosexuality. It is by much the most important psychosexual abnormality with which the psychiatrist has to deal. This is shown by the statistics given by Whitener and Nikelly. In 30 months they examined 39 male deviants. These were 3 exhibitionists, 3 transvestists, 1 voyeur, 2 multisexual opportunists, and 30 homosexuals.

This is about the usual proportion one would expect to find in an unselected series.

HOMOSEXUALITY

Definition

It is usual to define homosexuality as the attraction between those of the same sex. This is undesirably vague since it includes the slightest of friendships. Homosexual behaviour should not be regarded as perverse unless it leads to ejaculation through stimulation from the other partner.

CAUSATION

In the past it has been usual to speak of inborn and acquired homosexuality. Such terms are meaningless and only lead to confusion. Similarly with facultative and inborn homosexuality. They have been invented and used by those who have had little or no clinical contact. There seem to be four possibilities regarding aetiology: (1) Homosexuality is a genetic aberration. (2) It is an endocrine disorder. (3) It is a psychological disease. (4) It is a combination of two or more of the preceding factors.

The conception of homosexuality as a genetic disorder is a fascinating one, and has been worked out to a considerable extent in insects. For example, Goldschmidt demonstrated that he could produce various stages of intersexuality with different types of butterflies. In a series of cases he was able to effect a gradual transition from complete male down through feminized males by a complete set of intersexes to the female. Similarly he was able to work back from complete female via a set of masculinized females to the male.

The intersexual male or female exists in animals as well as insects and can be found, of course, in the human in such diseases as adrenogenital virilism. The theory is therefore an interesting one and naturally has led to further research. This has been performed notably by Lang. He states:

There are two possibilities. Male homosexuals may be regarded either as more or less feminized males or as real male sex intergrades, which are genetically female but have lost all morphological sex characteristics except their chromosome formula. If it is true that a proportion of male homosexuals are actually transformed females, then an undue preponderance of males must be found amongst the siblings of male homosexuals.

Lang therefore investigated the relatives of male homosexuals in Munich and Hamburg. He found that there was a shift amongst their brothers and sisters in the ratio of male: female, 121·1: 100 (normal male:

female rate is 106:100). It therefore looked as if there might be something in the theory. Unfortunately in the actual children of homosexuals, in contradistinction to the proportion of the brothers and sisters of the homosexual fathers, the ratio was found to be 106·9:100, which is normal. It is obvious that the theory falls to the ground to a large extent.

It is generally admitted that belief in the genetic causation rests more on faith than proof. The Memorandum of the British Medical Association on Homosexuality stated, 'It must be admitted, however, that the case for a genetic basis is not acceptable to all observers. Homosexuality is in fact an unsuitable trait for precise genetical study because its character is complex, it does not show clear segregation, and it is much influenced by environment. In so far as it can be regarded as a symptom of psychopathic disorder its genetics may be studied by implication when the familial incidence of a more inclusive disorder is being investigated.'

This is surely an incredible statement. If homosexuality is to be considered as a sign of psychopathy then every psychosexual abnormality should be so regarded, and that makes nonsense of psychopathy as a clear-cut antisocial or asocial personality disorder. Moreover, since Kinsey found about 50 per cent. of all middle-aged Americans had had some homosexual experience does the Committee consider that half America consists of psychopaths? Such statements make learned committees merely look ridiculous.

The work of Kallman on homosexuality in twins is always quoted to support the genetic basis for homosexuality. He collected 85 homosexual men who had each a twin. Of these 45 were binovular and 40 identical twins. The binovular one showed 50 per cent. and the identical twins 100 per cent. inversion. Kallman himself states: 'Procedurally it is especially impedient in a twin family study of the kind that the road from the point of procuring the name and recorded history of an apparently homosexual twin, subject it to the establishment of a formal acquaintance with the given person or his relatives, is an incredibly long, rugged, and sometimes perilous one. The subjects are astute in disguising their identities, shifting whereabouts and family connections. They usually live far from their families, and they are rarely able or willing to discuss more than their family histories.'

I have studied this work very carefully. The actual clinical data are very sketchy and unsatisfactory and most of the paper consists of three case histories. The others are not given because he states that the patients were still subject to New York laws. Although the paper gives elaborate statistical analysis the basic clinical facts must be completely determined to be of any value at all. I comment in my monograph on homosexuality: 'Obviously one cannot go up to a man and say, "Excuse me, I understand your twin brother is homosexual: do you mind telling me if you are?" It is here that the perilous part comes in and it seems possible that sometimes he went more on hearsay than actual investigation.'

Kallman has now retracted his 100 per cent. concordance in identical twins, and stated that it was an artefact. His change of mind was, no doubt, due to the harsh criticism which his work encountered on all sides. For example, Heston and Shields, on the basis of a great deal of research, state, 'There is no evidence that monozygotic twins *per se* are particularly prone to homosexuality' (which they would be if there was 100 per cent. concordance). Moreover, Kallman's work has been contradicted by what other workers found with such twins. I have seen identical twins in at least one case, where one was normal and one was homosexual. Lange had published a case of identical twins showing similar disparity. West also claims to have seen identical twins, one of whom was homosexual and one normal. Parker reports three cases from an unselected series of homosexuals in which twins, two monozygotic and one dizygotic, occurred. There was no evidence that the homosexuality of one was shared by the other twin. He admitted that in an adequately documented case the homosexuality was due to the mother's attitude.

So much for the 100 per cent, concordance in monozygotic twins which is still being claimed by some, for example Eysenck, in 1964.

Kallman's paper therefore stands suspect because: (1) his clinical material is not satisfactory; (2) it is contradicted by the experience of others; (3) it is unusual in medicine to obtain 100 per cent. results, and one usually encounters some omission or contradiction; (4) his work has never been confirmed by others; and (5) the final blow to the geneticists is the fact that a good percentage of homosexuals can be cured by suitable psychotherapy. If this is an inborn disease it thus behaves differently from every other genetically caused condition. Yet so pertinacious is this idea that as recently as 1962 the suggestion was still being made. For example, Hauser stated, 'Homosexuality is possibly inborn in a small number of people' but gave no facts whatsoever to support such a belief.

In concluding this discussion on genetics it may be worth mentioning a review in *The Times Literary Supplement*. The reviewer states 'Both psychiatrists who are ignorant of analytic therapy, and homosexuals themselves, have a vested interest in preserving the idea that homosexuality is a genetic variant—for the former can assure themselves that the psychotherapy that they are not equipped to practise is bound to be ineffective, whereas the latter can console themselves with the belief that their abnormality is neither a reflection on their upbringing nor a failure on their part to reach emotional maturity.'

It is impossible to add to such a succinct summary.

The possibility of homosexuality being an endocrine disease is, of course, a popular conception. If only this could be proved true we should have something tangible in this most puzzling of diseases. After all, the laboratory worker is inclined to argue that here we have a male behaving in a feminine way. There are male and female hormones. Surely this feminine behaviour *must* be caused by the female endocrine being present in the male. This view is a perennial one; for example, in a leading article the editor of a medical journal states:

For our part we are reluctant to believe that there is no organic aberration. When we consider the tremendous compulsion which must lie behind this perverted impulse to drive these individuals onwards in defiance of the savage penalties which lie in wait for them, to say nothing of the attendant personal disgrace, and when we remember that they are often men of great intelligence and ability, of sound judgement, and outside their perversion, of the highest character, it is impossible to believe that they are not victims of some freakish alteration in that obscure but compelling chemistry that plays so large, if unsuspected a part, in shaping our personalities and destinies.

With the discovery of tests for the androgen and oestrogen excretion in urine a whole host of endocrinologists and biochemists plunged into the field in the hope of settling the problem once and for all time. Wright, Glass, Deuel, Bauer, Neustadt, Myerson, and many others attempted to find the basic hormonic imbalance in the abnormal conduct.

At first, as so often is the case, reports were optimistic and it appeared possible that homosexuals could be differentiated from normal by hormone assays of the urine. Soon, however, this was contradicted. Rosensweig and Hoskins published a paper on the ineffectiveness of sex hormone medication, and Kinsey gave most valuable criticism of the endocrine point of view. Kinsey has demolished the assumptions of the endocrinologists. Firstly, he showed that the results of Glass, Deuel, and Wright were statistically unsound and the standard errors in their small number of cases were too great for their results to be conclusive. Then that their technique was faulty, and finally that the methods of sampling were erroneous and led to wrong conclusions. Similar criticism can be applied to all the similar assertions.

In spite of the repeated demonstration that there is no endocrine basis for homosexuality one finds perennially fresh assertions that this or that hormone can be found excreted in the urine. The latest is that of Cossa who states: 'With R. Rivorie we have shown that if the homosexuals of the first type (i.e. psychogenic) have normal urinary hormone excretions, those of the second type, on the contrary, sometimes excrete an excessive quantity of ambivalent oestrogens (oestrone), and sometimes even a notable quantity of oestradiol, that is to say an oestrogen that we should never meet in the male.' (My translation.)

Such research work is always honest and no doubt in a few cases (about

1 or 2 per cent.) endocrine abnormalities are discoverable, but they are to be found in those who are not abnormally orientated, and it is to be expected that the work of Cossa will, like similar previous research, not be confirmed. Other organic research negatives such assertions. Surely, for example, where there are conditions, dependent on genetic factors, producing endocrine abnormalities, such as intersexuality, hermaphroditism, agonadism, and Klinefelter's syndrome, we should expect to see homosexual reactions, if genetic or hormonal factors have any validity at all. In a recent book edited by Overzier on intersexuality not one single author of the eighteen specialists who contributed to it reported anything of the kind. Every variety of physical condition was reported, but no single case of homosexuality was found to result. Those who support the genetic or hormonal causation of homosexuality must explain why this is so.

We can accept with confidence the assertion made by Swyer that: 'There is no convincing evidence that human homosexuality is dependent on hormonal aberrations.'

I am reluctantly driven to the conclusion that there is, so far, no evidence upon which any reliance can be placed that there is any endocrine difference between 'normal' and homosexual. This is in accordance with the clinical finding that castration does not cause a man to be homosexual, nor does it even, in all cases, cause cessation of heterosexual intercourse. Moreover, injection of female hormones fails to make a man behave homosexually if he has previously been normal. The endocrine factor may be ancillary but is not the basic cause.

Hirschfeld's insistence on the physical intersexuality of the homosexual has been proved unreliable and untrue by numerous authors. Weil's data appeared to support Hirschfeld's view, but they have been re-analysed by Wortis who found them valueless. *I can state with confidence that there is no discernible difference between the physique of the homosexual and heterosexual by any tests, microscopical, macroscopical, biochemical, or endocrine of which we are aware at present.* As far as I can discover it appears that the view of Wortis, which is that the homosexual appears effeminate because he wishes to look feminine, is the correct one and that there is no physical differentiation present in the average case.

This view has been supported by work on oral smears to determine the chromosomal sex. Dixon and Torr in tests on 260 normal individuals found the method was accurate and then applied it to 60 cases of abnormal physical and psychological sexual development. They state: 'The present series includes cases of true and pseudo-hermaphrodites. The method has been particularly useful in separating out those cases with definite physical abnormalities—for example, Klinefelter's and Turner's syndrome—from those of an essentially psychological nature, without resort to laparotomy. *In the psychologically maladjusted group it has been our invariable experience that the physical sex diagnosis is borne out by the chromosomal sex findings'* (my italics).

Similar conclusions were reached by Barr and Hobbs who examined 194 male homosexuals and 5 male transvestites. These invariably gave masculine readings. Raboch and Nedoma stated that it is likely that, in any group of homosexuals, the proportion of those having a chromatin sex status inconsistent with their apparent sex is no greater than amongst those with normal sexual leanings. This has been confirmed by Pritchard who investigated the problem very thoroughly, and stated that over the past twenty years nuclear sex has always been proved to be consistent with phenotypic sex. In a series of six male homosexuals the study of somatic chromosomes confirmed the sex chromosome constitution as male in each case. He added that Lang's hypothesis can no longer be regarded as tenable.

Such work appears to dismiss effectively Slater's suggestion that homosexuality is sometimes caused by chromosomal abnormality, but many still have a singular reluctance to abandon the idea.

Anthropological investigations confirm the views of Wortis that there is no physical indication of homosexuality. Coppen, for example, stated, 'The androgyny score (i.e. $3 \times$ biacromal $= 1 \times$ bi-iliac diameters, in centimetres), however, did not differentiate the homosexuals from the controls any better than did the biacromial diameter, which is less in these patients. It was concluded that homosexuals have a body-build similar to that found in patients with other psychiatric disorders and that it could not be specifically related to their sexual disorder.'

Ellis, in America, has recently examined the available data and has come to exactly the same conclusions I have been stating for the past 20 years. He writes:

Several hypotheses concerning the possible innateness or direct constitutional causation of confirmed homosexuality have been examined, including the theories that it is genetically caused, is hormonally based, is directly connected with an individual's body-build, is almost completely untreatable, is the result of brain damage, and is historically and culturally uniform in incidence. When critically reviewed, all these hypotheses are found to be distinctly lacking in objective, confirmatory evidence of a scientific nature. What has been found, at most, is that certain genetic, hormonal, and anatomic factors may well help *in*directly to produce homosexuality in some subjects, and particularly, perhaps, in those with tendencies towards severe emotional disturbance, hormonal imbalance, and physiologic immaturity.

It would be wearisome to labour the point. No investigations in any sphere indicate an organic basis for homosexuality, whether physical, chemical, cellular, microscopic, or macroscopic.

Yet in spite of such overwhelming evidence, the persistence of the idea that homosexuality can be divided into essential (genetic, inborn, innate, &c.) and environmentally determined types is incredible. Thus the Memorandum of Evidence prepared by the Special Committee of the British Medical Association for submission to the Wolfenden Committee states: 'The genetic basis of homosexuality is not entirely accepted by everyone, but doctors do see patients whose homosexual tendencies appear to be so fixed that they seem inborn.'

The view that a fixed tendency must be inborn is surely surprising, and depends entirely on the efficacy of treatment available. A man remains homosexual because he is not correctly treated and therefore it is concluded that his tendency is inborn. However, many homosexuals respond to proper therapy and if he is one of these he recovers—therefore his condition is acquired! Surely it is time that we abandoned such arguments.

The psychological basis of homosexuality is one which has been a long time coming to the front. It is only with the great developments of psychiatry in the past fifty years that dynamic explanations have been possible. Yet there is no doubt of the importance of this factor.

Firstly, it is always assumed that homosexuality and heterosexuality are diametrically opposite conditions. There is absolutely nothing to prove that this is so. It is not so in the behaviour of apes. I have stated elsewhere:

When we study sexual abnormalities from the psychological point of view we see that the laboratory worker finds the problem artificially simplified. To him it appears that homosexuality is a clear-cut clinical entity and contra-distinguished from heterosexuality. To the clinician this is not the case. Homo-sexuality is mixed inseparably with a whole host of other perversions (i.e. abnormal ways of obtaining sexual pleasure). The writer has seen cases in which it has been mixed with sadism, masochism, exhibitionism, voyeurism, frotteurism, and transvestism. They may practise cunnilingus, fellatio, inter-mammary intercourse, anal intercourse, with both sexes, and bestiality. Other rarer perversions such as urinary and urethral perversions and pygmalionism may be part of the syndrome, as well as various fetishisms. Anyone who can explain these perversions by an endocrine abnormality will earn the clinical psychologists' gratitude and a certain fortune.

This point of view is supported by the researches of Kinsey on the basis of great experience. His data were drawn from a large series of 5,300 males and 5,940 females, all white, in the United States over a period of fifteen years. Thus he was provided with an enormous series of 11,240 individuals which gave a general view of human sex behaviour.

His statistics showed that male exceeded female homosexuality by roughly half as much. He states:

The incidence and frequencies of homosexual responses and contacts, and consequently the incidence of the homosexual ratings, were much lower among the females in our sample than they were among the males on whom we have previously reported. Among the females the accumulative incidences of homosexual responses had ultimately reached 28 per cent.: they had reached 50 per cent. in the males. The accumulative incidences of overt contacts to the point of orgasm among the females had reached 13 per cent.: among the males they had reached 37 per cent. This means that homosexual responses had occurred in about half as many females as males, and contacts which had proceeded to orgasm had occurred in about a third as many females as males. Moreover, compared with the males, there were only about half to a third as many of the females who were, in any age period, primarily or exclusively homosexual.

A much smaller proportion of the females had continued their homosexual activities for as many years as most of the males in the sample.

A much larger proportion (71 per cent.) of the females who had had any homosexual contact had restricted their homosexual activities to a single partner or two: only 51 per cent. of the males who had had homosexual experience had so restricted their contacts. Many of the males had been highly promiscuous, sometimes finding scores or hundreds of sexual partners.

Kinsey states further: 'In brief, homosexuality is not the rare phenomenon which it is ordinarily considered to be, but a type of behaviour which ultimately may involve as much as half the male population. Any hormonal or other explanation of the phenomenon must ultimately take this into account.' He points out, moreover, what most psychiatrists specializing in sexology had already found, that there are very few homosexuals who have not had some, and in many cases a great deal of, heterosexual experience.

Kinsey has much the same views as those I have put forward in the past. He states categorically:

The literature constantly makes a sharp distinction between incidental and exclusive homosexual experience, between so-called 'acquired, latent, and congenital (constitutional) homosexuality' and between 'true inverts' and 'normals'. But although we have more detailed data on a larger number of cases than are recorded in any of the published studies, we fail to find any basis for recognizing discrete types of homosexual behaviour. An analysis on any basis will show every type of intergradation between the extremes of our series. There are individuals who have had a lone and more or less accidental experience; there are cases which have had as many as fifteen or twenty thousand homosexual contacts. But between these individuals there are cases which involve all points between one and twenty thousand.

It is a little difficult to credit the statement that some had had as many as 20,000 homosexual contacts, since this means a daily contact for approximately 60 years. If the young man started his homosexual career at 15 he would have to continue steadily until aged 75! Although it is possible to have intercourse daily for a long time one is entitled to doubt if it can be maintained for quite such a period. It would seem that the patient exaggerated and his story was accepted uncritically.

In spite of the work of Kinsey and others there has been an attempt to divide homosexuals into 'inverts' and 'perverts'. This was put forward in the Church of England's *The Problem of Homosexuality* in 1954, and was used by the counsel in the Montague trial. It was suggested that 'an invert is a man who from accident or birth has unnatural desires . . . whereas a pervert is a man who either from lust or wickedness will get desires for either natural or unnatural functions.'

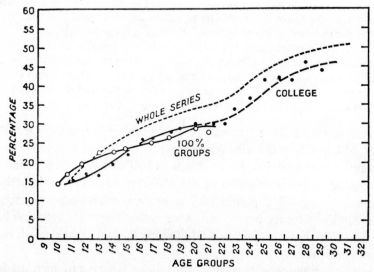

Homosexuality. Incidence. *After* Kinsey. This graph shows the number of homosexual contacts increasing with age until by 30 some half of the subjects had had homosexual experience. It is to be noticed that the college students, presumably more intellectual and better educated, differ little from the whole series.

I must point out with all due respect that this view is quite untenable no matter how much it may seem important morally. Behaviour, in this case, is merely a measure of either the strength of the urge or the power of the controlling force. If the urge is weak and the controlling force is strong no behaviour may result but if the desire is strong and the repressive forces weak then sexual conduct breaks out. It may be compared to the pressure of steam in a boiler. Whether this can be held in check or whether it blows up the machine is immaterial as far as the nature of the steam is concerned.

That a large number of homosexuals never give way to overt sexual activity is without doubt. These form a large group of bachelors who drift through life without forming any connexions. Naturally all bachelors must not be regarded as homosexual since there are men who prefer not to marry for various reasons, but who find some sexual outlet by keeping a mistress, visiting prostitutes, and so on. Nevertheless many are homosexually inclined and if it is desirable to divide them from practising homosexuals the inactive may be nominated 'inverts'. However, con-

sidering that Kinsey's statistics (see table below) show such a large number of men have had homosexual experience the number of bachelors
who are inverts must be very small indeed. It is felt, in any case, that the
whole categorization of homosexuals in this way is a mistake and has been
done only to show that some are morally pure.

AGE	ESTIMATED FREQUENCY		PERCENTAGE HOMOSEXUAL	
	HOMOSEXUAL	HETEROSEXUAL		
				HETEROSEXUAL
24	0	450	0	
22	4	550	1	
19	30	1000	3	
22	15	200	7	
24	30	266	10	
31	200	200	14	
22	21,400	10,000	19	
25	150	600	20	
22	30	100	23	
34	800	2,250	26	
19	150	300	33	
27	1,400	2,400	37	
26	350	475	43	
26	150	180	50	
26	200	200	50	
22	200	150	57	
24	3,000	2,000	60	
26	1,200	700	63	
22	100	50	67	
21	500	150	77	
29	15,000	4,200	78	
21	800	200	80	
31	1000	200	83	
25	700	100	88	
27	1,250	100	93	
29	2,000	100	95	
41	3,000	100	97	
19	500	4	99	
24	1,600	0	100	
			100	HOMOSEXUAL

Homosexuality. Graduations between heterosexuality and homosexuality. *After* Kinsey.

Another classification which Kinsey's experience tends to undermine
is the division into passive and active homosexuals. He says: 'A popular
opinion bases a classification on the technics involved in the physical
relation, and makes a sharp division between the so-called active and
passive partners in the relation. Many of the so-called "passives" regularly
show that they can respond to homosexual stimulation by coming to
climax in the (active) relation.' He finds that out of 108 individuals 55
(i.e. 51 per cent.) have made distinctly successful heterosexual adjustments. He found that exclusively homosexual or heterosexual behaviour

may be replaced in a later period of life by more or less exclusive behaviour in the opposite direction.

We must accept that although there is no hard-and-fast division between 'active' and 'passive' homosexuality there is some use in the distinction, since most of those physicians who have studied these cases find that some homosexuals do *generally* take a passive role whereas others usually behave actively although there is nothing to stop them changing their behaviour, as, for instance, when an active pervert meets a more dominant partner and behaves passively. The terms therefore are useful although by no means hard and fast.

Statistics from Sweden suggest that a much lower percentage of the population are inverted. They show that at least 1 per cent. of men are exclusively homosexual and 4 per cent. bisexual. However, the Swedes themselves doubt the validity of these figures and believe them to be higher.

If Kinsey's statistics are valid in England with its population of 18,000,000 adult males then we have some 900,000 men exclusively and 5,400,000 partially homosexual. Even if the Swedish statistics alone are valid there are 180,000 exclusively and 720,000 partially homosexual.

It is unwise, therefore, to accept the statement of the Wolfenden Committee which says: 'Our conclusion is that homosexual behaviour is practised by a small minority of the population, and should be seen in proper perspective, neither ignored nor given a disproportionate amount of public attention.'

One cannot help wondering if the Committee would be so calmly judicial if such a large percentage of the population—somewhere about a million—were affected by some other chronic disease.

It is obvious from the work of Kinsey and others that the genetic and endocrine factors cannot be other than ancillary, if active at all. Some other and more powerful causation must be at work. This I believe to be the psychological one.

PSYCHOPATHOLOGY

It has been seen that if frogs are unable to find a suitable partner at their mating time they will attempt to mate with pieces of wood. So strong is the instinct to copulate that an animal, and presumably a man, will attempt to perform sexual congress with unsuitable partners if no suitable ones are available. This was shown very clearly by a valuable piece of research which was performed with almost mathematical exactitude by Jenkins. He found that if rats were segregated sexually so that the males and females were confined in separate places and no possible contact with the other sex allowed, then, after some time, homosexual behaviour would commence. This grew in proportion according to the length of segregation. He then found that if he waited until a proportion of his animals were attempting to make homosexual 'matings' and introduced animals of the opposite sex they showed little heterosexual interest and were not attracted to each other. The number of those which remained homosexual and the number which regained their heterosexuality was strictly dependent on the length of time they had been segregated. If this time was short only a small number of the animals were affected, but by prolonging the temporal separation it could be made general. The longer the segregation the greater the number of rats which showed diminished heterosexuality on mixing with the other sex. These results have been confirmed by reliable investigators. The rule appears to hold for other animals as well as rats.

It is not surprising, therefore, if the same rule holds for human beings as well as for other mammals. In our civilization everything possible is done to discourage sexuality, as William Brend has so brilliantly shown in his book. Under such conditions it is inevitable that a large percentage of the population (different observers have calculated from 2 to 10 per cent.) should be thus abnormal. Looked at from this point of view homosexuality seems to be merely the substitution for a heterosexual mate. Nevertheless, there is more in the matter than this. Strong conditioning appears to be able to have an effect, as is shown in the very interesting case of the Big Nambas, a cannibal race which lives in Malekula in the New Hebrides. Harrisson says:

The first thing which one notices among the Big Nambas is the way the men go around behind the boys and the boys are the fond servants to the men. This homosexuality system is ancient, with its own technique and nomenclature, relationship regulations as to which boys you may like. Each man has his boy, if he can get one; he guards him more jealously than his female wife. The two often grow very fond of each other. Men who have boys have one or more wives and children. There are more children per head in this area than any other part of Malekula. The women have a parallel pleasure system.

It is noticeable that this curious system is traditional, that there is no impotence such as one frequently finds in homosexuals who attempt to mate with females under our European code. Real circumcision is done and the initiation rites or 'manhood rites' at puberty are severe and end in a terrific heterosexual orgy.[1] This seems to show that homosexuality can be in some cases an ancillary to typical heterosexual behaviour and the result of environment. The real clue to the matter appears to be that the man takes on a father position and he himself is used by the boy as a substitute for the mother. The remarkable thing is that the boy loiters in

---

[1] An orgy demonstrates weak heterosexuality rather than strong instinctual desires since it means that it is necessary to whip up the feelings by special circumstances.

the stage of homosexuality until puberty and then suddenly swings round to heterosexuality (although, of course, the system allows him to retain an active homosexual outlet). Unfortunately Harrisson does not mention the nature of the homosexual practices these people use. This form of social homosexuality is curiously akin to that which was practised by the ancient Spartans. There the friendship was rather between men and adolescent boys. The association was essentially for instruction; as Plato says, 'its aim is to educate'.

Fenichel gives a very clear account of homosexuality from the psychoanalytical point of view. He writes:

In certain situations where there are no women—at sea, in prison, &c.—a man who under normal circumstances would be sexually normal establishes homosexual relationships. This fact proves first of all the general distribution of the 'latent' perversion, which we call psychological bisexuality. Without the latter such a transient turn to homosexuality would be unthinkable. This leads us to the question whether all types of homosexuality might not be the result of similar circumstances, i.e. a situation in which the absence of a woman determines the inversion, except that instead of external circumstances, internal ones might exclude one from contact with a woman. In other words, it might be that for some problematic reasons no woman exists for the homosexual. Two facts lend extremely strong support to this hypothesis. First of all, a number of homosexuals when questioned closely admit that, despite their original assertion, they are not indifferent to women; or on the contrary, they assume towards them a resistive attitude, they consider the woman or the female genitalia as horrible or disgusting. Just as so-called unmusical people are not indifferent towards music but perceive it as something unpleasant and thus show that with them it is not a matter of absence of musical capacity but that of a psychogenic inhibition, so do homosexuals show that the choice of a woman as the object of love became impossible to them on account of some inner psychological circumstance. The second account which appears to corroborate our hypothesis is observed in those individuals who turned to homosexuality following an acute disappointment in a woman, as if they said to themselves: I shall never have anything to do with the sex at whose hands I have had so much suffering; as far as I am concerned there exist no women. It is quite probable that such a sharp turn towards homosexuality as the result of a disappointment would not take place, were it not for the fact that the disappointment in some way becomes connected with another one, which is deeply seated and which occurred in childhood and was repressed.

We thus assume that homosexuals are men who in some way experienced a very deep disappointment which turned them against the female sex. Psychoanalysis also confirms the following rule, which was formulated for the neurosis: whenever the difference between genitalia of the sexes (which in itself is, in reality, of relatively little importance) is found to have an outstanding meaning in the unconscious of the individual, whenever we find that a person's relationship to a fellow human being are unconsciously determined by the other person's sex, we may be certain that we are dealing with the castration complex. This is in accordance with the fact that the rejection of women by the homosexual is a distinctly genital one: a number of homosexual men make good friends with women and respect them highly, but any genital friendship frightens them away. Psychoanalysis of homosexuals has heretofore always brought out the fact that homosexual men suffer from repressed memories, from castration anxiety arising from the perception of female genitalia. Freud formulates this attitude in the following manner; the homosexual man, he says, is so insistent on the idea of a penis that he refuses to miss it in his sexual partner. One could also give a negative turn to this formula; homosexual men are so frightened at the sight of a being without a penis, that they reject any sexual relationships with such a partner.

The sight of the female genitals may arouse in a boy a sense of disappointment or anxiety reactions connected with the castration complex in the following two ways; first, as Freud pointed out, the actual absence of a penis in a woman, i.e. the recognition of the fact that there are actually human beings without a penis, leads to the conclusion that one actually might also become such a being; in other words, old threats of castration might be revived by such observations. Secondly the female genitalia, through the unconscious connexion of castration anxiety with old oral anxieties, is perceived as an instrument of castration, an instrument which might bite or tear off the penis. Quite frequently the combination of both trends is met with.

There are many reactions to such a castration shock provoked by the sight of female genitalia. This shock is in no way pathognomonic of homosexuals; it may be found quite frequently in many heterosexual men. Only the reaction to this shock can be characteristic to homosexuals. Following the loss of an object or following the disappointment in an object, all persons tend to regress from the level of object love to the preliminary phase of this love, i.e. to the phase of identification; in other words, they become psychologically the object which they cannot possibly possess. The homosexual individual, also, identifies himself with the woman following his disappointment in the latter, but what determines whether he will become homosexual is how and in what respect this identification takes place and in what particulars this identification is manifest. In a homosexual individual this identification takes place in regard to object choice; following his disappointment in his mother, like her, he loves only men.

I have taken this long quotation from Fenichel because it demonstrates so well the psychoanalytical point of view which is so important in this connexion. I do not, however, believe that this is the complete picture. It seems to me that homosexuality can be produced by the persistence of excessive emotion, either negative or positive, which has been aroused by the parents in the past. I will take, for example, the case of the man, since sexuality in the male is more clear cut and easier to study. I believe that homosexuality can be caused by one of four ways:

1. Hostility to the mother.
2. Excessive affection for the mother } Oedipus complex.
3. Hostility to the father
4. Affection for the father when the father himself does not show sufficient heterosexual traits; introjection of an abnormal father.

Hostility to the Mother

Affection for the mother (or some mother substitute) forms as it were a psychological bridge by which the boy is able to transfer his love from her to other women. In general one may say that human beings tend to transfer emotion from the parent of the opposite sex to the mate. Thus in obsessional women one sometimes finds fears of killing the husband which conceal deep-seated hostility towards the father and so on. It is inevitable in all persons that the emotion they transfer from the parent of opposite sex should be ambivalent to some slight extent. Nevertheless, there does appear to be a certain number of men who have never been able to develop affection for the mother. It is not unusual, for example, to find that homosexuality springs up in the institutional child who has had little or no contact with a woman until he leaves the home at puberty. Although these children may be compared with the segregated rats of Jenkins which became homosexual, there is a more complex psychological factor in their case. The child who has unconscious hate for its mother, or who has never had a woman to love, cannot learn to transfer affection to other women because it has never developed any. The process of falling in love heterosexually in such cases must be comparable to the 'mannering' of a savage horse by slow conditioning—and even then the product may be unstable. However, in these men there is often a substitution for the mother in some convenient male, particularly so when affection becomes allied with surreptitious sexual practices such as we find in institutional life. A patient once said to me: 'One has to be taught how to love (i.e. women) and I have never been taught how to do it.'

The type who has persistent hatred, sometimes for good reasons, for the mother finds it difficult to approach women. They represent to him someone he hates and if he does mate with them it is rather a woman he can dominate, or thinks that he can do so, such as a prostitute. More often he drifts into homosexuality and finding it pleasurable becomes more and more conditioned to it.

This hatred for the parent of opposite sex is, in my experience, the mechanism *par excellence* for homosexuality in the woman by lack of what I call 'emotional bridging'. In females the process of moulding the personality seems less important in the formation of psychosexual abnormality than the ability to love the father, and so form an emotional bridge by which she can transfer her love to other men. If she hates her father she is unable to do so and is left in a state of deprivation, which allows her to be an easy prey to other women eager to intruct her in the ways of inversion.

One can sometimes detect women of this type because they do not dress in an excessively male manner, although they may wear trousers, but are usually neglected, dirty and rather like an uncared-for child. The basic unhappiness of her condition often makes her willing to co-operate in treatment which is frequently successful.

Negative conditioning seems to produce a more active revulsion. For example, Hadfield has recorded cases which suggest a definite example of this mechanism. In one case a serving woman a man slept with as an infant, stimulated him sexually and then put his hand on her vagina, which disgusted and frightened him. The result was he grew up very homosexual with no interest in women. The other patient was an illegitimate child and the mother tried to smother him, by first overlaying him, and later with a pillow. In his forms of childish play he 'suffocated' himself with a pillow, and removed it just in time. As Hadfield says, this is typical of a child working out its problems in play. Both these cases responded to psychotherapy.

Excessive Love for the Mother

This is, of course, only one side of the Oedipus complex, but frequently this side is developed with very feeble hostility towards the father. It is as if one 'leg' of the complex alone had appeared. The father is, as far as the child is concerned, a nonentity. This occurs when the father dies whilst the child is an infant, or when he is forced by circumstance to spend long years abroad. The boy has no one to mould himself upon, no masculine person to introject, and so identifies himself more and more with the mother. Often a boy picks out some admirable male in the environment and uses him as a father surrogate, but sometimes this is impossible. For example, it is commonly noticed that there tends to be a wave of homosexuality following wars. This was very evident in Germany after the First World War. It would be exceedingly difficult to explain this on the basis of homosexuality being inborn. The only explanation on this basis could be that the hunger and hardship which almost invariably occur in war-time influence the women in some way so that they bring forth children with this inborn peculiarity. Since one of the theories explaining the increase in *male* children in war-time is the effect of such hardships on the parents, it is obvious that this theory cannot be applied to homosexuality except with regard to females. But as a matter of fact it seems that the increase is in male homosexuality, so obviously there must be some other reason. I believe that the increase in male homosexuality after wars is because the fathers and elder brothers are away fighting and so leave the young boys without any proper males to use as unconscious models upon which to mould themselves into masculinity. The boy has only his mother; his teachers are, in war-time, often women; his father is away and too shadowy an object for identification; the result is inevitable. This view is, of course, contrary to the psychoanalytical one that introjection takes place only in infancy and childhood: but I believe that this is too narrow.

I have already pointed out in Chapter 3 that this moulding of the personality, which is probably akin to conditioning continues, at least until puberty, when the boy tends to rebel against his parents. It appears instinctual, but much more fluid, like all human responses, than imprinting in birds (which takes place in only a brief period). Once it is effected, however, it tends to be difficult to eradicate.

This point of view is supported by the work of Bieber *et al.*, although based on psychoanalytical work. They were able to produce statistical evidence that the part played by the mothers of homosexuals in their lives was much more than those of normal men. In general it seems at least twice as much.

The unfortunate child, then, who is brought up with no male element in the environment becomes excessively attached to the females and identifies himself with them. This may be the explanation of the widespread homosexuality in the East where the child is brought up in the harem until puberty and has few male contacts. Identifying himself with women he feels himself feminine and can love only males. The manifestations of homosexuality which follow are the results partly of physical limitation, partly of conditioning, and partly of the psychosexual development so stressed by Freud and his followers.

(There is another factor, mentioned here for completeness, which causes an increase of homosexuality in war-time and that is the confinement of men in prison camps and otherwise segregated from females. I have pointed out that the work of Jenkins shows the inevitable increase in homosexuality which results. Many of these male homosexuals return to civilian life and do not revert to normality. Boys are assaulted by them and turned into abnormal channels.) There may be other factors which are ancillary which we do not yet understand. The fact that there is a war in every generation is sufficient to renew the pool of inverts before the disease has a chance to die out spontaneously.

Hostility to the Father

Hostility to the father is the other side of the Oedipus complex. It is very common in the study of homosexuals to find that the father is unsuitable, that he is alcoholic, brutal, and ill-treats the mother. It is as if his behaviour had perpetuated and aggravated the Oedipus hatred and turned the boy more towards his mother. There is clearly no urge to identify himself with the father but rather the opposite—he turns away from what he feels is bestial masculinity towards the kinder and more desirable femininity. Masculinity to the boy represents brutal domination, cruelty, and often alcoholism, he spurns it and accepts the gentler mother as the ideal and more desirable mould upon which to shape his personality. This is, of course, not simply a conscious choice but controlled also by deeply unconscious factors. Nevertheless, the conscious feelings in the matter are not to be disregarded. The conscious element also may complicate treatment inasmuch as the patient has no wish to be like the brute he has known as a father. The grown man represents the father to him and so he chooses young men of his own age or boys, instead, as a sexual object.

O'Connor regards the effect of the relationship with the father from a more behaviouristic point of view. He examined 50 homosexuals and 50 neurotic patients he saw in the R.A.F. and concluded 'that emotional rapport between father and son delays maturation of the instinct of self-reproduction'.

Gebhard et al. in their large series of sexual offenders, 2,274 in all, found that in general all types of homosexuals (those who interfere with children, minors and adults) had had poor relationships with their fathers and a greater attachment to their mothers. Moreover, there was inter-parental friction in 35 per cent. of cases.

Eva Bene in a sample of self-confessed homosexuals and 84 married men found that previous results were confirmed; that is that homosexual men more frequently than normal men had had bad relations with their fathers. She did not find, however, that they had been more strongly attached, over-indulged, and over-protected by their mothers.

In female homosexuals, in a series of 37 lesbians and 80 married women, the lesbians were more hostile to, and fearful of their fathers, and they felt more often that their fathers were weak and incompetent. The results also pointed to a relationship between the parents' wish for a son and the homosexuality of their daughter.

Kay et al. made a study of female inverts and found that 'Homosexuality in women, rather than being a conscious volitional preference, is a massive adaptational response to a crippling inhibition of normal heterosexual development.' They believe that 'the heterosexual drive is interfered with or blocked, by anxiety, inhibition or threat'. This is caused by (a) a significant history of threats or punishment for sex play with boys, and (b) fear of or aversion to the male penis, scrotum or ejaculate. They believe that the fathers of homosexual females tend to be puritanical, exploitive and feared by their daughters.

This type of father was found also by Apperson and McAdoo, who believe that he produces homosexuality in the female child because he is critical, impatient, and rejecting.

Important though it is, such research does not preclude the influence of the mother, but may merely mean that the subtler relationship is not so easily revealed.

Novelists and dramatists, who by necessity examine human beings with a dispassionate eye, sometimes observe things which others pass over. Thus Tennessee Williams in his play *Cat on a Hot Tin Roof* depicted this type of homosexuality, and moreover, showed the victim steadily drinking himself into chronic alcoholism. The father was depicted not as necessarily a bad man, but overwhelming and one who had never given his son the affection and love which he craved.

Excessive Affection for an Insufficiently Male Father

A great show of affection may sometimes conceal a deeply seated hostility, but there is no doubt that in some cases affection which is not over-compensatory is sometimes a cause of homosexuality. In this case we believe that it causes the introjection of an insufficiently masculine personality. For example, a man marries a woman and because he is not sufficiently masculine she leaves him after the birth of a son. The father brings up the child and the boy moulds himself unconsciously upon his father. The result will be that he introjects his father's personality *in toto* and is not completely masculine as a result. As well as this the mother's desertion has produced hostility to her and the boy is told constantly that all women are vicious. There is little surprise that he grows up homosexual. I have seen a case in which a father surrogate produced this sort of thing. The father was a fussy type of man but not undesirable, the mother was a normal woman. At the age of 11 years their son was seduced by a homosexual schoolmaster who came to live with the family. The boy worshipped this man and undoubtedly moulded himself, consciously and unconsciously, upon him. The result was that he, also, became homosexual.

A curious point which is not always clarified is that not only is the patient identified unconsciously with the mother but the sexual object has also undergone a similar identification. When one analyses a patient one invariably discovers that the *homosexual love object is only the mother in disguise.* This is, of course, entirely unconscious and the patient is entirely unaware of it. By means of this curious identification of the love object various attributes of the mother become metamorphosed into parts of the male. Thus, for instance, the breast is transmuted into the penis and this explains the frequent fellatio which occurs with homosexuals. Similarly it may be identified with the buttocks and is the reason for homosexual sadism falling upon the buttocks. In exactly the same way the maternal vagina is symbolized by the anus or mouth and vice versa. (This is shown by the fantasy of the vagina having teeth.) The anal intercourse is only unconscious incestuous behaviour, although it has undergone considerable transmutation. Perhaps the diagram will show what has happened more clearly than a description.

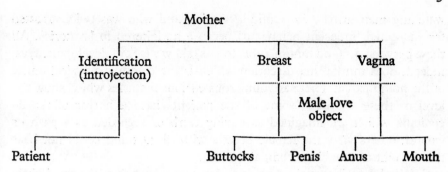

It is difficult to understand why, for instance, homosexuals are frequently attracted to men in tight breeches until one realizes that the buttocks beneath the stretched cloth represent breasts. Once one has understood the psychopathology beneath all this behaviour the whole thing becomes comprehensible. This important mechanism—the identification of the mother with the homosexual love object—is not stressed by the psychoanalysts, perhaps because it does not fit in easily with the Freudian idea of introjection as the basis of identification.

I have pointed out its reality for many years, although others occasionally deny it. Nevertheless, it is always present and only those who do not look fail to find it and deny its reality.

Homosexuality is the most complex of all the sexual neuroses and I do not pretend for one moment that the various combinations and permutations of the causal elements which have been given here exhaust the genesis of it. There is no doubt that evidence can be produced to show that homosexuals have fixations anywhere along the avenue of emotional development. For example, the frequency of fellatio in them shows that oral fixations, that is, over-attachment to the mother and particularly to the breast, are of importance. The anal practices are indications of a fixation in that stage in some cases (Havelock Ellis says that 15 per cent. and Hirschfeld believes 8 per cent. of inverts indulge in this form of sexual congress). Freund concluded from a series of 222 male homosexuals that the sexual outlets were oral, anal, interfemoral, and manual in that order of frequency. We must remember, however, that these perversions do not occur in all cases since some homosexuals are disgusted at the thought of anal or oral indulgence (Havelock Ellis states that 20 per cent. of homosexuals never indulge in sex of any kind, and 30–35 per cent. masturbate so that at least half of the homosexual population never indulge in oral or anal sexuality).

Homosexuality may be tied to almost any other perversion. I have seen homosexual sadists, homosexual masochists, homosexual infanto-exhibitionists (exposure of a man to young boys), and a curious case of a homosexual ondine voyeur—a man who obtained sexual pleasure from watching men urinate in public lavatories, and who was twice arrested for suspected 'indecent behaviour' because he loitered in lavatories. All these perversions (and innumerable others) show a lack of development, as, indeed, does mutual masturbation which is the common physical outlet of the homosexual. There are numerous curious fantasies which show the level of these fixations; some of the patients have a horror of female genitalia which are imagined as having teeth or regarded as a gash or wound, others view the female breasts with disgust and could not bear the thought of touching them, and so on.

Fenichel describes various types of development such as the narcissistic homosexual who loves young boys who appear to him as he thinks he appeared in youth, and who treats them as he would have wished his mother to have treated him. Also the anal type 'who strives to submit himself to his father genitally' (i.e. anally). He thus explains the active and passive behaviour of the homosexual. (I have pointed out that although this active and passive behaviour is by no means fixed, undoubtedly at any given time the protagonists do usually accept one or other role.)

It is unfortunate that the psychoanalysts, to whom we owe so much of our knowledge of sexual abnormality, have tended to disregard the importance of emotional metamorphosis which occurs at puberty. Ernest Jones demonstrated that the boy at this time passes through the earlier psychological phases in a truncated recapitulation. It seems to be that this time is one of particular danger as far as sexual trauma is concerned. This is the age when a boy is most attractive to the adult invert and when he is most likely to be subject to interference.

The Ministry of Education must be given due praise for appreciating the danger of homosexual schoolmasters and for taking precautions to prevent the tragic events of the past. Private schools are now inspected and masters who have been prosecuted for sexual misconduct are frequently told that they must see a psychiatrist and if necessary be under supervision to make certain that they are safe to continue teaching. This should greatly diminish offences since, although no psychiatrist can pretend to foresee all possible lapses in such cases, he can often help patients to avoid dangerous situations, or inform the authorities if the man is quite unsuitable.

In spite of the fact that the Ministry of Education and the officials of the Scout movement realize the dangers, and will not willingly allow homosexuals access to boys, yet they still obtain access and interfere with them.

At the expense of being repetitive it must be emphasized that to deliberately seek out a position where one, as a schoolmaster or Scout-master, is placed *in loco parentis*, is to aggravate the offence and the law takes this into consideration. The man who uses his position to assault boys will be, rightly, given a much heavier sentence than the unfortunate who is faced with sudden temptation for which he made no provision and who is unable to withstand his abnormal urges.

The result of allowing abnormal men to occupy a position of authority is that almost invariably, sooner or later, they succumb to their inverted urges and interfere sexually with those in their charge. Nor must we conclude that this sort of thing occurs only where the male sex is concerned. Schoolmistresses, female employers of girls, and even hospital sisters occasionally instigate homosexual behaviour with the young girls in their care.

The result of such acts, particularly with a boy or girl about the age of puberty, is that the emotional stage through which he or she is passing becomes accentuated because of the sexual pleasure resulting from the behaviour. It has been observed again and again in experimental psychology that pleasure 'stamps in' a form of reaction and makes its repetition more likely to recur. At puberty the homosexual stage in both sexes is most evident and boys and girls eschew the opposite sex. The pervert excuses himself because his victim is homosexual and thinks he does no harm. It is just because all boys and girls are homosexual at puberty that such conduct is particularly dangerous since it is likely to make them remain so the rest of their lives. Boys and girls are more homosexual than heterosexual before puberty, and this phase is only the zenith of the danger period. *Any perverted interference before manifestation of well-marked heterosexual behaviour must be regarded as likely to have serious consequences.*

Again, when we analyse a man who has had such trauma in youth we discover that it has produced deeper 'faults' in the strata of his mental development. The schoolmaster, or whoever it is who interfered with him, frequently takes on the position of a father surrogate so that the boy introjects the man's personality and identifies himself with him. He thus moulds himself and shapes his personality on a man who is abnormal and who frequently glorifies homosexuality (to justify himself to the boy). This, to minimize the position, is unfortunate and gives a wrong perspective, but in actual fact produces a distorted and inverted man.

Again and again in analysis one discovers in homosexuals a tremendous desire to be loved. This must be present throughout their development and it is this seeking for affection which places the youth in such a dangerous position. It is essential that all who have dealings with boys and young men should realize how dangerous it is to allow their friendly feelings to become overtly sexualized and what havoc this can produce in youthful development if it does occur.

I cannot accentuate too firmly the necessity for proper parental interest in the child, particularly from the parent of the same sex, the necessity of the boy seeing much of his father so that he 'can learn to be a man' from him. At school a boy should be taught by a master of good personality (and of course a girl by a similar mistress). No boy should be subjected to abnormal interference by choirmasters, clergymen, or anyone else, no matter under what cloak of holiness and sanctity nor however disguised. Puberty must be regarded as a difficult period and the boy or girl should be helped to find heterosexuality by the encouragement of dancing, and similar heterosexual amusements. Probably co-educational schools are beneficial, but this is a point which is not yet determined.

Even when the boy is not markedly inverted, but immature (not having progressed beyond puberty), he may still drift into homosexuality. I find that a large number of timid, shy men who have drifted into homosexual relations have done so *because they are afraid of women.* They have never developed the male aggressiveness, and literally do not know how to make love to a girl. They feel that if they do she will be shocked. As women seem inaccessible to them they have sexual relations with a similar timid man as a *faute de mieux.* It comes as a revelation to such men that girls, also, wish to be loved, that they are seeking a mate, and want a man to take them out and show them affection. Even when this is not quite so severe and the young man has been out with a girl often he has not been able to regard her as a sexual object. He has taken her to cinemas or restaurants and treated her as if she were another man. Similarly the idea that she might be willing to respond to him sexually and not scream for the police if he kissed her never seems to have crossed his mind.

It was wrongly suggested by the Wolfenden Committee that left alone such men would soon become mature spontaneously, and this shows lack of clinical knowledge. I have seen men of this type who have attained the age of 35 years without it happening, but pressure of the right sort and superficial analysis soon change them.

These cases are important since a very large percentage of men who state that they are homosexual are merely immature and do not know how to help themselves to attain adult sexuality.

It would not be proper to close this account of the psychopathology of homosexuality without a brief discussion of the relationship of homosexuality to the psychoses. That this exists there seems to be little doubt. Perhaps the most striking, if only because of its violence and unexpectedness, is what Kempf described as 'acute homosexual panic'. These are brief sudden psychoses which are characterized by the overwhelming nature of the fear and blind intensity of the reaction. The content of the psychosis frequently demonstrates the psychological basis for it. The illness is characterized by its acuteness, and Kempf believed that if the patient could form some friendly feeling or transference relationship to the doctor this helped a great deal in his recovery.

If Kempf's psychosis is to be regarded as an acute homosexual insanity there exist chronic psychoses which are obviously based on inverted behaviour. A large number of the persecutory schizophrenic psychoses of a paranoid type are homosexual in nature. The persecutor is often easily demonstrable as the beloved and the paranoid feelings are erected as a defence, much as in the anxiety neuroses fear is used to prevent the forbidden wish. A similar mechanism is seen in many of the psychoses released by alcohol and which have been believed in the past to be caused by the organic effects of this drug. It is impossible to discuss these psychoses in full, but since Freud originally showed the mechanism involved, experience has confirmed his demonstration in a very large number of cases.

Freund, however, denies that homosexuality is in any way related to psychosis. One must accept his conclusions with caution since they are so contradicted by daily experience of the content of psychotic delusions and hallucinations. Only 9 of his 222 cases came to his clinic complaining of neurotic illness. It is improbable of course that homosexuality *per se*, when it is conscious, is a cause of neurosis, or psychosis.

Closely related to the homosexual psychoses is suicide, often in a curious or ritualistic manner. I do not know of any extensive statistics (since they are difficult to obtain) but from the literature I have the impression that it is much more common for homosexuals to develop a psychosis or to commit suicide than it is for normal people. For example, Connor expresses the view that in 90 per cent. of suicidal depressions the sexual life was unsatisfactory to a marked degree, either in the direction of weakness of the heterosexual urge, or of strength of the homosexual urge, or both. No doubt the self-destructive tendencies are due to the abnormal introjection which occurs in their case.

Homosexual murder is common. This is usually the result of one of two causes: jealousy appears to be much stronger and violent in the homosexual than in the normal and often suddenly bursts into action. This one might expect when one realizes that the invert is the product of a great deal of unresolved hatred for another man (i.e. the father) in many cases. Under stress this hostility is released with the result that the beloved is killed. Whatever the cause of the patient's homosexuality there is little doubt that the average invert has strong ambivalency in his emotional relations which make his affections a source of danger to the loved one.

The other cause of murder is the ever-prevalent blackmail. Just as prostitution is haunted by the lurking figure of the *souteneur* so is homosexuality shadowed by the blackmailer. Naturally sooner or later the homosexual is pressed too far and in desperation tries to rid himself of his persecutor by killing him.

It must not be thought that all homosexuals are weaklings or spineless, flabby creatures. Some are determined, strong-willed men—I have met fighter pilots who admitted to homosexuality but who had performed acts of calculated bravery. It is little wonder that when a blackmailer meets a man of this type he is ruthlessly exterminated and a large number of unexplained murders must be of this kind, since the motive is often concealed, and difficult to detect.

TYPES

In writing of homosexuality one can hardly help oneself at times falling into the fault of writing of inverts as though they were a single simple group. However, this is entirely wrong: there are a large number of different types which are important not only because they have a different psychogenesis, either in nature or degree, but because they are more or less responsive to therapy. I do not pretend to be able to exhaust all the possibilities here, but the following types have been encountered and treated by me in the course of clinical work.

1. The shy, nervous immature man, as described above, who is too afraid of women to approach them and who drifts into homosexuality, often with a man of similar character, as a result. In my experience this type is the most common of those patients seeking treatment and, fortunately, most responsive to it.

2. Homosexuality associated with neurosis. The neurosis is most commonly hysteria or anxiety states, and this is fortunate because it compels the patient to continue treatment. As Harry Stack Sullivan points out, often during the treatment of the neurosis the homosexuality melts away.

3. The compulsive homosexual who has periodic overwhelming urges to have relations with other men. This is obviously different from the inversion with a concomitant neurosis because here *the homosexuality is the neurosis*. This type is quite different from the man who falls in love with other men. In fact, he often has considerable aggression in his make-up and does not wish for love. He is responsive to treatment.

4. Deprivation homosexuality. Although this is common in prisons and other situations when men are deprived of women (or vice versa) it may occur in ordinary life as in the case of an officer in the Mercantile Marine I treated. He developed homosexual urges following the death of his wife because he felt that it would be disloyal to find another woman. Such cases are often helped merely by a discussion which removes their emotional barriers to living a proper sexual life.

5. The so-called bisexual whom I regard as a partially developed

heterosexual with sufficient homosexual residue to prevent normal behaviour. He, also is responsive to therapy.

6. The homosexual whose personality is otherwise normal. Such men often lead useful social lives and, apart from their sexuality, cause no trouble. Their response to therapy depends on their wish to be cured more than anything else.

7. The homosexual in whom there is an ancillary endocrine deficiency. This is usually testicular failure due to undescended testicles, old orchitis, eunuchoidism and so on. Such cases are difficult and are not cured merely by giving testosterone or androsterone. They lack the proper male drive, and even if one corrects their deficiency may not respond well to psychotherapy.

8. The homosexual whose inversion penetrates the whole of his personality: he talks in a falsetto voice, dyes his hair, wears extravagant clothes and is generally exhibitionistic. Although not a common type he is quite unresponsive to any therapy at present and, indeed, the last thing he wishes is to be cured.

9. The homosexual psychopath. He, like all psychopaths, feels no inhibitions to any form of conduct no matter how antisocial. He has a special tendency to drift into crime associated with homosexuality—blackmail and the like. Such men sometimes go with wealthy homosexuals merely to rob them because they know that no charge will be made against them by the unhappy victim.

10. Homosexuality is frequently complicated by alcoholism and 'the drinking homosexual' forms a clinical problem. I have seen a man of this type who experienced two attacks of delirium tremens and only avoided a third because he consented to take sedatives and vitamins. He firmly refused to stop drinking; and when seen by another physician was thought to be on the edge of a further alcoholic psychosis. Usually with such types more or less symptomatic treatment for their alcoholism is all that they will tolerate.

11. Homosexuality associated with psychosis. In such cases the psychosis is often the presenting feature. This may take the form of Kempf's 'acute homosexual panic' (described on page 216) or, more usually, in a chronic schizophrenic illness. Although some psychiatrists deny any relationship it would seem, as Freud first pointed out, that there is a tendency for homosexuality to be associated with paranoid psychoses. For example, Moore and Melvin examined 205 male schizophrenic patients receiving intensive psychotherapy to determine the relative estimate of homosexual orientation between 128 paranoid schizophrenics and 77 non-paranoid ones. They found that the paranoid schizophrenics had a statistically greater incidence of past overt homosexual acts, preoccupation with homosexuality and were judged latently homosexual more often by the

psychiatrists treating them. In such cases, obviously, the treatment is that of the psychosis and the homosexual element is not available for therapy. If the patient recovers from the psychosis he may benefit from psychotherapy.

12. Homosexuality released by cerebral damage. Patients with various forms of dementia, or amentia, may behave homosexually. Similarly following haemorrhages, thromboses, or trauma to the brain behaviour may become aberrant. These cases are not responsive to any form of therapy and treatment consists in attending to the primary illness.

There are many other types less common which I have insufficient space to describe. For example, Berg, a very careful analyst, described a fetishistic type. Hauser gives an elaborate classification of homosexuality but it does not seem to have any logical basis. His types are: (1) the bisexual, (2) the married man, (3) the upper class married man, (4) the middle class married man, (5) the working class married man, (6) the demoralized married man, (7) the young bisexual, (8) the self-isolated homosexual, (9) the fully sublimated homosexual or bisexual, and (10) the homosexual prostitute (the young volunteer, the 'call-boy', the 'cottage type',[1] the 'club and pub prostitute', and 'the roller'.[2] His sub-classes are even less enlightening. It is easy to make objections to this classification— the position in society to which a homosexual belongs has no relation to his illness, although it might control his social behaviour to some extent, for example, whether he indulges in prostitution or not.

THE SOCIAL PROBLEM OF THE HOMOSEXUAL

The confirmed homosexual forms a social problem which is peculiar to himself. Other perverts, such as the sadists, may, by their behaviour, cause social anxiety but not in the same manner as the homosexual. This is because the invert alone tends to band with his fellow sufferers and form a community within the structure of society. No doubt this is partly because he is rejected by many of his fellow men as a monstrosity unfit for congress with the community, but it is partly because social life (as Zuckerman has shown in apes) is based on sexuality and the homosexual develops his peculiar brotherhood by common attraction. The invert forms a life of his own: he frequents certain restaurants and cafés, he dresses in a manner peculiar to himself, he even walks and talks, individually.

The suggestion has been made by Armstrong that 'there is no doubt that active male homosexuals recognize passive male homosexuals by some means unknown'. The idea being that they have some sixth sense.

[1] 'A cottage' is slang for lavatory hence 'cottage' types are those who frequent lavatories to pick men up.
[2] 'A roller' is a decoy used by blackmailers to trap homosexuals.

Thody points out that Proust, who was himself homosexual, describes such a meeting in *A la Recherche du Temps Perdu*, and says that according to Proust the recognition is both instinctive and mutual.

I would strongly refute the suggestion that such a recognition is in any way due to a sixth sense or anything of the sort. Surely it is of the same nature as when a man knows whether he is likely to meet success in making an approach to a woman. He knows this 'instinctively' or 'intuitively' (but really he has interpreted trivial signs of interest which would otherwise be unobserved). He looks at her, she glances up, drops her eyes, smiles. He looks again and smiles, and so on. The homosexual does the same sort of thing to his fellow. It may be, as Hauser suggests, that the interest is not so innocently aroused but slightly suggestive gestures may be used. In both cases the slightest negative response puts a stop to the comedy.

It is not necessary to be homosexual to be able to detect inverts in casual social life. Although I am normal I have seen many homosexuals and am able to observe them in a crowd by minute gestures, tones of speech, and so on. Even on the wireless one can tell them by their speech which is either excessively soft and slightly slurred or else grating and harsh.

There are some trades and professions which are the homosexual's province—dress designing, interior decorating, acting, ballet dancing, and so on. Often he is successful and wealthy; unless he more or less challenges the established order (as, for example, Oscar Wilde did) he is left alone. This is not always the story as Henry and Gross show in their interesting study of one hundred under-privileged homosexuals. They divide them into three classes:

1. *Respectable*. These are men who live a quiet, decent life, and apart from their sexuality do not behave abnormally.

2. *The Prostitute*. This type is not only abnormal but uses his abnormality as a source of profit to himself.

3. '*The Hoodlum*.' This is the bullying blackmailer who frequently works with the prostitute type to entice the respectable homosexual into his clutches.

I have pointed out that homosexuals may be driven to violence by threat of exposure. Henry and Gross draw attention to the fact that the homosexual lives in fear of being blackmailed. His mind is so perpetually haunted by the thought of falling into the hands of the authorities that he is an easy subject for the blackmailer. Once he has been trapped into a compromising situation he is unlikely to go to the police because he knows that even if his tormentors are caught the publicity will lose him his position in society, his work, and so on.

This is shown in a particularly shameful case recorded in the Wolfenden Report. It is disgraceful inasmuch as a man who went to the police complaining of blackmail was punished for the very offence for which he asked protection—which is contrary to common justice and, indeed, except in the case of homosexuality, also contrary to police practice. The details are as follows:

A., aged 49, met B., aged 35, in a cinema. Afterwards they went to A.'s flat and committed buggery.

For a period of about seven years B. visited A.'s flat regularly, and the men committed buggery together on each occasion.

B. then commenced to demand money from A., from whom, in the course of about three months, he obtained some £40.

A. finally complained to the police. The facts were reported to the Director of Public Prosecutions, who advised that no action should be taken against B. for demanding money by menaces, but that both men should be charged with buggery.

Both men were thereupon charged with two offences of buggery committed with each other, and, after pleading guilty, were sentenced to nine months' imprisonment. Neither man had any previous convictions, nor were any other offences taken into consideration.

The Wolfenden Committee comment, rightly, that 'Blackmail is a pernicious social evil, and we regret that any unnecessary obstacle should be put in the way of bringing it to light. We feel that, except for some grave reason, proceedings should not be instituted in respect of homosexual offences incidentally revealed in the course of investigating allegations of blackmail.

'At present, extortion by threat to accuse of buggery and certain other crimes carries a specially heavy penalty. From the point of view of blackmail, we see no reason why the law should differentiate between buggery and other homosexual acts, and accordingly recommend that Section 29(3) of the Larceny Act 1916, be extended to apply to all homosexual offences.'

However unattractive the normal man finds the behaviour of the homosexual, most people will agree that blackmail is a greater social evil. In the past judges have termed it 'Murder of the Mind' and 'Mental Torture'. There is no doubt that it can drive a man to desperation. The homosexual, as I have pointed out, is not always the gentle effeminate type of man. Driven to desperation the more aggressive type may find murder preferable to torture. I have already shown that murders are often the result of homosexuality. Surely it is common sense that we do not increase the circumstances leading to homicide.

It is deplorable enough if the law drives a man to commit murder but, perhaps, more deplorable still if, by failing to give him protection, it allows him to be slowly driven to suicide.

It seems to me that it is a matter of common justice that everyone who lives in society is entitled to legal protection unless it is proved that he is injuring others by his behaviour. It is improbable that the victim is injuring the extortioner, and however distasteful his behaviour may have been to normal people, he deserves legal protection. It is to be hoped that now, after so many years of insisting on the uselessness of punishing homosexuals, the law has been changed so that it is no longer a crime to indulge in homosexual behaviour between consenting adults in private, that the threat of blackmail will be diminished, if not completely abolished.

There is, of course, still the possibility that the blackmailer may try to frighten his victim by threatening to reveal his behaviour (i.e. by photographs) to his employer, if the employer is known to be hostile to this abnormality. Nevertheless, the threat to the homosexual's happiness is greatly diminished now that he no longer lives under the daily shadow of imprisonment.

Ignorant people are still agitating to reverse the new law and bring back imprisonment. This is worse than useless. Prison, with its sexual deprivation *is the ideal place to produce homosexuality.* Medical officers in German and Japanese prison camps noticed an increase in it. In penal prisons a homosexual is often as welcome as a woman from the sexual point of view. To deprive men of the company of women for months and years at a time and provide them with only a homosexual outlet is almost as good as forcing them to be homosexual.

Karpman, who has had valuable experience as a psychiatrist to gaols, states that:

Sexual irregularities are flaunted daily in prisons: they are almost universal. The sexual urge is too elemental to be controlled by confinement. The prisoner may struggle to maintain heterosexuality but opportunities for sublimation are impossible and the physical environment favours abnormalities. Masturbation, which derives its value from accompanying fantasies, which give it an abnormal or normal character, becomes compulsive. Transition to more abnormal expressions takes place gradually. Many undergo severe conflict before yielding; some never succumb but develop neurotic or psychotic reactions.

In many cases homosexuality is indulged in freely. If masturbation and homosexual practices continue they become fixed; the individual on release may find himself unable to return to normal sexual activities. The entire personality is disturbed. The youth still in the formative period is likely to remain single, and lead a bisexual or homosexual life. Those led into homosexual prostitution are likely to continue this on the outside.

Taylor published a paper which gives valuable facts regarding the incidence of homosexuality amongst the prison cases. He found during 1946 that 96 persons were charged with homosexual offences. During the same time the total number of remand and trial prisoners was 5,023 so that the percentage of homosexuals was 1·91 per cent. In the same period the total number of men charged with heterosexual offences was 198. Of the 96 homosexuals 39 were charged with indecent assaults on boys, 24 with importuning, 17 with gross indecency, and 16 with buggery.

Taylor divided his cases into 'pseudo-homosexuals' (which were mainly cases where 'the homosexuality was in the nature of a substitution for the normal heterosexual act'); 'bisexuals', 'in whom strong heterosexual as well as strong homosexual tendencies were obvious'; 'prostitutes' who were 'characterized by the fact that the homosexual acts were carried out for gain'; and 'true inverts'. All the 'prostitutes' had had previous convictions.

He gave the following tables:

Classification

	Indecent assault	*Impor- tuning*	*Gross indecency*	*Buggery*	*Total*
Pseudo-homosexuals	34	13	11	8	66
Bisexuals	5	1	2	4	12
Prostitutes	0	2	1	2	5
True inverts	0	8	3	2	13
Total	39	24	17	16	96

It is interesting to notice that Taylor found that the incidence of offences rose not in the spring, as suggested by Walker and Straus, but in September. This is curiously similar to the statistics for juvenile delinquency recorded by Cyril Burt who suggested that the rise was due to the long summer evenings which gave greater opportunity for misbehaviour.

The following table given by Taylor gives valuable facts on the previous convictions and shows the slight effect of punishment:

Previous Convictions

	Nil	*One previous conviction*		*Two previous convictions*		*Three or more previous convictions*	
		Same offence	*Other offence*	*Same offence*	*Other offence*	*Same offence*	*Other offence*
True inverts	7	4	1	0	0	1	0
Bisexuals	4	4	0	2	0	2	0
Prostitutes	0	2	0	1	0	2	0
Pseudo-homosexuals	44	3	5	1	6	0	7
Total	55	13	6	4	6	5	7

This can be compared with the previous convictions in males convicted of unnatural offences:

	Nil	One previous conviction	Two previous convictions	Three or more previous convictions
1939	93	27	16	51
1940	116	35	17	45
1941	156	35	20	39
1942	196	44	18	43
1943	213	60	32	75

Taylor found the commonest single environmental factor was seduction in early youth or childhood. Unfortunately he does not seem to have studied the home life and makes no mention of the relationship of these patients to the parents. He found androgynous physique in six cases but this is abnormally high and would not be encountered in private practice in similar cases.

He discovered that the dreams accompanying nocturnal emissions were frequently homosexual in nature. This accords with my experience and contradicts the findings of Hubert and East. It shows how difficult it is to obtain the truth from those who are suffering imprisonment since these were experienced investigators.

There is considerable homosexuality in the armed forces. This has been suspected by psychiatrists for many years but was recently openly admitted in the report of a Select Committee. A Rear-Admiral stated that there are quite a lot of homosexual offences in the Navy, and an Air Commodore said that homosexuality had been a constant problem in the R.A.F. It seems significant that no statistics were given. No doubt the Service life, with its frequent isolation from home and women, tends to produce isolation homosexuality, as well as attracting men who are consciously or unconsciously homosexually inclined.

There is no denying that there are a number of homosexuals who contribute a great deal to the community. Henry and Gross suggest that this is usually artistic rather than scientific. I cannot agree with this since I have often been asked to treat doctors and scientists. However, perhaps it is true that outstanding work of homosexuals has often been of artistic nature. Oscar Wilde, although much of his writing is derivative, produced a new type of comedy. Tchaikovsky has a definite place in music and Diaghileff helped to create modern ballet, to point to only a few who were undoubtedly abnormal.

Homosexuals sometimes claim that all genius is based on their particular abnormality. This, of course, is untrue. To achieve outstanding success in any branch of art or science it is necessary to pour out a great deal of energy as well as to have the necessary intellectual ability to attack the problems involved. The great source of energy is sex (as shown by the American experiments on rats running in revolving cages). The abnormal have difficulty in expending their sexual energy satisfactorily and do not release it so completely as the heterosexual. *Hence they have much more energy to use for their particular art or science.* The works of the muscian Bach (who had many children) and, indeed, Freud himself, show that if a heterosexual is willing to turn sufficient energy into his work he can be as successful as the homosexual—if not more so.

Those whose duties took them within the courts frequently heard judicial condemnation which placed the invert in the category of a fiend in human form. That this is not so and that the homosexual can show fine human feeling is shown by Oscar Wilde's efforts to release three little children who were imprisoned in Reading Jail for poaching rabbits.

It cannot be stated too clearly that the homosexual is neither a fiend nor a genius, but merely a sick man whose illness produces peculiar social problems. Except for those who interfere with children they do little harm to the community (unless persuaded to marry in the hope of cure) and, in some cases, produce work of artistic or scientific value. On the other hand, the homosexual does not propagate himself—a fact which in a world of rising population may be fortunate.

It is worth while dealing here with the problem of bisexuality. A great deal of nonsense has been written on this subject in the past and it is necessary to clear away many misconceptions. Firstly, bisexuality is only the case in which the patient has achieved partial heterosexuality—he has fallen between the two stools and is neither one nor the other. That is to say, that he has partly introjected his father and partly remains identified with the mother. Secondly, he is not a favoured individual who may obtain his sexual pleasure from man or woman as he wishes. He, being insufficiently developed, usually gains only a modicum of sexual enjoyment with either sex. This is the type of homosexual who sometimes succeeds in 'curing himself' by having relations exclusively with a woman. Unfortunately this is not a complete cure as could be seen by the fact that when such men were conscripted to the Services they frequently developed symptoms owing to the constant propinquity with other males and did not recover unless invalided. Since it is obvious that the less homosexual a man is the easier it is to cure him, this type of partial homosexual is usually very responsive to psychotherapy.

It is well known that alcohol will release sexuality which otherwise would remain controlled. It is, perhaps, for this reason that night-clubs, public-houses, and similar places tend to be frequented by prostitutes and homosexuals. There is probably a deeper relationship between alcohol and homosexuality, however, since one finds in certain homosexuals a strong tendency towards alcoholism. Moreover, since narcotics of any sort produce regression this accentuates the condition. It is difficult to know what is the realtionship since there are many theories and probably no single one is explanatory. For instance, the homosexual is usually an unhappy person since he is trying to live in a world adapted to normal heterosexual persons. Alcohol may in some cases therefore be used simply as a drug to dampen his misery and temporarily shut out unpleasant reality. In other cases it is used to release the inhibitions and help the shy homosexual make contacts which he would not dare when sober. Possibly there are deeper roots also and alcoholism is symptomatic of hidden oral cravings. There is no doubt that in dipsomania the emotional drive is overwhelming and insatiable for a time. How closely this is related to homosexuality it is impossible to say, but I do not subscribe to the doctrine of the analysts that it is invariably a homosexual trait. In women loose sexual conduct, as Ovid pointed out, is frequently a concomitant of alcoholism, but its relationship is not yet fully determined.

It is interesting to consider the response which the homosexual makes to members of the opposite sex. This is by no means a matter of indifference—frequently the feeling is extremely negative. I have heard homosexual men who have expressed disgust at women, whom as sexual partners they have regarded as filthy and abhorrent. In a similar way lesbian women describe men as brutal, animal, and unfeeling. It is obvious that there is strong feeling repelling the patient from the normal sexual partner as well as impelling him or her to the abnormal one.

This repulsion seems to be linked with the fear of intercourse. Many homosexuals express a vague fear of having sexual relations. This is sometimes because there is a vague idea, in the case of men, that the vulva can hurt in some way; sometimes that it is provided with teeth so that obviously it is confused with the mouth, more or less unconsciously of course. Probably the fear of intercourse goes deeper than this. All women are confused with the mother and identified with her to some extent. This means that intercourse falls under the prohibition of incest and is tabooed. It is only by making a further identification of the mother with a man that the sexuality can be released. Sometimes the possessive mother aggravates the sexuality between her and the boy by saying, 'If only you were twenty years older or I were twenty years younger I could be your wife', &c. We have known the case in which a woman said this to her son and he actually had sexual fantasies, which occurred in full consciousness, regarding her. This young man never had sexual dreams of women and his nocturnal emissions were always related to dreams of men, yet on one occasion he did dream of a woman sexually—his mother lying naked on a bed.

Homosexuals of both sexes often feel disgust at cosmetics. This may be partly because they are identified with excrement—they call them 'filthy muck' and object to 'smearing themselves all over with that stinking stuff' and so on—but this may also be related to the mother and the reaction depend to some extent on whether she used or did not use cosmetics.

In a similar way I have seen a homosexual who disliked women's underclothes which he said were ugly. Yet perhaps at no epoch has women's lingerie been so beautiful as at present, with easily obtainable nylon, artificial silk, and so on. This again we have found related to the mother since she was by necessity often seen in underclothes when the patient was a child.

In spite of all these repulsions the homosexual often does form a relationship with those of the opposite sex. The girl tries to become 'the jolly pal' that men regard without sexual feeling and with whom they can sail, ride, play golf, and so on without emotion. The homosexual man is often tolerated by women because he has good taste, and has similar interests, and can be made to fetch and carry without masculine attempts at domination.

In concluding this section it may be pointed out that homosexuality is *par excellence* the perversion in which the original impulse becomes replaced by later gratifications. An example of this is shown by the fact that a homosexual neurosis is frequently the seeking of a disguised form of the mother at the onset, but later the driving force is not maternal at all, but the immediate sexual pleasure obtained by this form of behaviour. It is as if the perversion has become autonomous and indeed autonomy would be a good term for it in this stage. The original impulse remains strong enough to direct the channel of sexual conduct, however, but the immediate driving force is sexual satisfaction. It is this autonomy which explains the great difficulty which one may meet in treating established homosexuality. Although it is often easy to unearth the symbolism, and even to evoke emotion which has caused it, the patient remains obstinately uncured since one is not touching the moving principle of his illness. This autonomy can be undermined by various motives: I have, for instance, seen a man abandon homosexuality, or rather homosexual behaviour, because of strong religious feelings—he considered his behaviour wrong and intolerable. Similarly it may be hindered by fear, and some homosexuals sought treatment because they knew that their behaviour was punishable by imprisonment, although as a general rule this tends to instil caution and a determination not to be caught rather than a wish to be cured. Often the idea that his abnormality is not approved of by society will force a man to turn away from it. No doubt the much larger number of men who seek treatment compared with women is due to this attitude of society. If this is so it is an argument against the social acceptance of adult homosexuality which the homosexual of today is eager to establish.

Be this as it may there is no doubt that public opinion is turning against the cruel pillory of the invert which made behaviour harmless to society into a crime carrying with it a sentence of anything up to life imprisonment.

Many homosexuals suppress all sex and live a bleak, loveless existence. Such a case was that of the poet, A. E. Housman, who had a childhood which explains his deviation.

His mother, to whom he was over-attached, died when he was twelve years old (a vulnerable time) and his father, who had been more interested in sports than in his family, deteriorated and took to drink.

Housman turned all his interest into scholastic work, and when he went to Oxford it was thought that he would take an excellent degree. Unfortunately he developed a homosexual attachment to a normal man there, and this interfered with his studies. He failed and spent the rest of his life overcompensating for his fiasco. Although he succeeded in holding chairs in Latin in London and Cambridge he remained a sad, unapproachable, friendless man whose suppressed emotion rendered him liable to grimaces which made his students think that he might start weeping at any time. It is small compensation for his unhappy life to know that his poetry, although not perhaps supreme, occupies a small niche in literature.

The homosexual, unless he is particularly adroit, walks in danger all his life. He must avoid his own weaknesses such as alcohol and drugs, pick his way skilfully through the waiting blackmailers, thieves, and others, who do not hesitate to impose on his fear of calling for the protection of the law to their own ruthless profit. In the face of such contant stress it is not surprising that he has a tendency to psychosis and suicide.

However, no matter what his ability in his work or his skill in conquering his difficulties, there is one enemy he cannot subdue—age. Little by little he grows old: the bright attractions of his youth pass, he becomes middle-aged and balding. Now he is no longer courted by older men and it is his turn to buy affection by gifts, privileges, and even money.

This lasts but a short time and he finds that he has fewer and fewer friends. The married man has always the company of his wife, and if he has them, his children. He has social contacts through his marriage which fill his life, but the homosexual finds his friends fugacious and inverted love transient. The lonely old bachelor, if we but knew it, has only too often been the gay youth in his young homosexual days.

Sooner or later the invert dies, not surrounded by relatives and friends, but in lonely lodgings, or small hotels, solitary and neglected.

CASE NO. 10

A Case of Homosexuality in a Woman

This case is one described in my monograph on homosexuality. It was that of a young woman aged 24. She complained that she was depressed, could not study and was homosexually attracted to other girls. Her parents were alive and well. The father was a dour, bad-tempered Scotsman. Her mother was tolerant and motherly. There were two brothers and two sisters. Her home was not a happy one—the father knocked her about and was unbearable. She was in consequence nervous as a child and very shy. At school she did badly but was good at English and needlework. She says that she was a failure at the rest. On leaving she was apprenticed to millinery but 'got sick of it after a few years'. She had left home and was working as a petrol pump attendant when first seen. Her sexual life had been somewhat confused. In spite of her homosexual feelings she had lived with a young man who kept a bookshop for the past four years. This was not happy and she did not wish to marry and have children. In fact this affair was only a defiance to her father whom she wished to outrage. She was not completely homosexual since she had obtained satisfaction from her lover but she dressed in trousers, wore unattractive sweaters, and was grubby and unkempt. She had attractions towards women, but had never had any relations with them. In the past she had had treatment in a mental hospital voluntarily for her sexual difficulties but had seen the doctors only a few times and no real effort had been made to investigate her case. Then she had served in the A.T.S. but had become depressed and was invalided out. She said firmly that 'I don't like men as a sex'.

Treatment consisted in unearthing the hostility which she bore to her father. This was not difficult and she was willing to talk freely of his misdeeds (he seems to have been a most unpleasant type) at length. As she improved she commenced to become more feminine. It was amusing to see her slowly swing round, and instead of wearing a dirty unbecoming sweater to change to a more attractive one, and to little feminine additions such as a powder-blue chiffon scarf. She revealed hostility to her mother for her passivity, and for not leaving her father: and after this the patient became more feminine in her dress and behaviour. She finally said that she felt perfectly normal, and was inclined to marry her lover instead of tolerating him, and her clothes became completely feminine. When last seen she wore a canary-yellow sweater and a brown corduroy skirt, and used cosmetics. She said that she had no interest in women sexually and was finding a more womanly job than working on petrol pumps. Her treatment consisted of one weekly session for six months.

This case is not exceptional, and others, Hadfield for example, record similar ones.

CASE NO. 11

A Case of Homosexuality in a Man

This was a particularly difficult case and one which I feel especially happy to have brought to a successful conclusion. It was that of a man aged 30 years who was an officer in the Army. He complained that he had never had any attraction to women, but periodically he had a strong impulse to have anal intercourse with men. Men wearing tight trousers attracted him and so he was excited by those in battle dress (the English battle dress exposed the buttocks because the man wore a blouse and not a coat). However, he had always avoided having anything to do sexually with men in his own regiment.

Owing to his duties and the fact that he was stationed abroad nearly all the nine years he was being treated it was only during his annual leave, and once for a few months when he was stationed near London, that he could be seen. This naturally complicated and prolonged treatment.

He gave the usual story of an unfortunate home: his father was a drunken failure and his mother a neurotic obsessed with her bowels. He had an older brother who had inspired his dislike. At school he did well and on leaving worked in an office. The war gave him a chance to escape from this into the Army, where he was promoted and elected to stay in the Service afterwards. He was an over-conscientious officer and took his duties very seriously. He looked after his men efficiently, but his over-scrupulousness made him unpopular with the other officers.

When he was first seen he had never had anything to do with women and the idea was distasteful to him; but he was afraid that he would finally get into trouble with the police because of his sexual activities. This was not altogether unfounded, since he had had narrow escapes, been swindled, and robbed, and caught gonorrhoea in his activities.

At first he did not seem likely to respond, but after the first month's treatment said that he felt less anxious. It was not expected that he would return, but eleven months afterwards he asked for further therapy. He admitted that he had relapsed in the interval. Little by little his homosexual neurosis was broken down. The reason for his excitement by tightly clothed buttocks was found to be caused by early memories of the breast, and when these were unearthed he no longer felt them attractive (I have already pointed out that this attraction is due to memories of the maternal breast under a tight dress). He found that he would like to have an interest in girls but was nervous and shy with them. Finally, he started to have a relationship with a girl who had been his brother's mistress. No doubt there were emotional reasons for his choice but this was not discouraged. He then discovered that he was in love with this girl and, since he was potent, married her.

Unfortunately as he progressed sexually he found that the Army interested him less and less: his duties appeared irksome and he clashed badly with his fellow officers. It was obvious that his interest in Army life had been founded, as it so often is, on his homosexuality and he was now unsuited for it. He left and entered civil life. There he obtained a suitable post as a London manager of a provincial firm and was able to adjust himself to his new occupation satisfactorily.

He was seen some ten years later and complained of a minor depression. This had an interesting cause. He and his wife had had a pet budgerigar which was a cock bird. He had become tremendously attached to it and was terribly upset when his pet caught a form of avian pneumonia and died.

His depression responded rapidly to an hour's psychotherapy during which he released a great deal of emotion about his dead pet which seemed in some curious way to represent his mother. This, like other cases which ended successfully, seemed to be a symbol of his previous homosexual attachments but so diminished that it was difficult to realize its significance.

CASE No. 12

A Case of Homosexuality in a Woman

A girl aged 23 stated that she was not sexually attracted to men and was involved in a sexual relationship with another girl who was a cripple. She had applied to an endocrinologist for treatment but no glandular abnormality was discovered. It was remarkable that this young lady resisted men so easily since she was very pretty, and no doubt found plenty of men who wished to be her admirers.

She stated that her home was not a happy one because of her domineering and aggressive father. He was excessively strict and she admitted she was terrified of him. At school she had been a timid girl and on leaving worked in a factory. Her looks attracted men, but she was too frightened to go out with them. Some years before she saw me she had met the crippled girl (who was in no way attractive to men) and formed a sexual relationship with her. However, as time passed she felt that she was getting older and should do something regarding marriage.

Her difficulties were investigated and she was told that she was equating all men with her father. She was expecting men to behave in the domineering way he did. This was not so and most men would be happy to be tender to such a pretty girl as herself. She was encouraged to break off her friendship with the cripple (who was holding her back) and go out with men when asked. This she did and finally fell in love with a man who was trying to get a divorce from his wife with whom he was not happy. She admitted that she was strongly stirred sexually by his love-making and would have liked to have had intercourse with him but for her strict moral standards.

CASE No. 13

A Case of Homosexuality in a Man

This patient was a man 34 years old, married with one child. He complained of urgent homosexual feelings which sometimes became overwhelming. There was no conscious desire to be abnormal and the feelings intruded unwanted into his normal way of life.

He came from a normal family. His father, a surgeon, died after the First World War and he was brought up mainly by his mother. The family consisted of four brothers and one sister, the patient being the youngest. It was one which was very much ruled by tradition—for example, all the boys went to a famous public school, and thence to the same college of a certain university. The males excelled in sports and not to like them was to declare oneself a pariah and untouchable. The family did not understand that anyone might enjoy anything else, and they looked askance at intellectual pleasures.

The patient was a nervous child and in early life showed a violent temper. He did not do well at his preparatory school, hated his headmaster, and to the horror of all failed to enter the family public school. All this produced contempt and dislike. His father was away in the First World War and he saw little of him. Apart from memories of being teased in a kindly manner he had little memory of him. As a result of his school failure his mother regarded him as a queer freak and his brothers thought him odd and peculiar. After his father's death his elder brother took on the paternal mantle and started to order him about. The patient, although only a schoolboy, resented this and hated him as a result.

At another public school he was seduced by bigger boys and had sodomy practised on him. He was very feminine and liked to indulge in amateur acting in which he took girls' parts when he could do so. He was not good as an actor but persisted in his hobby. He did fairly well but again did not like the headmaster.

He said that his mother was a snob and he had no sexual instruction as a boy. This was never discussed in the family circle. He detested his eldest brother and did not mould himself on him at all.

When he went to his university he tended to go to parties of the masculine type where there was much beer-drinking. He had gathered the impression from his snobbish family that it was beneath his dignity to flirt with shop-girls and typists when he was an undergraduate. Consequently he missed the valuable experience of mixing with women as a young man. He said: 'I had a taboo on women: I was told it was wrong to have anything to do with them except a Victorian approach to the one I eventually married.'

The patient went abroad for two years after he left the university. Then he returned to England. He married in 1938 and sexual intercourse was normal. His wife gave birth to a daughter. No doubt if he had been allowed to live his life unhindered from then on all would have been well but he might have developed into abnormality just as easily.

He joined the Army at the onset of war and was eventually sent to North Africa. He fought with distinction throughout the whole campaign but the isolation from women—he was separated from his wife the whole time and had no home leave—produced depression and he started to have waves of homosexual feeling. How far this was produced by the news that his wife had fallen in love with someone else it is impossible to state.

His homosexual feelings became violent and he indulged in sodomy, often at great risk, whenever he had an opportunity. The urges came at about fortnightly intervals and were overwhelming.

Finally he was demobilized and able to resume his normal life. He returned home to discover that a large sum of money which had been left to him to start a business had been entrusted to the man his wife had wished to marry. This unscrupulous scoundrel had made love to her and got his hands on her finances. The wife discovered that she wanted her husband and legal proceedings were started to recover the funds.

Unfortunately return to normal sexual life did not abolish the abnormal impulses which had become established. The patient still had sudden desires to commit sodomy on men and, although he did his best to resist them, occassionally they did overwhelm him and he indulged them. He realized the gravity of his behaviour and the serious consequences which discovery would entail but this did not stop him. He decided to have treatment and came to me.

He responded well to psychotherapy and soon lost his feelings of depression. He brought up terrific hate for father-surrogates, headmasters, and his eldest brother, and a great many early memories. He stated that when he was a child he showed a desire to dress in his mother's clothes, and used to put on her hats to go out in the road. Coloured things pleased him best. People said that he should have been a girl. He was nervous of mixing with boys when he was small because he thought that he had a small penis (actually physically he was normal in every way with no genital, nervous, or endocrine abnormality).

He produced considerable hate for his eldest brother and spoke a lot of how he was bullied by him. Once his brother tied him up and covered his face with petroleum jelly. Once he took him into a wood, took down his trousers, and made the patient take down his also but nothing further happened.

He used to steal money from his mother because she gave it to his brothers and not to him. This memory showed how he resented not receiving affection from his mother and such a reaction, of course, often results in later criminality.

His homosexuality resolved itself into hatred for his eldest brother (the other brothers did not make the same impression) and a seeking for affection from his mother. Of the latter he said: 'I had the feeling that everyone else got more than I did.'

He responded well to treatment and after three months felt that he had lost his homosexual urges. Against my wishes he ceased treatment and the subsequent history shows that this was unwise. He quarrelled with his mother and had a violent return of his homosexual feelings. He gave way to these and had further sodomy. This resulted in a urethritis for which I sent him for treatment. It was discovered to be non-specific but frightened him considerably. Owing to the summer holidays treatment was interrupted and he was not heard of until he wrote the following letter:

'I am feeling most ashamed of myself for not writing to you sooner—not only to say thank you once again for all the trouble you took with me but also to tell you of my progress. I am most happy to tell you that things seem to be going progressively better with me—I have finally been able to arrange that I should not see my mother at all for the next four months, by telling her that I suffer from bad shell-shock dreams, which my doctor advised would only be cured if I kept away from my family. She has appeared to swallow this, and I am sure that I am benefiting from the result. It is almost uncanny how a meeting with her brought its almost inevitable result. I would even be as bold as to suggest that should you have other cases like mine you should try to arrange this separation from mother as early as possible. It seems to be the main thing and the whole problem. I would not suggest that I do not still find the problem hitting me, I do think I have now reached the stage when I can say "No" to it and that is of course a tremendous advance. Also it seems to hit me less often; more if I get tired and I do seem to need a lot of sleep.

'I was horrified at all the publicity given to the recent C—— court martial —how cruel the press can be. While it is probably inevitable that such a person should be removed from the Army it seems inexcusable that still the means of removal and results of it should be so drastic and so lasting. I wonder if there is anybody who tries to reform this aspect of our penal code.'

Three years after the cessation of treatment he wrote stating that he had remained well and said: 'Both my wife and I are so much better now, and it is really wonderful how our lives have changed.'

CASE No. 14

A Case of Homosexuality in a Woman

This patient was a rather beautiful woman of 31 years of age, who was Canadian in origin. She complained that she was depressed, could not trust anyone and did not wish to have anything to do with others. She was tremulous and her hands shook. Although she was married she had had nothing to do sexually with her husband for over a year, but had fallen in love with other women; she was in love with one when first seen. Physically she had a normal feminine physique.

Her parents appear to have been normal; she was attached to her father, who was an engineer, but did not much like her mother who was 'a club woman' and did a lot of work for societies like the Red Cross. There were no other children of the marriage.

She was a nervous but friendly child. At junior school she did well because she had a good memory. At high school she failed in French and showed some rebellion, smoked and misbehaved. She then took a secretarial course and became secretary-receptionist to a diamond drill firm. It was here that she met her future husband who was, like her father, an engineer. She said she made a 'silly marriage' with him. Hardly anyone liked her husband; the men who worked with him called him 'the stupid engineer' and she felt sorry for him but did not love him. She said, 'I have fallen in love only twice in my life; once with a man and once with a woman, but when I fall in love it is always with the wrong people. Sexually I am drawn to people but they always hurt me.' At high school she had four or five affairs—'I wanted to try out sex but it never meant anything to me.'

She had married some twelve years before she saw me and had had two children, both girls, now aged 11 and 9 years. Her husband came from wealthy parents, his father was reputed to be a millionaire, but he was cold and self-contained and never demonstrated affection for her. She felt that after their children were born he lost interest in her and she felt lonely and neglected. The result was that she had drifted into affairs with other women. These were older than she was, 43 and 44 years old. The one she was attached to when she came for treatment had taken her to lesbian clubs in London and tried to involve her in a prolonged affair. However, the patient felt that there was no future in this and willingly came for treatment.

She expressed hostility to her mother and said that she found her 'bossy', 'a back-seat driver' and one who never had a good word for anyone. Her husband was mean and spiteful and nagged her like her mother had done. Six months after they were married she met another man, and fell in love with him, but then it was too late.

As treatment progressed it was obvious that she hated her mother and her husband had become linked with her in a common hatred. She expressed considerable hostility for both; her husband was undemonstrative, never kissed her, or told her he loved her. He got annoyed if he thought her housework was not up to standard. She then expressed hostility to her mother and complained about her a great deal. She was a good woman but inept and dominant. Indeed it became apparent that her life had been to a great extent a revolt against her mother.

Her husband was interviewed and it was suggested that he should show her more affection, and try to save the marriage, but it was obvious that he had found someone else and did not wish to co-operate. There had been hints of divorce from the first; she had left her husband six months after their marriage to consult lawyers, and had repeated this several times. This now came to a head and they decided to separate. Her husband confessed that he had lost interest in her and would like a divorce. This was finally brought about; and, curiously enough, she met the man she took for her second husband at her lawyer's office whilst waiting in the reception room. At first they did not like each other very much, but later fell in love and she remarried.

When seen after the treatment of the wife had ceased for two years, they both said how happy they were. She had no homosexual longings at all and to test whether this was so her husband had taken her to the club where she had gone with her lesbian friend, but they both found it boring and the homosexual women there uninteresting.

They were both very much in love when seen and looking forward to emigrating to Canada. The only difficulty was the children who had been placed in her first husband's custody, and she was trying to obtain possession of them.

There is no doubt that this woman was unable to identify herself with her mother, acquire a completely feminine personality, and somehow had used her husband as a target for her hate for her mother. This had caused tensions between them and having found heterosexuality with him unsatisfying she had drifted into homosexual affairs. These had been unsatisfactory and she realized that she was not living a completely happy life.

She co-operated well and, although her treatment lasted only a few months, it was possible to release the hostility to her mother and husband so that she could form a proper attachment to a more suitable man. She was much more feminine when last seen, dressed well, had her hair beautifully arranged, used perfume and looked a normal happy woman.

This was admittedly an easy case to treat successfully; she was bisexual before she drifted into lesbianism, wished to be cured of her homosexual tendencies, responded well to the short treatment she had had, and was fortunate enough to meet a suitable man as soon as she was free to remarry.

REFERENCES

ALLEN, C. (1958) *Homosexuality; its Nature, Causation and Treatment*, London.
APPERSON, A. B., and McADOO, W. G. (1968) Parental factors in the childhood of homosexuals, *J. abnorm. soc. Psychol.*, **73,** 201–6.
ARMSTRONG, C. N. (1955) Diversities of sex, *Brit. med. J.*, **2,** 1173.
BARR, M. L., and HOBBS, G. E. (1954) *Lancet*, i, 1109.
BAUER, J. (1940) Homosexuality as an endocrine, psychological and genetic problem, *J. crim. Psychopath.*, **2,** 188–97.
BENE, E. (1965) On the genesis of male homosexuality, *Brit. J. Psychiat.*, **3,** 803–13.
—— (1965) On the genesis of female homosexuality, *Brit. J. Psychiat.*, **3,** 815–21.
BIEBER, I. *et al.*, (1962) *Homosexuality*, New York.
BREND, W. (1936) *Sacrifice to Attis*, London.
BRITISH MEDICAL ASSOCIATION (1955) *Homosexuality and Prostitution*, London.
CHURCH OF ENGLAND (1954) *The Problem of Homosexuality*, London.
CONNOR, W. (1948) Some notes on suicide, *Brit. J. med. Psychol.*, **21,** 222–8.
COPPEN, A. J. (1959) The body-build of male homosexuals, *Brit. med. J.*, **2,** 1443–5.
COSSA, P. (1959) *Approches Pathogéniques des Troubles Mentaux*, Paris.
DAILY TELEGRAPH (1954) Trial of Lord Montague.
DIXON, A. D., and TORR, J. B. D. (1948) Chromosomal sex and abnormal sexual development., *Brit. med. J.*, **1,** 222–8.
ELLIS, A. (1956) The effectiveness of psychotherapy with individuals who have severe homosexual problems, *J. cons. Psychol.*, **20,** 191–5.
—— (1963) Constitutional factors in homosexuality, in *Advances in Sex Research*, ed. BIEGAL, G., London.

Eysenck, H. J. (1964) *Crime and Personality*, London.
Fenichel, O. (1934) *Outline of Clinical Psychoanalysis*, London.
Freud, S. (1925) *Collected Works*, vol. 3, 255–68, London.
—— (1930) *Three Contributions to the Theory of Sex*, New York.
Freund, K. (1963) *Die Homosexualität beim Mann*, Leipzig.
Gebhard, P. H., Gagnon, J. H., Pomeroy, W. B., and Christenson, C. V. (1965) *Sex Offenders; An Analysis of Types*, London.
Hadfield, J. (1966) Origins of homosexuality. *Brit. med. J.*, **1**, 678–700.
Harrisson, T. A. (1937) *A Savage Civilisation*, London.
Hauser, R. (1962) *The Homosexual Society*, London.
Henry, G. W. (1950) *Sex Variants*, London.
Henry, G. W., and Gross, A. A. (1938) Social factors in case histories of 100 under-privileged persons, *Ment. Hyg.* (*N.Y.*), **22**, 591–611.
Hestoo, L., and Shields, J. (1968) Homosexuality in twins, *Arch. gen. Psychiat.*, **2**, 149–60.
Jenkins, M. (1928) *Genetic Psychological Monographs*, vol. 3, 457–571.
Kallman, F. J. (1925) *J. ment. Dis.*, **115**, 283–98.
Karpman, B. (1954) *The Sexual Offender and His Offenses*, New York.
Kaye, H. E., Soll, B., Clare, J., Eliston, M., Gershwin, P., Kogan, L., Toada, C., and Wilbur, C. (1967) Homosexuality in women, *Arch. gen. Psychiat.*, **17**, 626–34.
Kinsey, A. C. (1941) Criteria for hormonal explanation for homosexuality, *J. clin. Endocrin.*, **2**, 424–8.
Kinsey, A. C. *et al.* (1948) *Sexual Behavior in the Human Male*, Philadelphia.
—— (1953) *Sexual Behavior in the Human Female*, Philadelphia.
Lang, I. (1940) Studies in genetic determination of homosexuality, *J. nerv. ment. Dis*, **92**, 55–64.
Lange, J. (1931) *Crime as Destiny. A study in Criminal Twins*, London.
Moore, R. A., and Melvin, L. S. (1963) Male homosexuality, paranoia, and schizophrenia, *Amer. J. Psychiat.*, **119**, 743–7.
O'Connor, P. J. (1964) Aetiological factors in homosexuality. *Brit. J. Psychiat.*, **110**, 381–5.
Overzier, C. (1963) *Intersexuality*, New York.
Parker, N. (1964) Homosexuality in twins; a report of three discordant pairs, *Brit. J. Psychiat.*
Pritchard, M. (1962) Homosexuality and genetic sex, *J. ment. Sci.*, **108**, 616–23.
Proust, M. (1941) *Cities of the Plain*, London.
Raboch, J., and Nedona, K. (1958) *Psychosom. Med.*, **20**, 55.
Special Report from the Select Committee on the Armed Forces Bill (1966) London, H.M.S.O.
Swyer, G. I. M. (1954) *Practitioner*, **172**, 374–9.
Taylor, F. M. (1947) Homosexual offences and their relation to psychotherapy, *Brit. med. J.*, **2**, 526–9.
Weil, A. (1924) Sprechen über anatomische Grundlagen für Angeborensein der Homosexualität, *Arch. Frauenk.*, **10**, 23–6.
West, D. (1955) *Homosexuality*, London.
Whitener, R. W., and Nikelly, A. (1964) *Amer. J. Orthopsychiat.*, xxxiv, **3**, 486–92.
Wolfenden Committee Report of the Committee on Homosexual Offences and Prostitution (1957).
Wortis, J. (1940) *Amer. J. Orthopsychiat.*, 567–9.
Wright, C. A. (1958) *Med. Rec.* (*N.Y.*), **147**, 449–52.
Wright, C. A., Glass, S. J., and Deuel, H. J. (1940) Sex hormone studies in male homosexuality, *Endocrinology*, **26**, 590–4.

10

INFANTOSEXUALITY, BESTIOSEXUALITY, AND AUTOSEXUALITY

INFANTOSEXUALITY

Definition
The use of an immature person as a sexual object.

Psychopathology and Occurrence
The choice of an immature sexual object is not infrequently found in perverts. We must admit that the suggestion made by Freud that this is due either to external or internal inhibitions is probably correct. The child has been conditioned that his mother is sexually unapproachable by the mother herself and by others, particularly the father, who implies it by his possessive manner. Sometimes, when children are brought up in an environment in which sex is considered 'dirty' or taboo, the external inhibition is sufficient to make them avoid the manifestation of adult sexuality. The orientation towards the child as a sexual object may be produced by the fact that at an early age it performs sexual experiments with other children. (As a matter of fact, all children play sexual games and this is so particularly amongst savages, as Malinowski found amongst the children of the unspoiled Trobrianders. It can also be seen in the primates, as pointed out in the chapter on monkeys and apes.) Through its conditioning the child never seeks the normal sexual object.

Apart from this mechanism, that of fixation, an infantile sexual object may be chosen either from transference of emotion or from identification. It is common to find emotion transferred from a neurotic's mother to her little girl—hence the reason why some obsessionals fear they will kill their child; it is their mother they really wish to kill. When this mechanism occurs in sex the man transfers an ambivalent feeling from his mother on to some small female child. The result is a sadistic attack. The identification occurs more frequently in homosexuality. For example, a homosexual I analysed first of all loved men of his own age, but as he grew older he started to love younger and younger children, and had a compulsive desire to lavish excessive affection upon them. It was revealed that he had a hard, unaffectionate father and never had any love from him as a boy. Now that he was adult he sought to give the boys he loved that which he had himself missed. He was identifying himself with them and seeking to give them (as symbols of himself) the tenderness for which he had always longed.

However, I must stress that except during treatment is is almost unknown for the homosexual attracted to other men also to be interested sexually in children. The view, popular with ignorant people, that there is a type of rake's progress in which a man indulges in sex with those of his own age, then with youths, and eventually with boys (ultimately with babies?), is unknown clinically. In almost every case there is a clear-cut type, adult, youth or boy, which is attractive. This makes the statement by the Special Committee of the British Medical Association in the Memorandum of Evidence submitted to the Wolfenden Committee even more incredible. Paragraph 114 states, '*Relatively intact personalities otherwise well socialized.* These include young men who have little scruple in living partly at the expense of older homosexuals and their older counterparts who are promiscuous, but they usually know how to avoid blackmail or contact with the law. They appear to be happy and can hold useful jobs successfully. Homosexuals in this group are the most effectively deterred by the threat of punishment, which may persuade them to avoid socially dangerous activity (e.g. with children).'

Such men are almost never attracted to children and this is so well known to the clinician that one wonders whether the members of the Committee have ever seen a homosexual, let alone treated one! In practice the commonest types who assault children are: (1) the mentally subnormal, (2) the chronically inhibited pervert, and (3) the precariously adjusted heterosexual who tends to regress towards infantile behaviour in times of stress. The assault is usually caressing and not violent.

From the psychoanalytical point of view the seeking of an immature sexual object is the result of an unresolved Oedipus complex. The mature female suggests adulthood and this implies the mother. The prohibition is against sex with an adult woman, and the child is used as a substitute. As we have pointed out (under homosexual perversions), when the immature sexual object is of the same sex as the patient there is doubtless a great deal of narcissism, since then the pervert is seeking one who is as he would like to be—i.e. a beautiful child. Again, it may have homosexual roots since in loving a child the pervert is identifying himself with his mother. This is most obvious, of course, when the child is of the same sex.

The celibate 'Lewis Carroll' (Charles Dodgson), the author of *Alice in Wonderland,* with his passion for photographing little girls in the nude, is probably an example of infantosexuality. This appears to have been sublimated to a large extent since there is no evidence that he did more than take photographs and tell the children entrancing stories. His interest appears to have been directed only towards little girls.

Kopp evaluated the personalities of 100 sexual offenders seen at the New Jersey Hospital, Trenton, U.S.A., and concluded that such men who interfered with little girls fell into two classes. The first were timid, passive, immature men who lacked the courage to attempt sexual contacts with mature women. The second were men who posed as being very much the man of the world, self-important and self-righteous with an air of arrogant independence. Their lives are characterized by one or more marriages, some success in business, and an active role in the adult community.

Kopp's findings have not been confirmed by others but are probably true. The psychiatrist without special facilities sees too few of such men to be able to criticize his work with any confidence.

It is not unusual when patients are being treated for homosexuality or impotence for them to pass through a stage of infantosexuality (the sexual object being of the opposite sex) as they slowly become heterosexual. This no doubt shows the slackening of the bonds of the Oedipus complex and a release of the attachment to the mother. In this case the new sexual object may represent a sister or other less closely related person.

Mulcock made a valuable study of the men who commit sexual assaults. He found that out of 314 children between the ages of 4 to 17 years, 73 were girls and 241 boys. Thus three times as many boys as girls were involved. There were a larger number of girls than boys sexually assaulted at the lower end of the age scale. Mulcock thought that this was due to the earlier maturation of girls who 'offered a curious attraction for the infantosexual offender'. He feels that the actual chronological age may be of less importance to the offender than the development of the child concerned. The most vulnerable ages in both boys and girls was found to be between 10 and 12 years. (Obviously when one writes, as Mulcock does, of assaults on girls of 17, it seems an exaggeration of the term to regard a willing girl of that age as being assaulted or considering the man as necessarily abnormal. This is all the result of our exaggerated view of immaturity.)

Mulcock found that out of 100 offenders 39 to 50 years offered the most dangerous age for offences against boys and 33 to 44 years for those who interfered with girls. Married men formed 32 per cent., divorced or separated men 8 per cent., and single men 60 per cent. of all offenders. He states: 'Married men figure largely amongst the offenders and therefore non-marriage as an excuse for abnormal outlet is fallacious—as marriage is to correct it.'

Work or profession seemed to have little relationship, the 'white collar' workers being nearly equal to the trade or manual occupations. Manual workers formed 36 per cent., school teachers 21 per cent., priests and parsons 14 per cent., youth leaders and scoutmasters 14 per cent., miscellaneous trades 9 per cent., welfare workers and miscellaneous professions 6 per cent.

The punishments inflicted varied from probation and fines to 15 years imprisonment. Well might Mulcock conclude, 'Sentences were most disproportionate to the type of offence. These ranged from a £10 fine and probation to 15 years' imprisonment, the lesser sentence being in the case of girls.'

The victims of infantosexual assault—being often children of a tender age—naturally arouse great sympathy. Many perverts, particularly homosexuals, claim as extenuation for their abnormality that they were interfered with in childhood. Judges are more severe in punishing those who make a child a sexual object than those who have adult relations. How far all this is justified is difficult to say. In some cases the child is provocative and seeks the assault, in others, as Gibbens and Prince discovered, two-thirds had been sufficiently willing participants to co-operate in assaults more than once or by more than one assailant. Doshay (quoted by Ahrenfeldt) found among 108 unselected cases of children between the ages of 7 and 16 who had been involved in sexual delinquencies there was no single case of known sex violation in adult life. Of 148 cases of the same age-group involved in sexual and other delinquencies only 8 per cent. committed known sexual offences of a minor kind in adult life whereas no less than 25 per cent. committed non-sexual misconduct. Doshay was of the opinion that sodomy, which was the most usual sexual offence committed by older men or boys upon young boys or girls, should not be regarded too seriously. Out of 256 cases only 2 revealed such deep interest in sexual practices. Bender, Blau, and Rasmussen have done similar work on girls which confirms these findings.

I do not believe, however, that in all cases infantosexual practices are harmless. Conditioning continues throughout life and may have particularly strong effects when the child is passing through a particular phase, as, for example, throughout the homosexual phases of childhood and puberty. Moreover, when the environmental conditions are such as to induce particularly strong homosexual cravings (when there is excess of maternal affection and an unsuitable father, when there is complete lack of maternal or feminine influence, and so on), then the child may be swayed into abnormal directions much more than if it had been left alone. I believe that if a child is found to be indulging in sexual practices it should be weaned from them by providing more healthy influences since otherwise, if the sexual desires are suppressed forcibly by threats, these desires may appear in later life and the adult seek the satisfaction in children he failed to obtain when a child himself.

There is a curious tendency at the present time for fashion to try to make those who accept it not merely look young, but infantile. Girls are wearing excessively short skirts ('mini-skirts') which give the appearance of little children, who are sometimes dressed in that way. Some young men wear their hair at shoulder-length in a Little Lord Fauntleroy style.

The exact psychological meaning of this is not clear, but it seems to be related to infantosexuality in some manner.

In some nations infantosexuality has been regarded as normal in the past. In India, for example, mating between grown men and little girls—which most people would regard as quite immature—of 10- to 12-years-old was approved. It is interesting, however, that the average age of marriage of Indian women has slowly risen over the past 30 years, although not more than about 3 years in all that time. The following table indicates the trend.

Average age at marriage of Indian women according to various censuses

	1921–30	1931–40	1941–50	1951–60
Assam	14·1	16·3	16·5	18·54
West Bengal	10·6	13·8	14·3	15·86
Bihar & Orissa	11·2	13·8	14·1	14·81
Maharashtra	12·1	14·5	15·2	13·74
Andhra Pradesh	10·2	11·4	11·8	15·26
Madhya Pradesh	10·6	14·2	14·1	13·87
Madras	14·7	16·2	16·8	18·14
Mysore	14·8	15·9	16·0	16·33
Punjab	14·6	15·3	16·1	17·46
Rajasthan	12·3	13·6	14·0	14·22
Kerala	17·2	19·2	19·4	—
Uttar Pradesh	11·4	13·4	13·6	14·43
Jammu & Kashmir	15·0	16·2	—	19·97
India	12·0	14·9	15·4	—

After Karkal (1968).

CASE No. 15

A Case of Infantosexual Fetishism

The patient was a man aged 52. He was a chartered accountant and successful in his business. In spite of the fact that he knew that treatment would be entirely confidential and there was no possibility of any leakage of information he preferred not to give his address and insisted on paying for his treatment on each occasion at the end of the session. Physical examination revealed nothing abnormal.

He complained that he was sexually attracted towards small girls aged about twelve to fourteen years. It was essential that the girls wore their hair in plaits, and in his fantasies he imagined them to be in a state of wanting to urinate, but being unable to do so because of social circumstances. Sometimes he had placed himself in jeopardy because on occasion when he saw a girl who excited him he masturbated under his mackintosh in public places. He had never harmed the small girls and was content merely to look at them. No attempt had ever been made to interfere with them sexually or to let them know what he felt about them. He was an enthusiastic nudist and published a book on nudism for children.

His father had been a dominating man, but the patient had seen very little of him since he had passed most of his life abroad. In fact, except for an occasion when he was at home for two or three years, there had been practically no contact at all. His father died in Tasmania apparently of an acute intestinal obstruction at the age of 70 years.

His mother was a much more normal figure and displayed nothing unusual. There was one sister who was the eldest in the family, the patient had an elder brother and one younger than himself.

His childhood was normal except that he was a nervous boy, bullied at school in spite of the fact that he was good academically. On leaving he was articled to a chartered accountant and qualified without trouble.

He had married at the age of 32 and when first seen had a daughter aged 16 years. No sexual instruction had been given him as a boy and he knew nothing until the age of 12: at first he had had the idea that girls and boys were physically the same, but then conceived the thought that girls were concealing something. This gave him the desire to see girls urgently wishing to urinate, but being prevented from doing so, in order to humiliate them. He retained the idea that urinating was 'sex' until he reached the age of 20 when he started to masturbate. He felt that the girl in his fantasy might represent his sister who was dominating and aggressive, or else a cousin who teased him sexually.

Part of his wish to be analysed was to make it possible for him to say the letter 'R' which he associated with anxiety about passing urine.

As his treatment progressed it became apparent that the young girls represented himself as well as being identified with his sister and cousin. He said that he had had the fantasy that he, himself, was a little girl passing urine and whilst imagining this he remembered that he had had a lot of anxiety as a little boy wanting to pass water. There was a taboo on sex in his home when he was a child: the passing of water lifted the taboo and allowed it. His attraction towards plaits seemed to be based on the fact that his mother used to plait his sister's hair, when she was a small girl, before she went to bed at night.

He had married twenty years ago and when he was engaged had asked his fiancée to grow her hair long: however, after marriage he persuaded her to cut it short again. The attraction towards plaits (not little girls) had appeared only in the past four years.

He felt the trouble with his fetishism was that as it grew he tended to drift away from his wife and found her less attractive.

The association of plaits with the breasts was shown by the fact that he spontaneously identified them. Apparently he thought of the clefts between two tight plaits as the same as the cleft between the breasts. He admitted that he had always felt a desire to bite the plaits and had fantasies of small girls with penises urinating into his mouth or sucking the penis like a child suckling at a breast. Clearly his fantasies of plaits were reminiscent of infancy and breast feeding. He realized that he had never wished to have intercourse with young girls and appreciated with some part of his mind that they had normal sexual organs. But he felt that he wished to humiliate them because they had deceived him. Women kept their genitalia secret although he felt that they knew he wished to see them. He said 'as a little boy I could not hold my water,

I wet my clothes and was humiliated'. In spite of the improvement with treatment he still found young girls exciting.

He then brought up curious memories of his sister sitting on his lap and urinating whilst he sat on the lavatory. He admitted that in all his fantasies he was a small boy with an elder girl. He went on talking of these and talking of the clefts between the breasts and I noticed that his symptoms were becoming less intense. He lost his obsession for plaits and started talking of fantasies of hurting little girls who would not show him their genitalia, of being a schoolmaster and forcing little girls to expose themselves and so on.

As he realized that his wish to see girls' plaits was really indicative of a wish to see their genitalia and that the little girls represented his mother (perhaps with his sister and cousin), he found his symptoms disappearing. Finally, three months after he started treatment, and after about thirty interviews he felt completely freed from his symptoms. He was seen a year later and said that things had improved amazingly. The obsession with girls' plaits, and indeed with little girls themselves, had disappeared. His personality had not changed and he was still a nudist. Five years later there had been no reccurrence.

This was a very satisfactory case. Fetishism is not always easy to cure and East and Hubert suggested that there was a danger of releasing sadism in treatment (I have never found that this theoretical possibility occurs in real clinical work) but the analysis was uneventful. Nothing was suggested to him and his discovery that the cleft between the plaits represented the cleft between the breasts came as a surprise to me since I had never read of a similar finding. There is too often the suggestion made by those who have never done any analytical psychotherapy that the analyst suggests things to the patient. This is quite untrue and the most satisfactory patient is, like this present case, one who discovers things for himself—often to the analyst's astonishment.

It would seem that this man's fetishism was built on a chain of associations. Thus mother's breast—mother—sister—cousin—linked with hostile feelings based on sexual curiosity—frustration—wish to humiliate—humiliation by wetting himself—wish that small girls should be humiliated by having to hold their urine until they wet themselves—wish to look at small girls.

Such a case should encourage others to treat fetishism which even in this patient of the relatively advanced age of 52 responded to proper psychotherapy.

REFERENCES

AHRENFELDT, R. H. (1947) Homosexuality and 'sexual trauma', *Brit. med. J.*, 2, 795.

DOSHAY, L. J. (1943) *The Boy Sex Offender and His Later Career*, New York.

FREUD, S. (1924) *Collected Papers*, London.

GIBBENS, T. C. N., and PRINCE, J. (1963) *Child Victims of Sex Offences*, Institute of the Study and Treatment of Delinquency, London.

KARKAL, MALINI (1968) Age at marriage, *J. Family Welfare*, xiv, 3, 50–6.

Kopp, S. B. (1962) The character structure of sex offenders, *Amer. J. Psycho-ther.*, **16**, 64–70.

Malinowski, B. (1929) *Sexual Life of Savages*, London.

Mulcock, D. (1954) A study of 100 non-selected cases of sexual assaults on children, *Int. J. Sexol.*, **7**, 125–8.

BESTIOSEXUALITY

Definition

The use of an animal as a sexual object.

Psychopathology and Occurrence

The same factors are found to produce this perversion as we found caused infantosexuality, in so far as they are both the common result of prohibition. Opportunity is also important, as is shown by the fact that bestiosexuality is not uncommon, as Freud pointed out, amongst farmers and others who have contact with animals. This was later confirmed by Kinsey *et al.* The prohibition against a normal sexual object is usually an inner one, and the pervert seeks his secret satisfaction because he is prevented, by fear or distaste, from seeking a woman. (Those who practise bestiosexuality are sometimes found to be mentally defective and their prohibitions are external ones—they are unattractive to women so have no hope of finding a normal mate.)

No doubt a great deal is explicable by the fact that a child does not easily distinguish between the animal and the human and that it tends to treat animals as if they were equals. It is only after prolonged conditioning and maturation that it begins to treat them differently from itself. Probably a considerable amount of abnormality can be attributed to this cause, since children, moreover, frequently show a great deal of affection to animals. If this is so it implies a great deal of immaturity or a fixation in the personality of the pervert.

The whole psychopathology of bestiosexuality has not been clearly developed as yet. It seems that the animal is used as a maternal substitute and to avoid the Oedipus situation which a woman would evoke. Possibly, also, there is often a considerable amount of castration complex in bestiality, since by the avoidance of a woman the bestiosexual pervert is symbolically, or by his behaviour, enacting a castration situation.

Many animals are unsuitable for a sexual approach except sadistic ones, but doubtless multitudes of animals have perished for this reason. It is characteristic of such perversions that they frequently occur under the influence of alcohol and those who normally would not perform such acts do so when inebriated. Gebhard *et al.* in their large series of 1,500 sexual criminals discovered only five cases involving contact with animals. Those used were dogs, cows, chickens, and a mare. The ages of the men ranged from 16 to 38. They all denied their acts. Four came from broken homes, and four adults were heavy drinkers who indulged in antisocial practices and were thieves.

Bestiosexual sadism commonly occurs in boys and youths who torture animals without appreciating why they are doing so. Such cruelty is notorious and is often accepted as a more or less normal phase in development. Sometimes it appears to be obviously pathological as in the following case:

Boy Admits Maiming 11 Horses

A boy, aged 15, admitted at Dorking Juvenile Court yesterday that he stabbed 11 horses in or near their left eyes. He said: 'I don't know why I did it at all. I was very sorry afterwards.'

Mr. David Hodges, defending, said: 'I understand from a psychologist that the left indicates evil. There may be something there that a psychologist ought to be able to trace and cure. It is not a sadistic trait because it is done only to horses.'

Detective-Inspector Frederick Messenger said: 'This boy comes from a good home and well respected parents. Without any apparent motive he has deliberately inflicted terrible wounds on horses and caused them untold misery.' Inspector Messenger produced a tool called a fish disgorger such as anglers use to take hooks out of fish. He said this instrument and a ball-point pen were used by the boy to maim horses. . . .

The boy's father said: 'This is so completely alien to his character. We have kept the whole galaxy of animals. We have had snakes, lizards, everything, and there has never been any cruelty. The boy is always pleasant, helpful, and friendly.'

It is not easy to make reliable psychiatric deductions from such an account but it is obvious that horses were symbolic in some way whereas other animals were not (and so were not harmed). The defending solicitor is at fault in thinking that sadism cannot be applied to horses or other animals. Possibly the boy, by always being so pleasant and friendly has repressed a great deal of aggression. Boys should be rough and unruly at times. No doubt the attack on the horses' eyes represents some sort of castration situation referred to above.

Certain nations have the reputation for indulgence in bestiosexuality. This is said to have been so of the Chinese. If it is true one may be fairly certain that it is the result of customs and prohibitions which prevent the young man from mating or make the normal love object undesirable.

It is sometimes suggested that bestiosexuality is practised by women with large domestic hounds and dogs. If this occurs it must be very rare and I have never treated a case, nor seen one before the courts. That it is physically possible is shown by the case of *R.* v. *Bourne* mentioned in the medico-legal section on page 456. It probably has the same psychological basis as we have noticed in men—that is, either some internal prohibition due to complexes or fixations; or else something external prohibiting normal sexuality—lack of ability to attract a mate through deformity or some similar cause.

Kinsey and his co-workers have drawn attention to the fact that animal contacts frequently form the first source of sexuality for a certain number of children brought up in rural conditions, the highest number being amongst those in the middle educational levels between the ages of 16 and 20. These may show as much as 1·08 per cent. finding their sexual outlet in this way. Usually the contacts in other levels form under 1 per cent. and in any case tend to diminish with increasing age.

Bestiosexuality is of extreme antiquity, as one might have expected, and indications have been found of it as far back as remote times. Anati, for example, found a picture in the Camonica Valley, in the Alps, which shows a man with an erect penis penetrating a donkey, which was probably drawn in late Neolithic or early Bronze Age times (2100 to 1200 B.C.).

Since animals were not domesticated before Neolithic times bestiosexuality must have been impossible previously, owing to lack of opportunity.

Kinsey draws attention to the Hittite code, from which the Hebrew legal system was drawn to some extent. In the Hittite laws not all animal contacts were considered reprehensible. For example, he quotes Barton as giving one of the laws as follows: 'If a bull rear upon a man, the bull shall die, but the man shall not die.' 'If a boar rear upon a man there is no penalty.' 'If a man lies with a horse or mule there is no penalty, but he shall not come near the King and he shall not become a priest.' The reason why some animals were regarded more severely than others does not seem to be apparent.

In mythology bestiosexuality is often stated quite frankly. The wife of King Minos, Pasiphaë, for example, mated with a bull. The King had asked Poseidon to send a bull from the sea for him to sacrifice. The bull was so handsome that Pasiphaë would not kill it. So Poseidon caused her to fall in love with it, and with the help of Daedalus she was disguised as a cow and attained her end. The result was that she gave birth to the Minotaur (Minos, after the legendary king of Crete, and tauros, bull). The excuse that a god intervened to make one do what one wished to do is common in Greek history, but does not conceal the underlying impulse. Modern archaeological researches have shown that the basis of this legend was in bull-fighting which was a sport of the Cretans, but this does not invalidate the psychological importance of the story. The fact that bulls are often symbols of the father in dreams and legends would support the fact, stated previously, that probably the significance of bestiosexuality is related to the Oedipus complex. The association of fear with this may explain the fact that during the last war many famous Continental artists—Picasso, for example—were preoccupied with Minotaurs. The fear is, of course, unconscious fear of a terrifying father.

A similar myth is that the first king of Ceylon, Vijaya I, was the grandson of a lion (also a big savage animal symbolic of the mighty father).

About 600 B.C. the king of Bengal had a daughter who apparently suffered from hypersexuality. She was so maddened by lust that she descended secretly at night from the upper storey of the palace and seduced a passing lion. He responded to her advances and from this union she gave birth to a son and daughter. The hands and feet of the son were formed like the paws of a lion. When he became adult the son slew his leonine father. In this case the animal really does seem to indicate the forbidden father and bestiosexuality becomes a method of evading the Oedipus complex.

It is interesting to notice that bestiosexuality is sometimes related in fairy-tales but is 'de-sexualized' so that the fantasy appears harmless. Usually it speaks of 'married' and no progeny is mentioned—e.g. the sort of fairy-tale which starts 'There was once an old woman who was married to a large grey wolf', &c. Again it was a common idea from medieval times that the Negro nation was the result of the mating of a woman with an ape. (Fortunately the author of the Tarzan stories provided a human mate!) It is evident that bestiosexual fantasies are common although perhaps rarely put into practice in urban life.

Probably the worship of animals was related in some manner to bestiosexuality and Pan was represented by the goat because of that animal's sexuality. Herodotus wrote regarding it:

The veneration of the Mendesians for these animals, and for males in particular, is equally great and universal: this is also extended to goat-herds. There is one he-goat more particularly honoured than the rest, whose death is seriously lamented by the whole district of the Mendesians. In the Aegyptian language the word Mendes is used in common for Pan and for goat. It happened in this country, within my remembrance, and was universally notorious, that a goat had indecent and public communication with a woman.

Where the animal represented the god, as in the national fantasy of such peoples as worshipped beasts as gods, no doubt it was not only considered natural, but even honourable and desirable, that a woman should accept the condescension of the deity. We know that animals which were previously worshipped later became hated. No doubt this repugnance reinforces the 'natural' disgust at the thought of a human mating with an animal.

Female animals were sometimes religiously, ceremonially, bestiosexually mated as in the following example which horrified the Welsh chronicler, Giraldus Cambrensis (quoted by Gelling and Davidson) in Ulster in the twelfth century.

When the whole people had assembled a white mare was led out in front of them and the chosen ruler in full view of everybody approached it in bestial fashion and with no less imprudence than shamelessness showed he also was an animal. The mare was immediately killed, cut up and boiled, and a bath prepared for the king in the water in which it was cooked. He sat in it and ate pieces of meat which were given to him, while the people stood around and ate with him.

He also drank the water.

CASE No. 16

A Case of Bestiosexuality

This was a young man aged 32 years. He came from a normal family with both parents alive and well, one brother and one sister, all normal. He was not a nervous child and although at first he did not do well at school later on he improved and passed his General Certificate of Education. He then went to university on a three-year course studying forestry. He did not complete the course because he had sexual pre-occupations partly of the buttocks and partly of having sexual relations with animals—mares. The pre-occupation with the buttocks started at the age of 9 but the interest in mares later.

At university he became attracted to the woman he later married and by whom he had two children. However, since he could not finish his course he started teaching, partly because that provided a means of livelihood for an educated man and partly because he was able to obtain work near his future home. The school was a mixed one and his sexual pre-occupations led to assaulting the female pupils. This was discovered and he was discharged and barred from teaching in any school in England. His sexual interest in horses increased and led at first to masturbation and finally to actual sexual intercourse. He realized that this was very dangerous and he might have lost his life but said that he did not mind taking the risk and could sense whether the mare was receptive or not. He had had this sexual urge for twelve years when seen.

It seems that the sexual attraction towards buttocks is related to the urge to have intercourse with mares. The mares' buttocks are the sexual stimulus. Thus the behaviour is closely linked.

Although no opportunity was possible to study this man, as far as could be determined it seemed that the buttocks (as in most similar cases and first pointed out by Hadfield) represent the mother's breasts under her dress, the outline being very similar. He realized at once that the mares' buttocks were exactly similar although larger and distorted.

It would seem, therefore, that this man was really fixated to his mother. He was able to have sexual intercourse with his wife but unconsciously desired his mother. This attachment to his mother came out in the longing for buttocks (as symbols of her breasts) and thence to mares. His intercourse with mares was therefore really symbolic intercourse with the mother. The fact that he could have been killed by an irate mare seems to have had no deterrent effect, nor did the possibility of having a severe sentence had he been discovered and reported to the police.

REFERENCES

ANATI, E. (1964) *Camonica Valley*, London.

COTTRELL, L. (1954) *The Bull of Minos*, London.

DAILY TELEGRAPH (1958) 10 September.

GELLING, P., and DAVIDSON, H. E. (1969) *The Chariot of the Sun*, London.

GERHARD, P. H., GAGNON, J. H., POMEROY, W. B., and CHRISTENSON, C. V. (1965) *Sex Offenders*, London.

HERODOTUS, *Euterpe*, vol. i, 369 (Beloe's translation, 1806), London.

HOLDEN, L. (1958) *Ceylon*, London.

KINSEY, A. C. et al. (1948) *Sexual Behavior in the Human Male*, Philadelphia.

AUTOSEXUALITY

Definition

Perversions performed on oneself.

Psychopathology and Occurrence

The four preceding perversions all had sexual objects which represented the mother. How are we to reconcile this view with perversions performed upon oneself? From the psychoanalytical point of view this is the result of primary narcissism—that is, the emotion which Freud believes is directed first upon the self. It is, however, with the greatest of caution that I regard this primary narcissism. I have shown overleaf that the instinct is but the elaboration of the simple reflex, and this simple reflex is designed to deal with the *outside* world. We may say that the somatic reflexes are somewhat in a special case and that the body is, mentally, regarded as the outside world. The instinct which results from this elaboration of reflexes therefore must retain its external adaptive qualities. It seems probable, therefore, that the instinct is first turned outside and attempts to deal with external stimuli. *If this fails, as I have shown in the experiments of Zuckerman and Tinklepaugh, then instincts tend to get reversed. This, I believe, is the true explanation of the use of the self as a sexual object,*[1] and which Freud has described as narcissism. This sometimes takes on a frankly sexual tone as when a patient treated by me stated that as a child he attempted to practise oralism upon himself, and, indeed, Kahn and Lion have published a note on a self-fellator. It is significant that in my case the child was brought up in one of the most loveless homes one could imagine and obtained no affection from either mother or father. In any case it is inevitable that a certain amount of self-love should be produced, since it is unlikely that the child is ever able to reach such a perfect environment that all its instinctual urges are able to reach their proper objects. Some of its instinctual desires must be deflected back and this is, I believe, the primary narcissism which Freud describes.

The psychoanalytical point of view, however, is that the emotion is all primarily directed on to the child and only as it develops through the various stages is it able to detach this emotion from itself. The degree and amount of this emotion which it is able to direct to altruistic ends shows the amount of development towards complete adulthood.

Szasz suggests that autosexuality is sometimes the basis of apparent homosexuality. He states:

The notion of 'homosexuality' has occupied an important position in the psychoanalytic theory of psychosis and in the explanations put forward to account for all types of withdrawals from the outside world. Although this

---

[1] I have never heard of any psychoanalyst who has attempted to explain the objection to this point of view—unfortunately it is too late to lay it before Freud himself for criticism.

view is of some value, revisions and refinements are necessary, among them the need for clarification of the misleading impression that the notion of 'homosexuality' creates—namely, that the patient is (sexually) interested in another person who is of the same sex. *Observation often shows that the patient is interested only in his own body* (my italics). An ego orientation to the body might readily appear to be homosexual to the observer, particularly if it is a manifestly projected form. What is meant by this is that the patient might treat another person—man or woman—as if this person were his body. If the person in question is of the *same sex* (his italics) as the patient, the observer usually concludes that this is 'homosexuality', whereas if the person with whom the patient interacts in this manner is of the opposite sex the psychological meaning here suggested often escapes the observer's notice altogether.

It is obvious from this, with which I agree, that autosexuality can form the basis of many psychological states which are not easily discerned and are frequently overlooked entirely.

The chief autosexual perversion is masturbation. Now there has been a great deal of misconception about it in the past because there is always considerable superficial guilt associated with it. Masturbation has been described as seriously injuring the physical health and as the cause of every variety of psychosis, but the association with mental disease has been finally abolished by Haire who demonstrated its absurdity. It is worthwhile examining it therefore to see how much is true. Firstly, masturbation frequently appears in the infant (as the behaviourist J. B. Watson observed) towards the end of the first year. Can it be that deprived of the comfort of suckling the child turns its emotions back upon itself and attempts to obtain pleasure from the only thing like a breast it possesses, viz. the penis? Even later, when it is long past the stress of weaning the child may start masturbating when faced with other strains, and modern paediatricians, such as Davison and Levinthal, for example, in their excellent book, accept that it is, with other behaviour disorders of childhood, the response to stresses of normal development, such as the arrival of a new sibling, illness, moving, school, &c. Self-stimulation usually passes away but starts again at puberty (when the child again seeks affection of a more adult kind). It also occurs in those who have been deprived of normal heterosexuality through environment.

The psychoanalytical view of masturbation confirms what we know from observation. This is that masturbation shows attachment to the mother and that it is a regression to a phallic stage of development which causes it to appear. There is no doubt that it is frequently accompanied by incestuous fantasies, as in the patient of mine who had conscious fantasies throughout his whole childhood of his mother masturbating him when he indulged in onanism and then, after puberty, of intercourse with her.

Masturbation is unlikely to be harmful either physically or

psychically. Firstly from the physical point of view: the genitalia consist of the penis and testicles. These are activated by the nervous system. Does any one of these organs become damaged by masturbation? The penis is a piece of muscle which has become specialized. Now we know that muscle, far from being injured by exercise, is improved. The penis is no exception, so that rather than injuring it masturbation should make it stronger and more virile. Again, the testicles are glands and use does not injure a gland, in fact it makes it hypertrophy. (The only exception to this seems to be the pancreas, and causes of diabetes are probably more than overeating.) We can conclude with some reason that masturbation does not injure the testicles. Does it injure the nervous system? This seems improbable, since it is almost impossible that the number of impulses which form the spinal reflex could do any such thing. Moreover, it is a spinal reflex and the spinal cord has been proved to be almost inexhaustible as a reflex centre. Numerous physiologists have shown that it is impossible to exhaust a normal nerve-fibre. Where could masturbation cause damage? The only possibility is that by its concomitant fantasies it could strengthen the maternal fixation and make it more difficult for the individual to fall in love with another woman. No doubt it can form a vicious circle in this way, since the more the boy is fixated on his mother the more he tends to masturbate, and so on. Nevertheless the vicious circle is usually easy enough to break by environment or by psychotherapy.

We might then ask the paradoxical question: 'Does masturbation have any useful function?' One could produce a good case for the fact that it has. We know that disuse causes atrophy. Every other muscle and gland in the body tends to atrophy if not used. Why should the genital organs form any exception? The truth is, however, that they are never allowed to atrophy. If the individual is deprived of normal sexual outlets, sexual urges arise which drive him to utilize his sexual organs in abnormal directions, the chief of which is masturbation. It may be that this is to preserve the integrity of the sexual organs until they can be used normally. Myriads of saints and ecclesiastics in the past have tried to suppress sex but have found that their battles were in vain—it has always burst out either in voluptuous dreams with an emission, or else by an overwhelming compulsion to masturbate. It needs more than a vow of celibacy to abolish the sexual instinct.

If we are to regard masturbation as a perversion (and it has no biological end to fertilize the female) then it is the most trivial and least serious. In my experience those cases in which it appears as a grave feature always have a whole host of more serious symptoms hidden away. This leads us to the much-discussed 'psychic masturbation'. This is the bugbear of all those who write on sexological subjects. It is said that ordinary masturbation can change into the very serious psychic masturbation. Psychic masturbation is, of course, the production of an orgasm without physical stimulation. In my experience this phenomenon is very rare indeed, and when it does occur it is not through ordinary masturbation changing into psychic masturbation. It is part of sexual hyperversion and this itself is sometimes the outward symptom of a psychosis—usually schizophrenia. (An example of psychic masturbation is recorded in the case of Peter Kürten on page 138.)

It must not be thought that in diminishing the alleged evils of masturbation I am necessarily approving of it and encouraging the habit amongst young people. Masturbation is only a substitute and should as early as possible be replaced by normal heterosexual intercourse. Its dangers, such as they are, reside in the fact that it allows gratification in solitary fantasy instead of urging the young man to go out and seek a mate. The guilt feelings engendered often make the young man, or woman, more self-conscious and shy, thus leading to further resort to masturbation and less to that social life by which the young meet suitable partners. Masturbation is only to be considered abnormal when the patient deliberately turns from heterosexual intercourse to it for satisfaction. Where there is an impossibility of normal intercourse it is inevitable that it will arise or persist. In this case, when it is present *faute de mieux*, it can do little harm and cannot be regarded as abnormal.

The relationship of masturbation to anxiety can be twofold. Not only does masturbation produce anxiety, but frequently it is used from infancy to allay worry and fear (we have noted that masturbation often starts in children during the trauma of weaning when no doubt the child is in a state of fear). When this occurs in other children it is easy to see how a vicious circle is produced. The child is cautioned regarding the evil effects of the habit and this produces anxiety. This anxiety is dispelled by masturbation, but only for a time. The guilt feelings produced by the masturbation recur and this leads to fresh onanism. The vicious circle continues; anxiety—masturbation—more anxiety—more masturbation, and so on. This vicious circle is easily dispelled by psychotherapy and the sometimes miraculous results of treatment occur in a short time once the anxiety is removed.

Masturbation also occurs at the other extreme of life—in old men. This may be because their diminishing sexuality makes them unresponsive to women, or because age has made them less attractive and they are unable to find a woman willing to have intercourse with them. Curiously enough, as we have noticed, the psychological urge tends to appear before the individual is physically capable of intercourse in childhood, so in old age the psychological desire may persist long after the body has lost its capacity to satisfy it.

REFERENCES

BERNE, E. (1944) The problem of masturbation, *Dis. nerv. Syst.*, **5**, 301–5.

DAVISON, W. C., and LEVINTHAL, J. D. (1957) *The Compleat Pediatrician*, 7th ed., Durham, N. C.

GAREISO, J., and PETRE, A. J. (1938) Onanismo infantíl, *Rev. argent. Neurol. Med. leg.*, **3**, 142–51.

HAIRE, E. H. (1962) Masturbatory insanity, *J. ment. Sci.*, **108**, 1–19.

HUHNER, M. (1944) Masturbation in both sexes, *Med. Tms (N.Y.)*, **72**, 188–90.

HUSCHKA, M. (1938) Incidence and character of masturbation threats in a group of problem children, *Psychoanal. Quart.*, **7**, 338–56.

LEES, H. (1944) The word you can't say, *Hygeia (Chicago)*, **22**, 336.

LUYS, G. (1937) Les dangers et les complications de l'onanism chez l'homme, *Bull. Soc. méd. Hôp. Paris*, **141**, 663–9.

MEHTA, P. M. (1943) Autoerotism—a case and some reflections, *Med. Bull. (Bombay)*, **2**, 165–7.

SAL, Y., and ROSAS, F. (1939) Un caso de histeria surgida a raíz de supresión brusca de la masturbación y curada por el choque cardiazolico, *Rev. méd. peru.*, **2**, 175–84.

SPROCK, B. (1942) Notes on the psychology of circumcision, masturbation, and enuresis, *Urol. cutan. Rev.*, **46**, 768–70.

STIRT, S. S. (1940) Overt mass masturbation in the classroom, *Amer. J. Orthopsychiat.*, **10**, 801–4.

11

NECROPHILIA, GERONTOSEXUALITY, INCEST, AND RAPE

NECROPHILIA

Definition

The use of a dead body as a sexual object. It may be one extracted from a mortuary or stolen from a cemetery, or else a living person murdered in order to provide a corpse to be used sexually.

Psychopathology

I must confess to considerable difficulty as to the classification of necrophilia. Psychopathologically this might be considered from different points of view. It might be regarded as: (1) a fetish; or as (2) sadism carried to the extreme; or of course (3) as a mixture of these two (i.e. a perversion-fetish[1]); or (4) an obsessional compulsive neurosis possibly with sadistic elements.

Can necrophilia be considered as a fetishism? There is a strong suggestion that it might be so. Nobody can claim that the dead body of a woman can be regarded as a normal sexual object, and by definition a fetish is the substitution of some object totally unfit for a normal sexual aim for the normal one. If it is not a pure fetishism then it might be claimed that this is a factor. However, Karpman, whose opinion is always valuable, states: 'Necrophilia is intimately associated with extreme sadism. The defencelessness of the corpse is an important factor. The necrophiliac is usually psychotic, frequently epileptic.' One wonders whether this illness is really more common in epileptics or whether this is only a residue of Lombroso's exploded ideas.

[1] What is called here a 'perversion-fetish' would be called by Freud a perversion. The writer feels, however, that when the sexual object is an unbiological one (i.e. a perversion) which is attractive because of some abnormal point of attraction—such as coughing—then the coughing is a perversion-fetish. The whole product stands midway between perversion and fetish and is best known as a conjunction of the two (i.e. as a perversion-fetish). This is both convenient and explanatory. It is important to realize that almost any combination can occur; e.g. I have seen a transvestist who liked his wife to wear high-heeled shoes and heavy make-up—a shoe fetishist in fact. He periodically practised mutual masturbation with her when he was dressed as a woman and she wore the high-heeled shoes. At other times they had normal intercourse, but he was less excited than when he practised his abnormality. This is carried to even further lengths in another case of a man who had uncontrollable urges to bite the lobes of other men's ears. Here the sexual object was unbiological—i.e. another man—and the aim similarly unnatural. An illuminating case was mentioned by Waugh in his autobiography: a schoolmaster who was sexually excited and had an emission when he placed a boy's naked foot inside his trousers. Here is homosexuality combined with foot fetishism. Such a condition could only be classified as a perversion-fetish.

Can necrophilia be considered as the extreme limit of sadism? This again seems probable, but against it is the fact that sadists usually lose interest in the victim once he or she is dead and do not usually return to the body and assault it when it is cold. They do, it is true, sometimes return to the scene of the crime, but then only to excite themselves with the thought of the expiring agonies, the flowing blood, and so on.

I must confess to a lack of pathological material to clarify the psychopathology. Necrophiliacs are very rare, some are insane and inaccessible, and infrequently consult the psychiatrist. I have never seen it in a sane person, and the literature is very sparse indeed. London mentions a man who, amongst other symptoms, had necrophiliac desires during his psychosis, but gives no suggestion as to the psychopathology of this perversion. In the whole recent literature on sexual abnormalities (out of some 300 references) there are only one or two papers on necrophilia, such as those by Brill and Rapoport.

The possibility that necrophilia is strongly obsessive-compulsive is suggested by the case of Christie which will be described overleaf. There is no reason why a compulsion should not be sadistic, and carried to the extreme it could comprise killing and violating a woman. In favour of compulsion is the repetition of the act and other obsessional traits which necrophiliacs sometimes show.

Like all perversions, necrophilia is as old as mankind. For example, Herodotus states that the ancient Egyptians took precautions against it. He writes:

The wives of men of rank, and such females as have been distinguished by their beauty or importance, are not immediately on their decease delivered to the embalmers: they are usually kept for three or four days, which is done to prevent any indecency being offered to their persons. An instance once occurred of an embalmer's gratifying his lust on the body of a female lately dead: the crime was divulged by a fellow artist.

It is said that certain Parisian brothels cater for this perversion. The prostitute is made up like a corpse with a pallid appearance, dressed in a shroud, and lies in a coffin. If this is so perhaps this perversion is more common than it appears to the psychiatrist. Even if it is a wish-fulfilling fantasy it suggests that it is not infrequent.

The following case shows that occasionally such a patient falls into the hands of the police and it is significant that there is a strong element of psychosis in this man's personal and family history.

D. R. P., singer, 24, was sentenced by Timaru Supreme Courts to two years jail, with hard labour, for having improperly interfered with the body of a young girl aged 12, which was taken from a hospital morgue on December 20.

On earlier pleas of guilty to three thefts charges, P. was sentenced to $2\frac{1}{2}$ years hard labour, all sentences to be cumulative, making a total of $4\frac{1}{2}$ years hard labour. The jury reached a verdict in 95 minutes.

'History supplies us with examples of the astounding nature of this very type of offence', Mr. Justice Fleming said in summing up. 'It is stated that one of the greatest military leaders—not of British origin—was a glaring example of this monstrous type of offender. I will not even refer to what he was accused of in history, because it is so frightfully revolting. But it is true that there is a type of person in this world who indulges in this type of thing.'

Concluding, Mr. Justice Fleming said that the only point the jury really had to decide was whether P. was really sane enough to know that what he did on December 20 was wrong in the eyes of the law. Seeking leniency, the defence counsel said that P.'s mother was admitted to a mental hospital at an early age whilst P. himself was admitted at the age of 14.

One cannot help being struck by the fact that both the patient and his mother had suffered from a psychosis, and also the judge's complete lack of understanding of this man's condition. Whether the military leader was of British origin or not seems somewhat irrelevant, but the fact that he was a soldier might suggest a sadistic element in the origin of *his* necrophilia.

The most terrible case of necrophilia, at least in English legal history, was that of John Reginald Halliday Christie who committed the so-called 'Rillington Place Murders'. These shocked everybody, not only because eight murders were done in this humble house in the poor district of Ladbroke Grove, but because two, that of Mrs. Evans, and her daughter, Geraldine, previously discovered, had been attributed to Timothy Evans, her husband. Timothy Evans had been tried, found guilty, and hanged. In spite of the fact that a judicial inquiry conducted by a prominent lawyer, Scott Henderson, had upheld this verdict, most people now believe that poor Timothy Evans was guiltless, and that Christie, a witness at his trial was the murderer.

Multiple murders of such a nature are uncommon in English medico-legal practice and the only previous case of the same sort (without the necrophilia) was that of John George Haigh, who killed six people by shooting, and destroyed their bodies in acid.

The Rillington Place murders were discovered by a Jamaican, Beresford Brown, who occupied the flat previously inhabited by Christie. Beresford Brown was sounding the walls in order to find a solid place to put up a shelf for his radio when he noticed a hollow portion. He stripped off the wallpaper and found a cupboard underneath. Using a torch he looked in and saw the naked body of a woman. He summoned the police at once. On opening up the recess they saw not one body but three hidden there.

The police decided that the whole house must be examined and the inside of it was literally taken to pieces. A further body, later identified as that of Christie's wife, was found under the floorboards of the front room.

The discovery of these bodies led the police to examine the garden. There, after much effort in which every single grain of soil was sieved, two skeletons, one of which lacked a skull, were unearthed. It is a point of drama that one important bone was discovered not only in the very last plot (into which the police had divided the garden) but in the very last sieveful of earth removed.

On 31 March 1953 Christie was arrested. He had been wandering about London and was found on the riverside near Putney Bridge. He made a number of not very reliable statements, but confessed to the murder of the four women found in the house. His wife he admitted strangling with a stocking because, he said, she was dying of barbiturate poisoning with which she had attempted suicide. This was untrue—there was no barbiturate found in her body. The others he said he strangled after he had had intercourse; except one, Malony, who was drunk and attacked him so that he had had to kill her in self-defence. He later admitted that he had killed the two women whose bodies had been buried in the garden and whose skeletons were found later by the police.

One curious point is that a tobacco tin was discovered in the house. This contained bunches of pubic hair, apparently deliberately collected and arranged by Christie, for some unknown purpose. The bodies found in the cupboard also revealed a curious similarity inasmuch as they were each wrapped in a blanket which was secured round them, the head was covered with a pillowcase, the sexual parts were covered with a diaper, the lower clothes had been removed but the stockings left on.

The pathological examination revealed that sexual intercourse had taken place at or shortly after death.

Christie stated that he had killed these women by making them drunk, then gassing them with coal gas supplied by a tube behind the chair in which they sat, and strangulation.

Psychiatric examination revealed a great deal about him. He was the youngest boy of a family of seven children. One brother and three sisters were older than he, and one sister was younger. These were all alive and well, but one elder sister had died. There was no family history of mental illness but the father was a very strict man: all the children were frightened of him and he had to be approached through the mother.

Apart from the father the home conditions were good and Christie got on satisfactorily with his brothers and sisters. Similarly he was a good scholar at school and got on well with his companions but made no friends. He was never in trouble at school, enjoyed sports, and played in the school team. Moreover he was a King's Scout and became an assistant group leader. In his spare time he worked in his father's garden.

He left school at the age of 15 years and was employed as a cinema projectionist. This he did until 1915 when he was conscripted into the Army and sent overseas to France in the First World War. There he remained until 1918. He was never in the firing line, but claimed that he lost his voice for three and a half years after being gassed. He was awarded a disability pension for this, but his voice later came back when he became angry and swore. The disability was therefore hysterical. He seems to have been rather boastful about his service stating that he could have had promotion had he wished; that he had been a marksman, had won shooting competitions and so on.

Christie had a long history of sexual inadequacy both before and after marriage. He said that he had had no sexual intercourse with his wife for two and a half years before he murdered her.

After he left the Army in 1918 he rested at home for some months and then became a clerk. He held various posts of short duration but was with one firm for five years.

He registered as a War Reserve Police Officer before 1939 and served as a special constable for four years, then as a a full-time reserve constable from 1939 to 1943. He was considered a useful officer and was twice commended. On leaving the police force he was employed with British Road Transport and did this work until December 1952 when he gave notice and disappeared. He did no more work until his arrest.

He never smoked or drank to excess. His first sexual experiences were when he went to a district near his home frequented by girls of loose morals. He was teased by them, and by the two boys with whom he went, because he was not able to have intercourse, and he acquired the reputation of being too slow. He had intercourse with a girl when he was 17 and occasionally went with prostitutes when in the Army.

Christie had a long history of hysterical symptoms: not only the loss of his voice in France, but loss of his vision for a time when this occurred. He also had diarrhoea which proved intractable, pains in his back, and 'fibrositis'. In 1950 he had depression and defective memory.

In prison Christie was meticulously clean and tidy. He was egocentric and kept a photograph of himself in his cell. In addition to this he was found to be a great talker and enjoyed discussing his own case.

At the trial the psychiatrist for the defence, Dr. Hobson, stated: 'I regard Christie as one of the most severe hysterics I have met with in my psychiatric practice. In my opinion these severe forms of hysteria should be regarded as "disease of the mind" of the Macnaughton Rules.' The prison doctor, who was not a psychiatrist, expressed the opinion that Christie was sane and had not suffered from hysteria.

The psychiatrist for the prosecution stated: 'I would regard Christie as the possessor of a highly abnormal character rather than as a victim of disease.' He added naïvely, 'Nor am I completely satisfied that the murders were necessarily sadistic. There is nothing, for example, to suggest that a sadistic motive entered in the murder of his wife. Christie himself repudiated any sadistic motive, emphasizing that to hurt anybody was the last thing he ever wished to do or have done.'

It is curious that no emphasis was placed on the obsessional way in which the bodies were trussed up, nor on the curious clumps of pubic hair arranged in the four corners of a tobacco box. Christie was obsessionally clean and tidy in prison. Moreover, he described a typical obsessive-compulsive feeling when he stated: 'When I had done one I dismissed it from my mind. I seemed to feel as if I had to do it.' He said that he was really glad he had been arrested as he felt he would have continued to go on doing these things had he not been caught.

It is a thousand pities that a more detailed study of Christie was not made but the psychiatrists involved were, naturally, more employed in investigating his mental state from the point of view of his trial rather than the cause of his condition.

Why did he indulge in the appalling violation of women he had just killed? It is not easy to state with certainty the source of his impulse. Firstly, we can say that it was not due to schizophrenia since none of the doctors who examined him found that he suffered from that disease. One might suspect that his frustrated sexual impulse (he had never been very successful) was the fundamental cause of his behaviour. Probably there was unconscious sadism, and even some consciousness of it. We must not be so simple as to believe that because a man derives sexual pleasure in hurting others that he is not a sadist. Particularly a man like Christie who stated what he felt would be of advantage to him. If he were sadistic then he probably would be sexually inadequate. His psychopathy, if he were an inadequate psychopath, was probably related to it. The psychic drive manifested itself in an obsessional urge to kill and violate. Once this was done then he felt a sense of relief and was able to put the matter aside, much as a normal man feels a sense of relief after normal sexual intercourse; and not until mounting sexual urgency turns his thoughts to those channels does he become preoccupied with such an outlet.

In terms of conditioning his father brought him up to be fearful, he was unable to have normal sex because of it, and he found an outlet which permitted sexual success but at the expense of murder. The Freudian would suggest that his behaviour showed a mixture of sadism, obsessionalism, and hysteria.

It is impossible, on the meagre basis of information which this case provides, to give a satisfactory psychological explanation for his behaviour. Whatever it is everyone will agree that it is fortunate that such a conjunction of circumstances arises so rarely.

One might suspect that necrophilia is, psychopathologically, a type of aggression with the victim representing the mother. If this is so one can find a homosexual counterpart in the Aztecs, who seemed to specialize in religious sadism.

They indulged in a curious ceremony called *Tlacaxupehauliztle* (flaying-the-man feast) in which, according to Peterson, 'the warriors who captured prisoners led them by the forelock in front of the temple of Huitzilopochtli. The prisoners' hearts were cut out, their skins removed and worn in a grisly dance by their captors or the priests.'

Soustelle in *La Vie Quotidienne des Aztecs à la Veille de la Conquete Espagnole* (based on Fray Bernardino de Sahagún) describes a ceremony performed in honour of Zipe Totec (the flayed god) in which the prisoner 'was fastened to a kind of frame, shot with arrows and then flayed—the priests dressed themselves in the skin. In most cases the victim was dressed, painted and ornamented, so as to represent the god who was being worshipped and thus it was the god himself who died in his own image.'

Pottery and statues show that *the priest was actually laced in the dead man's skin*, presumably to enhance the identification.

I have never heard of anything similar in our culture, although some patients have had wild fantasies of this nature. It is difficult to know how sexually connected the Aztecs' behaviour may have been; it could have been sadism of the first type showing no sexual evidence, but no doubt it caused sexual excitement in some cases.

The interesting fact is that the victim impersonated the god, and psychoanalysis has shown that the god represents the father, so in this case the aggression was directed to him and not to the mother; but whether there was some deeper psychopathology, with the father symbolizing the mother, and the behaviour representing some sort of return to the womb cannot be known now.

REFERENCES

BRILL, A. A. (1941) *Journal of Criminal Psychopathology*, **2**, 433–43 and **3**, 50–73.
CAMPS, F. E. (1953) *Medical and Scientific Investigations in the Christie Case*, London.
CASO, A. (1953) *El Pueblo del Sol*, Mexico City.
HERODOTUS, *Euterpe*, vol. 89, 428–9 (Beloe's translation, 1806), London.
KARPMAN, B. (1954) *The Sexual Offender and his Offenses*, New York.
LONDON, L. (1946) *Libido and Delusion*, Washington, D.C.
MELBOURNE HERALD (1948) 6 February.
PETERSON, F. (1959) *Ancient Mexico*, London.
RAPOPORT, J. (1942) *Journal of Criminal Psychopathology*, **4**, 277–89.
SOUSTELLE, J. (1955) *La Vie Quotidienne des Aztecs à la Veille de la Conquête Espagnole*, Paris. (Translated by O'Brian, Patrick: *Daily Life of the Aztecs*, London.)
SPOERRI, VON TH. (1959) Nekrophilie, Strukturanalyse eines Falles, *Bibl. psychiat. neurol. (Basel)*, Fasc. 105.
SZASZ, T. S. (1957) *Pain and Pleasure*, London.

GERONTOSEXUALITY

Some authors describe 'gerontosexuality' which is defined as the seeking of an elderly person as a sexual object. I have not considered this extensively here partly because it is so rare as to be inconsiderable and partly that it is impossible to know when it starts. It is not unusual for young men who are mother-fixated to choose women older than themselves as sexual partners. At exactly what age are we to consider this a perversion? Since we have defined a perversion as some sexual behaviour which does not lead to the possibility of fertilization perhaps it would be considered perverse if a young man mates with a woman over the menopause. Yet sometimes young women seek old men. What is to be the limit here? It is indefinable unless we define it as mating with a man so old he is unable to have intercourse. It is felt that gerontosexuality is really a special form of heterosexuality or homosexuality and, particularly as it is so rare as a real form of behaviour for a young man to behave sexually to a very old woman, or a young woman to a very old man, it is negligible, although in very exceptional instances it may explain the sadistic attacks made upon old people. In my very extensive practice in these cases I have never seen a real case of gerontosexuality.

Ancillary Considerations

It must be stressed that it is rare to find a perversion in pure culture—it is usually admixed with some other perversion; or, indeed, with a neurosis or psychosis. In my opinion, and it is very difficult to discover reliable statistics on the matter, it is much more common to find psychoses amongst those who suffer from perversions than those who do not. This, of course, accords with Freud's view of the origin of the psychosis and the perversion in a fixation in the earliest years. Whether Freud's views are correct, or not, there is no doubt that perverts often become insane, and in the psychoses we frequently find evidence of the perversions (in fact Rosanoff suggests that schizophrenia is only the exhibition of chaotic sexuality, and produces interesting facts to support his beliefs). I have already pointed this out elsewhere and stated that in a series of seven early psychotics treated by me one was a sado-masochist, one had had two homosexual episodes but at the time was behaving heterosexually, and one was a fetishist.

Freud at one time believed that there was a common relation between the perversions and the psychoses. He said:

But psychoanalysis teaches better than this. It shows that the symptoms do not by any means result at the expense only of the so-called normal impulse (at least not exclusively or preponderantly) but they represent the converted expression of impulse which in a broader sense might be designated as *perverse* if they could manifest themselves directly in fantasies and acts without deviating from consciousness. The symptoms are therefore partially formed at the cost of abnormal sexuality. *The neurosis is, so to say, the negative of the perversion.* (His italics.)

To this he adds in a footnote:

The well-known fancies of perverts which under favourable conditions are changed into contrivances, the delusional fears of the paranoiac which are in a hostile manner projected on to others, the unconscious fancies of hysterics which are discovered in their symptoms by psychoanalysis agree as to content in the minutest details.

Without necessarily agreeing with this completely it cannot be denied that the two conditions are more or less related.

This alone should make us realize that, if the neuroses and psychoses are to be regarded as disease processes, the perversions must be so regarded also.

Apart from the tendency to psychoses it is not unusual for perverts, as I have pointed out under various sections, to commit suicide. In fact reports which show that the victim of suicide was perverted in his sexuality are not uncommon, but such details are suppressed in most newspaper accounts. It is unlikely that the pervert commits suicide because he finds that he has difficulty in adjusting himself to a world made for normal people, although that is usually the excuse for his end. It is much more likely that he tends to commit suicide for the same reason that the psychotic does—that is, because he is compelled by unconscious forces to take his life. Undoubtedly, frequently the sufferer does not intend suicide but takes his life accidentally. This results in those cases in which a patient ties himself up in a locked room. A slipped rope obstructs his breathing and owing to his trussed-up condition he is unable to release himself.

It is, perhaps, characteristic of the pervert's tendency to reverse emotion back upon himself that, apart from the sadists, suicide is much more common than murder. He is, in general, much more dangerous to himself than to others.

From whatever point of view we regard the sexual perversions we must admit that they are traceable, like the neuroses and psychoses, back to childhood, and far from being the result of an innate refusal to live normally and enjoy the sexual pleasures of the majority, or an attempt to gain secret and sinister gratification, they are the production of disease processes which have affected the mental life of the pervert. These processes are intimately connected with the growth of the child and its environment from earliest times. We shall see that in certain cases, it is possible by psychotherapy to reverse the process and allow the patient to return to normality.

Related Conditions

It is by no means easy to fit incest and rape into the classifications I have given here. This is not because it is an unnatural one, but because our customs make them unacceptable. In incest the sexual object is not one prohibitive of reproduction, neither is it in rape.

Rape may have been the more or less usual way of acquiring a mate in some primitive cultures, as instanced by the examples in anthropology where it was customary to pretend to steal the wife away from her people against her will. Obviously in such a case this was only enacting in a playful way something which was once serious; seducing the girl forcefully would have been the next, inevitable step.

In neither of these cases can it be suggested that the sexual object is not the biological one, but these instances have been put here as the most suitable place.

INCEST

Definition

Sexual relations between those with the forbidden degrees of relationship.

Psychopathology

Incest differs from most sexual abnormalities inasmuch as it is a more 'natural' act which has for various reasons, psychological and otherwise, become forbidden. Animals have no feeling in the matter and willingly mate with brother or sister, father or mother, and so on. The Freudian view of the primitive horde and the behaviour of the strongest male capturing the females until killed by the young males is somewhat upheld by the researches of Zuckerman on apes. From this point of view the young males were expelled from the group and incest started from it inasmuch as the old male would not tolerate sexual approaches to his females. This, however, does not explain how the horror which it attached to sexual relations between father and daughter came about. There is no doubt that the elaborate taboo which exists amongst savage tribes is to a great extent, consciously or unconsciously, devised to prevent the possibility of incest.

Incest was tolerated in ancient times, although it appears to have been mainly brother-and-sister rather than father-daughter type. For example, Herodotus states that Cambyses[1] asked the royal judges in Persia whether there was any law which forbade a brother marrying his sister. The judges wisely replied that they could find no law which would permit a brother

[1] Cambyses was said to be epileptic, alocholic, and finally insane.

doing so but they had discovered that there was one which permitted the king of Persia doing what he pleased. He therefore married his eldest sister at once and shortly afterwards married a younger one as well.

Frazer gives an intersting explanation of the incest which appeared in royal lines in early times. He states:

He (Cinyras, ancestor of the ancient priestly kings of Paphos) is said to have begotten his son Adonis in incestuous intercourse with his daughter Myrrha at a festival of the corn-goddess, at which women robed in white were wont to offer corn-wreaths as first-fruits of the harvest and to observe strict chastity for nine days. Similar cases of incest with a daughter are reported of many ancient kings. It seems unlikely that such reports are without foundation, and perhaps equally improbable that they refer to mere fortuitous outbursts of unnatural lust. We may suspect that they are based on a practice actually observed for a definite reason in certain special circumstances. Now in countries where the royal blood was traced through women only, and where consequently the king held office merely in virtue of his marriage with an hereditary princess, who was the real sovereign, it appears to have often happened that a prince married his own sister, the princess royal, in order to obtain with her hand the crown which otherwise would have gone to another man, perhaps to a stranger. May not the same rule of descent have furnished a motive for incest with a daughter? For it seems a natural corollary from such a rule that the king was bound to vacate the throne on the death of his wife, the queen, since he occupied it only by virtue of his marriage with her. When the marriage terminated, his right to the throne terminated with it, and passed at once to his daughter's husband. Hence if the king desired to reign after his wife's death, the only way in which he could legitimately continue to do so was by marrying his daughter, and thus prolonging through her the title which had formerly been his through her mother.

Such circumstances were present in ancient Egypt. It was thus that Cleopatra, one of the most beautiful women the world has ever known, was the product of many incestuous marriages, and married her own brother.

The Romans were terrified that incest would cause famine and Frazer has something interesting to say of this, also. He states: 'Hence, too, we can understand why an ancient Roman law, attributed to the king Tullus Hostilus, prescribed that when incest had been committed, an expiatory sacrifice should be offered by the pontiffs in the grove of Diana. For we know that the crime of incest is commonly supposed to cause a dearth: hence it is meet that atonement for the offence should be made to the goddess of fertility.'

The Greek laws appeared to permit incest in certain cases. At Athens a man was allowed to marry a sister by his father but not by the same mother. In Lacedaemon he was allowed, on the contrary, to marry a sister by the same mother but not by his father. Modern law appears to have been influenced by Hebraic codes which forbid incest under any condition.

S—PSY. D.

Formerly it was not a crime under English law although if the attention of the ecclesiastical courts were drawn to it punishment might be administered. However, by the Incest Act of 1908 it became a misdemeanour, punishable by imprisonment, for a man to have intercourse with his grand-daughter, daughter, sister or mother. Half-brother and half-sister are taken to be the same as brother and sister. This Act has been consolidated by the Sexual Offences Act of 1956.

Incest appears under modern conditions only when circumstances are strong enough to undermine the very rigid taboo which is imposed against it. It is felt more probable that this taboo is based on deeply seated psychological grounds than upon a knowledge of eugenics.

Incest occurs: (1) between defectives who are unable to comprehend the prohibitions against it or whose feelings are too strong to inhibit them behaving in this way; (2) where alcohol removes the sense of prohibition; (3) in cases of cerebral disease such as general paralysis, senile cerebral degeneration, and so on; (4) in more normal persons where a brother and sister have been separated since childhood or for a long period and meet later as strangers; lastly (5) where there is great propinquity and close relations have to live in intimacy. This is sometimes produced by poverty, and other causes of overcrowding. It is obvious that various causes operate in different circumstances—e.g. cerebral degeneration is more likely to be a factor in father-daughter incest whereas separation or propinquity is in brother-sister forms.

There have been some studies of the fathers concerned in father-daughter incest. Weinberg, for example, describes three types: (1) Endogenous; men who live socially and sexually within their families, and have little extra-familial social life. (2) Those with paedophilic tendencies. (3) Those who are simply indescriminately promiscuous. On the other hand, Gebhard, Gagnon, Pomeroy, and Christenson divide incestuous fathers into those who offend with children, those with minors and those with adults.

These may be useful for description, but the classifications throw little or no light on the production of the behaviour.

Almost all authors consider that alcohol is a factor in causation, and some suggestions have been made which throw the blame mainly on the daughters. Wolffs, for example, believes that the 'victim' often provokes the offender. Weinberg thinks that incestuous fathers are sometimes encouraged by their daughters' promiscuity and submissiveness. Howard considers that it may be the daughter's wish to revenge herself on the mother.

There is no doubt that the fathers are often abnormal. Medlicott, for example, compared actual incest cases with those in which there had been false allegations. The following table shows his findings:

Psychiatric State of Fathers Involved in Incest

Condition	Actual Incest Series (N.17)	Falsely Alleged Series (N.10)
Psychosis	6 per cent.	0 per cent.
Severe character disorder	47 per cent.	10 per cent.
Immature personality	41 per cent.	30 per cent.
No gross abnormality	0 per cent.	40 per cent.
Unknown	6 per cent.	20 per cent.

On the other hand, the daughters are often found to be suffering from psychiatric disorders, although how far this is due to their experiences or to their having initiated them one cannot say. Medlicott gives the following table showing his findings in his series:

Psychiatric State of Daughters Involved in Incest or Referral

Condition	Actual Incest Series (N.17)	Falsely Alleged Series (N.10)
Schizophrenia	0 per cent.	30 per cent.
Affective disorder	30 per cent.	10 per cent.
Neurosis	35 per cent.	20 per cent.
Character disorder	35 per cent.	40 per cent.

It might be reasonable to conclude from these two tables that incest probably never occurs where both fathers and daughters are normal. Where the father is abnormal it is likely to occur only when the daughter is frightened and dominated by the father, but is much more likely to occur and continue when there are abnormalities in both parties.

Since we do not know the circumstances regarding the cases in which incest was falsely alleged it is not possible to generalize regarding them.

Bromberg (quoted by Karpman) states: 'Incest offenders do not have the neurotic reactions of other sexual criminals: responses are less clouded by evasion and complete denial. They seem to consider incest as essentially normal, not so reprehensible as perverted sexuality but a mature form of heterosexuality.' It must be admitted that some cases certainly support Bromberg's views. For example, Raphing, Carpenter and Davis describe a case of incest in three generations. The fathers encouraged their sons to utilize the daughters for sexual purposes. The conclusion which is drawn from this case is that 'There can be no doubt that the ultimate factors which determine the adherence to, or transgression of the incest barrier are related to the conscious or unconscious communication between parents and child'. There seemed to be little shame or concealment in this case.

I do not believe that this is always true. I have seen cases in which there was denial of the act and considerable evasion; others displayed neurotic clouding and refusal to accept that the behaviour had occurred. Some patients insist that society is at fault. Perhaps the very fact that their mentality has tolerated such behaviour as incest shows that they have a poor super-ego, inhibitions, or conditioning (or whatever terminology one wishes to use) and in such cases one would not expect much, if any, guilt feeling.

If I be permitted to draw on my own experience I can quote cases which throw some light on the psychology of those concerned. One was an 'alcoholic' case—a woman was separated from her husband. Her son, aged 12, complained that she drank to excess and when drunk enticed him into bed with her and seduced him. She firmly denied it: but there seemed no reason why a boy, who might have boasted of his sexual prowess with a maid-servant or other girl, would admit of such a relationship. There was no evidence that he had suffered psychological harm, but he was observed for less than two years. No opportunity was afforded to study the mother.

This case is curiously the opposite to that of the lovely Ninon de L'Enclos. That she was indeed beautiful can be seen by her portrait now in Knowle House. Epton states:

> One day her ex-lover, the Marquis de Gersay, of Brittany, announced that he was sending his son of 22—their son, but the origin of his birth had been kept secret—to be introduced to the polished circle of Ninon's friends. On no account, he stressed, was their relationship to be revealed. Ninon attached herself to her son but soon a terrible thing happened; he fell madly in love with her. When Ninon realized this she forbade him to return to her house, but he insisted on a final interview during which he declared his passion. As he approached to embrace her, Ninon withdrew, and hiding her face in her hands, sobbed: 'I am your mother!' The young marquis stopped and stared at her, speechless. Then he rushed into the garden, drew out his sword and stabbed himself. Ninon ran after him and caught him as he fell: he died in her arms.

Although there was no incest obviously the impulse was there on the son's part and his suicide was directly the result of it.

Another case in which an apparently normal individual had incestuous impulses, which he did not quite put into action because of unfavourable circumstances, was that of a man aged 37, who put his hand on the sexual parts of his daughters, aged 12 and 9.

The wife discovered what he was doing and informed the police. The reason for his behaviour, of which he was tremendously ashamed, was that he was a strict Roman Catholic, and his religion forbade the use of birth control. He already had six children and was fearful of having more. Intercourse with his wife was therefore restricted to three or four times annually, and even then was not satisfactory because he withdrew. He was thus in a state of constant sexual deprivation without a satisfactory chance of alleviation.

When he was first seen he was suffering from severe anxiety and depressive symptoms. He stated that he had little memory of what he had done and appeared in a condition of dissociation. His relations with his wife had not been satisfactory at any time, and there was no doubt that his sexual life had been chaotic.

The poet, Lord Byron, was a case of 'brother and sister separation' incest and after seeing his half-sister, Augusta Leigh as a boy he did not meet her again until a young man. A similar type of case was that of a man aged 30 whose sister had been brought up in America so that he had not seen her since they were children. He was being treated for an obsessional neurosis with strong guilt feelings at the time when his sister came on a visit to England. When he stated that she was coming he was warned that he must be careful in his relations with her because of the danger of sexual attraction. In spite of this he fell violently in love with her and would have committed incest if she had permitted it. Fortunately she saw the hazards of remaining in England and left hurriedly for the United States. The young man admitted that had she been willing, so strong was his feeling, that he would have lived in incestuous relationship with her no matter what the consequences might have been. The result of this attachment was psychologically disastrous. He had been improving but rapidly became considerably worse, refused further psychotherapy, and found a surgeon who did two leucotomies on him. When seen some years later he appeared unchanged. The wish for leucotomy was no doubt a punitive one and possibly had some castration significance.

Another case was that of a woman aged 28. She had had a most unfortunate childhood. Her father appears to have had an incorrigible impulse towards his girl children. He terrorized his wife so that she was afraid to interfere with his behaviour. First he cohabited sexually with the patient from the age of twelve until she was sixteen when he turned his attentions to one of her younger sisters who replaced her. The patient, when she discovered what he was doing to her younger sister, and that there was a law against it, went to the police. He was arrested, charged and tried. The patient gave evidence against him and he was imprisoned. Although she later met a man who fell in love with her (she was an attractive person) and married, she slowly developed an insidious type of paranoid schizophrenia and deteriorated in spite of treatment. It would seem that in her case this was caused by the fact that a great deal of guilt had been engendered, not by what had occurred at her father's hands but that she had had sexual pleasure from it. This, to me, seems to be one of the major problems of incest. The trouble is not so much that conventional morals have been flouted but, horrifying though it may seem, once the first shock has passed the girl only too often obtains sexual pleasure from the intercourse.

To those who are willing to face what is truth, rather than what should be, this is not shocking at all. Animals, as I have pointed out, feel no guilt at incest. Why therefore should we expect anything different, at least in the unconscious minds, of human beings when faced with compulsion, particularly from one of the beings from whom they should obtain their prohibitions?

The progression when incest occurs in the case of father and daughter seems to be somewhat as follows. The father, usually because he has lost control due to alcohol, assaults his daughter. The girl is shocked, hurt, and horrified. She is often forced to keep silent through threats and says nothing, even to her mother. Then, once the prohibition has been broken, the behaviour tends to continue. The girl becomes more and more acquiescent. Finally a relationship almost comparable to that of a normal marriage is established. This is, of course, at once upset and destroyed if the behaviour becomes known to others, and the natural horror shown by them immediately produces terrific guilt. The girl then plays the part of the victim of a relationship which she had not only endured but enjoyed. It is this, rather than the fear of the father, that so often allows an incestuous relationship to continue so long without complaint. It is noticeable, for example, that it was not until the patient described above was replaced by her younger sister that she went to the police and complained. No doubt her willingness to give evidence was partly a form of revenge.

Possibly the last case gives a clue to the prohibition of incest in modern legal systems. It is not that it is so biologically undesirable—it does accentuate all traits, good and bad, of the parents in the offspring—but the fact is that it may make the participants unsuitable for normal marriage. There is no doubt that in our society it may have very severe psychological results, including schizophrenia, and this, in itself, makes its illegality rational.

One might point out that it is useless to imprison incestous parents and then, after serving the sentence, allow them to return to their children, so that they can repeat the offence. Where it exists the impulse appears to be overwhelming (in spite of the refusal of the law to recognize that impulses can be irresistible) and to allow the offending parent to have control of his children again is asking for trouble. They should be taken permanently out of his control and care. The cases where incest occurs in brothers and sisters after a long separation are truly pitiable and, indeed, usually the courts are able to recognize this. It is wise, as is usually done, to separate, but not to punish, them.

The word incest can be extended to include homosexual relations between blood relatives, but how far this is included in the modern meaning of the word it is not easy to say. It originally meant unchastity.

For example, Langsley, Schwartz, and Fairbairn describe a case of father–son incest in which the father masturbated the son after they had stripped to practise weight-lifting together. I have had a similar case in which the father felt that the son was insufficiently interested in sex and did the same. The young man subsequently developed schizophrenia, but how far this was due to the father's behaviour one cannot say, although it was undoubtedly productive of psychic trauma.

Medlicott described a case of mother–daughter incest in which the mother slept with her teenage-daughter and indulged in sexual play with her. The daughter was disgusted and rejected her advances.

The legal and clerical critics of artificial insemination by donor (A.I.D.) have suggested that one of the gravest objections to this procedure is that it may lead to incest without the participants knowing. Needless to say such a possibility may also occur due to adultery or, indeed, to adoption where brother and sister are unknown to each other and possibly have not met since earliest childhood.

This fear, in my opinion, is a grossly exaggerated one. The numerical possibilities show how remote it must be. If there were 8,000 children resulting from artificial insemination by one donor in London (and the probability is that this estimate is excessively high) the likelihood of half-brother mating with half-sister (through having had the same paternal donor) would still only be one in a thousand.

The biological effects of incest are by no means negligible; although it must be appreciated that, since it is much commoner amongst mental defectives who find it difficult to obtain a mate outside the family, we must expect it to produce more untoward results than would occur amongst normal people.

Examples of the bad physical effects have been recorded by Adams and Neel. They reported that of 18 offspring from incestuous unions between first-degree relatives only 7 were normal, one died at 6 hours, and one at 15 hours, one died at 2 months from 'glycogen storage disease', one had a bilateral cleft lip and two were severely mentally retarded with seizures and spastic cerebral palsy, 5 were mildly retarded (I.Q.s 50–70).

Carter recorded the conditions seen in 13 incestuous children; only 5 were normal, 3 failed to reach the age of 9 years (dying at 13 months of cystic fibrosis, at 21 months from progressive cerebral degeneration with blindness, and at 8 years from congenital heart disease). One was severely mentally retarded and four mildly so (I.Q.s 50–76).

Thus in these two series 12 out of 31 were subnormal.

Roberts has analysed the work which has been done on the inhabitants of Tristan da Cunha, where there is considerable inter-marriage, at various times by Woolley, Munch, and Loudon. This amply confirms the fact that in-breeding has a bad effect on mental capacity.

There is therefore sufficient evidence that incest has the effect of deteriorating the offspring, although probably the stock was not good to start with since on Tristan da Cunha, for example, the more intelligent move away.

Studies of the offspring of incestuous unions amongst those of more normal intelligence are probably impossible to obtain since they do not occur with any frequency.

It is time that we took a mature view of this problem and, as Dr. Johnson said, clear our minds of cant. Incest is so distasteful to most normal people that the thought of committing it is inconceivable. It is something we cannot consciously envisage in our wildest fantasies. Yet, since the psychological effects are based on the guilt feelings aroused, there can be no psychic trauma if there is no knowledge of any blood relationship. Oedipus himself was happy until his dreadful secret was revealed to him.

REFERENCES

ADAMS, N. S., and NEEL, J. V. (1967) *Pediatrics*, **40, 55.**

CARTER, C. O. (1967) *Lancet*, i, 436.

EPTON, NINA (1959) *Love and the French*, London.

FRAZER, J. (1922) *The Golden Bough*, London.

FREUD, S. (1916) *Introductory Lectures in Psychoanalysis*, London.

—— (1918) *Totem and Taboo*, New York.

GEBHARD, P. H., GAGNON, J. H., POMEROY, W. B., and CHRISTENSON, C. V. (1965) *Sex Offenders, An Analysis of Types*, London.

HERODOTUS, *Thalia*, 179, xxx (Beloe's translation 1806), vol. ii.

HOWARD, M. S. (1959) Incest. The revenge motive, *Delaware med. J.*, **31,** 223–7.

KARPMAN, B. (1954) *The Sexual Offender and his Offenses*, New York.

LANGSLEY, D. G., SCHWARTZ, M. N., and FAIRBAIRN, R. H. (1968) Father-son incest, *Comprehens. Psychiat.*, **3,** 219–26.

MEDLICOTT, R. W. (1967) Incest, *Aust. N.Z.J. Psychiat.*, 180–7.

RAPHING, D. L., CARPENTER, B. L., and DAVIS, A. (1967) Incest, *Arch. gen. Psychiat.*, 16, **4,** 505–11.

ROBERTS, D. F. (1967) Incest, inbreeding and mental abilities, *Brit. med. J.*, **4,** 336–7.

WEINBERG, S. K. (1955) *Incest Behavior*, New York.

WOLFFS, C. (1962) Inzestsituationen, *Nge. Pol.*, **16,** 154–7.

RAPE

Definition

Rape is sexual intercourse with a female by force or trickery. It is rape to induce a married woman to have intercourse by impersonating her husband, or when a woman is unconscious, or mentally defective. The essential factor being that the woman does not give her consent.

Psychopathology and Occurrence

There is singularly little authorative literature on this subject. The definition being a legal, and not a medical one, is very extensive and covers a number of different types of behaviour. These range from more or less normal behaviour to the grossest aberrations. They are extraordinarily difficult to classify. I shall use here the classification put forward by Brancale, Ellis, and Doorbar for all sexual crimes, but the examples given to amplify it are my own. The types suggested are:

1. Normal, well adjusted men who behave abnormally when under the influence of alcohol.
2. Sexually deviated but psychiatrically non-deviated offenders. Well adjusted apart from abnormal sexual activities.
3. Sexually and psychiatrically deviated offenders. Compulsive and emotionally disturbed.
4. Sexually non-deviated but psychiatrically deviated offenders. Psychotic, defective or suffering from brain damage and so on.

Type One

The apparently normal man who misbehaves under the influence of alcohol is probably the commonest type of rapist. The typical story is that the man, who shows no evidence of abnormality, goes to a dance and takes a certain amount of alcohol. He sees a girl there and sometimes asks to be allowed to accompany her on her way home, or sometimes merely follows her without permission. He may be allowed by the girl, if he accompanies her, to indulge in harmless love-making, kissing and so on, but when intercourse is refused knocks the girl down, and assaults her. The man who follows the girl may come up to her and assault her without more ado.

Usually it would appear that alcohol is the main cause of the behaviour by releasing emotions normally under control. However, in some cases the girl is somewhat to blame, by permitting everything except intercourse when the man has become so excited as to be unable to control himself.

The reason for this behaviour may lie in immaturity of the man. A normal man can so easily find a sexual partner in some complaisant young lady, a prostitute, &c., that it is difficult to understand that some men feel frightened even to approach a girl, but this is the case. He feels so inferior as to be afraid to make proper advances, but under the influence of alcohol he attempts foolish and clumsy manoeuvres which terrify her, she tries to get away, he becomes angry, and obtains sexual satisfaction by force. In at least 25 per cent. of cases the man has been drinking but is not drunk.

Are we to consider such men normal as the definition suggests? This is improbable. The fact that symptoms, for example, in neurosis or in homosexuality, appear only under the influence of alcohol does not mean that the man is psychologically healthy, but merely that his illness is capable of suppression. The same is true of this form of rape. Many of these cases, when the behaviour has not been too gross or the girl is partly to blame, are probably capable of psychiatric help which will do more to prevent future misconduct than the sentence of a year or so in prison.

Type Two

The sexually deviated but psychiatrically non-deviated offenders are found in rape as well as other sexual neuroses. Dr. Karpman, a psychiatrist of unrivalled prison experience, who has analysed many dangerous criminals, in a personal communication, informed me that he has had under his care some rapists who experience sexual pleasure only when obtaining intercourse by force. This is undoubtedly true of the brutal assailant who is incorrigible in his behaviour: he never seeks out a woman normally, and does not need to be intoxicated to rape one. He continues his career until captured.

There is undoubtedly a strong sadistic element in these cases which may sometimes be traced back to a miserable childhood, a drunken parent and so on. Others are trying to break through early prohibitions by violence. Most are attempting to work out some psychological situation.

Type Three

The sexually and psychiatrically deviated offenders who are compulsive and emotionally disturbed probably form a large number of men who commit rape. Thus Ellis found in a study of 300 sex offenders in America that about one-fourth (27 per cent.) of the total examined were so mentally disturbed as to be committable (i.e. certifiable), but they were 'impulsive, poorly controlled, infantile individuals who, especially under the influence of alcohol, give way to their sex urges in an uncontrolled antisocial manner'.

It is often difficult to classify this type of person from the psychiatric point of view. He is obviously inadequate and poorly adjusted to life but yet not sufficiently antisocial to be classed as a psychopath. Often he is capable of doing ordinary work and to pass unnoticed in society until he starts drinking.

Clinically one rarely sees men who feel compulsive urges to rape women. There are undoubtedly individuals who feel insatiable sexual desire, but usually they are able to satisfy themselves with prostitutes or with complaisant females.

Type Four

Sexually non-deviated but psychiatrically deviated offenders are usually obvious. The schizophrenic, often considerably deteriorated, may assault a female without understanding of what he is doing or else because he has been 'told' to do so by hallucinations.

Mental defectives and those of low intelligence also get into trouble in this way. Ellis suggests that they are more frequently caught and punished by the law than normally intelligent men because they have insufficient initiative to escape. East states: 'Among mentally defective persons received in prison, sexual offences in England and Wales come second in frequency. Acquisitive offences take priority. Usually the sexual crime is of minor character, but murder and rape occur.'

The frequent association of murder with rape may indicate that there is, as I have suggested, a close sadistic relationship between the two. In some cases it will be considered that the motive is to prevent the girl giving evidence against the assailant, but this is probably merely ancillary since a normal man would never go to such lengths.

Most psychiatrists believe that the rapist[1] is not a particularly normal person. Karpman points out that in some men only the resistance of the woman makes them potent. He quotes Guttmacher who divides rapists into three classes: (1) those in whom assault is an explosive expression of pent-up impulse: this is the true sex offender; (2) sadistic rapists: masculine sexual activity is aggressive, in some this is exaggerated and dominates the picture; and (3) the aggressive criminal, not a true sex offender, who is out to pillage and rob and for whom rape is just another act of plunder.

Karpman points out that the sexual drive is stronger in paraphiliacs (and presumably so in rapists who can obtain satisfaction only in these peculiar situations) because 'the avenues of release are limited'. It is usual in situations where the instinctual drive is very confined that it will suddenly explosively burst out and this certainly seems to be the case with rape.

Gebhard *et al.* divide rapists into two classes: (1) the majority which

[1] There is no medical term in English for one who rapes and I have used here the American terminology 'rapist' which saves unnecessary verbiage.

are criminally inclined men who take what they want, and (2) the minority which appear rather ordinary citizens suffering from a personality defect which ultimately erupts into a sex offence.

Kopp describes two types of rapists which probably coincide with the classifications already given. The first is a cold-seeming, unfeeling man who has always taken what he wanted from others without apparent concern for the feelings of his victims, or the consequences of his acts. For him rape is just another instance of aggressive taking except that in this case he steals sexual satisfaction rather than property. This man is similar to Guttmacher's aggressive criminal. The second type is markedly different; he is a very compliant person who rarely asks for what he wants because he feels that he does not deserve satisfaction from others. He spends most of his time trying to please other people in order to earn their appreciation and affection, and often cannot accept anything which is freely offered without repaying it in some way. For such a man the act of rape represents a serious break in his character defences. This type is probably the same as Guttmacher's explosive rapist.

Both of Kopp's types feel that rape is a way of stealing love. This would suggest that they had insufficient affection in childhood.

The case of a man who had a compulsion to commit rape was recorded in the press. This was when Lord Parker, the Lord Chief Justice, refused to give a ruling in what he described as a 'difficult and in many ways tragic case'. It was that of a man, aged 23, a joiner, who apparently had uncontrollable sexual impulses. The court was asked to agree to an operation (presumably castration) being performed in prison. The court dismissed an appeal against consecutive sentences of two years' imprisonment. These were imposed at Surrey County Sessions on each of two charges of assaulting a woman aged 57 on the towpath at Barnes with intent to ravish, and of possessing an offensive weapon, a knife.

Lord Parker, who sat with Mr. Justice Salmon, said that the prisoner began receiving sentences for sexual offences when he was 16. He was put in an approved school, and in March 1956, was gaoled for a 'horrible rape'. Later, while cycling along the towpath, he stopped a hospital nurse, threatened her with a knife, and it was quite clear what he intended to do. Luckily for her there was a police launch nearby and she attracted its attention.

'One of the doctors,' his lordship said, 'at any rate, fears that if he is let out he may be guilty of a very serious offence, even murder.' Two possible solutions were that he should receive hormone treatment or an operation.

The court agreed with the doctors that an operation was probably the only hope. It could not accede to the request that it should assure the hospital authorities that such an operation would be lawful and not contrary to public policy.

Lord Parker said that at the moment the court could see no grounds for interfering with the sentence.

The law presents the judges, who are obviously humane and kindly men, with considerable difficulties. They have no power to alter the laws except by 'case law' in which they interpret the statutes in a wider way than formerly. However, here we have a man suffering from a compulsive condition which it is agreed could be cured by operation or hormone treatment. Most reasonable people would say that he was ill. The fact that his illness makes him liable to commit horrible crimes is by the way. Yet, instead of being able to attack the cause of his condition, in the hope that he might become a comparatively normal man, he has to be sent to prison from whence he will emerge in exactly the same state to do further horrible rapes on harmless women. No doubt, if he does so he will be given heavier sentences which will have no effect *except to release him in a state of sexual hunger and more likely to repeat his offences.* The most terrible thing is that the man is willing and eager that something should be done whilst he is in prison to prevent further disasters.

Even though I do not view castration of these men with enthusiasm surely he could be permitted to have such heavy doses of stilboestrol, during his two years in prison, that it would be a long period before he recovered his sexual competence.

REFERENCES

BRANCALE, R., ELLIS, A., and DOORBAR, R. R. (1952) Psychiatric and psychological investigations of convicted sex offenders: summary report, *Amer. J. Psychiat.*, **109**, 17–21.

DAILY TELEGRAPH (1959) 12 May, p. 15.

EAST, N. (1949) *Society and the Criminal*, London, H.M.S.O.

ELLIS, A. (1951) A study of 300 sex offenders, *Int. J. Sexol.*, **6**, 127–35.

GEBHARD, P. H., GAGNON, J. H., POMEROY, W. B., and CHRISTENSON, C. V. (1965) *Sex Offenders*, London.

KARPMAN, B. (1954) *The Sexual Offender and His Offenses*, New York.

KOPP, S. B. (1962) The character of sex offenders, *Amer. J. Psychother.*, **16**, 64–70.

MANT, A. K. (1956) The tow-path murder: the medical aspect, *Med.-leg. J. (Camb.)*, **24**, 1–4.

WAUGH, E. (1964) *A Little Learning: An Autobiography*, London.

PART FOUR

DISORDERS OF THE SEXUAL STIMULUS

12

TRANSVESTISM, TRANS-SEXUALISM, AND FETISHISM

TRANSVESTISM

Definition

The assumption of clothes of the opposite sex for sexual purposes.

Transvestism appears to be a deep-seated and abnormal impulse of great antiquity. It is easy to discover in history examples of men who dressed as females and women who dressed as men—Caligula and Assurbanipal (Sardanapalus) immediately come to mind amongst the males and the Chevalier d'Eon and George Sand amongst the females. Again, in some religions it has been the custom for priests to assume a quasi-female or even completely female garb, and I point out elsewhere in this book that this usually occurred when the deity was a goddess rather than a god.

This abnormal impulse appears just as prominently in modern life. Nevertheless, women do sometimes not only assume masculine clothes but in doing so pose as men and even attempt to marry, thus showing that this perversion is as common in the female as in the male.

Psychopathology

Those ignorant of the deeper currents of the human mind are likely to jump to the conclusion that transvestism is probably caused by the child being forced to wear clothing of the opposite sex; the boy being brought up as a girl or vice versa. Occasionally one finds that parents have treated children in that way and *conditioned* them to behave as if they were of the wrong sex. Although I do not believe that this is the whole causation it is probably of importance in some cases, but in my studies of hermaphrodites with Broster's team I have only once seen a case of a patient who had rudimentary male testes and a female psyche. This is confirmed by Albert Ellis, who studied all the cases of hermaphroditism recorded in the English medical literature. Not one of those who had been brought up as male became homosexual or behaved as a transvestist. Nevertheless it is a curious thing that some cases, in which there is undoubtedly deeper psychological causation, have been dressed as of the opposite sex mainly 'for fun' when they were children, or because their parents wanted a girl or boy, as the case may be. London recorded a case of this kind, and it is to be noticed in the one described by Fenichel.

This may be a strong ancillary factor in canalizing the behaviour into transvestist channels as is shown by the work of Stoller. He examined 32 transvestists and their womenfolk (i.e. mothers, sisters, girl-friends, &c.) and states:

The women all share the attributes of taking a conscious and intense pleasure in seeing males dressed as females. All have a common fear of, and need to ruin, masculinity. Very envious of males, such women revenge themselves either by dressing their males in female clothing or encouraging such dressing once it develops 'spontaneously'.

He divides these women into three categories.

1. The malicious male hater. She hates all males and humiliates them whenever possible.
2. The succourer. She does not initiate transvestism but supports it with sympathy.
3. The symbiote. These are mothers of boys who spontaneously and compellingly encourage to dress in female clothes as soon as they are old enough to dress themselves.

This work has not been confirmed by others but it must be admitted that in general the females associated with transvestists have not been studied widely.

It was not until 1910 that transvestism was clearly defined as a perversion by Hirschfeld. He recognized four types: (1) heterosexual; (2) homosexual; (3) narcissistic; and (4) asexual. Other writers have suggested a fifth type, bisexual.

I believe that there are fetishistic and exhibitionistic roots to this behaviour and that these are certainly more important than, for instance, Hirschfeld's asexual factor.

Heterosexual

I do not believe that transvestism is ever a manifestation of heterosexuality and I am of the opinion that these cases should be regarded rather as apparent heterosexuals. Transvestism must accord by definition with the usual habilimentary customs of the country; in China and parts of the East, for instance, it is usual for women to wear trousers, and for men to wear flowing robes. It would be just as much transvestism for a woman to wear flowing robes as it would be for a man to wear them in Europe.

Pettow believed that transvestism was a compulsion, but careful studies of cases do not support this view. Nor do they uphold Fessler's theory of endocrine, particularly testicular, dysfunction; or his idea that this abnormality is one which necessarily appears late in life—in fact frequently it is quite the opposite.

There is no doubt that a large number of these cases do appear to be heterosexual. The man is frequently married with a child or children, and has intercourse with his wife. Sometimes the perversion appears only when he is under the influence of a drug such as alcohol, which suggests that it has a homosexual basis, normally repressed, but appearing when repression is removed. In this way it may be regarded as the only manifestation of homosexuality. I have seen a strong, burly man who was an officer in the R.A.F., who played rugby football, and mixed normally with other men. He showed a normal interest in women, yet he liked to wear female clothes when he had intercourse with his wife and did not obtain satisfaction unless he did so. His wife was kind and sympathetic and allowed him to do this although it distressed her that he was so abnormal. He had on some occasions worn female clothes in the street and obtained great pleasure from appearing in public dressed in this way. In spite of the fact that he wore women's clothes, shoes, jewellery, &c. and made up his face with cosmetics, the idea of any form of relationship with other men was unattractive to him. He did not change his clothes to attract other men, but definitely obtained more sexual pleasure in intercourse with a woman if dressed as a female. In appearance he was a masculine type with a heavy frame, normal masculine hair distribution and no sign of feminine fat, male type of skin, and so on. In his ordinary clothes there was no evidence of homosexuality in his appearance or manner. That this type is common is shown by the fact that Olkon and Sherman have described a very similar one except that the man was more homosexual, and again the man in the Cornock case, in which the wife was acquitted of murder, lived heterosexually for a time and had had a child.

Liakos has published an interesting case of familial transvestism. In this three members of a family of eight, a father and two sons, were all transvestists.

The father seems to have been abnormal and made excessive demands on his wife, hid her underclothes in a cupboard, and apparently urinated on them, as well as smearing them with red soap and cutting them in various places. This started after his wife refused to have sexual relations with him. The neighbours complained then that he tried to interfere with young girls. Finally his wife divorced him because he tried to chloroform her, apparently in order to rape her. He admitted that he had always had a tendency to wear feminine clothes, but had not previously given way to it.

His son aged 32 was married, but known as a transvestite, and was serving a sentence of 3 years for assaulting his step-daugher. His mother had noticed that when he was living with her, after leaving his wife, he hoarded female underclothes stolen from neighbours' clothes lines, in a cupboard.

His trial brought his abnormal tendencies into the open, and he asked for eleven cases of stealing female underclothes to be taken into consideration.

The other son, who was apparently normal until aged 17 when he had behaviour problems, never kept his jobs more than a few days, His mother found he wore female underclothes in bed. He admitted he had a tendency to wear female clothes, and had wished to do so as long as he could remember. He thought that this would give him sexual satisfaction, and was disappointed that it did not do so, but still continued the habit.

The other two brothers (aged 14 and 25) and two sisters (aged 12 and 21) in the family were all apparently normal.

Liakos suggests that transvestism must be much more common than is usually thought since for the family incidence to be due to chance a high proportion of the general population must be affected. It is noteworthy as he points out, that there was no tendency for the parents to treat the boys as girls.

No doubt George Sand would be cited as an example of transvestism in a heterosexual. This lady wrote under a masculine name and wore male clothes, yet had a succession of lovers, including Alfred de Musset and Frédéric Chopin. Yet a careful examination of her psychological disposition made by Helene Deutsch shows that there were sadistic and homosexual elements present which drove her on from lover to lover and made her destroy them one by one. She was essentially bisexual and this was caused by the conflict between her grandmother and her mother and the idealization and loss of her father. I believe that similar unconscious motivation could be discovered in other apparently normal transvestists if only sufficient were known about their lives, and if they were obliging enough to leave a large amount of literary work to reveal the hidden springs of their behaviour.

Even when transvestism appears in the heterosexual there are always traces of other abnormalities present—in Olkon and Sherman's case there were sadistic and masochistic elements. In the Cornock case the man was a transvestist and masochist as well as having other perversions which the judge refused to make public.

Homosexual

This, I believe with Stekel, is the main or primary root of transvestism. Transvestists are usually found to be more or less homosexual, although in some cases the homosexuality is deeply repressed. The common form of transvestism, however, is when it forms only one manifestation of a generalized homosexuality. It is a curious fact that the homosexual who views a woman with horror frequently dresses as one. This may, of course, represent only an effort to attract other men with a view to prostitution. Naturally the men attracted must be homosexual also, since a heterosexual man discovering the 'woman' who had attracted him was a disguised male would retire with irritation and disappointment.

Apart from male prostitution the homosexual appears to derive a definite sexual excitement from wearing female clothes. That he will run considerable risks to do so is shown by occasional cases which appear in the courts and one can assume that for the one case detected many escape discovery.

The fact that the confirmed homosexual often wears feminine clothes goes to support the view that he has moulded himself upon a woman and is trying to appear like her. The woman, of course, is his mother, and although he has turned from other women with disgust he is still seeking to be like her, although his motive may be unconscious. It may be confirmatory of the homosexual basis of transvestism that Bender and Paster found amongst 23 homosexual children that 12 enjoyed dressing in the clothes and adopting the manners, gestures, etc., of the opposite sex. Their ages varied from 5 to 13 and they all came from broken homes. One cannot, however, regard such a small series in such young children as being of much significance.

Homosexual transvestism is not necessarily a part of homosexuality. The homosexual ranges down a vast scale from the man who would not dream of assuming feminine clothes, is an enthusiastic sportsman, football player, or cricketer, to the mincing, lisping, transvestist who carries feminine clothes as if he were born to them. In between are men who wear female underwear but never anything else and sometimes rationalize that the silk is more comfortable and does not cause a skin rash and so on.

Why exactly some homosexuals eschew feminine clothes and some long for them so strongly probably depends on the amount of conditioning, perhaps in relation with the degree of introjection or moulding which has occurred. In some there may be deep-seated introjection of the mother, but because the boy has been to a public school where an outward show of masculinity was insisted upon he rejects any idea of transvestism. In other cases the boy has had less superficial conditioning and is able to throw off the masculine element with greater ease.

Narcissistic

We have noticed that the psychoanalytical school has demonstrated a narcissistic element in homosexuality. The patient loves a boy who, he feels, is beautiful as he himself was beautiful in youth. It is probable therefore that we shall find some narcissism in transvestism as Hirschfeld suggests. Since the eighteenth century, when Beau Brummell abolished the coloured and elaborate clothing which preceded him and instituted black and white as de rigueur for well-dressed men, there has been little scope for the male to wear bright costumes. Nevertheless, there is still plenty of opportunity for foppery and dandyism for the narcissistic. (Beau Brummell, it is interesting to note, was obsessionally clean, as well as narcissistic, and used to spend literally hours every morning bathing and being dressed by his valet; invariably in male attire.) Narcissism, unless backed by a strong homosexual tendency, is unlikely to lead to transvestism, although it may be part of the motivation producing those cases in which men dress up in uniforms of Service officers, but often in such cases there is a concomitant desire to swindle, to impress a woman, and so on. With some twenty-five years' experience of abnormal persons I can state that I have never seen a case of transvestism in which narcissism was the sole cause. But when there is also a homosexual element it is easy to see that the assumption of feminine clothes, the wearing of elaborate silk underwear, the frills and laces, silk stockings, cosmetics, nail lacquer, perfumes, jewellery, and the like all give scope to a narcissistic element which is forbidden to the male.

I feel that it is reasonable to assume, therefore, that narcissism can be given an ancillary role in the production of transvestism but is unlikely to be the primary cause.

Asexual

The idea of asexuality, of course, is that the patient is not possessed of any strongly defined sexuality and so wears male or female clothing indiscriminately. This, I feel, is a mistake. In the case of males there are severe penalties for behaviour whereby a breach of the peace may be occasioned, which is taken by the police to include wearing clothes of the opposite sex; and even in females there may be ridicule for dressing too much like a man. The transvestist obtains a definite excitement, really a sexual excitement, in dressing in the forbidden manner. If a man is psychologically asexual surely he would obtain no excitement in putting on a woman's clothes and unless there were some strong urge he would not risk penalties to do so. That there are some individuals who feel little excitement in the sexual sphere, either normal or abnormal, I am willing to admit, but these individuals are content to continue a monotonous existence without taking any interest in others. They are the last persons to chance a risk without profit.

Bisexual

I have pointed out previously that bisexuality is, in my opinion, only a partial homosexuality. It is obvious, therefore, that transvestism due to bisexuality is exactly the same as that due to homosexuality, although probably not so strongly motivated. It is unnecessary therefore to discuss it further.

Fetishism

Some writers consider that the basis of transvestism is fetishism with the clothes of the opposite sex taking the place of the fetish. That there is an element of truth in this is probable in many cases. In fetishism the symbol is taken for the whole, some special attribute or peculiar garb (mackintoshes, for example) must be shown for the patient to obtain sexual excitement. In transvestism it is not the sexual object but the patient himself who must wear the clothes. This suggests that the patient is identifying himself with the sexual object—i.e. a woman. This woman on investigation usually proves to be the mother or possibly a mother surrogate. Thus we are led back to the fact that this is basically a homosexual illness. The patient identifies himself with his mother and so behaves like a woman to a greater or lesser degree—in pure transvestism only in his clothing, but in transvestism associated with homosexuality sometimes completely. An example of transvestism limited only to clothing has been given in the R.A.F. officer described above, and it should be noted that his behaviour was so circumscribed that it concerned only clothing and this was mainly associated with the sexual act with his wife.

We shall discuss fetishism later as a definite sexual malversion.

Exhibitionism

The exhibitionistic element in transvestism is obvious inasmuch as the patient is seeking affection by the assumption of the clothing of the opposite sex. The psychoanalysts believe that he is identifying himself with the phallic woman, but it could be explained just as easily by the view that he had accepted castration and was appearing as a female.

Curiously enough, transvestism of the exhibitionistic type is often found in the 'ritual suicides' which are common in this illness. Usually the patient is a man, and sometimes his friends and acquaintances are unaware of his peculiarity and shocked at the manner of his death. Before he commits suicide he dresses himself in most elaborate female clothing complete to the last item. He applies cosmetics, wears perfume, places on jewellery, sometimes wears a wig so that there is the perfect illusion of femininity. Frequently he seats himself before a mirror and then finishes the sad play-acting by killing himself. Ritual suicides of this type appear to be a rare in feminine transvestists (women sometimes commit suicide in a narcissistic manner—lying in bed with satin sheets, surrounded by flowers, gazing into a hand-mirror at their perfectly made-up faces—but infrequently dressed as a man).

No doubt, as I have suggested, some men parade dressed as women in order to prostitute themselves with other homosexuals, but in some cases it is done purely for exhibitionistic reasons—for the thrill of wearing female clothes in public.

As women are permitted to wear masculine garb publicly this type of behaviour is less common and less noticed than in the male and no doubt those who do wear men's clothing are usually frankly homosexual and possibly do not obtain the excitement which the transvestist man feels.

Probably the exhibitionistic motif is attributable to transvestism upon the stage—the lady who appears dressed in perfect masculine evening clothes and sings a song, and the man who performs dressed, usually as a blowsy charwoman. That this sort of thing is enjoyed by the audience suggests that they, too, have unconscious and perhaps weakly represented ideas of this nature.

It is common to find that transvestists like to indulge in alcohol (this would be a curious similarity with homosexuality if we did not believe that they were so closely related). As I have pointed out, people who are normally heterosexual and who usually dress according to their sex often show transvestist peculiarities after indulging in it. That homosexuality is more common in similar circumstances does not seem without significance.

Masson has pointed out in her thesis that transvestism is rare in psychosis but cases have been recorded—e.g. by Fortineau, Vercier, Durand and Vidart, by Levy-Valensi, Pequignot and Pasche, by Desoille, Durand and Vidart, and Yawger. Yawger's case is particularly interesting since the patient murdered a man in order to practise castration which he intended to do on himself.

It has been seen that accidental deaths are common in masochism in which the sufferer tends to tie himself up, slips, and is asphyxiated. [See also p. 164.] The following is a case in which a transvestist met his death in curious circumstances which were probably indicative of extreme regression. In general the transvestist is more likely to get into trouble with the police than suffer from such an accident.

Death in Bin 'Fantastic'. Accident Verdict

'Fantastic and appalling' was the description applied by Mr. C. L. Phillips Powell, the Hereford City Coroner, to the death of a woodwork master whose body was found in a dustbin at his school. The verdict on Malcolm Frederick Clarke, 23, who was dressed in woman's clothes, was accidental death.

'It may be difficult for some people to believe that such forms of perversion exist and are practised,' said the coroner. To all his friends, it was stated, Clarke was a rational and intelligent person.

Dr. C. A. Hunt, pathologist, of Bristol forensic science laboratory, said the clothing Clarke was wearing and the markings on his face were characteristic of a form of perversion. It was associated with a desire for confinement in a small space.

Clarke, who came from Frome, Somerset, died of suffocation. The position of the body was such that it could only have been achieved by a voluntary effort.

The fact that this man wished to be confined into a small space would be taken by some to suggest that not only did he wish to get into his mother's clothes, but into her womb as well.

Infantosexual Transvestism

There is a rare form of 'transvestism' (if one can call it such) in which the patient does not dress in the clothes of the opposite sex but as a child. This was first described by Pettow in 1910. I have never treated such a case but have seen very rare mention of them in the public press. The patient seems usually to be a woman and in one case actually went to school for a time. The psychopathology of this is that it is a reversion towards childhood, a most obvious regression. It probably appears in more or less normal adults who like to go to fancy-dress balls dressed as infants complete with feeding-bottle or dummy. (We have already noted, under infantosexuality, the curious fact that present-day fashion tends to give the impression of immaturity—the Little Lord Fauntleroy hair styles amongst young men &c. Possibly this is also related to infantosexual transvestism.)

It is only fair since we owe so much to the psychoanalysts in the matter of the causation of the perversions that I should try to summarize the views of this school as clearly as possible. Sadger thought that this was the unconscious thinking of the transvestist: 'As a female I should be loved by my mother and, indeed, by everyone. When I put on my mother's dress I feel as if I were she herself and so could arouse sexual feeling in my father and possibly supplant her with him. And, finally, a third person derives as much pleasure from a woman's clothes as from herself and looks on the putting on of clothes as a sexual act.' Boehm accentuates the castration fantasy which the analysts believe is so strong in all the perversions. His view is that the patient unconsciously thinks, 'In the clothes which they put on they represent the mother with the penis.' Fenichel puts it in this manner:

Normally, what conditions the disappearance of infantile sexuality (the passing of the Oedipus complex) is the dread of castration. Now the homosexual has no regard for any human being who lacks a penis, the fetishist denies that such beings exist, while the exhibitionist, the scoptophiliac, and the transvestist try incessantly to refute the fact. Thus we see that these perverts are endeavouring to master their anxiety by denying its cause. In so far as they succeed in maintaining the illusion that there is no such thing as a lack of the penis, they save themselves anxiety and can indulge in infantile sexual practices, *because*, just in proportion as they can effectively deny the grounds for it, their castration-anxiety, which otherwise would act as a check on such sexual behaviour, is diminished. We must, however, qualify this statement by saying that this process succeeds only up to a certain point. That is to say, such infantile activities are bound up with a simultaneous, incessantly renewed denial of the reason for anxiety, and it is this denial which is represented in the perverse practice. The behaviour of the pervert implies: 'You have no need to be afraid', and so long as he believes this himself, his infantile sexual activities can produce orgasm, which signifies the gratification of his Oedipus wishes.

It is true that this hypothesis makes the feminine perversions and the whole subject of the castration-complex in women all the more problematic. Indeed, one does receive the impression that they are different in character from, though akin to, perversions in men. This strikes us, for instance, when we think of female exhibitionists and recall Harnik's work on the differences between masculine and feminine narcissism. Female fetishists are extremely rare and female transvestists seem to be simply women who covet the penis, and out of desire to possess it, have identified themselves with men.

Beigel and Feldman suggest that transvestism is a manifestation of immaturity. They made a study of ninety-three stories written by trans-vestists and concluded that: 'In its daydream state, trans-vestism combines with the security in mother's love the fulfilment of the dependent child's social aspirations. Since he knows himself to be ineffectual among boys, he conjures up a change of sex in his fantasy. His yieldingness, gentleness, emotionality, and physical attributes will gain him all that he desires as a boy—if he were a girl.'

Segal holds a somewhat similar view. In his opinion transvestism is a defence mechanism against separation anxiety, and wearing feminine clothes (i.e. the mother's) brings the subject once more into an intensely enveloping relationship with her.

There is strong anthropological evidence that the basis of transvestism is, in the main, a homosexual one. Devereux has described the curious customs of the Mohave Indians. These people are extraordinarily tolerant to homosexuality and permit inverts, of either sex, to assume the garb of the opposite sex and even to indulge in 'marriages'. He says: 'The transvestite must attempt to duplicate the behaviour-pattern of his adopted sex and make individuals of his anatomic sex feel toward him as though he truly belonged to his adopted sex.' The voice, manners, and so on are assumed as well as the clothing. Often the first appearance of abnormality occurs at puberty.

A boy may begin to act strangely just as he is about to reach puberty. At that time other boys try to act like grown-ups and imitate their elders. They handle bows and arrows, ride horses and hunt, and make love to little girls. These boys, however, will shun such tasks. They pick up dolls and toy with metates[1] just as girls do. They refuse to play with the toys of their own sex. Nor will they wear breech-clouts. They ask for skirts instead. . . . Girls will act just the opposite. They like to chum with boys and adopt boys' ways. They throw away their dolls and metates, and refuse to shred bark or perform other feminine tasks. They turn away from the skirt and long for the breech-clout.

Their parents will eventually notice this strange behaviour and comment upon it. 'Well, he may be a boy, but he seems to be more interested in the

---

[1] Metates are curved stones used for grinding corn and maize in Mexico.

ways of women.' Corresponding comments are made about boyish girls. Parents and relatives will sometimes try to bully them into normal behaviour—especially the girls, but they soon realize that nothing can be done about it. 'If our child wishes to go that way, the only thing we can do is make it adopt the status of a transvestite.' They are not proud of having a transvestite in the family because transvestites are considered somewhat crazy.

There were certain ceremonies used to initiate the boy or girl into their new clothes and after this 'marriage' to one of the same anatomic sex was permitted. Boys who went through this ceremony naturally did not go through the male initiation ceremony since they were regarded as female. In some cases transvestites were believed to have special powers and assumed the functions of shamans. They were supposed to be able to cure diseases, particularly sexual diseases such as gonorrhoea or syphilis.

Devereux is of the opinion that the communal acceptance of transvestism was valuable. He says:

Socially speaking Mohave civilization acted wisely perhaps in acknowledging the inevitable. This airing of the abnormal tendencies of certain modes of atypical behaviour of the glamour of secrecy and sin and of the aureola of persecution enabled certain persons swaying on the outskirts of homosexuality to obtain the desired experience and find their way back to the tribal pattern without the humiliation of a moral Canossa.

Other tribes had customs of the same nature. Indeed, according to Gifford, amongst the Cocopa the female transvestites had their noses pierced like a man and fought in battles.

A somewhat similar custom is described by Carstairs. He states:

While in India, the writer had occasion to hear a great deal of malicious gossip about homosexual practices in castes other than that of his informant of the moment. In this Hindu society, homosexuality was abhorred and concealed, but constantly in mind—there was, in fact, an institutionalized form of homosexuality which was far from inconspicuous. This was the role of *hinjra* or male homosexual transvestite (Carstairs, 1956). In every group of villages of this district there were one or two men who dressed in women's clothes, and lived as women. They would appear at private or public celebrations where they performed a lewd parody of women's songs and dances, and of feminine gossip. Unlike most other traditional mendicants, the hinjras were viewed with loathing and contempt, and yet their antics were always watched by a fascinated crowd whose sniggers would easily turn into abuse when they carried their lewdness too far. Hinjras are not peculiar to North India. They have been studied and described as far south as Hyderabad by a professor of forensic medicine (Rao, 1955) whose photographs substantiate the fact that many of these hinjras literally castrate themselves in order to take up this role.

REFERENCES

BEIGEL, H. G., and FELDMAN, R. (1963) The male transvestite's motivation in fiction, research and reality, in *Advances in Sex Research*, ed. BEIGEL, H. G., London.

BENDER, L., and PASTER, S. (1941) Homosexual trends in children, *Amer. J. Orthopsychiat.*, **11**, 730–43.

CARSTAIRS, G. M. (1964) Cultural differences in sexual deviation, in *Pathology and Treatment of Sexual Deviation*, ed. ROSEN, I., London.

CAULDWELL, D. O., ed. (1956) *Transvestism*, New York. (Essays by various psychiatrists and patients on transvestism and trans-sexualism.)

DESOILLE, H., DURAND, C., and VIDART, L. (1941) Travestissement et démence précoce, *Paris méd.*, **1**, 165–7.

DEUTSCH, H. (1946) *The Psychology of Women*, Vol. 1, *Girlhood*, London.

DEVEREUX, G. (1937) Institutionalised homosexuality of the Mohave Indians, *Hum. Biol.*, **9**, 498–527.

ELLIS, A. (1945) The psychology of human hermaphrodites, *Psychosom. Med.*, **7**, 108–25.

FENICHEL, O. (1930) The psychology of transvestism, *Int. J. Psycho-Anal.*, **2**, 211–27.

FESSLER, L. (1933) Ein Fall von post-traumatischen Transvestismus, *Arch. Psychiat. Nervenkr.*, **100**, 332–6.

FORTINEAU, J., VERCIER, R., DURAND, C., and VIDART, L. (1939) Idées de transformation sexuelle et travestissement chez deux délirants chroniques, *Ann. méd.-psychol.*, **97**, 51–5.

GIFFORD, E. W. (1933) The Cocopa, *Univ. Calif. Publ. Archaeol. Ethnol.*, **31**, 294.

HORTON, C. B., and CLARKE, E. K. (1931) Transvestism or eonism. Discussion on two cases, *Amer. J. Psychiat.*, **10**, 1025–30.

LEVY-VALENSI, J., PEQUIGNOT, H., and PASCHE, F. (1939) Une observation de travestissement tardif, *Ann. méd.-psychol.*, **97**, 770–5.

LIAKOS, A. (1967) Familial transvestism, *Brit. J. Psychiat.*, **113**, 49–51.

LONDON, L. S. (1933) Psychosexual pathology of transvestism, *Urol. cutan. Rev.*, **37**, 600–4.

LUKIANOWICZ, N. (1959) Survey of various aspects of transvestism in the light of our present knowledge, *J. nerv. ment. Dis.*, 128, **1**, 36–64.

MASSON, J. (1939) Un cas de travestissement, *Ann. méd.-psychol.*, **97**, 132–9.

OLKON, D. M., and SHERMAN, I. C. (1944) Eonism with added outstanding psychopathic features, *J. nerv. ment. Dis.*, **99**, 158–71.

SADGER, W. (1921) *Die Lehre von Geschlechtsverirrungen*, Vienna.

SEGAL, M. M. (1965) Transvestism as an impulse and as a defence, *Int. J. Psycho-Anal.*, **2**, 209–17.

STOLLER, R. S. (1967) Transvestists' women, *Amer. J. Psychiat.*, **3**, 333–9.

YAWGER, N. S. (1940) Transvestism and other cross-sex manifestations, *J. nerv. ment. Dis.*, **92**, 41–8.

TRANS-SEXUALISM

Definition

The wish to change sex: sometimes this is manifested by the delusion that a change of sex is taking place, or has taken place, spontaneously.

Psychopathology and Occurrence

Every psychiatrist of experience has seen one or more of these cases. The patient, usually a man, but occasionally a woman, most often young, but not invariably so, complains that either a strange change is taking place and an alteration of sex is occurring; or else he or she had always felt as though their physical sexuality was unnatural and there was a sensation as if he or she were occupying a body of the wrong sex. The purpose of the consultation being that either the spontaneous change, which the patient believes occurring, should be expedited by treatment; or else, if nothing is believed to be happening naturally, an operation should be performed to produce the alteration so that the body coincides with the mentality. It is not unusual for the patient, if a male, to insist that menstrual bleeding occurs from the urethra or anus, but sometimes periodically from the nose or elsewhere. Examination shows that the patient has a perfectly normal physique and there are no signs of metamorphosis. It is not unusual to find that the patient is a transvestist, also, and, if a male, wears feminine underclothes more or less permanently; or, if a woman, dresses in male costume. The usual excuse being that it is more comfortable clothed like this. Such cases are not uncommon and I have seen well over a hundred in the past twenty-five years.

What is the explanation for such an occurrence? I have always considered that homosexuality, transvestism and trans-sexualism were closely related. Briefly, it has seemed that the homosexual identifies himself with the mother in sexual behaviour (he identifies his sexual partner with the mother, also, but that is not important in the present connexion). The transvestist identifies himself with the mother only as far as her clothes are concerned, but does not do so sexually and, indeed, is sometimes normally sexed. The trans-sexualist identifies himself with his mother bodily but not sexually. In fact he does not want to be changed into a woman for sexual reasons, but merely to have a female body.

It is interesting to examine the literature and see what are the opinions of others. As is usual in such cases there is always the physician who discovers a physical basis. Vague believes that both in homosexuality and trans-sexualism there is an abnormal physique. This, he thinks, is not visible in the hair distribution but can be detected by measurements of the shoulder and pelvic girdles, and the fat distribution. This is entirely contary to the findings of others, and I do not need to stress the difficulties inherent in accurate measurement of small variations in the shoulder and pelvic structures.

Benjamin cautiously suggests that both organic and psychological factors may be at work and, of course, brings in intersexuality, which is not relevant, because in my experience the intersexual is not seeking a change of sex.

It is not unusual for schizophrenics, both male and female, to develop the delusion that their sexual organs are changing size or shape, or that they are changing their sex. Gittleson and Dawson-Butterworth found that this occurs in roughly the same proportion in both sexes.

No doubt this is only an exaggeration of the ideas which the more normal trans-sexualist develops; but even he persists in his supposition that he is changing his sex with delusional intensity and is not open to argument.

Hamberger, Stürup, Hertstedvester and Dahl-Iversen operated on an American soldier who afterwards became known as Christine Jorgensen. The operation, which was shrouded in mystery in the daily press was merely a complete castration (removal of the penis and testicles with the scrotum) and the administration of oestrogenic hormones to develop the breasts. A great deal of publicity resulted and it was stated in the newspapers that 'a man had been changed into a woman' (this was entirely wrong—what had been done was a man had been mutilated and treated with endocrines). However, a large number of trans-sexualists (455 in all) wrote to Hamberger asking for similar operations to be performed. Hamberger has published an analysis of the letters he received. These show that a desire for change of sex is most apparent in patients suffering from transvestism. Roughly three times as many men as women wish for the operation. The average age of the men was 28½ and of the women 26 years. He found that 'a homosexual libido plays a considerable if not a dominant role' in the wish to change sex.

The figures given by Hamberger were:

No information	50
Always wanted to be a girl ⎫	
Cannot live as a man ⎪	
Life history like reported case ⎬	116
Feminine psyche in male body ⎭	
Homosexual	75
Other causes (wants admission to a Buddhist nunnery!)	1

These confirm my own clinical impression that transvestism and homosexuality are related conditions.

The most valuable paper on the psychopathology of this condition is that published by Worden and Marsh. Although this is only a preliminary report it throws a great deal of light on the motivation. They state:

Certain personality and behaviour characteristics have been observed in men seeking surgery to remove their genitals and modify the perineum so that it has a female appearance. These findings, based on preliminary pilot studies may be summarized as follows. These men offer a simple stereotyped explanation of their condition, frequently stating that they are really women with male bodies. Our data contrasts sharply with the formulation and point to a high degree of complexity of the problem. All of the subjects show a marked impairment in the ability to give an adequate history of their past lives. The memories they offer initially with composure are restricted in numbers and content, and when pressed for further details they become emotionally disturbed by significant but painful recollections that they are reluctant to think about.

It would seem that commonly, according to Worden and Marsh, these patients had an unhappy childhood and as they say 'no warm friendly family life'. The result was that they began at an early age fantasying that they were girls.

Worden and Marsh did not think that these patients had any conception of the duties and responsibilities entailed by being a woman: but rather were wrapped in fantasies of being beautifully dressed, and embellished with sparkling jewellery, wonderful coiffures, cosmetics and so on. This was clearly shown in the fantasy given at length by one of these patients. The aim was a narcissistic one rather than normal adult feminine sexuality. The authors state: 'the idea of surgery seems to represent an escape from their sexual impulse rather than a wish for female sexual life.'

Randall in a paper on transvestism and trans-sexualism examined 50 cases (37 male and 13 female). The 13 female were all transvestites but 10 wished to be masculinized. The 37 male patients consisted of 15 married, 2 divorced, 4 separated and 16 single.

He thought that two large groups emerged from his cases: (1) homosexual; and (2) obsessive-compulsive. The second group was proportionally larger amongst the male patients. He thought that homosexuality is not necessarily present in every case of transvestism. The homosexual groups demanded to be changed by operation but the obsessionals were satisfied by wearing clothes of the opposite sex.

Lukianowics has reviewed the literature of transvestism and trans-sexualism and his conclusions confirm those which have already emerged regarding these related conditions. They are:

1. Transvestism is a sexual deviation, met in all ages, and in all cultures.

2. It is most often confined to a desire to cross-dress only; less often there is a wish to cross-dress and to be socially recognized as a 'woman'.

3. Trans-sexualism is characterized (apart from the desire for cross-dressing) by a morbid urge for an anatomical 'change of sex'.

4. If this urge is frustrated, it may precipitate severe psychoneurotic reactions, self-mutilation, and even suicide.

5. It is important not to confuse transvestism with other related sexual deviations (such as homosexuality, fetishism, masochism, exhibitionism, &c.), although the traits of some of these deviations may be found in almost every case of transvestism.

6. It is also important to adhere to the division of the phenomenon into two separate clinical syndromes, one of transvestism and one of trans-sexualism. This facilitates the understanding of the problem, and its prognostic and therapeutic evaluation.

7. The course of transvestism is self-limiting; that of trans-sexualism incessant.

8. A male transvestite is usually capable of making a fairly satisfactory marriage, provided he meets with an understanding and sympathetic attitude on the part of his wife. It seems that all female transvestites are homosexual and unable to adjust themselves to heterosexual marriage.

9. Genuine transvestism and trans-sexualism appear to be male sexual deviations exclusively brought about by a pathological female identification.

10. Cultural factors are of utmost importance in the development and social status of transvestism.

11. Neither transvestism nor trans-sexualism is hereditary.

12. The attitude of the social environment towards a transvestite should be sympathetic and permissive, and psychotherapy may help him to achieve a compromise between his transvestite cravings and the social prohibitions. There is at present no satisfactory treatment for trans-sexualism.

The constant demand for operation which I meet in these patients may conceal the possibility that the castration complex is behind trans-sexualism and the wish to change is really the hidden impulse to lose the genitalia. This probably forms the main urge behind sexual mutilation dealt with below.

Even if surgery were the answer to this problem it would be unwise to undertake it light-heartedly because, although the operative risks are not high, there are other possibilities which have been recorded. For example, Symmers has published two cases of carcinoma of the breast in trans-sexual individuals after treatment by operation and hormones. The procedures included; castration, amputation of the penis, construction of a pro-vagina and mammoplasty. Oestrogens were given by inunction of the breasts, by implantation and orally. The result was, in each case, the appearance of a primary mammary adenocarcinoma 5 years later.

If one refuses surgery in these cases the patient will sometimes resort to castrating himself. I have had patients who have attempted this, sometimes with very dangerous results. One, who used to attend my out-patient department for many years, was very schizoid and had cut off not only his testicles, but most of his penis as well: he very nearly died of haemorrhage. This had occurred before I saw him.

Blacker and Wong discovered five such cases in the literature, and recorded two of self-castration and two of severe laceration of the penis. All the patients came from disturbed homes with dominant mothers, and three had absent fathers. The sort of homes were similar to those which I have described as typically producing homosexuality.

These patients before they attempted surgery on themselves had a long period of intense sexual confusion associated with depression. They repudiated their genitals at first symbolically, and then in reality.

Books by those who have had their sex 'changed' have been published by Roberta Cowell (a former pilot in the Royal Air Force) and by an ex-naval Surgeon Lieutenant, but although their experiences are interesting, it is unwise to accept the theorizing of sufferers as valid because of the intense need to rationalize their behaviour.

Obviously mutilating surgery is not the solution for such patients. The aim should be not to make the *normal* body fit the *abnormal* psyche but vice versa. The problem, however, is that these patients will listen only to the promise of surgery, and only too often fall into the hands of ignorant surgical enthusiasts who are eager to show their skill. It is, perhaps, a good thing that such operations as that performed by Hamberger *et al.* are now forbidden in Denmark except to Danes who have obtained a certificate issued by the Government. In England and America the operation is *mayhem* in law and may result in legal proceedings. If the patient can be persuaded to accept psychotherapy this is the treatment of choice, but in such cases in which it is refused, or in which it has failed (and very few patients are willing to accept it or to persevere) then the use of oestrogens is permissible.

Although the Registrar General was apparently willing to change the sex on the registration certificate of Roberta Cowell (a patient who had the same procedure as that used by Hamberger) it is understood that this is only allowed now to those patients in whom there was a mistake of sex *at birth*. Thus, even if such an operation is done at the present time the patient remains legally a male and if he wears clothes of the opposite sex he can be regarded as masquerading.

The bizarre, and indeed amateurish, views on transvestism and transsexualism expressed by medical men unacquainted with psychosexual diseases sometimes reach beyond astonishment. The following extract shows to what length they can go. It must be remembered that this was evidence in a court of law, not the gossip of ignorant patients.

Medico-Legal

Earlier this year (*British Medical Journal* (1958) 2, 1187) we reported a case in which the judge held that the behaviour of a husband in dressing up as a woman with the knowledge that it would cause his wife distress, a course of conduct which would ultimately have a serious effect on her health, amounted to cruelty. The wife was granted a decree of divorce. On May 22, Mr. Justice Davies (*The Times*, May 23, 1958) had to deal with the petition of another wife. She was married in April 1950. In May 1951 a child was born of the marriage, but apparently the husband had started shortly after the marriage to develop female characteristics, at any rate mentally. After consulting psychiatrists in 1952 and 1954 he was sent to hospital for treatment, and was given hormones with the express intention on the part of the doctors to accelerate and facilitate the development in him of female characteristics. The endocrinologist who, with the psychiatrists, had advised this treatment said it was plain that the husband was suffering from a mental illness which made him to some extent like a woman and want to be a woman.

In 1957 the husband left his wife because of his desire to become a woman and because he could not stand living with her, and now dressed as a woman and was employed as a woman clerk. This naturally caused his wife revulsion.

Mr. Justice Davies held that the husband's consent to undergo hormone treatment for his mental illness was not cruelty on his part, since he could not help his illness any more than any other illness. He added that if the wife waited until May 1960 she might get a divorce on the grounds of desertion.

Most informed psychiatrists will feel that this judgment was unsatisfactory. The treatment—to facilitate the metamorphosis of the husband into a female—was misguided and the female hormones could merely suppress his masculinity. It would have been more satisfactory if the judge had followed the precedent and allowed the wife a divorce for cruelty.

A case such as this is not similar to that in which the patient is hermaphroditic and possesses glands relating to both sexes. In this condition the external genitalia are indeterminate and the patient is usually sterile. When we are dealing with hermaphroditism, and I have seen a certain number of such cases, the operative means are used to clarify and accentuate one set of sexual characteristics rather than to produce a change. Every effort was made with these patients to determine their psychosexuality and to remove the sexual glands which were inappropriate. This is the most satisfactory practice.

The trans-sexualist presents a pitiable problem, and one which we have not yet solved, but surgery does not provide a solution. The patient usually refuses to accept an explanation that his desires are impossible, and goes on from one doctor to another, until he finally meets a surgeon who promises to change his sex, and ends up mutilated. In most cases it is best to explain that some characteristics of the opposite sex can be produced by hormone treatment, and persuade him to be satisfied with that. The diminished sexual drive which results gives a feeling of relief and many patients are satisfied with this measure.

In conclusion I must emphasize that every particle of evidence appears to support the view that I have already given that homosexuality, transvestism and trans-sexualism are very closely related; that the male homosexual, for example, identifies himself with his mother in sexual behaviour, the transvestist does so as far as apparel, and the trans-sexualist wishes to have a body like his mother's. The transvestist and the trans-sexualist do not necessarily wish to indulge in intercourse, and are often content merely with the apparent evidence that they are of the opposite sex.

REFERENCES

BENJAMIN, H. (1953) Transvestism and trans-sexualism, *Int. J. Sexol.*, **7**, 12–14.

BLACKER, K. H., and WONG, N. (1963) Four cases of auto-castration, *Arch. gen. Psychiat.*, **8**, (2), 169–76.

BRITISH MEDICAL JOURNAL (1958) 9 August, 394, Medical Legal Notes.

CAULDWELL, D. O. (1956) *Transvestism*, New York.

GITTLESON, N. L., and DAWSON-BUTTERWORTH, K. (1967) *Brit. J. Psychiat.*, **113**, 491–4.

HAMBERGER, C. (1953) Desire for change of sex as shown by personal letters from 455 men and women, *Acta endocr. (Kbh.)*, **14**, 361–75.

RANDALL, J. B. (1959) *Brit. med. J.*, **2**, 1448–9.

SYMMERS, W. S. C. (1968) Carcinoma of breast in trans-sexual individuals after surgical and hormonal interference with primary and secondary sex characteristics, *Brit. med. J.*, **2**, 83–5.

VAGUE, J. (1956) Le désir de changer de sexe; forme épidémique actuelle d'un mal ancien, *Presse méd.*, **64**, 949–51.

WORDEN, F. G., and MARSH, J. T. (1955) Psychological factors in men seeking sex transformation, *J. Amer. med. Ass.*, **157**, 1292–8.

FETISHISM

Definition

Freud defines fetishism as 'those cases in which for the normal sexual object another is substituted which is related to it but which is totally unfit for the normal sexual aim'. I would define sexual malversion as a disease of the sexual stimulus, or that part of the object which excites sexual feeling.

Psychopathology and Occurrence

The normal sexual object for a man is a woman, yet, although a man working in a city may see as many as a thousand attractive women in the course of a day only one or two may stir his sexual interest. It must be that these one or two women possess something which excites him, and this point of attraction is called here the sexual stimulus. This sexual stimulus may be the colour of the hair, the conformation of the face or figure, or even some characteristic garment, mode of dressing, or cosmetic. It is not the whole object which is the point of attraction so much as a characteristic of it. Now when this point of sexual stimulus is detached from the object so that the woman is of no importance but the characteristic all-exciting we speak of a fetishism. Common examples are mackintosh fetishisms, foot fetishisms, hair, shoe, fur, and similar things.

Let us take, for example, a mackintosh fetish. In this case the fetishist is attracted only by those women who wear mackintoshes, and if he can steal or obtain a mackintosh from a woman it will still excite his sexual feeling and he will use it for looking at, or wrapping himself in, while masturbating, and so on. But any mackintosh will not do—the waterproofs worn by men, for instance, have no magic power to stir his sexual interest: it is only the mackintosh of a woman that is attractive. In the case of 'dummy fetishism' which will be given in the representative cases, the patient went from chemist's shop to chemist's shop to find one where there was a pretty girl serving behind the counter, and from her he would buy a 'dummy' (a baby's comforter). He also had vague affairs in which the woman placed a dummy in his mouth, but it was the dummy rather than the girl which captivated him. Again, in the case of another fetishist the attraction was of girls smoking. It was the act of smoking rather than the girl which formed the centre of sexual attraction. It is, therefore, not the whole object, but that part which forms the sexual stimulus which is detachable from it and can, in these illnesses, form an independent sexual object. The presence of some characteristic sexual stimulus, no matter how bizarre, may be taken as normal as long as it leads on to relations with the woman, who forms the sexual object, culminating in coitus. It is only the detachment or inhibition of the sexual impulse which is abnormal. Again it is curious that fetishism rarely occurs in women. This may be because the woman takes a more passive role and it is the very activity of the man which stirs her: in the case of the man it is some point of attraction in the woman which stimulates him. Being stirred more by the masculine activity than by any particular point of attraction it is harder for her to develop a fetishism. The woman has little freedom in sexual choice, and although she can seek or refuse and so accept men who present the type of sexual stimulus which excites her, she cannot detach the sexual stimulus so easily as the man. The psychoanalytic explanation is not so simple as this as we shall see below. The fact that fetishism rarely occurs in women was noted by the older writers, but they were unable to account for it other than by degeneration.

The great problem is how the sexual object acquired this particular stimulus. How is it that some men are attracted to fair women, some to dark, and so on? How is it that some desire the women to perform some action such as smoking and find a woman who does not perform this action unattractive? How is it that some men are excited by a woman only when she wears furs, high-heeled shoes, or corsets?

Binet first pointed out the great influence of the first sexual impression in relation with fetishism. Thus he offered an explanation which has been supported by the behaviourist doctrine of conditioning. This invaluable mechanism is completely explanatory. It has been pointed out that the sexual object in abnormal sexuality appears to represent the mother and is the result of the conditioning which the child receives from her at an early age. It becomes, therefore, sexually excited only by those who display the characteristics which appear in the mother. From the behaviourist point of view, therefore, the fetishist represents some attribute of the mother to which the child has been conditioned. It is important to appreciate this because it is contradictory to the Freudian view.

Again, I have pointed out already in a previous chapter that in homosexuality the partner of the same sex is only representative of the mother.

Now, curiously to note, it is possible in rare cases to discover homosexual perversion-fetishes in which the homosexual partner is attractive because of some particular attribute. One of my patients was attracted to men who had large, brown, dog-like eyes, and such men he described as his ideal 'dream man'. Now this is equivalent to the characteristics which we who are normal seek in those of the opposite sex—the brunette who is attractive to some men whilst the blonde is not so desirable and vice versa. This is sometimes carried to the limits of a perversion-fetishism, however, as in the case mentioned by Howe of a man who was only able to obtain sexual excitement when he could encounter a man who had severe paroxysms of coughing. He would follow this man for miles and become sexually excited at the apogee of the paroxysm. The key to this curious homosexual fetishism is to be found in the fact that his mother suffered from a severe cough. She had conditioned him to coughing as a sexual symbol, or symbol of femininity, and he had retained this even though he abandoned all other attributes. It would appear, therefore, that my view that a fetishism is the point of sexual stimulus of the object has strong grounds for its support. It is upheld by the fact that every fetish is found to be something associated with the mother. High-heeled shoes, corsets, furs, silk stockings, braids of hair, underclothes, ear-rings, and other jewellery, or some act like smoking or using cosmetics are common festishisms which have either become detached from the sexual object, or form the attraction of the object, and show the derivation from the mother.

The point of view that fetishisms are produced by conditioning has received strong support from a most interesting paper by Juan Marin on the 'foot-binding' of the Chinese ('Los "pies vendados" de la mujer china y el fetichismo del pie'). This custom, which is supposed to have been originated by the club-foot of the Empress Ta-Ki (A.D. 1100), was in reality a national fetish. It is improbable that it began through this lady's deformity. The fetishistic element is shown firstly by the poetic manner in which this artificial talipes equinovarus was regarded—it was compared to the 'golden iris flower'. But much more important, psychologically, than mere poetizing is the fact that the woman's foot was regarded as sexually exciting as a girl's breast is to an occidental. As Marin says: 'All the feminine modesty, in China, had concentrated itself upon the diminutive foot.' A woman, for example, would never dream of exposing her foot to other than her husband, and European doctors who treated Chinese women had the greatest difficulty in attending to diseases which involved the feet. Chinese men were not excited by a show of calf or leg but solely by the foot. 'It is in the foot, and only in the foot is rooted the secret Eros of the Chinese and it is well known that the kiss and the breast take no part in sexual intercourse.'

No doubt (as Marin points out) this fetish was reinforced by other factors—men kept a number of wives and concubines in Old China and there was always the possibility of them being attracted elsewhere. The foot-binding limited their activity and the difficulty in walking certainly made excursions outside the house almost impossible. The theory that the lack of activity due to the foot-binding increased the size of the mons veneris (and presumably the pleasure of intercourse) Marin scouts as nonsense, and unsupported by any of those physicians who have had experience of the Chinese.

It is obvious that once such a major fetishism was started in a nation it would tend to be perpetuated. The boy would be conditioned to the idea that his mother's feet were deformed, and would be sexually excited by women whose feet had been treated in this way. He would be attracted only to such women. Those who had not been deformed would not be acceptable. Since only those whose feet had been deformed would have children and these children would again grow up with an attraction for mutilated women and so on round the vicious circle. It is obvious that if one accepts the view that foot-binding was a fetishism then one must accept the possibility of conditioning as the basis for it.

If fetishes can arise from imprinting, as I have previously described on page 5, and they are a special form of conditioning occurring at the moment of maturation of an intinct, it is not surprising that they are so often connected with the mother. The baby is in contact with her, usually from birth until later infancy, and if the moment of maturation comes during that time, as it may well do, then the circumstances will be set for the imprinting to occur. (It will be remembered that in ducklings the critical time was only about the third or fourth day and the condition was irreversible.)

Imprinting would have special opportunity to occur with the Chinese foot-binding because the tiny child could hardly fail to notice the mother's bound feet, her hobbling gait, and the general emphasis on the foot. Apart from this special case it can explain many other fetishes; such as fur (pubic hair), buttocks (breasts), mackintoshes (waterproof sheets used for bathing babies) and the like.

Freud says 'the substitute for the sexual object is generally a part of the body but little adapted for sexual purposes, such as the foot or hair of an inanimate object which is in demonstrable relation with the sexual person, preferably with the sexuality of the same (fragments of clothing, white underwear)' and suggests that this is due to the 'psychological overestimation of the sexual object which encroaches on everything associated with it'.

The Freudian explanation of fetishism is obsessed by the castration complex and the denial of it. The child, according to him, attributes its mother with a penis, and when it discovers that she has none makes desperate efforts to deny its discovery. Fenichel says:

As in homosexuality, here too the crucial etiological factors—Oedipus complex and castration complex—do not make up part of the manifest clinical picture; instead, they are repressed in a typical and specific fashion by the perversion itself. The process of partial repression, which makes it possible for a *pars pro toto* to be retained in consciousness, while the *totum* remains repressed, is best seen in cases of fetishism. The total object is replaced by the fetish that stands for its most important part, the penis.

Freud believes that fetishes most frequently encountered represent the penis: feet, long braids of hair, he believes symbolize it. Fur represents the pubic hair which hides it and leaves open the question whether the penis is present or not, underclothes perform the same function, and so on.

He advances the fact that fetishism is rare in women to support his view and says that: 'The fetish in these cases (i.e. women) also represents a penis, simultaneously feared and desired, the penis which the woman wishes she possessed by virtue of an identification with the father.'

Freud says:

Psychoanalysis has filled up the gap in the understanding of fetishisms by showing that the selection of the fetish depends on a coprophilic smell-desire which has been lost by repression. Feet and hair are strong-smelling objects which are raised to fetishes after the renouncing of the now unpleasant sensation of smell. Accordingly, only the filthy and ill-smelling foot is the sexual object in the perversion which corresponds to foot-fetishism.

He seems to discount entirely the fact that the foot might be representative of the mother. From his point of view the case of the man who found his sexual pleasure in sucking a dummy is to be explained as an unconscious symbolism for fellatio. From my point of view the dummy represents the mother's breast both in symbolism and as it does in real life.

In seeking a dummy he was merely seeking his mother, or in neurological terminology, he had been conditioned to the dummy, by his mother, when he was a child and continued constantly to seek it because of his conditioning. I have already mentioned that Fenichel suggested that there was a certain amount of fetishism in the perversion of transvestism. This, he suggests, means that the patient who obtains sexual emjoyment from wearing clothes of the opposite sex is doing so because there is the unconscious fantasy of copulation with the clothes. He says:

Transvestite coitus is proved by analysis to have two meanings: (1) an object-erotic, fetishistic, one—the person cohabits not with a woman but with her clothes: and (2) a narcissistic, that is, a homosexual meaning—the transvestite himself represents a phallic woman (i.e. the mother with a penis fantasied by children) under whose clothes a penis can, in fact, be found, and whose clothes therefore represent a penis symbolically.

This point of view is upheld by other psychoanalysts—e.g. Lorand gives this interpretation in the observations upon a child who showed 'fetishism *in statu nascendi*' and was attracted to women's shoes which he liked to fondle. This child showed considerable interest in women and put his head up their clothes in order to discover their construction.

An interesting case of fetishism in a girl is recorded by Dudley and is worth reproducing here. He states:

A 17-year-old school girl was fascinated by the smell and feel of rubber mackintoshes, 'About once a week,' she said, 'I undress and slip on my mackintosh. I spread a rubber sheet in the bed and dream of sexual experiences. I am going to have my tonsils removed. Another girl who was operated on told me that she wore a rubber cap and that there was a mackintosh sheet underneath her. I have woven this into my dreams, I imagine I am going on the operating-table when I get into bed. I see the rubber breathing-bag filling and feel the mask pressed on my face. I put my hands in my mackintosh pockets and rub my thighs while I pretend to breathe the chloroform. I struggle and a nurse in a rubber apron holds me tightly. Then as I go under the anaesthetic the sexual climax comes. I hate myself for doing it. Ordinary ideas of intercourse just don't appeal to me. I know there is bound to be a lot of mackintoshes, rubber aprons, &c., about when I have my operation and I am so afraid I am going to give my secret away.

This case is valuable because of the rarity of fetishism in women. It shows a mixture, also, of masochism (having an operation, being held down and so on). Moreover, it seems to have displaced ideas of normal intercourse completely. Dudley believes that the fetish is associated with repressed infantile experiences and the mackintosh may be a substitute for the mother's breast, or for the rubber teat of the feeding bottle.

Odlum states that in her experience fetishism occurs in women. She says:

One of my patients—a woman in the forties of the highest character and a teacher of English—was deeply disturbed because she had a definite orgasm whenever she saw a pair of eye glasses on a table or in any place where light reflected on them. She found it a great temptation to put glasses in such a position and from time to time did in fact do so, but her most satisfactory orgasm came when the situation arose by chance. In another case a woman had strong sexual sensations whenever she touched certain types of fur, notably sealskin, moleskin, or squirrel, or when she handled certain types of velvet. In another case orgasm always resulted from the sight of a riding whip or cane, associated with masochistic fantasies. None of these cases were suffering from any kind of emotional disturbance and they were all making a good adjustment to life. I have also known of other cases where the women were happily married and were all well adjusted to their husbands and children and life in general. The condition is not necessarily due to a morbid tendency due to a lack of emotional satisfaction but rather represents an alternative or supple-mentary form of sexual gratification. I have also seen cases where some girl children as well as boys had obvious orgasms when they were sucking a blanket before they would settle down at night, and a number of children of both sexes obviously show rudimentary orgasm when they smack or hug a doll or teddy bear. I have not heard of a case in which a woman has practised fetishism in public, but in the cases which I know of they are extremely loath to speak either because they feel guilty about it or because they realize that it would give rise to moral or social condemnation even though they themselves do not feel any guilt. This may be the reason why its existence has not been generally recognized.

Whether fetishism is as common as Odlum believes the fact that it arises in a few women contradicts the Freudian view of it being a castration symbol. It supports the idea that it is due to some early memory, such as of the breast. In my experience the castration element arises in this manner. The child, for some reason, perhaps because it is not fed as often as it wishes, develops hostility to the breast and wishes to bite it off. This is reversed, as such hostility frequently is, and so it fears that it will have its penis bitten off by the mother—that is, be castrated by her. It thus arises long before the Oedipus situation, actually at the second oral stage of emotional development. This, more or less, supports the descriptions first given by Melanie Klein.

Sylvia Payne believes that fetishisms are produced by very early, pre-genital components and this accords with my own view. She believes that they are the product of a sadistic impulse, however, and that the repressed aim is to kill the love object. There may be considerable truth in this since it is not unusual to find that the patient destroys the love object after he has used it for his sexual purposes. For example, mackintosh fetishist may cut up or burn the rainproof, which he has taken so much trouble to obtain, after having used it.

This point of view is supported by Gillespie who recorded a mackintosh fetish in which anal, urethral, and oral material were intimately connected. Of this he says: 'The fetish may thus be regarded, in Freud's phrase, as a memorial not only to castration fear but also to the trauma of weaning.' Again he emphasizes that there is a deeper basis than castration fear when he says: 'There were a number of fantasies of attacks on the interior of the mother's body with a view to finding the penis; and it was clear that these fantasies were motivated only partially by castration anxiety—another important factor was the fantasy of the penis as a source of food.' (It is clear from this that the patient equated the penis with the breast and that what he really sought was the mother's breast and was only using the fantasied penis as a substitute.) He concludes his paper with an interesting summary:

Finally, reverting to the problem of phallic *versus* pregenital, I should like to make the following suggestion with regard to the aetiology of fetishism. May it not be that what we have actually to deal with is neither the one thing nor the other, but a combination of the two? I do not simply mean that I want to have it both ways—what I am suggesting is a specific constellation, to use Dr. Glover's conception. I feel that there are points about this case which give strong support to this view: in particular, the extraordinary compound (for it is much more than a mere mixture) of phallic, oral, and anal aggressive and erotic fantasies.

To put it another way, I would suggest that fetishism is the result of castration anxiety produced by a strong admixture of certain oral and anal trends.

All analysts do not take such a broad view as Gillespie, and Kronengold and Sterba record two cases of fetishism (one in which the patient tied himself, rouged his face, and was nude except for polished shoes, and the other in which a rubber apron was the stimulant). These writers agree with the formula for transvestism proposed by Fenichel (this is that it is an attempt to deal with the discovery that woman has no penis) and say:

The fetishistic act has the significance of an identification with the woman who keeps her penis in spite of her masochistic role. In both cases, the penis was twice represented in the manner which Fenichel considered specific for transvestism. On the one hand, the penis is particularly felt in the fetishistic act of pressing the fetish against the genital region, so that its presence is clearly proven to the possessor: on the other hand, the fetish, which becomes connected with the body during the act, itself represents a penis. It has frequently been observed elsewhere that, as in this instance, duplication serves the purpose of a vigorous denial of deficiency. In both cases the same formula may be applied which Fenichel adopted for transvestism.

Now why clothes should 'represent a penis symbolically', as Freud says, he does not state. One might conclude that these, without a single point of resemblance, would be the last things chosen. I accept that long-pointed objects from hypodermic syringes to factory chimneys may be phallic symbols—in fact anyone who has cared to examine a few dreams must be forced to realize that this is so—but clothes I cannot accept: neither can I agree that coughing represents a penis, nor does a mackintosh sheet. I can only conclude that to force them to do so is a flight of logic which has been made to bring the facts into line with the theory.

It seems much more probable, as Hadfield has suggested, that the fetish represents the child's first love object—the breast—and that is it things connected with, or substituted for, the breast that become fetishes. He says: 'We find in fact that in all cases of fetishism the objects are substitutes for the mother's breast, which is the child's first love object.' It seems likely that the penis which Freud has suggested is the origin of the fetish is really itself a substitute for the breast and that he has not carried his analysis far enough. This is probable, since Melanie Klein has shown that children soon substitute the penis as a symbol for the breast and have fantasies about it which they had for the breast. This has recently been supported by Fairbairn who had a patient who stated, 'I made my penis into a breast'. (Really, of course, it was vice versa.) An objection is sometimes made, when the importance of the breast in the unconscious life of the child is described, that a large number of babies are bottle fed, and have no experience of the maternal breast. This objection is invalidated by the fact that the child undoubtedly does consider the bottle as a breast or at least emotionally equates it with it. The fact that bottles have rubber teats may, in some cases, be the reason why rubber so often forms the basis for fetishism. The transition of the bottle to the Freudian penis—if there is any basis in this in the formation of fetishisms—appears easier than from the breast.

Even with this clue it is not always easy to unravel the curious fantasies which we meet. For example, what possible relationship with the breast can be the sight of a girl smoking? Yet in the analysis this was discovered to be partly a sadistic element—the patient thought that smoking was harmful to her, and, of course, the sucking of the cigarette could be related back to breast-sucking. Again, I once saw for a few sessions (unfortunately the treatment was interrupted and never resumed) a patient who obtained sexual excitement only when he saw a horse cruelly reined-in by the rider. This the patient easily related back to suckling— he felt that the breast was uncontrollable—and revealed the inner nature of the fetish. It is again obvious in these fetishes (as in the Chinese foot-binding) that there is a strong sadistic factor and this upholds Payne's suggestion that it is usually present.

A large number of children find breast substitutes, varying from the thumb to such things as curtain-fringes, cot-blankets, and similar things which they suck. They resent any change in them and are passionately adherent in their choice. Winnicott has called these substitutes, 'transitional objects'.

In my experience they do not form a basis for fetishisms and I have been told by many different patients that they had this passion for sucking everything from door-knobs to bits of clothing, but they have shown no evidence of fetishes. Indeed, I suspect that it is by some different mechanism than mere passive substitution, no matter how strongly favoured, that they arise and possibly this very substitution may be a protection against the development of a fetish. If, however, I am mistaken and they do, at least occasionally, form the basis of fetishism, it is possible that fellatio could be regarded as such a condition and the penis—even if, at first, only in fantasy—is one of Winnicott's 'transitional objects', and so forms the mechanism in which this is prominent.

A psychical disease which is regarded here as a fetishism (i.e. an abnormality of the sexual stimulus) is known as pygmalionism. This is the sexual attraction of a statue or statues. This form of abnormality is sometimes classified as a perversion (i.e. abnormality of the object and sexual manifestations towards it). In any case it is very rare in its pure form—although it is not unusual for pictures to be used as adjuncts in masturbatory activity, and when it does occur it takes the form of over- whelming attraction to the statue. Like other forms of fetishism it can be heterosexual, homosexual, infantosexual, or bestiosexual, but the object instead of being living is the statue. Perhaps the best representation of this illness is shown in Oscar Wilde's poem 'Charmides' in which a young man had relations with the statue of a goddess. Such a fantasy throws light on Wilde's own mentality and suggests that he was more polymorphous than homosexual. The difficulties associated with the actual relations with sculpture make this fetishism commoner as a fantasy than as a reality. No doubt as in other fetishisms the statue is attractive as an embodiment of some of the attributes of the mother (goddesses particularly often represent maternal characteristics). Masturbation before pictures or statues which occur in childhood but which may persist in later life perhaps forms a latent or intermediate form from which the true pygmalionism may have been derived.

Probably many phobias have a negative fetishistic basis. Thus most, if not all phobias, are formed psychopathologically on a repressed wish. Fear of underground trains is due to an unconscious wish to throw one- self under them and so on. It would seem that aversion to worms and snakes, for example, that one finds in women is sometimes accompanied by sexual dreams which clearly indicate that they symbolize the penis. These have been called fetish-aversions and it is easy to see them in different forms in various patients. Their presence shows how easily our classifications shade into each other and how unwise it is to try to be too rigid in nomenclature.

Fetishism, as I have pointed out with different psychosexual abnorma- lities, often appears in conjunction with other conditions. The following case is of interest:

This was that of a gentleman, a Mr. S. S. aged 57, who was Chamber- lain to the City of London. He was found lying dead on the floor of his bedroom in his home. A rope with a slip-knot was round his neck. He was dressed in a black sweater and black ballet tights pulled up only to the buttocks. There was a small gold-coloured chain round the left ankle underneath the tights. On the bedside table and elsewhere in the room were a leather gaiter, a chain with a padlock and key, three webbing straps, a sack made by sewing two large sacks together, and two small padlocks, with a key, which appeared to fit the gaiter.

The end of the rope was secured to the handle of a door leading to a bathroom. The rope passed over the door, which was 6 ft. 10 in. high. The loop could have been at that height from the floor, but was, in fact, only 4 ft. 6 in. from the floor. Mr. S. S. was 6 ft. 4 in. tall so he could have stood up with the loop round his neck, with no tension on it. There was no danger if he stood up with the rope round his neck. The floor was polished.

An electric fire was still switched on, but the double bed had not been slept in. The dead man's son had been called by a servant when no answer could be obtained from knocking. He climbed a ladder and entered the window. There was no note left in the room. The day previous had been his father's birthday and he was quite happy.

The wife was asked if she had noticed anything unusual about his behaviour before the occurrence and stated that her husband had been reading books on the Inquisition.

A pathologist said that death was due to asphyxia caused by hanging. He agreed with the coroner that the dead man had been engaged in some sort of elaborate ritual, and added, 'I think that sometimes they get into such a state that, having produced anoxia, and intending to release the apparatus causing it, they find that they are unable to do so, and they lose consciousness'.

The coroner gave a verdict of accidental death and said kindly, 'It would be indiscreet for me to say more. What goes on in a man's bedroom, which harms only himself is nobody's business but his own.'

It is worth while considering this case since such occurrences are not unusual and this one presents many interesting points. Firstly, undoubtedly the man's death was an accident, as was found by the coroner, but the other elements, such as the chain, padlock, gaiter, with small padlocks, webbing straps and the sack indicate an obvious masochistic element. Now masochists often commit suicide (because masochism is aggression turned back on to oneself) so there may be a possibility of an *unconscious* suicide here. The masochist often 'dices with death', as it were, and the nearer he gets to suicide, and escapes, the greater apparently is the thrill he feels. It does seem extravagantly risky to tie ropes round one's neck, attach them over a moving door, and stand on a polished floor, whilst indulging in some sort of fetishistic manoeuvre. This brings us to the fetishistic element in his behaviour. He had dressed himself in ballet tights and a black sweater. The ballet tights were not pulled up, presumably in order for him to indulge in self-stimulation. The wearing of the gold-coloured chain round his left ankle is another element. It was fashionable, some thirty years ago, for girls to wear gold chains round their ankles and this may be representative of such a fashion. His books on the Inquisition confirm the diagnosis of masochism.

Why should a man of this mature age indulge in such behaviour? He was wealthy and presumably could have kept a mistress had he wished.

I think that the answer is something like this (although one must admit that it is somewhat speculative). This man was aged 57. Possibly his wife had passed the menopause and so was no longer interested in sex. He was happily married and had had a normal sexual life (or he would not have had a son). Finding the normal sexual outlet closed to him he regressed to some earlier point and indulged in a fetishistic ritual which, combined with a masochistic element, gave him some relief. Such men often prefer this to keeping a mistress, since the discovery of a second *ménage* would be distressing to their wives.

It is difficult to help these patients who rarely come for assistance, but the psychiatrist can suggest that they should avoid this masochistic trussing up, particularly with ropes round the neck, which sooner or later, ends in fatality.

HETEROCHROMOPHILIA

A curious condition related to fetishism which might be called 'heterochromophilia' is to be found in those men who are capable of being sexually attracted only by women of another colour. Such men are uninterested in women of their own race, no matter how lovely or attractive they may be, and fall in love with coloured women whom they make their mistresses or even their wives. Such a case was that of the American mining engineer, Clarence King, who came from a more or less aristocratic family and had the entrée into the best society. Although he could easily have married a rich and beautiful white American girl he lived with a succession of coloured mistresses.

This curious condition occurs in those who have had coloured nurses and is to be found often in white inhabitants of the West Indies, the Southern States of America, South Africa and so on. The fact that in some of these countries coloured people are looked down upon sometimes creates a serious dilemma. A compromise may be made and one man under my care married a swarthy woman with markedly negroid features although apparently of white blood.

One can hardly call this a fetish since an abnormal sexual object is not substituted for a normal one, but there is a strong fetishistic tone about the attraction. Possibly it may be caused by imprinting, but so little is known of this condition in human beings that it must be purely speculative.

Many white children brought up in tropical countries must have coloured nurses yet very few develop this condition. The causal factor is not easy to determine and whether these are breast fed by the coloured nurse or not cannot be discovered. If they were it might throw more definite light on the causation of fetishisms.

Gluckman has described an interesting case of lesbianism in a Maori girl which he believes was due to the fact that she was adopted at an early age by parents who disliked coloured people. She was abused and called 'a nigger bastard' &c. This apparently gave her a dislike of others of her own colour. The result was that she not only grew up homosexual, but was attracted only to white women. He calls this heterochromophobia and feels that it is contrary to heterochromophilia, which is based on affection, but is caused by hate and hostility.

Case No. 17

A Case of Foot Festishism

The patient was an intelligent young doctor aged 32. He complained that until five years previously he had been leading a normal sexual life, but that since then everything had been abnormal. He had been going out with a beautiful young mannequin who was his mistress for two years but who had finally given him up because he would not marry her. This he was not able to do without considerable domestic upheaval since he was dependent on his grandmother who disapproved of his marriage. It was found when he was treated that his affair with the mannequin was not completely normal since they indulged in sexual play in which she was tied up. She delighted in displaying herself in diaphanous clothes which he found very sexually exciting, and he was also attracted by her feet which were very beautiful and adorned with nail lacquer and so on.

After he broke off from this girl the patient deteriorated. His potence had always been a source of pride for him but the last time he attempted intercourse with her he was impotent. Since then he could not develop a normal erection and although he had been with prostitutes it was masturbation, not intercourse, in which he indulged. He continued to masturbate twice weekly but felt depressed and unhappy all the time. In 1943 he joined the Army but after a year, since he was so near qualification, he was released and returned to his studies. He met a girl and fell in love with her but was refused when he proposed. In the year before he consulted me he had lost much of his sexual feeling and noticed that his fantasies were sado-masochistic. He imagined he was with a girl—always the same girl—who was tied up, helpless, and humiliated by him, or else himself was tied up and humiliated. He was kissing her feet. Many of his day-dreams were of potence. He had indulged in mutual masturbation with other men but this was purely as an expedient and *faute de mieux*.

He said that he had been brought up at first by his mother. She had asked him if he played about with himself and told him that such conduct caused insanity. He saw little of his father who was abroad. At the age of 7 years he was taken to Australia. At 10 years a scoutmaster interfered with him, placed the patient's penis in his mouth, and placed his penis in his hand. This the patient found boring. A year later the same thing happened with another man. Then he was circumcised. A year later he started to tie himself up and masturbated. He also started to take an inordinate interest in feet and the foot fetishism appeared. He had intercourse with a prostitute at the age of 19 and noticed that the foot fetishism was firmly established.

Treatment released great hostility to his mother who had apparently been a heavy drinker at some period of his life. There was also hostility towards headmasters at school. He had not really known his father, who was abroad, until later life. The masochism was not related to this but to a wish to be humiliated by his mother, which was itself an inverted wish to humiliate her. This was understandable since he had never had any affection from her and was definitely hostile to her.

He had dreams which revealed the causation of his fetishism. He dreamed that he saw his uncle lying in a ditch. He had a penis two to three feet long and the patient started to lick it. He said in association that he always associated the penis with the feet of a woman. He had practised oralism with the feet, the vagina, and sometimes the anus.

Treatment revealed that the penis and the foot were only symbols of the breast, and a great deal of emotion was released. This was a vague homosexual feeling towards the uncle (perhaps as a father substitute and the basis for his 'faute de mieux homosexuality'). There was also hostility towards the mother and grandmother with a great deeply unconscious longing for the breast.

He improved a great deal and after four months' treatment appeared perfectly well.

REFERENCES

ALEXANDER, R. (1930) Fetishism in the female, Med. J. Rec., 131, 402–5.

BALINT, M. (1935) Contribution on fetishism, Int. J. Psycho-Anal., 17, 481–93.

DUDLEY, G. A. (1954) A rare case of female fetishism, Int. J. Sexol., 8, 32–4.

FAIRBAIRN, W. R. (1964) A note on the origin of male homosexuality, Brit. J. med. Psychol., 37, 31.

FREUD, S. (1928) Fetishism, Int. J. Psycho-Anal., 9, 161–6.

GEBSATTEL, V. E. (1930) Über Fetishismus, Nervenarzt., 3, 8–20.

GILLESPIE, W. H. (1940) A contribution to the study of fetishism, Int. J. Psycho-Anal., 21, 401–15.

GLUCKMAN, L. K. (1967) Lesbianism in the Maori, Aust. N.Z. J. Psychiat., 2, 98–103.

KRONENGOLD, E., and STERBA, R. (1936) Two cases of fetishism, Psychoanal. Quart., 5, 65–70.

LORAND, A. S. (1930) Fetishism in statu nascendi, Int. J. Psycho-Anal., 11, 419–27.

MARIN, J. (1941) Los 'pies vendados' de la mujer china y el fetichismo del pie, Crón. Méd. (Lima), 58, 145–53.

ODLUM, D. (1955) Brit. med. J., 2, 302.

PAYNE, S. (1939) Some observations on the ego development of the fetishist, Int. J. Psycho-Anal., 20, 161–70.

VENCOVSKY, E. (1938) Psychosexual infantilism: Fetishism with masochistic component, colostrophilia and lactophilia, Čas. Lék. čes., 88, 469–73.

WILDE, O. (1913) Charmides and Other Poems, London.

WILKINS, T. (1958) Clarence King, London.

WINNICOTT, D. W. (1953) Transitional objects and transitional phenonema, Int. J. Psycho-Anal., 34, 89.

PART FIVE

DISORDERS OF THE INSTINCTUAL STRENGTH

13

ABNORMALITIES OF THE SEXUAL URGE

Apart from diseases which may affect the sexual stimulus, more of instinctual expression or manifestation, and the nature of the sexual object, there are conditions which affect the strength of the sexual urge itself. It is obvious that this can be either in a positive or in a negative direction in both males and females. The sexual desire can be diminished to complete negation, forming impotence in the male and indifference (which is usually concealed under dyspareunia) and frigidity in the female.

On the other hand, the sexual urge may appear much greater than usual, so that it appears to be impossible to satisfy it however frequently the patient seems to do so. This produces a condition which is known as satyriasis in the male and nymphomania in the female.

In spite of the manifold classifications which different authors have attempted to make, we can conveniently describe three types of abnormality of the sexual urge:

1. Sexual Aversion—impotence in the male and frigidity in the female.
2. Sexual Hypoversion—weak sexual desire in either sex.
3. Sexual Hyperversion—satyriasis and nymphomania.

Before we discuss the matter at length, however, it is important that we should recognize the factors which can cause increase or diminution of the strength of an instinct. All the factors are probably not known but those given here will be sufficient to explain a great deal.

FACTORS CAUSING INCREASE IN INSTINCTUAL STRENGTH

1. Organic Factors: Inherited or Acquired. These organic factors are not sufficiently known to discuss them at length. They probably depend on the endocrine basis of instinctual behaviour, and as such are related to the whole hormone orchestra and its proper functioning. Again, there is probably a nervous factor, since certain drugs such as strychnine are known to increase sexual desire. Injections of testosterone proprionate *do not* increase the urge in normal people (but they do so, as well as improve the sexual performance, in eunuchoids). Increase of metabolism due to hot climatic conditions and slight fever will accentuate sexual desire and performance. Thus it is well known that sexual desire is increased with the approach of warmer weather in the spring and summer, and those who inhabit tropical and sub-tropical zones are more desirous. Again those who suffer from slight continued fever, as in tuberculosis, are often very sexual.

2. *Youth*. It is obvious that the instincts and emotions are stronger in youth than they are in old age. The passions are more violent and tend to overcome the restrictive influence more when the subject is young. Erotic emotions are certainly strongest at adolescence: this was confirmed by Kinsey's work.

3. *Partial Obstruction*. Partial obstruction, or complete obstruction for a short time, to an instinct tends to increase its force, but long complete obstruction is deleterious to it.

4. *Certain Attributes of the Object*. The attribute of suitability is a very strong one in increasing the strength of an instinct. The young man is normally more sexually exited by a young woman than by an old one or an immature child. The hungry man is more attracted by good food than stale and rotten food and so on.

5. *Reciprocal Responses from the Object*. These are very important in increasing the strength of the instinctual responses. The normal young man is attracted still more to the girl who loves him in return. The strongest hate is produced by those who return it.

6. *Certain Conditions in the Organ Affected*. These are not properly known. It is appreciated that variations occur in the appetite in diseases of the stomach, however, and possibly they may occur in other instinctual responses with variations in other organs. There does not appear to be any certain knowledge if this occurs in sex but it might be conjectured that some of the sexual urge depends on the tension in the sexual channels. If these are more or less empty, as after recent ejaculations, there is little desire, but if full the drive to find a mate is intense. It seems that after prostatectomy, when the sexual channels are disorganized, desire may be greatly diminished and sexual capacity disappear. It is often stated that prostatectomy does not make the sufferer impotent, but it is unusual to find a man who has had this operation retaining much of his potency. It must be remembered, however, that it is performed only on men after the age of fifty and the sexual powers are usually diminishing in any case. Perhaps the alleged increase in sexuality which is supposed to follow irritation of the urethra after taking cantharides is of this type. Similarly the variations of sexual desire which occur periodically and are related to the menses in the female are probably of this nature; perhaps due to the congestion of the pelvic viscera.

7. *Psychological Factors*. Undoubtedly the psychological elements are of great importance in controlling the strength of the sexual drive. A man

may be quite unable to respond to a woman who disgusts him, or who he thinks may be diseased.

It would seem that the process of falling in love is the binding of libido, or sensuous feeling, on to the object, apparently by a process of association. Although Freud never clarified his views on the matter completely it seems that the transfer of emotion must occur with each association until nearly all the subject's thoughts and emotion are attached to the love object. This is not a restatement of the old associational psychology, which failed because it was too intellectual a matter, and it was not realized that with every concept, or thought, there was an emotional change as well.

The function of falling in love seems to be that in this condition one instinctively wishes to get as close as possible to the loved one; hence the cuddling, caressing, stroking, &c. which occurs. This, carried to its ultimate conclusion, means that the male wishes to get inside the female (i.e. penetrate and have intercourse) and the female wishes for such penetration. The stronger the emotion the more powerful the urge to do this.

What the basic factors which control falling in love may be, apart from fetishistic ones such as attraction to peculiar shades of hair &c. is not really known. In general the work of Terman and others suggests that it is probably a matter of conditioning occurring in one's development; since most people are attracted to those of the same nationality, social type or class, religious practices and the like. (This does not explain why sometimes an exotic person may arouse intense feeling, as Rudolf Valentino apparently did when he first appeared on the films.) Propinquity, which offers a chance to become familiar with someone of the opposite sex, is also important. Presumably biologically it is desirable that human beings become adjusted to those of the opposite sex who are available, and so tend to fall in love with those near them.

It must be admitted that in the present state of our knowledge we are unable to explain the psychological factors completely, but must state merely that this intense emotional feeling of being in love will greatly enhance the sexual drive. No matter how much it may distress those who have a romantic view of life it seems possible that, from the biological point of view, the whole value of falling in love is to initiate the sexual behaviour which will ultimately lead to reproduction. Hence the enhancement of the sexual drive which accompanies it.

FACTORS CAPABLE OF DIMINISHING INSTINCTUAL STRENGTH

1. Organic Factors: Inherited or Acquired. The diminution in sexuality which follows castration, the adrenogenital syndrome, and other endocrine diseases is well known. Diseases of the brain will sometimes diminish or abolish sexual desire, and in such disorders as cerebral syphilis there is often impotence. No doubt other organic factors can be inherited as in such conditions as dystrophia myotonica in which there is atrophy of the testicles, frontal baldness, cataracts, and myotonia with wasting. Starvation diminishes sexual desire (as those who suffered in prison camps noted) and exhausting diseases frequently leave the patient less desirous.

2. *Age.* The emotions tend to be diminished in old age though not always as much as one might expect. I have seen an old lady of over 80 years who complained of the strength of her unsatisfied sexual feelings, but no doubt such cases are rare. Usually the emotions diminish so that in extreme old age there is more or less apathy.

3. *Satiation.* After an instinct has fulfilled its aim and achieved its object there is a lessening of tension and a reluctance to seek the object again until some time has elapsed and tension has reaccumulated. This may account for temporary impotence after frequent copulation. It is, however, physiological and quite harmless.

4. *Attributes in the Object.* Unsuitable objects may diminish the instinctual responses. Many men would lose their desire at the thought of a woman of different race—e.g. a white man with a Negro woman or vice versa. Great discrepancy in age or class and so on may produce the same result. To some extent (as in difference in class) this is obviously due to conditioning.

5. *Lack of Reciprocity.* This may, of course, act as a stimulant as we have seen in the case of monkeys and apes, but prolonged indifference acts as a long deprivation of the sexual object and causes diminution. Even the most ardent lover grows tired of an unresponsive mistress and looks elsewhere.

6. *Certain Conditions in the Organ.* The conditions of the organ which cause diminution are just as unknown as those which cause an increase in instinctual responses. In hunger, for instance, gastritis can cause a sense of fullness which diminishes the appetite. Exactly what factors in the organs cause diminution in sexuality are not definitely known, except that it is usually believed that the tension in the vesiculae seminales has some influence. Lack of tension produces in some animals an absence of sexual feeling whereas desire increases *pari passu* with the filling of the vesicles until copulation takes place, as I have noted previously. Women who have never had sexual intercourse do not usually feel sexual desire as strongly as those who have had it. In fact, sexual intercourse produces psychical as well as physical changes in the female.

7. *Sublimation.* Sublimation, by which we mean the voluntary deflection of sexual energy into non-sexual channels, is very important. Everyone knows the lack of sexual desire when engaged on preparation for higher examinations. That this can be continued almost indefinitely is

certainly true for some people, if not for all. It is believed that if this is continued too long it is productive of neurosis and certainly damages normal sexuality. For instance, Terman and Miles found that there was lack of psychical sexuality in boys who had concentrated excessively on intellectual progress. I believe that over-sublimation can cause considerable abasement of sexual desire.

8. Other Psychological Factors. There are other psychological factors which are difficult to classify in the sections given above. For instance, if the emotion is concentrated on one woman, i.e. the man is in love with her, he is less likely to be sexually aroused by another. This may not be impossible, of course, but in general it usually is so. In such a case any woman will not do because the concentration leaves no emotional drive to be aroused.

Separation, which undoubtedly weakens the emotional attachments, will weaken the sexual drive towards the desired woman (hence the Victorian hero who went to Africa to shoot lions after being rejected).

Legal sanctions if sufficiently fearful may weaken sexual desire; although men and women will risk terrible punishments, as in the German youths in Hitler's time who had intercourse with Jewish girls, knowing that if caught they could be executed; and the South African men who receive long terms of imprisonment, apart from considerable contempt, for sexual congress with coloured girls.

Religion may have a very inhibitive effect for those who believe that transgression may mean punishments in the hereafter. The fear of venereal disease may suffice to prevent those who are desirous from seeking prostitutes; or, if they do, inhibit erection.

THE SEXUAL ACT

Normal sexual behaviour has been described from the psychological point of view on page. 53, but the reader is asked to reconsider the sexual act itself so that its abnormalities can be classified and described. Sexual intercourse consists of two parts: (1) the psychical factor which is the sexual excitement, tension, or desire—this is the driving force which urges the individual on to copulation; and (2) the physical act. This is a psychical reflex which is closely related to the excrementary and urinary reflexes. Although not completely under the control of the will it is initiated by cortical activity, usually by the sight of a desirable sexual object. It can be inhibted, to some extent, if not completely, in most persons—although this may be difficult if the excitement is allowed to progress too far. Once excitement has been aroused, however, I am extremely sceptical regarding the alleged power of the male to control the moment of orgasm in order to make it coincide with that of the female. He is constantly urged to do this by writers on popular sexology, but the exact way in which it is done is never explained except that it is by 'will-power'. The failure of the husband to do it often leads to unfounded accusations of selfishness on the part of the wife.

In the male excitement produces turgescence and erection. Contact, friction, and growing tension due to stimulation of the special senses (sight, smell, touch, &c.) cause the spinal reflexes to become prepotent with the result that the sexual channels discharge their contents into the urethra and, from thence, are finally expelled into the vagina by the muscles acting upon them.

In the female there is vaginal turgescence as a result of excitement, with discharge of secretion from local glands, producing moisture to lessen friction, combined sometimes with muscular movement to draw the penis into the vagina. After penetration the vaginal muscles grip the male organ. It is believed that at the moment of orgasm the uterus may be drawn down by muscular force to approximate to the end of the penis and so facilitate the entry of sperm into the cervix. Some sexologists believe that the uterus develops some peristaltic movement to draw the sperm into it and there is a certain amount of evidence to show that this may occur.

Obviously then sexual diseases can result in four possibilities in the male.

1. Anomalies of sexual desire: excessive or diminished.
2. Abnormalities of erection: mostly failure (chordee, or excessively prolonged erection is usually an organic condition).
3. Abnormalities of ejaculation: premature or failure.
4. Anomalies due to failure from the psychical side which result in diminution or lack of pleasure from the sexual act. (I have never heard of any patient complain of excessive or too much pleasure!)

In the female similarly we can have:

1. Anomalies of sexual desire: excessive or diminished.
2. Inability to tolerate entry.
3. Lack of response although entry has been effected.
4. Lack of pleasure although orgasm may occur.

In practice the anomalies of erection and ejaculation are so intermixed with diminished sexual feeling and desire that they are better considered as sub-classes, and this I intend to do. Similarly in females lack of response and inability to feel pleasure are combined in most cases.

14

SEXUAL AVERSION

Definition
Complete lack of sexual desire, or inability to have intercourse through psychical causes.

Psychopathology and Occurrence

It is only within recent years that it has been realized that a vast number of neurotics are more or less impotent and that those who are neurotic rarely, if ever, reach the height of orgastic pleasure attained by the normal. Even if a man appears perfectly normal, as most of those complaining of impotence attending fertility clinics, &c., seem to be, there are psychical reasons for his failure. It must be accepted therefore that these are the main reasons for sexual aversion. In doing so I do not discount the enormous importance of the endocrine factor which has not yet been fully explored or exploited. These can be of paramount importance when needed. I have seen eunuchoid men who were completely impotent restored to normal sexuality by testosterone propionate. Used without indication it is a waste of time and money, as well as preventing the patient having psychotherapy which would help him. The importance of proper diagnosis, and so of adequate treatment, whatever the cause, cannot be stated too emphatically. For example, impotence sometimes occurs due to cerebral damage caused by tumours &c. Out of 76 patients complaining of impaired sexual potency Johnson found 2 who had impotence due to intracerebral tumours. One had a temporal lobe neoplasm and the other a tumour of the frontal lobe.

If a man states that he does not feel sexual desire and is impotent, yet has no endocrine or cerebral abnormality, we may be sure that his illness is due to psychical causes. He is usually: (1) a sufferer from neurotic anxiety, whether he appears so or not; (2) a pervert or fetishist; or (3) either of these but unconscious of his mental trends or concealing them. The fourth possibility is that he is in love with someone other than his sexual partner. This latter is not really to be regarded as aversion. Patients who feel perverted or fetishistic urges are naturally reluctant to discuss them and superficial questioning is often very misleading, since a patient may be under treatment some time before admitting his abnormality.

Impotence and hyposexuality can be regarded from the behaviouristic point of view as being due to two causes: (*a*) diversion of the instinctual energy into other channels or (*b*) negative conditioning.

The diversion of sexual energy may occur, and usually does, as a temporary phenomenon during states of exhausting mental toil, as when students are working for higher examinations and so on. Moreover sexual intercourse is a function which needs all the instinctual energy available and most animals (though not perhaps the sub-human primates as shown in Chapter 2) prefer solitude, and any interruptions are likely to interfere with the successful function. *In all cases with any animal fear is the most dangerous emotion to potence,* and the one which is most likely to inhibit the function. This is clearly shown in those cases in which sexual congress has been interrupted as in the case of 'illicit' intercourse in unpropitious spots where the parties are disturbed by a policeman or a gamekeeper, &c. Frequently after such an experience temporary impotence

Chart showing the Frequency of Normal Intercourse
(from various statistics)

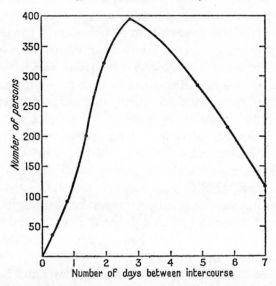

Owing to the scarcity of reliable data such a chart as this cannot be absolutely reliable. It will be seen that the average is about once in 2–3 days, but a certain number of people feel desire as frequently as three times daily without being abnormal. Based on 1,000 persons.

occurs, and not until the patient has been successful under better circumstances can he be sure of being potent again.

Fear is, of course, a frequent cause of frigidity in women after being introduced to sex in a painful manner, and indeed, this is believed by some to have been the cause of the frigidity of Queen Elizabeth 1. Others have suggested in her case the fear came from a different source—her mother, Anne Boleyn, had been beheaded for supposed adultery, and her stepmother, Katherine Howard, dragged screaming to the block for the same crime. Jenkins states: 'In the fatally vulnerable years she had learned to connect the idea of sexual intercourse with terror and death: in the dark and low-lying region of the mind where reason cannot penetrate, she knew that if you give yourself to men they cut off your head with a sword, or axe.' It would be an interesting piece of research if those girls who were known to have been criminally sexually assaulted in the past could be examined thirty years later and the result obtained, but as far as is known this has not been done.

Negative conditioning is a most common cause of hyposexuality. This is usually found in excessively narrow religious families where sex is particularly taboo. In many such families the parents so nag and bully the child when he shows any sexual interest that he finally surrenders and shows none at all. This is comparable to the conditioning of rats quoted previously, in which a male rat was given a painful electric shock whenever it attempted to gain access to the female, or the electrical aversion therapy described in the section on treatment in this book. As a matter of fact this conditioning from the mother does not usually succeed in abolishing the sexual impulse entirely, and the boy often allows it to appear in excessive flirting and interest in females, and it is only when he attempts the sexual act that the conditioning has an inhibitive effect. Sometimes the negative conditioning succeeds too well and then the man grows up with no normal sexual response. He may be diverted into homosexuality because he feels that women are prohibited. The suppressed sexual impulse bursts out into morbid religious activity, and if it does not develop into some abnormal sexuality—which it frequently does in the morbidly religious—it ends in paranoid schizophrenia or some other schizophrenic manifestations such as Rosanoff's 'chaotic sexuality'.

It is believed that in some cases where there is some prepotent mental activity, as in musical geniuses, mathematicians, and similar folk, all the sexual energy seems to be voluntarily diverted into their avocation. The result is that there is sexual aversion and impotence because there is nothing left to activate the instinct. Such cases of over-sublimation probably have a deep-seated emotional inhibition, but there does seem to be a superficial volitional diversion of sexual emotion into the art or science which interests them. A complete lack of sexual interest results. This appears to have been so in the case of Sir Izaac Newton who never displayed any sexual interest in his whole life.

The psychoanalytical school believes that impotence and frigidity are the result of infantile modes of reaction. Menninger gives the main causes as unconscious hate. This may be the result of an unconscious wish for revenge against the woman who represents some previously loved woman who has treated the patient badly. This woman is, of course, representative of the mother. Again, envy of the woman's pleasure (or in the case of the woman the man's pleasure) is often present. Many women have been brought up by their mothers to believe that men are 'disgusting' and 'bestial', and revenge what they imagine must have been ill treatment to the mother by refusing the man sexual pleasure. Of course, if the man unconsciously regards the woman as his mother (many mother-fixated men do equate all women with the mother) all the sexual prohibitions attached to her will be displaced on to the woman, so it is not surprising if he does not feel sexually excited with her.

Conscious or unconscious homosexuality is a frequent cause of impotence, and it is unusual for a homosexual to be able to have proper intercourse with women. In my experience the 'bisexual' individual is someone who is more or less homosexual, and who does not obtain proper pleasure from the members of either sex (although often they like to boast that it is entirely different).

Anxiety, which the psychoanalysts attribute to the 'castration complex' (the unconscious wish to castrate the father and fear that it will be revenged with talion punishment by him), is a common finding in impotence and frigidity. This anxiety is, of course, rationalized by finding various 'causes' for the sexual difficulties. For example, the woman frequently tells one that she had great difficulty with a previous pregnancy and she fears intercourse because if she becomes pregnant again she will have a similar experience. This is not dispelled by the fact that adequate contraceptive measures have been taken and there is no chance whatsoever that she will again become pregnant. In the case of the man it is commonly shown by fear of doing himself some injury by intercourse, of weakening himelf or 'draining away his energy'. This, of course, is quite impossible. I have never encountered anyone who was made ill by 'sexual excesses'. Long before any physical harm could be done the patient temporarily loses the sexual desire and the capacity of erection. Another common fear is of catching venereal disease, although proper measures make this a very remote danger.

It is not uncommon in my experience to find that a man may describe how he became impotent after a love affair with a girl which came to an unhappy termination. Whether this girl represents the mother or not may depend on the case, but until his emotion has been released from her, as long as he is craving for her and constantly thinking of her, it is inevitable that he will remain in a sexually suspended condition without even slight sexual desire for other women.

It is not only through over-attachment to the mother at the oedipal stage that impotence is caused—earlier fixations may produce the same result. Two oral erotics were treated by me: one who obtained sexual pleasure from sucking the udder of a ewe and the one who obtained it from sucking babies' comforters; both showed no interest in girls until they had been cured.

The fantasy of the vagina having teeth has already been described. Curiously enough this sometimes causes impotence based on oral sadism. It would seem that the baby may have a strong wish to bite the breast. This is reversed and there is a fear that the mother will bite back. The penis is equated with the breast and so there is fear that the penis will be bitten. The maternal mouth is equated with the vagina with the fear that intercourse will damage the penis. Naturally, those who have never analysed a case will regard this as amusing nonsense, but in my experience it is real enough to cause impotence.

It is a curious fact, and confirms to some extent the Freudian symbolism, that women who are frigid frequently show great fear of snakes and often dream of them. That the snake in such cases represents the penis seems certain. Fears do undoubtedly represent a defence against unconscious wishes so that it would appear that these women strongly desire the phallus (i.e. intercourse), but this has been prohibited in some way and so repressed. This may be due to parental taboos and probably usually is so, but there may be a much deeper-seated repression due to developmental, or incestuous, influences.

Menninger in the work quoted above regards impotence and frigidity as a form of 'focal suicide' brought about to solve unconscious conflicts. These conflicts are those caused by fear of punishment, fear of reprisals, and fear of unconscious hate, 'together with deficiencies in the erotic investment of the act due to conflicting aims'. This seems to be a good summary of the whole problem. (For a full psychoanalytical account of this matter the work of Hitschman and Bergler should be consulted.)

As far as the male physical manifestations, as distinguished from the psychical ones, are concerned these are two: (1) lack of erection or failure to maintain it; and (2) failure to ejaculate. In my experience the patient who has never felt any sexual feeling at all, who has never had any desire to masturbate, or have sexual intercourse, and in whom the most seductive siren can stir no response, is the most severe form of this disorder. He is the least likely to benefit from treatment and the most difficult to analyse, even over a long period. In him the causes are buried deeply and difficult to elicit—frequently he is homosexual, or has some similar abnormality. Sometimes one suspects an endocrine deficiency but rarely finds evidence to demonstrate it.

The patient who fails to ejaculate is usually suffering from a psychological condition, although naturally if he is a victim of a disease such as disseminated sclerosis and the sexual symptoms are a mere concomitant the condition is organic. However, it has been suggested that incoordination of the sphincter mechanism of the neck of the bladder can be at fault with the result that the semen passes into the bladder instead of distally along the urethra. This condition is supposed to be diagnosed by finding spermatozoa in the urine voided after orgasm. It must be of extreme rarity since I have never seen one.

A normal man should be able to reach an orgasm and the expulsion of seminal fluid should occur without difficulty. In some conditions, mainly where there is excessive anxiety, the reflex mechanism may not work adequately and ejaculation then does not occur. This is most often combined with other sexual difficulties, particularly when the wife has lost patience with her husband and reproaches him for his inadequacy. After repeated failure and wifely abuse he ceases to feel roused; and if he does attempt intercourse and attains orgasm the final stage of ejaculation fails.

Sometimes this condition appears as a residue when one has cured the other symptoms of hypoversion or aversion. I have found it in cases where a boy has been told that masturbation will have a grave effect on him because 'a drop of semen is equal to a pint of blood'. The unfortunate youth has no way of knowing that this is the wildest nonsense, without a shadow of truth.[1] (If it were true every time a man had intercourse he would be performing the feat of almost depleting the body of blood!) I have had patients who have been told this sort of untruth in order to make them avoid self-stimulation with the result that they have felt the sexual urge so strongly that they have masturbated to the very verge of ejaculation, but avoided reaching an orgasm. The result seems to be that the fear is repressed only to reappear in later life when intercourse occurs. The psychiatrist is then faced with the difficult task of unearthing the condition which caused the trouble. Sometimes the boy has been told that ejaculation drains away not the blood but the spinal fluid and this, also, is alarming to him. Unfortunately for the physician to tell the man in later life that neither of these ridiculous theories is true is insufficient to cure him and usually prolonged psychotherapy is necessary. Fear that the woman may be impregnated in extra- or pre-marital intercourse may have a similar effect.

In some cases a much deeper psychopathology may be present—sometimes a castration complex due to experiences as a child: the sight of female genitalia or threats of 'cutting it off' when the boy has been seen masturbating and so on. There is often an ambivalent attitude towards

---

[1] Masters and Johnson in their valuable study of human sexual responses state; 'The superstition that mental or physical deterioration results from excessive masturbation is firmly entrenched in our culture. . . . Every male questioned expressed a theoretical concern for the supposed effects of excessive masturbation, and in every case "excessive levels" of masturbation, although not defined specifically, were considered of a higher frequency than did the reported personal pattern. One man with a once-a-month masturbatory history felt once or twice a week to be excessive, with mental illness quite possible as a complication of such a frequency maintained for a year or more. The study subject with the masturbatory history of two or three times a day wondered whether five or six times a day wasn't excessive and might lead to "a case of nerves".'

females. In this case ejaculation is unconsciously equated with giving the woman something valuable and this is resented by the patient and refused.

In other deep-seated cases there seems to be strong unconscious incestuous wishes. Quite possibly in some cases this is linked with the castration fears just described. It is not suggested that these deep-seated causes are present in every case but, since they are unconscious, it is quite easy to overlook them.

The prognosis, except in the gravest cases, is usually good and the patient, in superficial conditions, may recover quite easily. In the more serious ones a course of psychotherapy under someone familiar with these conditions should be started as soon as possible. If incoordination of the sphincter muscles is suspected, and this should only be considered if there are no other more possibly psychological symptoms, then the urine should be examined after orgasm. However, the condition is rare and in any case treatment of it is said to be ineffective. In my experience the vast proportion of cases of failure of ejaculation is due to psychological causes and often curable.

This section would be incomplete without a brief note upon what might be called 'contraceptive impotence'. This one frequently finds in men who have used a sheath for long periods. The man often finds that in making love to his wife he becomes sexually excited but has no sheath at hand (often for reasons of privacy these have to be kept in a drawer away from the bed). He has to get up and perhaps cross the room to obtain one. By the time he has returned and applied the sheath erection has passed away; he is frustrated and unhappy. Let this occur a number of times and he realizes the impossibility of success. Anxiety becomes associated with the sexual act and can be displaced only by the use of other methods, such as oral contraceptives and by appropriate treatment.

Similar conditioning may produce impotence—for example, I have seen a man who was previously potent fail badly after a painful operation in which a cystoscope was passed down the urethra.

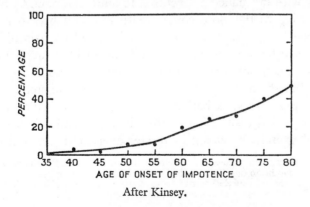

After Kinsey.

Any failure in the man may be complicated by an understandable irritation in the woman who has been deprived of sexual pleasure. Since women are always watching for evidence that their charms are fading, which is indeed an abiding fear in the mind, they may suspect themselves and this appears to produce additional anger against the husband.[1] At other times the husband's faithfulness is suspected, and divorce is threatened. All this drives the situation from bad to worse, and the marriage may actually be destroyed unless proper intervention is made.

Ageing is a process which tends to diminish penile erective powers, yet it is by no means inevitable that the man becomes impotent. According to Masters and Johnson, 'in most instances, secondary impotence is a reversible process for all men regardless of age, unless there is a background of specific surgery or physical trauma'.

Yet most psychiatrists (for example Kinsey et al.) would agree that sex does die down with advancing age and the urge and physical response is not so strong as previously. Often this is due to the ageing partner, and the fact that the older man cannot attract such exciting young females as he once could.

In women sexual aversion is shown by a refusal to permit the man to penetrate: this may show itself by a conscious refusal, or by vaginism which is due to an involuntary contraction of the pelvic muscles, adductors of the thighs, &c., and really signifies an unconscious refusal. Frequently the woman insists that she does not know why she is so fearful, and the basic causation is only to be found in the deeper levels of the mind. The unconscious factors will be discovered to be much the same as those which we have given as producing sexual aversion in men. Not all women will admit the reality of the unconscious motivation and rationalize that the sexual act is 'dirty', bestial, and so on. Since in cases of this sort penetration is not permitted orgasms and pleasurable sensations do not come into the picture. Haslam describes two cases of dyspareunia due to sexual aversion. The first was that of a woman aged 22 who had enjoyed sexual play with her fiancé but refused to allow intercourse. She became pregnant owing to the close contact with him and had to get married. She remained very afraid that intercourse would be painful and at the critical moment became so tense that she was unable to allow penetration.

The second case was that of a woman aged 23 who had been married for 2 years but the marriage had never been consummated. It existed on the basis of mutual masturbation, which both parties enjoyed. The wife had had congenital dislocation of the hip joints and this had entailed a long period of immobilization in plaster as a child. The hip joints were

---

[1] There is a description of sexual aversion in the *Satyricon* of Petronius which shows a similarity to the condition one finds to-day and, moreover, is complicated by this considerable irritation on the part of the woman, who suspects her own charms. This shows how little this condition has changed since the time of Nero.

normal when she married. She had also had a vaginal examination by a general practitioner when she was very young and had been very afraid of it.

Cases like these show a fairly easily understandable causation. The first must have had considerable emotional disturbance when she discovered herself pregnant and was, perhaps unconsciously, fearful that subsequent intercourse would be followed by similar painful results. The second had been conditioned not to open her thighs by the prolonged plaster fixation and the painful vaginal examination led her to expect discomfort rather than pleasure from intercourse.

I know of no extensive research on the sexuality of women which gives a reliable percentage of sexual aversion but the recent studies made by the French Institute of Public Opinion on the sexual responses of French women may be of interest. They were asked: 'In your opinion, are sexual relations an important part of marriage for women?' and replied; for nearly all, 68 per cent.; for a minority, 22 per cent., and no answer was given by 10 per cent. Asked if 'In your opinion, are women generally satisfied by physical love in marriage, indifferent to it, or disappointed by it?' they answered; satisfied, 46 per cent., indifferent, 15 per cent., disappointed, 22 per cent., no answer, 17 per cent., Only about half the women in France appear satisfied by their husbands, and the French are supposed to be erotic by temperament! The work of Kinsey and his co-workers show that impotence increases steadily with age, for example, in their series at 15 years 0·05 per cent. were impotent, at 20 years 0·1 per cent., at 25 years 0·4 per cent., at 30 years 0·8 per cent., at 35 years 1·3 per cent., at 40 years 1·9 per cent., at 45 years 2·6 per cent., at 50 years 6·7 per cent., and at 55 a similar figure. At 60 years 18·4 per cent., at 65 years 25 per cent., at 70 years 27 per cent., and 75 years 55 per cent. Finally at 80 years 75 per cent.

Kinsey agrees with the statements made in this book that in his experience practically all cases of impotence, excluding damage to the sexual organs, are due to psychological disturbances.

Psychic Emasculation

This condition is found in boys who have been brought up by the delicate, 'nice' type of woman who assumes a sort of pseudo-refinement by which any form of sexuality is considered 'not quite nice'. She frowns on rough play and rude words; takes her son away from schools where other boys use 'bad words' and, if possible, sends him to 'better schools' where well-brought-up boys attend in the hope that he will be protected from coarseness. Such boys are not allowed to partake in rough games like football, or masculine youthful activities like the Boy Scouts or Cadet Corps.

Y—PSY. D.

Usually this sort of woman attracts the man who is noisy and outwardly masculine, but who is really rather uncertain and feminine underneath his boisterous exterior. The result is that the boy has a poor model on which to mould himself in the father, and the mother has undue influence which is often unappreciated even by the young man himself.

When he is old enough to take an interest in girls the mother gently dissuades him because she feels that 'She isn't good enough for you darling'. He is made to feel that going out with girls is 'not quite nice', and any suggestion of sexual activity is regarded by the mother, and consequently by him, with horror.

I have been consulted by many such patients and had an opportunity of watching four over a long period. Two managed to emancipate themselves from their mothers sufficiently to attend strip-tease clubs (a curious way of safely enjoying vicarious sexual activity), the third goes to parties and takes girls to their homes afterwards, but makes no advances. The fourth is withdrawn, and never makes contact with girls although he would like to do so. Two have had schizophrenic episodes, and are odd in their behaviour. These young men, if they are able to meet girls, are too shy, nervous and inexperienced to arouse the girl's interest and cannot even kiss them. The girl, instinctively and intuitively, realizes his incapacity and subsequently avoids him.

Such young men remain immature and in a pre-pubertal emotional condition so that although they may like mixing it is always in a childish way; they do not regard gatherings as an opportunity to find girls, but as exciting events like a child's birthday party.

Young men of this type may drift into homosexuality, but usually they grow up emasculated and become old bachelors; or marry when past sexual life. Unfortunately as they have no insight they are not responsive to attempts to assist them to a normal life.

Novelists, whose work depends on their observing people and describing their lives, naturally have noticed this condition; and, Fiedler in a review of American literature, lists a number of books where characters show this form of emasculation.

It is not pretended that there is not a great deal of unconscious emotion in the relationship of such men to their mothers. Naturally the young man often replaces his father in the mother's emotion, and various situations arise even if not appreciated by either.

The situation is a tragic one since the young man is unable to adjust himself to normal adult sexual life and, owing to the overwhelming influence of his mother, ever to benefit from treatment.

CASE NO. 18

Although the obsessive and fetishistic elements in some cases may be so fantastic as to appear slightly amusing to people who are normally sexed these illnesses are by no means funny to the sufferers. Moreover, they frequently produce severe impotence which wrecks the marriages and which is sometimes difficult or impossible to cure.

This is shown in the following case. It is that of a schoolmaster aged 45. He stated that he was obsessed by girls and women with thin legs. The rest of the woman's figure, breasts and so on, evoked no interest or excitement. The whole attention was concentrated on the thin legs.

The patient's parents had been unhappily married for eighteen months before his birth, but he never knew his father because his mother left him and went to live with her parents and the father died shortly afterwards. The mother's parents were alive for the first six years of his life. The mother 'was incredibly nervous and hysterical' and the patient was over-protected and over-valued. As a child he was nervous and from the age of six onwards, until the age of 12, he was terrified of having an enema. He then had an operation in hospital and was given one. This ridded him of his fear. At the age of 15 he started to become obsessed with women's thin legs, and it has steadily got worse. He looks at women in the street to see whether their legs are thin, and at advertisements where exaggerated thin legs fascinate him. Recently he has noticed that Indian and Negro girls have them and these occupy his interest.

At school he was successful and won a scholarship to Cambridge where he succeeded in obtaining a double first in classics. He then devoted himself to teaching which he was still doing when seen.

In 1946 he had what he described as a 'breakdown' and felt 'physically strange'. This occurred after he had taken his degree. A year later he had psychoanalysis for twelve months but without much relief. In 1958 he married and needed further psychoanalysis but was impotent. He consulted another psychiatrist who told him he ought never to have married. In 1959 his wife left him because he was completely impotent and had never consummated their marriage.

He stated that since early adolescence he thought of himself sometimes as a female and felt that if he had had attractive thin legs he would be an attractive girl. If he were a beautiful girl he would have no need to work. At other times when he went out with a girl who had the sort of legs he found attractive he thought that other men were envying him his companion. He was fascinated by court shoes with high heels but there was little sexual excitement in his interest.

He had tried to have sexual intercourse with a girl whose legs were thin but failed because he had a premature ejaculation. If he could once succeed, he thought, he would lose his obsession as he had lost his fear of enemas.

This young man's sexual life was completely spoiled by his obsession and it was unlikely that his marriage would ever succeed unless he were cured. However, since he had had two years' analysis this was most unlikely. Since he was not anxious to have further psychotherapy he was given sedation in the hope that successful intercourse would cure him but little improvement was anticipated.

The analysts seemed to regard the thin legs as symbolizing penises but the patient did not subscribe to this view. There is no doubt that a homosexual basis existed for his illness—his identification with girls—and this was derived from the fact that he had no contact with his father. His mother played the dominant part in his life. Probably the obsession with thin legs was derived from her in some way (actually she was plump until the age of 45 and then very thin) but the case was not studied enough to make any certain statements. The salient point in this case is that, like many patients with sexual deviations, he was quite impotent.

CASE No. 19

This patient was a foreigner who had settled down in England and was earning his living here. He complained that he found difficulty in thinking and could not have successful intercourse with his wife. He suffered from poor erections and these often failed before orgasm. In addition he sometimes had premature ejaculations. Physically he was a normal healthy man and the prematurity indicated the psychological nature of his condition.

His father had been an invalid from the First World War and had died nine years before the patient was seen. He had been a psychopathic failure and drank heavily. His death was apparently due to cancer. The patient's mother was a dominant woman and was still living abroad. There was one brother alive and well.

His childhood was unhappy because of parental quarrelling and his father's heavy drinking, but the patient did well at school. On leaving school he went to a university but unfortunately the war interrupted his career and he fought in the Army against the Germans. Taken prisoner he escaped after a time and managed to reach France, and finally England. He fought in Normandy after D Day.

In 1948 he married but this was not happy because he felt unsatisfied and his wife was not contented. They had two children who appeared to be normal but were troubled by parental discontent.

He has seen other psychiatrists previously without effect and it was decided to treat him by psychotherapy. This was prolonged and he needed three years' psychotherapy. However, it revealed a great deal about his state of mind.

Following the First World War his family were forced to live in refugee camps and he had a traumatic experience in one as a child. There was one communal bath for the males and one for the females. He wished to go with his father to the men's bath but his father did not agree and he was taken by his mother into the women's. The females there objected to a boy being admitted and he was faced by a horde of naked protesting females all shouting at the top of their voices and pointing to him. He was confused and terrified. Not unnaturally he thought that there was some threat to his genitalia.

This fear was revived later on when at the age of 13 a pretty young female cousin came to stay with them. She was gay and lively and her beauty aroused him sexually. He was discovered by his mother masturbating in bed when daydreaming about this cousin. His mother was horrified and dragged back the bed-clothes, leaning over him and threatening that she would 'cut it off'. This threat terrified him. He realized that he could only gain acceptance by his mother by repressing sex completely. This was impossible and he could not keep sexual thoughts out of his mind. At the age of 16 he had an ejaculation by what he described as 'sheer will power' and this frightened him further since he felt that if it could happen once it might occur again and he would go on losing valuable semen indefinitely. He was his mother's favourite and she seems to have disregarded his brother. A conflict was produced between his sexual urges and his wish to retain his mother's affection. He solved this by repressing sex until his marriage in 1948.

Psychotherapy revealed a terrific castration complex. This seemed based on his hostility to his father for his drinking and neglect. The father's behaviour might have been due to the fact that he found the mother impossible to live with because of her dominance and resentment of his masculinity. Whether this was so or not the patient was hostile to him. He felt that for most of his youth he had tried to identify himself with his mother and resented that he had done so. He said 'I am sick to death of playing my mother. I am not myself—I am my mother. I do everything in my power to emulate her'.

The experiences, first of all in the refugee camp where he saw a number of hostile naked women aroused his fear of castration (he thought they had lost their genitalia) and secondly when his mother actually threatened him with castration, focused his fears on his genitalia. There was the conflict of wishing to please his mother and mould himself on her, but this entailed rejecting his masculine genitalia which he wished to retain. He was frightened of the vagina and said that why it was frightening was that 'there was no penis'.

It was not surprising that he had had sexual difficulties when there were so many conflicting emotions at the back of his mind and such fear of the woman's genitalia.

REFERENCES

EISENSTEIN, V. W. (1957) *Neurotic Interaction in Marriage*, London.
FIEDLER, L. A. (1960) *Love and Death in the American Novel*, New York.
GRIFFITH, E. F. (1957) *Marriage and the Unconscious*, London.
HASLAM, M. T. (1965) The treatment of psychogenic dyspareunia by reciprocal inhibition, *Brit. J. Psychiat.*, **111**, 280–2.
HITSCHMAN, E., and BERGLER, E. (1936) *Frigidity in Women*, New York.
JOHNSON, J. (1965) Sexual impotence and the limbic system, *Brit. J. Psychiat.*, **111**, 300–3.
KINSEY, A. C., POMEROY, W. B., MARTIN, C. E., and GEBHARD, P. H. (1953) *Sexual Behavior in the Human Female*, Philadelphia.
MASTERS, W. H., and JOHNSON, V. E. (1966) *Human Sexual Response*, London.
REMY, J., and WOOG, R. (1964) *Patterns of Sex and Love, A Study of the French Woman and her Morals by the French Institute of Public Opinion*, London.

15

SEXUAL HYPOVERSION

Definition

Diminished sexual desire. This definition unfortunately leads to complication, since it necessitates the definition of what is normal sexual desire. Biologically, no doubt, in monogamy, intercourse a few times a year would be amply sufficient to propagate the species, but such infrequency would be quite insufficient to satisfy an average man. It is impossible to give an accurate definition of normal sexual desire any more than it is possible to give an exact definition of normal appetite for food. Bulimia and anorexia are usually described as excessive desire or lack of desire for food without further discussion. I would, however, try to go a little further than this and describe sexual hypoversion as a disorder in which the sexual desire is lower than that found in other men and women of the same physique, and which is insufficient to satisfy an average normal healthy sexual partner. In practice I find that sexual hypoversion shows itself in infrequent (perhaps less than once monthly), and in unsuccessful, sexual intercourse which gives little pleasure to either party.

Psychopathology and Occurrence

It is not unusual to find that impotence and frigidity do not exist in full force but are diluted down, as it were, to partial failure of sexual function. The patient manages to have some sort of ejaculation but it is either too rapid (i.e. ejaculatio praecox) or too delayed. If this is not so, then intercourse may be unsatisfactory because of a poor erection, or failure to maintain erection. Havelock Ellis, of course, has divided the sexual function into two 'instincts' (they are in reality reflexes), that of erection and that of ejaculation. This does not seem of great importance, since it is often found that both disorders exist together, or even alternate, to spoil intercourse. Frequently difficulty starts by premature ejaculation and later, for some unknown reason, progresses to failure of the erection. Why it should happen in this way is a complete enigma.

As Menninger has pointed out, these unsatisfactory states frequently exist and are treated by physicians by the injection of various hormones or by excitants such as strychnine, or too often not reported or treated at all. Although I have seen a large number of impotent and frigid patients I have rarely seen any of these benefited in this way. Too often patients feel that nothing whatsoever can be done to help them and drift on until their marriages end in the divorce court. A large number of cases of infidelity on either side are caused by unsatisfactory sex life.

This is all very tragic since sexual hypoversion is a very curable condition and easily treated if the causation is properly understood. In order to appreciate the problem it should be compared with the functional disorders of the urinary system. This is particularly relevant since these both have the same nerve supply—S. 3 and 4.

It is obvious that there are two disorders of urination which are comparable with premature ejaculation and with failure of erection. These are: the involuntary passage of urine—usually when in a state of fear—and the inability to pass water. This latter occurs when there is slighter agitation, perhaps because there is a strong inhibition acquired by education against wetting oneself, whereas there is no such inhibition against holding one's urine. The common occasion when a man finds that he is unable to pass water is when he is trying to urinate in the presence of others as after a football match, or on coming out of a cinema, and is being told to hurry up by those behind. The slight anxiety produced causes a complete inability to urinate, although a few moments before the patient may have been extremely eager to do so.

It is obvious, therefore, that anxiety can cause similar derangements in the sexual as well as the urinary apparatus. Fear, anxiety, worry, perturbation, or whatever name is given to it, is potent enough to affect the reflexes. It is therefore in that sphere that we have to seek the cause.

The story is usually a common one. A young man with no previous sexual experience gets married and is very eager that all should be well. Or he may have 'illicit' intercourse and fear that the girl will become pregnant, or they may be interrupted. Whatever it may be there is fear attached to the act. This causes, very frequently, a premature ejaculation. The young man may not be perturbed, in which case it may correct itself, but more usually he is very upset at what he fears is an indication of a serious disease. Possibly he had been told, as a youth, that masturbation is a cause of impotence; he harks back to the past and fears that in his youthful masturbation he has produced incurable and hopeless disease. He cogitates upon it and looks forward to the next occasion of intercourse with a mixture of hope and dread. This fear in itself is enough to produce a further premature ejaculation and this confirms his worst fears. He now ruminates upon his supposed impotence most of his time and so starts a vicious circle: fear—premature ejaculation—more fear—more premature ejaculations—still more fear, &c. The same thing can occur with failure of erection which may be substituted for, or follow, repeated prematurity.

Now another factor appears. His wife, or sexual partner, obtains little or no pleasure from his intercourse, and becomes irritable. Often she is understanding and helpful, but frequently she becomes angry and says, 'There you are again, you're no good, obviously you don't love me', &c., and this upbraiding exacerbates the condition. Some wives feel that the husband should have an erection whenever they desire it (just as some husbands think that their wives should always welcome them sexually) and do not appreciate that they are asking for impossibilities. Probably the worst thing is in those cases when the woman expects to be satisfied on one particular night, say Firday night, or some other time. The man, who has had a strenuous and anxious day, is quite unable to be emotional, and the wife, feeling that he no longer loves her, becomes resentful and angry. Finally the man dreads to have intercourse because he *knows* he will fail (and the fear makes it certain that he will do so). A great deal of quarrelling in marriage comes from sexual dissatisfaction without either of the couple realizing it. The husband resents his wife's coldness and nags her, the wife hates him for his impotence and finds fault over trivialities. The husband starts looking at girls in the office and the wife becomes friendly with other men. Sooner or later one or the other starts a liaison and the marriage breaks up. This could be prevented if they had realized their 'incompatibility' was only resentment due to sexual dissatisfaction which could have been corrected.

CASE No. 20

A Case of Sexual Hypoversion

This case was one of a young man aged 25. He complained of being out of harmony with himself, shut off, shy, and self-conscious. He was worried by masturbation and impotence.

There was a family history of alcoholism on both sides, but when the patient was treated both parents were alive and well. His eldest brother was killed in the First World War, but he had two brothers living, one twelve years older and one three years younger. His sister was alive, but married to a man many years her senior. The elder brother was married, but he had himself been impotent for some years. The younger brother had shown no interest in girls and apparently no heterosexual or other sexual interests. The patient was physically well except for slight unimportant mitral disease.

He said that he had had an affair with a foreign girl some four years before and had not had successful coitus although he felt physically desirous. He said: 'The desire was there but I could not translate it physically.' He had noticed this particularly when he had had further sexual attempts a few months previously. He was worried about the results of masturbation, about which he had heard terrible things. Although he had been interested in little girls as a small boy he found the segregation of preparatory and public schools led him to take a sexual interest in boys. Similarly, when he attended a university. When he went abroad he fell in love with a girl, but owing to various circumstances he was separated from her. He was attached to a young man at a place where he worked, but had no relations with him. When he masturbated he had both heterosexual fantasies (of the foreign girl) and homosexual ones (of the man where he worked).

His first dream was of particular interest psychologically. It forms to some extent the key to his whole illness. He dreamed: 'I was going to a fancy-dress ball. I was shocked and horrified by a large middle-aged woman who was naked with large breasts. She had a male organ added on. I was very much frightened by this dream.' Although it was not clear to the patient and was not interpreted to him, there is no doubt from the material which was unearthed later that the woman in the dream represented his mother. She had always dominated the family, including his father, and taken on the male role. She was not only 'wearing the trousers' but wearing the penis, and so represented what Ernest Jones calls: 'The terrible mother with the penis.' His mother, it appeared, had always regarded sexuality very seriously, and he had a frightening memory of her nearly catching him masturbating as a small boy. This had terrified him, and his fear of masturbation was greatly increased by the fact that his brothers had told him terrible things which resulted as the consequence of this habit. He felt full of fear but could not stop it. He confessed a horror of breasts and says that he was revolted by them. When he was small he saw his brother at the breast and felt jealous. He was apparently in consequence of this attracted by the back view of a woman and by her buttocks, and repelled by her front. This he associated with an incident in which he indulged in sexual play with a small girl at the age of 7 in which they smacked each other's buttocks.

He confessed that although he was interested in women and had had two unsuccessful affairs with girls, he was also attracted to a young man, who was homosexual, at the place where he worked. This streak of homosexuality had appeared at school and persisted through university life, but he had never been able to display any overt homosexuality and was as impotent with a man as with a woman.

He then produced some sado-masochistic fantasies of horses being injured (although in real life he became very indignant at anyone ill-treating animals, and once at a racecourse swore at a jockey who hit a horse). These fantasies he spontaneously connected with his mother. After this he tended to turn his feelings of attraction to the homosexual young man at his work into a display of hostility and felt that he wanted to hurt him. As is usual in cases where there is strong negative emotion attached to the mother, he began to work out an Oedipus situation with this emotion as it was displaced. He started to express hostility to his older brother. His fantasies, which had been purely passive, tended to become more active. He expressed his interest in the anus; he felt that when as a little boy he smacked the child's bottom the vagina (or he felt perhaps the anus) opened and shut. His attention had been called to the anus by the fact that when, as a child, he had been constipated, his mother had placed soap suppositories in it.

He produced memories of being tremendously sexual as a boy at his preparatory school and even until puberty. (This is very usual in cases of impotence.) Even after one month's treatment he felt much better, much less self-conscious, and much less homosexual.

He then started to dream of a girl with whom he had been in love. For convenience this girl is called 'G'. He started to reminisce and fantasy about this girl, who was the first girl he had really loved. He also fantasied about another girl he had been fond of whom we will call 'A'. It became quite apparent

that these girls had been confused with his mother, and he tended to be repulsed from them by anything which reminded him of his mother—for instance,
once when kissing one of these girls he noticed that the curve of her cheek was
like his mother's and he lost his emotions immediately.

His homosexual emotion appeared traceable to his brother, and he remembered feeling sexual emotion to this younger brother at the age of 7, and as
these emotions and memories appeared he felt less and less attracted to him
although some of the negative emotion still remained. A certain amount of
castration material came up—particularly in the form of injuring the eyes.

At this time, about four months after beginning treatment, he received a
rather unkind letter from the girl 'A' who had got married. This upset him and
filled him with fantasies about her. Moreover, he went away for a short holiday
with his parents, and this caused a brisk reversal in his sexuality so that he lost
interest in girls for a while. This shows how important it is in these cases to
control the surroundings, although it is only the environment as far as the
causal family situation is concerned which is important.

About this time he started to become attracted to a young girl who was aged
15 years. This is not unusual in such cases, and in my experience is a good prognostic sign. It shows that the homosexual attraction is being changed to a
heterosexual one, although the love object is chosen as far different from the
mother as is possible. Unfortunately he had an attack of influenza which,
although it did not reverse his feelings, made him very weak and hindered his
progress.

He then brought up a certain amount of excremental material as is shown
in the following dream: 'I was very busy swilling faeces down three lavatories.
My father and sister were looking on and throwing down pieces of paper into
the lavatories. My mother was in bed (my father told me later) and had been
given some wrong pills which gave her terrible diarrhoea. I felt disappointed
that she was not going to die.' He confessed that in his childhood lavatories
had played a great part and he had spent a lot of time reading and masturbating
there. With this excremental material he brought up more hostility to his
mother (in fact the dream given above shows how important this is and how
inextricably confused is the hostility and this material). He felt much more
cheerful, however, and found his work more interesting than ever before. He
gained half a stone in weight. He found that his fantasies were all heterosexual,
and thought of homosexuality as boring. He then dreamed that he was having
intercourse with 'A' but failed, although the penis was erect. This was the first
time in which he had had even this amount of success in a dream. It shows,
however, that there was a strong unconscious wish *to fail*, and no doubt this
was located in the confusion of the girl with his mother.

He started to have sexual excitement with the girl of 15 and found her breasts
exciting. This was the first time he had noticed breasts in this manner. This
was an important change, since previously his reaction to any signs of physical
maturity in a woman was complete impotence both physically and mentally.
He then found this girl was attracted to another man and regressed in consequence and felt 'fiendish jealousy'. It became apparent that he had always
linked the idea of cruelty and intercourse together. When he had felt tender to
'G' he found that he was most impotent. He began to appreciate that his
previous horror of breasts really concealed an unconscious attraction for them.
This was part of the reason why he wished to have intercourse *a posteriori*. He
then felt that the girl aged 15 was causing him to regress—he could not have

intercourse with her because of her age and decided not to see her again. This girl (who was very sexual) did see him again and said something about having intercourse with someone else. This upset him, and as he expressed it, 'made him feel dead in the penis'.

He produced a valuable dream which he remembered having at the age of 12. 'A large middle-aged woman came into the street and pulled two kittens about and started to torture them to death. A small man without a waistcoat attacked her but he failed to prevent her.' The man he associated with his father, the woman with his mother, and the kittens with his testicles. Evidently even at the age of 12 he was so tortured with the feelings of guilt regarding sex which his mother had driven into him that he wished to be rid of it; or, alternatively, at a deeper level he felt castration feelings to her (hatred to the breasts) and reversed them on to himself. He remembered then that he had always felt sexual attraction to his mother—particularly her breasts and the 'middle part of her body'.

He went for another holiday with his parents without any dire results after he had had six months' treatment. He was still very fixated to the anus, however. He said: 'Until I came to you I had much more interest in the anus than in the sexual organs. The anus had always been the physical love object to me. I can remember as a child the sexual acts and fantasies were connected with it. I used to love being in the lavatories where a little girl I was fond of had been. When I was about 7 I used to get constipated and my mother used to put ointment in my anus. I used to hate it, and I felt like a young girl who has been raped.' He then had another dream of a woman with a penis, but it did not cause so much emotion. He confessed that he still felt some fear of seeing a woman naked. He felt attracted by the hairlessness of a woman's buttocks. It was suggested to him that this might be because they resembled the breasts. He accepted this suggestion with eagerness and *said he felt that the anus represented a nipple*. After this discovery he felt a great longing to examine the nipples of the young girl. This young girl, who was by this time aged 16, did entice him into bed. He did not have intercourse, however, but got a strong erection. He was disappointed with the fact that 'her bottom felt rough'. (This shows the persistence of emotion transferred from the breast to the buttock.) He felt unselfconscious, and this was a great advance, since, when a few years before he had gone to bed with the girl 'G', he had been revolted at the vagina and had had no erection at all. He did not feel this with the young girl. The idea of the vagina produced a memory which he had of a dream occurring frequently when he was ill as a child. 'It was of a bush swelling until it grew to enormous size.' There is not much doubt that this 'bush' really represented the pubic hair perhaps seen in early childhood. He spontaneously brought up ideas which confirmed this. He said: 'Until I was 16 the sight of the sexual parts was tremendously exciting, they had no pubic hair. After puberty the sight of pubic hair was horrible. As a small boy I was horrified by my father's and his friends' pubic hair and their old man's breasts. I feel I did see a woman's pubic hair. I felt it was my mother's, yet I do not know. The little girl told me that her sister was covered with hair. I was horrified. I saw my father's pubic hair when I was in bed with him. When I dream of the woman with a penis there is no pubic hair.' It was suggested, following the analogy of his horror of the breasts, that this again concealed a tremendous attraction.

He produced a great deal of horror of diarrhoea (it will be remembered that in the dream given previously he dreamed that his mother had diarrhoea), and said that he hated the idea of liquid and liked the idea of solid excreta. He added that, 'Diarrhoea and the idea of fluid coming from one's body is associated with my mother.' It became apparent that this horror of fluid really represented milk (i.e. the anus represents the nipple, and therefore the fluid coming from it must represent the milk). This again was horrifying to him and he said: 'Suckling is as revolting to me as diarrhoea. I hate the thought of breasts filled with milk.'

He had a dream apparently resulting from this: 'The girl "G" had my penis in her mouth. I was doing something of the same nature to her vagina.' Obviously this is really a dream which shows an intense desire to suckle, but, as has been pointed out, the sexual organs have been confused with the breasts.

At this time, nearly a year after he had commenced treatment, he tried again to have sexual intercourse with the young girl, but unfortunately a tough hymen thwarted him. His mother tried to get him again under her influence, but he greeted her advances with intense hostility and refused to allow her to dominate him. He had another try at intercourse and was more successful and had an ejaculation. Curiously enough this depressed him, and he felt ill and had diarrhoea afterwards. His mother had always assured him that the consequence of masturbation was illness, and no doubt this was caused by the constantly repeated suggestion.

At this time he went abroad for a holiday and while there had intercourse with a prostitute. This was successful, although the woman had to produce the erection by a certain amount of fellatio. The penetration and ejaculation were then quite normal and he felt tremendously elated about it afterwards. There were, however, still a certain percentage of dreams which showed a wish to be impotent and a certain number of fellatio fantasies. He was in spite of this much more masculine, but when he again tried to have intercourse with a prostitute he failed. He felt that was because she refused to encourage him with fellatio as a preliminary. This seemed to be because of her vagina also, since he felt a certain amount of horror at it still. He had a fantasy which must have been a memory of touching his mother's pubic hair as a little child, and asking what it was: he was tremendously abused for this. He said that his mother had always made him think that failure was inevitable. 'She was incompetent. She was never able to nurse us [he and his brothers were bottle-fed]. She is the epitome of failure.' He had some time ago given up the young girl, but had found another girl who was complacent and fond of him.

The analysis continued rather monotonously by displacing hostility from his mother, and as it was displaced it was used to work out his Oedipus complex. His sexual life had obviously been complicated by the fact that his mother had been much too masculine and his father much too feminine in make-up. He tried again (just over a year after he had commenced treatment) to have intercourse with this girl. This was not very successful, but immediately afterwards he felt much better; the next day he felt ill and depressed. He had lost his horror of the vagina, and this was a great step forward. He tried again after a week or two and succeeded in having intercourse *a posteriori*, and then again in another week and was successful in the normal way. It was then found that the analysis was stationary because of negative transference from his mother, and this was resolved. He again had more or less successful intercourse and noticed that his interest was passing from the breasts on to the vagina. He said he feared that the girl would feel contempt for him through his failing sexually. This was apparently the result of displacement from his mother, since she had always expressed contempt for his sexual functions and made him feel that failure was inevitable.

He formed another friendship with a girl but felt too much tenderness to her to be successful and this friendship failed. It seemed that he 'could not get the penis to work' because it was identified with the breast, and this had happened when he had tried to suckle at the breasts. At the beginning of his analysis he felt hostile to his penis, but slowly this passed away and he felt that he wanted to cherish it. He said: 'I feel I want to have my penis ill-treated as if I hated it. I do hate it in a way because it does represent to me bitter disappointment. I felt when I was a child that my mother *hated* my penis. She loathed sexuality when I was a child—she does now. I feel that my mother having failed to feed me felt angry about it and got back at me.' He then went abroad and met 'G'. He found that he was still fond of her and made up his mind to marry her. He proposed to her and was accepted, and a marriage was arranged. At the last moment he became rather panicky, but went through with it without trouble. He did not succeed at once in having successful intercourse and needed a few months' more treatment. He still tended to have intercourse *a posteriori* but slowly overcame this. He produced some fantasies or memories of suckling at the breasts and having a foul taste in his mouth. (This is very common in these cases.) In spite of these residues, however, he succeeded in overcoming his impotence and when last heard of had been leading a normal happy married life for some years.

This case is very important inasmuch as it shows the roots of impotence. Firstly the continued conditioning from the dominant mother on the impossibility of success and the wrongness and dangers of sex. The masculinity of the mother and the lack of it in the father are also important. Then the deeper unconscious motifs—the failure to suckle, the identification of penis and breast with the resulting displacement of emotion on to the anus and protective horror of them. Impotence of this type is usually considered the most obstinate and difficult of all the sexual neuroses. This case, however, which took over two years to cure, shows that it is not incurable and that persistence is rewarded in some cases.

CASE No. 21

A Case of Impotence

This case is typical of the rapidity in which uncomplicated conditions of impotence are curable provided that they are approached properly, and the vicious circle of anxiety and inhibition can be broken by careful examination, reassurance, sedation, and encouragement. The patient was a young man aged 36 who complained that he failed to get an erection with a girl with whom he was in love. He came from a normal family but his mother died from some unknown cause when he was aged 3 years. His father married again and his step-mother, who was kind, brought him up. His relations with her were excellent. There was one brother and one sister both alive and well.

Possibly as a response to the early loss of his mother (in spite of his happy home) he developed asthma and this continued until he was aged 21. At preparatory school he got on well but he was at his public school for only two years because his parents wished to evacuate him away from the air-raids. He later went to a university where he lived a normal social life and took a degree.

On leaving he became a journalist and was a leader writer to one of the biggest national newspapers.

He stated in his sexual life that he was not given wrong information about masturbation and it never worried him. At school he had the usual homosexual 'crushes' on older boys but this passed away after puberty. There were never any physical relations with it. He had tried heterosexual relations with girls but failed to obtain erections. That this was due to anxiety is evident because it was sometimes replaced by premature ejaculations.

Physical examination showed that he had nothing organically wrong to cause his symptoms. It was found that his fiancée was abroad (she was not English) and he saw her rarely. His work in the provinces made it even more difficult for him to visit her than if he were working in London (where he wished to obtain a transfer).

He was reassured that there was no reason why he should not be potent and given a sedative and strychnine. Nothing further was heard from him for a year when he wrote saying that he had married and his potence had become normal. His marriage was happy and his wife was pregnant. He appeared delighted with the result.

Such a happy termination might not have resulted had he been given hormones, or some other useless treatment, until he had lost confidence and reached the depths of despair that he would ever be a normal man.

The deeper-seated factors which cause partial failure of the sexual act are the same as those which cause complete failure. There may be one exception here, inasmuch as ejaculatio praecox is sometimes found in those who have been forced to abstain from intercourse for some time and presumably are suffering from excessive excitability. In those cases although premature ejaculation may occur a few times it usually disappears as soon as the patient regains his sexual adjustment. He may, however, be frightened that something is wrong, and this fear tends to keep up his prematurity. Simple reassurance will often restore normality. It is not unusual for those who have partial failure of their sexual functions to use alcohol as an aid to their hyposexuality. This is not, however, of any value and is more likely to lead to failure than otherwise. Those who suffer from sexual aversion or hypoversion often show a reflection of their difficulties in their ordinary life (since one may take it as a truism that if the sexual life is deranged one's whole life is disorganized). These people are usually of a very intellectual type, yet it is rare to find that they have attained the position in life to which their intellectual ability entitles them. Moreover, as soon as their erotic differences are corrected the subjects frequently improve, not only in the sexual sphere, but in their everyday life also.

Occasionally one sees what may be regarded as a reversal of this principle—that is, that anxieties usually associated with the everyday life become so great that invasion of the erotic side occurs. I have seen an increasing number of men in whom the worries associated with business, world disturbances, threats of war, and so on have caused premature ejaculation, erective impotence, and so on. The 'tired business man' is not altogether a myth, and the fact that he prefers a musical play, a vaudeville show, or a revue in which there are girl dancers in a state of more or less undress shows not excessive sexuality, but a diminution which needs such exhibitions to whip it up to normality. The increasing pace of normal life in civilization, the greater anxiety in daily work, and the constant threat of war undoubtedly tend to have a deleterious effect on a percentage of male sexuality. The effect of this was observed clearly in a case of mine in which a middle-aged 'jobber' on the Stock Exchange had rapidly lost all his sexual responses owing to the increasing tension he felt due to the constantly falling markets. Finally he was unable to show his wife, or anyone else, any sexual interest at all.

Many men noticed a similar effect during the bombing of London. That this did not always occur was shown by the fact that some men seemed sexually stimulated, but ancillary factors may have been at work in such cases—for example, they were brought in contact with different and more desirable young women, and so on.

There is a type of patient who complains that he obtains no sexual pleasure from intercourse (no doubt what Chodalos de Laclos, in Liaisons dangereuses, calls 'the manual labourers of love'!). Fenichel gives the factors which cause insufficiency of orgasm as two: (1) there is no current possibility of satisfying the infantile sexual wishes (for example, the sexual partners are not the real parents); and (2) the defensive forces—in the form of anxiety and guilt that pertains to infantile sexuality.

It is probable that often there are more superficial reasons for lack of desire or satisfaction. For example, it is not uncommon for some attribute of the object to cause it. Many men would be impotent with a woman of another race and many women would be frigid for the same cause (although this is by no means always the case). This appears to be the result of conditioning and it is often found, for example, with white men in the tropics, that a woman who has been distasteful to a man at first sight can later become attractive—particularly after lack of opportunity to relieve the desire with one of his own colour. Many white men living in Africa finally live with native women, and Europeans often mate with Chinese after residence in the Far East. Again, the normal partner is one of the same age and excessive differences in age may damp desire. Lack of response in the sexual partner (e.g. frigidity in the woman) will frequently lead to diminution of sexual pleasure. It is doubtful, however, whether we should class these failures as true sexual hypoversion, or aversion. These are factors which may affect any normal man and cannot be regarded as unusual. A patient is not said to suffer from anorexia because he has no desire to eat strange food—koumiss or shark's fin soup!

I have discounted in this section the production of impotence or sexual hypoversion due to old age. It is usual for the desire to die down with increase of age, but this does not always occur. I have already mentioned that I was once consulted by a lady, of over 80 years of age, who complained that she was kept awake by unsatisfied sexual desire. She had led a full sexual life and enjoyed it before the death of her husband. (See diagram in section on Aversion showing onset of age of impotence.)

Again, impotence (which is purely temporary) may follow satiation, but unless the patient is frightened by what he fears are the results of excessive intercourse, normality invariably returns after a short rest. It cannot be too strongly reiterated that *it is impossible to damage the sexual functions by use*. This diminished response can be usefully employed by encouraging patients with premature ejaculations to have intercourse as frequently as possible since if they do so they find that the prematurity decreases until they attain normality, particularly if assisted by proper physical and psychological treatment.

Prolonged suppression of the sexual functions, as many soldiers who remained 'faithful' to their wives discovered on returning home, may diminish the response to erotic stimulation. It was a frequent complaint that they found it difficult to become sexually aroused by their wives. This is a purely temporary condition and if the woman is encouraging soon passes off. In any case it is responsive to proper treatment.

Sexual desire may be diminished or absent in cases of depression—particularly in severe depressions of the manic-depressive type. The patient feels no sexual urge and even if capable of performing the sexual act obtains no pleasure from so doing. Often 'paradoxically' the desire remains more or less unchanged. In schizophrenia the sexual desire is frequently present, but the patient makes no effort to satisfy it other than by masturbation. Again, in this disease it may appear to be completely absent or very weak. This is, however, in the earlier stages since later, particularly when there is deterioration of personality, the desire is often increased enormously.

Frigidity and sexual aversion in women are, of course, the happy hunting-ground of the psychoanalyst, and an enormous amount of work has been done upon these conditions. Consequently a large number of causes have been ascribed to the fixations and regressions which can be found in the hypoverted woman. Much over-classification has been done on this subject. For example, Hitschman and Bergler give as the types: (1) Total frigidity with vaginal anaesthesia. In this the woman shows no trace of pleasure and wishes to get over the coitus as soon as possible. (This I consider to be sexual aversion.) (2) Total frigidity with vaginal hypo-aesthesia. In this type there is slight emotion, slight vaginal secretion, slight clitoric sensitivity, no involuntary muscular contractions.

(3) Relative frigidity with vaginal hypo-aesthesia. This type shows relatively strong excitement at the thought but less excitement at the deed. (4) Relative frigidity with vaginal sensitivity but sudden cessation of excitement before the orgasm, no orgasm. (5) Clitoric orgasm with vaginal hypo-aesthesia. In these cases the woman attains orgasm only through clitoric stimulation. There is no vaginal orgasm, although excitement and glandular secretion are sufficient. (6) Frigidity of the nymphomanic type. In these women there is strong excitement but no orgasm; insatiable seeking after men and promiscuity. (7) Obligatory and facultative frigidity. In obligatory frigidity the disorders described occur regularly with all men. In facultative frigidity they can disappear under special conditions (in defiance of prohibition, in situations of contempt—such as prostitution, in special coital positions). (8) True frigidity and pseudo-frigidity. Types 1 to 7 are true frigidity due to psychic causes. Pseudo-frigidity is due to ignorance and incorrect technique.

I feel a more useful classification is: (1) refusal to permit penetration —this is regarded as sexual aversion and has already been dealt with; and (2) lack of orgasm or pleasurable sensation—this is regarded as sexual hypoversion. This is almost always due to *anxiety* in some form or other. It may be easily unearthed or may need a deep analysis to discover its nature.

I cannot fail to note here the very valuable paper by Malleson on vaginismus, in which she states:

Clinically, the term 'vaginismus' denotes a condition of vaginal spasm varying from a constriction at the beginning of coitus (so slight that it may merely discomfort the woman herself) up to the extreme case in which the spasm causes acute pain to the woman and entirely prohibits any penetration by the husband: indeed, the introitus may be so constricted that even the tip of the examining finger can gain no entrance. The spasm may affect the perineal muscles exclusively or may be felt as a varying constriction of the levator ani right up to the vaginal fornices. Accompanying this spasm there is usually a definite cramp-like spasm of the adductor muscles, and invariably the lumbar spine is extended in the position of lordosis. In severe cases the posture is one almost of opisthotonos. A concomitant of the syndrome is a greater or lesser degree of hysterical hyperaesthesia. Rarely, this may be absent, but in some cases it may be more prominent than the spasm itself. The hyperaesthesia is usually of the 'glove and stocking' variety, starting exactly at the vaginal introitus, but in extreme cases it may be registered all over the vulva and even over adjacent parts of the abdomen and thighs. Vaginismus need have no relation to an unstretched hymen, and can occur with equal severity in the woman who has borne children as in the virgin. It is known to appear as a secondary protection to some physical lesion (such as urethral caruncle, salpingitis, &c.) which would otherwise cause dyspareunia, but such cases are rare compared with the 'ideopathic' vaginismus, and will not be dealt with here.[1]

[1] When in doubt the psychiatrist must obviously obtain gynaecological confirmation that there is no organic factor present. This applies particularly to dyspareunia due to obscure causes, as in that described by Eton where there is pain after intercourse, either at once or on

It is important to realize that a true vaginal spasm cannot be voluntarily produced—that is, it cannot be consciously employed by a woman to evade coitus—and it may appear in spite of the utmost *conscious* willingness to accept the coital act. Fortunately it can very largely be modified by conscious control.

Malleson points out that it is always psychogenic and states that in her wide experience conditioning plays an important part in causation. With regard to this she says:

Many of them have during infancy been 'conditioned' to expect pain in the pelvic region by the insertion of a foreign body, the offending object being usually the enema, the suppository, or the old-fashioned soapstick so much employed in Victorian nurseries for the treatment of constipation. Anyone who has witnessed such a procedure will recognize the extreme pain to which the child is subjected. Soap is painful in the rectum as in the eye, and as the infant screams and flings itself into opisthotonos the rectum is instantaneously emptied. The baby who is repeatedly treated in this way will scream and stiffen at the very sight of the attacking object. Here, surely, we have a 'conditioning' at the age which is most susceptible to permanent impression.

At first sight it may appear improbable that experience of rectal pain should lead to anticipation of vaginal suffering. To understand such a possibility it is necessary to recapitulate facts of great importance in medical psychology. The rectal, vaginal, and urethral orifices are developed from the original cloaca and possess the same innervation. In very young children the sensations arising in these organs are largely undifferentiated: hence the difficulty in learning sphincteric control and the fact that any of these organs may—and normally to the same extent do—receive erotic stimulation during stretching and friction. Thus when a young child experiences pain in either the rectum or vagina the resulting impression of the attack will be very similar whichever of the cloacal organs actually received the stimulation.

It is not difficult, therefore, to realize how a child who has come to dread the forcible introduction of a rectal object responds with fear and shrinking, first in childhood to the vague instinctive ideas of coitus, and then in later life to the actuality of sexual penetration.

This clear account of the causation and nature of feminine hypoversion shines like a light in the mephitic obscuration in which some writers delight. It is not surprising that in such cases the woman responds with a defensive reaction, but, even where penetration is accepted, a lesser degree of fear sometimes remains and this is sufficient to diminish the crescendo of feeling which aggregates until it bursts into the change of emotion we know as orgasm. This is shown by the fact that I frequently encounter women who say that when they first married they were 'very small'. They visit a gynaecologist who examines them with some difficulty—sometimes under an anaesthetic. After this they are reassured that all is well and timidly permit coitus. They manage to accept the physical procedure but then find that they cannot respond, and feel no emotion.

the following morning. He believes that this is due to uterotubal spasm caused by coitus and is relieved by giving antispasmodics.

Sometimes when they have gained confidence, or after the birth of a child, they find that an orgasm occurs; in other cases the woman's sexual response has been spoiled, and will not become pleasurable without prolonged and elaborate treatment.

Related to this type of hypoversion is that found in the woman who marries and has a more or less normal sexual life until she gives birth to a child. Possibly because of poor obstetric attention she had great pain, or because she is one who is excessively sensitive to pain, she is terrified of having further pregnancies. She may try to refuse intercourse, even with satisfactory contraception, but if she permits it she is so fearful that she inhibits any sexual response. I find similar cases in unmarried girls who have become pregnant and had abortions performed upon them. The anxiety and fear of their experience tends to inhibit pleasure when they have intercourse even if they know that no pregnancy will occur.

Deutsch states that female inhibition

can be strengthened as a result of her narcissism, masochism, tie to former objects, and motherliness; and each of these four factors, if present to an excessive degree, can become a source of frigidity. Especially in favour of the last-named component does the feminine woman often renounce orgastic gratification, without in the least suffering in her psychic health. But even if motherliness is not involved, she often tolerates her sexual inhibition without losing her all-embracing warmth and harmony.

American authors have done considerable research on the lack of sexual response in women, and the general opinion seems to be that if a woman feels emotion—either pleasurable or otherwise—at the first coitus she will tend to have sexual feeling in the future.

We have, in the past, produced frigid women by the wrong sort of education and by the inculcation that sex was unclean and even dangerous. In fact it was not understood that a woman should respond; a Victorian judge once said that the suggestion that women obtained sexual pleasure from coitus was a slur on their sex! This tradition has undoubtedly made many tend to inhibit and suppress any emotion which they have felt. The horror of masturbation in the female child demonstrated by the parents has often had a decided effect.

This is not to state that there are no deeper factors but only that there are many superficial ones to be considered before we delve deeply into the mind. For example, female homosexuality can result in complete frigidity. I have treated a homosexual woman who had never felt any orgasm. As treatment progressed and the roots of her homosexuality were unearthed she felt more and more normal until she ended by obtaining a healthy climax.

The older traditions of female education have passed away and it is now generally recognized that women should enjoy sex as much as men, and probably this will have a beneficial effect upon the coming generations. It is to be hoped that frigidity from superficial educational causes will disappear completely. That this could be so is shown by the fact that amongst the Polynesians in the days before great contact with white races there was said to have been no frigidity at all. In their case promiscuous sexuality before marriage was encouraged and the social consequences of children born before the marriage rites were, in many tribes, absolutely nil. Indeed, in the Tuomotuas this still exists.

CASE NO. 22

A Case of Sexual Hypoversion

It is believed that all functional sexual hypoversion is acquired, but it may be taken as a general rule that the earlier the acquisition the more difficult it is to cure. When, for some reason, it occurs in adult life for the first time it is usually, as in the present case, easily cured.

This case was one of a man aged 41 years. He was an Army officer and showed the usual virile physique and mentality of his type. He did not complain of hypoversion when first seen, but said that he had a lack of concentration, poor application to his work, loss of self-confidence, and dislike of being alone. Such symptoms as these are, however, frequently only a reflection of the sexual life.

His family history was very bad. He had a half-sister who was described as 'a completely seductive nymphomaniac' (!), but who had settled down to married life and become a rabid theosophist in later life. The patient's mother, who was married to his father a few years after his first wife's death, was very religious but otherwise normal. The patient's sister was secretary to an engineer and had a liaison with him which resulted in a 'breakdown' from which she recovered and was able to run a dress shop, but collapsed and needed treatment in a mental home in Kent. When she 'recovered' she, her mother, and her sister went on holiday, and she and her sister tried to strangle the mother. Soon after both sisters were certified. One of them died a year later.

The patient's father died when he was an infant and his mother died of carcinoma the same week that he lost his wife, eighteen months before he was seen by me.

His childhood was not an easy one. His father died and left his mother penniless and the patient had been educated partly by his father's brother's generosity and partly by his mother's own efforts. He managed to attend a small public school and later passed through Woolwich and so entered the Army. He was fairly successful in his career and reached a fairly high rank. He married in 1922 and had two children, one aged 14 years and one aged 4 years.

He appeared to have been a normal man until the death of his mother, which was followed tragically by the death of his wife who developed general peritonitis and died a few days later. For a year after his wife's death he worried a great deal and complained of insomnia. This made him feel that he might develop insanity like his sisters.

This was all that could be elicited in the first interview, but although he was hostile to any further investigation he did consent at his doctor's urgent request to consult me again. He then confessed that since his wife's death he had been much worse, but even before her death he had felt very depressed and had noticed a falling off and diminution in his sexual life. He needed more stimulation to make him feel sexual and prolonged intercourse to bring about ejaculation. It then became apparent that his sexual life with his wife had not been particularly happy. She had returned from abroad some nine years previously and said that she had fallen in love with someone else. She did not wish to continue living with him, but finally decided it was better to live in comfort with someone who had a certain amount of money than to live alone in poverty. She continued to live with her husband, and four years before had had another child. Twenty months previously she had become pregnant again and had had an abortion done. This apparently left some septic parametritis and resulted finally in peritonitis and death.

Apparently the cause of the patient's hypoversion was due to two factors. Firstly, when he had relations with women since his wife's death he felt that he was being disloyal to her memory. Secondly, and much more important, was the fact that he had felt a great deal of hostility to his wife due to her falling in love with other men (actually she had fallen in love twice with someone else) and for some time, nearly a year, they had no sexual relations and as a result he felt disgruntled and hostile to women. He was able to discuss the whole matter freely. This led to immediate relief and made him realize that he was being foolishly sentimental in regarding a normal sexual life as an act of disloyalty to his wife, and, secondly, that his partial impotence was due to hostility to his sexual partner who symbolized in his mind his dead wife. Put simply in neurological language, his wife had done her best to condition him to regard sex as something unhappy and miserable. His physician was advised regarding the nature of his trouble and a suggestion was made that his condition would probably be helped by the action and suggestion of strychnine. He was therefore given Easton's syrup. The simple superficial analysis, the suggestion, and the strychnine worked a miracle with him, and three months later the patient delightedly told his doctor that he was now perfectly normal and had no complaints to make regarding the sexual functions. He has remained since perfectly well.

This shows that there are certainly cases in which a prolonged analysis is not only unnecessary but undesirable. No doubt those who advocate prolonged analysis in all cases would have unearthed interesting complexes, but in such cases as these it is better that the patient should be allowed to respond to superficial analysis followed up by strong suitable suggestion than that any attempt should be made to discover why he met unfortunate circumstances by such a reaction.

CASE No. 23

A Case of Premature Ejaculation

This case would not have been recorded, so commonplace is it, and like the many hundreds one sees in practice, but for the fact that it nearly led to complete disruption of the marriage. The patient was a brilliant young pathologist. He came from a normal family: the father had died from prostatitis and anaemia, but the mother, who had a dominant personality, and a younger brother were alive and well. The family was not well off and this threw a strain on the patient from his earliest years. As a child he walked in his sleep, was afraid of the dark, stuttered, and was left-handed. At school his record was exceptional and he worked his way through medical school by means of scholarships. He had no money to spend and said that he existed on seven shillings and sixpence a week. During his whole life he worried about money. This prevented him doing posts as house physician, which spoiled his career. He obtained minor posts as a pathologist and slowly worked his way up. He was haunted by fear of illness as well as lack of money and at 17 had tachycardia. Ten years before he was seen he had an attack of depression. He was not happy in his work, which was salaried, and gave no scope for his ambition. Three years before he was seen he developed ulnar neuritis and again had tachycardia. He had been married for thirteen years and had one child.

This patient was sent to me by his private doctor who had treated him for 'virus pneumonia', but who discovered that he had threatened to leave his wife and go off with his secretary. Fortunately before he could do this he found that the secretary had been living with various men and was an extremely loose woman. He cancelled the rooms which he had booked for them and returned to his wife.

The key to this man's marital problems was easily found to be premature ejaculations. His own physician very sagely attributed this to the strain of his work—six or seven post-mortems, with written reports, and coroner's court evidence, a day. The tension of his life had reflected itself on his sexual activities and resulted in prematurity. This had been complicated by the fact that his wife had found the unsatisfactory intercourse a strain and felt hostile about it.

The patient, who was 38, and had a dominant, aggressive, ambitious personality, needed careful handling, but when his confidence had been won was co-operative and helpful in his attitude. In spite of the fact that he was a pathologist a careful physical examination was done according to routine and the normality of his physique demonstrated. The mechanism of his sexual neurosis was pointed out to him: his powerful ambition driving him on to overwork and nervous strain, this anxiety reacting on his sexual responses and causing premature ejaculations, and thus antagonizing his wife. It was explained to him that he would have to take a more easy-going, sans-souciant attitude to life, to realize that his sexual difficulties were due to worry, and to take a sedative for a month or two.

The wife as well as the patient was interviewed. She said that sex had always been taboo in her home and so she was ignorant of what had happened with regard to her husband and was upset. She thought that it was the result of his falling in love with someone else. It was possible to make her see that the husband's arrangements to go off with the secretary were more to prove that he was normal than that he loved this woman. If I cured him and he regained his sexual life with the wife all would be well. She agreed to co-operate in every way in her power.

Four months later he wrote the following:

'I owe you an apology for not having written you before, but I have been rather occupied with various matters, medico-political, professional, secretarial and others. So that although the intention has been there the opportunity has not hitherto materialized. I am very pleased to inform you that the matter about which I consulted you is better (I might say, infinitely better) and with the minimum of treatment. I should like to express my sincere thanks for your advice. I only wish I had consulted you before, &c. . . .'

His improvement, in spite of the fact that his letter shows that he really had not relaxed the pressure of his activities, suggests that he had managed to deal with his anxiety and adjust himself to life without being so worried. This case is very typical of the whole class of sexual hypoversion. He shows the dominant, intellectual, ambitious personality, the terrific activity, with partial suppression of sex, to obtain his ends, and the price of anxiety and fear which he had to pay. Finally the appearance of prematurity with the reaction of the wife—what the husband described neatly as 'glacial acquiescence' as a result. The vicious circle of ambition—fear—prematurity—more fear—more prematurity—more fear, and so on is, very clearly shown.

REFERENCES

COURTENAY, M. (1968) *Sexual Discord in Marriage*, London.
HITSCHMAN, E., and BERGLER, E. (1936) *Frigidity in Women*, New York.
MALLESON, J. (1935) *Principles of Contraception*, London.

16

SEXUAL HYPERVERSION

Definition

Excessive sexual desire and inability to satisfy it no matter how frequently intercourse is attempted. This again leads to the complication of defining what is normal sexual desire. We would refer the reader to the definition given under sexual hypoversion, which states that it is that which is found in normal men and women of the same physique and age and which satisfies an average normal healthy sexual partner. The inability of a normal partner to satisfy the sexual appetite, and the presence of sexual desire so strong that it is difficult or impossible to do so, suggests the presence of hyperversion.

Psychopathology and Occurrence

Those who display excessive sexual desire have always attracted attention. Presumably because it is generally supposed to be accompanied by an equal capacity for pleasure. It is difficult to know why this should be, since the diabetic gets not one whit of pleasure from his excessive thirst, although quenching thirst is a pleasurable sensation to many people. Those who are driven on by excessive sexual desire, as a matter of fact, seem to have to go, like the perverts, to a superlative amount of trouble to get what most of us are able to obtain much more easily. Fenichel says: 'An accurate anamnesis by itself often shows that the nymphomanic women are by no means the most excitable sexually, and do not readily or regularly have an orgasm. Even when they have an orgasm, it is not true end pleasure and gives them no satisfaction.' This is also more or less true of men suffering from satyriasis.

No doubt there are a number of factors which can increase the sexual desire such as we have given above. Raised temperature seems to have a stimulating effect and often occurs in those who have a prolonged very slight fever—hence the well-known enhanced desire of the tuberculous. For example, Leonard Williams says:

Very considerable importance is attached in France to a sign of pretuberculosis, which is presumably the direct outcome of irritation of the nervous system, of which in this country we hear very little—namely, an exalted sexual appetite. The toxin of tubercle would seem, especially in young men, to exercise a very decided aphrodisiac influence, and our French friends contend that in the many cases in which the disease appears to supervene as a fitting nemesis upon a licentious adolescence, the real truth lies in the fact that when the unfortunate patient embarked upon his immoral career he was already the subject of tuberculous invasion—that it was, in fact, the action of the toxin which impelled him to the unbridled gratification of his passions.

(There is no evidence that it is *Myco. tuberculosis* or any toxin which increases the desire in such cases and I believe that the effect is due to the slight rise in temperature. I have seen a case, for example, in which a tuberculous man lived in a hot part of Africa. He was so desirous that he insisted on his wife having intercourse four or five times during the day and a similar number of times during the night. Not unnaturally she complained of feeling worn out.)

Tropical countries probably do not in themselves increase sexuality and the hot moist climates of West Africa and the West Indies make one feel languid and less sexually excitable. The slight infections common to such places increase the effects. On the other hand shortage of women (as in other factors which slightly obstruct instinctual outlets) may increase sexual feeling when they are encountered. Moreover, conditioning regarding 'romantic' surroundings—palm trees, star-lit nights, rustling surf, and so on may in themselves be suggestive. Obviously all these minor factors may act as an influence and together be important.

It is rare to find excessive sexuality due to endocrine causes. The child with adrenal tumours who becomes an 'infant Hercules' is said to show excessive sexuality, but it appears to me to be rather a premature normal sexuality due to the acceleration of the emotional development by the hormones.

We do not know a great deal about the behaviouristic factors which can influence sexuality. How much an animal can be conditioned to be sexual has never been properly worked out. It would appear, however, that any form of pain tends to act in a negative direction, so that it might be reasonable to conclude that the more pleasurable sexuality has been made to appear primarily the more it will be sought. Milton Harrington has suggested that conditioning is really the result of a law of confluence, by which he means that any two simultaneous responses tend to become linked. No doubt if this is so, sexuality can be very widely conditioned and almost anything and everything can be used as a stimulus. Thus a vicious circle could be established so that the patient was in a constant state of sexual excitement and tended to become more sexually excited still.

Organic disease of the brain can produce hypersexuality. Thus Klüver and Bucy performed some experiments on monkeys in which they removed the temporal lobes on both sides. This produced, amongst other symptoms, a marked increase in sexual responses. The monkeys had frequent erections, with oral and manual manipulation of the penis. On some occasions they copulated almost continuously for half an hour.

Terzian and Dalle Ore reproduced this in a youth who had both temporal lobes removed for epileptic seizures. He had, as well as an insatiable appetite, spontaneous erections, followed by masturbation and orgasm as well as homosexual attraction to various of his doctors, to whom he made homosexual approaches and suggestions. Two years later he was masturbating twice a day and was still homosexually orientated.

This work has been repeated and confirmed by Van Reeth and his colleagues, who discovered four cases of temporal lobe tumours with epilepsy and hypersexuality.

Some psychiatrists have considered that this discovery is of importance regarding hypersexuality but, although it is interesting, it must be admitted that temporal lobe tumours are infrequent, and hypersexuality is not often encountered. A combination of both is excessively rare.

Perhaps it implies clinically that when one meets a case of hypersexuality one should make sure that the patient has not suffered bilateral temporal extirpation.

(Curiously enough Kolarsky, Freund, and Machek thought that organic brain injury was more common in homosexuality. They state 'A history indicating the age of probable brain damage could be found significantly more often among sexual deviates than non-deviant subjects.' It is difficult, therefore, to understand the relationship in such cases.)

Psychoanalytically hyperversion is shown by the behaviour of Don Juan. Fenichel says of him:

Don Juan's behaviour is no doubt due to his Oedipus complex; he seeks his mother in all women and cannot find her. But the analysis of Don Juan types shows that the Oedipus complex is of a particular kind; it is pregenital and pervaded by narcissistic conflicts, and tinged by sadistic impulses. The pregenital quality that accompanies the love of the mother here appears to be not merely a regressive distortion. The Don Juans' Oedipus complex from the start is coloured by their strong pregenital fixation; their relationship with objects is always attended by strong unconscious narcissistic relations, their love is always mixed with a certain amount of hostility; and their love and hate include a certain amount of unconscious 'incorporation' of the object. Their sexual activities are often primarily designed to settle conflicts regarding their self-esteem and elevate their self-regard . . . or it appears to be the covert sadistic and pregenital aim in their unconscious desire for the mother that cannot be satisfied through coitus. The sadism in question is not always directed towards objects but often against their own ego, so that their vigorous sexual activity includes a masochistic or self-punitive effort at self-destruction.

From the psychoanalytical point of view, therefore, the excessive sexuality is partly due to sadism—a wish to injure the woman—partly to vanity, and partly to self-punishment. This seems to be true, since these patients often hurt themselves either by losing their work through their evil reputation, or else by their sexual excitement which gives no opportunity for protection against venereal disease, which sooner or later they contract.

There is no doubt that there are a number of ancillary causes which may increase sexual desire; such as youth, partial obstruction to achievement, and the very desirability of the object, but these usually do not lead to persistent excessive desire nor to the constant seeking of new sexual objects which is so characteristic of hyperversion. Indeed the patient suffering from this condition is obsessional in his behaviour and constantly repeats the act without satisfaction and only a temporary, even momentary, diminution of tension. Incidentally there is no aphrodisiac which increases sexual desire; although strychnine and yohimbine sometimes help to restore sexual feeling to those who are physically jaded they do not increase it more than normal.

Hypersexuality in the man is rare but in women it is less common still. Yet the insatiable woman has appeared in legend throughout history. I suspect that frequently she is to be regarded as a wish-fulfilling fantasy because in reality so many women have been frigid and unresponsive. It is possible that different nationalities and climatic conditions have effect. Burton, for example, traveller and translator of the *Thousand and One Nights*, who had unique knowledge of the sexual customs of the East, said: 'As usual in damp-hot climates, for instance Sind, Egypt, the lowlands of Syria, Malabar, and California, the sexual requirements of the passive exceed those of the active sex.'

In most cases sexual hyperversion in women is psychogenic. The woman is frequently to some extent homosexual, and thus behaves in an active rather than a passive way. She is, from the psychoanalytical point of view, seeking a father-surrogate, and her intense sexual urge is unconsciously incestuous. In addition to this there is often an obsessional element which we have noticed in the male so that the act is repeated again and again without appreciable lessening of tension. It is almost inevitable that the hyperverted woman drifts into promiscuity, and often alcoholism as well. Illegitimate children frequently occur until venereal diseases cause sterility.

Ellis and Sagarin suggest that nymphomania should be confined to a syndrome in which the woman seeks constant sexual relations due to (1) compulsions and (2) self-hatred. These produce an uncontrollable impulse to repeat the act again and again. The nymphomaniac will have intercourse with anybody, no matter how dirty, repulsive or diseased he may be. This, Ellis and Sagarin feel, differentiates her from the woman who shows selective promiscuity, and has frequent intercourse; but who is not troubled by an uncontrollable compulsion, and so can select her partners at will. They feel that the suggestion that nymphomaniacs rarely experience orgasm, and their behaviour stems from their constant search for it, is not true; some do feel a climax.

Elsewhere in their book they give a different classification which is: (1) nymphomaniacs who have a compulsion due to brain lesions, hormonal imbalance or other physical abnormalities; (2) nymphomaniacs suffering from hypomania; (3) physically hypersexed woman with an exceptionally strong innate sexual drive (these he calls Donna Juanitas); (4) a class of females who have normal sexual drives, but for psychological reasons compulsively force themselves to have indiscriminate relations with males.

Since writers in recent times have become fascinated with the concept of nymphomania, and one can hardly open a novel without meeting a character suffering from this condition, it might be as well here to state that it is clinically very rare. Usually novelists depict women who are sexually loose which they imagine is hypersexuality and have no conception of the tragedy and misery of the real condition.

It is essential to point out here the relation of sexual hyperversion to the psychoses. Just as sexual aversion or hypoversion is frequently the product of depression of the manic-depressive type (or indeed most depressions), so it is common to find increased sexual desire in cases of mania, and, moreover, the irresponsibility of the manic patient makes his desires more difficult to satisfy and his behaviour asocial. No doubt the alcoholism which is sometimes found in such cases is the result of increased sexuality. The patient finds the emotions difficult to satisfy and tends to repeat the act again and again. I have seen a hypomanic girl who developed her very mild psychosis following adrenalectomy. How far her condition was endocrine and how far psychogenic it was impossible to say. She had previously been a quiet, well-behaved girl who lived a stable, perhaps monotonous, life with her parents. When she developed the hypomania and sexual hyperversion she started to use cosmetics excessively and to be exhibitionistic—lying about on the lawn where she could be seen clad in the briefest of 'sun-suits'. She spent much of her time telephoning young men with whom she sometimes had had the slightest of acquaintanceship, and leading the conversation into channels of sex and marriage. Finally she enticed a young student into becoming engaged to her and, although he was studying theology, soon seduced him. It was with some difficulty and considerable sedation that she was tided over this illness but she finally recovered and behaved normally. The exact reason why excessive sexual feeling should be associated with mania is not known, but no doubt the excitement, and exultation of feeling, combined with the increased metabolism of manic states have a great deal to do with it.

Sometimes this association of sexual excitement and mania has very tragic consequences. There is the common case of the young girl who appears to be perfectly normal until she meets a young man who attracts her, and who appears to like her. After going about with him for a few weeks she gradually becomes more and more excited and finally develops mania. This may be so severe as to necessitate the patient's removal to a mental hospital where, after a time, the psychosis dies down.

The reason why this occurs is difficult to say. Here we have a girl who seems on the point of attaining her heart's desire and wrecks everything by becoming psychotic. It may be the obverse of the condition described by Freud in which a young man covets a position held by an older man who blocks his promotion. He wishes the older man to die so that he can step into his shoes. At last the senior does so but the young man plunges into a deep depression. Freud suggested that this was due to unconscious death wishes against the older man and when these wishes are fulfilled guilt and self-punishment result. If this is so by analogy in the case of young girls who develop mania in this way one might think that there were tremendously strong sexual desires which had been long held repressed. Then when marriage appears about to fulfil the unconscious longings they burst out in the form of mania.

Again, it is not uncommon to find exaggerated sexual desire in the schizophrene who has the disease at the stage when it is already showing signs of florid development. In the earlier stages this type of patient is usually rather sexually averted, but in the later stages, particularly when there is considerable deterioration of the personality, sexual desires may appear and be insatiable.

Epilepsy has been blamed for excessive and violent sexual desires in the past, but probably its influence has been exaggerated. No doubt, it is responsible, if manic depression and catatonia are excluded, for those cases in which sexual desire shows a periodic increase in strength. The association of epilepsy with psychopathic personality may also be partly explanatory.

Excessive sexual desire occurs in any of the perversions, but we have no right to regard it as true hyperversion. It may be quite as overwhelming as in true 'normal' hyperversion. It is frequently found in homosexuality, and in such cases the results may be pitiable. I had as a patient an eminent solicitor, who had such strong attacks of homosexual desire that he spent whole evenings wandering from one public lavatory to another trying to encounter some homosexual with whom he could find a sex outlet. The explanation for this is found in the fact that we have already seen that the homosexual partner represents the mother, to some extent, and probably excessive sexuality in cases of this perversion is but the child's longing for its mother sexualized and felt to excess. In infantosexuality there is frequently an excessive sexual desire which leads the patient to commit crimes which may result in severe penalties.

These facts regarding perversions have been noted for completeness and not because it is meant that a perversion with excessive desire should be regarded as true hyperversion, although it is obvious that the sexual urge in their case can vary just as in normality.

I have tried to give the descriptions of these diseases as simply as possible, and by adopting a clear terminology to make it as easy as I can to appreciate their nature. Anyone may complicate the subject by adopting an exotic terminology and describing minute differences by Latin names. For example, one can speak of erective impotence, ejaculatio ante portas, ejaculatio praecox, ejaculatio retardata, and ejaculative impotence. All this, however, means that the sexual instinct has been inhibited or diverted so that the psychical component is insufficient to activate the physical machinery. To use one simple terminology such as sexual aversion or sexual hypoversion is to my mind the best way of describing the matter. After all, we do not describe physical diseases so minutely and classify scarlatina into a dozen different diseases according to the intensity of the rash.

DISORDERS ASSOCIATED WITH INVOLUTIONAL CHANGES

The menopause in women may be accompanied by various physical and psychological symptoms which are too common to be recorded here and are to be found described in every textbook of endocrinology. However, there are a few psychological ones which are of interest. Some women seem to have a last upsurge of sexual desire and it becomes apparent by their dressing extravagantly, and inappropriately—they wear clothes suitable for girls rather than mature women and use cosmetics unwisely. This upsurge of emotion may lead them to make advances towards younger men and may even make one think that they have some sexual hyperversion for a time. Their own sexual desires may be projected on to their husbands so that suspicions, or even, in the case of psychosis, delusions of unfaithfulness may occur.

In general there seems to be some diminution of sexual desire after the menopause although some women still seem able to enjoy a normal relationship. Some women on the other hand seem to miss a normal sexual life without altogether being aware of it. This manifests itself in complaints of the worthlessness of life and a vague sense of unhappiness not amounting to depression.

In men increasing age usually leads to diminishing sexuality although some men seem to retain their potency to a great age. This diminished potency may cause anxiety and even panic; as in women this can shade off into involutional psychoses. Just as some women dress extravagantly to attract younger men so ageing men often seek much younger women. In both men and women old dissatisfactions with the sexual partner may be allowed to appear, and these, with the urge to prove that attraction is still possible, may lead to the destruction of the marriage. Possibly in a very small number of cases prostatic enlargement may cause irritation and so give the appearance of increased sexuality, but this is by no means so important as used to be thought.

Just as the female may suffer from flushes the male may complain of erections. These may occur at night so that the patient states that he always has an erection when he wakes, and feels that it is present all night. I have had patients who have found this so uncomfortable that it has been necessary to give oestrogens to diminish the sexuality.

The difficulty which increasing age causes the patient in finding an attractive sexual partner may cause an increase in masturbation. Unable to obtain an erection with a woman he seeks satisfaction in this way instead. It may be possible to obtain an orgasm by masturbation when intercourse is prevented by impotence.

Similarly, increasing age may cause the appearance of psychosexual responses which would previously have been suppressed. The commonest of these is the exhibitionism which is seen in old men. This was formerly attributed to prostatic enlargement but this is improbable. Exhibitionism in old men sometimes appears very pathetic when some distinguished gentleman of advanced age appears tremulously in the dock charged with this offence after a lifetime of honourable service to the community.

The failure of potency with women and the fact that manual stimulation by another male is successful in eliciting an orgasm may cause the patient to turn to homosexuality. It is improbable that he will do so unless there has previously been suppressed homosexual attractions, but this is difficult to prove.

Other psychosexual disorders, such as sadism may appear, and I have described elsewhere in this book the case of an old man who developed a psychosis and killed two small girls to eat.

The treatment of these cases differs with each, but in general some response can be obtained from appropriate hormone therapy. Where necessary complete suppression of libido, as in the case of men with the use of stilboestrol, may be of great service.

REFERENCES

BERGLER, E. (1937) *Die Psychische Impotenz des Mannes*, Berne.
BURTON, R. (1860) *The Lake Regions of Central Africa and Zanzibar*, London.
ELLIS, A., and SAGARIN, E. (1965) *Nymphomania*, London.
FENICHEL, O. (1934) *Outline of Clinical Psychoanalysis*, London.

FREUD, S. (1924) *Collected Papers*, London.

HADFIELD, J. A. (1933) *Proc. roy. Soc. Med.*, **26,** 1023.

HARRINGTON, M. (1938) *Biological Approach to the Problem of Abnormal Behavior*, Lancaster, Pa.

HITSCHMAN, E., and BERGLER, E. (1936) *Frigidity in Women*, New York.

HOWE, E. G. (1931) *Motives and Mechanisms of the Mind*, London.

JENKINS, E. (1958) *Elizabeth the Great*, London.

KLEIN, M. (1932) *The Psychoanalysis of Children*, London.

KLÜVER, HEINDRICH, and BUCY, P. (1939) Preliminary analysis of function of the temporal lobes in monkeys, *Arch. Neurol. and Psych.*, **6,** 979.

KOLARSKY, A., FREUND, K., and MACHEK, J. (1967) Male sexual deviation, *Arch. gen. Psychol.*, **17,** 737–43.

MALLESON, J. (1942) Vaginismus : its management and psychogenesis, *Brit. med. J.*, **2,** 213.

MENNINGER, K. (1938) *Man Against Himself*, New York.

TERZIAN, H., and DALLE ORE, G. (1955) *Neurology*, **5,** 373.

THIONOT, L., and WYSSE, A. (1916) *Medicolegal Aspects of Moral Offenses*, Philadelphia.

VAN REETH, P., DIERKENS, J., and LUMINET, D. (1958) L'hypersexualité dans l'épilepsie et les tumeurs du lobe temporal, *Acta neurol. belg.*, **59,** 194.

PART SIX

PROSTITUTION

17

FEMALE PROSTITUTION

Definition

The dictionary definition is promiscuous intercourse practised by women for gain. It is derived from the Latin word *prostituere*—to set forth in public, to offer for sale. Legally it is for a woman 'to offer her body to indiscriminate lewdness for hire'.

There is usually some difficulty regarding such definitions since there is no doubt that many cases are border-line. For example, wealth is an attraction and some women will marry a wealthy man purely for the advantages he has to offer, sometimes with no intention of remaining his wife. Some women will remain the mistress of one man for some time, then pass on to another and so on (as in the case of Nelson's Lady Hamilton). I have no wish to confuse the issue and I accept the Latin derivation of a prostitute as a woman who actively hires herself for intercourse more or less promiscuously.

Psychopathology and Occurrence

It is impossible to estimate the increase in prostitution recently, if indeed it has occurred, because, since the Street Offences Act of 1960, prostitutes have been driven off the streets. They still practise and advertise in shops as photographic models, or masseuses, and act as hostesses in night clubs. Probably their number has increased rather than diminished. Moreover, it may be that the newer situations are to their advantage, since in a recent court case a night club hostess admitted that she was really a prostitute and was able to charge £25 for a night with a client. It is improbable that a prostitute could have usually obtained anything like that sum before the Act. An extensive psychological investigation of prostitutes does not appear available and few psychiatrists could claim to have analysed many. Probably, like other psychosexual problems, prostitution has a number of roots. Thus in a number of professions sexual looseness is regarded as natural. A woman in whom this led to prostitution was treated by me as a hospital out-patient. She had been first a stage dancer and had minor 'affairs'. Unfortunately she had mitral stenosis and the strenuous activity of the stage was too much for her. She then became a cabaret dancer in a night club, but could not stand this stress either, and so became a night club hostess. But the ballroom dancing this entailed was too tiring for her weak heart; she drifted into prostitution as a side line and finally became a prostitute with a more or less private clientele. No marked psychiatric abnormality appeared until she developed schizophrenia. She then commenced complaining to the police that men were assaulting her in the street, which no doubt revealed a deep-seated hostility to them.

A case which describes how a girl can drift into promiscuity is recorded by Stockwell. No doubt if no intervention had occurred she would have ended up as a prostitute. He states:

Another girl, left to herself by a promiscuous mother in the home of a grand-mother who worked at night, had developed at the age of 14 the pattern of entertaining boys in the home while her grandmother was away. The 'enter-taining' consisted in giving each of the boys a chance to have sexual relations with her and sometimes she would pose in the nude for them to take snap-shots. When some of these pictures fell into the hands of the grandmother the story came out and the juvenile authorities with the grandmother's aid had the girl committed to an approved school. This girl explained in detail how she got started in 'giving' her sexual favours and how she felt about it. To her it had been a means of getting attention and the feeling of being wanted by someone—something she had never received from her mother or grandmother. She said that she had no particular interest in sexual activity as such, in fact she simply agreed because it seemed to please the boys. There was also a succession of older boys during one year to whom she gave her favours. The whole idea of sexual relations had become so casual and so commonplace yet such a habit to her by the time she became a student at the school—with never a suggestion of pregnancy at any time—that she was beginning to believe that she was destined to follow this pattern for the remainder of her life and she would be denied a normal home and children.

I have treated successfully a similar girl of the same age who was drifting into promiscuity but responded to psychotherapy and the introduction to a girls' club where she mixed with respectable girls and learned a happier mode of life.

The British Medical Association Special Committee considered that there was no single cause for prostitution but stated that: 'It is, however, our considered opinion that in most cases of habitual prostitution there is an innate deviation of temperament which amounts to a perversion of the normal female sexual impulse.' This seems a remarkable statement since 'innate' means 'inborn' or 'inherent'. Surely the Committee cannot believe that prostitution is inherited?

However it also stated:

Important factors which tend to lead to prostitution are:

1. An unsatisfactory home background or a broken home with lack of parental love and security. In many cases the girls have been subject to too harsh a discipline or allowed too much licence. Frequently, the parents have failed to set a good example, and are often themselves dishonest or amoral. In

such homes there is often a complete lack of moral or spiritual values or any sense of social responsibility.

2. Laziness, self-indulgence and a deliberate intention to earn easy money.

3. Desire for glamour and excitement which persists beyond the age of adolescence, and is associated with emotional immaturity and a failure to accept reality.

4. Adolescent rebellion against authority, especially in the 14–18 age group. Frequently there is a history of persistent truanting from school and of minor delinquencies dating from a relatively early age.

5. Minor degrees of mental deficiency or mental sub-normality associated not only with intellectual inferiority but with social inadequacy.

The extent to which one of these factors predominates will depend largely on the social structure. For example, full implementation of the Mental Deficiency Acts would retrain most of those persons influenced by factor 5 above.

Whilst I would agree with the various factors the Committee has given it is difficult to see how any could be 'innate' other than mental deficiency. It seems to most psychiatrists that prostitution is almost wholly environmental in origin.

The factors given by the Committee, however, seem much more likely than those suggested by Norman Haire, a writer who had an inclination to exaggerate both his experience and his insight. His conclusions are:

1. Economic reasons. Poverty, or the financial rewards of prostitution.
2. Hypersexuality.
3. Frigidity.
4. Homosexuality.
5. Inadequate sexual satisfaction in married women.
6. Upbringing in the case of children of prostitutes.
7. Seduction and abandonment.
8. To save money for the future (i.e. marriage) when the life of prostitution is abandoned.

Economic reasons seem to me to include the wish to save money for the future and also seduction and abandonment. Although no doubt these were cogent in Victorian times women are now so much more emancipated and adequately paid that they probably have little influence. We must not, however, forget that prostitutes do tend to mix in a higher class of society than that in which they were born and, for a time at least, it may lead to a financial rise in the world. Thus prostitutes, under the guise of night club hostesses, may consort with aristocracy and wealth. Although in certain societies—such as those in North Africa the women prostitute themselves to save for a dowry—such prostitution may occur but it does not seem to do so in civilized life. Again, although seduction and abandonment may have been a frequent cause in earlier times there are so many charities now to help the abandoned mother that this is unlikely to be a serious factor today.

I do not believe that prostitutes live this sort of life because of sexual hyperversion although this view is constantly put forward by those without psychiatric experience, and is a hall-mark of their ignorance. For example, Henriques, who is not a psychiatrist, has again resuscitated it. Most psychiatrists are of the opinion that they do not enjoy the sexual act, and probably frigidity is much more likely to be a cause in most cases. I must not disregard the fact, however, as I have pointed out in the chapter on endocrine influences in sexuality, that soon after puberty there is an uprush of sexual feeling which leads girls to hang round Army camps and so on. Such an overwhelming urge may lead a girl to start a life of prostitution but most of these girls seem to marry and settle down after the initial instability.

The frigid woman may cynically take to prostitution feeling that since she is unlikely to obtain pleasure from sex she might just as well obtain money. It would seem to me that frigidity, inadequate sexual satisfaction in marriage and possibly homosexuality are all related.

Upbringing in the case of children of prostitutes may be a strong factor. In such cases it would seem that neglect and a sordid environment produces this result rather than 'training'. The child observes the mother's behaviour, moulds herself on her parent, and drifts into a similar life. This was found to be so by Hollender who had the opportunity of analysing two girls: one a 'call girl' and one who had been an inmate of 'a call girl house' (a brothel). Both their mothers had been promiscuous and they had never been able to develop a normal adult affectionate relationship. Greenwald in his study of 'call girls' (prostitutes) noticed the same thing in a number of cases.

Such a result is not invariable; I have had a singularly beautiful patient, an actress, who was brought up, like Collette's Gigi, with the idea that she should use her looks to become the mistress of a rich man, as her mother and grandmother had, but who went on the stage instead. She was, like some actresses, rather loose in her sexual life, but not for financial gain.

Krisnaswamy studied in India 50 sex-delinquent girls and 50 prostitutes and this research, modest though it is, gives more information than the speculations of others. He used 50 non-delinquent girls as a comparison. He found that the sex-delinquent girls and prostitutes had more severe illnesses during childhood; they were moody, obstinate, assertive, selfish, and short-tempered. In addition they felt inferior and insecure due to neglect in their homes. In some families they hated their mothers and loved their fathers and in others vice versa, although the majority had an unfavourable attitude to both. The non-delinquent girls had a more normal home atmosphere.

The non-delinquent girls were more intelligent and artistic and the sex-delinquent girls were superior to the prostitutes. The sex-delinquent and the prostitutes were more impulsive, fickle-minded, and emotionally immature. The non-delinquent girls were less lethargic and more active.

A large number of the sex-delinquent girls and prostitutes showed no ambition in life. They had no interests, no recreations, and did not think of their employment. The non-delinquent were just the opposite, they worked better and were more efficient.

The sex-delinquent and the prostitutes were more assertive and aggressive. They were also unreliable, dishonest, ungrateful, argumentative, quarrelsome, immodest, impious, less helpful, and less sympathetic. They were also secretive and suspicious. Although suggestible they were also more incorrigible. The non-delinquent girls were more sociable, sincere, and gay.

Of the 100 offenders studied more than 90 per cent. were non-virgins though only 36 were married at the time. On the contrary only 36 per cent. of the non-delinquent girls seemed to have had sex-relationships. Some of the sex-offenders were markedly coquettish and some had homosexual tendencies. Despite their numerous experiences the sex offenders had never loved anybody in their lives. The maternal instinct was dominated and in some cases even eclipsed by the sex-instinct. It would seem from such studies as this that *prostitution in women tends to be the counterpart of criminal psychopathy in men.* If this is so it suggests that the girl has never developed the mental barriers, prohibitions, and inhibitions against things which are considered socially reprehensible. For example, prostitution seems related to a lack of morality in other matters than sex: these girls frequently steal from their clients if circumstances allow. Moreover the inability to learn from experience seems common to both states.

The deeper causes of prostitution suggested from the investigations of analysts are: (1) a flight from homosexual repressions into pseudo-heterosexuality; (2) a form of female Don Juanism due to an unresolved Oedipus conflict; and (3) displaced hostility to the man (usually arising from the father).

Caprio, a well-known American psychiatrist who has made an almost world-wide investigation into prostitution, writing from the wealth of his extensive experience, states:

The prevalence of lesbianism in brothels throughout the world has convinced me that prostitution, as a behaviour deviation, attracts to a large extent women who have a very strong homosexual component. Through prostitution, these women eventually overcome their homosexual repressions. I am further convinced that prostitutes, by and large, are victims of unresolved bisexual conflicts, and that their flight into sexual intimacies with many men, rationalized by the profit motive, is symptomatic evidence of their fear of their own unconscious homosexual desires. As one might surmise the majority of prostitutes come from homes where there existed parental incompatibility. Having been deprived of a normal love relationship during childhood with their mother and father, their basic feeling of insecurity inspires them to seek out the affection of both sexes via intimacies with both men and women.

Since all prostitutes are frustrated they attempt to find consolation for their feelings of insecurity and basic need for affection by seeking the love of some member of their own sex. They will either assume the role of feminine-passive, love-starved daughter seeking the love of an older mother-surrogate, or they will take on the role of the mother-lesbian, and seek out the love of some young girl who becomes their daughter. In the latter case the older woman is bestowing upon the younger girl the amount of affection she was deprived of as a daughter.

It is interesting, in view of Haire's statement that some women take to prostitution because of hypersexuality, that Caprio found prostitutes were frigid. He quotes Polly Adler, author of *A House is not a Home*, mistress in a brothel, who wrote: 'Actually, of course, despite all the feigned transports of ecstasy (for the purposes of increasing the tip) to ninety-nine out of a hundred girls, going to bed with a customer is a joyless, even distasteful experience.' This might appear, at first sight, to contradict Krisnaswamy's suggestion quoted previously that the maternal instinct is dominated and in some cases eclipsed by the sexual instinct but this does not, of course, imply heterosexuality—homosexual and other abnormalities may be the dominating factors.

Glover puts forward the psychoanalytical point of view and, like most other writers, stresses the homosexual element. He states:

Amongst experienced types, an extremely common factor is that of *sexual frigidity*—in other words, an absence or marked diminution of either physical or psychical pleasure in the sexual act, and in particular an incapacity to achieve sexual orgasm. But although this factor is highly significant it should be remembered that in one form or another frigidity is common both in neurotic and apparently normal women. Obviously, then, its significance in cases of prostitution depends on its association with other elements. This is true of all mental abnormalities. There is always a *constellation* of causal elements, some of which are plainly manifest, others unconscious. In the case of prostitution, the factors most closely associated with frigidity are those of *unconscious homosexuality* and *unconscious antagonism to the male*. (His italics.)

Glover divides prostitutes into three main groups:

The first consists mostly of street-walkers of the 'drab' type, who in most cases practise prostitution as a life-long profession. They are apathetic and hopeless in attitude, some mentally disordered, others mentally backward; others, prone to form associations with criminals. They incline to excessive use of alcohol.

The others are the 'young' prostitutes—unstable adolescents (which I have already described as girls who hang round Army camps &c.) and what he describes as the 'flourishing' professional. She is usually a girl of better intelligence who is sensible enough to avoid police interference. This group shades off into the 'discreet' type who becomes the short-term mistress and often ends apparently respectable.

Gibbens has studied juvenile prostitutes and out of a group of 21 girls (selected from 400 girls 'beyond control' and 'in need of care and protection') he found 8 were bright and highly intelligent, 6 were average, and 7 extremely dull. This contrasts with Krisnaswamy's findings which have already been given.

The factors Gibbens considered important in causation were unconscious homosexuality, sexual maladjustment between the parents, over-attachment to a weak father, almost incestuous attachment on the part of the father, hostility and contempt for men, jealousy of brothers, a narcissistic and mercenary personality, excessive fantasy, emotional instability and often an undersexed temperament.

Maerov on the basis of twenty cases of prostitution states that: 'The plight of a great percentage of prostitutes is a complex emotional aberration. Prostitution is a symptom, manifest as an abnormal expression of sexual behaviour, which shields the personality disturbance pervading every facet of the psychic operation and its development.' This seems a far cry from the simple 'easy money' theory so often put forward.

Prostitutes themselves do not always have a clear notion why they took up the profession. Polly Adler seemed to think that it was mainly due to laziness, attractive looks, opportunity and possibly by being assaulted. On the other hand, Majbritt Morrison, a woman who was a prostitute for four years, and who wrote a book on her life in the West End, states that 'One ponce in four in London is a lesbian and at least half of the prostitutes have had lesbian experiences, although probably only half of these are truly lesbian. Homosexual women persuade attractive young girls to enter lesbian relationships—and then get the girls to keep them by working as prostitutes.' Moreover, she says that 'There is nothing crueller nor more savage than a butch lesbian forcing the younger girl to work for her. No man can beat up a young girl with the same ferocity as an old lesbian.'

How far such conclusions can be confirmed by others it is difficult to say since prostitutes rarely write much about themselves, and their experiences seem to vary with different districts and levels of society, but to me they appear to have the ring of truth.

In some forms of prostitution the woman seems to be the counterpart of the male Don Juan. Just as in his case he is forever seeking the unattainable mother with whom he can have incestuous sexual satisfaction, so the girl goes from one man to another profiting financially, but really wanting more than money. She is obviously seeking a father and the terms used by such women—for example 'Sugar Daddy'—indicate the unconscious realization that this is the case. Women of this type are less likely to become inhabitants of brothels, but become the mistress of an older man, move on to the protection of another, and so on continually. Nelson's Lady Hamilton, robbed of the romantic nonsense which has surrounded her, was the perfect exemplar of this sort of prostitution.

Deutsch believes that prostitutes are psychologically infantile. She says:

Even the simplest moral laws have absolutely no influence on these women, because these sanctions express values that are completely alien to them. In their eyes, moral laws conceal unbearable wrongs and are full of the most contradictory requirements. To moral indignation, to every attempt to influence them to change their ways, they react with cynicism. And why should they accept moralistic proposals, if the tangible social norm is represented for them only by the police and the authorities whom they hate and struggle against? The promise of happiness in an orderly family life does not tempt them because, according to their ideas, family life is only a source of unhappiness and disappointment, or deadly boredom.

Their psychic infantilism makes of the entire world a nursery in which social institutions are personified by their representatives, and their emotions are turned against these representatives. Many investigators of the problem believe that prostitutes are 'born' as such, and to prove it they argue that whenever a prostitute is removed from her milieu and placed in a new, more favourable one, she returns to her previous way of life out of her own desire and impulse. We grant that in these cases a powerful urge is present that proves stronger than everything else. The motives operating here are of course psychologic, but they are acquired, not innate.

It is easy to become moralistic and incensed regarding prostitution, but it is well to remember that this may be based on deep-seated reactions which go back as far as the sub-human primate and in the chapter on monkeys and apes we noticed that they sometimes presented sexually in order to obtain favours and food. This was called by Kempf 'prostitution' because of its similarity to human behaviour.[1] Whether this is so or not it is evident that prostitution is founded on psychological reactions developed during infancy: probably a large number of factors lead to such behaviour. In any case it is obvious that moral lectures, religious sermons, and imprisonment are unlikely to affect such fundamental distortions.

The prostitute with a heart of gold is mainly a fiction of sentimental novelists, yet it is wise for us to remember that a prostitute is a woman, too, and able to feel as other people. When the poet, Francis Thompson, author of *The Hound of Heaven*, was destitute, and taken ill in the street with pneumonia it was a prostitute who took him to her back-street room and nursed him until he recovered.

According to Oliven (who gives no detailed references):

---

[1] The proffering of food should be regarded with a great deal of caution as a sign of prostitution in animals. Male birds, for example budgerigars, feed their mates before and after covering. This is to be regarded rather as a sign of affection than anything else.

Estimates from various parts of the American and European continents seem to be agreed that a minimum of 20 per cent. of prostitutes are prepsychotic, psychotic, mental defectives, or frank psychopathic personalities. Among typical examples one may mention the simple-type of schizophrenics, the very early arrested hebephrenics, unrecognized in the teens, with their sometimes marked antisocial tendencies (Hess, Kahlbaum), and some with a tendency to provide frank psychotic episodes (Stuempel's *schizophrene Engleisundstendenz*) although they often manage to stay clear of mental hospitals: and the affect-blunted unadjustable schizoid (Willmans). Also the restless dissatisfied, brazen type of psychopath, with her proneness to perversity and addiction yet relatively great resourcefulness: the irresponsible psychopaths, drifting, erratic, impulsive rather than impulse-ridden: the dull 'toilers' whose semi-alcoholized existence is punctuated from time to time by epileptoid excitement states: and others more. Contrary to what one would expect, these individuals do not seem to furnish the bulk of the 'degraded' prostitutes, i.e. the women with a long record of appearance in police courts and the accelerated downward drift to derelict status.

Within my own admitted very limited clinical experience this appears to be correct.

It is easy to become exasperated with the obstinate incorrigibility of the prostitute, and many people are constantly urging more severe penalties against her. This has been the case with the Wolfenden Report. However, severity in the past has proved useless and no doubt will be as valueless in the future if it is re-introduced. Those who wish to abolish prostitution must start with the abolition of the causal factors. They must prevent parental cruelty and neglect, bad environment, lack of adolescent amusement of the right type, and abolish night clubs, all-night cafés and other dragons' teeth which, allowed to burgeon, produce prostitution and similar evils. The Child Guidance Clinic and the Marriage Guidance Council are more likely to affect the incidence than savage legal sanctions which only drive it underground to augment out of sight.

It is not wise to become too indignant regarding prostitution for, although it is undoubtedly an evil and distasteful to most people, it should be recognized that this is not so everywhere nor has it always been. Marco Polo, for example, describes how in Kaindu (probably Ning-yuen in the Kien-ch'ang valley of the Sze-ch'wan province):

There are residents in the villages and homesteads perched on crags by the wayside who have beautiful wives and offer them freely to passing traders. And the traders give the woman a piece of fine cloth, perhaps a yard or so, or some other trinket of trifling value. Having taken his pleasure for a while, the trader mounts his horse and rides away. Then the husband and wife call after him in mockery: 'Hi, you there—you that are riding off. Show us what you are taking with you that is ours! Look at what you have left to us—what you have thrown away and forgotten', and he flourishes the cloth they have gained from him. 'We have got this of yours, you poor fool, and you have nothing to show for it!' So they mock at him. And so they continue to act.

If this occurred in England now the woman would be prosecuted and fined £10 for the first offence and £25 for subsequent offences. She could be sent to prison for three months as well. Moreover the husband could be convicted for living on the immoral earnings of a woman, an offence which is punishable on indictment with two years' imprisonment; causing prostitution in a woman, punishable with a further two years' imprisonment, and permitting premises to be used for prostitution, punishable, if the offence is committed after a previous conviction, with six months' imprisonment and £250 fine, or both!

The Romans, the Greeks, and other nations which had fertility religions regarded sex as almost holy, and thought nothing of prostitution, which was, in some cases, an established custom in the temple. This is shown by the following poem, from the Greek Anthology, translated by F. L. Lucas, and quoted by Charles Seltman:

> *Rose girl, fair as a rose, what do you sell?*
> *Is it yourself, or your roses? or them and yourself as well?*

On the other hand it would be wrong to be enchanted with the charm of such a poem and forget the sordidness, the misery, the commercialization by business interests, the brutality and unhappiness which are the inevitable accompaniments of prostitution in our civilization.

THE PROSTITUTES' CLIENTELE

This section would be incomplete without a brief reference to those men who resort to prostitutes. There is not a great deal in the literature on this matter but, from the experience of patients who do so, one can make certain deductions. Those that resort to them include: (1) the shy, nervous man who would not dare to approach a respectable girl: (2) the frustrated man, whether married or single, who can find no other outlet; (3) the man whose sexual urges are released by drink and who seeks immediate release; (4) the psychosexually abnormal man who cannot be satisfied by normal relations; (5) the old man who still retains some libido.

The Shy Nervous Man

This is the type of young man who fears that he may fail to be sufficiently potent or who is frightened to approach a girl for some other reason, usually because he feels that he is unattractive physically (often due to such trivialities as acne vulgaris), or because someone has told him that his organ is insufficiently developed. Astonishing though it may seem such young men often suffer a great deal of anxiety and misery: it is only because the sexual urge is so strong and they feel a great compulsion that they seek out someone who will not jeer and (even though paid to do so) will accept their advances. Moreover, they frequently obtain reassurances that their penises are of the proper size and that their sexual performance has been normal. The disadvantages of such relations (apart from such dangers as venereal disease) are that often the prostitute is not particularly attractive, she may be impatient and merely wish to get her hands on the money, so that the young man is further discouraged and made to feel yet more worthless. The anxiety engendered may cause premature ejaculation or impotence so that he fears that he will not be successful in better circumstances, whereas in reality he almost certainly would have no difficulty. Benjamin suggests that prostitution allows the adolescent boy to find an outlet and prevents the youth wavering between homosexuality and heterosexuality.

The Man Whose Sexual Urges are Released by Drink

Prostitution and intemperance are closely related; often prostitutes frequent public houses and night clubs, and many men will admit that they would not have had intercourse with a street woman had they not been drinking. Such men, if they cannot find a prostitute, will assault some harmless girl going home from a dance. One can hardly open a Sunday newspaper of the 'popular' type without seeing two or three such cases. All the time that alcohol is available and there is no real limit to how much a man may drink there will be cases where men feel a need for an urgent sexual release. It is mere hypocrisy to pretend that this does not occur. I do not believe that the prostitute is the protector of the pure woman, as the Victorians insisted, but she may, in such cases, prevent assaults which might occur otherwise.

The Psychosexually Abnormal

Prostitutes provide an outlet for many men who suffer from some psychosexual abnormality which is harmless to others. Such cases are those men who have a sexual malversion—such as a mackintosh fetish—which makes them impotent with a woman who cannot excite their abnormality. The ordinary woman is upset and disturbed by such a request whereas the prostitute accepts it merely as one of the necessities of her trade. Similarly the masochist who desires to be whipped—and the whips and cords sometimes exhibited before a disgusted and horrified magistrate show that this is by no means rare. It is difficult to see what harm is being done in such cases. Obviously it is better for the man to have treatment and be cured (if this is possible) but there seems to be no injury to others either by the prostitute or her client.

The Old Man who Retains Some Libido

Prostitutes are often frequented by ageing men who still have some libido. Such men include those widowers who either do not wish, or cannot afford, to re-marry. Such men frequently lead solitary lives, and their loveless existence is alleviated by outlets they find in this way.

Other Types

This is not meant to be a complete list and doubtless there are many other men who have relations with prostitutes for reasons which are not immediately obvious. There are immature men who cannot face the responsibilities of marriage, men who through their upbringing find that they cannot love a woman yet wish for sexual relations with one, the Don Juans who are insufficiently physically attractive to find seduction easy, business men away from home, ship's officers and sailors in foreign ports after long voyages, and the like.

Gibbens and Silberman did some research which gives valuable information regarding these men. They interviewed some 230 patients who had contracted venereal disease with prostitutes. These showed a preference for full-bosomed motherly types and disliked 'hard-faced' girls. Only 15 per cent. went with the same girl twice and only 15 per cent. were friendly with the girl. The majority of men were between 20 and 40 years of age, and half of those who went with a prostitute had done so first when under the age of 20. The population which visits prostitutes rises steadily with age and 41 per cent. were over the age of 40 when seen. About one-third were married: the married men had usually gone with prostitutes before marriage, and started again after the birth of the first child because of the competition for affection.

Roving types of work encourage relationships with prostitutes and Gibbens and Silberman ask: 'What causes men to take up such work in the first place?' In some 10 per cent. of the men there was a physical defect which made them unattractive, and some who had no such defect felt that they had one. Sexual perversion was not common, but there was an element of sadism, masochism and voyeurism present.

They found that the men who went with prostitutes were either inhibited, passive individuals with steady jobs, living at home with a mother to support, and frequently a dead father, or one of little account, the mother being a domineering woman, sometimes of high moral code. Some men being rovers, sailors, &c., seek a 'sexual mothering'.

The other main type was self-assertive, often from a broken home or one in which there was parental discord. They show strong dependence on the mother. Such men have no preference and go with prostitutes, or 'pick-up' girls indifferently, but as they grow older they gravitate more and more to prostitutes because they are less attractive.

Gibbens and Silberman thought the cause was: (1) Conflict of dependence and independence starting with the mother and extending to all women. (2) Lack of identification with the father or inadequate identification with him.

The inhibited group go with prostitutes because it needs the least effort and the impulsive group because they are temperamentally unable to maintain stable relationships.

Over 25 years' experience with sailors at the Dreadnought Hospital taught me that the ordinary man 'before the mast' was usually an unstable type, preferring an environment which he could change every voyage in many cases; but usually wanting a fixed point he could return to, and which was provided by the mother. Sailors usually carry a pocket-book in which the mother's photograph is almost invariably present. There is strong mother-fixation in their choice of prostitutes because of their choice of the 'full-bosomed' type of girl and their longing for 'sexual mothering'. The rejection of the, perhaps more beautiful, 'hard-faced' girls in preference for the motherly ones is surely indicative of this.

In general, if one had to generalize regarding prostitution one could say that the prostitute is basically homosexual, tolerating the man for money and inclined to punish him as a symbol of the hated male; on the other hand the client is seeking a mother-figure who will give him incestuous affection and satisfaction, without more claim on him than the bank-notes he leaves on the mantelpiece.

There are those who would punish the man who goes with a prostitute, as well as the prostitute herself. It is not always easy to follow the reasoning behind this since the prostitute is not punished because she sells herself; but because she offends the law and makes herself offensive to others. The client cannot be held to offend against the public unless in his relations he offends against common morals (as having relations where he may be seen by others). The whole position seems to be one of considerable legal complexity, but I suspect that many who would hound those who are not injuring society have other, perhaps unconscious, motives apart from the public good.

REFERENCES

BENJAMIN, J. (1951) Prostitution re-assessed, *Int. J. Sexol.*, **4**, 154–9.
CAPRIO, F. S. (1957) *Female Homosexuality*, London.
DEUTSCH, H. (1946) *Psychology of Women*, London.
EAST, N. (1949) *Society and the Criminal*, London, H.M.S.O.
GIBBENS, T. C. N. (1957) Juvenile prostitution, *Brit. J. Delinq.*, **8**, 3–12.
GIBBENS, T. C. N., and SILBERMAN, M. (1960) The clients of prostitutes, *Brit. J. vener. Dis.*, **36**, 113.
GLOVER, E. (1960) *The Roots of Crime*, London.
GREENWALD, H. (1958) *The Call Girl. A Social and Psychoanalytic Study*, New York.
HAIRE, N. (1948) Prostitution: abolition, toleration or regulation, *Marriage Hyg.*, **1**, 220–6.

HENRIQUES, F. (1962) *Prostitution and Society. Primitive, Classical and Oriental,* vol. 1, London.

—— (1963) *Prostitution and Society. Prostitution in Europe and the New World,* vol. 2, London.

HOLLENDER, M. H. (1961) Prostitution. The body and human relatedness, *Int. J. Psycho-Anal.,* **42,** 404–13.

KRISNASWAMY, A. K. (1954) A study of sex delinquents, prostitutes and non-delinquent girls, *Int. J. Sexol.,* **7,** 97–9.

LUCAS, F. I. (1951) *Greek Poetry for Everyman,* London.

MAEROV, A. S. (1965) Prostitution: a survey and review of 20 cases, *Psychiat. Quart.,* **4,** 675–701.

MORRISON, M. (1965) Lesbianism, *New Statesman,* London.

POLO, MARCO (1958) *The Travels of Marco Polo,* trans. LATHAM, R. E., London.

SELTMAN, C. (1956) *Women in Antiquity,* London.

STOCKWELL, S. L. (1953) Sexual experience of adolescent girls, *Int. J. Sexol.,* **7,** 25–7.

THE SPECIAL COMMITTEE OF THE COUNCIL OF THE BRITISH MEDICAL ASSOCIATION (1955) *Memorandum of Evidence on Homosexuality and Prostitution,* London.

18

MALE PROSTITUTION

HETEROSEXUAL

Definition

Intercourse by the male with a woman to obtain financial or other benefits.

Psychopathology and Occurrence

This, like female prostitution, was common in the sophisticated civilization of Rome. It was thought in those days that intercourse spoiled the voice, consequently actors, singers, players on the cithara, and other public performers were infibulated and wore a metal ring, something like a modern safety pin, through holes in the prepuce. This was supposed to prevent sexual desire and intercourse. However, the belief existed that because of their abstinence these men had exceptional sexual powers and the wealthy ladies of that time bribed them to remove their metal ring and satisfy them. Under such a circumstance it was not surprising that often the infibulation and metal ring were merely a sign of the male prostitute. No doubt there were other forms of heterosexual prostitution which time and the coyness of scholars have concealed.

It is also stated that in Tzarist Russia brothels existed in which men of exceptionally fine physique were available to satisfy lonely women, but it is difficult to confirm such statements.

The modern form of male prostitute is the *gigolo*.[1] This is a young man who lives with, usually, a much older woman, selling his favours for an enhanced social or financial position. It seems that such behaviour must be accepted as a form of male prostitution although often practised with discretion. Indeed at times it is concealed under the cloak of secretary or chauffeur. This, like the similar cases in women, shows the difficulty in defining this form of behaviour since such men occupy a similar position to the woman who lives as a mistress to one man but easily moves on to another if circumstances change.

I cannot claim to have many opportunities of examining such men since they rarely ask for treatment unless there is some ancillary condition such as a neurosis. However, it would appear that the usual motivation is

---

[1] The linguistic origin of this word is obscure. It does not appear in French, Spanish, or Italian dictionaries. The nearest word to it is the Italian *giglio*—a lily. Whether this was first applied to the beautifully dressed young man and became distorted it is difficult to say. The *Oxford English Dictionary* on the contrary states that it is the masculine correlative of the French *gigole*—a tall thin woman, which is a good description of the type.

due to immaturity. The young man rationalizes his behaviour by the financial advantage he obtains, but unconsciously there is often the seeking of a mother-figure. He thus appears to obtain the best of both possible worlds, gaining the satisfaction of his unconscious urges and being paid for it at the same time. Obviously, though, he is abnormal because a normal man wishes a mate of approximately the same age, and finally marriage, with, if possible, a family. A normal man may find difficulty in being potent with a woman much older than himself.

HOMOSEXUAL

Definition

Intercourse in some form or other by a male with another man in order to obtain financial or other benefits.

Psychopathology and Occurrence

Homosexual prostitution is also of extreme antiquity. It was common, with its female counterpart, in the ancient fertility religions when sex was regarded as something magical which formed part of the ritual. The Hebrews, in their original religion, appear to have had homosexual prostitutes called Q^{e}dheshīm (although this view is disputed by some authorities). In any case homosexual practices were later forbidden by the codes in Leviticus.

Throughout history—particularly English history—it would seem young men, euphemistically described as 'the King's favourites', were really homosexual prostitutes kept by him as, for example, Mme Du Barry and Mme de Montespan were kept by their respective monarchs.

Modern homosexual prostitution exists because the homosexual is incapable, in nearly all cases, of a prolonged attachment. This makes the relationship transient and unstable. It thus gives the opportunity to young men willing to respond for money or favours.

There do not appear to be homosexual brothels but homosexual young men meet others in certain public houses, cafés, and restaurants which constantly alter in popularity.

It is not easy to discover the psychology of the homosexual prostitute. They certainly appear superficial young men, eager to profit from anything which benefits them—and hence with poor super-ego structure, and so poor morality, but not grossly psychopathic in the sense of being actively dangerous to society. These young men usually have personalities too deviated to respond to any form of psychotherapy and, in any case, they do not wish for a cure which would make their lives more difficult and arduous. The fate of boy homosexual prostitutes is not as bad as one might suppose. Doshay found out of 256 boys between 6 to 12 years of age that only 86 appeared later in court and only half of them were accused of sexual offences.

Jersild, Chief of Copenhagen Morality Police, investigated 300 boys and young men convicted of prostitution. He found that only 7 per cent. were 'real' homosexuals and 13 per cent. bisexual. He followed up 228 of these over 5 years and found 112 imprisoned, but only 5 (2 per cent.) convicted of sexual offences.

Craft also investigated a very small series of homosexual prostitutes but the numbers were so small as to give no proper information.

The later life of the homsexual prostitute is a mystery since I have never seen middle-aged, nor old men, who admitted to this form of activity in youth. No doubt, once they have lost their looks and can no longer attract other men, they must return to earning their living by work. If one considers it, very rarely is a woman encountered who admits that she has been a prostitute in her youth, so it is not surprising that men are just as reticent.

THE SOUTENEUR

Definition

A man who cohabits with and lives on the earnings of a prostitute.

Occurence

There is no adequate literature which I can discover regarding the psychology of the souteneur. Even physicians with great prison experience, such as Norwood East and Karpman, have recorded little about them. Yet in England about 100 to 200 men are annually prosecuted for living on the immoral earnings of women. With such a sparsity of information I can only use such facts as it is possible to unearth and make deductions which, although they are inadequate, are the best I can provide.

It would seem that the souteneur's relation to the prostitute may be on various bases. These are:

1. He may have a genuine emotional relationship to her. This, however, may not be the normal affectionate love relationship, but appears sometimes to be based on a sado-masochistic feeling. The souteneur is the sadist who beats the woman unless she obtains adequate returns and she accepts the position consciously or unconsciously because she enjoys her subjugation. This explains why for no apparent reason she meekly hands over the money she gains instead of leaving him and 'working' for herself.

2. The souteneur may blackmail the woman into working for him under the threat that he will injure her, slash her face with a razor and so on, unless she does so. Since street-walkers are often out late at night when it is easy to do such things they are often intimidated. There was a

case of three Maltese brothers, named Messina, who behaved in this way and one even possessed a Rolls-Royce on the proceeds. It is known that sometimes rival souteneurs endeavour to make the same woman work for them and gang fights break out. Only in such a way does the matter become public since the woman is afraid of going to the police for protection.

3. In some cases there appears to be a pure business deal without any emotional relationship. Neither the man nor the woman think of prostitution as wrong or antisocial and regard their behaviour as purely mercantile. For example, the man provides the woman with a flat or house, furniture and a maid, and the woman pays for what he has provided out of her earnings. Hersh (quoted by East) states that in 1924–5 in ex-Russian Poland souteneurs were twice as many amongst Jews as non-Jews, and 40 per cent. of the Jews condemned for offences against sexual morality and the family were souteneurs, against barely 5 per cent. of the non-Jewish condemned prisoners. It seems probable that this was not because the Jews were of a lower sexual morality than the non-Jews but because, being a mercantile community, they regarded the whole thing as a purely business matter. Thus, amongst the Jews, the merchants were twenty times as many as amongst the ordinary population.

Coloured men seem to be attractive to some prostitutes and many have been accused of living on the immoral earnings of women; but how the percentage relates to white men doing the same thing it is impossible to say. The reality of the matter can be seen by anyone driving round the Porte Saint-Denis district of Paris, where coloured pimps can be seen keeping a close watch on their women openly soliciting in broad daylight.

Repugnant though the souteneur may be, he may serve a useful purpose. A large number of prostitutes are murdered; sometimes in lonely streets, as in the case of Jack the Ripper; but more often by a client when she is asleep in bed and by strangulation so that no sound is heard. In some cases the souteneur is in the same flat or house and can truly fulfil his function of protector to the unfortunate woman.

East states:

The prostitute appears to many as lazy, shiftless, avaricious, untruthful, selfish, and faithless. But the absence of virtues we are accustomed to regard as essential does not necessarily exclude others which are estimable. Some courtesans are charitable, kindly, sympathetic, and affectionate. If a man lives on her earnings and is utterly despicable, he may be the only person for whom she had any tender feeling and her only anchor. She may be blind to his faults and dissociates him from the men who are her clients. In his company she can relax and be her natural self and throw aside the arts and devices of her calling. He acts as her champion in a dispute and her protector in a scene of violence. He forms a bridge which unites what she is with what she might have been.

He supports her artificial self-reliance and the weakness of her position. He satisfies her inherent desire to be owned, although he may exploit her cruelly and callously satisfies her masochistic cravings. Hence it may be particularly difficult to influence her in other directions as long as her masochistic submissions afford her emotional gratification.

This shows a compassion and insight which all East's experience as a prison doctor did not blunt. However, we must not let our sense of pity blind us to the fact that a great deal of the sordidness of prostitution stems from the souteneur behind the scenes and his constant pressure on the woman in his grip which may reduce her to less than a slave.

REFERENCES

BAILEY, D. S. (1955) *Homosexuality and the Western Christian Tradition*, London.
CORY, D. W. (1955) *The Homosexual Outlook*, London.
CRAFT, M. (1966) Boy prostitutes and their fate, *Brit. J. Psychiat.*, **112**, 1111–4.
DINGWALL, E. J. (1925) *Male Infibulation*, London.
DOSHAY, L. J. (1943) *The Boy Sexual Offender and His Later Criminal Career*, New York.
JERSILD, J. (1953) Den Mandlige Prostitution—Arsager, Omfang, *Dansk Videnskabs Forlan*.

PART SEVEN

THE PREVENTION, TREATMENT, AND PROGNOSIS OF THE PSYCHOSEXUAL DISORDERS

19

PREVENTION

There is no doubt that the paraphilias cause a terrific amount of biological waste, inasmuch as many desirable types fail to reproduce themselves, so that the problem takes on a national or even international importance. I do not subscribe to the view so often put forward by perverts themselves that genius is the product of perversion, but it must be admitted that sexual abnormalities do, in the main, occur in the more intellectual and artistic types whose abilities are so worth preserving in the future representatives of the race. Apart from the eugenics of the matter, however, there is an enormous amount of suffering caused by sexual anomaly. The pervert is rarely a happy man no matter how much he may show a façade of contentment. He has to take a devious course to satisfy an instinct which most of us enjoy without difficulty, and even when he obtains satisfaction it is rarely that he reaches ecstasies which a normal man accepts as his due. Moreover, innumerable men and women suffer from impotence and frigidity, so that either the partner has to live in a state of constant sexual hunger which many find unendurable, or else they abandon the pretence of marriage and indulge in 'infidelities' which sooner or later lead to its dissolution. In spite of the ill-advised dicta of exalted clerics, there is no doubt that normal sexuality and sexual enjoyment in married life is of immense importance, and no marriage is worthy of the name in which it does not exist.

If we disregard those clergy who would make marriage such a rigid sacrament that on no account can it be broken except by death—and some, even outside the Roman Church, still insist that this is so—most sensible people feel that marriage in which the sexual side is spoiled (although possibly it may once have existed more or less satisfactorily for a time) can hardly be regarded as happy or worth preserving. Moreover, the sexual dissatisfaction in such a union inevitably leads to irritability, quarrelling, and sometimes alcoholism or cruelty. In such an atmosphere the happiness of the children—which is always put forward as the necessity for preserving a marriage—can hardly exist.

Children, more than adults, intuitively know that their parents are detesting each other. There is often a leaning towards the parent of opposite sex, who is considered in the right for emotional reasons. *The child thus grows up in the very environment likely to distort its own normal sexuality and make it into an adult suffering from psychosexual disease.*

Sixty per cent. of divorces occur in marriages which have persisted for more than 10 years and 35 per cent. in those which have existed for 15 years. Thirty per cent. of the couples are childless also. The harm done in such cases cannot be so grave as the clerics, for their own reasons, maintain.

This does not say that one must rush to divorce before all is lost. Many people's sexual failure can be corrected and should be treated by sensible advice and, if necessary, medical therapy. Divorce is the surgery necessary when medicine has failed.

This point of view has recently become appreciated by the Church and a strong effort has rightly been made by it in encouraging the Marriage Guidance principle to assist people in the problems of their sexual life. This cannot be fostered too much.

It is imperative, therefore, that everything possible should be done to prevent sexual abnormality, since it is always easier to prevent than to cure. It will have been seen from the preceding parts of this book that I believe that abnormality in the sexual sphere is due to abnormality in various parts of the instinct itself. It is essential therefore that the child should be allowed to develop normally. Now the psychoanalytic school has laid down that sexuality begins with suckling at the breast, and there is a great deal of evidence to show that suckling is or may be sexualized. I do not know whether or not the psychoanalytic school will be proved correct, but it can do no harm to pay attention to what it teaches: that is, that the child should be breast-fed and the mother show her love for it by feeding it properly and unemotionally. It should not be fed irregularly because it gives the mother sexual pleasure, nor should she make feeding a form of titillation for the child. I have encountered women who have never attained an orgasm because they had been educated to regard sex as 'animal and beastly' and who gained much sexual pleasure from the suckling infant. Such women, particularly if they give overt expression to their pleasure, endanger their children. Again, suckling is a mode of nourishment and not a remedy against unhappiness, so that the child should not be put to the breast the moment it shows signs of pain or discomfort. Moreover, as far as possible the conditions such as epithelial abrasions, inverted nipples, engorged breasts, and so on, which make feeding difficult and the baby unhappy and resentful, should be treated before they cause difficulties which may have an unfortunate effect on the child's emotional life.

The child should be weaned, not by painting the breast with aloes and such methods, but properly at the right time by giving it other food before it is given the breast so that it is satiated and tends to abandon the breast by itself. Since we protect ourselves against unwarranted desires by the expression of hostility, it is unkind to force milk puddings and milk too much on the infant who is trying to suppress its desire for the breast by hating milk and its analogues.

Again, when it develops its teeth it should be given hard food so that it can externalize its biting activities in a natural way. A child who bites others should not be bitten back 'to show that it hurts' (it will reverse its instincts only too easily) but discouraged by being made to realize that such behaviour is 'babyish' and not grown up. It should not be fussed over its bowels but they should be treated as any other human activity. A child with proper food and exercise is unlikely to have much trouble, but undue maternal anxiety is likely to derange its functions. If constipation does occur it should be treated by gentle vegetable purgatives and not by suppositories and enemas (unless ordered by the physician) which direct the attention too markedly to the anal regions, and may make the procedures too emotional, especially if pain or discomfort are produced.

It has been shown by Bowlby and his school that separation from the mother during the period of 6 months to 2 years of age has a grave emotional effect on a child which may produce severe depression, either at the time or later. Indeed, I have seen adults who have developed impotence in adult life due to this experience. It is reasonable to exert every effort to avoid such occurrences. Those who scoff at this as a fantasy may be impressed by the fact that a bird, such as a budgerigar, for example, separated from his fellows, will mope in his cage and refuse to eat for some time, due to separation anxiety. This fact is, therefore, supported from the behaviouristic side. If separation can affect a bird how much can it upset a tiny baby?

When the child develops an interest in its body (the navel is usually an interesting problem to it), the answers should be given to its questions unemotionally and calmly; as simply as possible—so that it will understand—but truthfully. If the child is fobbed off with lies it only invents fantasies which are often dangerous to its future development. If it shows sexual interest in itself or its companions it should be allowed to do so, no comment being made. Above all, it should be taught to appreciate that sex is normal, desirable, and not some monstrous activity which only exists to be condemned. The most essential thing is that it should be surrounded by an environment which contains affection, but not slobbering sentimentality. It should be treated consistently and, when in doubt, as one would prefer to be treated oneself.

The work of Whitener and Nikelly confirms the immense importance of the attitude of the parents to the child, and this may be influenced by parental quarrelling as well as preferences resulting from the personality and emotional orientation of the parents. In quarrels the child is sometimes used by its parents as a useful pawn to gain advantage over one or the other. The love-starved woman will use her son as a substitute for his

father, and smother him with affection; the father may spoil the daughter.
Both parents may denigrate each other, and ask the child to make an
emotional choice between them, which may be impossible at an early age.
Parents with some psychosexual difficulty, such as homosexuality, may be
unable to provide a proper environment for children, and many similar
situations may occur. Parental influence must be accepted as of supreme
importance in forming the orientation of children.

One knows from clinical experience that a large number of abnormally
sexed persons come from unhappy homes. Since the sex life of its members is of prime importance to the nation, it might be expected that it
should cast its laws so that those who are unhappily married should be
enabled to readjust themselves (and their children) by leaving their
partner who cannot win affection and marrying someone who is loved,
instead of living miserably with one who is hated, in constant tension,
so that married life becomes miserable and the children grow up abnormal.
It is better for a boy to grow up with a healthy mother and to mould
himself—introject—on the best masculine characters in his environment
than for him to develop in an unhappy family caused, for example, by the
presence of a brutal and drunken father who does his best to make him
hate masculinity and everything associated with it. This, of course,
holds good in the reverse sense for the girl with an unsuitable mother.
Most clinical sexological psychiatrists agree that the undesirable parent
of opposite sex is a prime element in the production of homosexuality
and there seems no reason to discard the deductions from what is a
common finding. By these statements it must not be thought that I
approve of divorce for every and any disagreement. Obviously quarrels
may arise in any marriage, but they are usually soon resolved and in any
case they should not be conducted before the children. It is the perpetually
unhappy marriage to which I refer here. There are signs that the legislators
are at last beginning to appreciate the importance of these matters and
divorce is slowly getting easier in suitable cases.

The Freudian believes that the harm or good is all done before the
child reaches the age of 5 years, but for the behaviourist one is never too
old to be conditioned. It is essential, therefore, that the child should
have normal contacts both in its school life and after. I believe that the
unmixed public school in which young men remain until 18 or even 19,
until they pass on to college, is a source of a great deal of homosexuality.
Numerous novelists (e.g. Alec Waugh and Bruce Marshall) have depicted
the fact that older boys, their sexual impulses frustrated by the unnatural
restraints and the prudishness of schoolmasters, turn to younger boys as a
sexual object and seduce them into perversions. This type of novel would
not be tolerated unless it was to a large extent true and clinical findings
show that it does represent a reality. It is to be hoped that sooner or later

public schools will be replaced by co-educational institutions. In the past battles may have been won on the playing-fields of our public schools, but numerous lives have been broken in the dormitories. Similarly it is never desirable that bigger boys should be allowed to cane smaller ones, nor should masters cane boys before the class or the school 'as an example'. I have repeatedly encountered sadists in whom the first stirrings of their perversion have occurred following such an exhibition. In any case there are many better methods of punishing unruly boys than by caning them—no matter how much corporal punishment provides an outlet for the sex-starved schoolmaster. Yet in spite of this the present Minister of Health has stated that he will leave it to the school-teacher whether not only normal but handicapped children should be caned.

The avoidance of sexual assaults on children by adults is a matter of primary importance, and it is certainly not wise to allow a child to enter an environment where this is likely to happen, however much it is surrounded by an aura of piety. Too often one finds that the child with homosexual tendencies, for example, has been permanently diverted into those channels because it was assaulted by someone who should have been its spiritual guide and director.

Mulcock, in a valuable study of 100 non-selected cases of sexual assault on children, pointed out that nearly 75 per cent. of men assaulting boys and girls between the ages of 4 and 17 years were already known to the parents and had gained the confidence of the child by contacts established as schoolmasters, scoutmasters, and so on. Of these 21 per cent. were school-teachers and 14 per cent. clergymen.

The assaults took place in indoor sites or places familiar to the child in 75 per cent. of cases and the men committing them were almost as often 'white collar' as manual workers.

It is obvious, therefore, that it is useless to warn children 'Don't speak to strangers', 'Keep away from rough men', and 'Mind where you go' because assaults are less likely to be committed by unfamiliar men in strange places. (We must not disregard, however, that sadistic assaults may be quite a different matter and children are sometimes killed by strangers in out-of-the-way places.)

For some reason which is not entirely clear almost three-quarters of the assaults were on boys. The age when such assaults were likely to take place on either sex was found to be between 10 and 12 years. The homosexual assault being the commoner should lead to most vigilance.

It is true, as a homosexual schoolmaster once told me in excuse of his behaviour, that 'all boys are homosexuals', but it is just because of this, because they have to develop into something else, that we must do our best to see that nothing is done to hinder their journey along the path of heterosexuality. It has been suggested by Ernest Jones (and I have quoted him at length in Chapter 3) that the child repeats the Freudian scheme of development at puberty. The possibility of some obstruction to its normal sexuality is probably greater then than at any other time. It is often about this period that the young boy or girl starts to show interest in the opposite sex. This should be encouraged, and frequently is by sensible parents, by such activities as dancing, swimming, skating, and the like. Sometimes, however, one finds a great deal of teasing and chaffing is turned on to the sensitive adolescent, so that he feels that in his flirtations with the desirable young lady in the fifth form at the neighbouring girls' school he is doing something wrong or ridiculous. Sexual interest is regarded much more seriously in the girl, whose potential fertility carries the danger of unwanted and unexpected pregnancies. The mother or teacher frequently tells the girl exaggerated lies about sexual intercourse, and the nature of men, so that she will not stray from the fold and embarrass them with an illegitimate child. (This in itself is an indictment of their upbringing!) It may be doubted that such descriptions could do anything to damage the sexuality of a girl who has developed normally until puberty, but not every child has grown up in an atmosphere of completely normal emotion. It is such children who may be harmed seriously, so that in later life they can never enter happily into marriage. Not only may such descriptions damage a child at puberty but they can affect apparently normal individuals at an even later age. I have seen a man of nearly 30 years of age who had been told a lurid tale about the dangers of venereal disease and the awful results accruing from it whilst in the Army. He had been so frightened by the medical officer's lecture that when some time later he tried to have sexual intercourse with a woman he felt too anxious to obtain an erection. After reassuring him that what he had been told was untrue he recovered completely.

Parents are at last being educated to the harmlessness of masturbation, but one still encounters men who have been told that this produces impotence and sterility. It should be stated, once and for all, that the best way to make a man impotent is to tell him that masturbation as a boy will do so. The sexual organs are never damaged by use and to pretend that they are is a crime and an outrage. More pompous nonsense has been preached about this in the past than it is possible to imagine.

The worst type of parent the child can have is the one who tries to stamp out all sex as a manifestation of the devil. Too often he or she succeeds and the child grows into an impotent man or a frigid woman.

It is difficult to know all the roots of fetishism, but it is doubtful if it ever appears in those who have developed in a normal emotional atmosphere. It is probably an off-shoot from over-attachment to the mother in spite of the elaborate analysis which Freudians have described. This partial attachment is not so complete as in transvestism, where all the clothes, for example, are the fetish but only one article of clothing or something similar, is unconsciously selected. Thus buttock fetishes derive from the mother's breasts under tight dresses, high-heeled shoes from her own footwear, and mackintosh fetishes from the mackintosh she used to protect her knees when bathing the little child. It is thus somewhat comparable to homosexuality which is caused by identification with (or moulding upon) the mother. In such cases the mother has not shown a consistently affectionate attitude to the son, but by being alternately cold and affectionate, or by being neurotically over-affectionate or indifferent to the child, has made him seek an affection which he has never enjoyed. It cannot be stated too strongly that the duty of the mother is to help the child along the path to adulthood, not to draw him or her back because of over-attachment, nor to use him or her as a substitute for the lack of affection from the husband, but to make willing sacrifices that growing up may be easy and painless. Jealousy between parents is, of course, the cause of much unhappiness in the child. Thus when the boy reaches the age when he wants to go fishing with his father it is a selfish woman, and indeed, a foolish woman because the son will ultimately hate her, who tries to keep him back to join in her own activities.

All the blame must not be attributed to the mother—it is sometimes attached to the father. With a son often the father is too busy, or too interested in his golf, to show much affection to the child, and instead of taking it for walks, showing it the local railway engines, talking to it, and really giving it a chance *to know* him so that it can form its character upon him, he leaves its education to others, often with inferior person-alities, or of the wrong sex, and is surprised and horrified when in later years the child shows some sexual abnormality which brings him un-desirable publicity and the young man to ruin. In the case of the girls the father is often too indulgent (perhaps because the daughter reminds him of her mother at the time when he loved her most), and perhaps by seeking her company too much tends to condition her into too masculine a manner so that she grows up homosexual (as in Radclyffe Hall's novel *The Well of Loneliness*). If he does not do this he may, by adopting an over-bearing manner, convince her that the tales of her mother or teacher regarding the horrible ways of men in sex are true, and by transfer of her fear of her father on to other men she becomes frigid and miserable.

Children at puberty should be allowed to indulge in those things which are proper to their sex. A girl is much less likely to damage her complexion by face powder and lipstick than the parent or teacher is to injure her sex-uality by forbidding any normal manifestations of the outward sign of sex.

In the past parents have tended to be afraid that such signs would indicate the danger of the boy 'getting a girl into trouble' and of a girl running after men and becoming pregnant. These dangers in a properly brought up child are negligible.

It is useless to elaborate the whole theme. Parents should be glad when they notice signs of normal sexual interest in their children, and should take them to have treatment when such signs are absent instead of regarding them as being good children. It is doubtful whether any definite suspicion of abnormality can be confirmed before puberty, but any lack of proper sexual interest after puberty is pathological and needs treatment. The boy who likes 'dressing up in girls' clothes' and vice versa, the boy who takes no interest in girls, the timid boy who will not speak to girls, and so on, are all pathological, and if correction of their environment will not help (and it often will) something more must be done. This usually takes the form of psychotherapy.

I would mention here the great importance that the cinema and television have had in the development of the adolescent. It is improbable that any child or adult is perverted by reading a book, no matter how 'bad' it may be, nor by seeing a play or a film. Nevertheless it is felt that a constant diet, an unending reiteration, of one theme may have effect; just as the continuous propaganda of war finally influences the mind of even the most balanced and impartial. There are two undesirable themes which permeate the modern cinema and television in spite of the ridiculous precautions of the avuncular censorship, which is usually valueless if not pernicious. These are violence and the exploitation of sex known as 'glamour'. The constant ill-treatment of women on the screen certainly has an undesirable effect on the adolescent mind and may lead to sexual advances which appear to be more of an assault than a gesture of affection. Moreover, these films give the impression that to be manly a man must be 'tough'—that is, brutal and vicious—and disregard the gentler, protective, and kinder aspects of masculine love entirely.

There is no reason at all why feminine beauty should not be accentuated in the cinema and on television and, in fact, this may be a good thing. Probably the universality of the film has done much to rid women of the drab clothes which the poorer once wore and has allowed them to see more tasteful things. Unfortunately this has often led to the 'glamourizing' of the demi-mondaine and the suggestion that the pinnacle of feminine success lies with the courtesan rather than with the mother. Maternity is shown as a wearisome burden spoiled by anxiety over the children's welfare and overwork in their upbringing. This, of course, is pernicious nonsense. We obtain our greatest possible happiness in giving freedom to normal instincts and living as we were meant to live. A woman attains the greatest stature when she displays her maternity, and in the development of her children. Those who would cramp women into the confines of the home no doubt do her wrong, but most normal women would cheerfully exchange the excitements of the *poule de luxe* for the happiness of a husband who loves her, healthy children, and a contented home. Unfortunately, the cinema ideal tends to encourage narcissism and incidentally amateur prostitution, perhaps leading on to professionalism.

It is essential that the first introduction to sex should be a normal heterosexual one, and, although at this stage of civilization it is hardly possible to introduce the child to heterosexuality like one can perform an experiment in the laboratory, yet by encouraging normal sexuality and by seeing that it has the right environment such a happy result can hardly fail to be achieved. Too often the child is treated as if it were an idiot unable to understand the meaning of sex or of proper behaviour from the fear that sexual knowledge will bring inevitable disaster. It is far more likely to do the opposite. Some parents do timidly tell the child 'the facts of life' but spoil this by doing so at some particular time—usually puberty, when the child is unstable and likely to react emotionally, instead of answering its questions at any period when it asks them. Moreover, such parents often tell the child that it must not discuss what it has been told with others. This again is fruitless. Children, and youths of both sexes, invariably do sooner or later discuss sex. Why bring an element of guilt into the matter? If what has been told is the truth there is no fear that discussion will unsettle the child. It is easy to discourage premature experiments by the simple argument that if they are indulged in there is the danger of pregnancy, and it is unfair to oneself and to the child to have one without economic security. This is an argument which everyone can understand and better than a list of 'Thou shalt nots' which often will not stand critical examination—and the adolescent is acutely discriminating.

It is essential for the health of the individual that normal sexual contacts should be made as soon as possible. We know that a normal adult in whom the proper sexual responses have been developed is in danger of regression into abnormality—usually homosexuality—if deprived of a sexual outlet in adult life. How much more is this likely to occur in young people, in whom sex is much more violent and urgent, if he or she is too long kept in a state of hunger! Yet it is a most unfortunate fact that the economics of our civilization tend to delay longer and longer the age when young persons can marry. Once, e.g. in Elizabethan times, it was usual for a young man to marry at about 17 and for a girl to be a wife by 14 or 15 (see *The Paston Letters*). No ill seems to have resulted since these were the days of large families, even if nearly always depleted by a high infantile death-rate. Now most young men, particularly of the professional classes, find it difficult to marry before the age of 30 or 35 because of the exigencies of their studies and the necessity of establishing themselves in their avocation. The result of this is that girls cannot marry until much later. One result of this custom is the establishment of a law making carnal

CC—PSY. D.

knowledge of a girl before the age of 16 punishable by imprisonment, although many girls are capable of reproducing much before this, and can be married and have intercourse younger, although such intercourse would be illegal outside matrimony.

The postponement of normal sexual outlets before such an advanced age as 30 to 35 leads either to illicit relationships and thence to promiscuity —no doubt this has resulted in the slackening of the rigid moral codes of the Victorians—or else to an outlet by perversion. This may be such behaviour as homosexuality (concealed under a cloak of good-fellowship and heavy drinking) or else allow some half-obliterated perverse trend, such as sadism, or voyeurism, to become manifest.

We have been told *ad nauseam* by cleric and moralist that continence does no harm to anyone: that the moral character is strengthened by abstinence and so on. This I do not believe. The sexual organs consist of gland and muscle co-ordinated by the nervous system. No other organs are improved by disuse, so why should these be exceptions? Again, the nervous system does not benefit if some instinctual urge is obstructed and, indeed, we know for certain that the obstruction of strong instinctual urges leads only to their breaking out in some abnormal channel, as when the starving man chews bits of wood or leather to allay his hunger. I believe that the same is true for the erotic instincts, and would argue strongly that *continence is definitely harmful* and should be avoided as far as is humanly possible. It is not unusual for a psychiatrist who works with cases of sexual abnormality to encounter men, often of good intellectual and moral principles, who for ethical reasons have never had any sexual outlet—even youthful masturbation has been avoided, and premarital intercourse abhorrent. These men for financial or other reasons have married at a late age, 40 or older, and find to their horror that they are impotent. Moreover, such impotence is by no means easy to cure since it is the result of complete suppression of instinctual impulses from a very early age. Again, I have seen a strong man reduced to a severe anxiety state by marrying a frigid woman and losing his normal sexual activities. I am not alone in this view. Lydston says: 'No man or woman at adult age is in perfect physiological condition unless the sexual function is naturally and regularly performed.' Similarly von Schrenck-Notzing gives the same warning as I have given above. He says clearly: 'Likewise in man enforced abstinence may endanger the freedom of the will and lead to perversity of the sexual act.' That this is evident is shown by the fact that in prisons, or on the old sailing-ships, which were often months away from land, perversions frequently occurred. In normal people continence is not only difficult—it is impossible—if they are to remain normal.

The correctness of this view—that continence is harmful—was shown by the results of the last war. There were a large number of men stationed abroad, in places like the Western Desert, where they rarely saw a woman, and had no leave for long periods so that they could see their wives. Moreover, many of these men felt it was morally wrong to commit adultery with some other woman when they were happily married and had a wife at home. The unfortunate result was that they suppressed their sex for as long as three or four years. The result being that after the war I treated a large number of men for impotence on return to their married life. The ironical thing was that often, because he could do nothing sexually, the wife believed that her husband had been leading a riotous life abroad and was now 'worn out'! The rakes who had not been continent retained their sexual capacity and the poor faithful ones lost theirs (fortunately only temporarily).

It is for these reasons that I would plead for earlier marriage and a national attempt to prevent the slowly widening gap between puberty and marriage. The sad fact is that often the manual labourer can marry young and have a large family; whereas the intellectual professions demand long periods of study and difficult examinations with the consequent delay in establishing a normal marriage. I believe that every young person should have the economic right to marry before the age of 20, although for many reasons it might be wise to delay the establishment of a family until a little later. Unless this is possible it would seem that civilization shows a grave danger of subsiding in a wallow of promiscuity and perversion.

It is too much, perhaps, at this moment to ask *homo stultans* to cease warring, but if wars must be fought surely it is possible to prevent men being separated for years from their wives. To do so is tempting the gods too far.

It has been evident again and again that perversions tend to become manifest after the consumption of alcohol. No doubt, in young persons, if this had never occurred there was at least a chance that normal sexual responses would have been established and a normal sexual life have resulted. I feel therefore that the excessive consumption of alcohol, amongst young persons particularly, should be discouraged by social custom and convention.

In short I believe that a certain amount of sexual perversion and abnormality could—and would—be prevented by treating the infant in a proper biological way from its birth so that fixations tend to be avoided; by giving it as healthy an upbringing as possible during childhood and youth, so that it develops socially and is able to mix freely with its fellows of either sex; by a wise management of puberty—particularly with the avoidance of unhealthy sexual contacts, no matter under what aura of sanctity, and by proper sexual instruction given without emotion (in fact, this should be given by answering questions sensibly at any age); finally by making it possible for the young man and girl to marry when their sexual instincts are most difficult to confine.

It should never be forgotten that the psychologically healthy adult tends to have mentally healthy children, whereas those who have been cribbed, cabined, and confined into abnormality have twisted children. Each child which grows up normally and is able to have a normal marriage adds to the sum total of national happiness, each child who develops perverted detracts from it. The happiness of a nation can never be supported on the pillars of individual misery.

REFERENCES

MULCOCK, D. A. (1954) A study of non-selected cases of sexual assaults on children, *Int. J. Sexol.*, **7**, 125–8.
WHITENER, R. W., and NIKELLY, A. (1964) *Amer. J. Orthopsychiat.*, xxxiv, **3**, 486–92.

20

TREATMENT

GENERAL PRINCIPLES

If one reads the earlier sexological literature, particularly that of the German physicians, it is evident that little in the way of therapy was considered possible. Indeed the physician was inclined to stand back in wonderment at the bizarre behaviour of human beings and content himself with describing their antics. Sexual abnormality was in general regarded as a legal rather than a medical responsibility. Indeed, had the earlier psychiatrists wished to treat the sexually abnormal they would have had little in the way of resources to do so. Endocrinology was in its infancy so that there was a confusion of the physically abnormal with the psychologically ill. Psychotherapy consisted of hypnosis, which was regarded with a certain amount of suspicion, and Weir Mitchell's 'rest-cure'. The physician was inadequately equipped to face one of the most difficult of all psychotherapeutic problems.

We can claim to have made many advances since those times, yet the attitude of nihilism still lays a shadow on the treatment of sexual anomalies. This is particularly so in the case of the psychiatrist whose experience has been with hospital out-patients rather than with psychotherapy under more favourable conditions. Pressure of out-patient work necessitates a large number of patients being seen in a short time, and the physician is, frequently, forced to resort to organic treatments, such as sedation, rather than proper investigation of the unconscious causes. It is obvious that little can be done with such intimate illness in the brief interviews, often before students, which such circumstances necessitate. Wilder points out that the results of such treatment in psychoneurosis are not so satisfactory as those following treatment given elsewhere, and says 'Clinics seem to have the poorest results', so it is not surprising that in the more difficult paraphilias the out-patient psychiatrist is not impressed. Moreover, not all physicians are psychologically suited to treat the sexually abnormal. Many of those who feel that they are dealing with wickedness, or are disgusted by something which they feel is outrageous, would be wiser to turn their attention to work which they find more attractive to them.

Their attitude may be, and probably is, due to their own sexual anxiety. This will be hotly denied, but Woods and Natterson examined a large number of medical students and found that nearly half had anxiety over sex which would interfere with the treatment of patients. The majority of these had some sexual conflict as a major concern.

It may be a *sine qua non*, then, that the psychiatrist treating the sexually abnormal, should be sympathetic and as helpful as possible, and never regard them as outcasts, no matter how bizarre their behaviour. Any sign of hostility or ridicule will make treatment impossible.

There are schools of psychological thought which advise a prolonged treatment for every sexual abnormality. Yet it is doubtful whether this is necessary, or advisable, except in special cases. The medical psychologist, like every other physician, must adjust his therapy to the patient, and use whatever means he feels are best for the particular case. To do anything else is not only bad medicine, but shows a rigid mental attitude which precludes any advance of knowledge.

It should be an axiom, however, that no case of sexual abnormality should be treated until one is quite sure that no endocrine or other abnormality exists. I have shown elsewhere that the normal sexuality tends to be maintained because of the constant stimulation of the endocrines, and that any falling off of this stimulation leads to a lessening of the sexuality. I believe that this is not only a matter of the sexual hormones but of the whole endocrine orchestra. The preliminary for any psychotherapy should be, therefore, a thorough physical examination to observe the signs of glandular disease such as the hair and fat distribution, shape of hands, enlargement of palpable glands, and so on as well as any other physical abnormality. In doubtful cases it is worth while having the male and female hormones estimated. *I would emphasize most strongly that it is not to be assumed that there is any hope of benefit from giving testosterone propionate or any other sexual hormone to cases of psychosexual abnormality in which the sexual hormones are found present in normal amounts.* This invariably leads to disappointment and results in no benefit. In fact the exact contrary is the case, since to administer testosterone propionate to a normal male over some time can result in testicular atrophy. Psychotherapy is useless unless the hormones are normal and, in fact, it is often difficult enough to treat severe psychosexual abnormalities in those who are normal physically without the added disadvantage of endocrine dysfunction. Nevertheless, it is essential that the importance of proper harmony should be stressed, although it is not to be treated at length here. I have shown elsewhere the importance of this. In a series of sixteen homosexuals suffering from adrenogenital virilism 50 per cent. showed heterosexuality after adrenalectomy, and in a similar series of sixteen who were heterosexual 50 per cent. showed increased heterosexuality.

Again, Foss and others have shown the tremendous effect testosterone propionate can have on a post-pubertal eunuch whose condition was due to wounds of the testes through war. This man, aged 38, lost practically all his libido (presumably he had become, as I found in similar cases, auto-sexual), but injections of testosterone propionate produced good erections and even priapism, with desire for coitus lasting through the day and night. Hamilton noticed a similar state of affairs with another patient. There are now many similar cases in the literature and I have myself had successful cases with eunuchoids. These results have been quoted to show the tremendous effect that proper endocrine therapy can have with suitable cases, but it must not be forgotten, as previously stated, that most cases of impotence (not due to endocrine lack) make no response what-ever to hormone treatment.

It would be impossible in a book of this character to exhaust all the neurological possibilities which may cause sexual complications, but obviously cord lesions are the most important. The reader must consult neurological textbooks if he is interested. A thorough physical examina-tion will usually reveal if anything abnormal exists in the central nervous system. The rarity of such discoveries is inclined to make one careless in sexological practice, but the physician will be wise to see that this does not occur. However, I must admit that I have seen few cases where neurological disease could have caused the symptoms of which the patient complained. Usually those who have such lesions as spinal tumours have more obvious symptoms than sexual failure, which tends to be overlooked amongst the presenting paralyses, incoordination, and so on. I can remember a girl, for instance, who complained of sexual anaesthesia but whose real illness was disseminated sclerosis, and doubtless a few similar cases could be discovered if one searched one's records carefully enough.

Such organic cases will be detected by a proper physical examination, which is not only helpful by excluding such conditions, but also impresses the patient. For instance, whilst performing the neurological part of the examination it is wise to test the cremasteric reflex. The reaction should be pointed out to the patient. Most lay people have no idea that such a reflex exists. The fact that one can demonstrate visibly that there is nothing wrong neurologically may provide a cogent indication that the trouble is 'only emotional', and a very strong suggestion of cure in cases of hypoversion. I have often noticed the look of relief come over a patient's face when shown that the positive cremasteric reflex proved that he had no organic disease causing his symptoms.

Excessive libido sometimes occurs when there is loss of inhibition in the case of cerebral tumours, general paralysis of the insane, and similar diseases. Patients showing extravagant sexual behaviour, sometimes accompanied by heavy drinking, should be suspected at once and sub-jected to a thorough investigation.

It is a good rule in treating psychosexual diseases that if one is not entirely happy regarding the physical condition one should, as in other types of medicine, enlist the help of a specialist in endocrinology, a neurologist and so on, but even that will not always be accepted as an excuse if something hidden appears during treatment.

A simple point regarding the physical side which one would regard as self-evident yet is often neglected. This is the examination of the sexual organs themselves. It is true that in the vast majority of cases nothing is found, but in a certain number one does discover something of importance. For example, I have seen in one week two young men who complained of inability to perform the sexual act. One had an excessively long foreskin which when rolled back produced such a cincture as to prevent penetration. The other had such a tight foreskin that it would not retract at all, in fact the opening was almost a pin-hole. Obviously neither of these men could have normal intercourse and needed circumcision. They had both seen physicians without benefit. The repeated failure of intercourse was already producing neurotic symptoms and in time would produce a sexual neurosis. Naturally where the fault may be in the woman a proper gynaecological examination should be performed.

Preliminary Investigation

Before one considers attacking a sexual abnormality it is a wise thing to give the patient a thorough psychological investigation. No doubt everything one can discover by questioning could be obtained by analytical psychotherapy, but that information may be a long time coming to the surface. Many sexual abnormalities are of recent orgin and follow some psychical traumatic event. I have known young men become impotent after hearing exaggerated accounts of the horrors of venereal disease, after being discovered having intercourse in compromising positions, &c. Again, I have known of young men who became homosexual after catching gonorrhoea, or after similar disasters. The psychopathologist will no doubt insist that these minor traumata should not have produced this result had the patient not been in a state to respond in this way. Probably this is true, but it does not alter the fact that many of these cases are easily treated and will readily respond if approached in the right way. If the particular causal trauma is thoroughly investigated, and the patient is encouraged fully to describe everything which happened and so rid his mind of the fear which filled it at the time, it is easy to give him enough strong suggestion so that he is able to go off and attain at least partial success, and this partial success can be utilized to prove that there is nothing much wrong with him and so lead him back once more to the path of sexual health. If this is neglected, abnormal habits are allowed to become fixed, the patient becomes a million times more difficult to treat, and his chances of successfully attaining normality are greatly jeopardized.

Apart from the actual traumatic incident, if such a one exists, it is wise to note the family history. This gives one some idea of his background as well as mental and physical make-up. It is possible that the strength of the sexual instinct is inherited, or depends on inherited factors, so that one can judge something of this by the forebears. Neurosis, alcoholism, suicide, and the like in the parents may all throw light on the patient. The religious, social, and intellectual background is of importance, and may give a clue to the basis of the patient's illness.

What the patient consciously remembers of his sexual development is also of supreme value in the examination. One should try to determine the date of onset of his sexual impulse and its nature: whether he was introduced to sexual matters by others and in what manner. The sexual manifestations in youth, and the first introduction to heterosexuality should be noted. Finally his adult sexual life, and his emotional reactions to it, should be elicited. Not only does such a history throw a light on the conscious responses but often, to an experienced worker, shows the unconscious reactions also. One can see the effect of the background of the young man who has never taken a girl out because his father does not approve, the youth who is emotionally bound to his mother, the girl who has been so terrified by the consequences of sex that she is afraid to allow herself to be kissed, and so on.

Apart from the very valuable information obtained in this way such an investigation is essential since it gives the patient a feeling that here, at last, is not someone to condemn him as a monster, but who is willing to listen to his difficulties and understand them. Often the problems are much less than he has imagined and even the most difficult cases are helped by wise understanding.

METHODS OF TREATMENT

The psychotherapist has at his command eight methods of treatment. These are:

1. Explanation and education.
2. Manipulation of environment.
3. Suggestion (which includes hypnosis, persuasion, and progressive muscular relaxation).
4. Superficial analysis.
5. Deep transference analysis.
6. Conditioning (including aversion therapy by drugs, or electric shock).
7. Medicinal treatment.
8. Sublimation.

Explanation and Education

In most branches of medical knowledge the public lags behind, and this is particularly so with regard to sex. Probably the gap is wider in sexual knowledge because of the difficulty in obtaining proper books. Sexology is the quacks' delight, so that not only is there ignorance but deliberate perpetration of untruths. For example, many books devoted to the alleged cultivation of health and strength advertise courses of exercises to prevent masturbation, 'night losses', and to cure poor erections and premature ejaculations. This we know from physiology to be utter nonsense, yet the poor unhappy wretch who thinks that he is ill because he has an occasional nocturnal emission (and is too fearful to consult anyone about it) pays his guineas for a useless set of contortions which can achieve nothing. Let it not be thought that this is a solitary example—such young men exist in thousands. Again, many books written by the unqualified, often with a hypocritical religious veneer, lay down the law for young married people. These seem often to be produced by those who are sexually abnormal themselves, and convey all manner of wrong information. Sometimes, even, one encounters patients who have been misinformed by those who should know better. For example, I once saw a young woman who had recently married. She was complaining of various anxiety symptoms for which she had consulted her general practitioner, who had, incidentally, a local reputation for gynaecology. He had asked her regarding the frequency of intercourse with her husband and she had told him this occurred once nightly. This is, of course, well within the bounds of normality. Yet she was told that it was too frequent and her symptoms were due to excess. On investigation it was found that she had been in love with another man shortly before her marriage and had taken her present husband *faute de mieux*. The other man had since written (after which her anxiety symptoms commenced) and this had thrown her mind in a turmoil. The nature of her symptoms were explained to her, she was given a sedative, and told to live a normal life. The symptoms disappeared and troubled her no more.

It is mainly regarding masturbation and the frequency of normal intercourse that most people are ignorant, but some people need education regarding birth control. I have seen a couple who had been 'married' for twenty years, but the husband had never penetrated his wife because she was 'delicate' and an invalid who could not have children. He had masturbated himself between her thighs, all this long time, whenever he sought sexual relief. There is little wonder that finally he developed depression.

Manipulation of the Environment

This is very important since a careful examination of the case will sometimes show that there is some obvious factor which is preventing normal sexual outlets. I have seen, for instance, cases of exhibitionism in which the man has behaved in this manner because he has been brought up to the idea that normal sexuality was prohibited. In fact, this prohibition of sexuality which so many parents think will safeguard the boy is often the cause of the young man becoming abnormal in later life. It is necessary to break down such confining ideas and encourage a normal life. The mother, by over-protection, often cramps a young man from normal outlets and her influence must be broken. This is frequently not difficult and the young man will be only too glad to receive sufficient support to follow the inclinations which have been prohibited. I have seen young men drifting into homosexuality because they have felt that a normal life was barred to them, owing to the wrong ideas which had been instilled into their minds. This does not mean, of course, that I have encouraged such young people to frequent brothels and seek prostitutes. This would be bad practice and wholly unwarranted. It is enough to persuade the young that when the bird grows its wings it should fly from the nest; that dances, ice-skating, hiking, and social activities of every sort are consciously or unconsciously designed by society so that young people can meet their potential mates. In social concourse between young people there is often considerable harmless sexual relief—as, for instance, in dancing—and the pliable mind orientated into the right channels.

Again, I feel strongly that it is a most important part of treatment to break up the environment which every homosexual tends to build around himself. The association with other homosexuals, the use of the language of abnormal people (many people do not realize that these patients have a strange jargon in which perverts are 'queers', lavatories are 'cottages', &c.), the use of restaurants, public houses, and similar places used by others suffering from the same illness, all these must be abandoned and a normal environment with constant mixing with healthy people of both sexes substituted for them.

It is obviously unwise for the exhibitionist to frequent the environment where he has misbehaved previously, at least until psychotherapy has solved his difficulties and released the driving force of his perversion.

Suggestion

With the invention of analytical psychotherapy suggestion tended to fall into disuse. It had always smacked somewhat of quackery and it was felt that 'anyone could do it'. If the suggestion of a bottle of medicine failed, of what value was hypnosis? This is, of course, a wrong idea, and if we abandon suggestion we tend to lose a very valuable mode of treatment. It might reasonably be asked, therefore, what type of case should yield to suggestion? Many of the older writers considered that serious

sexual abnormalities responded to suggestive treatment, and Milne
Bramwell and others did not flinch from the gravest perversions. It is
doubtful, however, whether such a severe illness as homosexuality would
often respond (in spite of Bramwell's successful case), but cases of mild
impotence, caused by fear, such as frequently follow being surprised
when having illicit intercourse, and so on, are often easily cured. Owing to
lack of interest in hypnosis at the present time I have had to go back over
sixty years to find a suitable case for demonstration here. It was recorded
by Milne Bramwell.

Case No. 49. In one still more striking case, sent to me by Sir Victor Horsley,
on October 31st, 1903, the patient's sexual instincts from earliest boyhood had
been homosexual and unnatural sexual connexion had frequently taken place.
He married hoping that this might cure him, but when I saw him there was
complete impotence as far as his wife and any other woman was concerned,
during the whole of his life. The attraction of his own sex was a veritable
obsession, while the idea of touching his wife was as repugnant as the idea of
touching his sister. After prolonged treatment by suggestion, he entirely got
rid of his morbid ideas and his sexual relations with his wife became normal.

This is a truly remarkable case, and by suggestion Bramwell seems to
have done everything a modern analyst could have done. The patient was
a lifelong homosexual (the most difficult type), he was one who had
practised it frequently (again the most obstinate sort), and he was impotent (also a crippling complication). Yet in spite of all these obstacles
Bramwell cured him and he became normal.

This is by no means an isolated case. Other hypnotists give a number
of instances of treatment of psychosexual disease which has been successful. It is not in the treatment of severe sexual abnormalities, however,
that I have found suggestion to be of value, but in minor cases such as
sexual hypoversion in the newly married.

As I have pointed out one often comes upon a case of a young man
who has been warned of the supposed grave consequences of masturbation,
or who has caught gonorrhoea in the past and has been told that it produces impotence. This young man marries and finds that through anxiety
he has impaired potence. In such cases to discuss the matter with him and
unearth the cause of his condition will often do a great deal to help him.
If this is followed up by the strong suggestion that he will be successful,
it will frequently do a great deal to bring about the desired result. The
man has produced the vicious circle that through previous events he may
be impotent. This fear—as all fear—tends to weaken his sexual feelings,
and does make him sexually averse or hypoverse. This makes him dread
that his worst fears are true. He becomes more and more anxious and less
and less potent. Once he has been induced to have normal intercourse and
has had sensory proof that he has nothing to fear he will be normal for the

rest of his life. No doubt the enthusiastic analyst could discover a castration complex (as no doubt everyone's appendix has been inflamed at times) and possibly, if he could afford it, such a man might benefit from five years' treatment, but from the point of view of practical therapeutics such is unnecessary and wearisome for both patient and physician. From the Freudian point of view we all have castration complexes, just as we have appendixes, but it is only when they become grossly inflamed that they need to be cut out, and to excise every appendix which gives a twinge of pain is as rash as to over-treat a complex.

Hypnosis can also be used to elicit unconscious material, using a combination of it with analysis. I cannot say that I find this very satisfactory except for rare solitary traumatic events such as one found in war neurosis, and these have little or no relation to the perversions and other sexual abnormalities. It can be used, also, to recover the memory in fugue states which are not uncommon after broken homosexual love affairs.

Narco-analysis, which is closely related to hypnosis, since the somnolent state is induced by sedatives instead of suggestion, is similarly useful for unearthing solitary traumatic memories, and clearing up fugue states, but it has little or no value in the treatment of sexual abnormalities which have been induced through a multitude of minor irregularities in the course of development, and by continuous environmental pressure.

Frequently waking suggestion, combined with education and explanation, is enough and no attempt need be made to use the deeper forms of suggestion with sleep so favoured by the older psychotherapists. Probably a great deal of the technique to induce such sleep-states has fallen into abeyance, and it is for that reason we do not achieve such successful results as Bramwell. Nevertheless we have a very potent weapon in analysis.

Progress Muscular Relaxation

This was first developed by Wolpe, and is based on the idea of reducing the effects of the sympathetic autonomic nervous system which is causing the manifestations of anxiety, and consequently the sexual symptoms such as impotence. This is done by increasing the parasympathetic activity.

Treatment is performed in a darkened room; the patient lying on a couch or sitting in an armchair. He is instructed to close his eyes and relax his toes, his legs, arms, &c. Instructions are given in a drowsy voice; after a time he feels more peaceful, his pulse becomes slower, and he is generally more tranquil.

The next move is for him to relax in bed with his partner who excites him sexually. He should not attempt intercourse until he is able to sustain a strong erection and feels sufficiently undisturbed to have a reasonable chance of success.

It is obvious that this method is closely related to hypnosis and probably the successes claimed by it could be induced just as easily by hypnotizing the patient and making suitable suggestions. This being so it is obvious that it will be most efficacious with conditions such as sexual aversion which are likely to respond to suggestion.

It is not much more than reassurance in some cases, as when larger and larger bougies are inserted into the vagina with the encouragement that they will not cause pain.

How far all this is to be regarded as reciprocal inhibition or simple deconditioning remains a matter of opinion. Nor is it of importance if the patient is able to respond and improve.

Superficial Analysis

If the case is too severe for suggestion, the next method of attack is analytical psychotherapy. This does not necessarily mean that one must embark on a full-length Freudian psycho-analysis. It is worth while to try either a superficial technique with considerable interpretation and explanation for a few weeks, or else to utilize Groddeck's or Hadfield's elaboration of Freud's original cathartic analysis. In this the patient is put to rest on a couch in a quiet room in semi-darkness and asked to associate on his symptoms. A train of thought is thus started which brings up one traumatic incident after another, and it is often possible to drive, as it were, a shaft into the deeper strata of his mind, and to bring out the causal emotion without excavating the whole area of his emotional life. This method is more likely to be successful with those who suffer from isolated symptoms like the milder forms of sexual aversion, or fetishism, rather than a fully developed condition such as homosexuality or sado-masochism. There is little doubt that it can be used very successfully to eliminate such symptoms as fetishes, but it does not (and probably no one would claim that it does) eliminate the whole of the emotional abnormalities as those which frequently occur in impotence when the patient is not only sexually impotent but his whole life is a reflection of his abnormal sexuality, and one complete or partial failure.

The advantage of this method is that, being more directed and concentrated, it tends to produce quicker results as far as the actual symptoms are concerned so that fetishes, for example, may respond rapidly to it. The disadvantage is that profound character changes which occur with transference type of treatment cannot be expected. This is not to say that changes in the personality do not occur—obviously they do— but there is no fundamental personality change such as the Freudians can justly lay claim to. Moreover one of the greatest difficulties is that, at least in my hands, by making too abrupt an attack on the resistances, it stirs up terrific barriers and transference. This almost inevitably leads to a slackening of the technique, which must then follow different lines. Again, in superficial analysis there is little regard paid to the transference, and this easily accumulates so that there is great hostility to the physician, or else the patient becomes suicidally depressed. The physician is then forced to start interpretation of the transference, lest the analysis ceases abruptly, and the cathartic analysis changes into the more passive transference type.

With regard to deep transference analysis, it is impossible for the complications of this method to be discussed here at length, but since there are gross misconceptions regarding this form of treatment it may be worth while to write a short account of it.

Deep Transference Analysis

As in more superficial methods it is usual to have the patient lying on a couch in a darkened room: this is not for any reason of hocus-pocus, but because he is able to allow thoughts to enter his mind if he is in a state of relaxation and undisturbed by external stimuli. He is asked to speak of anything which enters his mind, and usually does so by expressing hostility to some relative or person with whom he has made contact. He releases emotion, and after a shorter or longer period comes to a full stop. On the contrary, he may never start and be unable to say a word from the beginning. Whether he cannot speak from the first, or comes to a disjunction, it is obvious that he cannot have exhausted his thoughts. A human being can do only three things: think, or feel, or move, as Wundt pointed out long ago. If he is lying still on a couch he is not moving to the exclusion of thought. He insists that he can think of nothing. *Therefore he must be feeling.* This is explained to him and he is asked to say what he feels. It is invariably found that he is thinking of the doctor but sometimes this is not directly observable. He may say 'I feel as I used to feel when in the headmaster's study at school, when I was to be punished', or 'My father was a colonel in the Army, I never liked him, and I couldn't say anything to him when he came home', and something of the sort. It is then explained to him that only he and the analyst are in the room. If he feels something like this it must be because he is transferring emotion which he has felt previously to someone else on to the analyst. Caught in the web of such relentless logic he is forced to accept the explanation (which, indeed, is the true one), and is often silent for a few minutes. The analyst must, as a principle, never intrude, and sits quietly waiting for the interpretation to take effect. After a while it does so and the patient, being freed from his emotional barrier, bursts out with the expression of what he feels—usually regarding the offending schoolmaster (father-surrogate), or father himself. He then continues talking, perhaps for a session or two, until the same emotional situation recurs. The barriers are again removed in the same way and the analysis continues. It must not be thought that emotional barriers are only negative—sometimes affection and love come into play also, and these are traced back by exactly the same method. The emotion, which is known as the transference, is derived from the emotion which he has released in his talking and displaced on to the analyst. He is using him as a substitute for the person he hates or loves, just as the angry business man in kicking the office cat is using it as a substitute for the typist whose error has cost him a business deal. Often the way the patient shows this transference is most subtle. He may say: 'I feel you are bored with what I have been telling you.' This obviously means that he feels the doctor is hostile to him. He should be asked who it was in the past who seemed bored with him and the emotion traced to its source. He may say: 'My father used to get bored when I asked him questions, &c.' *Transference must in every situation be traced to its origin.* It is obvious that in every case it is not so simple as this, but such a crude example gives some idea of the process.

The question may be asked why such transference appears. This can be answered simply enough. Firstly, what we feel towards anything depends to a large extent on what we have felt towards similar things in the past. The first people the patient has experienced have been his father or mother (or surrogates) so that what he feels towards other people —including the analyst—will depend on these former relationships. Again, no animal makes a sound unless it feels emotion. No bird sings, no animal growls or whines, unless moved by love or fear or hate. Human beings, in their cunning, have elaborated these emotional sounds into language but they remain, however, disguised as a conveyance of feeling. In ordinary speech there is usually not much emotion released and this is broken by the ebb and flow of conversation (although to the careful listener it is still there). In analysis nothing is done to hinder its appearance and sooner or later it accumulates. The method of interpretation used here is not quite that used by the orthodox Freudian but it is so simple, so scientific, and so uninfluenced by the personality of the analyst that it is to be recommended. All that is needed when a blockage of speech occurs is that the analyst examines what the patient feels and asks where before such a feeling occurred. The emotion can then be referred back. Obviously one never accepts the patient's statement that he has never felt this emotion previously—he must have felt it before. Insistence will always succeed in finding its origin.

It is this breaking down of transference which forms the whole technique of deep analytical psychotherapy, and a good psychotherapist should never interfere with thought processes other than when necessary to dissolve transference. By correct use of this technique it is possible to bring up earlier and earlier memories which may appear in the form of fantasies. For instance, a patient does not show hostility to, let us say, the breast in a simple statement, 'I want to hit my mother (or my mother's breast)'; instead he has fantasies of chopping off door-knobs or something similar. Slowly he gathers an inkling as to the meaning of the fantasy, and finally expresses his emotion with the basic ideas as such. It is obvious that by this method one can help the patient, without influencing other than the transference, to 'work through' the whole of his affective history and relive the emotional episodes which have determined his behaviour. Indeed, in a successful analysis, he may gnash his teeth and scream at something which happened years previously.

This release of emotion is, of course, the basis of cure, but whenever it is brought to consciousness it produces transference. The secret of analysis is a constant vigil to discover and resolve it by pressing the patient to unearth its source.

There is one form of response which seems to puzzle some who analyse psychosexually abnormal patients, and that is their tendency to become depressed. Now the aggressive and hostile emotions which are repressed in these cases are often very violent, which makes them more akin to psychotics than neurotics.

The cause of depression in such patients is that the transference may not be on to the analyst, *but the emotion directed on to the patient, himself.* This means that he hates himself, and hate directed on to oneself is the basis of depression. The patient may become more and more depressed and, unless this is dealt with energetically, he may become suicidal or the analyst become frightened and stop treatment.

The way I have always found successful in such cases is to treat this reversed transference in exactly the same way as emotion displaced on to the analyst. It should be brought to the patient's attention that he is depressed because he is hating himself, but that the person he really hates is his father, mother, or whoever it is. If he has suicidal fantasies they should be turned back by telling him that the throat he wishes to cut is not his own but his father's &c. Often the patient can realize, without assistance, that this is so, but where he is depressed one may need to point it out.

This may sound extravagant, but I have always found that it succeeds, unless one has chosen a psychotic patient. If one has been unwise enough to try to treat a psychotic in this way—and I have attempted a number in the past—one finds that the problem is not that he is inaccessible, but that one cannot control the transference: he either attacks one or else becomes suicidal. It is easy, however, to detect the unsuitable cases either before one starts or after a session or two. Psychotic homosexuals, or other paraphiliacs, should be avoided for this reason.

DD—PSY. D.

It is just as dangerous in another direction to allow hostile transference to accumulate on to the psychotherapist as it is to permit its reversal on to the patient. The moment he expresses, no matter how obliquely or guardedly, hostility to the analyst its origin should be discovered, and it should be dissolved. Failure to do this may, in some cases, cause the patient to break off treatment, or even lead to a personal assault although this is unlikely except in the pre-psychotic or psychotic.

Naturally, in some cases where strong hostile emotion has been released it may take a session or two to dispel completely the transferred affect. One should always be observant in any case where aggression or depression appears to be building up, and the moment it is observed resolve it as I have suggested. It is unwise to waste time once one is sure what has happened; since the patient will be out of one's view for the interval until the next session; if he is allowed to go away depressed he may become worse and disasters can happen.

I would strongly recommend this technique to those, even if experienced in analysing neurotics, who are unfamiliar with paraphilia, and can point to my own freedom from patients who have committed suicide by its use.

It can be seen that, correctly used, this method is essentially scientifically sound but is not in every detail the orthodox Freudian one, although it approximates to it in most respects. The Freudian doctrine that the analyst should maintain silence and help the patient to talk by destroying the accumulating transference is essential; but I do not feel that it must become an unalterable dogma. Those interested in the purely orthodox psycho-analytic technique should consult the classical works of Glover and Forsyth, or the valuable books by Charles Berg, *Clinical Psychology* and *Deep Analysis*, or the many scattered papers in the *International Journal of Psycho-analysis*.

In spite of certain inherent difficulties and frailties, the deep transference analysis is the sheet-anchor of treatment of the perversions and sexual aberrations. It is necessary to point out, however, that such mental surgery, like physical incision, is not a method without danger in unskilled hands, and if wrongly handled the patient may react in unexpected ways—e.g. a patient who responded well under me had been under a clergyman who practised 'analysis' on him with the result that he (the patient) made two attempts to commit suicide. It stands to reason that the analyst, himself, should be a stable person, preferably one who has had a personal analysis—not for treatment but for didactic reasons—since for some reasons, perhaps because psychiatry attracts unstable persons, unsuitable analysts frequently take their own lives.

There are two schools of thought regarding the treatment of the sexual aberrations. Some analysts attempt to produce complete mental change by release of libido and do not allow the patient to have sexual intercourse until they feel convinced that he or she is completely heterosexual and freed from fixations and regressions. There is another school which believes that the patient should attempt sexual intercourse as soon as he feels capable and should keep on trying if his efforts are only partially successful or even fail. I have had successes with both methods. I feel, however, that cure is likely to be hastened if the patient has partial success but retarded if he fails completely, so that the wise psychotherapist awaits the proper time before encouraging him to try his luck. In any case it is a good thing for the patient to press in the direction of normality as far as he can as long as he avoids the distress of complete failure.

It is important that the analyst does not take too passive a role indefinitely in such cases. I can easily remember a number of cases where a patient has been treated for some time (two for three years or more) under another psychiatrist and appeared to make no progress. Pressed by me to make friends with the opposite sex he had done so, found that he was potent, and in a month or two made more progress than he had done in the preceeding two years. Once the analyst has found that the patient has made sufficient progress he must press him to more active behaviour or he may find that treatment has come to a standstill because he enjoys the state of being nursed along by the therapist, or fears to make the plunge into heterosexuality.

I have developed a technique of accelerating and accentuating the effect of deep analysis by making it wish-fulfilling. This is done by allowing the patient not only to say what he wishes in the consulting-room but to do anything he wants to do also. This means that the fetishist is allowed to wrap himself in his mackintosh, the transvestist puts on his female clothes, the exhibitionist lies naked on the couch, and so on. This obviously has its limitations, since one could hardly allow a sadist to turn one's consulting-room into a slaughter-house, but this has never—so far —been required! On the other hand, to allow the patient to have freedom in this manner brings up a terrific flood of emotion which accelerates the treatment to a surprising degree. The analyst need have no fear that he is likely to have any actual attack on his person if he adopts this technique— in fact it is a good plan to encourage the patient to show his hostility to the analyst, since he will never put his emotions into serious action if this is done. For example, a patient felt at times that he wished to attack me. He was encouraged to do so and gave me a gentle tap on the jaw (as a token) and then hit the arm of the chair a savage blow. Another sadistic patient who, elaborating in fantasy what he would like to do to me, was striding about the room in his excitement and accidentally tripped over my foot. At once he said: 'Oh, I am sorry, have I hurt you?' He was evidently full of alarm. It is important in using such technique that the emotion is used to carry the analysis forward and the patient is not allowed to use the sessions merely as a means of obtaining his sexual pleasure in a symbolic way—but this has never happened in my practice. It can be done only by proper arrangement of the intense transference which is aroused by this method.

Some psychiatrists are enthusiastic regarding group therapy and appear to use it very successfully, but not many statistics have been published. Kopp, for example, states; 'I believe that group therapy is often the treatment of choice for sex offenders. Most of them have kept the secret of their sexual behaviour from others for a long time, and it is tremendously helpful for them to share them with others in the same position. It is only after a while that each member reveals he has chosen some other offender's act as representing a worse crime than he himself has committed. It is particularly helpful to assemble a group which includes consonant and dissonant types of character for each offence. They are wonderfully sensitive to the underlying hypocrisy of the opposite type. Because of this group resistance is minimized and one is never without auxiliary therapists.'

No doubt, as in other forms of psychotherapy, success depends a great deal on the experience and personality of the psychiatrist and his skill in managing the group.

The treatment of homosexuals by this means is outside my experience. However, no doubt some of the timid shy types may be responsive to it, although little has been published on this form of treatment in such cases. One tends to see only the failures. The criticism which can be made from them is that there must inevitably be passivity on the part of the therapist in charge of the group. The patient seems sometimes to drift along without making proper efforts to contact girls. One such case treated by me had been attending a clinic for two and a half years without any change. After three sessions of more active psychotherapy he found an attractive girl and had normal relations with her. This was enjoyable and he lost his interest in men, wondering why this had never happened before.

Conditioning

There is no doubt that this is very important in the treatment of sexual aberrations, since the pervert frequently surrounds himself with others who are abnormal and rarely tries to live a normal life mixing with people who are heterosexual. It is essential, therefore, that the first step to cure those suffering from abnormal sexuality is to wean the patient from his abnormal friends. The average homosexual, for instance, surrounds himself with a circle of homosexual friends who tend by their talk and behaviour to condition him to homosexuality. He should, on the contrary, if treatment is to be a success, be encouraged to attend dances, to mix with women as a man, and to form friendships with men of a masculine type as an equal. If he will indulge in manly sports and pastimes so much the better. This is particularly important when the patient is young. The young man who is somewhat abnormal will often adjust himself to heterosexuality by living in a normal environment, and the great difficulty in curing the confirmed pervert is that he has built up an unhealthy world from which he refuses to be freed. It must be appreciated that a great deal of homosexuality is in itself due to conditioning. Anal intercourse, for instance, does not come freely to the passive party and is produced by prolonged experience. Many homosexuals have said that they could not permit it because of the pain produced and have never submitted to such conditioning. If a thing can be produced by conditioning, surely it can be helped to be removed by the same methods? In any case to persuade a man who is abnormal to behave as normally as possible can do little harm, even if it does no good, and there is every reason to believe that it is beneficial. Similarly, although perhaps not quite by the same method one can use as an adjunct to psychological treatment, the fetishist can be persuaded to adopt conditioning. The fetish can be diminished as a mode of attraction so that the man who cannot have intercourse except with a woman in a certain garb &c., can slowly reduce his fetish by his sexual partner using it less and less. Every indulgence in a perversion, fetishism, or other abnormality tends to 'stamp it in', whereas every normal intercourse tends to reduce its dominion over the mind.

A form of conditioning which has claimed to be successful is a form of aversion therapy. This has, of course, been used for some years in conditions such as alcoholism, but not for sexual abnormalities. It was first reported in a Czech journal in 1953 by Srnec and Freund. They describe the treatment of male homosexuals conditioned by the following means. The patient was given coffee or tea with emetine, and then, ten minutes later, given injections of a mixture of emetine, apomorphine, pilocarpine, and ephedrine. He was shown films and slides of men dressed up in bathing suits and in the nude. A quarter of an hour after the beginning of the session he felt unwell and started to vomit. In the second phase he was shown films in which women appeared in situations likely to rouse the sexual appetite in normal men. This was done before bedtime and he was given an injection of 50 mg. of testosterone. This was repeated five to ten times.

The results were excellent. Twenty-five persons went through the entire procedure and of these 10 achieved predominant heterosexuality, 3 adapted in such a way that their homosexual activity receded almost entirely with insignificant heterosexual activity. In the remaining 12 the condition remained exactly as before. Four of the patients who had turned predominantly heterosexual relapsed, and of these two had a further course and regained heterosexuality. The third attended one more session and disappeared. The fourth remained relapsed and made no further effort to be cured. One of the incompletely adapted patients relapsed and refused to repeat the treatment. In four of the twelve who showed no change at the completion of the procedure there had been an improvement at the beginning, but later relapsed so it was felt that it had had some therapeutic effect.

This work was repeated by Raymond in 1956. The case was that of a married man, aged 33, who had been in trouble with the police twelve times for damaging perambulators. He had been in mental hospitals twice and had been repeatedly fined for malicious damage. The urge to damage perambulators had arisen at the age of 10 years. In the past he had had psychotherapy which traced the origin of his fetishism to an incident when he knocked a toy boat against a perambulator and caused feminine concern. Another time he felt sexually aroused by his sister's handbag. In spite of these revelations the attacks continued. His family history revealed that his mother had been a paraphrenic who was certified at the age of 54. His father died when he was aged 15 years. He had served in the R.A.F. for ten years and was discharged for his fetishism. At the age of 27 he had married but could have intercourse only with the aid of fantasies of perambulators and handbags. There were two children of the marriage and his wife said he was a good husband.

He was treated by aversion therapy: this was by means of injections of apomorphine two-hourly day and night, and by being kept awake by amphetamine. When he felt nauseated he was shown perambulators, handbags, and pictures of both. No food was given. At the end of a week treatment was suspended; he returned after eight days and reported that he had been able to have intercourse with his wife without the aid of the old fantasies. Treatment was re-commenced with emetine hydrochloride. After five days the mere sight of the objects made him sick. At the end of nine days he begged for the handbags and perambulators to be taken away and sobbed uncontrollably. After six months he had another further course.

Nineteen months later he still had no need of the old fantasies to make him potent, his wife was relieved of the constant worry that he would be in trouble with the police, and the Probation Officer said that he had made noticeable progress. He had been promoted at his work.

This case confirms my view that there is no danger of releasing homosexuality or sadism, which East and Hubert thought was one of the hazards of treating fetishism.

In 1960 Freund reported further cases treated in this way and found that success depended, as one might have expected, on how much the patient sought help voluntarily.

James recorded a homosexual successfully treated by aversion therapy in 1962, but it had been followed up only for 20 weeks.

Coates quoted a case, communicated to him privately by Stead and Cohen, of a 'dummy fetishist' who improved, but apparently needed considerable psychotherapy and behaviour therapy as well.

Raymond and O'Keefe have recorded a case of a man who suffered from what they called 'a pin-up fetishism'. The patient, a married man, had the compulsion to cut out pictures of nude or semi-nude girls from newspapers or magazines in order to secret them under carpets. He was treated by the injection of apomorphine gr. 1/20 twice a day for 2 weeks and shown pictures of semi-clad girls just before the vomiting commenced. He reported himself cured from his fetishes 2 years later and had had no relapses.

The disadvantages of apomorphine aversion are that the unpleasantness of the nausea can discourage a patient from continuing treatment; moreover, since some people show idiosyncrasy to it there is slight danger. This has led psychiatrists to seek a better method.

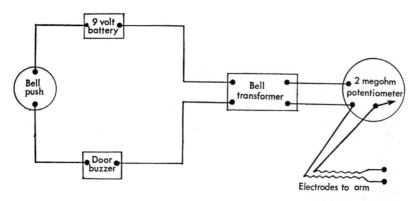

Wiring for apparatus used by McGuire and Vallance for aversion therapy by electric shock

The circuit consists of a buzzer which interrupts a circuit from the battery through a switch and transformer. In this way the D.C. voltage (9 volts) provides an A.C. current which is then stepped up by a transformer to provide an A.C. voltage (about 70 volts). Components are: (1) One push-button switch. (2) One 4-8 volt buzzer (miniature type). (3) One small transformer (about 50:1 ratio). (4) One grid-bias battery (9 volts). (5) One potentiometer (2 megohms, log track). (6) One knob for above. (7) One box as container. (8) One armband with electrodes.

In 1963 Blakemore and his colleagues gave a faradic current to a man suffering from transvestism. He dressed and undressed in female clothes 400 times in 6 days, and at the same time was given electric shocks from an electric grid in the floor. He lost his symptoms and remained well for a year, except for a relapse on one occasion. This appears a success since the man had had psychotherapy for 6 years previously without any effect on his abnormality.

In 1964 McGuire and Vallance described a very suitable technique. They used an electric shock from a simple apparatus which is under the control of the patient. This was given when he was immersed in fantasies and saved the wearisome activities of Blakemore's method.

In the cases described by McGuire and Vallance, amongst others, were 14 who were sexually abnormal. Three abandoned treatment, 1 showed mild improvement, 4 good improvement and 6 lost their symptoms. There were 6 homosexuals (3 of whom were those who discontinued), 3 compulsive masturbators, 2 transvestists, 1 sadist, 1 fetishist, and 1 who interfered with children.

The treatment was not very prolonged and appears to have consisted of three sessions daily for a few weeks, and then the patient was allowed to take the apparatus home and continue treatment himself. Success, even if in only 50 per cent. of cases, is very valuable; and, the fact that the patient can treat himself, saves both his own and the psychiatrist's time.

MacCulloch and Feldman treated 32 homosexual patients by faradic aversion and found that a follow-up from 3 months to $2\frac{1}{2}$ years showed that one half were actively heterosexual, and a further sixth were utilizing only homosexual fantasy instead of active intercourse.

In a further communication they recorded the treatment of 43 homosexual patients by faradic aversion therapy. This series had a minimum follow-up for a year. The authors pointed out that the best previously recorded statistics showed under 25 per cent. recovery. In their new series of 45 patients, 36 completed treatment and of these 25 were significantly improved (14 Kinsey 0, 9 Kinsey 1, and 2 Kinsey 2). This figure (58 per cent.) is unusually successful and according to the authors was partly due to learning techniques which were used.

Marks and Gelder made a careful study of two fetishists and three transvestists who were treated with success by electrical aversion therapy. They noted that fairly specific changes occurred in these selected patients. Fantasy images of deviant behaviour were first suppressed and then partially extinguished as aversion proceeded. Deviant images became indistinct and transient, lost their pleasurable quality, and ceased to be accompanied by erections. Images which were not shocked did not show these changes.

The discovery of Srnec and Freund that homosexuality responds to aversion therapy and its elaboration by Blakemore and his colleagues makes it possible to treat obstinate cases which would otherwise have to be abandoned as hopeless. It is, moreover, suitable for clinics and even in prison if nursing facilities are available. In prison, no doubt, it would best be given shortly before the patient's discharge so that he could be normal on release and reinforce his normality by ordinary sexual relations.

Apart from frank perversions there are often what may be called postural sexual habits in intercourse which frequently occur through mild abnormality in one of the partners. These may vary from some slight deviation from the usual positions to the most grotesque postures. No doubt these habits are sometimes established in the lesser degree because one or both of the partners obtain more pleasure or success in intercourse in some special posture when in a state of worry or fatigue. The more bizarre positions usually are indicative of some unconscious abnormality and even of a frank perversion. It is, to my mind, a *sine qua non* of treatment that the patient should be encouraged to establish a normal habit as far as possible. Not because the more usual posture has any particular virtue in itself, but that if one is attempting to direct a patient into the paths of normality the sexual posture is of great importance psychologically. It is, moreover, as the patient becomes more and more normal, conducive to greater pleasure and success. The establishment of a more normal posture can often be produced by encouraging the patient to penetrate and then indulge in 'love play' while in the normal position. This results in an increase of sexual excitement which may terminate in intercourse in the ventro-ventral position. It may even occur if one of the partners is very abnormal. The effect is as though a wave of sexual excitement carried him or her past the obstruction, and naturally the more frequently this occurs and the more the resulting pleasure the easier it is attained. When there is lack of erection such a method is not applicable, but even in such cases the conjunction of the sexual organs without penetration may result in erection and penetration which finally produces the wave of excitement which I have described above. It is probable that patients will not succeed in attaining this alone, but it is, in my experience, a valuable adjunct in the treatment of these cases and a method of reconditioning patients which should not be rejected.

The alteration of environment acts in a similar way and can be of tremendous importance. The abandonment of the protection of the doting mother and the pampering of home will often lead to an increase of sexuality and independence in the man (or girl) with an increase in the capacity for normal sexual feeling. There is always a resistance to any such course, but it is often necessary. The breaking of the abnormal world, which everybody suffering from sexual abnormality creates, is essential. The impotent man is too often unconsciously enjoying the humiliation of his position produced by a nagging wife. The frigid woman is deriving pleasure from the exasperation of her husband when she provokes him to quarrels which end in him beating her, and so on. Often the partner is sensible enough to understand the position and do his or

her part in correcting the environment. In those cases, where the partner
is not understanding, it is useless to suggest divorce as a method of cure,
since the new partner will behave in exactly the same way as the old. The
partner in marriage must be educated as to how to behave in order to
help the patient and actively assist in the cure. It is obvious that every
necessary adjustment to the environment cannot be suggested here, but
the therapist must keep careful observation and advise where necessary.

Medicinal Treatment

The medicinal treatment of sexual abnormalities is not very helpful
except as an ancillary. No specific treatment by drugs is known except in
such cases as impotence due to endocrine insufficiency. It is bad medicine
and useless to give endocrine preparations to every case of hypoversion
without determining its basis (yet I have seen over many years two or
three cases of loss of erection a week and all have been pumped with
testosterone propionte). I have stated previously, however, that every
case should be examined physically to determine the absence of proper
endocrine stimulation, and if hormone abnormality is present it must be
treated before psychotherapy is even considered.

Apart from endocrinology medicinal treatment is not very satisfactory.
In cases of excessive sexual desire it has been advocated in the past that
cortical sedatives, such as bromide or phenobarbitone, should be given.
This is reasonable enough until one had a chance to obtain some influence
over the patient, but no patient should be kept drugged indefinitely. Some
psychiatrists suggest that it is a good plan to give a quick-acting sedative,
such as *Nembutal*, in cases of exhibitionism when the patient feels himself
becoming sexual. This may be used but it is more satisfactory to cure
the patient by psychotherapy—which can usually be done.

In sexual hypoversion or aversion a sedative, such as sodium amytal,
should always be used to reinforce the strong suggestion. Where there is
mainly anxiety—such as a man may develop after being disturbed when
having intercourse in inauspicious circumstances—it should be used
alone, or if necessary in conjunction with strychnine. Where the patient
has premature ejaculations it is not useful to give strychnine since this is
sometimes found to accentuate them. There is a logical basis for such
treatment since the sedative, usually phenobarbitone or sodium amytal,
acts on the cortex and removes the anxiety. The strychnine (or yohimbine
preferred by some) acts on the spinal cord and facilitates the reflexes.

Local treatment is said to be of value in premature ejaculations, but in
my experience is not satisfactory except in rare cases to restore confidence.
An ointment containing a harmless analogue of cocaine applied to the
corona of the penis will sometimes delay the ejaculation. A useful ointment for this purpose is *Nupercaine* (made by Ciba products). Such treat-

ment is useless, of course, unless the ejaculation occurs after penetration. An ordinary sheath will usually do just as well and delay ejaculation a reasonable time by diminution of friction. When ejaculation is caused by adjustment of the sheath it should be applied if possible *before* erection. These methods are merely adjuncts and usually useless apart from psychotherapy.

Vasodilators improve the erection and may be used when the patient complains that this is inadequate. This is probably one of the factors when alcohol increases sexuality (apart from the sedative effect on the cortex). A better result, however, is produced by such substances as nicotinyl alcohol (3-pyridylcarbinol) tartrate (*Ronicol*) or tolazoline hydrochloride (*Priscol*). One tablet is sufficient taken before intercourse. The effect of alcohol, a transitory one, can be produced by giving one of the higher alcohols, such as methylpentynol carbamate (*Oblivon-C*). The difficulty of this is, however, that some people find it nauseating and difficult to retain.

It has long been held that cold baths diminish sexuality whereas hot baths tend to increase it. These facts are not usually of great value, but it is reasonable to prescribe a suitable régime in appropriate cases. The application of heat or diathermy to the testicles themselves is not recommended since it has a deleterious effect.

The wise physician does not pin his faith to any one particular line of therapy but uses what he considers necessary. To disregard psychotherapy is to abandon the most valuable form of treatment, but on the other hand, to disregard medicinal treatment is to lose an ally which may turn the scale and make a case successful which would otherwise be a failure.

I do not use appliances other than those necessary for birth control. Some physicians do utilize a 'splint' in cases of impotence. This is a metal support which is fixed along the penis. It can act only by suggestion since a limp penis is unlikely to penetrate properly or receive sufficient friction to behave normally. I have no experience of this method but see no reason why it should not be used if the patient wishes to try it, but probably a case in which it would be successful would be cured just as easily by other means. Loewenstein, who invented this apparatus, has written a number of papers on it and advocates its use in what he describes as the following conditions: (1) primordial impotence; (2) temporary impotence; (3) involutional impotence; (4) ejaculatio praecox; (5) homosexuality; (6) wedding night impotence; and (7) as an alternative to artificial insemination.

Unfortunately he does not give any statistics so it is impossible to judge how successful his appliance is in practice.

However, it is significant that the use of splints has, like all new methods which are not satisfactory, not found general acceptance and has tended to fall into abeyance. It must call for exceptional patience in both the man and the woman and it is not surprising that the tendency has been to abandon it.

Sublimation

The favourite cry of those who regard sexual anomalies from the moral point of view, instead of from the point of view of illness, is that of 'sublimation'. It is as though sublimation is the mystic key which makes the whole of abnormality easy to manage from the physician's position and facile to bear from the patient's. This to my mind is utterly untrue. By sublimation we mean the more or less conscious inhibition of the abnormal sexual object with the substitution of an asexual one in its place. The manifestation of the instinctual force, and the aim, may be altered or retained unchanged (as in hunting as a sadistic outlet). It is worth while examining sublimation and seeing what are its advantages and disadvantages. Firstly its advantages are that it reduces an antisocial force into a social one (even though very unstable), but at the same time allows the sufferer to obtain some sexual pleasure more or less disguised at the same time. We may confidently say that the nature of the force never changes. This leads us to its disadvantages. These are, firstly, that there is always a danger of the sublimation breaking down and the real object being substituted for the asexual one. This frequently occurs, as can be seen when scout-masters and school-teachers become involved in sexual behaviour with young boys who are entrusted into their care. The other disadvantage is that sublimation is always a second best even at its most satisfactory, and the individual obtains little of the pleasure and relief of tension which real outlets bestow. Sublimation is contrary to treatment inasmuch as it leaves the original condition entirely unchanged and the individual suffers from the concomitant disadvantages of it—e.g. the homosexual is still impotent with the opposite sex and the fetishist unthrilled by anything other than his fetish.

There is no doubt that sublimation is useful where the condition is not amenable to treatment, as in some obstinate cases of chronic homosexuality; but in these cases it is advisable to encourage the patient to concentrate, if a male, on dress-designing, interior decorating, and housework, or if a female on acting as a chauffeur, farm-worker, and so on.

It is absolutely wrong, however, to take the view sometimes taken and regard homosexuality as incurable by psychotherapy and to consider sublimation as the first point of attack. Such a 'treatment' leads to dangerously pent-up emotions and lays the patient open to an outbreak of his perversion sooner or later.

I believe that sublimation should be encouraged when other forms of treatment have failed, and that it is very useful only in certain perversions: mainly in homosexuality. One must be doubtful whether deliberately to encourage a sadist to become a butcher is likely to be very successful, nor is it likely to be a kindness to the animals he slaughters. One might feel the same about encouraging such pastimes as hunting in these people, although doubtless from the utilitarian, but not from the ethical, point of view it is better to mangle an animal rather than a human being. It is possible to regard such professions as surgery as a form of sublimation, but if one is to stretch one's net so widely any form of human activity can be included. To my mind this is unreasonable, and only those activities in which there is some close relation between the manifestation and object should be regarded as sublimations.

Sublimation may be regarded as a psychical drug which it is convenient to administer to the incurable, but only to be used as a last resource and then not very reliable. Moreover, in many illnesses (such as fetishisms) it is utterly useless.

It is, perhaps, permissible here to discuss religion although we do not regard this necessarily as a form of sublimation. Religion 'works' from the psychological point of view partly as a sublimation—e.g. the masochist obviously can obtain some satisfaction from helping the poor and wretched; incidentally living in dreary and unhappy surroundings to do so. In addition to this it is also a form of repression—the religion tells the adherent what he may and what he may not do. The psychotherapist has in religion a very valuable aid if he cares to use it and one which should not be scorned, but it is, of course, only a valuable ancillary when the patient is initially religious. Many perverts find it easy to cheat the law but cannot escape their Church. It therefore forms a driving force which tends to impel the patient to come for treatment, and continue it even against the temptations of abnormal inclinations. When the patient is a religious man or woman there is every advantage in co-operation with his spiritual adviser—providing, of course, that this is a sensible and helpful person. If the patient is not religious it is useless to try to force unwelcome views upon him and in any case the psychotherapist should leave his religious beliefs alone—these are the province of his spiritual adviser—and outside medicine, unless they are contrary to normal life, as where a man regards sensuous dreams accompanied by nocturnal emissions as being wicked and sinful. In such cases sound advice can usually be given to him by the priest, particularly if the psychotherapist takes him into his confidence and asks his help.

Various Organic Expedients

There are certain operative measures which we mention mainly to condemn. Firstly, the use of castration. This was used extensively on the

Continent about twenty years ago although it seems to have fallen into disuse now. This was advocated by Naville, Kandou, and Speyer, Kopp, Ley, and others, and is still used in Denmark by Stürup.

The statistics from Denmark, taken uncritically, appear at first sight to be convincing. In the Herstedvester psychopathic prison men convicted of a sexual offence on a child may choose between castration and long imprisonment. It is stated that out of 175 released prisoners 117 had been castrated and 58 had not. Of the former only 5 (4·3 per cent.) were convicted of renewed offences. All of these were homosexuals associating with boys. Of those without castration 25 (42·4 per cent.) were convicted of renewed offences.

One might conclude that there was about ten times the chance of an uncastrated man committing a further offence. However, there are fallacies in such a conclusion. The decision to be castrated is voluntary and no doubt those who ask for it are very different from those who refuse it: indeed *they may be men who would have avoided further misconduct in any case even if they had not been emasculated.* The man who had the determination to serve a long term of imprisonment rather than be castrated is not comparable to the man who submits. The statistics are comparing two entirely different types of men, and are not valid.

It is, perhaps, a little more permissible in trans-sexualism where the patient begs for a physical change. For example, Hertz *et al.* treated 5 cases of transvestism and trans-sexualism in 2 males and 3 females, by hormones and surgery. The two men had the penis, testicles and scrotum removed, and then had oestrogens. The females had the ovaries, tubes, uterus, and breasts removed and were given androgens. From $3\frac{1}{2}$ to 16 years later 3 cases were satisfactory and 1 definitely good. The fifth, a man, was satisfactory until an attempt was made to make an artificial vagina which failed. This produced an attack of depression.

One wonders, however, with such cases whether as satisfactory a result might have been obtained with the use of hormones alone without the mutilating surgery.

Mainly castration is used for chronic antisocial sexual behaviour, such cases as exhibitionists, repeated sexual assailants, and so on. This we feel is morally, ethically, and medically wrong. Certain patients will welcome castration. Some homosexuals ask for it so as to 'be made into a woman'. Masochists look at it with fearful longing. In any case it has a punitive rather than a curative flavour. Many of the recorded successes one feels would have responded to psychotherapy, with the threat of punishment if necessary, rather than a mutilating and terrible operation. In homosexuality it seems probable that it may convert the active and rather more curable type into the passive and less treatable pervert. Castration does not entirely abolish the sexual impulse nor the sexual capacity so there is always the danger of the patient breaking down in the future.

Bremer gives some statistics regarding castration which may be of interest. 'Out of 157 cases: 74 were asexualized shortly after castration; 23 in the course of the first year; 54 (almost one-third) showed a certain sexual interest and reactivity for more than a year, 4 cases were reported for suspected recidivism.' He states, 'Sexual practices which could have been of a criminal nature if committed outside the institution were encountered for a period of 1 to 16 years after castration in 8-10 per cent. of the material'. (One wishes he had been less coy in telling us what exactly was done.)

Moreover, 'In 13 cases potent activity was retained for 1-16 years after castration'. He found that in homosexuals the sexual direction was unchanged and the older the patient the less the effect on the sexual urge.

That it is still considered here as a form of treatment is shown by the following case.

Voluntary Submission to Castration (From our Legal Correspondent)
The Court of Criminal Appeal dismissed on May 11, 1959, an appeal by a young man aged 23, against sentences of imprisonment passed on him for an assault with intent to ravish and for being in possession of an offensive weapon. (*The Times*, May 12, 1959.) The appellant was a psychopath with several convictions for sexual offences.

The Lord Chief Justice stated that there were two possible forms of medical treatment for the appellant, by hormones or by an operation. The Court could not order probation or a reduced prison sentence, conditional on submission to hormone treatment, because such a condition could not be enforced. The alternative treatment was castration, which might be successful, and which the doctors had said was probably the only hope. Counsel for the appellant has said that the appellant was willing to undergo the operation. Counsel asked the Court to give a ruling that it would be lawful for the prison doctors to perform the operation. The Court refused to give any direction in the matter.

As Glanville Williams points out in his excellent book, *The Sanctity of Life and the Criminal Law*, castration is held to be a maim, and maiming is unlawful because it is what Mr. Justice Swift defined as an act *malum in se*.

The whole problem of this case depends on the rule that hormone treatment must not be given in prison. I had a case in which an elderly homosexual was placed on probation on condition that he resided in a mental hospital and had treatment under me. This was devised to allow him to have stilboestrol treatment. When he arrived in the mental hospital he refused the hormone therapy because he said he was a Roman Catholic. On being told that he was breaking his probation and would have to appear again before the court for sentence he rapidly changed his mind and religion.

In conclusion it is well known that there is a danger of insanity following castration and it is morally wrong to expose a patient unnecessarily
to such a risk.

This use of stilboestrol and/or female sex hormones in older men (those
past the age of 50) has become an accepted treatment and, indeed, in the
Report of the Wolfenden Committee it was suggested that prisoners who
wished might have it whilst serving their sentence. This is a method of
'chemical castration' which inhibits spermatogenesis and if continued
long enough will cause atrophy of the genitalia with swelling of the breasts.
It is possible that patients with litigious tendencies might sue one for
malpraxis unless warned of this occurrence. It is better, therefore, to give a
warning and, to circumvent such a possibility, have a document signed
stating that this is appreciated. The technique is to give stilboestrol or
other oestrogens (five to ten milligrammes of stilboestrol daily) until
spermatogenesis ceases and the patient no longer secretes sperm. Some
atrophy of the genitalia occurs. Then a suitable maintenance dose is found
on which the patient can continue. There is no doubt that in many cases
libido is lost and the patient is able to continue his life without being
troubled by abnormal sexual urges. Unlike actual castration insanity does
not appear to follow its use.

The disadvantages of such a treatment are that after a time fertility is
lost. This may be of little moment since such patients rarely wish to
marry. A much more serious objection is that even though the organic
sexuality is destroyed—the genitalia atrophic, spermatogenesis absent
and hypertrophy of the breasts apparent—the psychosexuality may
persist.

The other difficulty of the treatment is that it is dependent on the
patient's continuance. If he stops taking the stilboestrol he is in danger of
relapsing. However, in criminal cases this can sometimes be avoided by
asking for him to be under prolonged probation and treatment during
which the genital atrophy is usually sufficient in an older man to ensure
that it does not recover.

In my own experience if a man is given heavy doses of stilboestrol for
two years it is some long time before he recovers his sexual capacity—if at
all. Castration is therefore unnecessary and undesirable in these cases and
if the rule regarding this treatment in prison were altered it would be of
immense value to sexual offenders. There is only one possible objection to
its use in prison. Some physicians have noticed that with the large doses
given in the treatment of carcinoma of the prostate stilboestrol may cause
irritability, and if this happened in prison the man might break the rules
and get into serious trouble. No doubt if the medical officer were aware of
such a possibility he would give suitable sedation or prescribe tranquil-
lizers to prevent it.

I feel strongly that although hormone treatment may be of value in older men unsuitable for psychotherapy it is not clinically good practice to use it on young men likely to respond to psychotherapy. Although it is easier for the psychiatrist to prescribe hormone treatment, and hope for success, it is negligence on his part not to do his best to correct the patient's sexuality if this is possible.

Banay and Davidoff noticed that sexual psychopathy was cured in one case by cerebral lobectomy. It is to be hoped that the enthusiastic psychiatrists who are so eager to submit cases for leucotomy (which may be valuable in suitable psychotic patients but should be used only as a last resort) will not start using lobectomy on every sexual abnormal. This is less likely now that psychiatric interest in such treatment is much less than it was a few years ago when it had a greatly exaggerated praise.

In America *Metrazol* has been used by Owensby who believes that perverts are latent schizophrenics. He claimed a number of cures of homosexuals, but no one has succeeded in confirming his results, and this suggested treatment has fallen into abeyance. It is improbable that it would be successful in even carefully selected cases.

Again it has been suggested that male hormone is useful in some cases of homosexual anxiety. There is no suggestion that it cures the homosexuality but merely that it removes the anxiety. This can be performed much more effectively by psychotherapy and the removal of tension without the trouble of repeated injections, or implantations, and the possibility of damage to the testicles through prolonged endocrine therapy, so that it is obvious that psychotherapy is a much more desirable form of treatment for these cases.

Operative treatment to the ischio-cavernosus muscle has been advocated by some for the treatment of impotence. This is ridiculous since impotence, when due to poor erection, is not a muscular but a psychical matter and those who fail to obtain a good erection awake often find that their penis behaves normally with a nocturnal emission. Such operations can only succeed by suggestion and suggestion can be administered much more easily than by sewing up muscles.

The Wolfenden Report suggests that imprisonment is a form of treatment. Now with the greatest of respect this is a view to which no honest psychiatrist can subscribe. Imprisonment may be, and indeed, often is, necessary for the protection of the community. This is shown by the fact that about 58 per cent. of homosexuals in prison are there for offences against boys. Obviously to let them loose would be to release a corruptive influence which society could not tolerate. However, let us not conceal this behind a screen of cant. These men have been sent to prison, not from any hope of curing them, but because they are dangerous to youth.

The Report says: 'There are some men for whom a prison sentence is

EE—PSY. D.

in itself a salutary shock, as an expression of society's disapproval of their behaviour: and although there are some homosexual offenders—as there are burglars or embezzlers—to whom prison does more harm than good, yet there undoubtedly are others to whom it teaches an important lesson.'

I wonder what important lesson is taught to a homosexual man confined in a prison where a large and increasing number of prisoners sleep *three to a cell*, where the psychosexually abnormal never see a woman and where 21·6 per cent. have had four or more previous convictions and 10 per cent. seven convictions or more? I have seen patients, not psychosexually ill, who have stated that Borstal had changed them from young thieves to honest men; I have seen men who have changed after a brief prison sentence and have readjusted their lives, but I have never seen, in some thirty years of medical practice mainly devoted to psychiatry, a patient who stated that his psychosexual illness had been influenced (except for the worse) by confinement in a prison. This view has also been put forward by Karpman who has had enormous experience in American prisons. Mr. Greenwood in a debate on homosexuality in the House of Commons stated, in our view truly, 'One is as likely to cure a homosexual of his perversion by sending him to prison as of curing a drunkard by incarcerating him in a brewery'. Such common sense agrees with the findings of all experienced psychiatrists.

The Dangers of Treatment

In a recent book it has been suggested that the treatment of the sexually abnormal is not without its dangers. I must confess that I had not thought that their therapy was in any way different from those suffering from neurosis.

The suggested dangers are that patients may become so depressed as to be suicidal, or that a psychosis may emerge during treatment. Scott states: 'Thus suicide is a possibility, especially where intensive psychotherapy is undertaken in out-patient departments. Several therapists have reported the precipitation of psychoses by treatment. Too enthusiastic a start, permitting the patient to succeed in making the doctor angry, failure to recognize deeper problems behind "cover" symptoms, may drive the patient away and justify him in decrying medical aid ever afterwards.'

It seems to me that these occurrences are due to unwise psychotherapy, too active and too urgent, instead of commencing very passively, as one should. They may, also, be due to unsuitable psychotherapists: surely physicians who allow themselves to become angry are unsuited to this sort of work, and should be persuaded to choose a laboratory career where they have no contact with patients. A passive therapy will, sooner or later, reveal the deeper material under 'cover' symptoms.

I think that I can claim to be a pioneer in treating these patients but, although I have had the odd suicide, like any other psychiatrist, and I can remember four, they were in schizoid and depressive patients and not paraphilics. Such *contretemps* must be regarded as similar to those the surgeon experiences with embolism. A proper control of the transference will minimize the risk; indeed, it has always seemed to me that the danger with analysing the pre-psychotic is to the analyst rather than the patient.

Mackwood's suggestion that psychotherapy may induce the patient to act out impulses which would otherwise be suppressed is valid and patients who show any such tendency should be, as he states, treated in an institution where they are under some control.

Scott records one of his homosexual patients who was told under hypnosis that he would enjoy intercourse with his wife and subsequently blamed him for the fact that doing so made her pregnant. Here it seems that one must learn from experience; and, if one wishes to use this form of treatment, suggest that enjoyment will occur only if adequate preventative measures are taken.

It seems to me that in the hands of a suitable psychotherapist giving proper analysis the risks are minimal, and should not deter one from attempting its use in suitable cases. The occasions where patients become suicidal, or develop overt psychoses, are no more frequent than one encounters in the neuroses. Moreover, the alternative, which is doing nothing, means that the patient has little hope of recovery, although Scott says with much reason, 'with some of the milder cases there is practically no method which will not succeed, while at the other end of the scale there is practically nothing that will'.

Surely such a statement implies that one should attempt treatment in every suitable case in the hope that some will respond, and disregard the almost negligible dangers.

INDICATIONS FOR TREATMENT

It may be helpful to consider indications for treatment for the more prevalent sexual abnormalities, although naturally no rigid rule can be given. Everything depends on the individual case.

Masturbation

Anyone who practises sexology will find himself constantly consulted by young men who demand to be cured of masturbation, nocturnal emissions, sexual fantasies, and their believed ill effects. It is unwise to be trapped into trying to do so, and the right thing is to determine how far this is a normal condition in the patient. If it is discovered to have no association with perversion or psychosis he or she should be told that since this is a sign that the sexual glands are functioning in a healthy way it cannot be cured and must not be regarded as a disease. Where masturbation is caused by a vicious circle, that is to say, when it is used as a psychical relief from anxiety but in itself produces more anxiety, then clearly psychotherapy is needed to remove the deep-seated anxiety which is the cause. If masturbation is associated with a psychosis then the treatment is that of the psychosis in question. Nocturnal emissions unless associated with dreams of some perverse behaviour—sadistic, masochistic, fetishistic, &c.—should be disregarded as normal no matter how frequently they occur. If there are abnormal dreams with the emission then psychotherapy should be given. Where there is excessive anxiety a sedative is indicated whether the masturbation or nocturnal emission is obviously associated with the anxiety or not.

The only danger of masturbation is that the patient will lose himself in day-dreams and fantasies instead of facing life and overcoming his difficulties. The patient who is worried about it should then obviously be encouraged to go out and do practical things. Often such a patient fears that he is tainted with some terrible disease and will inevitably be impotent. He cannot therefore ask a decent girl to marry him and feels that he is doomed to misery all his life. No doubt many suicides in young men are from this cause. If the patient is made to realize that this is not so, that marriage with some girl he loves will end his misery, he will often confess that there is a female he wishes to marry. He should be told to go and propose to her forthwith. The cause of his masturbation in these cases is his lack of a proper outlet and what could be better than the girl he loves? To end the vicious circle of fear which prevents his marriage, and masturbation because he is not married, may not be elaborate psychotherapy, but it is common sense. When masturbation is used as a refuge from life and its problems the patient should be persuaded to tackle his difficulties and spend less time thinking about them.

It is obvious therefore from what I have said that the indications for treatment in masturbation exist only when it is a sign of some abnormality; whether a concealed perversion, a psychosis, or a fear of living. When this is so treatment is necessary but in the vast majority of cases explanation is all that is desirable.

Homosexuality

Norwood East, in and old but useful paper, suggested that this should be treated when: (1) the environment is the exciting cause of overt abnormal behaviour; and (2) the presence of modifying personality or neurotic factors have discouraged heterosexual interests. Clearly there are other important indications—when a patient is eager for cure, when he is more or less bisexual, when his homosexuality has only manifested itself under the influence of alcohol, when it is strongly against his ethical and religious beliefs, and when he is very young. East suggests that the contra-indications to treatment are: (1) when repeated overt acts have been present over a number of years; (2) when there are friendly relations with women without indication of sex awareness. It is also obviously useless to try to treat patients when there is no desire to be cured (such as those who are persuaded to see the psychiatrist because of parental pressure &c.). Also when there is an established feminine character—the patient who wears female underclothes under his male outer garb and who dyes his hair, uses face powder, and so on—is quite hopeless. The older a patient is the less likely is he to be cured, so patients over 35, particularly if they have built up a homosexual environment, are particularly unlikely to respond. The homosexual who has strong aversion to women is less likely to respond than the one who has occasional mild interest in them. East also believes that treatment is less likely to be successful when there are other well-developed perversions, in addition to homosexuality, and if there are anti-social trends present. This must not be taken too literally since I have already pointed out that it is rare, if not unknown, for a perversion to appear in 'pure culture'. Anti-social trends naturally complicate the problem because patients with them cannot be treated satisfactorily except in hospital and even there with difficulty.

If treatment is by analysis Beiber *et al.* give as favourable prognostic signs:

(*a*) Patient was bisexual at the beginning of analysis.
(*b*) Patient began analysis before the age of 35.
(*c*) Patient continued analysis for at least 150 hours, preferably 350 hours or more.
(*d*) Patient was motivated to become heterosexual.
(*e*) Patient had a not-detached, and at least an 'ambivalent' father.
(*f*) Patient's father respected and/or admired the patient, was affectionate, was more intimate with patient than with other male siblings, and liked women.
(*g*) Patient 'idolizes' women.
(*h*) Patient has tried heterosexual genital contact at some time.
(*i*) Patient had erotic heterosexual activity in the manifest content of his dreams.

Unfavourable signs were:

(*a*) Patient was exclusively homosexual at the beginning of analysis and had never attempted heterosexual genital contact.
(*b*) Patient began analysis at 35 or older.

(c) Patient undertook analysis for a reason other than the desire to alter his sexual pattern.

(d) Patient drops out of analysis in fewer than 150 hours.

(e) Patient had close-binding intimate mother and a detached hostile father.

(f) Patient's mother openly preferred patient to father.

(g) Patient had effeminate voice and gestures during childhood.

Recently the clinical psychologists have tried the use of various tests in the hope of determining which cases are most likely to be responsive to treatment. Coates, for example, suggests that those patients who had had previous heterosexual experience, and who gave 'a catastrophic reaction to the Rorschach card II', were of better prognosis in a series of 45 cases treated by analysis.

Machover claimed that in the Draw-a-Person test some degree of homosexuality was detectable in those who drew first someone of the opposite sex. (One would have thought on clinical grounds that it would be someone of the same sex.) These claims have been disproved by Grygier and others.

The failure to find tests valuable in such cases as homosexuality is probably because it never occurs in pure culture, and it is useless to try to detect types of abnormality until we have certain tests for emotional immaturity. Nevertheless such research may finally lead to something very useful and should be encouraged.

In the section on homosexuality I have described a number of different types and briefly indicated which are likely to respond. It is useless to write or speak of the homosexual as if he were always exactly the same individual. There are at least a dozen different types. The suitability for treatment and the likelihood of success depend on careful selection. The reader should, therefore, turn back to this section (p. 218) and study these different forms of inversion. To generalize too widely is only to invite failure in such cases.

Exhibitionism

East suggests that treatment is indicated when: (1) the practice is infrequent; (2) there is an absence of other perversions; and (3) there is a strong desire for relief. I concur with these factors and would add the presence of some environmental element—e.g. Rickles found that there was frequently a strong mother or wife who dominated the patient. The removal of such a condition is often the deciding factor in treatment. Where the patient has exhibited himself in spite of other normal sexual outlets (e.g. in a married man) the outlook for treatment is less favourable than when the patient is deprived of normal sexuality. East makes this point when he suggests that the contra-indications to treatment are: (1) when there is a failure of the normal sex life to substitute for exhibitionism; and (2) when the patient is over 30 years of age. Cases with concomitant organic disease are unsuitable for psychotherapy.

It is improbable that the commonly blamed enlarged prostate has much to do with exhibitionism; but if the patient is found to suffer from such a disability—and in old men who exhibit themselves it is not an unusual coincidental condition—then obviously prostatectomy should be performed. It is unwise to rely too much on the operation eliminating the exhibitionism, however, since some sexuality is often retained after it.

Sadism

I agree with East that sadism must in all cases be treated with caution. There must be no mistake, however, since this obviously depends on the degree of perversity. The patient who has sadistic fantasies, but feels anxiety and fear at the idea of putting them into practice is usually safe. An experienced psychiatrist can, in most cases, detect the drive behind the behaviour, and if there is any suspicion that the patient may break out in savage acts obviously he is unfit for treatment except in a mental hospital, and he should be persuaded to enter one as a voluntary patient forthwith, or if necessary he should be certified. A large number of those who have sadistic fantasies are perfectly safe to treat, but it is wise to remember that such patients, although unlikely to injure anyone else, may commit suicide unless transference is dealt with properly during the whole of the analysis. Cases of the Heath or Kürten type never, in my experience, ask for treatment and so do not form a problem.

Fetishisms

I do not agree with East that cases of fetishism must be undertaken with the utmost caution since a perfectly harmless fetishism may be transformed into a strong homosexual or sadistic drive. Those cases which I have treated have never shown these manifestations, although plenty of sadism can be discovered in the composition of the disease. Where there is a variation in sexual behaviour, the patient is reasonably young, under 35, and there is a strong wish for cure; also where other unpleasant neurotic elements, anxiety, or pain exist, the chances are good with psychotherapy and it should be undertaken. In long established and difficult cases which are unlikely to be cured with psychotherapy faradic aversion therapy is said to be valuable and this should certainly be tried.

Sexual Hypoversion

Treatment is indicated in all cases of this except perhaps in those who have never felt any sexual desire of any type—the man who as a boy never masturbated, never felt any interest in girls at adolescence, never had any interest in women in adult life, and so on. The superficial type due to anxiety needs treatment by explanation, suggestion, and sedation as well as reassurance of the sexual partner. Severe types—prolonged impotence, 'congenital impotence', &c., need psychotherapy, usually of the deep analytical kind. These latter should not be accepted except after careful consideration since they are always a very difficult problem and if treated without sufficient caution may be subjected to a prolonged analysis which has little or no chance of success. Frigidity in women is well worth analysis but in many cases, as Malleson points out, superficial causes can be discovered and the illness easily cleared up. In all cases of hypoversion the physician should be certain that the patient is really in love with his sexual partner and has not married her for ulterior reasons, such as money, since naturally affection is a necessity for prolonged successful intercourse, and few people are capable of happy sexual life with someone in whom they have little emotional interest.

Sexual Hyperversion

This obviously needs treatment as soon as possible since the girl obviously runs the risk of being impregnated and both sexes are in danger of venereal disease. If the sexual urge is very strong hospital treatment is indicated, but if it is not overwhelming sedation and psychotherapy can be tried. These cases sometimes respond to endocrine therapy as I have described previously—progesterone in the case of the woman and stilboestrol in the case of the man—but this should not be continued indefinitely. In every case the patients should be discouraged from forming rash marriages and, indeed, they should not form a permanent union until the condition is mitigated. Marriage in this condition does not cure, and it may lead to a great deal of unhappiness in both partners. Where there is an underlying psychosis it is obvious that this must be treated rather than the sexual manifestations.

It is worth while considering here the use of oestrogens—such substances as oestradiol and stilboestrol—in the deliberate production of impotence and diminution of the libido in homosexuals. It is true that in a certain number of such cases the exhibition of these substances produces a marked fall in the libido. The driving force of the endocrines is diminished and often disappears. This is purchased, however, at the expense of testicular activity and at first causes inactivity but later atrophy from which there is no recovery.

There is, although it is not generally appreciated, a much graver disadvantage in this form of therapy. It is a fact that in a percentage of cases endocrines reduce the capacity but not the desire. For example, I have given evidence in the case of a schoolmaster who was given enormous doses of oestradiol and stilboestrol in order to remove his homosexuality. These caused considerable atrophy of the testicles and a biopsy showed that the Leydig's cells (which produce the internal secretion of testosterone) had disappeared. The man's penis was reduced to half its size and the whole structure lost its turgidity. It is improbable that he could have maintained an erection for any length of time. On the contrary his breasts became greatly enlarged and almost as big as those of a woman. Unfortunately his libido was not affected and he interfered manually with a number of the boys under his care.

He was finally charged and tried at Winchester Assizes in 1953, accused of anal intercourse as well as masturbation. The Court was not convinced that he was capable of penetration and he was discharged on the more serious count but given five years' imprisonment on the lesser one. This is not an isolated case and I am familiar with a similar one in which doses of stilboestrol were given sufficient to cause mammary enlargement, but the man complained that instead of diminishing his libido the endocrine increased it. A prison doctor has informed me that in a case of a man who complained of a compulsion to rape women large doses of endocrines (in this case stilboestrol) had an exactly similar effect and the man discovered that his desire was not diminished but became uncontrollable. It is obvious from these cases that libido (whether normal or abnormal) is at least partly psychological and no amount of organic treatment is certain to affect it.

I would point out here that it is deplorable to use stilboestrol or progesterone to diminish the sexual desire in *normal* people. It was suggested once in the *British Medical Journal* by a correspondent that stilboestrol might be used to diminish the sexual desire in a young man. This appears to me to be a terrible proposition—young men should be desirous and only too soon will age diminish emotion and love no longer be 'all a wonder and a wild desire'.

I would emphasize here regarding treatment that no matter what line of approach we take it is essential that the physician's outlook be optimistic. Those who regard all sexual abnormalities as hopeless only too often infect the patient with their own dreary outlook and spoil the chances of cure. In perhaps no other branch of medicine do occasional unexpected miracles occur and these have the circumstance of happening to those who believe them possible. Therefore no case should be abandoned as hopeless unless it has been carefully considered from every angle and every suitable treatment tried.

REFERENCES

BERG, C. (1945) *Clinical Psychology*, London.
—— (1955) *Deep Analysis*, London.
BIEBER, I. *et al.* (1962) *Homosexuality*, New York.
BLAKEMORE, C. B., *et al.* (1956) *Beh. Res. Ther.*, **1**, 29–30.
BRAMWELL, J. M. (1909) *Hypnotism*, London.
EAST, N. (1939) The modern psychiatric approach to crime, *J. ment. Sci.*, **35**, 647–66.
EYSENCK, H. J. (1960) *Behaviour Therapy and The Neuroses*, London.
FORSYTH, D. (1922) *Technique of Psychoanalysis*, London.
FOSS, G. L. (1937) Testosterone propionate, effect on a post-pubertal eunuch, *Lancet*, ii, 1307–9.
GLOVER, E. (1928) *The Technique of Psychoanalysis*, London.
GRYGIER, T. G. (1958) Homosexuality, neurosis and normality, *Brit. J. Delinq.*, **9**, 59.
HADFIELD, J. (1958) The cure of homosexuality, *Brit. med. J.*, **2**, 1323–6.
HERTZ, J., TILLINGER, K. G., and WESTMAN, A. (1961) Transvestism, *Acta Psychiat. Scand.*, **37**, 238.
KANDOU, T. A., and SPEYER, N. (1936) Therapeutic castration of sexual perverts, *Med. T. Gennesk.*, **80**, 2482–7.
KARPMAN, B. (1941) Perversions as neuroses, *J. Crim. Psychopath.*, **3**, 180–99.
—— (1957) *The Sexual Offender and His Offenses*, New York.
KOPP, M. E. (1938) Surgical treatment as a sex-crime prevention, *J. crim. Law*, **28**, 692–706.
LEY, J. (1938) *J. belge Neurol. Psychiat.*, **83**, 344–56.
LOEWENSTEIN, W. (1947) *The Treatment of Impotence*, London.
—— (1951) Indications for coitus training apparatus, *Int. J. Sexol.*, **4**, 149–53.
MARKS, I. M., and GELDER, M. G. (1967) Transvestism and fetishism, *Brit. J. Psychiat.*, **113**, 711–29.
NAVILLE, F. (1935) La castration thérapeutique et préventive de délinquents et pervers sexuels, *J. Méd. Lyon*, **16**, 711–21.
RAYMOND, M. J. (1956) *Brit. med. J.*, **2**, 854–7.
SCOTT, P. D. (1964) Definition, classification, prognosis and treatment, in *Pathology and Treatment of Sexual Deviation*, ed. ROSEN, I., London.
SRENC, D., and FREUND, D. (1953) Treatment of homosexuality through conditioning, *Int. J. Sexol.*, **7**, 92–3.
STÜRUP, G. (1948) *Proc. Roy. soc. Med.*, **41**, 765–8.
WILLIAMS, G. (1958) *The Sanctity of Life and The Criminal Law*, London.

21

PROGNOSIS

In my opinion the paraphilias, or psychosexual disorders, are as capable of treatment as any other neuroses. There appears to be no inherent reason why a sexual neurosis should not be as treatable as any other neurotic illness except that it may provide pleasure which forms a secondary gain and causes the physician more trouble; yet such a gain is not unknown in other neurotic illness and is as frequently overcome. Where, of course, the patient does not wish for cure it is just as impossible to treat him successfully as it is to treat an unwilling neurotic.

This view is upheld by Karpman who says in a careful survey of Stekel's work:

Many physicians, not excepting practising psychiatrists, adopt a wrong attitude towards the paraphilias, and when the question of treatment comes up usually dismiss the problem with the statement: 'This man is a pervert; there is nothing we can do about it.' However, by stigmatizing the condition as a perversion one does not solve the problem, but merely gives vent to a sense of moral indignation that has no place in professional work. These patients should be regarded neither as perverts nor as degenerates, but as sick persons whose sickness is derived from environmental sources on the basis of arrested development (or perhaps maldevelopment) in the biologic and psychic evolution of man. They are no more responsible for that than a patient is responsible for having a particular disease. Rather than speak of these paraphilias as perversions or degeneracies it is much more proper to regard them as neuroses, for, as in neuroses, one is often able to trace much of the reaction to emotional factors which can be analysed for their individual components. While they differ from the neuroses in that they are established psychosexual reactions, one must remember that in neuroses paraphilic trends are often observed and the line of demarcation is not so sharp and clearcut as it might appear. On the other hand, one has no difficulty in observing in these paraphilias a large number of hysterical and obsessional features, so that by any definition these paraphilias are neuroses and should be treated as such. In disagreement with Freud who believes that paraphilias are not reducible, Stekel maintains that some of these are curable, as his case material shows, and that in many cases improvement, at least, can be effected. This is a decided advance. The fact that there still remain a large number of cases in which the paraphilia cannot be cured does not by any means signify that it is not curable, but merely that the proper avenue of approach has not yet been found. In the future psychotherapy will have to devise other methods and other technics for treatment in these cases.

It is obvious that unless we practise psychotherapy on every available case of perversion we shall never discover these 'other methods and other technics' which Karpman suggests may give better results.

The prognosis of sexual abnormalities is a difficult matter to determine statistically and there is very little literature on the subject. This is generally true of all the neuroses—and psychoses—but applies particularly to sexual neurosis. There is, however, a paper by Rees on the subject and various workers mention their experience in individual papers. Ross, in his book on prognosis, neglects altogether the sexual aberrations so that his valuable statistics are not helpful to us. Again Wilder, in an examination of prognosis and treatment, disregards sexual neurosis but some of his conclusions seem helpful. In a study of the figures published by various hospitals, clinics, psycho-analytical institutes, and private psycho-analysts he found: 'Clinics have the poorest results. The figures in general psychotherapy, including psycho-analysis, appear to be the best, but the number of cases is too small for definite conclusions in this article.' This suggests as far as the neuroses in general are concerned that there is no special advantage in psychoanalysis over many years although better results will be obtained with long rather than brief treatment, as one might expect. In my opinion what holds for psychoneuroses holds for the sexual neuroses as a general rule. Incidentally the poor results obtained from clinics explain why physicians whose work is in a busy out-patient department have such a pessimistic outlook for the treatment of paraphilia.

Rees gives a number of factors which he feels affect prognosis: these are age, duration of symptoms, intelligence, degree of desire for cure or change which the patient experiences, and his social situation. 'The severity of the coincident psychoneurotic symptoms may also play an important part in affecting the chances of recovery under treatment', and again (as we have stressed above) 'Environmental factors will influence the prognosis more than in any physical disorder. Social conditions are inevitably linked with these problems of sex.' I would like to stress the importance of the ancillary neurotic symptoms in the prognosis. This is also underlined by the orthodox Freudians, since it is believed that these show fixations at a later date, and therefore better opportunity of success because causal factors are nearer the surface. It is in my opinion a more simple view that if one has a perversion with no discomfort there is less compulsion to get well since one can obtain sexual pleasure with little inconvenience, whereas the addition of symptoms, particularly very painful ones, forms a driving force which compels the patient to continue treatment and his perversion is cured with the neurosis.

Ross divides the sexual abnormalities into two groups: (1) Those less serious and more susceptible of cure by comparatively simple treatment. These include masturbation, emotional (non-active) homosexuality, many cases of vaginismus, all cases of psychical impotence, mild obsessional states, and conditions of seminal emissions with anxiety. (2) In the second group he places active homosexuality, fetishisms, transvestism, masochism and sadism, and exhibitionism. These conditions are much more difficult to cure and do not respond to simple measures. A reductive analysis, of which the Freudian is most suitable, is necessary.

I would not agree wholly with this classification. In the first place most psychotherapists will agree that impotence is always difficult to cure if it is due to primary sexual hypoversion or aversion. Excluding the simple impotence due to anxiety which follows some psychic trauma or sexual misadventure, which is usually easily cured, most impotence is of this form. Sexual emissions with anxiety may be most difficult to treat and indeed form a type of impotence. Homosexuality, whether it has shown overt behaviour or is non-active, is sometimes difficult and needs prolonged treatment. This does not, of course, include unconscious homosexuality such as is unearthed during the analysis of neuroses.

Some types of psychosexual illness are usually responsive and it has been found that exhibitionism is one. For example, Rosen has reported the results in 13 male adult patients, of whom all except 2 have been before the courts. They were treated in two groups for some 23 sessions, after which there have been no more convictions reported in follow-up studies averaging 20 months. He concluded that 'There is no doubt that analytical group therapy is efficacious in the treatment of the adult severe phobic-compulsive exhibitionist'.

In adolescent patients he was much less successful. (They are in my own experience very difficult ones to treat.) Five patients, aged 15-16 attended, but their visits were irregular. Two boys with inhibited personalities showed personality improvement with later individual psychotherapy but the other three changed their offences to a non-sexual kind; two to stealing and the other to reckless driving. He stated: 'One must therefore conclude that whereas group psychotherapy can help the inhibited shy adolescent, it is of little benefit to the compulsive instinct-ridden patient; for these, intensive analytic psychotherapy and close supervision would be required.'

It is noticeable that those psychiatrists who advocate short treatments—e.g. Ross, do not give statistics regarding sexual neuroses or, again, if they do they give pessimistic ones, as those who say that it is useless to treat the overt homosexual by psychotherapy, and uphold this by the fact that there are no cures in the literature. Such a view has been accepted with avidity by many; but, as Albert Ellis points out, most of these, such as L. Allen Carpenter, Hirschfeld, Mercer, Vincent and Wildeblood, turn out themselves to be self-confessed, confirmed homosexuals. Ignorance of the law may be held to be no excuse, but ignorance of the literature is only too often used to support wrong ideas. We feel that it is a pity that some psychiatrists should have accepted Havelock Ellis's statement that 'he had not any knowledge of a case of congenital or fixed inversion in which a complete or permanent transformation has been achieved by psycho-analysis or any other psychotherapeutic method'. This is an unsatisfactory argument. If a case is shown to be cured it is, of course, not accepted as being 'a case of congenital or fixed inversion'. Moreover this places a premium on ignorance. What is not known cannot be. Many of us, unfortunately, are ignorant of India yet accept that it exists. The old parrot-cry that there are no successfully treated cases in the literature is constantly repeated by those who have not troubled to investigate it. Usually such statements are somewhat ambiguous and so qualified that it is difficult to pin them down. For example, Hemphill, Leitch, and Stewart in a paper in the *British Medical Journal* state: 'It seems to us that there should be more clear thinking about treatment. We have yet to find any evidence, in our experience or in the literature, that the direction of intensely homosexual drives can be successfully altered.' The operative qualification in this case being 'intensely homosexual drives'. If that means that the patient is so ill that he does not wish for a cure it is, indeed, correct and he is no more curable than any one else who does not wish to be normal: but, curiously enough, in the same issue of the journal in which this appeared there was an excellent paper by Hadfield which described four old cases, and five more recent ones, all successfully cured. These included a naval officer who might have been described as having 'an intensely homosexual drive' since he had no heterosexual interests and, indeed, avoided women. It was for that reason he had joined the Navy. Yet he was cured by psychotherapy, married and had children. He described his marriage as 'a great success'.

Hadfield has recently published, in addition to these cases, two further ones of practising and complete homosexuals, in one of which aversive therapy had failed, which were cured; one happily married, and the other heterosexual in his waking life and dreams.

Coates recorded a series of 45 cases; 33 over 21-years-old. After treatment 10 (30 per cent.) of the adults and 8 (67 per cent.) of the boys showed improvement. Ovesey, Gaylin, and Hendin recorded three cases treated by psychotherapy in which the patients attained complete heterosexuality confirmed by observation for some years.

Irving Bieber and his colleagues described a series of cases of homosexuality treated by psychoanalysis. Out of 72 patients who were exclusively homosexual at the onset of treatment, 19 per cent. became bisexual and 19 per cent. exclusively heterosexual; of the 30 patients who were bisexual when treatment started 50 per cent. became exclusively heterosexual.

This should silence those who insist that such cases never respond to analysis and accords with my own experience. Mayerson and Lief, in a series of 19 patients (14 male and 5 female) found that 47·5 per cent. were apparently recovered or much improved and 26·3 per cent. were improved, in comparison to their status at the beginning of therapy. In all the majority the follow-up revealed progress in behaviour since the beginning of treatment. In this series the mean duration of therapy was 1·7 years and the mean interval between the end of therapy and follow-up was 4·5 years.

I have described in my monograph on homosexuality 14 apparent cures and 4 social cures. *One may say that it is only those who have never treated a case of homosexuality, or have treated it wrongly, who have never had a cure.*

There are many older cases of cure or improvement in the literature: London, Naftaly, Lilienthal, Laforgue, Stekel, Serog, Frey, Virchon, Bircher, Sadger, Hadden, Sumaer, Sullivan, Ellis, Poe, Srnec, Freund, Karpman, Hadfield, Allen, and many others have published successful cases of the treatment of inverts.

Ellis's work is particularly interesting. He states that he treated 28 male and 12 female homosexuals who were seen for intensive psychotherapy.

These patients were treated for their homosexual problems or neurosis rather than for their homosexual desire or activity in itself. They were judged to be distinctly or considerably improved when they began to lose their fears of the other sex, to receive gratification from sex relationships and to be effective partners in these relationships, and to lose their obsessive thoughts and compulsive actions about homosexuality. It was found that of the male patients 64 per cent. were distinctly or considerably orientated towards heterosexuality after treatment, while 36 per cent. were still as strongly homosexual as before. Of the male patients (numbering 23) who had some desire to achieve heterosexuality, almost 80 per cent. became distinctly or considerably more heterosexual. *Every single one of the 13 males who had a strong desire to achieve heterosexuality became distinctly or considerably more heterosexual.* (His italics.)

Of the 12 female patients seen for intensive psychotherapy, all became distinctly or considerably orientated towards heterosexuality in the course of treatment, even though 2 of them had little or no desire to change when they first were seen.

Ellis's conclusions (which coincide with my own) are: 'It is felt that there are some grounds for believing that the majority of homosexuals who are seriously concerned about their condition and willing to work to improve it may, in the course of active psycho-analytically orientated psychotherapy, be distinctly helped to achieve a more satisfactory heterosexual situation.' Whitener and Nikelly state that in their experience good results depend on strong motivation for recovery, shorter time deviant, higher intelligence and the presence of other neurotic symptoms. Somewhat similarly Ross and Mendelsohn believe that successful treatment depends on the youth of the patient, the less homosexual his behaviour, the better scholastic record, the length of treatment possible, and the wish to change.

In spite of the fact that clinics have the poorest record for successes in treating psychosexual diseases, where the clinic is properly conducted with a chance for adequate psychotherapy the results can still be excellent. For example, the Portman Clinic (run by the Institute for the Scientific Treatment of Delinquency) in London is one which gives proper therapy.

Glover gives the results of treatment there of a group of 77 adults and 4 juvenile homosexuals. They had psychotherapy combined with hormone treatment in 74 cases, and hormone treatment alone in 2. The number of visits varied from under 5 (18·5 per cent. of the total) to between 50 and 170 visits (12·3 per cent.). The largest group (28·4 per cent.) attended between ten and thirty times. The total duration of treatment varied from up to 5 months to 5 years. All types of therapy from analysis to supervision and advice were given.

At the end of the treatment 36 of the 81 (44 per cent.) no longer experienced homosexual impulses: 21 who still had such impulses achieved discretion and conscious control (in 9 of these the impulse was diminished also), in 8 cases no change was noted; and in 14 treatment was interrupted or discontinued. None of the 9 exclusive homosexual patients lost his impulses after treatment, whereas this was the case with 51 per cent. of the bisexuals. Seven of the unchanged cases were persistent types. A 1- to 3-year follow-up showed that 19 were known to have made satisfactory adjustment and 34 were presumed to have done so on reasonable grounds.

The work of Ross and Mendelsohn supports the fact that I have asserted for 20 years. That is that deviant patients have as much chance of cure as those suffering from neurosis. These two workers compared a series of 15 male and 5 female homosexuals with a similar group of non-homosexual neurotics: they found no significant difference in the results of treatment. This refutes the pessimistic psychiatrists whose clinics do not give adequate psychotherapy and naturally have very meagre results.

There are plenty of cases of sexual abnormalities and the results of their treatment by psychotherapy in the literature, and taking the results of psychotherapy *en masse*, the prognosis is fairly good (I believe as good as any other form of neurosis). Rees gives the results obtained at the Tavistock Clinic as about 76 per cent. which appear to have benefited permanently. Whitener and Nikelly give an overall prognosis of 50 per cent. improvement in cases of all types of psychosexual disorder. The various clinics for psycho-analysis give similar or approximately similar figures. The point made by Rees that marriage should not be suggested as a therapeutic measure is a very important one. In fact it should be laid down as a general rule that *no patient should be encouraged to marry until sexual normality or approximate normality is attained*. This naturally arouses difficulty in experimentation, but it is better that the patient should patronize a prostitute than ruin the life of some unhappy woman who has been encouraged to marry him unknowingly in the hope that he will become cured. Such a hope is much too extravagant, in the absence of proper treatment, to entertain. Incidentally such marriages nearly always end in disaster, unhappiness, and divorce.

This problem of allowing the patient to see whether he is fit for marriage is one which the clerics refuse to face honestly. It is indeed one which presents us with an insoluble difficulty if one adheres to the view that in every case it is wrong to have intercourse before marriage. Here we have a patient who has had sufficient treatment to be interested in women, to be excited by them and to react normally in love making. Is one to permit him to marry? The fact that he is now responsive and has lost most of his interest in his old psychosexual abnormality is no guarantee that he will respond normally to the sexual act. Is one to encourage him to attempt intercourse before marriage? The cleric will say 'on no account'. However, if he marries and is not cured then he will spoil some unhappy woman's life. Moreover, since the cleric will tell us that marriage is 'till death do us part', the abnormal man and unhappy woman are tied together indefinitely. It is difficult to conceive any greater snare. One would have thought that the most sensible thing, and the kindest, would be to permit the man to try his luck before he commits himself irrevocably.

Fortunately in practice the patient himself usually cuts the Gordian knot. Once he thinks that he is capable of intercourse he goes off and attempts it. Only when he is pathologically meticulous morally does the problem arise.

In my own experience it may be expected that some more than 50 per cent. of cases of impaired potence can be expected to be cured or markedly improved. This seems to be the same as the results obtained by other workers. Stafford-Clark had 50 per cent. cures, although Tuthill claimed 84 per cent. No doubt the variation depends on the selection of cases. Others, such as Wallis and Booker, state that only 35 per cent. can be expected to be cured. Cooper reported that out of 54 patients he cured or improved only 20 (37 per cent.). He used various techniques, but not apparently sedation. His treatment consisted of muscular relaxation, provision of 'optimum' sexual environment, sex education and psychotherapy.

It would seem that undoubtedly suitable therapy, such as sedation in addition to psychotherapy, will produce results about, or better than, 50

FF—PSY. D.

per cent. in average cases, but the successes will depend to a great extent on the way the methods are used by the psychiatrist.

Some sexual abnormalities respond remarkably to proper treatment. For example, Gurvitz, quoted by Ellis, reports excellent results in the case of voyeurism and exhibitionism by using intensive psychotherapy. This was directed to unearth their underlying disturbances rather than concentrating merely on their sexual symptoms. Following up his cases from two to five years afterwards he was able to report that *'Therapy directed at this type of long term rehabilitation and ego building rather than specific symptoms resulted in sixteen of the eighteen sex offenders being free of sex offences at the present time.'* (His italics.)

In general, one cannot say that the perversions are any more difficult to cure than the hyperversions or hypoversions. The malversions form a different group. In every case the difficulty of cure depends on the criteria given by Rees: age, duration, intelligence, desire for cure, and social situation. It is only by full consideration of these that any one case can be assessed. Finally one can say that fantasy is less serious than action; that those who have enjoyed abnormal activities in thought only are more amenable to treatment than those who have fixed their tendencies by experience. Actions which approximate more to normality are better in prognosis than those which are bizarre, but one must realize that when we say normality we must include normal development: a patient practising bestiosexual oralism (suckling of animals' teats) may be more curable than a homosexual analist. In homosexuality mutual masturbation is less serious than anal intercourse, and activity in the male is better than passivity, and vice versa in the female. Homosexuality is more easily cured in the female than the male. In conclusion, it must be stated that if homosexuality is accompanied by alcoholism the prognosis is much more serious. It must be remembered that every case of sexual anomaly—particularly those which show considerable evidence of grave personality deterioration such as is found in some cases of hypersexuality (nymphomania) in which formerly respectable young girls have such an overwhelming sexual passion that they abandon themselves to those who are undesirable, and again in such serious perversions as overt sadism in which animals or human beings are injured—*there is a possibility of latent schizophrenia,* and in my experience if these cases are not treated early they frequently end in a grave psychosis. Anyone who has read the representative cases given here, however, will realize that this is not the inevitable result if the patient has sufficient treatment, and if, after being treated, they can settle down to normal useful lives.

An attempt has been made in this book to show that sexual abnormalities are capable of treatment and are likely to respond to it. The prognosis of those who cannot afford private psychotherapy nor obtain treatment at a psychotherapeutic clinic is very poor indeed. It may be instructive to examine the usual course of someone suffering from a sexual neurosis who cannot obtain some form of analysis. The young man, it is usually a young man, will discover in early manhood that he is definitely abnormal; perhaps his neurosis is one forbidden by law and so likely to lead to conflict with the police; and certainly dangerous to his marital happiness if he ever finds a mate. Frightened by his discovery he visits the psychiatric out-patient department of a general hospital. There he is seen in the hurly-burly of neurotics and psychotics. He is forced to discuss his problems, often of a most intimate kind, before students, sometimes of both sexes. If the psychiatrist is honest he may be referred to a special clinic which treats patients by deep psychotherapy. Even at such a clinic he will fall into the hands of a psychotherapist who is more familiar with the treatment of neurotics (who are more numerous than paraphiliacs) and who may find him technically very difficult to treat. If the psychiatrist at the hospital is not particularly honest he will refer the patient to a clinical assistant, that is, one who is learning psychotherapeutic technique, and he will 'treat' him. This is manifestly impossible considering the pressure of work, the constant interruptions, and the imposing difficulties of doing so at an out-patient department. The patient, feeling that he must persevere as his only chance of recovery may drag on wasting his time and money, until he feels that nothing is resulting. Finally he becomes cynical and gives up, only to relapse and perhaps fall into the hands of the law.

If such a patient comes into conflict with the police he will be treated by the officers with the greatest of kindness (a policeman sees too many abnormals to feel himself justified in showing hostility), but naturally the law must be administered. He is charged and goes before the judge or magistrates. If he is proved guilty a sentence of anything from adjournment *sine die* to fifteen years may be passed. The possibility of the prisoner obtaining treatment is literally infinitesimal. Moreover, the hope of cure will depend a great deal on the sentence which is given by the judge, who, no matter how wide his legal experience may be, is totally ignorant of psychotherapy. If the sentence is too short the prisoner will be discharged before he has had sufficient treatment to be effective, if too long he will have no chance in such an environment to respond normally and so will lapse back into his sexual neurosis, or whatever it is, *faute de mieux*. Such a situation would tax the clinical acumen of Freud himself. Yet judges promise that necessary psychological treatment will be given in prison. By pointing out these facts no criticism of the prison psychotherapist is suggested or implied; doctors who do this work are often struggling against official indifference or even obstruction. The whole trouble is that most of the prison medical officers are unqualified to do psychiatric work—certainly by psychotherapy.

The Wolfenden Report laments only too truly:

The prison medical service is understaffed and incompletely integrated with the National Health Service. Its members do much valuable and devoted work. But there are not enough full-time prison medical officers, not enough of them have had adequate psychiatric training—out of the forty-six full-time doctors at the time of our enquiry, only six held the Diploma in Psychological Medicine, though another twenty-two had had experience in mental hospitals or other fields of psychiatric medicine before joining the prison service—and in many parts of the country it is not possible for them to call on enough help from the psychiatric consultants of the National Health Service. There is a national shortage of psychiatrists: and it is to be expected that a substantial proportion of those who elect to take public appointments will prefer the wider and more varied experience offered by the mental hospitals and other psychiatric services within the National Health Service.

Things have improved, but not very much since the Report. This is the state of the existing Prison Medical Service as described by the Working Party set up to examine it which issued a Report in 1964:

There are at present 140 doctors in the Prison Medical Service. Sixty-two of these are whole-time medical officers, and 78 are part-time. The whole-time medical officers consist of the Director of Prison Medical Services, an assistant to the Director, and 4 Principal Medical Officers, 13 Senior Medical Officers, and 43 Medical Officers (39 men and 4 women). Most of these are employed at the larger prisons and a few at smaller establishments where special medical attention is provided. Most of the small establishments have only a part-time medical officer, who is normally a local general practitioner, and 10 part-time medical officers assist full-time medical officers. Two Principal Medical Officers, 11 Senior Medical Officers, 33 Medical Officers, and 13 part-time Medical Officers undertake court work.

The lower age limit for the appointment of full-time medical officers is 28, but the average age on appointment of the 62 now in post was $38\frac{1}{2}$ (few doctors under 35 are appointed to any branch of the medical Civil Service). Forty-one have had previous psychiatric hospital experience, and of these 11 possess the Diploma of Psychological Medicine.

It is pleasing to note that the number of prison medical officers holding the D.P.M. rose from 6 to 11 in 7 years. No wonder the Working Party asked for more psychiatrists and more clinics outside prison.

The Wolfenden Report suggests that prison is a form of treatment. Yet of 1,022 prisoners 211 (21·6 per cent.) had had four or more previous offences recorded against them and 102 (10 per cent.) had seven or more. The Wolfenden Committee states that these may not have been for sexual offences but may well have been. *If prison is a form of treatment it is singularly ineffectual.*

The passage of the 1967 Homosexual Act has put an end to the sad farce of sending adult homosexuals, interested only in other men, to prison; and given them a chance, if they wish to have proper treatment at some suitable clinic.

There will still remain those who have been imprisoned for some other psychosexual abnormality, often one socially more or less harmless, such as mild exhibitionism, which should be avoidable with a proper judiciary having insight into these conditions.

This is not to say, of course, that we should allow the deviants who are dangerous to society to wreck damage on it. Obviously, in the case of infantosexual homosexuals, sadists, &c. proper restraint must be applied and it is to be hoped that they will be given treatment, which should be much more available, now that the prison doctor is no longer to be burdened with the overwhelming weight of homosexuals.

Even so the prison medical officers themselves feel that they are battling against tremendous obstacles. In spite of the fact that they have to be so selective that the odds against a prisoner obtaining treatment are nearly one in two hundred they still have difficulty in obtaining results comparable with treatment outside prisons. For example, Young, quoted by Norwood East, states, concerning his work in Wormwood Scrubbs Prison: 'Psychotherapy is carried out under an unusual form of stress (in prison) in isolation from normal contacts, the encouragement of friends, and from opportunities to test the progress made, and in conditions which are often disadvantageous in other ways. On the other hand, the desire for cure has an added urgency to most prisoners, and the environment an abnormal freedom from extraneous distractions, though there is also an artificially heightened news value, both for the patient and other prisoners, which may injure co-operation and transference at a stage when the loss is not easily recovered.' East adds: 'In my view the psychotherapist should not occupy an administrative post in the prison, and he should be specially selected for the work.'

These difficulties are not peculiar to Britain. Pacht, Halleck and Ehrmann in their study based on treating patients in American prisons over 9 years came to the conclusion that, although they favoured the indeterminate sentence, prison was an unsuitable place for treatment.

It is felt that the suggestion which I have made above, that the prognosis of the deviant who cannot afford private or psychotherapeutic clinic treatment is somewhat gloomy, has been justified by the facts which I have given.

It might be objected that it is easy to make destructive criticism but what constructive measures might be taken? I would state definitely that it is most necessary to establish a clinic where patients suffering only from sexual neuroses could be treated. This would give the advantage that such conditions would be under psychotherapists who were familiar with them and skilled in treating such conditions. There should be a hostel attached so that patients could come from all parts of the country and live there; with proper supervision this could be beneficial since recovering patients always inspire those who are just starting treatment with the hope and desire for cure. It is believed that such a clinic is necessary, not only for treatment but for research. The great necessity is for us to know more of the causation, nature, and cure of sexual neurosis. This can be done only by intense study of clinical cases. *Yet in spite of the great social importance of the sexually abnormal there is no clinic devoted solely to the treatment of this illness anywhere in the world.* Even in London and the progressive cities of America the sexually abnormal have to be diverted to clinics for general psychotherapy. The New Criminal Justice Act offers a chance for treatment but provides no measures for the expenses or place for therapy. Perhaps, however, this slight recognition shows an awakening. We must treat sexual abnormality not as an object for pious admonitions and vicious prison sentences but as an illness. We have ceased to flog the insane; the leper is no longer an outlaw; the physical cripple is not considered comical. Perhaps humanity may soon find pity and help for the sexually abnormal.

REFERENCES

ALLEN, C. (1958) *Homosexuality: Its Nature, Causation and Treatment*, London.

BIEBER, I., et al. (1962) *Homosexuality, A Psychoanalytic Study of Male Homosexuality*, New York.

COATES, S. (1962) Homosexuality and The Rorschach Test, *Brit. J. med. Psychol.*, **35**, 177.

—— (1964) Clinical Psychology in Sexual Deviation, in *Pathology and Treatment of Sexual Deviation*, ed. ROSEN, I., London.

ELLIS, A. (1965) *Homosexuality: Its Causes and Cure*, New York.

GLOVER, E. (1960) *The Roots of Crime*, London.

HADDEN, S. B. (1958) Treatment of homosexuality in individual and group therapy, *Amer. J. Psychiat.*, **114**, 810–15.

HADFIELD, J. (1958) The cure of homosexuality, *Brit. med. J.*, **2**, 1323–6.

HEMPHILL, R. R., LEITCH, A., and STEWART, J. R. (1958) A factual study of male homosexuality, *Brit. med. J.*, **2**, 1317–22.

KARPMAN, B. (1941) Perversions as neuroses, *J. crim. Psychopath*, **3**, 180–99.

—— (1957) *The Sexual Offender and his Offenses*, New York.

LONDON, L. S. (1933) *Urol. cutan. Rev.*, **37**, 422–4.

—— (1945) *Libido and Delusion*, Washington, D.C.

MYERSON, P., and LIEF, H. I. (1965) Psychotherapy of homosexuals, in *Sexual Inversion*, ed. MARMOR, J., London.

NAFTALY, L. (1934) *Rev. Asoc. méd. argent.*, **48**, 424–6.

OVESEY, L., GAYLIN, W., and HENDIN, H. (1963) Psychotherapy of male homosexuality, *Arch. gen. Psychiat.*, **9**, (1), 19–31.

PACHT, A. R., HALLECK, S. L., and EHRMANN, J. C. (1962) Diagnosis and treatment of the sexual offender, *Amer. J. Psychiat.*, **118**, 802–8.

ROSS, H., and MENDELSOHN, F. (1958) Homosexuality in college, *Amer. Arch. Neur. Psychiat.*, **80**, 253–63.

SADGER, J. (1921) *Die Lehre von den Geschlechtverirrungen*, Wien.

STAFFORD-CLARK, D. (1954) The aetiology and treatment of impotence, *Practitioner*, **172**, 397–404.

TUTHILL, J. F. (1955) Impotence, *Lancet*, i, 124–8.
WHITENER, R. W., and NIKELLY, A. (1964) *Amer. J. Orthopsychiat.*, xxxiv, 3, 486–2.
WOODS, S. M., and MATTERSON, J. (1967) Sexual attitudes of medical students, *Amer. J. Psychiat.*, 124, 8, 1076–81.

PART EIGHT

THE MEDICO-LEGAL ASPECTS OF PSYCHOSEXUAL DISORDERS

22

THE LAW RELATING TO OFFENCES
DUE TO PSYCHOSEXUAL ABNORMALITY

The subject of maladjusted and abnormal citizens is one of vital importance to the community and since the law is devised primarily to protect
society against individual offences it is often unfavourable to the abnormal
delinquent. In the past laws were formulated when little was known of
mental disease and because of the conservatism of legislators have remained unchanged. For example, most of the laws regarding sexual
abnormality are at least ninety years old—so formulated long before the
discoveries of modern psychology.

The law of England discourages any public manifestation of sex; no
matter how normal it may be. Any transgression of this tends to be regarded as an act of indecency and may be punished accordingly. This has
not been rigidly enforced in more recent times, and such things as nudist
camps which, interpreted sexually, might be regarded as indecent, have
not been subject to legal interference. Again, the modern bathing costumes
which might have brought severe penalties in the past are now, in legal
eyes, regarded as healthy and natural. Even on the stage considerable
more licence is allowed in costume or nudity, as long as the motif is
artistic rather than sexual.

Innocent men are occasionally arrested in public lavatories for importuning. I have given evidence for a foreign film director who was accused
of visiting a lavatory four times in an hour. It was proved that he was suffering from diabetes mellitus, and an enlarged prostate. His diabetes had
been present for at least ten years. The magistrate dismissed the case.

The question of liability is just as much a bugbear in sexual abnormality
as in any other legal transgression. The psychiatrist is unfortunately unable to offer a magical solution: all that he can state is that the deviant has
the same impulsion as the normal man (although the direction is abnormal)
and suffers from deprivation as much as others when denied an outlet.
His evidence must, therefore, be mitigatory rather than a vindication.

The Criminal Justice Act, 1948 (11 & 12 Geo. VI, c. 58), modifies the
punishment for sexual and other offences, important alterations being
the abolition of penal servitude, hard labour, prison divisions, and whipping.

Probation is extended and the convicted person can be placed under it for a period of not less than one year and not more than three years, instead of being sentenced. The requirements of the court may be varied as to the circumstances of the case and may apply to the place of residence, treatment, &c. These requirements must be explained to the offender in ordinary language before the order is made. If he is over 14 years of age consent is necessary, Section 3 (5).

Where the court is satisfied, on the evidence of a duly qualified medical practitioner experienced in the diagnosis of mental disorders, that the mental condition of the offender is such as requires, and may be susceptible to, treatment but not such as to justify his being certified, the court may, if it makes a probation order, include therein a requirement that the offender shall submit, for such period not extending beyond twelve months from the date as may be specified, to treatment by or under the direction of a duly qualified medical practitioner with a view to the improvement of the offender's mental condition. Various forms of treatment (in-patient, out-patient, &c.) are permissible. Naturally the Probation Officer is required to supervise and see that the requirements of the order are met, but must not interfere with the actual treatment. If the physician in charge of the offender considers that treatment can be given more suitably or conveniently in hospital, he may, under Section 4b, with the probationer's consent, arrange for this to be done. The medical officer must inform the Probation Officer in writing of the arrangements, and this treatment shall be deemed to be treatment to which the probationer is required to submit under the order.

A report, signed by a medical practitioner experienced in mental illness, on the offender's mental condition (provided that the offender permits it or, if under the age of 17, his guardian agrees) may be received in evidence without proof of the signature, qualifications, or experience of the practitioner. This is an excellent thing and saves the futile waste of a medical man's time in attending court to give evidence of a purely formal character. When an offender is willing he can be ordered to submit to treatment but he can refuse to submit to any electrical, surgical, or other treatment if the court agrees that his objection is reasonable.

When a person is charged before a court of summary jurisdiction with any act or omission which is an offence punishable on summary conviction with imprisonment and the court is: (1) satisfied that the person did the act or made the omission as charged; (2) satisfied on the evidence of at least two duly qualified medical practitioners; and (3) also satisfied that he is a proper person to be detained, the court may, in lieu of dealing with him in any other manner, by order direct him to be received and detained in such institution for persons of unsound mind as may be named in the order.

This rough summary of the parts of the Act which affect to a large degree the sexually abnormal shows that the legislation is of considerable importance, the main factors being that offenders can be put on prolonged probation instead of being sentenced; they can be offered treatment and this is facilitated by the acceptance of a certificate without the physician wasting time in court. Offenders who are seriously ill can be sent straight to a mental hospital and not certified in prison. The main defect is that no arrangements have been made for the payment for private treatment and, as I have pointed out elsewhere, results are infinitely better when the treatment is given privately than when given at clinics. This is overcome to some extent because those offenders who are able to do so will eagerly accept private treatment.

Additional legislation, the Sexual Offences Act of 1956, deals with such matters as rape, incest, unnatural offences, indecent assault, prostitution, brothels, &c. It is an act to consolidate and amend the statute law previously in use.

The Mental Health Act of 1959 also applies to some guilty of sexual offences: if the offenders suffer from what Section 4 defines as mental disorder, by which is meant 'mental illness, arrested or incomplete development of mind, psychopathic disorder, and any other disorder or disability of mind'.

This very wide classification is further clarified by two more definitions, of severe subnormality and subnormality. The former is defined as 'a state of arrested or retarded development of mind which includes subnormality of intelligence and is of such a nature or degree that the patient is incapable of living an independent life or of guarding himself against serious exploitation, or will be so incapable when of an age to do so'. Subnormality means 'a state of arrested or retarded development of mind (not amounting to severe subnormality) which includes subnormality of intelligence and is of a nature or degree which requires or is susceptible to medical treatment or other special care or training of the patient'.

'Psychopathic disorder' is defined as 'a persistent disorder or disability of mind (whether or not including subnormality of intelligence) which results in abnormally aggressive or seriously irresponsible conduct on the part of the patient, and requires or is susceptible to medical treatment'.

Such a definition must include those who commit wholesale rape, the violent sadists, and those who injure animals 'for fun', as well as those who commit incendiary crimes as a sexual substitute, and similar cases.

The Act puts nothing in the way of these patients who wish to enter a mental hospital for voluntary treatment, but is especially concerned with compulsory treatment and guardianship of mentally disordered people. This is sometimes made to include such cases as homosexuals who need in-patient care and therapy.

Compulsory admission may be made for two reasons: (a) observation; and (b) treatment. These may be, based on an application to the mental hospital managers by the patient's nearest relative, or the mental welfare officer of the local health authority, and this application must be supported by the written recommendations of two medical practitioners, (one of whom should be a specialist) made in a specified form.

Patients admitted for observation are discharged after 28 days unless there is a further application or order made in that time. Those admitted for treatment may be detained for a year, but after that authority for another year may be made, and then for 2-year periods.

There is a proviso that no one may, by such an application, be compulsorily admitted for treatment as a subnormal or psychopathic patient after he has attained the age of 21, and all in these two categories admitted for treatment under Section 44 by application must be released upon reaching the age of 25, subject to certain safeguards. A Mental Health Tribunal consisting of lawyers, doctors and others is set up in the area of every regional hospital board to consider the applications, and to protect the liberty of the patient. Applications for discharge from relatives may be considered at any time during the patient's detention.

There is a further proviso, and that is for 'compulsory guardianship'. This allows patients, under the age of 21, to live outside mental hospitals under the care and authority of their guardian.

Courts of Assize and Quarter Sessions may, instead of sentencing, make 'hospital orders' or 'guardianship orders', if the medical witness can convince them of the desirability of such a course. There is, moreover, no limitation to the patient being under the age of 21; these orders can be made for any age.

Not only may the Court order a prisoner's detention in a hospital, but it may also, if it thinks that protection of the public is necessary place further restrictions on him, either of limited or unlimited duration. However, the Home Secretary may, if he considers that such a restriction is no longer justified, order the restriction's removal. Magistrates' Courts may also impose detention or guardianship on a prisoner where the offence is punishable on summary conviction with imprisonment.

Another Act which is of importance in the case of sadists who kill their victim is the Murder (Abolition of the Death Penalty) Act of 1965. This states that no person shall suffer death for murder and a person convicted of murder shall, subject to Sub-section 5 be sentenced to imprisonment for life. The exception is when the convicted person is under the age of 18, when he shall be detained during Her Majesty's pleasure.

Further sections make it possible for the Court to recommend to the Secretary of State the time which should elapse before the convicted person should be released on licence and that consultation should be had with the Lord Chief Justice of England or the Lord Justice General as the case may be and with the trial judge if available.

It is to be hoped that the abolition of the death penalty will allow the study of the aetiology of murder and its relation to sadism; that some psychiatrists will devote research to unravelling what occurs to set the train of events in motion, rather than that murderers will just serve their time unheeded in prison and be released at the end with nothing fresh learned which may prevent others behaving in the same way.

UNNATURAL OFFENCES

The offence of buggery consists of carnal knowledge contrary to the laws of nature and is either: (1) sodomy; or (2) bestiality.

Buggery

The Sexual Offences Act of 1967 states that a homosexual act in private shall not be an offence provided that the parties consent thereto, and have attained the age of 21 years, as long as not more than two persons take part and it is not in a lavatory to which the public has access. It must not involve mental patients, nor where the Acts concerning the Armed Services apply, nor with a member of a ship's crew.

The maximum punishment which may be imposed on conviction of a man for buggery with a man of or over the age of sixteen shall, instead of being imprisonment for life be (a) imprisonment for a term of 10 years except where the other man consented thereto; and (b) in the said excepted case, imprisonment for a term of 5 years if the accused is of or over the age of 21 and the other man is under that age, but otherwise 2 years.

The maximum punishment proscribed for an attempt to commit buggery with another man (10 years) shall not apply where that other man is of or over the age of 16.

Proof of the offence is usually given by the medical examiner who may observe irritation, bruising, fissuring, or other damage to the anus. The recovery of spermatozoa from the rectum of the passive party, and stains from the clothing, hairs, and fibres transposed from one party to the other, and excreta on the active protagonist's penis, form the best proofs in court. Injury may be expected where there has been violence or inequality between active and passive partners. In habitual sodomy no lesion at all may be left. Such cases, however, may be betrayed by the use of lubricant which can often be detected by ultra-violet light.

This crime is probably much more common than is generally realized since many cases never reach the courts because of the impossibility of obtaining substantial evidence.

Bestiality

This offence consists of intercourse (not necessarily with ejaculation of semen) between human beings and lower animals. It is not material whether the animals' anus or vagina is used[1]. Under the Sexual Offences Act of 1956 this is a felony punishable with imprisonment for life, and reinforced by the Sexual Offences Act of 1967.

In practice it is usually found that bestiality is practised by the mentally defective, or more rarely by normal men who have contact with animals—farm-labourers and similar workers.

Evidence in these cases may be that of eye-witnesses or circumstantial. In the latter hair from the animal found upon the person of the accused or human semen upon the animal will be regarded as evidence of unlawful contact.

An unusual case regarding this offence was that of *R. v. Bourne* (1952) 36 Gr. App. Rep. 125. Bourne was charged *inter alia* with compelling his wife under duress to submit to intercourse per vaginum with a dog. His appeal was rejected by the Court of Criminal Appeal.

GROSS INDECENCY BETWEEN MALE PERSONS

This is usually mutual masturbation, either manually or intercrurally, between two males. The Acts cover oral as well as masturbatory practices, as in the case of *R. v. Jacobs,* where a person forced open a child's mouth and inserted his penis.

The maximum penalty under the Sexual Offences Act of 1967 which may be imposed in indictment of a man of or over the age of 21 of committing an act of gross indecency with another man under that age or being a party to or procuring or attempting to procure the commission by a man under that age of such an act with another man shall, instead of being imprisonment for the term of 2 years, shall be for a term of 5 years.

This misdemeanour frequently occurs in the case of school-teachers, Sunday-school teachers, scoutmasters, priests, and similar persons in a position of trust and authority. *When this is so it is regarded as a reason for increasing the penalty. Aggravation is also found if the victim is infected with venereal disease* as a result of the behaviour or if the accused has *previous convictions* for lewd, or indecent, practices.

In several cases of this offence evidence has been admitted, for example, 'to show what the prisoner's practice was' (*R. v. Twiss,* 1918, 2 K.B. 853) and that certain indecent postcards were found on the prisoner, (*R. v. Gillingham,* 1939, 4 All. E.R., Depicting Dirty Sexual Acts). Whilst the admission of such evidence appears to be direct contravention of the

[1] It is to be noted that a domestic fowl has been held to be an animal within the meaning of the Act. (*R. v. Brown* (1889) 24. Q.B.D. 357: 54 J.P. 408.)

rule that 'It is undoubtedly not competent for the prosecution to adduce evidence tending to show that the accused has been guilty of criminal acts other than those covered by the indictment, for the purposes of leading to the conclusion that the accused is a person likely from his criminal conduct and character to have committed the offence for which he is being tried'. (*Makin* v. *Attorney General for New South Wales*, 1894, A.C. 57, 65.) Alcohol plays a part in the production of these indecent practices.

A large number of cases of gross indecency occur in public lavatories, usually in large towns, and any man loitering in one is likely to be taken in charge for importuning, or more likely observed until he commits an indecency with some man similarly engaged. It does not seem generally known that the police keep such places under observation, yet in spite of the continual arrests such fascination have they for certain men that offences constantly occur there.

RAPE

Rape consists in having unlawful sexual intercourse with a woman without her consent by force, fear or fraud. It is sufficient to prove penetration of the female organ by the male organ. Moreover, it must be proved that the intercourse took place without the consent of the female. To this end it is advisable to obtain evidence of consent: in the case of a young woman this is usually so. Apparent consent may, however, be negatived by duress or fraud. Thus if a woman's resistance is overcome by the administration of drugs or alcohol, or the man pretends (e.g. in the dark) to be her husband she will not have consented. In certain circumstances the consent of the female is irrelevant in law. It is a felony to have unlawful sexual intercourse with a girl under the age of 13, and the fact that she consented does not give a defence. It is a misdemeanour for a man to have unlawful sexual intercourse with a girl not under the age of 13 but under the age of 16. Here consent is only a defence if the man was under 24, has not been charged previously with a like offence and thought, having reasonable grounds for such belief, that the girl was over 16. In appropriate circumstances it seems that the prisoner may be charged with rape at Common Law even if the girl is over 13 but under 16. However, it seems that a boy under the age of 14 can never be guilty of rape and that a husband cannot rape his wife, so long as their marriage validly subsists.

If the woman submits to intercourse under a belief that a surgical operation is being performed this is not consent (*R.* v. *Flattery*, 1877, 2 Q.B.D. 410).

Inquiries into cases of this nature demand the examination of the scene of the crime, of the man, and of the woman. The scene of the crime may provide signs of a struggle. If this is not so there may be circumstances in particular cases which permit the offender to gratify his wishes without recourse to force. The existence of such circumstances in no way minimizes the gravity of the offence or removes it from the scope of the law. For example, a girl may be so drunk as to be incapable of consent or resistance. This type is the most common and cases of this kind should be given the closest possible scrutiny. A girl may have given her consent but, on recovery from the effects of alcohol, have entirely forgotten that she had done so. Again the woman may have submitted through fear and no signs of a struggle were made. The complainant should show distress from her recent experience, the clothing may be torn and there may be dirt, hair, and other matter for attention. The woman herself may show scratches, bruises, and hymenal trauma. Her vagina or clothes may be stained with blood or semen.

The accused may show signs of a struggle on his clothes or body, traces of blood or semen on his penis or underwear, and grass, soil, and so on from the scene of the crime.

Down the ages the crime of rape has been visited with the direst penalties, and castration and sometimes blinding were the lot of the offenders in bygone days. Whilst such a crime is wholeheartedly condemned we are not alone when we read with some misgiving (as to the righteousness of the penalty) of the execution of American soldiers who had been guilty of rape during the Second World War. In England rape is contrary to the Sexual Offences Act of 1956, Section 1. It is not triable at Quarter Sessions and the punishment is *imprisonment for life*. An attempted rape is also an offence and is punishable on indictment with 7 years' imprisonment.

INDECENT ASSAULT

Under Section 14 of the Sexual Offences Act it is an offence for a person to make an indecent assault on a woman. An exception is quoted by which where a marriage is invalid under Section 2 of the Marriage Act, 1949 or Section 1 of the Age of Marriage Act, 1929 (the wife being a girl under the age of sixteen) the invalidity does not make the husband guilty of any offence under this Section by reason of her incapacity to consent while under that age, if he believes her to be his wife and has reasonable grounds for that belief. Otherwise, the penalty on indictment is 2 years' imprisonment. An indecent assault on a man, Section 15, is punishable on indictment by 10 years' imprisonment.

The Act does not provide a definition of 'indecent assault' but to constitute the offence there must be: (1) an assault; and (2) circumstances of indecency. To the lay mind an 'assault' usually means the infliction by force, and against the will, of some bodily hurt. In law, an assault is usually thought to be committed by the mere offer to strike coupled with the ability to carry out the threat. There are also other circumstances which, whilst satisfying the law, are very far from assault as understood by the man in the street. 'Something offensive to delicacy and modesty' is apparently sufficient to supply the circumstances of indecency.

In order to provide an illustration of this offence it may be added that in the majority of cases a man or youth has, without invitation, put his hand up the clothing of an unsuspecting female.

That the indecent assault was committed with the consent of the person assaulted is a good defence when the latter is not under the age of 16 years or is not an imbecile to the knowledge or reasonable belief of the person charged. It has also been held that when the assault consisted of blows which would cause, or were intended to cause, bodily harm, the defence of consent can be of no avail. Such submission does not amount to consent.

In the case of *Fairclough* v. *Whipp*, 1951, 2 All. E.R. 839, the accused was found not guilty of indecent assault when he invited a young girl aged 9 to touch his penis and she did so. He could have been dealt with now under the Indecency with Children Act of 1960 which punishes the committing or inciting of gross indecency with a child of either sex under 14 with a maximum of 2 years' imprisonment on indictment.

INCEST

Incest has always been dealt with severely in most societies (but not in all; for example, the Ptolemies practised it in ancient Egypt and the Aztecs in America). Today in this country it is dealt with under Section 10 of the Sexual Offences Act of 1956. It is the unlawful sexual intercourse by blood relations and can be committed by a male person with his granddaughter, daughter, sister or half-sister, or mother, or by any female person with her grandfather, father, brother or half-brother, or son. It matters not whether the relationship is or is not traced through lawful wedlock. The penalty upon conviction is seven years' imprisonment. However, if the accused had committed incest with a girl under 13 (and this is so charged in the indictment) imprisonment for life may be awarded. No prosecution for incest may usually be commenced without the sanction of the Attorney General, except by or on behalf of the Director of Public Prosecutions. A male person who is convicted of incest (or of the attempt against a female under 21 years of age) may be deprived of all authority he may have over her.

The crime is usually detected by the complaint of the woman, who may be pregnant and frequently is under the age of 16 (the average age is 15 according to Glaister). The medical evidence in such cases is limited to evidence of defloration or pregnancy, and sometimes the discovery of seminal stains.

INDECENT EXPOSURE

The offence of indecent exposure falls within the province of both the Common Law and the Statute Law. Under the former it is a misdemeanour and procedure is by way of indictment, that is, by written accusation signed by the proper officer of the court of trial. The exposure must be indecent, public, and witnessed *by more than one person* to be indictable as a common nuisance. Bathing in the nude within the public view similarly offends the common law and it is no defence that the place has been so used within living memory.

The Vagrancy Act of 1824 and Town Police Clauses Act of 1847 each provide for the offence of indecent exposure. But with this difference—in the former it is necessary to prove that it was accompanied by an attempt to insult a female and in the latter that annoyance to residents or passers-by resulted.

It is presumably on the absence of these that nudist camps are permissible. The females who attend these are not likely to be insulted by nakedness and the camps are isolated from passers-by. Indeed, the nudists are more likely to be annoyed by prying intruders than the voyeurs by seeing what they have come to see!

Similarly the attempt to introduce topless bathing dresses and topless frocks as a fashion may produce interesting results. How far this will lead to the acceptance that women have the right to expose the breasts (as men are allowed to do) will eventually be fought out in the courts.

OTHER SEXUAL ABNORMALITIES AND LEGAL RELATIONSHIPS

Various perversion-fetishisms tend to bring the patient into contact with the law, particularly those which involve cutting girls' hair, pouring ink on dresses, and so on. These are punishable under the ordinary law regarding common assault.

If the patient is unable to consummate marriage on the grounds of impotence or frigidity the marriage may be made null (the judgment of the court is termed a Declarator of Nullity of Marriage). Except when there is some physical evidence this is not easy to prove. The wilful refusal to consummate the marriage is a ground for nullity. Similarly, recently it has been declared that the persistent use of contraceptives so that no children can result from the marriage is a ground for divorce.

The practice of sexual perversion may be legal cruelty and so can form a ground for divorce. I have seen occasional cases in which this has been used as a threat when nothing of the sort has occurred. Since sexual congress takes place between two people in private it seems almost impossible to prove one way or the other. Usually a perversion will be a cause for divorce by reason of cruelty, sodomy or bestiality, &c. However, in such cases the consent of the wife may be a defence in a divorce. Recently it seems that the courts may interpret the word 'consent' in favour of the petitioner. Turner and Armitage record (*T*. v. *T*., 1964, p. 85) a case where the wife petitioned for divorce on grounds of sodomy. The husband had represented to the wife that sodomy was a part of normal love-making and that submission to it was part of her matrimonial duty. The wife believed this although she did not think that it was a natural thing to do. The Court of Appeal held that the wife had not truly consented because of representations, albeit innocent, of the husband. It is, however, uncertain how far this ruling can be taken.

TRANSVESTISM

This is not an offence against the law either by males or females but is made so by the police—a fact which has been repeatedly pointed out in legal journals. To quote one eminently sensible article:

For some reason the courts never seem to be troubled with cases of the dressing by women in men's clothes. Hence, perhaps, the persistent popular delusion, found amongst persons who might be expected to know better, that whilst a woman may lawfully wear trousers it is unlawful for a man to wear a skirt in a public place. As we showed, . . . this 'cross-dressing' as it is sometimes called, or 'transvestism' in the barbarous jargon of more or less scientific persons, is never an offence against the law . . . it is a fundamental point which cannot be too strongly impressed upon police officers who, it seems, may be prompt to move when they are told about the practice, or upon clerks to magistrates if cases come before the Bench. Of course dressing up in any form —in clothes appropriate to the opposite sex, or like Michael Finsbury in windowglass spectacles and whiskers—may be strong evidence of unlawful intent in one direction or another. It may lead a person, who starts with innocent intentions, into conduct (such as using sanitary conveniences appropriated to the other sex) which is sometimes an offence against local bye-laws and may reasonably be sometimes thought likely to cause a breach of the peace. . . . In the metropolitan police district there is (for good or evil) an offence which does not exist elsewhere except under other local Acts, namely, 'On any thoroughfare or public place . . . to use any threatening, abusive, or insulting words or behaviour with intent to provoke a breach of the peace, or whereby a breach of the peace may be occasioned.'

When such cases have been brought before magistrates it has been a practice not to convict but to put the person on recognizances under the statute of Edward the Third—which is commonly called 'bound over to be of good behaviour'. This means that he is not convicted of misbehaving but must promise not to do it again! The appearance in court, the exposure to public ridicule is surely the last thing likely to be beneficial to someone ill, but binding him over is the most cruel thing. It is as good, in the public eye, as a conviction—most people have no appreciation that it is not the same thing. Fortunately this has at last been appreciated by the authorities and appeals are now allowed by the Magistrates' Courts Act 1956, Section 1 (Appeals from Binding Over Orders.) This abolishes a long-standing grievance.

SCOPTOPHILIA

In order to prosecute voyeurs it is necessary to go back to 1361. These men, who are usually described by the police as 'Peeping Toms' and stated to be behaving contrary to the Common Law and Justice of the Peace Act. Their behaviour is also likely to come under the provisions against behaviour likely to cause a breach of the peace where this is dealt with by local Acts. Usually the voyeur will be bound over to keep the peace and this was so in the case of a man who let flats for girls only. He had fitted the bathroom with a mirror which allowed him to see his clients bathing.

PROSTITUTION AND THE LAW

The Female Prostitute

Previously the punishment for prostitution was trivial considering the earnings obtained by this profession. Under the Town Police Clauses Acts of 1899 and 1947 any person, being a common prostitute, who in any street to the obstruction, annoyance, or danger of the residents, loiters or importunes for the purpose of prostitution was liable to a penalty not exceeding forty shillings for each offence; in the discretion of the court she might be committed to prison for a term not exceeding fourteen days. In a city such as Oxford prostitutes can be prosecuted under the University Act of 1825 which provides a maximum penalty of three months' imprisonment.

However, under the Street Offences Act of 1959 a prostitute can be fined ten pounds for the first offence and twenty-five pounds for subsequent offences. Moreover, after two convictions for soliciting she can be sent to prison for up to three months as well as being fined twenty-five pounds. In the past it was common for the police to caution a novice twice before taking her to court. Probably when she was charged it would be with insulting behaviour and only the next time would she be charged with soliciting.

No doubt the Street Offences Act will discourage novices and this may stop young girls taking to the life. However, the promulgation of a severer law against prostitution will in no way prevent the practice of it by the professional but will rather drive it underground. Systems of appointment by telephone (the so-called 'Call Girl'), picking up men by car, advertising in dubious newspapers, and tobacconists' windows, are being substituted for soliciting. One in a shop in Queensway, Bayswater, actually offered to provide 'individual strip-tease acts'! Indeed, the Act is already leading to much more serious offences than the trivial annoyance of being accosted by a street woman on a dark night. Clubs specializing in cheap vaudeville and strip-tease shows are being provided to allow the prostitute to meet her customer. These clubs are run by men of dubious character who no doubt live indirectly on the woman's earnings. This has led to gangs obtaining control of the clubs and to underground warfare of a serious kind.

The Street Offences Act broadens the meaning of 'loitering or soliciting for purposes of prostitution' since it is not only an offence for a woman to loiter or solicit in the street but in a 'public place'. It has been found that for a woman to be on a balcony or appear at a window is sufficient (*Smith* v. *Hughes*, 1960, 2 All. E.R. 859: 124 J.P. 430). 'Public place' is not defined and extends to more than a street; a field where the public were admitted for one occasion, a parking place behind an inn, &c., have been subject to prosecutions.

The Male Prostitute

These are punishable under the laws already described regarding homosexuality. They may be prosecuted for importuning, gross indecency, and unnatural offences. Under the Sexual Offences Act, Section 32, 'it is an offence for a man persistently to solicit or importune in a public place for immoral purposes. The penalty summarily is 6 months, or on indictment, 2 years' imprisonment.' The accused cannot claim to be tried on indictment under Section 25 of the Magistrates and Courts Act, 1952. It is also an offence under the Act to procure a woman to be a common prostitute, to keep a brothel, or for a landlord to let premises to be used for this purpose, and to live knowingly, wholly or in part, on the earnings of prostitution.

OBSCENITIY

I have pointed out that patients with coprophilic interests and sometimes for other reasons may write things which offend the laws regarding obscenity. The main law in the past was the Obscene Publications Act of 1857. This led to Lord Chief Justice Cockburn's definition in 1878. This I have already given on page 112. It was a description drawn so widely that it was used even to include advertisements for the treatment of venereal diseases.

Lord Chief Justice Cockburn's definition led to the condemnation of the works of such authors as Havelock Ellis, D. H. Lawrence, Shane Leslie, Radclyffe Hall, Pierre Louÿs, and Karl Huysmans. It received a blow when the American courts decreed that James Joyce's *Ulysses* was not immoral in 1934 and obviously the ban on it had to be lifted. Moreover in 1954 Mr. Justice Stable, in a famous summing-up, adopted a different definition for the purposes of the case before him and refused to accept that adults should be bound by what might corrupt a school-girl.

The Obscene Publication Acts of 1959 and 1964 prohibit 'any obscene article containing or embodying matter to be read or looked at or both, any sound record, and any film, or other record of picture or pictures.' This can lead to films and theatrical performances being suppressed and articles confiscated. The penalty on summary conviction is a fine not exceeding £100 or imprisonment for a term not exceeding 6 months, or on conviction on indictment to a fine or imprisonment for a term not exceeding 3 years or both. These Acts have strengthened the law regarding pornography—the deliberate sale of indecent literature—and made reputable authors much less likely to be prosecuted. An author is given the right to be heard before his book is condemned and in prosecution cases he and his publisher can plead that it is 'for the public good on the ground that it is in the interests of science, literature, art and learning'. On such points both sides can call expert evidence. Moreover, 'No prosecution can be brought more than 2 years after the commission of the offence'.

It is hoped that this Act will separate the genuine author from the patient suffering from psychosexual diseases who sends obscene letters to people he wishes to annoy, and allow the publication of scientific books, such as this present one, without fear of prosecution. However, there is still considerable fear amongst publishers and printers. For example in 1960 the firm of Penguin Books was prosecuted for publishing *Lady Chatterley's Lover* by D. H. Lawrence. The costs of defending such an action would have crippled a smaller firm. In 1964 copies of *Fanny Hill, The Memoirs of a Woman of Pleasure*, were seized by the police and the publishers asked to show why they should not be destroyed. This was under a different Act than that they used against the publishers of *Lady Chatterley's Lover*. Sir Robert Blundell, the Chief Metropolitan Magistrate, ruled at Bow Street that they were obscene and ordered their destruction. In 1967 a novel, *The Last Exit to Brooklyn*, was found to be obscene by a jury at the Old Bailey in spite of the fact that 18 defence witnesses had given evidence of its literary merit. The publishers were fined £100 and ordered to pay £500 costs. This was, however, quashed on appeal in July 1968 because the Court held that the trial judge had failed to put to the jury the defence case on obscenity or to give proper directions on law as to 'public good'. The fine and costs ordered were set aside and the company were awarded costs of the appeal. The cost of defending prosecutions of the book and launching appeals amounted to about £15,000.

NECROPHILIA

The law does not seem to make necrophilia punishable unless there is some injury to public morals by open lewdness, gross scandal, or outrage of decency. Only if it is performed in public or to insult a female would it be punishable under Common Law, the Vagrancy Act of 1924, or the Town Police Clauses Act of 1847.

The absence of definite legislation is probably due to the fact that such cases come before the courts so infrequently. (It would be interesting to know under what Act the case was tried in New Zealand, mentioned under the section on necrophilia.) It is probable, however, that if a case occurred which aroused sufficient public concern then some law would be found applicable.

SEXUAL PERVERSIONS FROM THE PSYCHIATRIC POINT OF VIEW

It is worth while dealing at this point with the responsibility of the pervert (and other sexual delinquent) from the psychiatric point of view, rather than the strictly legal. How far is the patient to be held responsible for his behaviour? I would state clearly here that the sexual deviant feels exactly the same about his sexual behaviour as the normal man. Now a normal man will go to great lengths to obtain heterosexual satisfaction. He will even risk his reputation, his money, or life, to gain his ends. On the one hand, his actions are volitional and conscious (in contradistinction to those of, for example, epileptic automatism). On the other hand, when a man is driven by instinctual demands he is forced by impulses which are not easily controlled—thus we are lenient to the starving man who steals to appease his hunger, the man who attacks another who steals his wife, and so on. The pervert is in the same position. The normal man would seek heterosexual satisfaction at all costs if it were declared illegal to obtain it. That this is so was shown in the Second World War when Jews risked severe punishments by having relations with German girls, and girls in occupied countries did the same, from subversive forces, when they had relations with the foreign soldiers. The same thing is found in South Africa where it is an offence for a white man to have intercourse with a coloured woman. Just as some normal men will risk all for sexual satisfaction so will the pervert. He is in the same boat, but his abnormal satisfaction is always illegal. He can avoid seeking it, but he is driven on

HH—PSY. D.

by terrible instinctual demands. What starving man can check his hunger by 'advice and resolution'? He may, for a short time, but sooner or later he is forced to do something to satisfy it.

In spite of our sympathy with those compelled by urgent instinctual drives, the function of the law is to protect the community, and although it is lenient to the starving man, he is not allowed to go on stealing. The pervert is a definite menace to the community, and this is particularly so when he is attracted to young boys and tends to interfere with them, and in so doing converts them into homosexuals. This is a very serious matter, and it is essential that such behaviour should be stopped even at the price of prolonged interference with the liberty of the offender. The present system of giving sentences of a few months, or years, after which the offender is released to go free is worse than useless. Statistics show that it has no deterrent effect. I would seriously state that imprisonment aggravates rather than cures perversion. This is particularly so with homosexuality, and cases such as that of Peter Kürten, the sadist, show that much of the enforced isolation in prison is spent in perverse fantasies. The work of Jenkins demonstrates that segregation from the opposite sex in rats tends to produce homosexual reactions, and that these reactions do not disappear after restoration of normal conditions. Yet we are performing Jenkins' experiment daily with human beings, for example, the Home Secretary states that the number of prisoners now sleeping three in a cell has fallen from 8,500 to just over 6,000. (The size of the regulation cell is 13 ft. by 17 ft. by 9 ft.) The idea of three sleeping in the same cell is possibly to prevent two men misbehaving alone. If this is so someone has little appreciation of the effects of sexual deprivation. Compared with the Mexican and Swedish system of allowing prisoners' wives and mistresses to spend week-ends with them our English prisons seem residua from the dark ages. We have, however, much stronger evidence that such segregation is harmful. For example, Fishman investigated the sexuality of a prison population in America and found that as many as 30–40 per cent. were homosexual. He stated that the worst thing was that many young men reacted to prison by being initiated, in the abnormal atmosphere, into homosexuality. Although I have no statistics, experience of homosexual patients who have served prison sentences here is that no improvement in their illness results without psychotherapy, and this is upheld by the high percentage of recidivists in these cases. It is true that the Sexual Offences Act of 1967 allowing homosexual acts between consenting adults in private may reduce the number of inverts in prison but cannot affect the argument that segregation with other men will aggravate the condition of those who are sentenced.

If the psychiatrist were asked exactly how he would treat the problem of the pervert, unhampered by existing laws, how would he answer? The question could be dealt with in this manner. It seems possible to divide these cases into three groups. The first group is more of a nuisance to the community than a serious menace—the fetishists, exhibitionists, frotteurs, and so on. These could be remanded for treatment and placed under surveillance of the Probation Officer for a long period, a year or two years, while attending a clinic or private psychotherapist, until regarded as cured. This is done frequently now in large towns with excellent results. (See, for instance, the reports of the Institute for the Study and Treatment of Delinquency.) This work is, unfortunately, hampered by the fact that there is nowhere in the whole of England (and indeed, so far as I know, in the world) a clinic devoted solely to the treatment of sexual abnormality. Those cases which did not respond to treatment and which caused distress and terror to sections of the community might be placed under permanent surveillance, or, if that failed, compelled to enter some permanent home where the nuisance could be restrained. It is useless to send such patients to prison for a short period since punishment does not deter them and they are discharged worse than when they went in.

The second group consists of those who are potentially dangerous to the community. This group includes the mild sadists and the infanto-sexuals whose desires are directed towards young boys. This is a more difficult group since they cannot be regarded as desirable at liberty and so any form of out-patient or private psychotherapy is, by definition, impossible. I feel that the best thing for those who are unsafe in the community would be detention homes: not prisons, but homes where they would be under discipline and able to have treatment. There could be a world of difference between these and a prison since there is no reason why comforts, books, cinemas, and everything except freedom should not be provided. It is essential that where treatment is to be attempted segregation from the other sex should be avoided, but that there should be opportunities for those of the opposite sexes to meet. I feel that prisoners of this type should be under much longer surveillance than at present, and some should be watched for many years.

The third group consists of those who are actually dangerous; such sadists as those of the Heath type. I feel that they should be treated as insane, certified, and sent to a mental hospital. Where they have committed murders and there is a previous history of psychopathic, odd, irresponsible behaviour the Macnaughton Rules should not be applied but the patient considered insane and unfit to plead.

I do not consider that every case, even of the apparently milder types, will necessarily respond to treatment (but then *they invariably fail to respond to imprisonment*). At present those who have been given opportunity of having treatment and who subsequently come before the courts may with some reason be treated more severely. No doubt the knowledge of this has considerable effect on the patient's desire to recover and will to do so. In my experience when a patient is given such an opportunity he often does try much harder to get well than if he has suffered a term of imprisonment and then comes for help. He is then cynical and hostile.

A large number of patients needing treatment are homosexuals and it is generally accepted by psychiatrists that, other things being equal, the younger a patient is the greater chance one has of curing him and influencing his future sexual behaviour. Imprisonment may not only make him cynical and hostile but wastes precious time which could be utilized in treatment.

Unfortunately, some of the societies which have been developed to protect the rights of homosexuals, such as the Albany Trust, are not satisfied with the new freedom provided by the 1967 Act and wish to extend the permitted age still further from 21 to 18 years. This is most undesirable.

In the previous edition of this book I have stated that I thought that 21 was too early and considered that permitting homosexual behaviour under the age of 30 was not wise. The reason for this is that many young men swing between homosexuality and heterosexuality at that time, possibly because of delayed puberty; if permitted to live a homosexual life too early they will miss the chance of becoming normal.

Remanding for treatment is a good thing. The patient has been frightened by his appearance in court. His disgrace has brought him brusquely against the facts of his life, and treatment appears like a ray of light in a dark world. Many patients have expressed to me their gratitude to the courts for compelling them to take a chance of recovery, and it is rare to find the case suggested by Rees when the patient is hostile to the help extended to him. Even if he is suspicious at first he soon comes to regard the psychiatrist more as a friend than as a warder.

In this book an attempt has been made to examine sexual abnormality in the same way as any other illness. It has been seen that it is the product of unhappy homes, unsuitable parents, and miserable childhoods. The sexually abnormal have to go to extraordinary lengths to obtain the pleasure that the ordinary man gains so easily and this frequently brings them into conflict with the law. It is easy to condemn, and violence towards the sufferers is aroused in the ignorant but this is as facile as it is fruitless. It is not justice, or even mercy—which is frequently a negative virtue—but wise understanding which is needed. We must achieve the ability of saying at the sight of these patients, 'but for the grace of God there go I', and do what we can to help them to achieve normality.

REFERENCES

ARCHBOLD, J. F. (1966) *Criminal Pleadings, Evidence, and Practice*, 35th ed., London.

CROSS, R., and ASTERLEY JONES, P. (1962) *Cases on Criminal Law*, 3rd ed., London.

DI FURIA, G., and MEES, H. L. (1964) *Amer. J. Psychiat.*, 120, **10,** 980–4.

EAST, W. N., and HUBERT, W. H. (1939) *Psychological Treatment of Crime*, London.

ELLIS, A., and ARBANEL, A. B. (1961) *The Encyclopedia of Sexual Behavior*, New York.

GLAISTER, J. (1962) *Medical Jurisprudence and Toxicology*, Edinburgh.

INSTITUTE FOR THE STUDY AND TREATMENT OF DELINQUENCY, Reports 1933–57, London.

JAMES, P. S. (1966) *Introduction to English Law*, 6th ed., London.

THE JUSTICE OF THE PEACE AND LOCAL GOVERNMENT REVIEW (1950) **114,** No. 3.

THE ORGANIZATION OF THE PRISON MEDICAL SERVICE: REPORT OF THE WORKING PARTY (1964) London, H.M.S.O.

REINHARDT, J. M. (1957) *Sex Perversions and Sex Crimes*, Springfield, Ill.

REPORT OF THE COMMISSIONERS FOR PRISONS FOR THE YEAR 1962, London, H.M.S.O.

ROLPH, C.H. (1969) *Books in the Dock*, London.

SEXUAL OFFENCES ACT (1956) 4 and 5 Eliz. 2 Ch. 69.

THE TIMES (October 1st, 1964) Report on a voyeur in flats.

TURNER, J. W. C., and ARMITAGE, A. LL. (1964) *Cases on Criminal Law*, 2nd ed., Cambridge.

WHITESIDE, J., and WILSON, J. P., ed. (1967) *Stone's Justices' Manual*, 98th ed., London.

WILLIAMS, GLANVILLE (1961) *Criminal Law*, 2nd ed., London.

INDEX